Isaac McCoy: Apostle of the Western Trail

Isaac McCoy

Apostle of the Western Trail

George M. Ella

Missionary Series

Particular Baptist Press

Springfield, Missouri

The Publication of this book
is made possible through the
shared vision of

Dr. Brian and Karen Whitson
Enid, Oklahoma

© Particular Baptist Press

2766 W. FR 178
Springfield, Missouri 65810

First Edition, September 2002

Typesetting by Mrs. Teresa Worley

Cataloging data:

Ella, George Melvyn, 1939 -

- McCoy, Isaac, 1784-1846
- Rice, Luther, 1783-1836
- Baptists - United States - history
- Regular Baptists - United States -
  missions
- Baptist Board of Foreign Missions -
  history
- Indian missions - United States -
  history
- Indian relocation - history

ISBN 1-888514-18-3   acid-free paper

Printed in the United States of America

Acknowledgements

I would like to acknowledge the fine assistance provided for me by the Librarians and Library Assistants of the Duisburg University Library who were particularly successful in obtaining American literature for me which I could not trace in German libraries. I would also like to thank the staff of the Gilcrease Museum, Tulsa, Oklahoma for giving us permission to reproduce the original paintings of George Catlin, the first and most famous of Indian painters who made portraits of many of the Indians who were ministered to by Isaac McCoy. The museum is also to be thanked for furnishing me with copies of photographs of McCoy's contemporaries and associates and also copies of original yet unpublished documents by McCoy in their care. In this connection I would like especially to thank Don Pearson, Preston Whitson and Paula Whitson for their expert advice and assistance. The Gilcrease Museum contains perhaps the greatest, and certainly the finest, collection of Indian artifacts and historical documentation anywhere in the world. Sitting in the Museum Restaurant, overlooking a breathtakingly beautiful wooded valley, eating a Buffalo steak and talking to Preston and Paula about Isaac McCoy and his missionary and surveying work was one of the highlights of my time of research. When Don uncovered the very documents that McCoy wrote, describing his planning and surveying of the Indian Territory which mostly covers present day Oklahoma, my joy was complete.

I am greatly indebted to Jack Armstrong, a Particular Baptist pastor in Woodward, Oklahoma for procuring for me a number of photographs of nineteenth century Indians. Indeed, I received from such kind supporters far more contemporary illustrations than could be used in this work but will, God willing, find a place for them in my future writings.

My most grateful thanks go out to Senior Pastor, Wade Burleson, and his assistant pastors and fellow-members of Emmanuel Baptist Church, Enid, Oklahoma who have hosted me three times while working on my books and have put many resources at my disposal. I am particularly grateful for their provision of microfilm copies of the entire McCoy Collection and also for fitting me out with copies of the unpublished writings of many other Baptist missionaries to the Indians. These documents, if printed out would make at least 60 large volumes of reference works so the reader will realize that there is ample scope for much further research into this field.

I would also like to thank Pastor Larry Vincent and his

fellow organizers of the 1998 Founders' Conference in Mansfield, Texas for the kind invitation and reception which they gave me. At this conference, I heard the doctrines for which McCoy lived and died preached faithfully. This was no accident as Isaac McCoy was one of those very Founders on whose testimony the widely appreciated Founders' Conference is built.

Above all, I would like to express my unbounded gratitude to Terry Wolever whose personal knowledge of Isaac McCoy is, I sincerely believe, far greater than mine. Indeed, I look upon this work as a hint to Terry to produce something far better, which he is well able to do. Terry has provided me with an enormous amount of literature on the subject and has carefully and patiently read through my manuscripts, suggesting points here and there, at times converting my too idiomatic Anglicisms and Germanisms into a language more palatable for American readers. I count it a great privilege to be able to preface this work with words from Terry's pen.

Finally, my deep thanks and affection go out to my wife, Erika, and Mark and Robin, our sons, for supporting me so well in this labor of love for the Great Commission and in my calling to reveal to the English-speaking public the life and testimony of one of America's greatest heroes.

George M. Ella
Mulheim, Germany

Dedication

This book is dedicated
to the work of the gospel amongst the Indians of North America,
many of whom, though still facing great adversity,
are finding peace of heart and mind in the Lord Jesus Christ.

"God often frustrates our plans, and disappoints our hopes, to teach us our littleness, and that He is sovereign....It may be said that, in a sense, [the missionary] does all his work upon his knees;"

Isaac McCoy
History of Baptist Indian Missions

Table of Contents

Illustration Credits

Fort Wayne, Indiana Territory: Charles E. Slocum, *History of the Maumee River Basin* (Defiance, OH: C. E. Slocum, 1905), p. 204.

Isaac and Christiana McCoy, John Calvin McCoy, Robert and Frances Simerwell, Jotham Meeker and Johnston Lykins: Courtesy of the Kansas State Historical Society, Topeka.

Evan Jones: Walter N. Wyeth, *Poor Lo! Early Indian Missions. A Memorial* (Philadelphia: W. N. Wyeth, 1896), frontispiece.

William Staughton and Spencer Cone: William Cathcart, editor, *The Baptist Encyclopedia* (Philadelphia: Louis H. Everts, 1881), pp. 1309 & 263.

Lucius Bolles: W. H. Eaton, *Historical Sketch of the Massachusetts Baptist Missionary Society and Convention, 1802-1902* (Boston: Mass. Baptist Convention, 1903), p. 20.

Francis Wayland, Jr.: Nathan E. Wood, The *History of the First Baptist Church of Boston, 1665-1899* (Philadelphia: A. B. P. S., 1899), p. 311.

John Mason Peck: Coe Hayne. *Vanguard of the Caravans; A Life - story of John Mason Peck* (Philadelphia: Judson Press, 1931), frontispiece.

Lewis Cass: Courtesy of the Library of Congress

Shawanoe Baptist Mission Station and Choctaw School: Joseph Tracy, et. al., *History of American Missions to the Heathen* (Worcester, MA: Spooner and Howland, 1840), pp. 541 and 248.

Hamilton Literary and Theological Institution: Courtesy of University of Rochester Archives, N. Y.

Silhouette of Luther Rice: Courtesy A. B. H. S., Rochester, N.Y.

Columbian University: *The National Cyclopedia of American Biography*, Vol. III (New York: James T. White, 1893), p. 151.

Indian tepee: Jesse Page, *David Brainerd the Apostle to the North American Indians* (Kilmarnock, Scotland: John Ritchie, 1910), p. 77.

Selected Indian portraits from the 1830's & 1840's by George Catlin (1796-1872): Courtesy of the Thomas Gilcrease Museum, Tulsa, Oklahoma.

Foreword

The story of Isaac and Christiana McCoy and their missionary associates to the American Indians has long been eclipsed in Christian literature by such notable worthies as John Eliot and David Brainerd. And while we would in no way wish to detract from their noble lives, yet the scope of what McCoy's missionary endeavors entailed and in the end what was achieved far exceeded that of his early predecessors in Indian missions and the comparative obscurity therefore is undeserved.

In Isaac McCoy resided the single greatest benefactor to the American Indian. Such a confident affirmation on our part will no doubt elicit more than a look of consternation from secular revisionists who decry what they term the "cultural devastation" brought about by decades of Christian missionary activity around our world.[1] But as it was so well stated by one many years ago, "facts are stubborn things,"[2] and when truthful objectivity and not political correctness is the aim of the inquirer, clearly no one accomplished so much good not only in his own day but for succeeding generations of American Indians as did Isaac McCoy. He truly *cared* for both their temporal and their spiritual welfare, and early on came to the realization that in order to preserve the various tribes from certain extinction they must be removed to the West and resettled within an Indian "state." McCoy later wrote that, "from that time [June 4, 1823] until the present I have considered the promotion of this de-

---

[1] As if, for example, the direct intervention of William Carey in ending the criminal practice in India of the burning alive of widows and the sacrificing of infant children to crocodiles was somehow "misguided." This "calling evil good, and good evil" (Isaiah 5:20) can be multiplied by many such instances

[2] Tobias Smollett (1721-1771), *Translation of Gil Blas.*, Book X, Chap. 1.

sign as the most important business of my life."[3] This was no mere paternalism on his part, but a compassionate and worthy goal to which he committed himself and his family, and one in which their devotion to Christ would bring them to experience in a large measure "the fellowship of His sufferings."

To make his vision of an "Indian Canaan" a reality required an amazing fortitude on the part of the McCoys and their co-laborers, facing as they did opposition and discouragement on every hand - even from within their own denomination. All of this is related to the reader in fine narrative detail in this present work.

There has been no sympathetic treatment of the McCoys and their heroic labors since Walter S. Stewart issued the first volume of his *Early Baptist Missionaries and Pioneers* in 1925, which contained a brief but admirable account of their ministry. Unfortunately more recent works have been disappointing, and in an effort to be "scholarly" have done something McCoy's contemporaries, those who knew him best, would never have done - impeach his character and impugn his motives. The contribution of Isaac McCoy to the spiritual life of the American Indian, and his influence upon generations of Indian people to date has not been fully assessed. And in secular histories McCoy has yet to receive the full credit for what was, essentially, *his idea*, the removal of the Indian tribes to what is now the State of Oklahoma. To him this movement owes its origins.

Until now, there has been no comprehensive biography written on the McCoys. A definitive appraisal of their lives and work is therefore long overdue. In other ways this exceptionally fine biography by noted author George Ella is a first. For example, it is the first to explore the embarrassing lack of competence and overall general mismanagement of some of the leaders in the early years of the Baptist General Convention's Board of Foreign Missions, which must now be considered as a major factor in fueling the anti-missions fervor by default in the early to mid-nineteenth century. On a more positive note, it is the first to relate just how spiritual and gentle a man Isaac McCoy was. He was never the instrument, in God's providence, of any great awakening among the Indians, but his great love for souls animated all of his earnest endeavors on their behalf, and they knew he loved them.

Many years ago Isaac McCoy's gravesite in Louisville, Ken-

---

[3] Isaac McCoy. *History of Baptist Indian Missions* (Washington, D. C.: William H. Morrison, 1840), p. 197.

4

tucky was paved over with asphalt, but on the campus of Bacone College in Muskogee, Oklahoma is perhaps the most fitting memorial to this great missionary friend of the Indians. Bacone College was founded in 1880 by Almon C. Bacone as "an Indian school that would place more emphasis on Christian ethics," and there in 1937 Isaac McCoy Hall, a dormitory for male Indian students, was dedicated in his memory. Here McCoy's name is associated as he would have desired it to be, with the betterment of the American Indian.

Terry Wolever
September 22, 2002

Tributes to Isaac McCoy

Isaac McCoy became one of the greatest factors in work for American Indians that Protestantism has ever produced. In sixteen years he visited Washington thirteen times from Michigan and the Indian Territory, interviewed three Presidents of the United States, Committees of the House and the Senate, and various cabinet officers. One result was the creation of the Indian Territory, officially ascribed to his efforts.

Barnes, Barnes and Stephenson

The most conspicuous monument to the memory of the McCoys was the marked advance in civilization and religion of those tribes whom they served. They had found the Indiana and Illinois Indians hedged in on every side by land-hungry whites and designing whiskey peddlers. Indian villages reeked in filth and squalor, and their inhabitants were despondent, debauched, and starving without hope of a better day. McCoy and his wife first taught them that Christ was the light of the world; then they showed them how to spin, weave, sew, clear away fields and plant corn, and the many other things necessary to advance them on the road to civilization. Obviously, there was much backsliding, much uncertainty, as the Indians moved forward. Sometimes the missionaries were so discouraged as to feel the utter hopelessness of success, but their Christian zeal, born of hope and faith, revived them and drove them on to final success.

Dr. Carl Coke Rister

"For nearly thirty years his entire time and energies were devoted to the civil and religious improvement of the aborigines of this country. He projected and founded the plan of their colonization, their only hope, and the imperishable monument of his wisdom and benevolence. Still his summons rings out." (Words on McCoy's marker).

Still the Indian continues to increase in numbers. Still many thousands of them have not even heard the gospel story. The challenge is not in past accomplishment but in present need. The daring of such consecration is a vital summons to Baptists. He who was willing to go on almost alone in his obedience to divine call, has put his impress on every loyal heart. Folks opposed him thinking that the Indian was doomed to extinction. People talked against the Indian Mission in his day, saying that it was unimportant. He never permitted himself to be drawn aside in vain debate over the question. He continued on

6

following Him whom he loved; only desiring that these Indians should hear of Him who is "altogether lovely, and the fairest of ten thousand."

W. S. Stewart

His was a heroic life and death, and he deserves a place high among the apostles and martyrs.

Henry C. Vedder

Isaac McCoy, Baptist missionary to the Indians, was an outstanding figure in the development of the Indian removal policy of the United States. He began his missionary work on the Western frontier of Indiana in 1817 and spent the twelve years following with the tribes of Indiana and Michigan. By 1823 he was convinced that the ultimate decline and ruin of the Indians could be avoided only by removing them from the encroaching whites and by colonization in lands west of Missouri. The following year he submitted his conclusions to the Baptist Mission Board and was authorized to present the matter at Washington. Secretary of War John C. Calhoun, whose department was at that time in charge of Indian affairs, approved McCoy's plans and became a supporter of the measure. McCoy worked unceasingly for the program and published in 1827 his Remarks on the Practicability of Indian Reform, in which he urged concentration of the perishing tribes in some suitable portion of the country under proper guardianship of the government.

Lela Barnes

This Association (American Indian Mission Association) was organized, chiefly through the influence of Isaac McCoy, one of the most zealous and devoted philanthropists that have lived and died in Kentucky. This self-sacrificing Christian minister, and devoted missionary, deserves to be "held in everlasting remembrance," especially by all the friends of the American Indians.

J. H. Spencer

Mr. McCoy and his wife entered upon this missionary work with all the zeal and strength of faith that characterized the life and labors of Mr. and Mrs. Judson. And their faith did not fail. Deprivations, sickness, and sorrows such as but few mortals know were not strangers to them. Mr. McCoy rode hundreds of miles through the wilderness, and swam the swollen streams, lying on the wet ground at night, for the sake of carrying forward his mission. He went on horseback to Washington several times to interest Congress in

7

measures beneficial to the Indian. Many months would be occupied in these journeys. One of the severest trials that Mr. McCoy was called to bear was that during his absence from home sickness and sometimes death would visit his family. Five of his children were called by death at different times while he was absent from home. Persons of narrow selfish views would readily call him cruel and indifferent, but men who could rise to his plane of devotion to the work that he believed God had given him can see that his loyalty to the Master was superior even to parental affection. No man loved his wife and children more than he.

Cathcart's Baptist
Encyclopedia

To alleviate their (the Indians') despair, God sent Isaac McCoy as His representative and their minister – a genuine friend in need. His sagacious analysis of the Indians produced a heartfelt concern that changed the entire life of Isaac McCoy. He determined to use his influence to civilize them. The Indians responded to the love of God made known to them by McCoy, and, in turn, loved, trusted, and had implicit confidence in their newly found friend, many even accepting the Christ he had revealed to them. An Indian, Quick, said they never had been treated with so much kindness. Many times tribes sent 'our friend McCoy' in their behalf to accompany letters and to intercede for them. McCoy was completely devoted to the task of Indian improvement, both temporal and spiritual.

Edward Roustio

He founded the missions among the Miamis, Ottawas and Potawatomis in Indiana and southern Michigan, drawing about himself a band of young workers, among whom were Johnston Lykins, Jotham Meeker and Robert Simerwell, who, inspired by their leader, devoted their whole lives to the cause of Indian reform, and afterwards formed the nucleus of the Baptist missionaries in Kansas.

McCoy's activities were by no means confined to the work of teaching. In 1823 he conceived the scheme of setting aside a large tract of land in the West, to which all the Indians of the United States should eventually be removed. This he thought to be the only way of saving them from destruction. Here, away from the baleful contact of white men, they could be raised to civilization. He had in mind a federation of all the tribes of the territory, and finally the formation of an Indian state.

It was not the scheme of a dreamer; it was formulated by one who knew the Indian character as scarcely any other person ever has, and it became his life work. Never once, to the day of his death, did he lose sight of his one great object— to civilize and Christianize the Indians. To this he devoted himself, unconditionally, all that he had — family, property and friends. Space forbids telling of his almost superhuman efforts to bring about success; of his oft-repeated trips to Washington and other cities of the East, through the wilderness in the dead of winter; of his frequent addresses in all parts of the country; of his lobbying at Washington. Suffice it to say, he won the support of John C. Calhoun, Secretary of War, and other influential men, members of both branches of Congress, and the result of his efforts was the act of May 26, 1830, providing for the removal of the Indians to the West.

Earl Leon Shoup

Your protracted labors in the cause of the Aborigines of our country, entitle you to the thanks of the philanthropic and the good. If the founders of Empires deserve to be remembered, surely his work is not less honorable who has saved a nation from decay.

Albert S. White

I know not how it is, my brother, but the sentiment is deeply imprinted upon my heart, that while the Elliots and Brainards are remembered, the name of Isaac McCoy, the red-man's benefactor, will not be forgotten. Let us think of him in our daily orisons.

Spencer H. Cone

He left the world with his face toward the Indian country. His ruling idea was supreme in death. Risking above all ordinary considerations, this hero of the wilderness and the camp, not forgetting the object of his sufferings, nor ignoring the importance of that to which he had devoted his manhood and sacrificed his all, passed from this life to the next with this message on his lips: "Tell the brethren to never let the Indian mission decline."

Dr. Walter N. Wyeth

McCoy's Time-Line

1784: Born near Union Town, Fayette County in Pennsylvania.

1790: Moved to Jefferson County, Kentucky.

1792: Kentucky becomes a state within the Union.

1801: McCoy baptized.

1802: Massachusetts Baptist Missionary Society founded.

1803: Moved to Silver Creek, Clark County, Indiana. McCoy married to Christiana Polke.

1804: Moved to Vincennes. Mahale McCoy born.

1807: Rice McCoy born. McCoy put on probation as preacher.

1808: Josephus McCoy born. McCoy licensed as preacher. Pastors Maria Creek church and some four others which he established.

1809: Delilah McCoy born.

1810: Ordained as minister by George Waller and William McCoy.

1811: John Calvin McCoy born.

1812: War with Britain and various Indian tribes.

1813: Elizabeth McCoy born. The Philadelphia Baptist Association calls a nation wide missionary convention for the following May.

1814: First Baptist General Convention.

1815: Sarah McCoy born.

1816: Appointed Association missionary to the Western Frontier. Indiana becomes a state within the Union.

1817: The McCoys thirteen-year old daughter Mahale dies. Second Triennial Baptist Convention, McCoy applies in March for missionary status to Indians. Accepted for one year. Mississippi becomes a state within the Union.

1818: McCoy sets up a mission station at Raccoon Creek working among the Weas, Kickapoos, Potawatomis and Delawares. Contacts Federal Government concerning his plans for Indian missions.

1819: Baptist Board encourage McCoy to continue under their patronage but without any formal contract. Corbly Martin employed as teacher and is converted under McCoy's ministry. Nancy Judson McCoy born.

1820: Johnston Lykins joins McCoy as teacher to replace Martin now an Ohio pastor. Establishes Fort Wayne Mission. First baptisms. Samuel Hill sent by Board to assist McCoy but he soon gives up the strenuous work.

1821: Eleanor McCoy born. Baptist Board formally resolves to

support Fort Wayne Mission to the Indians. The resolutions were only kept very sporadically. Financial aid granted the mission by Governor Cass of Detroit. Treaty of Chicago held in which McCoy was a major influence. The doors open for a work among the Potawatomis and Ottawas. Fort Wayne inspected by a Government Commission and receives strong praise. Missouri becomes a state within the Union.

1822: McCoy visits the Board at Philadelphia.

1822: Death of Elizabeth McCoy caused by an Indian attacker. A new missionary, Peter Clyde, gives up after only a few months work. Sears appointed as missionary and Jackson as blacksmith. Carey Mission founded. The mission's *Family Rules* compiled. Treaty of Chicago ratified and the mission promised large Government grants. McCoy asks for the Board to administer them. Johnston Lykins professes faith in Christ and is baptized. Daniel Dusenbury becomes a missionary. The Fort Wayne Church constituted and Articles of Faith drawn up.

1823: Maria Staughton McCoy born. Sears gives up missionary work and strongly criticizes the mission, especially the educational work, before the Board who give McCoy their full support. A work started among the Ottawas at Thomas. McCoy develops his plans for the Indian Territory. Members of the Government consider them and the Board forms a committee to study them. Keating reports favorably on the Baptist Indian Mission in his book on Major Long's expedition.

1824: Calhoun creates Indian Department within Secretaryship of War. McCoy again visits the Board and receives support in canvassing money and supplies for the Indian mission. War Secretary Calhoun accepts McCoy's plans for an Indian homeland. Sears tries in vain to stir up trouble between McCoy and Lykins. William Polke joins the mission but then gives up after a few months because of the hardships. Maria Staughton McCoy dies at the age of eleven months.

1825: Isaac McCoy born. Numerous conversions at Carey and Thomas. New missionaries Simerwell and Goodridge marry. The President makes McCoy's plans for the Indians Government policy.

1826: Columbian College run by the Baptist Board refuses to take in Indian scholars due to new policies with a newly elected leadership now situated in Boston. The Board supports non-Baptist Indian schools to the neglect of their own. The new leadership declares itself against higher education for the

Indians and refuses to educate missionary children free. Rice and Josephus leave Columbian College to study in Lexington. Nevertheless, the Board supports McCoy in resettling the Indians in the Indian Territory. Meeker, Crosley, the Slaters and Miss Purchase become missionaries to the Indians. Crosley backs out quickly.

1827: The new Board reject the *Family Rules*. They object to McCoy's plans to have Indians trained as doctors. Two of McCoy's scholars now study Medicine in Vermont at no expense to the Board. The Board does not meet its financial commitments. McCoy now works closely with the Government in drawing up treaties with the Indians. Slater complains that his fellow missionaries are too indulgent with the Indians. The Board believes that it should be relieved of all expenses concerning the Indian mission.

1828: Charles McCoy born. McLean puts forward a Bill to be enacted by the Senate and House of Representatives for financing the Indian colonization of land west of the Mississippi. The Board authorize McCoy to make a tour of the Indian Territory with a view to Indian removal. The Department of War elect McCoy as a Commissioner and Treasurer of an expedition to the Indian Territory with a view to relocating the Indians. A new station opened at Sault de St. Marie. Treaty with the Potawatomis held on Carey premises. McCoy's *Remarks on the Practicability of Indian Reform* published.

1829: McCoy reports to the Federal Government and the Board on his Indian Territory expedition. *Remarks on the Practicability of Indian Reform* goes into a second edition. A motion is put forward at the Triennial Convention declaring Indian missions impractical. McCoy succeeds in turning opinion towards Indian reform and gains the Board's full backing which they confirm in writing to President Jackson. McCoy's second tour of the Indian Territory. Rice and Josephus qualify as doctors from Transylvania University.

1830: Death of Dr. Josephus McCoy. Indian Bill for the colonization of the Indian Territories by the Indians passed. McCoy rejects high honors and Government appointments so that he can remain a missionary. McCoy seriously injured in a coach accident. McCoy, Lykins, Meeker and Simerwell discuss resigning from the Board's patronage. The Board ally with Presbyterian policies rather than with their own Baptists' opinions regarding the Indians.

1831: Charles McCoy dies. Another infant son, still unnamed, dies after living only five hours. McCoy and Lykins begin moving the Indians to the Indian Territory. The Board refuses to meet their promised commitments. Lykins must finance the first missionary station from his own pocket.

1832: Dr. Rice McCoy dies. First Baptist church in present day Oklahoma constituted by Isaac McCoy with Creek Indian John Davis as pastor.

1833: Slanderous opposition from the Roman Catholics. A Board report in the *Baptist Magazine* claims that McCoy 'is not in the service of the Board.' This is quickly rectified. Bolles, however, wishes to sever connections with McCoy but comes to respect McCoy as a missionary. Carey Mission moves to the Indian Territory. The Mormons begin to lay claims on part of the Indian Territory and gather on the border for entry and settlement.

1834: McCoy's mother Elizabeth and his brother Rice die. McCoy again in Washington. Meeker sets up a printing press in the Indian Territory. The Board rejects McCoy's plans to employ Indian teachers to instruct their own people in reading and writing their mother tongues. Rollin, Miss Rice, Miss Colborn and Bingham appointed missionaries.

1835: McCoy's first *Annual Register of Indian Affairs* is published on January 1st. The McCoys' daughter Sarah Givens dies. The Board refuses to allow the Indian Mission to appeal directly to the Baptist public for support.

1836: McCoy gains Government interest in plans for employing Indian teachers but is again opposed by the Board. Plans his *Indian Advocate* but cannot yet find a printer. The Cherokees begin to move to the Indian Territory but McCoy's colleague Evan Jones is against the move.

1837: The McCoys' daughter Christiana dies. McCoy becomes seriously ill. Publishes his *Periodical Account of Baptist Missions in the Indian Territory for the Year Ending December 31, 1836*. Meeker leaves Shawnee to work with the Ottawas and is replaced as printer by J. G. Pratt. Henry Skigget, an Indian, is appointed a missionary at McCoy's request but dismissed after a year by the Board though his work was very successful. Michigan becomes a state within the Union.

1838: McCoy appointed by the Government to visit the southern tribes and inform them of Bills before both Houses calling for their resettlement in the Indian Territory. McCoy is appointed by the Government to supervise their grants for Indian Improvement but the Baptist Board refuse to cooperate in revealing the amounts of money they receive from the Government. They are now suspected of misusing the money.

1839: The McCoys' daughter Eleanor dies. Missionary Rollin dies of tuberculosis.

1840: McCoy publishes his major work, *History of Baptist Indian Missions*.

1842: New Corresponding Secretary Solomon Peck informs McCoy that he is no longer a missionary. The Board now appoint a known adulterer with a criminal record as missionary and pastor of a separatist church in spite of massive protests from the older missionaries and the Indians. The Board force Lykins to resign by removing his missionary status and siding with the guilty party. The Board systematically close down their Indian work, supporting only a few younger missionaries, including the adulterer, who strive to increase membership by accepting known fornicators, drunkards etc. as members. They then merge their now very sporadic work with the Methodists. Sadly, Meeker supports these separatists. The Board inform the Government that McCoy is not in their employ so the Department of War give him no new commissions. Christian Indian chiefs and church leaders protest to the Board.

1843: The Western and Southern Baptist churches protest against the Board's policies and campaign for a new Indian Mission, inviting McCoy to become its Corresponding Secretary. The American Indian Mission Association(A.I.M.A.) is formed. Friends of McCoy's still on the Board strive to promote a union. Johnston Lykins, David Lykins, Simerwell and their wives, Skigget and eventually Pratt join the new mission with the McCoys. Former Board missionaries such as Posey and J. M. Peck now support the new mission. Other Indian missionaries cooperate with the exception of those mixed up in the adultery affair and Meeker who had obviously defended the offenders without knowing the true facts. A. I. M. A. missionaries are called and financed by their own churches. The main thrust of the mission is among the Weas, Potawatomis, Creeks and Choctaws. Now Stockbridge, Delaware, Potawatomi and Shawnee Indians whose churches had disintegrated through the Board's neglect, reconstitute themselves.

1844: The McCoy's daughter Delilah Lykins dies. Though often ill and feeble in body, McCoy travels thousands of miles canvassing for support and interviewing missionary candidates and agents.

1845: A council of Baptist churches denounces the missionaries involved in the separatist church and adultery scandal and exonerate Lykins, McCoy and Simerwell. The Baptist Board of Foreign Missions censored for appointing a man known to be immoral as a pastor and missionary. Meeker removes the Potawatomi Church Book with its account of affairs up to date. The new work prospers. Hundreds of conversions through the work of the A.I.M.A. among the Creeks and Choctaws, especially in the North Fork church in present day Oklahoma. The A.I.M.A. is represented by several Board members at the founding of the Southern Baptist Convention.

1846: McCoy becomes ill on a preaching journey and dies after a three-weeks' illness with the words, "Tell the brethren to never let the Indian mission decline" on his lips. He had lived sixty-two years.

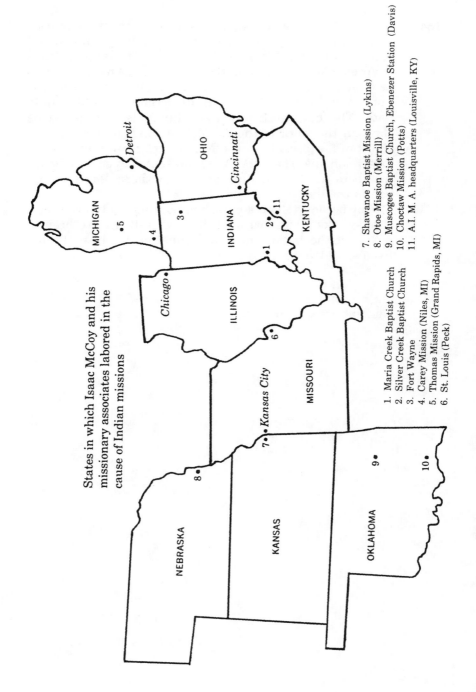

States in which Isaac McCoy and his missionary associates labored in the cause of Indian missions

1. Maria Creek Baptist Church
2. Silver Creek Baptist Church
3. Fort Wayne
4. Carey Mission (Niles, MI)
5. Thomas Mission (Grand Rapids, MI)
6. St. Louis (Peck)
7. Shawanoe Baptist Mission (Lykins)
8. Otoe Mission (Merrill)
9. Muscogee Baptist Church, Ebenezer Station (Davis)
10. Choctaw Mission (Potts)
11. A.I. M. A. headquarters (Louisville, KY)

Preface
The Search for a New Canaan

A story of unique significance

The story unfolded in these pages is of unique significance in the history of the United States of America. It is the tale of a man who was used by God to preserve the Indian Nations from certain extinction. It is the account of the opening of the Louisiana Purchase to colonization and the founding and settlement of Arkansas,[1] Kansas,[2] Nebraska,[3] and Oklahoma[4] which were to become bright luminaries in the star-spangled banner of the nation which has become the envy of the world. It is also the story of the founding of many great American towns and cities such as Kansas City, Grand Rapids, Chicago,[5] Niles and Paola which were built on former Indian mission sites and preaching stations. Above all, it is the history of how the West was won, not so much by the efforts of countless politicians, honorable as many of their efforts were, nor through the adventures of pistol-packing white pioneers who came much later. It is the history of a band of Baptist missionaries and their Indian friends who saw the writing on the wall in the northern, eastern and southern states and received the call to find a new Canaan where righteousness and peace could live side by side and where politics and social fair-play could be built on the Christian gospel.

---

[1] Received statehood June 15, 1836.

[2] Received statehood January 29, 1861.

[3] Received statehood March 1, 1867.

[4] Received statehood November 16, 1907.

[5] McCoy preached first sermon ever to a few believers who lived in a small collection of huts that developed into the town of Chicago.

17

White ownership initially through conquest, not purchase

On the whole, the European colonists to the New World, paid scant attention to the rights of the earlier settlers who had crossed the Bering Straits, split into many tribes and spread out over the vast stretches of North America. The Indians, as Europeans wrongly called these peoples, were thought to be dying pagan races and their lands free for the taking. It is true that a few lovers of every man's liberty such as Roger Williams (1600-1683) protested that no one had a right to take over Indian territory without permission from the Indians themselves and land must be bought honestly. Such protests earned the scorn of most of the European settlers and those who spoke in this way were quickly out-voiced and even punished. Williams was banished from the colony of Massachusetts for challenging the warped one-sided view of liberty adopted by the colonialists.

Initially, however, the Indians had shown great kindness to the European settlers and had given them the land they asked for. It was when land was taken from the Indians without their permission and by force that the trouble began. It was trouble caused entirely by the Europeans. After Independence from Britain, treaty after treaty was made with the Indians who were always "solemnly guaranteed" that no more inroads into their territories would be made. In spite of numerous such promises the Native Americans were cheated, robbed and murdered on a scale hitherto scarcely paralleled in the history of mankind. The whites' mentality was governed by the political philosophy of Europe which said lands can only be gained by purchase or conquest. As the Europeans argued that the Indians were not technically nations and thus could have no land rights to sell, they deduced that Indian territories might legally be gained by conquest. As a result, the Indians lost territory after territory to the whites who were governed by this rule of conquest. The new rulers allowed the former inhabitants none of the rights which they claimed for themselves. Even the right of citizenship in their former country was refused the Indians who were now unwanted foreigners on their own soil.

One of America's greatest heroes remains unknown

Isaac McCoy, the man who, to a great extent, put a stop to this inhuman practice, is still virtually unknown among American citizens and hardly ever mentioned in the history of missions. One looks in vain through the pages of Leonard's recent work, *Dictionary of Baptists in America* to find any mention of McCoy's name. This is more surprising as Leonard's work is obviously written from the point of view of a Southern Baptist and McCoy was present at the first Southern Baptist Convention and his work was eventually absorbed by that Convention. Other founding members of the SBC such as Humphrey Posey were members of the Board of Managers in McCoy's American Indian Missionary Association[6] and officially represented the Mission in the founding Conventions. Senator Wilson Lumpkin, ex-Governor of Georgia, one of the leading SBC founders, was an enthusiastic supporter of McCoy's work. Robert G. Gardner, in his history of the formation of the Southern Baptist Convention, shows how McCoy and his A. I. M. A. played a fundamental role in the early organization of the Convention.[7]

The Baptist Board of Foreign Missions plays down McCoy's important role

One of the first attempts to analyze McCoy's work as a missionary was drawn up under the superintendence of Solomon Peck in 1839 and published the following year.[8] Peck was at that time Foreign Secretary to the Baptist Board of Foreign Missions in whose services Isaac McCoy was employed. Peck traces McCoy's missionary activities up to 1827, always keeping a distance from him and stressing McCoy's cooperation with the Government, apparently not realizing that this connection was of a temporary, sporadic nature and, when it occurred, was under the strict authorization and command of the Baptist Board of Foreign Missions. Indeed, Peck is so totally unaware that McCoy is one of his own Board's missionaries

---

[6] Otherwise known as the A.I.M.A.

[7] Robert G. Gardner quotes McCoy as saying of the Convention, "We assembled with good feelings - we parted with better." *A Decade of Debate and Division*, p. 43. See also pp. 2-3, 20, 26, 29, 36, 37, 39-40, 42, 56-57.

[8] See *History of American Missions to the Heathen*, pp. 353-620.

that he even emphasizes that McCoy has no formal connection with the Board whatsoever though they admire his engagements on behalf of the Indians. All McCoy's great church planting activities, the tremendous work McCoy did for the Indian Mission in fund raising, public relations, recruitment of missionaries and endeavors to promote their spiritual and material state are not even hinted at after 1827. McCoy's great preaching and teaching ministry from 1827 to 1846 are left unrecorded and all McCoy's writings are commented on as if they were mere secular documents.

Indeed, McCoy's story exemplifies the fact that a prophet is never recognized in his own country. Thus an official history of the Baptist Indian Missions, prepared for the American Baptist Missionary Union, the successors of the Baptist Board of Foreign Missions, in 1849 by William Gammell,[9] less than three years after McCoy's death, also glosses over much of McCoy's work, ignoring the pioneer position he maintained, and attributing much of his accomplishments in the Lord's service, as, for instance, the founding of the first Baptist church in present day Oklahoma, to others who played far more subordinate roles.[10] The author erroneously believes that McCoy terminated his connection with the Board in 1830 by taking up an appointment under the Government's Department of Indian Affairs. The records, however, show clearly that McCoy was authorized to take this step by the Board so that they could profit from Government grants to finance the missions which McCoy superintended. Though an article in the June, 1833 edition of the *American Baptist Magazine* mentioned erroneously that McCoy was no longer under the patronage of the Board, this error was corrected in the following issue.

Gammell's acceptance of this wrong statement, however, leads him to ignore McCoy's major work between 1830 and 1846 and even gives the impression that others undertook it. Strangely enough, in the various lists and charts of missionaries to the Indians

---

[9] *History of American Baptist Missions.*

[10] The founding of Ebenezer Baptist Church is attributed to David Lewis with no mention of Isaac McCoy who constituted the church and moved the Board of Foreign Missions to appoint John Davis, a Creek Indian, as pastor. McCoy was instrumental in appointing Lewis as teacher at the mission's school. Lewis neither founded the church, nor pastored it and soon left the area in disgrace. Yet "official records" give Lewis as the founder and pastor of the church and call Davis his "native assistant." This matter will be dealt with in full as McCoy's story proceeds.

past and present appended to Gammell's work, neither McCoy's name is mentioned, nor that of his fellow pioneer laborer and son-in-law Johnston Lykins. The latter's name is mentioned but twice, almost by the way, in a twenty-three page account of a work in which he played a major part. Also, in an effort to show that everything in the Board's garden was lovely, Gammell does not reveal the tremendous suffering Evan Jones, Isaac McCoy and Johnston Lykins and their fellow missionaries had to undergo because of the mismanagement and intrigues within the Baptist Board. Likewise, missionaries appointed by the Board against the advice of the missionary family and who proved a great embarrassment to the Board, and hindered the work of the Indian mission, are also not mentioned. As these events were obviously major factors in putting an almost total stop to the American Baptist Board of Foreign Missions' work among the Indians, they must be seen as an essential feature of the Board's history and one of the major influences leading to the Board's bankruptcy and end. It is as if Gammell is carefully thwarting criticism from any side. Yet a history of missions is best written when its readers are allowed to make judgements for themselves. When mistakes are plainly shown to have occurred, future workers in God's vineyard are given the opportunity to learn from former follies and thus become better equipped as ambassadors for Christ. Skeletons in closets[11] are of no use to anyone.

Sometimes the omission of McCoy's name when portraying scenes in which he was obviously the driving force is most difficult to comprehend and one seeks in vain for a reason behind this silence. McCoy was one of the earliest campaigners for home Baptist missions, and Charles White in his *Century of Faith* argues conclusively that McCoy, along with Moses Merrill, was instrumental in founding the Baptist Home Mission. Yet, when Sidney Dyer, McCoy's successor as Corresponding Secretary of the A. I. M. A., composed the Home Mission's Jubilee Poem of 1882 to commemorate, among other things, the Baptists' work among the Indians, McCoy's name is conspicuous by its absence. On the other hand, Cone, Colgate, Going, Hill and Lincoln's names are mentioned in conjunction with the evangelizing of the Indians. Excellent as these men were in supporting an interest in Indian home missions, their work was chiefly done from the comfort of their New York and New England

---

[11] English: "Skeletons in cupboards." This is one of the few expressions which leads linguists to say jokingly that England and America are two countries separated by the same language.

homes, whereas the men and women at the front are left totally out of Dyer's poetic picture.[12]

Reasons for the neglect in recording McCoy's life and work

After McCoy's death, his family, missionary associates and friends decided that his work had been of such great importance that it was essential to the history of missions and to the personal testimony of McCoy that his biography should be written by an able man. To this end, the wider family, including the Lykins, collected together all McCoy's publications, sermons, lectures, missionary reports and private letters with the aim of placing them into the hands of a worthy biographer. On January 27, 1847, Johnston Lykins wrote to Spencer H. Cone, a close friend of McCoy's and a member both of the Baptist Board of Foreign Missions and the Board of Home Missions, seeking advice on the matter.[13] Cone, however, was now an old man, over-burdened with much work. It was also a very difficult time for the Baptist churches who were splitting up over the question of missions and slavery. Cone, a New Yorker, was in an anti-slavery area and his Board, based at Boston, had taken a mitigated anti-slavery stand. It was, however, their lack of interest in evangelizing the Indians which had compelled McCoy in 1842 to start up a new work. Ironically enough, the Board, though, on the whole, against slavery, had maintained their Cherokee missions, though the Cherokees were the largest slave-owners among all the Indian tribes. McCoy had never really taken sides on the question of slavery among the Indians as he argued that he was called to evangelize and civilize *the Indians*, so he must accept them as they were. He believed that when, with proper training, the converted Indians were able to play a leading role in Indian affairs, they would be able to tackle the problem of slavery themselves. Indeed, they did so in a manner far superior to the way the whites eventually solved the problem as will be explained later in this book. In 1820, however, McCoy joined an organization for repatriating freed African slaves back to Africa and took on a Negro student with the aim of preparing him for such a future. He also supported schemes whereby slaves were able to purchase their freedom. Nevertheless, McCoy, soon

---

[12] See *Patria Nostra Christo*, Baptist Home Missions in America, p. 280.

[13] McCoy Papers, Reel 11.

came to be branded by Northerners as a pro-slavery Baptist and a Southerner at heart. Thus no sympathetic biography could be expected from the Northerners and New Englanders under whose patronage McCoy had formerly worked.

In 1846, the year of McCoy's death, the American Baptist Board of Foreign Missions ceased to exist as a pan-American Baptist missionary organization. They reconstituted themselves as the American Baptist Missionary Union, representing the Northern and Eastern states only. However, the new Board gave the reason for the old Board's demise and especially their lack of interest in the Indians, plus the fact that they were over $40,000 in debt, as being the slavery issue alone. Southern states such as Alabama, they pointed out, had withdrawn their subscription and so the Baptist Board of Foreign Missions could not continue.[14] The Board, however, had begun to neglect their Indian missions a full decade before Alabama's protest at the Board's new politics and, as this study will show, the mismanagement of funds by the Baptist Board had nothing whatsoever to do with the slavery question. William Gammell, speaking on behalf of the new American Baptist Missionary Union and the one chosen as the organization's apologist, showed clearly that the new organization was to carry on the anti-Indian missions policy of their predecessors. Writing concerning the Missionary Union's lack of interest in the Indians, Gammell, explains that it is the unknown "distant shores of ancient heathenism" that attracts their main attention. He then comes nearer to the true reason for neglecting the Indians by saying, "This want of interest must also be ascribed to the particular barbarism of the Indians and their hopeless destiny as a people." Here again, were the very elements in the old Board's thinking against which McCoy had fought. He showed how the Indians were not more barbaric than foreign heathen and, indeed, they were more susceptible than other heathen to the gospel because of their lack of strong pagan religious structures which hindered their overseas counterparts in understanding the gospel. McCoy also argued that the Indians were only perishing because the whites were doing nothing to save them and, indeed, the whites were the very cause of their being degraded as a people. Gammell, however, as the spokesman of the new Baptist missionary organization, goes on to argue that the Indians "can never have a place among the nations of the earth," and that "the

---

[14] See Gammell's most one-sided account of the financial embarrassment of the old Board in his *History of American Baptist Missions*, p. 173 ff.

23

future opens before them no prospect of advancement - no hopes of ultimate greatness and power. It reveals to them only a descending pathway of decline and diminution, terminating at last in their utter extinction as a race."[15] It was such thinking in the old Baptist Board which caused McCoy to found the American Indian Mission Association. It might be considered an irony of history by some, but certainly the hand of God at work by others, that several years after McCoy's decease, his Indian mission was taken over by the Southern Baptists from whom the Baptist Missionary Union had separated themselves on the ground that they and not the Baptist Board of Foreign Missions, were racists.

Meanwhile, interest in Indian missions in general was at a very low ebb in the United States. Events which divided the Baptist churches also divided the Union politically and the country was about to enter into a bloody war in which brother was to fight against brother and matters concerning missionary biographies became questions of most subordinate importance. As a result, no Baptist was found in the antebellum period who had the ability and calling to record the life and works of Isaac McCoy for the public reader. Nor was anyone found in the period marred by the Civil War.

A Presbyterian looks at McCoy

William B. Sprague, the Presbyterian writer, began collecting material for his sixth volume of the *Annals of the American Pulpit* biographies around 1858 and completed the work in 1865, entitling it plainly and simply *Baptists*. Sprague's biography of McCoy leans heavily on the testimonies of those who knew McCoy personally and were in deep fellowship with him but also, for the sake of balance, those who were not always one mind with the missionary. The result is a fine all-round, objective view of McCoy which, nevertheless, reveals the author's deep admiration for the man and includes many a detail which had been missing from former commentators' works. Sprague must not have been widely read, however, by subsequent Baptist students of McCoy and his times since these details concerning his family, his childhood and his in-laws are not found in their later works.

Sprague includes the testimony of Joseph Chambers, a life-long friend of McCoy's and one who was baptized by him. Chambers

---

[15] *History of American Baptist Missions*, p. 342.

24

explains how McCoy came to be a "sensible, earnest, convincing" preacher who was "thoroughly Calvinistic" in his doctrine. Most interesting is the addition by Sprague of an account by Dr. Rufus Babcock, dated October 7, 1858. Babcock was on the committee governing the Carey Mission along with Dr. Cone and Dr. Wayland, but he differed from his colleagues at first in not sharing their almost boundless enthusiasm for McCoy's work. Nevertheless, Babcock was an honest and upright man and, after relating how the Board thought that McCoy put them in a bad light by his appealing for funds to the general Baptist public, so they grew to mistrust him,[16] he continues:

> In the endeavor to adjust these various difficulties, an excellent opportunity was afforded for learning McCoy's true character. Gradually but surely he rose in the esteem of us all, the various cross-examinations to which he was subjected, serving to bring out various good qualities, which would have otherwise been unknown, at least to us. How yearning his love for the mission family, - both the red and the pale faces; and what heroic toils and sacrifices he had been willing to submit to on their account! Subsequently, and in other places and relations, I heard him plead the cause of Christian Missions for our native tribes. Soon, too, we began a correspondence, which helped to ripen this acquaintance into a friendship which continued unabated till the close of his life.[17]

Baptists pay tribute to McCoy much later

In 1880, the Carey Mission which McCoy had founded, celebrated its fifty years' anniversary and Dr. Gilbert S. Bailey was asked to preach a sermon on the occasion by the St. Joseph River Baptist Association. The text he chose was Acts 11:4, "Peter rehearsed the matter from the beginning." Bailey did not preach a usual sermon but took the text to outline McCoy's life and works at Carey in a talk which covered 16 pages in its printed version. The account is not only most sympathetic in portraying McCoy's spiritual

---

[16] The Board had insisted that all funds should be sent to them to be used at their discretion.

[17] *Baptists*, p. 546.

achievements but also gives McCoy due credit for laying the foundations of political, social and economic freedom for future Indians.

It was not until 1895 that a full-length biography of McCoy was published. This was by the able and sympathetic hand of Dr. Walter Wyeth who designed his work as a tribute to both Isaac and his wife Christiana. Wyeth, however, could find no publisher for his work and founded his own publishing house to produce his writings on the "Judson of the West," as he called McCoy and other "Missionary Memorials," the name he gave to the series. Wyeth took up his pen to record McCoy's life, believing that, "Mr. McCoy's valorous doing for the Red Man must rank among the most heroic endeavors in our modern church activities, and the story of it will engage the attention and touch the heart of both old and young."[18] Wyeth had certainly a missionary calling in writing the book as he obviously wishes his readers to not only accept his story of one of the greatest missionaries of all time but to accept that missionary's Savior. Valuable and good as this book is, however, there is very much that is left out which is necessary to be known in order to fully understand the greatness of McCoy's. Wyeth, in his gracious way of writing, has toned down many a difficulty which faced McCoy. In particular, he glosses over the acute trouble McCoy had with a Missionary Board whose heart was almost closed to the needs of the American Indians. The Board, unlike McCoy who felt that charity must begin at home, felt that "missionary work" must begin abroad among the Asian Indians. Wyeth's account emphasizes the spiritual side of McCoy's work but does not equally stress the blood, sweat and tears and the sheer dirt and despair of life among the Indians of that time which called out that spirituality, with which McCoy was divinely gifted, to deal with what often appeared to be a hopeless situation. Nor does Wyeth deal adequately with the trials, rivalries and frustration which inevitably occur when a few whites are isolated from their accustomed culture and live together for years in cramped quarters, in inclement weather, often sick with fever and with little to eat and no decent clothes to wear. After saying this, however, this present writer must pronounce Wyeth's work to be the best of any work ever written on McCoy and it well deserves to be placed in the hand of any Christian who wishes to know how God works in fitting His people out for the task of obeying His Great Commission.

---

[18] Prefatory Note to *Isaac McCoy: Early Indian Missions, Isaac McCoy - Christiana McCoy.*

Twentieth Century estimates of McCoy and his work

During the twentieth century, there have been a number of short McCoy biographies such as W. S. Stewart's chapter entitled *Isaac McCoy* in his *Early Baptist Missionaries and Pioneers* written in 1925 and published by the Judson Press of Philadelphia. Stewart's 30 pages on McCoy are introduced with a most helpful time-line of his subject's life and, in a fine narrative style, depicts the main features of McCoy's life and calling. Stewart sees the benefit of recording the things that apparently often went wrong in the life of a missionary and does not neglect to describe the enormous financial difficulties the missionaries often experienced. Stewart also shows how that McCoy selflessly gave all the income he had through Government wages towards the work of the mission and indeed, became its main supplier of funds when the Board's purse was empty, or, more often, shut. As is fitting, Stewart sees the crowning importance of McCoy's work in his dream for a Canaan for the Indians being eventually turned into a United States law.

Another short, sympathetic essay on McCoy is to be found in John Cady's *The Origin and Development of the Missionary Baptist Church in Indiana* published by Franklin College in 1942. This work is important for showing how McCoy, who was a "thorough-going Calvinist,"[19] believed it to be every Christian's bounden duty to evangelize the unconverted. Cady also looks at the terrible anti-evangelistic, pseudo-Calvinism of the anti-missions lobby of McCoy's day. Then, highly influential agitators such as Daniel Parker (1781-1844) were arguing that missionaries were supplanting God's sovereign work by "human instrumentalities" and agency. If they had emphasized God's sovereignty in preaching the gospel, all might have been well, but these men, with their dualistic "Two Seed" theories which looked upon the devil and his seed as being virtually co-powerful with God, preached a Gnostic gospel in total opposition to the Biblical doctrines of grace in general and the doctrines of creation and rebirth in particular. Dr. William Cathcart sums up Parker and his Parkerism as:

> *The Man.*- Reared on the frontiers of Georgia, 'he was without education, uncouth in manners, slovenly in dress, diminutive in person, and unprepossessing in appear-

---

[19] p. 40.

ance.' His enthusiasm bordered on insanity.[20] In 1819 he came into Indiana from his home in Illinois, and at once began to attract attention. He opposed missions, education and Sunday schools.

The Motive, - He sought notoriety as a writer, and was anxious to use the columns of the *Columbian Star*, published in Washington City. His articles were rejected. In his revenge he attacked not only the paper, but all it advocated, such as missions, education, etc.

The Effect, - Scores of churches and hundreds of members were drawn away after him. And they went so far as to pass resolutions denouncing missions etc. But finally those churches died as a proper result of their heinous heresy. Parker was excluded from his own church.[21]

The effect of Parkerism on missionary evangelism

Parker's fantasies, viewed as positively as possible, have served to challenge the outward-going efforts of the early Particular-Regular Baptists who believed in preaching the full gospel of God's sovereign grace to the whole man, wherever the Spirit sent them. Seen as an alternative to such a Biblical stance, Parkerism merely served to show what depths of scurrility and warped imagination the Baptists could fall into when they left that gospel pattern. It showed the truth of Paul's words in 1 Corinthians 9:16, "Woe is unto me if I preach not the gospel." Parker's views against the dangers of parachurch organizations who set themselves up as denominational standards and dictators, are, however, worthy of note and a most positive warning to modern Baptists who seem all too eager to give up the administration of their churches to umbrella organizations and institutions, even to the extent of allowing them to elect their pastors for them and determine how they should use church funds. Sadly, however, Parkerism became little more than a parachurch movement itself with Daniel Parker as its uncompromising Managing Director. One of Parker's major errors was his inability to view the work of individual missionaries such as Isaac McCoy and John Mason Peck apart from the organizations with which they were associated. He just could not recognize the good work they were

---

[20] This might be considered and unkind reference but Parker boasted widely of his ignorance as if he considered it a profound Christian virtue.

[21] "Parkerism in Indiana," *Baptist Encyclopedia*, Vol. 2, p. 882.

doing, often in spite of their affiliations. This caused him to lose the distinction between true evangelistic work on the gospel front and the administrative New England committees of well-meaning but often incompetent administrators. Seen in its full negative darkness, however, Parkerism truly marred the work of the gospel on the Western frontier and in Texas and equally marred the reputation of orthodox Baptists in the eyes of other denominations who were shocked at such anti-evangelical stubbornness. Even today, among certain evangelical, non-Baptist denominations, when they think of the Baptists, they think of hardshell Parkerism which shuts them out of any positive influence those Baptists who preach the doctrines of grace could have on them. This writer, therefore, fully agrees with the conclusion of Byron Cecil Lambert in his excellent, balanced analysis of Parkerism when he says:

> As it was said of an earlier wanderer by the name of Ishmael, Parker became a wild man; his hand was against every man, and every man's hand against him; and he dwelt in the wilderness and became an archer.[22]

Rister ranks McCoy with Judson and Carey

The year 1944 saw the publication of Carl C. Rister's work entitled *Baptist Missions Among the American Indians* published by the Home Missions Board of the Southern Baptist Convention. Rister has some twenty-three pages on McCoy whom he sees as the first and most successful Baptist missionary to the Indians. Of his subject, Rister says, "Isaac McCoy ranks with Adoniram Judson and William Carey as one of the greatest American Baptist missionaries, if he were not one of the greatest missionaries of all time and of all nations."[23] Rister gives his readers insight into the many difficulties facing McCoy such as the Indians' addiction to strong drink, peddled illegally by the whites and the "bilious typhus fever'" which threatened to carry away the majority of the mission family at each fierce attack. He also succeeds in showing what labors and trials the missionaries had because of their isolation from the rest of the populated world, so that even the simplest errands for food and clothing necessitated hazardous journeys of hundreds of miles in

---

[22] Genesis 16:12; 21:20. *The Rise of the Anti-Mission Baptists*, p. 288.

[23] pp. 38-39.

most inclement weather. Rister sums up Isaac and Christiana McCoy's lives which were dedicated to the salvation of the Indians by saying:

> The most conspicuous monument to the memory of the McCoys was the marked advance in civilization and religion of those tribes whom they served. They had found the Indiana and Illinois Indians hedged in on every side by land-hungry whites and designing whiskey peddlers. Indian villages reeked in filth and squalor, and their inhabitants were despondent, debauched, and starving without hope of a better day. McCoy and his wife first taught them that Christ was the light of the world; then they showed them how to spin, weave, sew, clear away fields and plant corn, and the many other things necessary to advance them on the road to civilization. Obviously, there was much back-sliding, much uncertainty, as the Indians moved forward. Sometimes the missionaries were so discouraged as to feel the utter hopelessness of success, but their Christian zeal, born of hope and faith, revived them and drove them on to final success.[24]

A most useful source of biographical information

One of the most exciting sources of biographical information concerning Isaac McCoy is a work produced in 1948 in memory of Isaac's brother John, where Isaac appears as a mere "also ran."[25] Nevertheless, the authoress, Elizabeth Hayward, a direct descendent of John McCoy, succeeds in giving a most accurate and sympathetic account of Isaac's work among the Indians and his elder brother's faithful support throughout the years. Hayward has done a tremendous amount of research into the McCoy family and also gives a large number of tiny pen-portraits of the friends and not so friendly opponents of the Indian Mission. The amazing work of the pioneer Baptists in the Western Valley is portrayed so vividly that no reader will be in any doubt in understanding why the Baptists became so numerous in the Western and Southern States. Here we see sturdy pioneer farming pastors who refused to accept a salary

---

[24] p. 59.

[25] *John M'Coy: His Life and His Diaries.*

from their churches, yet pastored a plurality of churches - sometimes four or five - and, though they worked hard to provide for their very large families, managed to lead many souls to Christ and take part in many benevolent organizations. Hayward has provided one of the few books I have ever read in which browsing through the footnotes alone has proved informative instruction and spiritual blessing and even a source of real entertainment.

Post-Graduate work on McCoy

There have been a number of post-graduate theses covering the early history of the Baptists in North America and several of these have dealt particularly with Indian evangelization and the work of Isaac McCoy. The one that has interested this present writer the most is Edward Roustio's fine work entitled *A History of the Life of Isaac McCoy in Relationship to Early Indian Migrations and Missions as Revealed in His Unpublished Manuscripts*. Roustio is the first writer to base his work on a thorough study of McCoy's private correspondence and that of his friends and associates. As a result, much information is given that had not appeared previously in works on McCoy and many questions raised in older works, but never answered, have been dealt with. Obviously, Baptist writers acting from a position within the Northern successors of the antebellum Baptist Board of Foreign Missions have been averse to openly revealing the circumstances which led to the Board's breaking with the very missionaries who had spent the best years of their lives under their patronage. Such a hanging out of dirty laundry[26] in public was an embarrassment to them. Understandable as this is, such delicacy has spoiled McCoy's reputation and given rise to many theories which were harmful to McCoy's cause and were wind in the sails of those who preached a cut-down gospel void of evangelistic and missionary outreach. Thus readers never knew why the work of the Boston Board among the Indians after 1837 was reduced from some ten tribes to but one and why Isaac McCoy was dismissed from his services as a missionary in 1842 after twenty-five years of useful work. Nor did they know why Johnston Lykins, after over twenty years of devoted service under the auspices of the Board, was forced to resign. Nor was any explanation given as to why a number of commercial enterprises which were financed by the Board failed,

---

[26] English: dirty washing.

leaving them in great debt and why money reserved for the Indian Mission was obviously used by the Board for other means. Roustio delves gently but firmly into these unsolved problems, vindicating McCoy entirely of any blame on his side for the Board's mismanagement and failure to deal with younger, ill-qualified, rebel missionaries appointed by the Board against the advice of experienced men and women already on the field. Above all, however, this academic work testifies firmly to the faith in Christ and His Great Commission which spurred McCoy on to do great things for God and for the Indians. Summing up McCoy's missionary work, Roustio says:

> Like Moses of old, McCoy was a meek man of humble spirit, mild of temper, long-suffering, and patient under injuries. In the correspondence with the Board about terminating his service, his concern was not for himself, but for the Indians, lest harm befall the work and it decline. He labored with unselfishness and heroism in order that Christ might increase. He did not seek great things for himself, but labored sacrificially that God's will and way might be done for the Indians. For all victories and all accomplishments, he was careful to give God all the glory. His ministry to the Indians was characterized by earnestness and sincerity. He was filled with compassion for them, and his heart was burdened for their lost souls, as he yearned for their salvation. Four months before his death, McCoy wrote Lykins of his burden:
> 'The devil and his emissaries seem determined to destroy the aborigines. O that I had the power, they should all have a quiet home - O that I had the means - they should all have the Gospel - Thank God there is power in heaven, and there too is the source of good will towards men.'[27]

A highly unbalanced assessment of McCoy's character and labors

Whereas older works were usually written in approval of McCoy's faith, more modern times have produced works in which their authors strive to be scholarly and objective but allow their own lack of understanding of the Christian mind and disinterest of religious topics to present a most one-sided picture of McCoy. The

---

[27] pp. 228-229. Quote from McCoy taken from a letter dated January 30, 1846, McCoy Papers, Reel 11.

result is neither scholarly nor objective. Symptomatic of such works which maintain that objective biographical criticism can only be carried out when the subject's faith is disregarded, is Robert F. Berkhofer's 1970 *Introduction* to a reprint of McCoy's *History of Baptist Indian Missions*. Berkhofer, writing for the Department of History, University of Wisconsin, shares the awe that anyone might display on reading how this uneducated, unpolished man of the Western frontier could persuade generations of governments and succeeding Secretaries of War and Presidents to follow his plans. His most unlikely interpretation of McCoy's aim in thus guiding the future of his nation is displayed in the opening words of his Introduction to McCoy's *magnum opus*:

> Few missionaries ever dreamed of a task so large or a position so powerful in American Indian affairs as did Isaac McCoy. He sought nothing less than a portion of the trans-Mississippi West as a permanent Indian state with himself as ruler. In his mind, the welfare of the Indians was intimately bound up with the propagation of the Baptist religion, the establishment of a new country for them, and his own advancement. Church, state, and self were fused into one grand plan for Indian salvation through colonization. To achieve his scheme, he used whatever means came to hand, whether it was his Baptist mission patrons, the political furor over Indian removal, or the establishment of a new missionary society. All of these activities were but successive steps to his ultimate aim of power over Indian affairs for their and his own good.[28]

Thus Berkhofer describes McCoy as ambitiously planning and plotting to rule over an area as large as the Union of his youth with himself as the Big Chief of all the sixty-odd tribes and bands he gathered there. This quite ludicrous interpretation has so gripped Berkhofer that he goes on to relate how everything that McCoy ever wrote was "naturally harnessed" to this goal. Yet for all his insistence that whatever McCoy did, it was for his own personal grandeur, Berkhofer still fails to explain how it was possible for such a lowly figure to actually reach so high and live to grasp his materialized dreams. Though Berkhofer claims he has received his superior insight into McCoy's true character by reading far wider

---

[28] Berkofer's Introduction to McCoy's *History of Baptist Indian Missions*, p. v.

than McCoy's *History of Baptist Indian Missions*, it is such a reading of all the thousands of McCoy's extant written records that has moved this present writer to view McCoy as the truly selfless, gracious, loving character he really was, whose one aim in life was that which he recorded in his dying words - the spiritual and material good of the Indians. McCoy's moving factor was simply that God had called him to do a special work and whom God calls, He equips.

Writing biographical background with little regard to the central subject

In 1972 there appeared the second full-length biography of Isaac McCoy, a century and a quarter after his death. This was written by George A. Schultz, whose biography is on quite a different level to the majority of the articles on McCoy which had gone before. In many ways, Schulz' work goes deeper and wider than Wyeth's. He places McCoy more firmly into his historical background dealing with the expanding Western frontier as white settlers swarm over new lands, forcing the Indians to flee. He also spends more thought on McCoy's pressing call to create a new land of peace and freedom for the Indians. Hence the fitting title to his book which is *An Indian Canaan: Isaac McCoy and the Vision of an Indian State*.[29] One major advantage of this work is that it provides the reader with far more sources which can be looked into for further reading and study. The one major weakness in Schultz work is that, in spite of all his praiseworthy research, he never discovers McCoy as a person and thoroughly fails in summing up his motives for his actions. This lack of understanding is revealed to the reader in Schultz' Foreword which he ends with the words:

> McCoy emerges as a supporter of the Indian at a time when support of the Indian was a minority and unpopular position. He had no special favorites among the tribes but helped all of them in any way that he could. He had personal contact with many different groups, and he maintained a sincere interest in their way of life - even to the point of recording customs, beliefs, and the like. I believe that as a missionary he would have been considered a failure by his contemporaries. As a human-

---

[29] University of Oklahoma Press, Norman.

itarian sincerely concerned with the Indian's welfare, today there can be no question about his worth.[30]

Schulz fails to appreciate McCoy's motives

Schultz never grasps what made McCoy to be the humanitarian he was. McCoy's spiritual testimony leaves him cold. It is hardly ever mentioned. He does not appear to see it, never mind understand it. Whenever McCoy thinks, speaks and writes as a Christian, Schultz misinterprets him in a worldly, negative manner. This is seen in the minor things of life as well as the major. Whenever, for instance, McCoy says that he is disappointed with the way things are going, as when John Mason Peck wrote to say that he had decided not to follow the Board's advice and join McCoy at Fort Wayne, Schultz says that McCoy took offense.[31] Yet no such offense was meant by Peck or taken by McCoy and the two men remained the best of correspondents and friends. Similarly, Schulz speaks of McCoy being personally "affronted" at the Board's not paying his bills when in point of fact the passage which Schultz quotes shows McCoy truly worried about the future of the mission and certainly not concerned with his own personal pride.[32] Schultz argues that McCoy wished to enforce a military form of education upon the Indian children which "made little sense in their lives". This contradicts the various extant letters from Indian parents and children which impressed McCoy with the longing among the Indians to be educated. It also contradicts Indian accounts of the lenient methods he used. Indeed, one rebel missionary, who refused to follow McCoy's friendly method of teaching and ways of "correcting" unwilling pupils, accused McCoy of trying to make himself popular with the pupils by accommodating himself to their wishes.[33] Schultz even contradicts himself as, though he speaks without documentation of McCoy's alleged military rule over his pupils, he says of the pioneer missionary's treatment of his pupils, "McCoy

---

[30] pp. x-xi.

[31] p. 39.

[32] p. 43.

[33] See Leonard Slater's letter to McCoy dated July 21, 1827, McCoy Papers, Reel 5.

wrote that they were so "jealous of freedom: that "the course of conduct we must observe . . . must be such as will not in their estimation breathe the slightest appearance of an infringement on their liberties."[34] Schultz never allows himself to show any understanding of or sympathy with McCoy's situation. When McCoy, for instance, is left without the comfort of his wife and says, "I must now realize the toils, and anxieties of my forlorn situation, without the sympathies of a kindred bosom to console my griefs," Schultz's unkind and harsh comment is that McCoy's "chief lament was for himself."[35] Perhaps the author did not realize how much in love with Christiana McCoy he was even after many years of married life. A love which grew deeper though they were bereft of eleven of their fourteen children because of the terrible conditions which they endured for the Indians' sakes. Even when McCoy is a guest in the relatively luxurious home of the Secretary for War, yet misses the greasy blanket in a smoky bark hut of his missionary life, Schultz can only comment that this is, "a real failure of ego" on McCoy's part.

The main criticism which may be leveled against Schultz's work is that he maintains all along that McCoy did not understand the Indian and strove to foist on him a white man's fancy. Striving very hard to be objective in analyzing McCoy's tremendous efforts and success in his work as a missionary to the Indians, Schultz concludes his book by saying:

> The Indian State, which Calhoun had hinted at and for which McCoy surveyed a seat of government, of course never materialized. In spite of McCoy's sophistic arguments that the Indians for the first time had a legal claim to the lands they lived on, the titles given in the region beyond the Mississippi proved less substantial than those in the East, for they had no foundation in antiquity. Before the primary removals were completed, the secondary ones had begun. But McCoy's vision of an Indian Canaan cannot be entirely dismissed as chimerical. Eighty-eight years after McCoy's death, President Franklin D. Roosevelt signed the Wheeler-Howard Act, a measure designed to extend to the Indians the right of self-government and the opportunities of education and economic assistance so that they could attain 'a wholesome American life'. Nor can McCoy's goals and methods

---

[34] p. 41. Dots to mark words omitted supplied by Schultz.

[35] p. 47.

be wholly rejected. Much like McCoy's Indian nationalism, a twentieth-century Indian-inspired Pan-Indian movement in the United States has deemphasized tribal distinctions. The federal government of Canada, after sponsoring local schools in Indian and Metis villages in the Mackenzie District for many years, is again encouraging the development of McCoy-type residential schools. Here the students can be given supervision in what is considered a preferable environment.

And yet McCoy's bucolic vision of settled Indian life and his dreams of an organized Indian political state with all the trappings of representative government and written codified laws was typically early-nineteenth-century white America. It should be added that while most contemporary missionaries to the Indians were dispiritedly groping along conventional paths, adding a lone convert here or there to their denomination rolls, McCoy proposed a radical solution for the Indian problem which was only partly religious, and which in its grandiosity was somewhat breathtaking.[36]

An attempt to evaluate Schultz' account of McCoy

A number of comments must be made here to clarify the matter. Schultz appears to maintain that the colonization of the Indian Territory was, in the main, Secretary of War John C. Calhoun's idea, McCoy being merely one of his agents in carrying it out. Actually Calhoun's interest in the future Indian Territory came some years after McCoy's and he was initially only interested in finding the source of the Red River to which end he equipped Major Stephen Long in 1821 with an expedition. Calhoun established his Department of Indian Affairs in 1824, some seven years after McCoy began lobbying him on behalf of the Indians. Furthermore, the suggestion to survey the proposed Indian Territory and plan a site for the future Indian Government came solely from McCoy who was then commissioned by the Government to carry out his plans. Moreover, when Government representatives finally wrote to inform McCoy that plans for Indian colonization of the territory west of the Mississippi had been approved by Congress, these representatives assured McCoy that it was all thanks to his initiative. Schultz's "of course" in reference to the part-failure of McCoy's plans for the Indian

---

[36] p. 37.

Territory was certainly not because the plan was impractical. McCoy's great energies had made it possible and many tribes had been saved from extinction before McCoy's death. It was, however, this death that hindered developments. After McCoy, there was no one to command the ear of the Government for the cause of the Indians. There has never been an American Elisha to take up McCoy's Elijah-like mantle. Here, again, Schultz is self contradictory as he declares McCoy's efforts to be those of a typical early nineteenth century white American, yet he mentions the Indians' own pan-Indian dream. That such a dream is clearly Indian rather than white is shown by the present day success of the Inuits of northern Canada who, after centuries of campaigning for self-rule have been granted land six times the size of the present reunited Germany, which is to be called Nunavut (Our Land) and will be occupied by 22,000 people, 18,000 of whom are Inuits. The Inuits will have their own capital at Iqaluit on Baffin Island which is already inhabited by some 3,600 people. A similar development is at last taking place among the Same People, commonly, and wrongly, called Lapps, a people very close to the Indians in origin, traditions and culture. The various countries in which they live have now granted them leave to unite as one people under the same flag with their own political representation.

Clearly such an account as Schultz's has its advantages in examining how human factors might have influenced his human life, but its defects are all too apparent. Because the "one thing needed" in the life of a missionary to give that life purpose, i.e. his spiritual calling and equipment to that end, is, on the whole, ignored in Schultz's work, it must be considered too secular to give readers a true idea of who McCoy really was and what he truly believed. This present biography of McCoy is an attempt to redress the balance and present McCoy the man and McCoy the Christian as seen from a wide use of his own works, those of his fellow missionaries and the secondary literature of the past century and a half.

A word of caution to my readers

This work may come as a shock to those who harbor romantic views of Missionary Societies carefully choosing mighty men of God to go out as spiritual heroes to work unflinchingly in gathering a harvest of souls, with the Society faithfully supporting the missionaries in prayer, and in providing them with equipment and funds. Sadly, the reality of the American Baptist Board of Foreign Missions was often quite the opposite, although there were always sound men on the Board who maintained that such ideal views were workable. Spencer Cone with his strong character and unflinching testimony was one of them. Luther Rice, with his unwavering loyalty and evangelical zeal, was another.

Likewise, this book may put individuals and churches off the idea of supporting parachurch organizations in their efforts to evangelize the world. This author, though admitting that much good has been done by such organizations, also admits that they are far from the examples given in Scripture and the experience of two thousand years of Christian outreach. McCoy found out that a church's authorization of a member to do the work of a pastor, evangelist and teacher, and that church's individual calling and pledge to support that missionary in new fields, was a better way.

A note on eighteenth century Indians and contemporary spelling

Throughout this book, background information will be given concerning the various tribes who featured in McCoy's story so that the reader may obtain some knowledge of the Indians' situation during the nineteenth century. A fuller description of the various tribes and their relationships to McCoy will be given in an Appendix and may be referred to for further information while reading the book.

Spelling the names of the Indian tribes is a special embarrassment as so many forms occur for the same name. An attempt has been made to keep to modern spelling but often such forms have little to do with the original names. This is illustrated by the Tiaukakeek River which is now rendered 'Kankakee River' on American maps. Even more of a change is seen in the modern place and river name 'Tippecanoe', famous for the battle in 1811 which started when 1,000 men of the Vincennes area attacked Tecumseh's Indian Braves at Prophetstown. The original name was Ke-tap-e-kon, which had nothing to do with "tipping a canoe"! As native Indian speakers have assured the present writer that they differ among themselves in the way they spell their own names, he trusts that no Indian will be offended at his orthography. The spelling of English causes further problems which have been solved as follows. Spelling in quotes has been kept consistent with the originals except in places where ligatures such as 'fs' as in "mifsionary" or "im-

39

prefsion" for "missionary" and "impression" have been used with which the modern reader is unfamiliar. Likewise old forms of spelling the definite and demonstrative articles and their abbreviations such as "y^e" and "y^t" have been altered to "the" and "that" etc. respectively. Other common abbreviations such as "sho^d" for "should" have been given their longer form. Where I have quoted from modern publications of McCoy's works etc. where the spelling has been modernized, I have kept to that spelling. Concerning the "ou" spelling of words such as "favour" and "colour," as an alternative to "o," McCoy used both forms which have not been altered by the author.

Finally, I must add that, in writing this biography, I am fully satisfied that I have recorded the life of one of the very greatest men of God and philanthropists and, indeed, skilled politicians, America has ever produced and a man who stands out clearly worldwide as one of the greatest missionaries of all time.

Chapter One
The Recruiting of a Missionary (1784-1817)

The circumstances surrounding McCoy's birth

Isaac McCoy was born near Union Town, Fayette County in Pennsylvania on June 15,[1] 1784. The very year of his birth was of great significance in the history of suffering for the Indian nations. It was the year Congress abandoned the agreed plan to bargain with the Indians as a people. They preferred to adopt the policy of divide and rule, entering into treaty after treaty with separate tribes in an effort to wrench their traditional territories from their ownership. It was the year politicians and the military forces began to drive the so-called Six Iroquois Nations[2] and their near relations (and often enemies) the Wyandot, the Delaware, the Chippewa and Ottawa tribes from their lands. The Iroquois do not feature centrally in McCoy's story but the other tribes all played a major part in McCoy's missionary endeavors.

1784 was also the year that Georgia extended her state territories to include Creek Indian lands, the latter eventually being resettled in the plains of Oklahoma. Georgia made $207,580 at this time through sales of former Indian territories to land development companies. The Creeks formerly held vast lands along the waterways of what is now Georgia and Alabama and had even established some 50 townships. Towards the end of the Creek War of 1813-14, U. S. forces under the command of Andrew Jackson, soon to become U. S. President, all but annihilated the Creek braves at Horseshoe Bend, Alabama, and confiscated much of their remaining land. Their last possessions east of the Mississippi River were taken from them in 1832. The Creeks were evangelized by the Baptists before their removal to the Indian Territory and were the first Christian Indians

---

[1] Other sources give June 13.

[2] The Onondaga, Oneida, Seneca, Tuscarora, Mohawk and Cayuga tribes.

to found a Baptist church on their resettlement. This was the first church ever to be founded in what is now the State of Oklahoma.

Isaac's grandfather, James McCoy, had come to North America around 1700 as a ten-year-old orphan from Scotland. Calvin McCormick, a distant relative of Isaac McCoy's, tells how the young boy, tempted by tales from the New World, boarded a merchant ship which was to set sail for Baltimore and worked his way across the Atlantic as a cabin boy. Another distant relative, Elizabeth Hayward, adds to the story by telling how orphan James fled from the wrath of an uncle and started out for the New World as a stowaway but he was discovered and auctioned off to the highest bidder as a servant.[3] After a time, James moved to Kentucky with a party of friends where he built a fort, which carried his name, for the protection of the settlers and married a Scot's girl of the Bruce clan. Eventually the family settled down in Uniontown, Fayette County, Pennsylvania The McCoys had six children, the third of whom, William, was born at McCoy's Fort in 1754. William became a Baptist pastor and married Eliza Royce in 1776.[4] The couple were also blessed with six children of whom Isaac McCoy was one. William and Eliza's children became active members of Baptist churches. James, Rice and Isaac were ordained but John also maintained a Christian witness after his fortieth year.[5] John's daughter, Eliza, was to join her Uncle Isaac as a permanent missionary to the Indians while her brothers Collins, William, Isaac and John helped their Uncle Isaac from time to time.[6]

McCoy's early life

In 1790, when Isaac was six years of age, the McCoys moved from Pennsylvania to Kentucky where, at first, William did pioneer

---

[3] The full story is told in Hayward's *John McCoy*, though she makes no claims as to its authenticity.

[4] Also spelled "Rice." Hayward writes that McCoy Fort came into possession of William who lost the Fort in a law suit. See John McCoy, p. 7. However Isaac McCoy and his brothers and sisters inherited several hundred acres of land from their father which he had received from the Government because of his services to the Revolution. See John McCoy, p. 7.

[5] See Hayward's chapter *Deacon McCoy*.

[6] See *The Memoir of Miss Eliza McCoy*, Calvin McCormick A.M., Dallas, 1892. Also, Hayward's *John McCoy*, Chapter VII, Indian Missions, pp. 63 ff.

work as a preacher among the settlers who had moved in from the east. Kentucky was just emerging as a separate State to Virginia (1792) and had recently been "freed" from the hands of the Indians. The McCoys settled on the Ohio River in Jefferson County some seventeen miles from Louisville, moving a short time later to Shelby County where William became pastor of Buck Creek church. An Indiana church by the name of Fourteen Mile,[7] four miles northeast of Charlestown, asked Buck Creek to provide them with ministers and McCoy preached there alternatively with George Waller also of Buck Creek. This church is thought to be the oldest Protestant church in Indiana as it was founded in 1798 and became a member church of the Salem Association in 1799. One interesting feature of its earlier years was a debate concerning whether or not foot-washing should be introduced into the church.[8] After carefully studying John 13, the church decided in the negative. In 1803 the Fourteen Mile Church decided to move to Silver Creek, Clark County, Indiana, about five miles west of Charlestown, as most of the members lived in that district. William became its pastor and stayed there for the rest of his life.[9] The church built a chapel directly opposite the Ohio Falls.

We know little about Isaac's early life on the Western frontier, except that he loved the studious rather than the outdoor life and became an avid reader of good books. We know nothing about how he came to profess faith in Christ apart from the fact that his mother was the chief instrument to this end. Isaac's father had him taught the trade of a wheelwright which he practiced for a number of years and which remained a continuous source of income for him when he needed funds to fit him out for his preaching journeys. Isaac was converted at sixteen and baptized a year later on March 6, 1801 by Joshua Morris and became a member of Buck Creek. Two years later, on October 6, 1803, McCoy was married to sixteen-year-old Christiana Polke, known to her dear ones as "Kittie." The young Mrs. McCoy's mother and three other members of her family had been held prisoners by the Ottawa Indians for several years. This had filled her with a longing to take the gospel to those

---

[7] Also called Fourteen Mile Creek.

[8] McCoy tells of experiencing a foot-washing ceremony in a circular letter to friends written in March, 1819, McCoy Papers, Reel 1.

[9] See McCormick's *Memoir of Eliza McCoy*, pp. 21-22 and Spencer's *History of Kentucky Baptists*, Vol. I, pp. 422-423, 681-683.

people, which, by God's grace, she and her husband were now called
to do. As Isaac prayerfully mused on his future calling, he began to
write down his thoughts in verse, outlining the tasks he believed God
had given him to do:

> In more than common pensive mood,
> As all alone I sat,
> Two men imagination viewed
> Nor this I knew nor that.
> At first they were obscurely seen,
> Anon they drew quite near,
> One asked the other where he'd been,
> And I resolved to hear.
>
> "I'm traveling through the world," he said,
> "To instruct the savage mind,
> To teach the poor to earn their bread,
> The wealthy to be kind;
> To show the blind the living way,
> To set the wanderer right;
> To make the sportive quit their play,
> The wicked to do right;
> To beat the swords to pruning hooks,
> That bloody wars may cease;
> To fill the world with holy books,
> Jerusalem with peace;
> To liberate the abject slave,
> To give the gasping breath;
> To disappoint the boasting grave,
> And starve voracious death."
>
> The other, with sarcastic smile,
> Said, "Sir, you've much to do."
> (I listened closely all the while)
> Indeed I thought so too.
> But still his mind seemed firmly fixed,
> I read it in his eyes,
> And as if grieved and almost vexed
> He sternly did reply:
>
> "Yes, sir, 'tis great things I attempt,
> And great things hope to do;
> They would be less were earth exempt
> From infidels like you."
> "Don't blame my unbelief," he said,
> "Since what you now propose

44

Was never done since earth was made,
Or man to being rose."
"And what of that? Jehovah's arm
Admits of no control;
He promised (and He will perform)
To execute the whole."
"Aye, true; God must the work begin,
And God the work must do;
In saving men from death and sin,
He'll not ask help from you.
Perhaps all nations will repent,
And joy like rivers flow,
But wait, pray sir, till you are sent,
'Twill then be time to go.
It is presumption now to start,
To go you know not where,
To grieve a tender mother's heart,
Or drive her to despair.
Your children will, like fugitives,
Be left in heathen lands,
Like slaves to spend their wretched lives,
Or worse employ their hands.
Amidst a scene of wretchedness
Your life will terminate,
And in some howling wilderness
Your widow mourn her fate."

And now I saw the briny tear
Come trickling down the cheek
Of him, who felt his children dear.
At length he tried to speak:

In Thee, Oh God, is all my might,"
He spake with faltering tongue;
I trust that Thou wilt guide me right,
If I should now be wrong."

And as he raised his prayer to heaven,
Joy sparkled from his eyes,
As if his God a smile had given
That moment from the skies.
Myself, my family, my all,"
Said he, "are no more mine.
I have resigned them at Thy call,

My God, they all are Thine."[10]

Preparation for the ministry

McCoy's initial calling, was to Vincennes, a former French trading post on the fertile banks of the Wabash River, capital of the Indiana Territory before its division.[11] Here the newlyweds arrived in April, 1804. A fellow traveler at the time was Elihu Stout, the former printer of the *Kentucky Gazette* in Lexington. He had dismantled his printing press, packed it with the type on to pack horses and journeyed to Vincennes to start a new life. Indeed, thousands were flocking to Indiana from the east and by the time McCoy was appointed missionary to the Indians, the population of Indiana had risen from a handful of Franco-Spanish settlers to almost the 200,000 mark.

Vincennes did not provide the opportunities for service the McCoys had expected and their health deteriorated living near that stretch of the Wabash. After about a year they joined William McCoy's church at Silver Creek which had just moved from Fourteen Mile Creek. McCoy now felt that he should start out on his ministry and be ordained as a Baptist preacher but his church told him that he was too young and advised him to carry out his trade as a wheelwright until they could officially approve of his calling. Young McCoy did not remain idle and busied himself with personal witness and raising interest in missionary work, whereby he did not distinguish between domestic and foreign missions. This work led speedily to his co-founding the Bruceville Missionary Society and the Bruceville Female Missionary Society[12] which were eventually merged within the Baptist Board of Missions with its seat at Philadelphia. On July 11, 1807, McCoy preached a "discourse" at the Silver Creek Church before the elders, George Waller, John Sutton, John Reese and his father William McCoy and was put on a year's

---

[10] A number of McCoy's poems and hymns are to be found on Reel 1 of the McCoy Papers.

[11] Called Indiana after the Indians who occupied it. Indiana Territory was divided up in 1805 and eventually became the states of Indiana, Michigan, and Wisconsin. Indiana became the 19th state of the Union December 11, 1816.

[12] Each society had around seventy founding members.

probation. McCoy persevered both in his faith and witness, as shown by the following accreditation given to him by his church in 1808:

> Clark County Indiana Territory
> Silver Creek Church
>
> Whereas our Beloved Brother, Isaac M,Coy hath Exercised a Publick Gift, in the Bounds of This Church, for the space of One Year, & we think this Gift to Be Profitable, also His Morral Conduct Being well known among us, And We Believe Him to be Sound, in the Doctrines, of the Divinity and Gospel of Christ We Do Hereby License Him, to preach The Gospel, wherever God in His Providence, may Cast His Lot - Hoping the Lord may Crown His Labours with Success. -
>
> Signed By Order of the Church, at our Meeting of Business, August the 13th. 1808. -
>
> Elisha Carr - Moderator -
> James M,,Coy -Clerk[13]

McCoy had to wait another two years before being ordained as a minister by his father and George Waller on October 12, 1810. He then became the first pastor of Maria Creek Church which he had helped to bring to life. Here we see sound church principles at work practiced according to the office of elders and pastors as outlined in I Timothy 5. These frontiersmen might have never set foot in a theological seminary but they certainly knew how to practice church order and discipline.

Pastoring at Maria Creek

The McCoys' spent eight years in the pastorate, farming a small piece of land with Isaac occasionally making wheels to keep them financially independent as the small church could not afford a pastor's salary. McCoy made sure that he had plenty of time to visit the surrounding districts on horseback, witnessing and preaching whenever he met up with either Indians or whites, covering much of

---

[13] Spelling as per the original. Spencer in his *History of Kentucky Baptists* gives July 11, 1807 but McCoy's accreditation is clearly dated August 13, 1808. Spencer's reference is obviously to the beginning of the probation time.

Indiana and Illinois. He was the first Baptist minister to preach in many areas and most likely the first preacher ever. It is generally claimed that he founded three churches on the frontier but his letters reveal that five or more new churches would be nearer the mark. McCoy's preaching duties among the churches he founded before becoming a permanent missionary to the Indians were immense. Writing to the Baptist Board on May 7, 1818, in one of his many letters to interest the Board in the evangelization of the Indians and plea for further workers in the Lord's vineyard, McCoy says:

> Although I have travelled more than 1,900 miles since the 17th of last October, and besides attending church meetings, &c. have preached more than one hundred sermons, yet I have not been able to preach one sermon in Edwards, Davis, or Dubois counties, the last of which was formerly part of Pike county. In less than three weeks, I expect to have the sole charge of five churches, which are situated as follows: from White River church to High Bank is twenty miles, thence to Wabash twenty-four, thence to Maria twelve, thence to Prairie creek forty, from Prairie creek to White river church is seventy miles. This extensive route lies through an immense population, all destitute of preaching by our ministers. There are also two or three places where I think churches might in a little time be formed, but there is none to blow the trumpet to 'assemble them.' Now if I attend to preaching to these people, the Indians must be neglected, and if I attend to the Indians, 'with whom shall I leave these few sheep in the wilderness?' Should I be so happy as to embrace a brother in this work, it would be my wish to form a family establishment, where, while one of us would be on a preaching tour, the other could be father to his children, and could attend closely to the ultimate object of the mission. I am very desirous to hear from the Board something on this subject.[14]

Accepted as an Association missionary

Wherever he went, he found the whites hostile and the Indians unfriendly, especially as the former were pushing their

---

[14] *Latter Day Luminary*, Letter from McCoy, near Vincennes, May 7, 1818, pp. 182-185.

borders deeper and deeper into Indian territories. Services were always held with armed guards at the door and each worshiper sat with a musket on his knee. This state of affairs was instrumental in urging McCoy to bring these two hostile people together in Christian fellowship. He felt that he was called to work with and for the Indians rather than the whites and received the idea of forming an organization for Indian evangelism and sent his ideas in writing to the Wabash Association. They contacted the Silver Creek Association of Indiana and the Long Run Association of Kentucky[15] for advice which proved favorable to McCoy's endeavors. McCoy, now thirty-four years of age, was accepted as a missionary by the Long Run Association, though at first for only a trial period of a year and in conjunction with his work at Maria Creek. His appointment is still extant and reads:

> Knox County Indiana
> Territory Ky
>
> To all whom these presents may Come Greeting
> Know ye that our Beloved Brother in the ministry, Isaac Mckoy being appointed by a Committee Chosen by the Long Run association for the purpose of patronising missionaries on the Western frontiers this is to Certify that our Brother has the Hearty approbation of this Church and that he is Regularly Ordained to preach the Gospel and administer the ordinances of our Lord Jesus Christ. Done at the Church Meeting of Busines held at our Meeting House Maria Creek Church Meeting March 16th 1816
>
> By order of the Church
> Signed Wm. Polke C.lk

The Long Run churches had adopted the *Philadelphia Baptist Confession of Faith* of 1742 at their inauguration on September 16, 1803. This was basically the declaration of Benjamin Keach's Goat Yard Particular Baptist Church, Southwark, London and was introduced to the Baptist Church in Philadelphia by Elias Keach (1667-1701), Benjamin's son. The creed was soundly Calvinistic but the Long Run church stressed that the creed should

---

[15] These associations were originally part of the Long Run Association which became so large that it was considered expedient in 1811 to form two associations dealing with the Kentucky and Indiana areas.

not be understood in a Supralapsarian sense and that churches in the association should be free to adhere to or ignore the 31st Article concerning the laying on of hands.

McCoy's Calvinism and missionary zeal

McCoy's new task was to labor among all peoples, red or white, along the Mississippi River. Speaking of McCoy's work at this time, Professor John F. Cady of Franklin College in his *The Origin and Development of the Missionary Baptist Church in Indiana*, says that there were so many conversions that two daughter churches were formed belonging to the Maria Creek mother church. [16] He goes on to say, speaking of the little sympathy among fellow-Baptists for McCoy's outreach:

> But there were few Isaac McCoys, and the quickening which appeared here as a result of a missionary purpose was an isolated case. Maria Creek church differed not at all in standards from the other Regular Baptist churches. McCoy was as thoroughgoing Calvinist in his theology, as the constitutions of the churches which he organized reveal. He was simply moved to action by the suffering and miserable friendlessness of the Indians, and could not continue in his Christian profession without making some effort to relieve their distress. [17]

Cady appears to be indicating here that, apart from an interest in alleviating human misery, Calvinists, on the whole, were not evangelically minded. He is probably associating Calvinism with Daniel Parker's[18] and Alexander Campbell's legal teaching which began to plague the churches of the Western frontier towards the end of McCoy's pastorate. This movement was as anti-Calvinistic as it was anti-evangelistic and anti-missions. Before this church destroying movement spread, in 1811, there had been 956 baptisms

---

[16] Little Village and Prairie Creek. McCoy had also to do with the formation or reformation of White River, also the formation of Highbank, Wabash and an unnamed church in Sullivan County.

[17] Franklin College, 1942, pp. 39-40.

[18] See William Polke's letter to McCoy on Parker's anti-mission strategy dated June 20, 1820, McCoy Papers, Reel 1.

and at least five new churches founded in the Long Run Association, all of which were Calvinistic and all of which were out and out evangelistic and missionary minded. Arminians had been gently disciplined in the church courts and shown that their views negated the gospel of God's loving grace. J. H. Spencer, in his *History of Kentucky Baptists*, gives the number of churches in the association at this time as 41 with 2,925 members.[19] Yet even more glorious days were to come. During the years 1816-1820 another 1,138 converts were baptized and added to the churches. In the churches that McCoy founded, he reported to the Foreign Mission Board on July 29, 1819 that there had lately been 84 baptisms and the Prairie Creek church had grown from 28 to 100 members in little over a year.[20] Relatively large sums of money were raised by these churches to further evangelism and missionary work along the Western frontier.

McCoy's Calvinism is evident from the name he gave his son, *John Calvin* McCoy, born September 28, 1811 during McCoy's Maria Creek pastorate. Indeed, McCoy usually addressed his son by the name of "Calvin," dropping the "John."[21] John Calvin McCoy[22] was trained as a surveyor and was to be of great assistance to his father in the future work of Indian colonization. He made his name in

---

[19] See vol. II pp. 150-192 for a detailed early history of the Long Run Association.

[20] *Latter Day Luminary*, vol. I, No. 10, p. 504.

[21] A further indication of the staunch Calvinist background of these early Baptist pioneer missionaries is found in the name of McCoy's fellow missionary Mr. Pratt whose first names were "John Gill," named after the influential Calvinist, Baptist scholar-pastor (1697-1771), famous for his commentaries, sermons and theological works.

[22] Isaac also called his son "Calvin" to distinguish him from the various other Johns in the family. Indeed, there are so many Johns, Williams, Rices, James, Delilahs, Elizabeths and Isaacs (six of the latter) in the McCoy family that often one does not know which is being referred to in the family's letters. There were at least two John C. McCoys in the wider family and often several children of the same parents had the same name due to the McCoy's tradition of naming new born children after their deceased brothers and sisters. John C. McCoy, John McCoy's son, worked for a year or so with the McCoy's at Westport and it is quite impossible to tell which references are to whom.

Missouri and Kansas history by founding the town of Westport with his father in 1835 and co-founding Kansas City in 1838.

It was obviously not McCoy's Calvinism that eventually caused his fellow church members to be cautious of him but his out and out optimism that the Indians could be evangelized. Walter Wyeth quotes one member of McCoy's church as saying, "I will not dissemble that, in the weakness of my faith, I feared that he had fallen upon a Utopian scheme."[23] That friend came to share McCoy's vision. The truth is that aversion to the Indians had nothing to do with Calvinist beliefs but with the basic racial conviction that European whites were a superior people. Elizabeth Hayward writes:

> Most pioneers looked upon Indians as somewhat less than human, putting them in the same category as panthers, polecats and other"varmints" of which the land needed to be cleared. They were hated, feared and despised. Isaac McCoy, who practiced the gospel of Christian brotherhood which he preached, saw them in quite a different light.[24]

The anti-mission movement grows

McCoy now began to have difficulties with the Wabash Association who were rapidly revising their missionary strategy because of anti-Board policies and the new dualistic "two seed" theories of nigh Gnostic Daniel Parker.[25] Indeed, the Regular Baptists were in danger of being totally remodeled as they adopted new views concerning predestination and bowed to the influence of the anti-missions, anti-creeds movements of splinter groups from the Presbyterians such as Barton W. Stone's New Light schism and the Campbellites' ideas for "reforming" the churches. There was also strong political anti-missionary feeling expressed at the time. McCoy relates:

---

[23] Isaac McCoy, p. 17.

[24] Chapter VII, *Indian Missions* in her *John McCoy*, p. 59.

[25] For a good survey of Parker's extraordinary speculations see Spencer, op. cit. Vol. I, pp. 576-579. It is alarming to note that Parker found his most fanatical backing in churches that were formerly sound in Calvinistic doctrine.

> In 1818, I met at the Silver Creek Baptist Association, in Indiana, a certain minister of that State, who violently opposed all our missionary operations, and, as I thought, needlessly provoked altercation, not to say strife.[26]

The Association therefore did not renew their contract with McCoy after the trial year ended. The Wabash churches were now in danger of stifling any sign of evangelical fervor which rose among them. It seemed that they had accepted the notion that the gospel had no message to sinners but was merely for the comfort of those who were already believers. These changed views were not shared by McCoy and the Maria Creek church and it is interesting to note that Dr. Cady states, "In all the area of the Wabash District Association, in the vicinity of Vincennes, only the Maria Creek Church, of which Isaac McCoy was the pastor from 1810-1818, seems to have made progress."[27] Such statements show that McCoy had proven himself to be a worthy missionary at home before endeavoring to go out to do pioneer work among the Native Americans. This blessed fact so angered Daniel Parker that he wrote one of his earliest anti-evangelistic pamphlets specifically against the Maria Creek church. When the church that McCoy had founded did not bow to Parker's tyranny, he settled down near Maria Creek and for almost four years brought forward motion after motion against the church and any Association that corresponded with her. John Mason Peck often visited the Wabash area and defended Maria Creek's stance. Indeed, it soon becomes obvious on consulting the records, that Parker's ire was directed to a great extent against both John Mason Peck who was one of the most successful evangelists and church planters on the Western frontier and Isaac McCoy who was the most successful evangelist and church planter among the Indians.[28]

This anti-gospel influence within the churches moved the Wabash District Association to withdraw their support for the Baptist Board of Missions in 1819. In 1822 the Association struck off the Maria Creek church from their list of members because of its

---

[26] *History of Baptist Indian Missions*, pp. 133-134.

[27] *The Origin and Development of the Missionary Baptist Church in Indiana*, p. 18.

[28] See especially Parker's *A Public Address to the Baptist Society*, p. 36 ff., *Baptist Life and Thought: 1600-1980*, pp. 208-211, and the Baptist histories covering this period in the Bibliography.

home and foreign missionary outreach. From now on, the winds of doctrinal change blew constantly around the Maria Creek church as the local Associations changed their minds time and time again concerning the legality of their action. This also reflects the influence of the Campbellites who were constantly changing their attitude to missions and education. It eventually dawned on the movement that their massive public propaganda and highly effective journalistic work was nothing other than a substitute for the evangelistic and educational activity that they condemned in others. Soon, however, the Campbellites were ranked with the Mormons as a heretical sect.

The "Calvinistic Baptist" anti-mission lobby was neither truly Calvinistic nor truly Baptist

Another obvious problem in the Western churches was allying the doctrine of predestination with the Great Commission and the call to preach repentance and faith to sinners. Many of McCoy's Baptist contemporaries were now taught that the one doctrine excluded the other so that there were those who emphasized *either* predestination *or* preaching repentance as if the two did not belong together. It thus became a new custom among the former Calvinistic churches, influenced by New Divinity teaching propagated by New England Presbyterians and Congregationalists, to leave out the doctrines of election and predestination from their preaching to sinners and reserve such teaching for the already saved. By degrees, a gospel was being preached which left out the atoning work of Christ for His people and merely stressed repentance and faith as human duties. This dilemma is reflected in Cady's work when he supposes that McCoy did not take his own doctrinal statement regarding the "doctrine of Eternal election" in the Fourteen Mile church's creed seriously as he believed in preaching repentance.[29] For McCoy, as Calvin and great Calvinists such as John Gill, preaching repentance and faith was God's means of calling

---

[29] *The Origin and Development of the Missionary Baptist Churches in Indiana*, pp. 84-85. See also McCoy's *Fort Wayne Declaration of Faith* given in full below.

His elect for whom Christ died to salvation.[30] This must be borne in mind in view of the opinion often voiced among church historians and theologians that the cause of the antagonism towards any form of missionary work whether at home and abroad was a too strong adherence to Calvinism.[31] McCoy was a Calvinist second to none, as were most of his co-workers and friends such as Spencer Cone, William Staughton, Luther Rice, and John L. Dagg. These were men who dedicated their lives to Christian harvest work.

On the other hand, one could hardly call Parker's speculative philosophy Calvinistic in any sense and many would have difficulty in associating it in any way with Christianity. Stone and Campbell were doctrinally reeds shaken by the wind and were Arminian to the core. Indeed, these anti-mission movements were really non-Baptist in principle, just as their New Divinity opponents were non-Baptists, though Sweet tells us that there were 68,000 anti-mission Baptists in the United States by 1846, the majority being in the West. It was traditional Baptist polity that each local church was sovereign and no other church could meddle in its affairs or have dominion over it. The Anti-Missionites, however, formed militant parachurch organizations acting under the name of an association, organization or periodical such as the *Christian Baptist* and seized power over individual churches treating them now as "parts" to a "whole" and excommunicating them from fellowship if they did not toe the party line exactly. They obviously interpreted Luke 14:23, concerning compelling sinners to come in, to mean compelling them to stay out! No one was more thorough than Parker in demanding that churches

---

[30] " The usual means and instrument of repentance are the word, and the ministers of it, as faith, so repentance, comes by, hearing the word; the three thousand were pricked to their heart, and were brought to repentance, through the ministry of the apostle Peter; and as all the apostles were ordered by Christ to preach repentance in his name among all nations, so they went forth everywhere, and God in and by their ministry commanded all men everywhere to repent; and when and where the command was attended with power it produced the effect; and so the apostle Paul declared to Jews and Gentiles, that *they should repent and turn to God, and do works meet for repentance;* and the hand of the Lord being with him, great numbers everywhere believed and turned to the Lord, Luke 24:47; Acts 17:30; 26:20." John Gill in *Of Repentance Towards God.* See also entries under "repentance" and "faith" in Calvin's *Institutes*.

[31] See Sweet's *The Story of Religion,* p. 257 and McLoughlin's *Cherokees & Missionaries,* p. 266.

over whom he had no jurisdiction whatsoever should follow his leadership as a duty and his efforts to this end even moved him to demand access to church business meetings to tell the members that they had to follow his will. Furthermore, fees were extracted from the member groups to pay for the negative propaganda machine which had nothing to do with the Great Commission, Thus the Anti-Mission people lost their main argument, however just, against the Missions Board, i.e. that it was overruling the wills of the local churches. They also lost their often-voiced argument that the initiator of the Baptist Foreign Missions Board, Luther Rice, was a modern Tezel and the Baptist Board of Missions a Pope. Also, it was a moot question whether such Presbyterian split-offs as the New Lighters and Campbellites, were really Baptist in their thinking or not. Their ideas of baptism completing regeneration were as far from the former General and Regular Baptist thinking as the Reformation was from the Council of Trent.

The war of 1812 and McCoy's calling to the Indians

President Madison, having received the support of both Houses of Congress, declared war on Britain on June 19, 1812 and very many of the Indians, including the famous Shawnee Tecumseh, supported the British. Young Pastor McCoy now found himself enlisted as a reserve soldier and had to penetrate deeply into Indian territory. It was while fighting with a rifle in his hand that McCoy realized that he must return with a Bible instead of a rifle. He saw how the white man's influence on the Indians had been mostly for evil. The trade in alcohol was making havoc of the Indians' moral and social life and McCoy was able to enter Indian encampments unobserved as the inhabitants were all rolling around in a drunken frenzy. He felt that the only way that the Indian nations could be preserved was to separate them fully from the whites and teach them of a Savior who did not save according to color. He therefore campaigned that the Indians should be allowed to live in white-free areas which they could administer themselves and though loosely placed under Congress, they would be represented only by their own people. He also realized that the Indians needed to have their languages put into writing and have the Bible translated into these languages and so lobbied the government to provide schools to this end. None of these views were entirely original and had been raised in the previous century but had either faded from view or had not spread because of the still isolated nature of the American settlements.

Nor did many of McCoy's fellow Baptists share his views. The Indians were now looked on as enemies to be defeated rather than needy souls to be helped with the gospel. The fact that they had assisted the British and still showed sympathy to the former colonial powers did not help their case. Furthermore, the idea that the gospel was designed merely for the spiritual element of man and not for the whole man was growing. Thus many came to believe that brotherly love actually excluded important matters such as education and social welfare. One preached to souls not bodies and stomachs! Christ's words in Matthew 25:34-46 had apparently not yet touched their consciences. Against such a background, McCoy was to emphasize more and more that the gospel must be to the whole man.[32]

---

[32] See McCoy's *Character of Indian Missions* in his 1836 *Periodical Account of Baptist Missions Within the Indian Territory* and passim.

Chapter Two
Looking for a Field of Service (1818-20)

The Campbellite threat

The Baptist churches on the Western frontier were now in disarray as offshoots from the 1800 Presbyterian "revival" in the form of the so-called "Christian Church" of the Campbellites and the "Millennial Church" of the Shakers were causing havoc among them. A movement featuring jumping, falling, jerking, rolling, dancing, barking and loud laughing was asserting itself in the name of revival which was thought to be evidence of the Spirit's work. Seeing how the wind was blowing, Thomas and Alexander Campbell skillfully combined anti-mission strategy with Millennialism and drew thousands from former Calvinist backgrounds and from those churches who refused to be bound by doctrinal statements. Once the Campbells had rejected covenant baptism for believer's baptism as a seal of faith, Baptists literally flocked to them for a while. The Campbellites so emphasized internal church work that evangelistic and missionary work became abhorred by many even outside of the movement. They so denounced any formal doctrinal statement, especially regarding predestination, that many non-Campbellite churches began to question their old Regular Baptist creeds which were based on the First and Second London Baptist Declarations of Faith. Sadly, the Silver Creek church succumbed to Campbellism and the remaining members of the McCoy family, one in faith with Isaac, now the Board's missionary to the Indians, had to leave the church in 1829 and had great difficulty finding a new church which had not succumbed to the new teaching. Even the Maria Creek church began to compromise, though several years after McCoy had left his pastorate there, stating that "believing or not believing in

Articles of Faith is no bar to fellowship."[1] Such developments were moving many more moderate people to say that the churches had so much to do in their own ranks that they could not afford the time or the money to support missionary work. First one's own house must be put in order. McCoy was sympathetic with such a view but stressed that the plight of the Indians was a home church problem. The whites were settlers on Indian land.

The early days of the Baptist Triennial Convention

Having started evangelistic work along the Mississippi River, McCoy looked for ways of continuing his activities. As his own Association would not back him, he looked for a representative body of evangelistically inclined Baptists who might be willing to offer him their fellowship and be prepared to support him in his work. Three years earlier, the General Missionary Convention of the Baptist Denomination in the United States had been founded in Philadelphia, Pennsylvania. This convention had grown out of a number of missionary societies, among which were the two founded by McCoy. The most important of these were the societies back East, most notably the Massachusetts Baptist Missionary Society (1802) with its organ the *Massachusetts Baptist Missionary Magazine* (1803), and the Salem Bible Translation and Foreign Missionary Society which was founded "To aid in the translation of the Bible then being made at Serampore, India, by William Carey and his companions, or if deemed feasible, to assist in sending a missionary, or missionaries from this country to India."[2]

In 1813, the Philadelphia Baptist Association decided to form a national society for missionary organization and called delegates from the entire Union and her territories to meet at Philadelphia to this end. Delegates from eleven states and the District of Columbia arrived at the founding meeting in May, 1814. One of the major aims of the convention was to promote a united Baptist opinion regarding

---

[1] Cady, p. 75. Readers are urged to study this excellent survey of Baptist churches and policies throughout this most troubled period of North American history. See also McCoy's letter February 8, 1818 for an example of how a once enthusiastic supporter could change his mind in a moment concerning missionary activity. McCoy Papers, Reel 1.

[2] See *History of Kansas Baptists*, pp. 7-9.

missions, to canvas support for Adoniram Judson and Luther Rice[3] who had become Baptists after setting off for India as Congregational missionaries but also, mainly through the wish of the Western frontier settlers, to promote the evangelization of those on the Western frontier and the Indian tribes. The second meeting of this Convention was arranged for 1817 and as the convention continued to meet once every three years, it received the name Triennial Convention.

McCoy applies to become one of the Convention's first missionaries

Believing that missionary work was the same, whether at home or abroad, McCoy wrote to the Board of Managers of the Baptist Missionary Convention on March 26, 1817, requesting them to place him on their list of missionaries under their patronage. He also explained how he was most definitely called of God to work among Indians and thus Indian evangelism must be his field of service. Unknown to McCoy at this time was that he had found an ally in William Carey, the famous British missionary to India. Carey was busy writing letters to prominent New England Baptists such as Dr. Thomas Baldwin of Boston, asking them why the American Baptists did not take civilization and Christianity to the American aborigines.[4] Luther Rice who had returned from the mission field to help set up the Board of Missions and become its General Manager had already met McCoy and told him he would find work to suit his calling in St. Louis.[5] McCoy found confirmation that he was in the will of the Lord in making this step when he discovered that a letter from the Board written by Luther Rice on April 2, 1817 had crossed his own letter and arrived via Maria Creek on May 6. After asking

---

[3] Rice wrote to McCoy on January 26, 1815, asking for his support in distributing circulars concerning the new venture. Further letters followed. McCoy Papers, Reel 1.

[4] Benedict, *Fifty Years Among the Baptists*, p. 113.

[5] Perhaps there was some blood relationship between McCoy and Rice as McCoy's mother was of the Rice family. Isaac and Kittie called their second child Rice (born January 26, 1807, died May 26, 1832). Rice had made a tour of the southern states in 1816-17 when he discussed Indian missions with McCoy. He returned to Philadelphia where the Board was then situated, with a favorable impression of McCoy's plans.

McCoy for more details of the mission societies he had founded, Rice wrote:

> I should be pleased to know also if you would be willing to perform missionary service under an appointment by the General Convention and what you would suggest as most agreeable to your views and wishes in the event of such an appointment. The missionary cause, never I think, wore a more prosperous aspect than at present.[6]

McCoy replied on the day he received Rice's invitation, accepting the Board's patronage at once and confirming that he would like to move to St. Louis with his family. Soon, however, a major disappointment occurred. McCoy received a letter from Litchfield, Connecticut, dated May 23, 1817 and signed by John Mason Peck, who told him that the week before James E. Welch and himself had been accepted by the Board for missionary work among the Indians and he was to be stationed at St. Louis. This was a puzzle to McCoy as it was well known at the Board through his dealings with Luther Rice, that McCoy wished to be stationed at St. Louis and Rice had encouraged him to that end.

Furthermore, he had applied to become a missionary before Peck and Welch. Peck had heard from the Board that McCoy was interested in the area and enquired if McCoy could give him some very detailed information which he listed in nine categories. A further puzzle was a letter from Board members William Staughton and Luther Rice, dated June 23 accepting McCoy as a missionary but without discussing McCoy's concrete suggestions as to where he wished to work and again asking him for his views on the matter. Staughton, recently elected as the Board's Corresponding Secretary, even suggested that McCoy might wish to stay at Vincennes, although McCoy had indicated that staying there would not be a useful proposition in view of the missionary work he wished to do.[7] McCoy's reply of July 28 reflects his disappointment, which is in no way disguised by the fact that he confesses that a better man had received the post. McCoy had been very ill for five weeks with the fever that was to plague him all his life. This is perhaps why he, after his initial disappointment, was not firm enough with the Board concerning his own plans and calling. Indeed, in his weakness,

---

[6] McCoy papers, Reel 1.

[7] McCoy papers, Reel 1.

McCoy did not realize that Staughton had only suggested Vincennes as a possibility and not a must and wrote to say that he accepted the Board's choice of that area of service. This initial two-way mis-understanding between the Board and McCoy was to continue for the next thirty years. McCoy was too polite by far to use any form of pressure or bullying and the Board was equally incapable of un-derstanding McCoy's true mind.

The result was that McCoy was asked to cover the Wabash and White River areas, taking Edwards and Crawford Counties of Illinois and Knox, Sullivan, Pike and Davis Counties in Indiana in his stride.[8] Here, however, Indian presence was much less and furthermore, the whites were swiftly encroaching on Indian lands, driving their inhabitants before them. His appointment was also only for a year with an option of a prolongation should both parties be of one mind. This would mean that he would have to move with his family and build accommodation some hundred miles away, without any guarantee that his venture would be permanent. Also the funds promised by the Board in no way covered the cost of such an undertaking.

The short-lived Western Mission of Peck and Welch

McCoy's disappointment deepened when he heard that Peck and Welch had soon given up work among the Indians and were concentrating on evangelizing white settlers. In 1820, less than three years after its start, their mission was closed down. Peck stressed that the reason for winding up the mission was the failure of the Board to meet their commitments but in his official report he wrote:

> July 9th, 1820. The missionaries received official intelligence from the Secretary of the Board that this mission was closed for the following reasons:
>
> 1. The want of ample funds for its (the mission's) vigorous prosecution.
> 2. A supposition on the part of the Board that this region would soon be supplied by the immigration into it of preachers from the Middle and Eastern States.

---

[8] See letter from Staughton to McCoy dated September 16, 1817, McCoy Papers, Reel 1.

3. The opposition in the West[9] was also urged as a
    reason for its being abolished. The Triennial Con-
    vention had accordingly recommended this course,
    which the Board, as in duty bound, thus carried
    out. Brother Welch is requested to continue his
    labours in St. Louis as a private minister and not
    as a missionary, no aid being promised him. Brother
    Peck is directed as speedily as practical, on the term-
    ination of the present year, to remove to Fort Wayne,
    and join Rev. Mr. McCoy in his labours among the
    Indians. Thus terminates the Western Mission.

Attest. J. M. Peck, Secretary.

Here the blame, however, cannot be placed wholly on the
Board as William Staughton in 1817 had advised all churches and
associations not to limit their work to the white settlers but also take
the gospel to "the aborigines of the West." Furthermore, Peck had
been specifically authorized by the Board to include Indian evangelization in his program and, indeed, they emphasized in their
initial instructions to Peck and Welch that "The Board is particularly
desirous that the Fox, the Osage, the Kansas, and other tribes of
Indians, should engage your peculiar zeal."[10] The two missionaries,
however, soon felt called to evangelize the white frontier pioneers
only. When the Board finally closed Peck's Western Mission, this fact
was not given as one of the reasons but must have affected the
Board's decision. Peck kept in touch with McCoy and often spoke of
joining him but this was not to be. Peck continued to be an ardent
supporter of Indian missions through his preaching activities among
the whites and he kept in close touch with McCoy's Wabash
Association and spoke at Maria Creek and the neighboring
associations against Daniel Parker.[11] As the Board rejected any
natural demands placed upon them to honor their financial commitments regarding the missionary buildings etc., the two missionaries found they had to work for many years to pay off the short-
lived mission's debts. Welch was hit the worst as he had initially laid

---

[9] The Campbell-Parkerite anti-mission lobby.

[10] See the Board's instructions to Peck and Welch found on page 174 in
Brackney's source book *Baptist Life and Thought: 1600-1980*.

[11] See Peck's letter of optimistic enthusiasm against Parker in his letter
from Maria Creek dated June 12, 1822, McCoy Papers, Reel 2.

out his entire fortune, including selling off his family estate, to further the cause of the Western Mission, believing that funding would soon be available from the Board. The Board's decision left him and his family penniless and homeless.

Though Peck was an initial disappointment to McCoy because of not eventually becoming his co-worker at Fort Wayne as the Board had planned, he was able to do McCoy a great favor twenty-eight years later when he chaired a Board meeting to discuss putting their entire Indian Mission into the care of McCoy's able hands. It is a great testimony to Peck's fine, friendly character, that he rarely made enemies (apart from Daniel Parker) and even after the breach with the Board in 1820, he remained good personal friends with Staughton, Rice, McCoy and their associates and his influence with the Board grew over the years. Peck became particularly active among the churches McCoy had founded in the Wabash Association.[12]

Making plans for a wider mission to the Indians

Meanwhile, McCoy was looking out for new venues in serving the Indians and applied for information to various Indian Agents and well-informed people. As a result of these enquiries, McCoy opened contacts with the Weas, Miamis and Kickapoos who lived in Indiana and Illinois. The tribes were introduced to McCoy by the Agent who was distributing their annuities. McCoy was quick to note that the Indians were being given goods alleged to be of a certain value, but they were not allowed to compare the goods received with the invoice stating their cost. From this time onwards, McCoy wrote letter after letter to the Board, urging them to petition the President and Congress so that laws would be passed to protect the Indians from being cheated by the whites.[13] At this meeting, some Franco-Indians[14] showed interest in missionary work among them and especially in the education for their children. As several half-breed

---

[12] See Rufus Babcock's chapter entitled *Close of the Western Mission* in his *Memoir of John M. Peck.* Here the full story of why the mission closed is told in detail.

[13] See, for instance, letter to Board dated July 30, 1818, McCoy Papers, Reel 1.

[14] Potawatomi-French and Wea-French.

youths could speak English, McCoy thought he could use them as interpreters until he picked up their Indian language. He quickly wrote down his plans concerning possible missionary work among these peoples and circulated printed copies of them at his own expense throughout Indiana, Illinois and Kentucky. Throughout this time, McCoy preached to the whites wherever he found them and was instrumental in bringing a number to the Lord and establishing his converts in churches. On these occasions, he told the Board, he was the first Baptist preacher ever to enter those areas.[15] Meanwhile, the French fathers of their half-breed children drew back from their request to have McCoy educate their children as they feared they would then lose their Roman Catholic faith. Similarly, when McCoy's Roman Catholic interpreters found out more about McCoy's convictions, they refused to interpret for him.[16]

The death of Mahale McCoy

While touring the Kentucky churches, the McCoys' eldest daughter Mahale, a fourteen-year old girl, caught Typhus Fever and soon died. McCoy was heart-broken, particularly as his child had died at Bruceville in his absence. Little did he know that he was to lose eleven of his fourteen children in similar ways. McCoy commented on the sad occasion with the words:

> We afterwards believed that the event was sanctified to our benefit, in inducing us with less reluctance to let go the hold which our affections had upon people and things in the regions of civilised society, and in enabling us to trust *all* - our children, ourselves, and all our interests - to God. In view of taking up our abode in the Indian country, we had felt great anxiety on account of this daughter; our other children were small, but she was of an age to make it particularly desirable that she should enjoy the benefit of a good school in the midst of good society. We could not think of keeping her with us in the woods, and it seemed not very convenient for us, in our frontier country, to leave her in a suitable place, especially as the mode of life upon which we were entering would likely deprive us of the

---

[15] See letter to Board dated May 7, 1818, McCoy Papers, Reel 1.

[16] See letter to William Staughton, the first Correspondence Secretary of the Board, written March 3, 1817, McCoy Papers, Reel 1.

means of meeting the expenses of a favourable situation. But our Heavenly Father, by one stroke, taught us not to feel undue anxiety for any thing on earth, not even for our children; and we afterwards, for our motto on the subject of our children; wrote in our journal the words of the Psalmist - "I have been young, and now am old, yet have I not seen the righteous forsaken, nor his seed begging bread." Our children may be injured by our residence in this Indian country, and so they might become worthless were they brought up in a good society. But the additional risk on account of their residence in the Indian country will be more than balanced by the mercy of Him who has called us to labour there. This confidence in God has not been disappointed; and we mention it here, for the encouragement of other missionaries who may realise painful anxieties on account of their children while resident among a heathen people. No parents were ever more happy in reference to the deportment of their children than we. Most of them have been taken from us, but we believe that they are in heaven.[17]

Life at Raccoon Creek

The initial preparatory work for the McCoys venture into Indian territory and setting up a mission station at Raccoon Creek had taken so long that nine months of McCoy's probation year had passed before openings to move materialized. This is no surprise when one realizes how difficult communications were in those days. Also a suitable site had to be found and paid for. Normal correspondence with the Board took at least two to four months providing both sides replied immediately. McCoy often received postal notification of coming events, appointments to be met or tasks to do at certain times, long after those dates, appointments or times had passed into history. His solution to this problem was often not to write seeking permission for a move but trust the Board would understand with hindsight.[18] McCoy, however, discussed everything carefully and in detail with his Maria Creek church members and only launched out with his family into an uncertain future of work among the Indians after his church's assurance that their prayers were with him and

---

[17] *History of Baptist Indian Missions*, pp. 45-46.

[18] McCoy discusses these problems in his letter to Staughton dated June 23, 1818 when he discloses his plans for Raccoon Creek. McCoy Papers, Reel 1.

that he had been called from among them. Before the party set off, the church met in the McCoy's home for prayer and gave their missionaries their valedictory blessing.

Meanwhile, the Board was secretly wondering what to make of this zealous man of God who had presented himself without a formal education and no means of support and had taken on the task of evangelizing a people who were scorned by most. Their initial references to his work were characterized by deep interest, praise and a sober portion of caution. In the newly founded *Latter Day Luminary*, run by Luther Rice, the editor wrote:

> Mr. McCoy appears actively engaged in arranging and entering on a plan of extensive and energetic operations among the Wabash Indians. The prospect appears inviting, especially to one whose vigour of mind, and zealous determination, become more prompt and decisive in view of difficulties and obstructions. In a recent letter, he observes, that he is sensible of his duty to communicate to the Board his plans, hopes and prospects, without reserve, and is determined to be governed by their instructions. He is aware that if his scheme fails entirely, he will, like many better men, upon attempting great things, be obliged to bear the sport of his enemies, and pity of his friends. But when foreboding and apparently insurmountable difficulties 'threaten to plunge all in ruin', he proposes going with Zerubbabel to see the great mountain levelled to a plain. When Sanballet and Tobiah, by insidious attempts and false rumours, would make him afraid, he proposes going in company with Nehimiah. When he realises pain and hardship, he will visit Gethsemane! And, should we have the happiness to see the fruit of his labours, it will be his joy to say, not unto us, not unto us, but unto thy name, O! Lord, be all the glory.[19]

Actually, before McCoy was set up and working among the Indians in November, 1818, his probationary year with the Board had run out. Nevertheless, acting in the belief that he was called to such work, Board or no Board, he began erecting two log cabins, one for the family and one for the school. He realized fully that, apart from a Presbyterian work among the Cherokees, there was little Christian work done among the Indians at this time by any denom-

---

[19] Vol. 1, May, 1818, article dated March 3, 1818, pp. 90-91.

ination. He believed, however, that the time had come in the will of God to change these circumstances. In order to do this, McCoy made a tour of the Weas, Kickapoos, Potawatomis and Delawares to sound them out on their willingness to have a missionary work among them. Still not having any knowledge of an Indian language, McCoy found himself having to use two interpreters, one to put his English into French and one to put the French into Potawatomi. One obvious problem was that the Indians were still suspicious of the American settlers, believing that they had had a better deal under the British. McCoy had to tread warily so as not to get tied up in politics. The missionary was not a little put out on hearing the Kickapoo chief tell him that he would rather have a dram of whiskey from McCoy than hear his talk about mission work and schools. McCoy's interpreters were Roman Catholic and they secretly opposed McCoy's plans of evangelizing the Indians so that the missionary could never be sure that his words were being correctly translated. Once McCoy was out of hearing, they swore with vulgar oaths that McCoy must be mad to think he could help the Indians. Finally, McCoy's translators refused to translate anything on the subject of religion. Another disappointment was that the Indian Agent had promised to give McCoy Indian interpreters and arrange for him to meet the Indian chiefs. These promises proved to be completely empty.

McCoy employs Corbly Martin as school teacher

Things went better with the school. McCoy employed a teacher for his handful of pupils called Mr. Corbly Martin who was an avowed disbeliever yet a conscientious man and a good worker. Martin was able to take many tasks off McCoy's shoulders so that in December, 1818, McCoy started to widen the area of his work, visiting Delawares and Shawnees on the Ohio frontier two hundred miles away. He took Martin with him, trusting that they would be able to find pupils for the school on the way. McCoy was now in some anxiety as the Board had not contacted him for many months and he still did not know if they planned to help support the new work or not. He began to think that his many reports were not getting through. On their way, miles from anywhere, McCoy was surprised to find a widow and her several children who professed Christ and put McCoy and Martin up for the night. This was a happy change as the two men had slept for many nights on bare, icy ground. The lady said that she would be willing to send four of her children to the school. McCoy does not say whether this good lady was an Indian or not but as he was speaking in the context of traders married to Indian women, it would appear that she was an Indian. Previously McCoy had found a Kickapoo who professed Christ.

As a result of his journeys and meetings with Indians, traders and Agents and correspondence with the War Department, McCoy decided that he was in the worst place possible for contact with the Indians and ought to move back to the Wabash to an area thirty miles square held by the Miamis through a treaty with the Government.[20] There the Government was planning to erect a smithy and flour mill. This plan was thwarted by an influx of white bootleggers into the area. On their way back home, the two men gained some insight into the plight of the Indians at the home of a friendly and hospitable Delaware chief. He told the two men how the Indian Agents had persuaded them to adopt the white man's ways, so they invested all their money in cattle and hogs, erected comfortable log cabins and became farmers. After only a year, however, they were told that the whites needed the Indians' improved land and they would have to leave. Soon after McCoy's visit, the Indians were forced to leave their homes in the middle of winter by order of Congress. McCoy returned home in freezing weather suffering from fever and delirium. He found his wife extremely ill with her eyes so swollen that she was almost blind. No sooner had McCoy arrived home than measles struck the family and they were all ill for a month. Meanwhile, Martin had six pupils, five whites and one Indian boy of the Brothertown Indians to teach. Soon another five Brothertown Indian children were added and a Wea child.

McCoy's employment by the Board was of a most unclear nature

At last, on January 9, 1819, McCoy heard from the Board. It was one of those many letters which McCoy was to receive which avoided answering any of his questions directly. All McCoy wanted to read were the words, "Yes, your contract with us is renewed," but such words were not written. The nearest Corresponding Secretary

---

[20] See McCoy's letter to W. Taylor dated January 8, 1819 in which McCoy discusses the above and seeks Government permission for establishing further missions. See also letter from John C. Calhoun dated February 15, 1819 concerning the War Department's interest in McCoy.

William Staughton approached to telling McCoy that he was still wanted, were the words:

> The Board is anxious to see the cause of the Redeemer spread through the nations and in a peculiar degree to hear of its influence on the Indian bosom. It also wishes its missionaries to be comfortable to the utmost extent of its ability.[21]

Instead of offering any kind of a contract to McCoy, Staughton praised McCoy for his hard work and success and wrote to him as if he had been a missionary for years and would continue to be so. The truth is that McCoy received no formal commission whatsoever from the Board and though they eventually gave him authority to commission missionaries himself, he was himself never officially appointed by the Board as a missionary. This caused McCoy much anxiety in succeeding years as when the Board were pleased with him, they called him their missionary, but when he did things with which they temporarily disagreed, then they temporarily disclaimed him as such.[22] It was very obvious that the Board wished to keep McCoy in their employment and he was told that his bills would be paid and an assistant would be sent, but he was not formally and officially appointed for a further period. There was also no special interest shown in the Board's letter for the general work he was doing apart from the fact that the Board said it approved. Nor was any special concern shown for the personal needs of the McCoys and those of their growing family, including their education. Nor was any concern shown for Martin and his pupils. This was the kind of strange relationship that McCoy was to have with the Board until 1842. He would often be admonished by the Board if they felt he was not following their interests meticulously enough but at other times they would act as if he were not their missionary at all on the grounds that there was but a "silent agreement," i.e. no formal contract, between them.

Furthermore, McCoy never quite knew where he stood with the Board financially. Even now, Staughton told McCoy that all his bills would be met whether for personal needs or buildings, or whatever, and he was encouraged to draw on the Board at any time.

---

[21] Letter dated Philadelphia, December 2, 1818, McCoy Papers, Reel 1.

[22] See McCoy's comments on his unclear status in a lengthy, undated report placed at the end of 1826 on Reel 5 of the McCoy Papers.

This generous statement was totally dampened by Staughton's adding that McCoy must bear in mind that he would only be allowed a maximum of $500 per annum. The cost of the great list of items for which Staughton said that McCoy could draw on the Board, however, amounted to far more than a paltry $500 per annum which was nowhere near enough to feed and clothe twenty-four people and more, and erect dwelling places and school buildings for them too. McCoy was also visited regularly by Indian chiefs and their braves who expected to be fed as was their own custom. Staughton was obviously interested in McCoy's suggestion that they should approach the Government concerning their grants for charity work among the Indians and he was told that the Board had set up a committee to discuss the matter. Actually, Staughton had already approached Governor Jennings on the subject based on a circular McCoy had sent out and had received a most favorable reply.[23]

The short-lived Indian work of Humphrey Posey and William Standige

McCoy also heard at this time that the Board had appointed Rev. Humphrey Posey of Haywood County, North Carolina, a man well-known to McCoy, to work among the Cherokees in North Carolina and Georgia. Just as McCoy had envied Peck and Welch, he must also have had a touch of envy at Posey's appointment to an area that was not pestered by anti-mission and anti-evangelism movements. Posey, however, became disappointed with the Board and left to take up itinerant preaching again in 1824.[24] Apparently, McCoy did not know at this time that the Sarepta Baptist Missionary Society were helping to support a preacher to the Cherokees, William Standige, in northern Georgia. Standige also resigned his position in 1824. Posey, too, was to remain a life-long friend of McCoy's and threw his weight behind him in 1842 when the Board began to run down their Indian mission. It must be confessed here that public opinion was always more on the side of the Cherokees, Creeks, Seminoles, Choctaws and Chickasaws than the more northern tribes among whom McCoy worked. The Board, indeed,

---

[23] Letter dated merely 1818 but with August written in another hand on cover, McCoy Papers, Reel 1.

[24] Evan Jones carried on much of the work after Posey left.

adopted the common way of referring to the former as "Civilized Tribes" and the latter as "Wild Tribes" and they were more easily persuaded to finance the "civilized" Cherokee and Creeks rather than the "wild" Potawatomis and Osages.

Turning to the Government for Indian development funds

As soon as McCoy recovered from a bout of severe fever which had struck again, he deepened his studies of the Miami language and was able to make more relaxed plans for the future of his mission, having now some assurance that he had a supporter. Sadly the whites were encroaching on the Raccoon Creek area, causing the Indians to flee. The Indians fled from the criminal whites without opposition.

On a visit to Vincennes, he found several Delaware Indians with whom he was acquainted now languishing in prison for manslaughter. They had been sold whiskey by the whites and had killed a man in a drunken fight. The Indians had not been given legal aid but also neither food nor clothing. McCoy prayed with the men and looked after their present material needs, determined more than ever to spend his life in the service of a people with no rights.[25] He had been seeking official approval of his work and free access to Indian territories for some time and had been greatly disappointed at delays in receiving a reply. Now McCoy heard that the Government were granting a $10,000 a year for Indian improvement so he contacted people of influence in Vincennes who applied to the Government on his behalf for a portion of the money to be used in missionary work. He made it quite clear that such funding must go through the Board and after McCoy had gained the Government's interest, the Board entered into successful arrangements with them.[26] Though McCoy received no money as yet, he was informed that his project had found favor with the Government. McCoy returned home to find his family ill again.

---

[25] See McCoy's report on this incident dated April 12, 1819 sent to Staughton, McCoy Papers, Reel 1.

[26] See Staughton's letter to McCoy dated September 22, 1819, McCoy Papers, Reel 1.

McCoy encounters the Delawares

Within a couple of days McCoy was on the move once more, visiting the Delawares with a most unreliable Wea Indian as interpreter. It was the rainy season and it was difficult finding dry wood for the fire. When John, McCoy's Indian companion found that the tinder and flint were useless for lighting a fire in the rain, he, unobserved by McCoy, simply threw them away so that throughout the entire journey, no fires could be made. Wherever the two men went, they encountered Indian after Indian intoxicated from the wares of the bootleggers. Once McCoy and the Wea were surrounded by drunken Indians of both sexes who demanded food with many a threat of violence but no harm was done to the two travelers. After a few days march, McCoy was able to buy tinder and flint from a French trader and confer with the principal Delaware chief, Captain Anderson. The chief said that he had nothing against the tribe's children learning at McCoy's school but reminded him that both of the Delaware children from his tribe who had been educated by the whites were later killed by them, one in his sleep. One chief wanted to know if the white man made a policy of first educating Indians, then killing them. Captain Anderson told McCoy straight that if the Indians had been settled, they would have nothing against having a missionary station in their midst but as they were a threatened people, never knowing if they could stay where they were or not, such a project would be futile. Hearing such tales must have wrenched at McCoy's heart as he knew that the Indians' judgement was sound and the threat of constant removal an evil truth.

References to McCoy's work left out of the Board's mission reports

A further disappointment came McCoy's way in the early summer of 1819. The Board regularly sent copies of their various magazines, circulars and reports for McCoy to distribute and canvas for subscribers. Rice sent him copies of his *Latter Day Luminary*, urging McCoy to collect money to support his enterprise. Now Staughton sent McCoy a pile of printed circulars to be distributed among the Wabash Association churches. The circular's contained a report on how the various missionaries were faring. Judson of Burma is mentioned first, then Peck and Welch are described as doing excellent work, though it appears that they are now working with whites and Peck had left St. Louis. The readers are told that Posey has had to give up his work for a time among the Cherokees because of the "unsettled nature" of that tribe and Henry George is described as going to work among the Indians for several months. There is not a word mentioned about McCoy, though his work was progressing very well and his school up and running.[27] Such behavior on the part of the Board never ceased to shock McCoy and the only explanation he could give was that the Board were frightened of publishing success stories of Indian evangelism because then readers would begin to fund Indian missions rather than missions in Burma.[28]

Corbly Martin's conversion

On June 2 and 3, McCoy had most constructive talks with the Delawares and Miamis, the latter smoking a peace pipe with him. McCoy became ill again but could not avoid being invited to a most uncomfortable council with a Wea chief named Stone-Eater and his chiefs, some of whom were highly intoxicated. They were joined by drunken Delawares who gate-crashed the gathering and a dispute arose which made McCoy fear that soon weapons would be used. The chief had removed the whiskey bottle away from the men and placed it by his side for safe keeping. His aim had been to keep the meeting sober. However, such was the temptation of the strong spirits that the chief found himself emptying the bottle and now bedlam was loose. McCoy and his companion silently stole away and left the intoxicated company to their own antics. The remaining journey home was marred by John trying to steal McCoy's horse and when home was at last reached, McCoy was suffering from a bilious fever which lasted for several months. During this illness, McCoy had to visit Vincennes on behalf of his missionary plans but had to break the long journey several times because of the fever. On his return, he was so ill that Mrs. McCoy spoke to him about his approaching death. McCoy told her that he knew he was about to die and that he could not expect the Lord to work a miracle on his behalf. This was too much for Mr. Martin who had been laboring under conviction for some time. He fell down on his knees at McCoy's bedside and prayed that his friend would be healed. Martin's prayer was answered and

---

[27] McCoy Papers, Reel 1.

[28] When the Annual Report was made, McCoy's plans for Fort Wayne were mentioned.

the faithful teacher received a heavenly reward himself on that day, for as he prayed, God's loving salvation was bestowed upon him.

Martin is replaced by Johnston Lykins

As two ministers Wilson Thompson and Aaron Frakes, were visiting at the time, Martin was duly baptized and straight away, he professed that he felt called to the ministry. Happy as this event was, it did not mean that McCoy had now a converted friend at his side and one who could lead the Indians to Christ. Martin left the mission school to pastor a flock of whites. He did however, keep in touch with McCoy and helped to make the needs of the Indian Mission known. McCoy found a replacement for Martin in young Johnston Lykins of Virginia. The fact that Lykins, born August 15, 1800, was not a believer did not trouble McCoy as he had seen what had happened to Martin. Indeed, Lykins not only professed faith in Christ before long but was eventually accepted by the Board and married the McCoys' daughter Delilah (b. November 24, 1809) on February 27, 1827, from which date on, he always addressed McCoy as "Father". Lykins qualified as a doctor and after years of missionary work which had ruined his health and body, he became the first Council President and Mayor of Kansas City.[29]

---

[29] William S. Gregory was voted in as Mayor in 1853 but was disqualified as he had not lived long enough in Kansas City to be eligible for the post. I am grateful to Wilda Sandy of the Kansas City Public Library for these details found in the library's Local History Biographies.

An artist's sketch of Fort Wayne, Indiana Territory and its surroundings

Chapter Three
Taking Over Fort Wayne for Heavenly Warfare (1820-21)

McCoy approaches Congress for permission to extend Indian missions

As soon as McCoy was able to sit up in bed and do a little writing after his long illness, he received a letter from the Government inviting him to apply for a portion of the $10,000 set aside by the President of the United States for Indian improvement.[1] McCoy was asked to state his missionary status and affiliation and explain how he hoped to benefit the Indians. McCoy lost no time in contacting influential people in Congress both to inform them of his plans and to seek information regarding extending the possibilities and outreach of his mission. As the U. S. Government had been officially at war with the Western Indians and there was no Government Department for Indian Affairs, McCoy wrote to the Secretary of War, John C. Calhoun, outlining his plans. Calhoun, from this time on, allowed himself to be strongly influenced by McCoy, viewing him as an expert on the matter of Indian settlement. In 1824, he established a Government Department for Indian Affairs under his own supervision as Secretary of War. This caused quite a commotion because Calhoun, fearing that Congress was not ready for such a move, had not asked their permission. Calhoun, however, gained the backing of the President, but it was not until 1832 that Congress officially backed the Department and created the office of Commissioner of Indian Affairs. McCoy also

---

[1] Letter from John Johnson, Government Agent to the Potawatomis, Delawares and several other tribes, to McCoy dated September 30, 1819, McCoy Papers, Reel 1. The personal details of this letter shows how well-known and respected was McCoy in Government circles and perhaps explains why Government officials invariably approached McCoy directly rather than through the Board, though their grants were paid directly to the Board at McCoy's request. McCoy forwarded Johnson's letter to Staughton. Johnson kept closely in touch with McCoy.

wrote to Congressman W. Taylor with whom he had been in correspondence for some time. He now asked Taylor to help him gain permission from Congress to set up mission stations among the Kickapoos and Delawares on their being removed to Missouri. McCoy also made preparations to evangelize the Miamis. All these plans were explained in detail to the Board who were asked to send more missionaries to take on the expanding work.

McCoy plans a new station at Fort Wayne

Next, McCoy planned to travel the 180 miles to Fort Wayne, twenty-five miles from where the St. Joseph River flows into Lake Michigan. He was to journey with his Delaware teacher, Ben Gray and another Indian to speak with the Indian Agent, Dr. Turner, but his bad health prevented him. Young Lykins, eager to prove his worth, asked to be sent instead and off he went to contact Turner and the Miami chief Pishewa. The agent received Lykins well and urged the Baptists to settle down at Fort Wayne where they would be able to take over public buildings rent free. The Agent said he could not allow the missionaries to live directly in a Miami village as drunkenness and violence was rife among the natives. Not being too happy with this news, McCoy made a trip to Fort Wayne himself on March 18, 1820 to have a meeting with Dr. Turner. He took a Delaware Indian, Silk Hembus, with him so that he could be taught throughout the journey. On the way, Hembus' horse became lame and McCoy's horse deserted him and was only found after a very long search. The ground was water-logged along the way and sleeping out was a most difficult and uncomfortable task. During their journey's adventures, McCoy was able to discuss deeply with Hembus and also learn something of the Delaware tribe's religion. Having had to travel most of the way on foot, Hembus became exhausted after about 120 miles but could find nowhere where he could sleep undisturbed. The area was now heavily populated with Indians almost all of whom were drunk and many threatening and dangerous. "Oh what a wretched people!" was McCoy's comment. Eventually the two travelers arrived at the home of Joseph Richardville, son of Pishewa. As was almost to be expected by now, Richardville and all his family and household were under the influence of what McCoy called "a bacchanalian revel." McCoy had to leave the exhausted Hembus behind and crossed the Wabash in a canoe, swimming his horse alongside him. Then the St. Mary's

River had to be swum and McCoy arrived safely but exhausted at Fort Wayne.

Once at Fort Wayne, McCoy proceeded with his plans to set up a station at Massinawa in the heart of Miami country. He was surprised when Pishewa told him he would be wasting his time there because of the state of his tribe. Indeed, McCoy could find no one who agreed with his plans in the slightest. As Fort Wayne was a major step in McCoy's missionary outreach and a decision to settle there was marked by problems that were to be with him for many years to come, perhaps it would be wisest at this stage to allow McCoy to give his own reasons for eventually choosing Fort Wayne as his next base and not Massinawa, as he originally intended. By way of explanation, McCoy wrote:

> But the Agent, the principle Miamie chief, and many others, were united to bring us to Fort Wayne, and I was under the necessity of consenting. True, it was a central point between Shawanoes, Putawatomies, Miamies, and others, a trading post to which many Indians resorted, and from which we could extend our acquaintance among the Indians in every direction; and as we could get buildings and a garden to occupy, without cost, I consoled myself somewhat, by supposing that we should lose little by stopping there, and we should, perhaps, while at that place, be able to make the most judicious selection for our permanent settlement.
>
> There were other considerations which weighed heavily in favour of accepting the invitation to Fort Wayne. We began to perceive that we had been mistaken in supposing that so much sympathy for the Indians could be excited in the Christian public, that a competent number of missionaries could be obtained. As yet, none had become willing to unite with us in our work. Our family had increased to the number of about twenty persons, and half of these were Indian children. No one female could be supposed to possess either muscle or mind sufficient to sustain the charge which devolved on Mrs. McCoy. In my absence, the care of everything without doors, as well as within, came upon her. She seemed to be sinking with fatigue and anxiety. At Massinawa, a place still more remote from supplies, and from places where labourers could be hired, and from which our circumstances would oftener carry me from home, these difficulties would be augmented. Moreover, the erection of buildings would be attended with considerable cost, especially so far from the settlements of

labouring people; and we were not quite certain that the Board would agree to meet the expense of erecting buildings, &c.

The chief attention of the board was directed to Burma and other countries beyond the seas, and missions to the Indians were a matter of no more than secondary consideration; and upon the mission begun at St. Louis, and designed to be extended to Indians west of the Mississippi, their favours for Indians would probably be exhausted. Neither the particular members of the board of missions, nor others, seemed to feel so much interest in the subject of Indian missions as to make themselves tolerably well acquainted with it. The public conjectured that a people so wretched as these Indians are would eagerly seize our offers to do them good, and were not prepared to make any allowance for the thousand disappointments and delays to which we were subject, especially when labouring under so many disadvantages.

We did exceedingly regret that we had not heard our patrons say to us, 'Seek out the most eligible site for your location, and study the most hopeful means and measures for accomplishing the designs of the mission; take time to confer freely with us; give yourselves wholly to these things, and we will take care that the necessaries of life shall he furnished you.' Had they given us this assurance, our course of proceedings, from the first, would, in many respects, have been different from what it was.

The hardheartedness of the frontier white inhabitants, and other causes, were driving the Indians further from our house, so that we could not hope to enlarge our school or improve our operations in that place. If our business should appear to the board to be stationary upon its present small scale, we should soon expect them to advise the discontinuance of our labours, especially as they had not, as we believed, felt altogether hearty in sustaining them. We were obliged, therefore, as soon as possible, to get to some place where we could increase the number of Indian scholars, and be able to make it appear to the public that our business was improving. Necessity, and not choice, compelled us to consent to go to Fort Wayne.[2]

---

[2] *History of Baptist Indian Missions*, pp. 68-69.

Doubts about the usefulness of missionary societies

McCoy was beginning to realize that his views of a missionary being sent out by a church supervisory body or missionary society had been more romantic than practical. He realized that no one could share his particular calling and the Board, at best, could only be of limited assistance in the work God had given him to do. Indeed, McCoy was going through the same situation that William Carey had experienced with the Particular Baptist Missionary Society. Both pioneer missionaries had to revise their views of missionary societies radically. Both had the closest friends on their missionary boards, Carey had Ryland, Fuller and Sutcliff and McCoy had Spencer Cone, Luther Rice and, eventually, the non-Board member but very influential J. L. Dagg. Both missionaries realized before much time on the mission field had passed that their societies could only organize a limited measure of publicity and prayer support for them and encourage a little financial help. The estimated two thirds to which extent Carey and his missionary friends supported their own mission in India can be compared to the amount of funds McCoy had to raise for his. Carey, as McCoy, often thought that the home committee's plans for the mission field were not according to knowledge and insight and were too patronizing. Carey fared better than McCoy in that British Baptists, on the whole, were theologically more open to missionary activity than their American counterparts. Indeed, those churches which had seen rapid growth in the new settlements on the Western frontier were almost fanatically anti-missions and anti-evangelistic which quickly led to their stagnation. Unlike McCoy, Carey received a good deal of support from non-Baptists, especially Anglicans. McCoy had an easier task than Carey in church planting as the American home board did not interfere with his drawing up of church constitutions and declarations of faith. The home board was often a millstone around Carey's neck as they strove to dictate his church polity from their isolation in Britain. Both missionaries suffered from the wrongs of wayward missionaries in their own circle,[3] both were accused of being too independent of their boards and both were

---

[3] See chapter 25, *The Schism* in S. Pearce Carey's book *William Carey*.

eventually moved to break off ties with their home committees and make themselves independent.[4]

Peck decides not to join McCoy as the Board had planned

After settling the matter of his establishing a mission station with the Indian Agent, McCoy set off for home, finding Hembus waiting for him where he had left him. The two men eventually also found the Indian's horse with all his belongings intact, though the travelers quite lost their own way in their search. They arrived back at Raccoon Creek on April 2. By this time McCoy was becoming more proficient in the Delaware language and was pleased to be visited by several Delaware Indians on his arrival. He was interested to note that the Delawares had no vulgar swear words in their language and was told that the Indians never cursed until they met English-speaking people. On his arrival back home, McCoy was disappointed not to find J. M. Peck awaiting him. After the missionaries un-successful attempts to contact the Indians at St. Louis and along the Mississippi River, the Board had answered McCoy's pleas for new missionaries by saying they would send Peck. McCoy had cor-responded with the gentleman for some months and was looking forward to his assistance. Awaiting McCoy was a letter from Peck saying that he could not continue the burden of missionary life and that his wife was in poor health. One of Peck's major reasons for not continuing among the Indians was that the Board just did not keep to their agreements with him and left him with no income so that he was continually forced to take up his occupation as a teacher so that he could look after his family.[5]

Peck, as also Posey, continued to be zealous supporters of McCoy's work. When the Foreign Mission Board lost interest in the evangelization of the Indians and began to fall apart through inter-nal differences of policy and politics, the two men maintained their strong friendship with McCoy. Then Peck, who became a Foreign Missions Board member, strove hard with a great measure of success

---

[4] Ibid, chapter 26, *The Woe*; also chapter 25, *Sorrow Upon Sorrow* in F. Deaville Walker's, *William Carey*, Moody Press, 1980.

[5] See Peck's letter to McCoy dated probably February 10, 1820, McCoy Papers, Reel 1.

to have the Indian work of his Board transferred entirely into Mc-Coy's hands.

The move to Fort Wayne

After a rest of only two days, McCoy was on the move again. This time to Vincennes, accompanied by Lykins, where McCoy made arrangements and bought goods, animals and equipment for their journey and mission to Fort Wayne. McCoy became very ill with fever and vomiting on the way and feared that his move to Fort Wayne would be delayed. Ten days after departure, McCoy and Lykins returned and McCoy was pleased to find himself fit again after very few days.

On 3 May, 1820, McCoy and his party set off for Fort Wayne in two groups. One group, setting out from Fort Harrison, punted a bateau[6] crewed by four men up the Wabash with five Indian children and most of the McCoy's and Lykins' private positions on board.[7] The McCoys with six of their children, Lykins, a hired laborer and an Indian pupil set off on horseback two days later. Two of the McCoy's children were left with friends in Indiana. Those going by land drove fifteen head of cattle and forty-three pigs before them. A group of Indians promised to accompany the party but they decided to turn back after only one night sleeping in the rain.

The travelers caused quite a sensation going through the Indian villages as many of the tribesmen had never seen either cows or sheep, nor a family of parents with their many children accompanying them. Usually, whenever the missionaries were on the move, they passed village after village of intoxicated Indians but this time McCoy felt that he had never seen so many people given completely over to strong drink. It was almost impossible to find a sober man anywhere. The Indians were too drunk to bother about the strangers who passed through, so this terrible state of affairs proved a blessing for the travelers. On the way through the Indian villages, McCoy's party heard that Stone-Eater, their Wea friend, had been

---

[6] A long, flat-bottomed boat. For the benefit of American readers, the English word 'punt' means to push the boat forward by means of long poles. It appears to be now obsolete in this sense in the American language.

[7] See McCoy's account dated May 19, 1820, McCoy Papers, Reel 1. For a description of this journey, also *History of Baptist Indian Missions.*

murdered but his murderer had been found and killed. Now both men lay in the same grave. McCoy paid an elderly Indian couple to tell Joseph Richardville that the group was under way and ask him to send some form of protection as the group still feared that their cattle and pigs might land up in an Indian cooking pot and their own lives might be in danger. The elderly couple took the money with thanks but after leaving the missionaries promptly decided not to carry out their request. On realizing that the couple had let them down, McCoy and Lykins went to seek protection. They left Mrs. McCoy and the children with the hired laborer in a sheltered spot and journeyed on to find Richardville. Only one threatening incident occurred on the way. A man attempted to strike McCoy and Lykins with a dog's carcass but the offender was quickly taken to task by his drunken friends. McCoy and Lykins found Richardville and the influential Indian assured McCoy that he would personally guide the travelers and send word around that they were not to be molested. He arranged with McCoy that he would meet his party the next day and escort them himself to Fort Wayne. This was very assuring news but, in his haste to get back to his wife, McCoy moved swifter than the Indian messengers who were supposed to prepare his way and he and Lykins were threatened. One young man seized the bridle of McCoy's horse in a great rage and began to draw his knife. A drunken French-Indian, however, rode up and prevented the young man from using his weapon and was able to pacify him. The man and his friend accompanied the missionary group some way until they were out of danger. At one time, they all had to gallop fast to rid themselves of an angry group of drunken Indians who were intent on no good. Now the two men were hemmed in by the Massinawa River on the one side and the Wabash on the other and were compelled to pass through a number of Indian villages apparently all full of drunken Indians, wasting away their annuities. McCoy now feared greatly for the wife and children he had left behind. When McCoy reached the camp, late at night, he found all were safe.

On the following day, Richardville failed to turn up, so the rather anxious missionaries set off without a friendly Indian escort. After a mile or so, they were met by two Indians who told them that Richardville was delayed because of the sudden death of a friend and the two would lead the missionary party. As now the Indians knew they had nothing to fear from the McCoy party, they greeted the whites with friendly gestures all along the way and the worst drunkards were kept in check by the more sober Indians. Dogs were kept at bay so that the cattle and pigs would not be frightened.

Meanwhile the rain poured down and the party found they would have to spend another night sleeping in soaking wet clothes. The party arrived at Fort Wayne on March 15, the boat party arriving a few days later. They found sturdy, habitable buildings waiting for them and two acres of freshly plowed garden, a gift from the Indian Agent Dr. Turner and Captain Hackley, which helped to make them feel at home quickly. They were, however, a hundred miles from any other white family and almost another hundred miles more from the next settlement.

A brief account of the fort's history

Fort Wayne was founded by General "Mad" Anthony Wayne in 1794 after he had defeated the Indians at the Battle of Fallen Timbers. It was situated where the St. Mary and St. Joseph Rivers converge to form the Maumee River. The fort was constructed as a military base to secure the territory of north west Ohio. In the following year, Wayne drew up a treaty with the local Indians whereby they gave up two-thirds of Ohio and part of Indiana to the United States. Wayne forced the Indians to agree to his building sixteen further forts in the remaining Indian territory. Ohio became the seventeenth state in the Union in March 1803. In the same year further treaties were signed, removing further land from the nine tribes living around Vincennes and along the Wabash River. By 1804 the Delawares had lost all their land between the Wabash and Ohio Rivers to Governor Harrison and were virtually a people without a home. The War of 1812 brought with it further strictures against the Indians, particularly those in the Indiana-Ohio region who had supported the British. This brought further loss of land, particularly in the case of the Shawnees and, further away along the Missouri, the Sioux. Indiana became the nineteenth state in the Union in 1816 and stage coach routes were set up in 1820, cutting up the remaining Indian territory. Thus, when McCoy reached Fort Wayne as his next step in his plan to evangelize the Indians, he found that the Indians had become a highly endangered species and were living on small pockets of land which had somehow escaped the eyes of the treaty-makers or which could be claimed from them at any time by the whites. It was at Fort Wayne that McCoy saw the fallacy of the Government's plan to buy land from the Indians or to reimburse them in money rather than kind under a project termed "Indian Improvement." As soon as the Indians received money, they spent it on alcohol which they consumed quickly, becoming exceedingly aggressive. Around Fort Wayne alone there were eight or nine murders committed by drunken Indians each time they received their annuities.

Establishing the mission station

Fort Wayne had now little to remind visitors of its former military state and was simply a village of Government officials, traders, retired soldiers and craftsmen of English, French, Canadian and Indian descent. The nearest other white settlement was in the State of Ohio some 100 miles away. The Fort Wayne school was opened on May 29 with 25 pupils, ten of them had an English background and six a French one. The French children came from Roman Catholic homes. There were eight Indians and one Negro. McCoy was pleased to find that there was a continual movement of Indians through the village and he hoped to persuade more of them to listen to his preaching and send their children to the school.

The McCoys were now without Lykins who had served the term arranged and now left to be rejoined with his family and to continue his studies. Lykins had not been employed by the Board but paid out of McCoy's own pocket. He had hoped to rejoin the mission in January of the following year but was delayed for several months because of the severe illness of his mother. McCoy had now to run the school himself but applied to Ohio for a man to assist him. Now Mrs. McCoy was looking after a household of twenty people whom she clothed, fed and lodged. Besides this she held classes for Indian women and girls in knitting and household duties. Whites and Indians, staff, laborers and pupils, all ate at the same table and lived as one family. On the weekends, services were opened to the neighbors and visitors as well as the mission station family. McCoy found he was eagerly listened to and was shown real friendship and kindness.

The first conversions and baptism

Mrs. Turner, the wife of the Agent and her sister Mrs. Hackley were half Indian and helped the McCoys greatly in contacting the local Miamis. It was not long before Mrs. Turner became convicted of her sin and professed faith in Christ. Apparently she had longed for the gospel to enter her heart and life but had thought that as she was an Indian, she was ineligible to be loved by God. Dr. Turner, however, had scruples about his wife being baptized but gave them up after several months. Meanwhile, Mrs. Hackley professed conversion and asked to be baptized. This was arranged for June 18. At ten a. m. on that day, McCoy gathered his family, workers and pupils, besides the newly converted and their families, on the banks of the Maumee River and preached on the subject of baptism. A number of whites and Indians not directly connected with the missionary base attended the meeting. At the river side, all sung a hymn McCoy had written for the occasion:

> Glad tidings, so the angels sung,
> Until the heavens with gladness rung;
> Glad tidings late my soul replied,
> For me my Lord was crucified.

> "The news shall spread through all the earth."
> So sang the host at Jesus' birth.
> Ye gentle waves, I call on you
> To say, is not this promise true ?

> This very stream was lately stained
> With blood from strangling soldiers drained;[8]
> Now, strange to tell, the Prince of Peace
> In it displays his sovereign grace.

> Ye oaks, which shook while cannons roar'd,
> Now bow your heads and praise the Lord;
> Tell the wild man beneath your shade
> Why Christ in Jordan's stream was laid.

> Those warlike towers on yonder wall,[9]
> Like those of Jericho, must fall,
> While deathful weapons dormant lie -
> Shout, saints, the Ark is passing by.

> Ye winds, which spread the news of death,
> No longer breathe offensive breath;

---

[8] In a former battle fought near Fort Wayne, the corpses were so numerous that they dammed the river.

[9] The fortifications around Fort Wayne.

> But the glad tidings loud proclaim,
> "Here saints rejoice in Jesus' name."
>
> Sure all who hear will join and sing,
>   Glory to God, our Christ is King.
> Still let the Gospel spread abroad,
> Till all the world shall worship God.

The baptism scene had a profound influence on the crowd and many were moved to tears. That evening many more people came to the service than usual and McCoy commented, "This was a good day to a couple of poor missionaries, who hoped that the blessing enjoyed might be but like a drop before a copious shower."[10]

McCoy's interest in world-wide evangelism

McCoy's heart was not only open to the spiritual and material needs of the Indians and the white settlers but he followed the progress of Judson in Burma with great interest. He was also keenly moved by the situation of the enslaved Africans. He therefore joined a society with his old friend and brother-in-law William Polke and others of his correspondents and friends which aimed to educate colored children, one of the intentions being to repatriate them in Africa where they could be of use to generally improve the conditions of the Negroes. To this end, McCoy began to educate a 20 year old Negro boy named Jesse Cox who seemed to be something of a public speaker and showed great promise as a Christian and as a scholar. He had come to faith under McCoy's care and had been baptized by him. When McCoy heard Cox singing of his faith with a radiant face, he told Staughton, "I am transported with the hope that the wilds of Africa will one day echo the melody of his voice."[11] Fearing that the Board might be too color-conscious to approve of this move, McCoy wrote fine reports concerning the young man's progress and assured the Board that they would not have to spend a penny on Cox.[12]

---

[10] *History of Baptist Indian Missions*, p. 78.

[11] Letter dated January 11, 1820, McCoy Papers, Reel 1.

[12] See the constitution of this society and the list of members in it, dated January, 1820, McCoy Papers, Reel 1.

New proposals from the Board

Meanwhile, the Board at Philadelphia were discussing McCoy's plans and proposals. Things were not developing quite as they had thought but McCoy had impressed the Board with his sincerity and success. They thought McCoy's ideas of setting up mission stations rather than doing itinerant work was too expensive by far, but they hoped that the government would come to their support in such matters. They were also finding that McCoy had a good business head on his shoulders and was able to sell off the Raccoon Creek buildings and property with profit. Though McCoy had invested a good deal of his own capital in the Raccoon Mission, all proceeds went to the Board. A committee was therefore formed to discuss McCoy's numerous suggestions and their own plans for the Indians. *The Latter Day Luminary* for May, 1821 gave the following report on the latest meeting of the Fort Wayne committee:

> The committee on the subject of the Fort Wayne Mission, under the Rev. Isaac McCoy, respectfully submit to the consideration of the Board the following resolutions.
>
> 1. That the Board view with pleasure the zeal, the piety, the diligence, and the economy of Mr. McCoy in the work assigned him.
>
> 2. That Mr. McCoy be directed to encourage agriculture, and all the arts of civilized life, among the Indians, to as great an extent as the amount of funds assigned him will any way admit.
>
> 3. That Mr. McCoy be authorised to draw upon the Board, from time to time, for such sums as may be necessary for the establishment, not exceeding $500 every two months, including the amount which may be received from government.[13]
>
> 4. That all expenditures of that mission shall be incurred under the authority and responsibility of Mr. McCoy.
>
> 5. That all monies received by Mr. McCoy for the benefit of the establishment, from agents or individuals, shall be placed to the credit of the Board.
>
> 6. That an agent or agents be appointed to travel and collect funds, for the purpose of aiding in the support of the mission under the care of Mr. McCoy.

---

[13] At the meeting, the Board proscribed the same method of financing Posey's Valley Towns Mission among the Cherokees. However, a gristmill and sawmill were also granted them.

7. That a farmer, a blacksmith and shoemaker, under the character of missionaries, be sent to Fort Wayne, as soon as they can be obtained.

8. That the thanks of this body be presented to the Female Benevolent Society of Xenia, for their undertaking the support of two of the Indian children; also to Mrs. Alexander, (widow 65 years of age) for 20-1/4 yards of homespun which she prepared with her own hands.

9. That the thanks of the Board be presented also to the numerous individuals who have contributed to the advance of the interests of the Fort Wayne mission, and that they be respectfully solicited to continue their offices of love, with a hope that others may be led to imitate so praiseworthy an example.[14]

The weaknesses in the Board's proposals examined

In spite of the kind words and display of appreciation, the growing Fort Wayne family were not too pleased with these resolutions. In plain terms, they meant that they would receive a mere $250 dollars a month to feed some 60-70 mouths, clothe a large number of pupils and run the school and training farm. Worse, this amount would include what they were due from the government, which they knew to be a far greater sum. Linked to this was a fear that the Board's demand that all gifts should be made payable to the Board and come under their administration seemed to mean that the Board would not be prepared to fund the mission with sums above the $250 per month, even if they were earmarked for the mission and were urgently needed. Also, the ninth point gave the impression that the mission was benefitting from a great number of generous donations which was hardly the case. McCoy had asked the Board to make the urgent need for funds clear, without which the mission could not function.

Throughout McCoy's dealings with the Board, he was always frustrated by the Board's hesitancy to lay the true nature of the mission before the public. In point of fact, even these stringent rules were never implemented. The Board never kept to their promise of bi-monthly payments to the mission and the only agents McCoy ever had were those who volunteered to help him privately such as Corbly Martin and George Evans of Ohio or those he paid out of his own

---

[14] *Latter Day Luminary*, vol. ii, May, 1821, pp. 286-287.

pocket for specific work. Evans was an authorized agent for the Baptist Home Mission and in this office often helped McCoy.[15] Meanwhile, we find McCoy saying, "I am now entirely alone! I cannot refrain from tears when I look through my window on those unfortunate beings who are passing yonder, and reflect that none is here to assist in their improvement, except myself."[16] McCoy must have felt that abandonment with greater pain when he looked into his copy of *The American Baptist Magazine* for July of that year. The Board announced that they had taken no less than ten thousand dollars from the missionary funds to assist in the erection of the Columbian College in Washington. This was money which had been sent to the Board especially earmarked for such work as McCoy was doing. Columbian College was initially built with the aim of preparing missionaries for the foreign field, including the Indian Mission. It was built on the empty stomachs of missionaries already on that field.

In spite of this loneliness, it must have been a real comfort for McCoy to know that the Roman Catholics with their massive financial backing, had failed over a period of years to entice more than a dozen Indian children to their schools while McCoy was already teaching far more and the school was continually growing.[17] In his report to the Board concerning this state of affairs, McCoy added, "We feel confident, dear sir, that God hath done this for us." [18]From now on, however, the Roman Catholics did their level best to arouse public criticism of the Baptists, even to the extent of printing bogus reports about them. McCoy's practice was always to be kind and courteous to such critics and invite them for a meal and a friendly talk which often broke down barriers.

Up to this time, McCoy had not received a salary, nor did he want one. He had hitherto, according to the Board's wishes, sent in the bills he accrued to be paid for by the Board. Later, he made out checks or drafts in the name of the Board, to be honored by them. This system

---

[15] See McCoy's undated Instructions for Bro. Elder G. Evans, Agent, McCoy Papers, Reel 2.

[16] Ibid., vol ii, August, 1820, p. 190.

[17] There were 15 children in the school at this time, about two-thirds being Indians.

[18] *Latter Day Luminary*, vol. ii, February, 1821 (report from previous December), p. 298.

had three disadvantages. It meant that the McCoys were always living in debt as it took months for a bill to be sent to Philadelphia and eventually be settled by a bank. It meant, too, that McCoy never quite knew if a bill would be settled by the Board or whether they would refuse to honor a check he signed on the Board's behalf. Thirdly, it meant that McCoy had always to pay more for goods as the traders would always give better value for money when cash payments were made. The Board, too, did not take into account the extent of the McCoys' financial commitments in their yearly budget. They wanted the missionaries to keep their own personal records of expenses separate from those of the mission. They suggested paying a wage for the McCoys' needs and maintained that McCoy should apply to them each time money was needed for the missionary work. This was most impractical as the McCoys lived as one family with their workers and pupils, so there was no practical means of separating family expenditure from that of the mission.

The Board's proposals were for the public eye alone

This situation made McCoy realize that he must seek for financial and material backing directly from the churches and individuals who supported him rather than from the Board alone. He thus had a circular printed which listed the work of the mission and its needs such as food, clothing and books. Martin was engaged "for a moderate compensation" to circulate this broadsheet. It was quite plain to McCoy that the mission could not be run on $250 a month, which the Board had told the Baptist public that McCoy was getting but which had not yet materialized. At times, the mission had hardly any expenditures due to a good harvest or work being done for no payment but, on other occasions, much more money was needed i.e. when school books or additional food and clothing were needed. The publication of the Board's methods of financing McCoy's mission, however, was only for the public eye. Staughton wrote a severe letter to McCoy on June 9, 1820, saying he was dropping his title of Corresponding Secretary in order to address McCoy as a friend and brother. Instead of addressing McCoy as such, he gave him a severe and, under the circumstances, highly unwarranted dressing down. Staughton then told McCoy straight that when the Board had told him at the start of his work that he would receive $500 per annum, it was determined that this should cover the entire expenditures of the mission, wages, buildings, school and all![19] The Board might consider going $200 above that but then the absolute limit was reached. Furthermore Staughton was shocked at the amount of pork (written in large letters and underlined twice) that McCoy's Indian pupils were eating and told McCoy that to receive tuition gratuitously was as much as the Indians ought to expect. Staughton told McCoy that the Board had not been in favor of his leaving Raccoon Creek without their express permission. This was strange news indeed as McCoy had discussed the move with the Board for many months and had received their blessing. Indeed, on the very Board of Managers' report on whose margins Staughton wrote his severe words, the following statement is made concerning McCoy:

> Brother McCoy has gone from his situation to Fort Wayne. The Managers recommended and approve of this change, as it will bring the mission more immediately into the centre of an Indian settlement and furnish him with the greatest prospect of doing good, by instructing and publishing the way of salvation.

Staughton seemed unaware that he was acting against the published policies of the Board. Yet the Board of Managers' report had been printed and circulated before Staughton wrote to McCoy on its margins to tell him that he was acting outside of the Board's will and his expenses were "disproportionate to his usefulness". Also in the report, the Board claimed that they had not only agreed to McCoy's move from Raccoon Creek even but they had initiated it. In the same circular, the Board also told their readers and supporters that Peck was to join McCoy and work with him, although it was known at the time that Peck had no such plans. They did not record that Peck had finally discontinued working among the Indians, his reason being expressed in the words, "The truth is, I have to exert myself every way to meet the expenses of my family as I have received no remittance from the board for a long time and for that purpose am obliged to teach school."[20] After being let down by the Board, Peck first taught

---

[19] McCoy Papers, Reel 1.

[20] Letter written to McCoy by Peck probably on February 10, 1820, McCoy Papers, Reel 1.

history at a college and then rented a farm which he worked for some years, giving generously of his profits to support evangelistic work.

It is ironic to note that Staughton penned his carping words on the back and margins of a Manager's Report which ended with the words:

> Permitted to live in an age before unparalleled for the wonders of grace, and called on aloud to stand in our lot and accomplish with our might whatsoever our hands find to do, God grant that we may none of us sink into slothful inactivity, degrading selfishness, or infidel despondency. Prophecy must be accomplished, and the Spirit of brightness effuse his living beams. If human effort, of itself, be imbecile, the Head of the church can render it effectual. Prove me now, saith the Lord of Hosts, if I will not open the windows of heaven, and pour you out a blessing that there shall not be room to receive it.

The Board's failure to understand circumstances at Fort Wayne

McCoy now made a journey into Ohio in order to buy provisions for those under his care and also to purchase much needed equipment such as a wagon, a spinning wheel and wool. As was his want, McCoy preached regularly on his journey and found many an isolated settler or Indian eager to hear the gospel. He was able to hire a Christian young woman who was willing to help his wife with the domestic chores. McCoy had to travel many miles to find food and material that he could afford. The fact that everything had to be transported at least a hundred miles to Fort Wayne ran up the prices considerably. Indeed, corn and other staple foods cost up to eight times as much as in the eastern states. This fact was never really appreciated by the Board who would receive bills from McCoy and compare them with the shop round the corner in Philadelphia, Washington or Boston and then judge McCoy to be extravagant. Indeed, the financing of the mission became a major problem with the Board which made them stop much of the planned work among the Indians as they could not understand the expenses involved and adopted the most impractical measures to keep costs down. This was one of the main reasons why the Board had given up most of its missionary outreach to the Indians on the Western frontier and not because of the anti-mission opposition there. Such opposition never troubled people of the caliber of Peck.

Conditions at the mission school

McCoy returned from Ohio very ill, as was usual when he made a lengthy journey. Though hardly able to walk, he baptized a man who had recently professed Christ and was pleased to enrol another eleven Indian pupils. The new teacher whom McCoy employed did not live up to expectations either professionally or morally. McCoy, as was his continuous practice, did not mention the names of the teachers he received either through his own efforts or those of the Board who proved ineffective. This was not to mar their future work. Soon another teacher was hired from Ohio. Sadly, the Indians had been told by the enemies of the mission that McCoy did nothing without charge and if the Indians sent their children to the mission school, one day they would receive large bills which would ruin them financially. Indeed, this was the open policy of most white schools for Indians and the method suggested to McCoy by the Board. McCoy, however, argued that the whites had taken so much from the Indians that they were duty bound to make up for this in some way. McCoy's way was by providing free tuition and board. In order to extend his school the more, McCoy decided to contact the Shawnees to see if they were willing to send children to his school. Thinking, perhaps rather naively, that all true professing Christians would find his plans acceptable, he wrote to the Quaker mission at Waupaughkonetta asking if he could visit the Shawnees under their care to invite them to place their children in his school. On receiving the Quakers' reply, McCoy commented with one of his typical understatements, "They preferred that we should not make any such propositions to the Shawanoes."[21]

The Indians come to love and respect the missionaries

Other journeys had to be made. Mrs. McCoy spent fifteen days away on a trip to Ohio in the missions' interest but also partly for her health's sake as she had been very ill and over-worked. In her absence, five of the McCoys and several of the Indian children became seriously ill with bilious fever which was an extra burden on McCoy. On September 20, he set out on the 270 mile journey to Vincennes with a

---

[21] *History of Baptist Indian Missions*, p. 80.

Miami interpreter. The two stayed at Indian villages on the way and were more than pleased to find that they were now treated with great hospitality and kindness. The Indians had by now found out that they had nothing to fear from Isaac McCoy. They knew he had come among them to give rather than receive and that he was not a Government spy but a trusted friend. Only five months before, McCoy's party had made the reverse journey through this territory fearing for their lives but now they only had to mention that they needed water, corn or a pumpkin and it was provided. Several times they were invited to partake of a meal of bear's meat or other such delicacies. McCoy was able, in turn, to assist the Indians in caring for the sick and attending to the condition of their hearts. McCoy was only sad that he could not tell them about Jesus the Savior in their own language.

The Board's relationship with the government concerning mission funding

Once at Vincennes, McCoy arranged for the sale of the land with the improvements on it which he had acquired at Raccoon Creek and, as became his custom, the amount he received was placed in the Board's name. McCoy and his fellow missionaries moved some six or seven times during their missionary careers up to the 1840's and each time they sold the land they had improved, and often partly or wholly paid for themselves, at a nice profit, and gave the entire proceeds to the Board. Similarly, the Government made sure that the Board came in for lucrative grants and preferences because of their work among the Indians. At first the Board made a point of stressing their team-work with the government in sharing a common aim to "civilize" the Indians. *The American Baptist Missionary Magazine* in its number for 1821 stressed this cooperation when commenting on Psalm 102:15, "So the heathen shall fear the name of the Lord, and all the kings of the earth thy glory," added, "Large societies are formed for their support, and our national government is contributing of its influence and funds to promote the glorious design. The convention has sought a share in this blessed charity." Later, after the *Latter Day Luminary*, the official organ of the Board, had ceased to exist amidst the scandal of misuse of government funds, this teamwork and the receipt of Government grants was played down by the Board, though they continued to hold out the same eager hand. For the grants the Board received in this way, their thanks were due almost entirely to the agency of Isaac

McCoy. But McCoy seldom received such thanks. Indeed, the Board rejoiced in the pork, butter, tea and sugar that came on their own tables but criticized McCoy greatly when they heard that he enjoyed a nice cup of tea now and then. The fact was that McCoy rarely saw tea and water was the most common drink on the McCoys' table. Yet, whenever their own projects began to fail because of their own bad stewardship and mismanagement, the Board turned to McCoy to ask him to use his influence with the Government to obtain new grants. Thus the Board, in time, came in possession of gigantic sums of money which, if invested back into the Indian mission, would have been a tremendous asset. Although McCoy and the missionaries kept meticulous account of their income and expenditure and forwarded this at regular set times to the Board, the Board never showed the mission the same transparency and the missionaries were often compelled to believe that monies given the Board for the Indian mission were indeed going elsewhere. It was obviously not being invested back into the Indian mission.

Dishonorable treatment of Jones

This was not merely the case regarding the improvements that Isaac McCoy made to his various mission stations before giving them up to follow the Indians westwards. When Evan Jones was at Valley Towns, he spent a good deal of money on improvements out of his own pocket, trusting that this would be refunded him by the Board. When Valley Towns had to give the mission up before the Cherokees were forced to move west, the Government estimated that Jones' improvements were worth $1,876. This was duly paid to the Board who kept quiet about it and left Jones thinking that he would never receive the money he had laid out. In the summer of 1845, Jones paid a visit to the Government archives at Fort Gibson. He looked through the files there appertaining to the financing of the removal and found that the $1,876 had been handed over to the Board on Jones' behalf seven years earlier.[22] He promptly put in a claim for the money and asked for an increase in his wages, but received the unexpected reply that not only was there no money forthcoming but the Board had decided not to honor any more drafts coming from him as they believed he was

---

[22] Letters dated August 11, 1845, October 16, 1845. Excerpts from Jones' letters are taken from the A.B.M.S. microfilm, Reel 99 and McLoughlin's fine work *Champions of the Cherokees: Evan and John B. Jones.*

using the money for a "dishonorable purpose." The Board apparently never judged themselves to be "dishonorable" in their treatment of Jones.[23]

The appointment of Samuel Hill as missionary to the Indians

On returning from Vincennes, McCoy discovered that his family had been very ill again but was pleased to find that another six Indian youths had joined the school. Now there were twenty-six Indian children at the school besides the English and French children. By this time, however, the Delawares had been driven away by the whites so McCoy began to learn Potawatomi during the little leisure time he had. The Board had at last reacted to the pleas of the missionaries and sent a teacher, Mr. Samuel Hill of Philadelphia, Pennsylvania in November 1820, so that McCoy could dismiss the hired teacher whom he was paying out of his own pocket. Oddly enough, the Board had sent a single man who had no calling to preach. Naturally, the McCoys had hoped for a married couple so that Mrs. McCoy would have some female company and assistance. McCoy also thought it odd that a missionary should be sent to him who could not share in the spreading of the gospel through preaching and Bible instruction.

The situation of the Indians and the mission family worsens

The missionaries now received ample proof that the Government's policy of removing the Indians from their land and paying them annuities in exchange was the worst thing that could happen to the Indians. The principle chiefs had asked McCoy to speak to the Miamis when the annual payment was made in Fort Wayne and warn them of the dangers of bootleggers who would be after their money as quick as lightning. The money was, however, paid out in the middle of November without due warning. Now ensued a long period of heavy drinking by the Indians until their money was completely consumed.

---

[23] Letter November 3, 1845. A younger missionary with a high opinion of his own talents as a leader was anxious to oust the now elderly Jones and had begun to spread evil rumors about him. One rumor had some background in fact as several of Jones' wife's relations had turned up at the mission and demanded free board and lodgings as they were "family."

There were the usual fights, brutal murders, and a number of people died through alcohol poisoning. The McCoys did what they could for many of the sick and wounded but many Indians were so drunk that they did not even think of eating and were in danger of perishing through hunger and cold. Though the McCoys shared what they had, they, too, were not far from starving at this time as no funds were available from the Board and they could not obtain nourishing food. Most of the McCoy family, including Isaac and Kittie, became ill through lack of decent food, clothing and want of rest. McCoy felt that they would lose much of their witness to the Indians as their pitiful condition, materially speaking, was now hardly better than theirs. To make matters worse, the Christian lady who had been hired in Ohio to help Mrs. McCoy felt compelled to leave the mission to seek more profitable employment. There were now more mouths to feed as the amount of Indian pupils were growing, there being thirty-two Indian pupils before the year was out. Food and money were both at an end and Mrs. McCoy was suffering intensely under the strain of maintaining such a large household almost single-handedly. It was thus decided that McCoy should travel the 120 miles to Ohio to find a lady willing to help his wife and to strive to buy food on credit at the store of a man called Phillips of Dayton who was not a Christian himself but felt that McCoy was doing a noble work. McCoy realized, too, that he would have to borrow money in Ohio, otherwise the mission would have to be given up within a few days. After much prayer and heart-searching, McCoy told Mr. Phillips all his problems and the good man gave him a substantial interest-free loan. McCoy was able to purchase three milk cows, flour, pork and other foodstuffs, material for the school and also hire a female home-help.

The Board's different attitudes towards Valley Towns and Fort Wayne

McCoy must have been wondering at this time why he, one of the very first Baptist missionaries to the Indians, was being treated in this way. He was aware of Posey's work among the Cherokees for which the Board were spending thousands of dollars and receiving enormous subsidies of two thirds of the cost from the Government. Stables, a saw mill, a gristmill and a large model farm were being set up with a small army of carpenters and craftsmen performing the work. In the case of Posey's Valley Towns mission, the Board advertized for a staff of missionaries, including a farmer, a blacksmith, a carpenter, a millwright, a miller, a shoemaker, teachers and unskilled workers. On September 26, 1821, the Board sent off a group of some 25-26 missionaries, among whom was Evan Jones and his wife, equipped with many luxuries that McCoy never experienced in his whole missionary career. All these people were to be paid wages befitting their occupations. Was this because the Board considered the "civilized tribes" more important than the "savages" to whom McCoy was called or was Posey somehow better at persuading the Board to part with money? Whatever the reasons, McCoy's faith, calling and sheer stickability triumphed and his witness and influence increased. After a very few years, only Evan and Elizabeth Jones were left of the original large team of Valley Towns missionaries. Most had given up out of dissatisfaction with the Board's financial policy or had decided to work among whites. The faithful Jones family were left to bear the complaints of the Board that the Valley Towns Mission Station had been built on too large a scale and was too costly. As Jones had had nothing to do with the founding of the mission, he felt that the Board were using him as a scapegoat to cover their own mistakes and told them so in plain terms.[24] McCoy, too, felt that Jones' complaints against the Board were just. Towards the end of 1824, he complained to Luther Rice that though the Carey Station missionaries, in compliance with their *Family Rules*, only asked for food and clothing as their material reward, agreed sums to cover these wants were withheld from them. Yet, the Valley Towns missionaries had been paid wages above their needs.[25]

The setting up of a preaching station at an Indian convert's home

One encouraging sign for the McCoys on the spiritual side was that a Delaware Indian who lived on the way to Ohio, had heard the gospel at Fort Wayne and become a Christian after returning home and corresponded with McCoy about her new faith. When McCoy called on her and Captain Shane, her husband, who was half Ottawa and half French and interpreted for her, the lady, Mrs. Shane, was able to tell McCoy the good news in person. From now on, McCoy was able to use the Shane's house as a preaching station. Mrs. Shane asked McCoy to baptize her but her husband, who was a Roman

---

[24] See William G. McLoughlin's *Champions of the Cherokees* for an excellent account of Jones' life and work.

[25] Letter dated November 20, 1824, McCoy Papers, Reel 3.

Catholic, objected, but more because of the delicate state of his wife's health than from religious views. On hearing that she had become a Christian, a religious body asked her to join them in Ohio but Mrs. Shane said that she would prefer to be baptized at Fort Wayne and join the Christians there as she felt she must witness to the Indians. Mrs. Shane was baptized on June 24 1820 and became a dedicated missionary to her own people.

Samuel Hill's short service

Samuel Hill, the new missionary, proved to be of less stamina and solidity in taking up his missionary tasks. He was a friendly young man but was unable to cope with his teaching duties and had no other talents which might have assisted the work of the mission. After hardly two months, Mr. Hill gave up the task and resigned from the mission field. It had been scarcely a wise move of the Board to send one so unqualified and inexperienced to work on the still wild frontier. Actually, the McCoys had not had the heart to tell Hill that he was of no help at all to the mission and was merely an extra mouth to feed. Hill, however, met Baptist minister George Evans, a friend of the Indian Mission in Ohio, and Evans was able to persuade Hill to be sensible and leave the work.[26] McCoy continually wondered why the Board made absolutely no effort to familiarize themselves first hand concerning the needs of the Indian mission. Another young man was hired locally who lasted but a few weeks. Then on February 7, 1821, Mr. Martin turned up and announced that he would help out until the Board provided a new missionary-teacher. McCoy's grateful comment was, "His services afforded great relief."[27]

Severe trials caused by both the Board and the Board's opponents

Now it seemed that the Board had not only cut off all supplies

---

[26] See McCoy's letter to Staughton on the subject dated May 2, 1821, McCoy Papers, Reel 1.

[27] *History of Baptist Indian Missions*, p. 89. See Martin's letters to McCoy dated July 19, August 1, August 15 and August 29, 1820, etc. which show what a work of grace had occurred in his life and how he strove to help the Indian mission. McCoy Papers, Reel 1.

to the Fort Wayne missionaries but they had ceased to have any contact with them. As a result of the circular that Mr. Martin had distributed, some income and provisions came in but not enough to feed and keep well over forty people. This was the time when Daniel Parker was engaged in distributing thousands of pamphlets arguing against missions and finding enormous backing among the Baptist churches on the Western frontier. Parker appealed to the feelings of independence of these churches, their mistrust of college trained ministers and their objections to paying ministers a salary. Parker appointed people to visit the churches and read out the charges that he had made against them. As Chambers and Polke, elders of the Maria Creek church, took no notice, Parker visited them himself, denouncing their support of their former pastor, Isaac McCoy. The church rejected his charges but then Parker brought charges against the whole church before their Association on the grounds that he had been wrongly criticized by the Maria Creek brethren. Parker demanded the right to appear before the Maria Creek brethren and read from his latest book to them.[28] Polke gave him the chance to do this in his own private home, providing that Parker's hearers would be given the freedom to reply. Parker rejected this proposal, insisting that he should be heard before the church and no reply was to be made. As a number of Parker's friends were members of Maria Creek, the elders were compelled to allow Parker to have his say but Polke told McCoy that Parker merely said what was in his book and the antagonist's friends were very disappointed at his performance. "The badness of his cause," Polke told McCoy, soon became apparent. Apparently the bone of contention that Parker had with Maria Creek was that they had approached McCoy on the subject and the missionary had read Parker's book and subsequently written to Polke, defending the cause of missionary outreach. Polke had passed on McCoy's comments to his church but Parker maintained that Polke had no right to do so. He ought to have shown Parker McCoy's comments first. This was, of course, a ridiculous accusation and goes to demonstrate the extraordinary high pedestal Parker had built for himself.[29] J. M. Peck was so disgusted with the way Parker perverted the Gospel and strove to

---

[28] *A Public Address to the Baptist Society, and Friends of Religion in General, on the Principle and Practice of the Baptist Board of Foreign Missions for the United States of America.*

[29] See Polke's letter to McCoy dated May 6, 1821, McCoy Papers, Reel 1.

gain authority over the churches that he wrote a pamphlet against him, printed in Washington, and distributed it in the Wabash area.[30]

Actually, at the time, the Board of Foreign Missions were stubbornly combating these objections and helping to drive the unwary Baptists into Parker's trap. The Board had become virtually a para-church organization, was striving to enforce a salaried missionary ministry[31] and was investing missionary funds in a college project aimed at training missionaries and pastors.[32] McCoy shared many of these Baptists' views and refused for many years to accept a salary. He was also very vocal in objecting to the misuse of donations and grants in fostering the Board's commercial enterprises and missionary training schemes. It took him twenty years, however, to realize that the Board was not indeed a consortium of separate churches but a self-appointed body to rule over the various independent churches, speak for them and dictate to them what their policy ought to be.[33]

Recognition and support comes from Governor Lewis Cass

One day, McCoy received a friendly letter from an entire stranger by the name of Mr. Hudson[34] who introduced himself as a Presbyterian but also a friend of the Indian mission. He suggested that McCoy should visit Detroit where he lived and speak directly with the Government representatives there about his plans for Indian improvement. McCoy set off straight away on the two-hundred mile journey to Detroit, sure that this was an opening from the Lord. At Detroit, McCoy met Governor Lewis Cass who became one of McCoy's

---

[30] See Peck's letter to McCoy on this subject dated April 17, 1822, McCoy Papers, Reel 2.

[31] This eventually became the Board's policy in 1826. See McCoy's long letter to the Board outlining his reasons for not creating a salaried missionary staff in his letter to Lucius Bolles dated July 22, 1826, McCoy Papers, Reel 5.

[32] Columbian College which eventually went bankrupt and had to be taken off the Board's hands.

[33] See William Polke's second letter on the subject of Parker in a letter dated July 8, 1820, McCoy Papers, Reel 1.

[34] Hudson's letters to McCoy can be found on Reel 1 of the McCoy Papers.

closest associates and always spoke of him with great respect. Cass listened to McCoy's story with sympathy and understanding and at once promised help in the form of money, clothing and food valued at $450. He also promised to send the McCoys a skilled agriculturist who would train the Indians in farm work and thus make them more independent. The Indians had long asked McCoy for such a help but no suitable man had been found. Further aids were promised McCoy such as use of the Fort Wayne smithy when McCoy needed to repair equipment.

Besides soliciting help from Governor Cass, McCoy had written to the Secretary for War concerning assistance for his plan to educate the Indians, commenting in 1840, "It was at this time, also, that I commenced arrangements for obtaining help from Government, which a few years afterwards became the principle part of the support of the mission."[35] McCoy was referring to the time when for years on end, the Board would make no effort whatsoever to care for the missionaries who were serving Christ in their name on the mission front. The result of this meeting with Cass won for McCoy an invitation to be present as advisor at the famous Chicago Treaty of 1821 concerning the future of a number of Indian tribes and the possibilities of a U. S. Government sponsorship for their education and improvement. Cass hinted that McCoy's presence would be of mutual value as the Government would benefit from McCoy's advice and experience which would be probably rewarded by McCoy receiving a more permanent and eligible site for his mission station.

McCoy helps found a church on the banks of the Maumee River

On his way back home, McCoy passed through a small white settlement near the Maumee rapids and found several Baptists there whom he gathered together and preached to. As the group of believers were without a shepherd, McCoy promised that he would do his best to find a pastor for them. He was very soon able to contact a Rev. John Mason of Ohio who felt called to join them as their spiritual shepherd. No one could say that McCoy had eyes for the needs of Indians only as he was permanently in the service of his Lord whatever the skin color of those with whom he came in contact.

---

[35] *History of Baptist Indian Missions*, p. 90.

This photograph of Isaac McCoy was made from a full length painting by the famous portrait painter Matthew Jouett of Kentucky, and is the only authentic likeness of McCoy. The location of the original portrait is unknown.

Christiana McCoy (1787-1851), wife of Isaac McCoy, from a portrait made sometime after that of her husband. She proved to be a true and faithful co-laborer with Isaac, sharing both the joys and sorrows of their missionary calling. "I could happily trust my family to the good Providence of God," Isaac McCoy wrote, and before his death in 1846, he and Christiana would be called to suffer the loss of 11 of their 14 children. Christiana died at the home of her son John Calvin (below) at Kansas City, Missouri in August of 1851.

John Calvin McCoy (1811-1889), the only child of Isaac and Christiana to survive his parents. He purchased some land from Johnston Lykins on which he built his home as well as a general store. These buildings situated on the Santa Fe Trail constituted the beginnings of both Westport and Kansas City, Missouri. McCoy is regarded as one of the 14 original proprietors of Kansas City. He is buried in Union Cemetery in Kansas City and there is a monument to him in Pioneer Park.

Dr. Johnston Lykins (1800-1876), Isaac McCoy's son-in-law and trustworthy friend. Of his dedication, McCoy wrote, "Neither the performance of the most disagreeable services for the sick, whether they were missionaries, their children or Indian children, nor their peevishness and unreasonable demands, nor the death-like discouragements which, in various forms, hovered around our abode, moved him from his noble determination to do *right*...It was not his amiable disposition alone by which we profited." (p. 162).

Right Evan Jones (1789-1873), McCoy's missionary counterpart to the southeastern Indian tribes. Born in Brecknockshire, Wales, Jones was appointed by the Board of the General Missionary Convention on July 24, 1821 as a missionary to the Cherokee Indians, and for over 50 years he labored as a preacher and teacher among them. It was said that "the confidence in which he was held by them was never impaired," while McCoy remarked that through perseverance Jones "had the happiness of reaping a rich religious harvest." Jones died at Tahlequah, Oklahoma on August 18, 1873.

The Missionaries

Robert Simerwell (1786-1868) and his wife Frances or "Fannie" (1789-1855). Mr. Simerwell began his missionary work in 1824 at the Carey Mission in Michigan and continued on faithfully for many years as a minister, teacher and government - appointed blacksmith among the Potawatomis.

Right Jotham Meeker (1804-1855), who was initially recruited by Simerwell to come to Carey, was 21 years old when he arrived at the mission. In August of 1827 Meeker left Carey to become Superintendent of the new Thomas Station among the Ottawas, and here he met fellow missionary Eleanor Richardson whom he married in 1830. Meeker eventually came to reside at the Shawnee Mission in Kansas primarily as a printer of Bible translations, Indian alphabets, spelling books, hymn books, tracts, and other materials relating to Indian missions.

John Mason Peck (1789-1858). Encouraged by a visit with Luther Rice
in 1815 to enter missionary service,
Peck and his wife Sally were appointed to the St. Louis area in 1817 where
they established a mission to the
Missouri Territory. Peck characterized Isaac McCoy as "an indefatigable
missionary among the Western Indians," and was a great encourager to
the McCoys in all of their endeavors.
Peck helped form the American Baptist Home Mission Society in 1832.

Lewis Cass (1782-1866) as he appeared
in this 1849 daguerrotype by Matthew
Brady. Cass as Governor of Michigan
Territory (1813-1831) was a firm supporter of McCoy's work among the Indians and was an important political
ally in McCoy's efforts to relocate the
various tribes to the Indian Territory.
After an unsuccessful bid for the Presidency against Taylor in 1848, Cass
served a second term as U. S. Senator
and would finish his career as U. S.
Secretary of State (1857-1860).

Left William Staughton (1770-1829), pastor of the First (1806-1811) and Samson St. Baptist churches, both in Philadelphia, and the first Corresponding Secretary of the General Missionary (Triennial) Convention's Board of Foreign Missions (1814-1826). So that Staughton could hold both the office of President of Columbian College and that of Corresponding Secretary, the Board was moved from Philadelphia to Washington, D.C. in 1823. It was the responsibility of the Corresponding Secretary not only to communicate with the missionaries in the field but also to see to it that both the missionaries and their missions were properly supported.

Right Lucius Bolles (1769-1844), pastor of the First Baptist Church of Salem, Massachusetts (1805-1827), and Corresponding Secretary for the Board from 1826 (when it again changed location from Washington to Boston) until replaced by Solomon Peck in 1842. Sharing the same general apathy and even disdain of the majority of his fellow Board members towards the cause of Indian missions, Bolles came to personally respect Mc-Coy, though he and treasurer Heman Lincoln, Sr. (1769-1869), throughout their long tenure on the Board were the cause of many grievous trials both to the McCoys and to their associates in the field.

Left Francis Wayland, Jr. (1796-1865), pastor of the First Baptist Church of Boston (1821-1855), like most of those who served on the Board, was much more enamored with the missions overseas than with those at home, and thus was not as strident an advocate for "the Judson of the West," as one writer referred to Isaac McCoy. Nonetheless, Wayland did support McCoy at critical times during his missionary career, for which McCoy was very grateful.

Right Spencer H. Cone (1785-1855), pastor of the Oliver St. Baptist Church (1823-1841) and First Baptist (1841-1855), both in the city of New York. Cone was actively involved in the work of the General Missionary Convention almost from its inception, and was elected President of the Convention for nine consecutive years beginning in 1832, declining the nomination to a tenth term. He was McCoy's best friend on the Board (on which he ably served in various capacities) and heartily supported the missions to the Indians. "Rev. Mr. Cone, of New York," McCoy wrote,

"was a friend who never forgot us, whether we were near or far off, who kept himself informed or our circumstances, and whose generosity was equal to his zeal." *History of Baptist Indian Missions*, p. 404.

A mission station

The Shawanoe (Shawnee) Baptist Mission Station as it appeared in this
1830's woodcut. After Isaac McCoy obtained permission from the chiefs,
Johnston Lykins and his family arrived at the nearby Shawnee Agency on
July 7, 1831 to found a mission for William Perry and Cornstalk's bands of
Shawnee Indians. The Board having failed to provide building funds that
year, Lykins bought "a small tract of U. S. land, immediately on the line of
the State of Missouri" and built a home for his family "at his own cost." The
site chosen for the new station was due west across the state line in Johnson
County, Kansas. In June of 1832, money was made available to begin construction of the mission buildings. Despite having kept meticulous records
of the expenses he incurred, totaling some $1500, and turning in his account
to the Board, Lykins was never reimbursed (see Chapter Twelve). McCoy on
visiting the station on October 3, 1832, wrote: "Their houses are not completed, but are so that they can be occupied except in [the] school house...They
will be substantial and comfortable buildings and are pretty well situated."

H. G. Phillips and George Evans again come to the mission's help

As soon as McCoy reached home, he reported all that had happened at Detroit to the Board and stressed that the mission was in dire pecuniary straits, especially as the school was growing and missionary advance progressing well. He also pressed the Board to send new missionaries who were equal to the task. As he had received no help from the Board for many months, McCoy had to face the embarrassing circumstance of having to travel again to Ohio and ask Phillips for an extended loan. This time, Phillips was understandably hesitant and asked McCoy to call again some days later. McCoy's journal entry for that day shows what anxiety he was experiencing:

> Spent the night in *painful* anxiety; reviewed my Christian experience, my call to the ministry, my exercises of mind on the subject of missions, my motives and my hopes, and the dealings of Providence under various circumstances. Has God, thought I, who has preserved my life, and in some instances almost miraculously, who has made me sensible of my unworthiness, and of my dependance upon him, who has comforted me often by teaching me to trust in him, and who has given me such an earnest desire to spend the only life which I have to live in this world in a way well pleasing to him, and who has taught me to pray that I might not materially err from the path of duty - suffered me to engage in the mission and to continue in it so long, and yet not required these labours at my hands? Have all my warm feelings on the subject been delusive? Have the prospects among the Indians brightened merely to confirm the delusion, to head me further from the right way, and to complete my downfall?" Never did I more earnestly beg, really beg, that God would save us from ruin, if he delighted in our course; and if the way was displeasing to him, to correct us in *mercy*, and set us right, without allowing any material injury to grow out of our error.[36]

McCoy was doubly in anguish as he had set off on the hundred and fifty miles journey without a penny in his pocket and had told the people where he had lodged on the way and in Lebanon and Dayton that he would settle his bills on the way back. Before meeting Phillips

---

[36] *History of Baptist Indian Missions*, p. 92.

again, at Lebanon, McCoy was met providentially by a friend who gave him five and a half dollars which just covered his accommodation bills. There was still, however, the question of supplies and equipment that had to be settled. McCoy visited Phillips once again and told him straight that he faced bankruptcy and that he had no guarantee that the Board would ever pay his debts. How Phillips reacted is found in McCoy's *History of Baptist Indian Missions*. The author, thankful to God, wrote:

> He very generously loaned me money to meet our immediate wants. I never borrowed upon interest. Matters were afterwards so arranged that he was not a loser by his kindness. The board afterwards did hesitate to pay those accounts; but Mr. Phillips was still my friend, and made a communication to the corresponding secretary of the board respecting our affairs, honourable to the mission, and perhaps to our future benefit.[37]

Actually, the Board refused point blank to cover these expenses in any way from their general fund and it was only through the kind and patient intervention of Mr. Phillips and a grant to the mission from Congress that opened the Board's hearts, pockets and, we trust, consciences. McCoy's requests to the Board to be told exactly the nature of the donations and Government grants which were earmarked for his work[38] remained unanswered.

At Dayton, Ohio, McCoy met up with his friend Rev. George Evans[39] who had occasionally worked for the Board as an Agent. Evans sympathized at once with McCoy and was shocked to hear how the Board was treating their missionaries. Evans sent off a report of his meeting with McCoy to the Board, urging them to take immediate precautions to ensure that the Fort Wayne missionaries were properly looked after. He, himself, then spent three weeks touring the churches, canvassing for support for McCoy's mission and was able to collect a substantial amount of money.

---

[37] Ibid, p. 93

[38] See, for instance, McCoy's letter to Staughton dated December 28, 1820, McCoy Papers, Reel 1.

[39] Evans' correspondence with McCoy can be found on Reel 1 of the McCoy Papers.

The continuing ministry of Peck and Welch

On returning home, McCoy found that his wife had been badly burned and the wound was very inflamed. He obviously heard more news from Peck and Welch on his arrival as he suddenly moves from his wife's burns to the careers of these two men in his account. He had corresponded with Peck for two years, hoping to win him once again for the Indian mission. He found that Peck was now working independently among white settlers and not for the Board. McCoy was full of praise for the work Peck was doing and felt that he would one day reap plentiful fruit for his labor. William W. Sweet says of Peck, "No other man in the early history of Illinois exercised a larger influence than did Peck, and it is stated that he did more than any other single individual to induce settlers to come to Illinois, through his publications *Guide for Emigrants* (1831) and *Gazetteer of Illinois* (1834)".[40] McCoy mentions that Welch had returned to New Jersey and was a zealous promoter of Sunday schools there and circulated Bibles and tracts. Though the men were lost to the Indian mission, which was really the Board's fault rather than theirs, they were certainly not lost to the gospel.[41]

---

[40] *The Story of Religion in America.* See pp. 248-249 on Welch and Peck.

[41] Peck left the work because of lack of funds and a stronger calling to the white frontiersmen and Welch was dismissed by the Board because of their lack of funds. See Staughton's letter to McCoy dated November 10, 1820, McCoy Papers, Reel 1.

Chapter Four
Witnessing to the Potawatomis (1821-22)

McCoy meets Menominee the Potawatomi

McCoy now heard that there was a group of religious Potawatomis who lived some 120 miles from Fort Wayne in a community led by their preacher, Menominee. As McCoy could not make such a long journey immediately because of ill health and duties at Fort Wayne, he wrote a lengthy letter to Menominee, inviting him to visit Fort Wayne. By way of reply, Menominee turned up in person with a group of followers on April 10th and the group stayed for several days. McCoy found the Potawatomis very pious and moral in their way. They held morning and evening worship each day during which their leader preached to them and they all prayed in chorus. The message, however was purely moral, dealing with excessive drinking, theft, murder and such evils but quite devoid of Christian doctrine. Yet, the Indians proved to be most open to the gospel, especially their leader. As the group had no easy task living among Indians who rejected such a moral life, McCoy wrote out a letter of recommendation for Menominee and his friends, asking their hearers and neighbors to treat them well as they wished all men the very best. McCoy was counting on his own popularity with the surrounding Indians to protect his new acquaintances from persecution. He had found out that the Indians were affectionately calling him their "father" and looked upon him as their guide and friend. This led the Indians to ask McCoy to arrange for help to be given to them in the form of a man who could teach them agriculture so that they could become self-supporting now that their hunting grounds were gone. Sadly, apart from lending them a plough and a few other tools, McCoy had no means of helping the Indians.

Life at Fort Wayne as the second year of the mission begins

During May, the first anniversary of their work at Fort Wayne came round. On taking stock of the situation, McCoy found that the work was growing, the McCoys were respected for many miles around and the school was going from strength to strength. However, both the McCoys were physically at a low ebb and Isaac McCoy found that he had to keep the true financial state of the mission from Kittie as her spirits were so low, it would have been too heavy for her to bear. McCoy reckoned that the mission could now employ three further male and three female missionaries but no help was forthcoming from the Board and McCoy was too ill and too busy to set up schemes for canvassing money. He merely adds that he cannot understand the Board's position as the Government had special funds to help missionaries in exactly the situation he was in. Little did he know that the Board was receiving such funds but putting them in channels for which they were not designed.

On May 7th, Martin announced that he could no longer help the McCoys out and that he must be about his further business. At this time, the mission family received some Christian company which raised hopes for a while that their missionary staff might be increased and their work eased. A retired minister by the name of John Mason visited them from Ohio and they shared such sweet fellowship with him and he proved so sound in the gospel that, in spite of his great age, the missionaries asked him to join them and serve the Lord with them. The gentleman found the offer tempting but his age and infirmity eventually forced him to decline. McCoy found a pastorate for him among the white settlers as described above (p. 104). A few weeks later, a correspondent of the McCoys from the Lake Erie region arrived to tell the missionaries that he had come to join them. McCoy employed the man for three months, paying his wages from his own pocket, his very last dollars, but it soon became evident that the man had two left hands in performing missionary duties and this hope on the McCoys' part also failed. McCoy's kind heart is always reflected in such reports. Whenever a missionary candidate had nothing to recommend him as a missionary, McCoy never mentioned his name so as not to cause him difficulties in finding other work.

Getting to know the Potawatomis better

By the end of the first week in June, the McCoys were rather better in health and Isaac decided to go on a tour of the Potawatomis, accompanied by three Indians, with the intention of seeing how an educational system could be set up for them and Government grants be obtained to that end. The rainy season had set in and after swimming across the swollen St. Mary's River, the party found the going tough. On June 10th, after three days' journey, McCoy's party met with Chiefs Topenebe, Chebass and Cheshaugen, with McCoy beginning his talk in the usual Indian way. First the peace pipe was smoked by the two parties, then the talking could commence. So as not to awake false hope in the Indians' hearts, McCoy spoke on every topic under the sun except education, preferring to feel his way gently. On the following day, McCoy proceeded to Menominee's village. The Indian had begun to feel that McCoy's promises of help were all mere show and had sent an envoy to him, asking if his promise to visit Menominee's village had been a lie. Now he was overjoyed and called out the whole village to greet his "father." He explained how McCoy had promised to come when the grass was a certain height and he had gone out daily to check it.

Now messengers were sent to the surrounding villages and crowds of Indians began to arrive. The ground was swept clean, the people sat down and were fed and McCoy was presented by Menominee's two wives with large boxes of sugar. Soon the Indians showed great disappointment. They had expected McCoy to make his permanent home with them but now heard that he was only paying them a short visit. Once such misunderstandings were out of the way, the large group of Indians spoke freely and openly with the missionary. McCoy was most embarrassed at the attention given him and hardly dared to look at the Indians who were regarding him with great reverence. Again the people begged McCoy to come and live with them. McCoy explained how he was committed to the work at Fort Wayne but the Indians merely said that Fort Wayne was only a stone's throw away and he had chosen a crooked route which took too long. He could thus look after their spiritual needs and those of Fort Wayne, too. The Indians explained how they had given up drink and other evil practices but needed a teacher to help them further. This was a great sign of Menominee's humility as he was the people's leader but not at all put out by the thought that McCoy would take his place. On the contrary, he welcomed it.

After the crowd was gone, Menominee came to McCoy and said he would like to talk about his two wives. He confessed that if this were against God's will, he must dismiss one of them. McCoy, thinking this was like cutting off a hand because it offended, told his Indian friend that he would like to think over the matter before replying but he would have an answer before he departed. McCoy knew that both Menominee's wives had children by him and if he cut off one with her children, they would become destitute. The Potawatomis persuaded McCoy to stay a further two days with them. He spent this time preaching, praying and singing hymns for them, going from wigwam to wigwam. He was thrilled on passing through the village, to hear prayer and praise coming from their communal house and rejoiced in the Lord at what he was experiencing. McCoy also experienced again Menominee's humility. The Indian had a large stick which he notched every time he preached. He showed this to McCoy who said that it was like his journal. He opened his book and showed Menominee where he had listed his preaching activities and the texts used. The Indian began to count the number of times each of them had preached and when he found that McCoy had outdone him, he spoke merely of his own inferiority as a preacher.

The next day, McCoy and his Indian interpreters went to visit the principle chief Pcheeko with Menominee where he was fed on hominy[1] and venison, though not at all hygienically prepared. Pcheeko anxiously approached Abraham, one of McCoy's older students and interpreter, asking him in a whisper if McCoy were not too partial to Menominee who, he thought, was not a very good preacher. Abraham replied diplomatically and truthfully that McCoy had come to meet all the Indians, not just Menominee. The interpreter then quickly outlined the duties of McCoy as a missionary and emphasized that he had no possessions of his own but everything belonged to the mission and to the school. He also explained, very tactfully, all the advantages of a basic education and practical skills, without giving the chief the idea that there were personal riches for him to be obtained from McCoy. The weather was intensely hot and everything was fly infested and the water and food dirty so that Abraham was now sick and McCoy was not feeling very well himself. The party decided it was time to return to Fort Wayne. On hearing this, Menominee called all the people together again and asked McCoy to speak to them. They received the promise that McCoy would return when the leaves begin to fall. Menominee accompanied the party half a mile on the way, promising always to endeavor to serve and please God. McCoy recorded the scene with the words, "And so we parted; when I was made to exclaim, 'O, compassionate Savior! didst thou expand thy bleeding arms upon Mount Calvary! and is there not room in thy

---

[1] McCoy calls it "hommony".

bleeding bosom for these dear people? and will not this desert begin to rejoice?'"

In his joy at what he experienced, McCoy was almost heart-broken. He realized what a great work was to be done and how there was such little enthusiasm shown by Christians and even his own denomination for the work. These thoughts are recorded in his *History of Baptist Indian Missions* and must touch the heart of every Christian as we recognize the sad truth they express:

> Here was an uncommonly favourable opening for doing good to these dear, artless people, who appeared ready to receive instruction in things relating both to this life and that which is to come ; but it was impossible for a solitary missionary and his wife, who already had much more upon their hands than they could manage, to improve the opening here presented. It was more properly the duty of the Baptist denomination to see to them, than that of others, because Providence had allowed us to become acquainted with them; but among three or four hundred thousand of our denomination in the United States, none manifested a willingness to make his home in the desert, and teach these poor anxious inquirers the path to heaven. Within a year after the time of which we are writing, the party, as such, began to dwindle, and long since it has ceased to exist as a religious party. Some have died, and some have returned to the vices which once they denounced; but, in the great day of accounts, will they not have cause to complain of the thousands of Christians who, though not far from them, neglected to hold out to them the lamp of life? They were left to wander in the dark, and have fallen. It is done; we cannot now go back to atone for our criminal neglect of the party of poor Menominee. We shall have attained our end in telling this sad tale of our injustice, if the narrative should induce a discharge of Christian duty to others within our reach.[2]

McCoy's party meet up with Sauks

On their way back home from Menominee's village, McCoy's party were oppressed by the heat and the flies and were feeling far from well. They met up with a party of Sauks who were on their way to Canada to receive their gifts from the British. Since the War of 1812, the British had treated those Indians who had assisted them

---

[2] p. 106.

against the U.S. forces as pensioners and many tribes made an annual trip to Canada to claim their benefits. This was thought politically unwise of the British and caused some hostile feelings among the U. S. whites against the Indians. No doubt, in their loyalty to their former allies, the British may have still harbored political motives. After losing two wars against American forces, one they caused themselves and one declared against them by the U. S. Government, it was hardly thought by either side that a third war would ensue. As the Indians were not legally U.S. citizens, and as the U.S. had hitherto denied them this right, they were still free to ally themselves as they wished. McCoy did not interfere in these political matters in any way but was glad for any assistance the Indians received, whether it came from Washington or London.

Comfort and discomfort among the Potawatomis

The Potawatomis on the St Joseph River welcomed the weary travelers and prepared food for them. The party, however, could not stomach the food which was prepared and served in extremely dirty vessels. They asked for a kettle so that they could make coffee but were given such a filthy can that McCoy's Indian traveling companions said that they would not drink anything prepared in it. One thing, however, the party ought to have tried for their health's sake. Several of the Indians built a hut of bark, put heated rocks into it, threw water on the rocks and sat among them sweating profusely before taking a dip in the cooling river. Perhaps as the day was hot enough and McCoy was so weary, he did not take part in this hygienic delight.

As the party moved on, the heat was replaced by cold pouring rain and both McCoy and Abraham weakened. After passing through three villages, making the aims of the mission known, they stayed for several days at the home of Abraham's half-breed relations who gave them comfortable lodgings and stocked them up with a supply of provisions. This was a welcome break as McCoy and his friends were now filthy and vermin infested and badly needed a rest and a clean-up. The Burnetts, Abraham's relations, were also related to Topenebe the Potawatomi chief and they had already contacted him about the Fort Wayne mission and were awaiting a reply. McCoy was wondering whether to set up a mission station among the Potawatomis or not. The member of the Burnett family present at a tribal discussion on the matter said that the principle chiefs had said it was a matter for the younger men to decide. These thought that there was no need for a mission among them. McCoy was not disappointed and thought it was wise of the Indians not to rush matters. A most positive sign was that Chief Topenebe's daughter gave McCoy two of her boys aged five and seven, asking that they would be educated at the mission school. A third boy joined the party a little later and McCoy had to hire Indians to carry the boys the many miles that still lay before them. It was providential that McCoy now had more men with him as they met up with an armed and drunken group of Indians, one of whom appeared to be raving mad and was striving to murder another member of their party.

An incident with a mad cattle-driver

It was also providential that McCoy now met up with a large group of men who were driving cattle through the wilderness to far a-way Chicago where they would be used to feed a large number of U. S. troops there. The troops were being gathered for the signing of the 1821 treaty with the Indians. One of the cattle-drivers had suffered so much from deprivations along the way that he had become quite delirious and even mentally deranged. McCoy at once offered his assistance and with great difficulty and the help of a kind and jolly Frenchman tied the poor man to his horse and set out for Fort Wayne with him.

The mad cattle-driver proved too wild for McCoy and the Frenchman to handle. McCoy was also now pressed for time and was urgently needed at the station. They thus left the sick man in an Indian hut with two of their party who were told to proceed as soon as the man was calm. The man died the following day and as the Indians had no means of digging a grave, he was placed Indian-fashion inside a fallen hollow tree which was then covered with other fallen timber. Meanwhile, McCoy's party moved on through swampy country in a violent storm and with great difficulty, crossed the St. Mary's River. When McCoy reached Fort Wayne, he described his homecoming in his usual understated fashion "(we) entered our own door very different from dry and comfortable."

Mrs. McCoy urgently in need of a doctor's care

Though ill and "uncomfortable" himself, McCoy found his wife much worse on his arrival back home. She was urgently in need of a doctor's care which could only be found well over three hundred miles away down the Wabash River in Indiana which was only navigable in an open canoe. The land route would have been an impossible task for the sick woman. The McCoys decided that Kittie must take the risk. The problem was that she had several infant children who could not manage without their mother's attention as there was no other female help of such kind in the mission settlement. At last it was decided that the three youngest should accompany their mother. McCoy could not possibly go with her as he was now alone with the forty-seven pupils and had to look after the entire household. He records how now he realized what a burden his wife had to bear when he was away on his journeys and left her alone to manage the station. Mrs. McCoy and her small children had to spend nine days of rainy weather on the river, camping at night on the mosquito-ridden bank without ever being able to get dried. It was hardly a journey to make a sick woman well, but complications in her pregnancy along with a general exhaustion and other unnamed ailments had made the journey a necessity. Mrs. McCoy returned via the land route on September 14. She had left on June 25th with three small children and came back with a new member of the family in her arms.

The Board resolves to give McCoy better treatment

A letter from Dr. Staughton dated July 2, 1821 brought with it a marked improvement in the disposition of the Board. Staughton wrote:

> The Board on commencing Indian Missions was quite inexperienced and you must attribute their resolves to their mistaken idea of the demands of the Indian Station. They had no idea and perhaps you had not yourself a full idea of what these missions would require. Your order for $630 given to Mr. Phillip has been paid. You will see that you are at liberty to draw for $500 every two months including the appropriation from government[3]

This was a noble gesture indeed from Staughton who became increasingly friendly to McCoy. Still, however, Staughton did not answer McCoy's oft repeated question as to how much of the money allowed him came from donations and how much came from

---

[3] McCoy Papers, Reel 2.

Government grants. Concerning the latter question, Staughton said quite surprisingly that he did not know. When Staughton found the full truth of McCoy's financial difficulties in July, 1821, he told him to draw on the Board immediately for $1,000.[4] Perhaps Staughton's growing interest in the Indian Mission became too obvious among the Board's members and proved to his and to McCoy's disadvantage as the Board replaced Staughton by Lucius Bolles in the great upheaval in the Board's policies in 1826.

More conversions and baptisms

Meanwhile, Mrs. Turner, the wife of the former Indian Agent, Dr. Turner, already mentioned, had asked to be baptized and she passed through the waters on July 8. She was followed a week later by another woman, a white, who had taken on temporary work in the family and had now come to profess Christ as her Savior. In the same month, McCoy was approached by several Potawatomi chiefs who affirmed that they were sympathetic to having a mission station set up for their tribe. The chiefs asked for whiskey to clinch the deal but McCoy pointed to a jug of water on the table and said that good water was all they drank. After trying in various unsuccessful ways to obtain spirits from McCoy, they at last gave him their hands and said, "My father, you are right. The Great Spirit will hear what you say, and protect you, for I feel that you are a good man." Perhaps the chiefs were only testing McCoy to see if his life was according to his doctrines. Whatever their motives, the chiefs were much impressed by McCoy and kept closely in touch.

Learning that hard work is honorable

It was now McCoy's turn to be truly astonished by his older pupils' conduct. In order to economize, McCoy had decided to plant some thirty acres of corn and go out into the plains to gather hay for the animals. With tools thrown over his shoulder, he set off for work, asking several of the youths to join him in this healthy exercise. He was surprised to find that the boys had nothing against their teacher doing manual work but it was beneath their pride to do such work as they were not slaves. With great patience, McCoy had to teach them

---

[4] McCoy Papers, Reel 2.

that hard work was honorable and also that unless the Indians learned to settle down, grow crops and breed cattle and pigs, there would be no hope for their future because their hunting grounds had now disappeared. McCoy always made sure that when the boys worked, he worked with them so that they and their parents would never be tempted to think that McCoy was using them as menial servants.

A further sign that the Board was out of touch with reality

McCoy's next surprise was a communication from the Board concerning the setting up of a Superintendent over each mission. The missionaries were told to select brethren of well known piety and discretion in the vicinity of their station and ask them to be their missions' Superintendents. As so often, McCoy felt that the Board was thinking that all mission stations were similar to the Cherokees' Valley Towns which was in the midst of several other settlements and one had only to travel a few miles to find a well-known pious person. It was obvious that the Board was thinking of appointing persons who were not directly involved in the mission's work, yet this would have meant for McCoy appointing some one who lived 150-200 miles away from the mission and so could not possibly exercise any oversight of it. Besides, such a person who lived far away from Indian presence and had no first hand experience of missionary work would be quite unqualified for such a post.

The Chicago Treaty of 1821

Ever since McCoy had met up with the party who were helping to prepare the logistics for the 1821 Chicago Treaty, he had been strengthened in his determination to accept Governor Cass' invitation and plead the spiritual and material needs of the Indians before the treaty partners. Finding his wife so ill and the fact that she was now absent had put an end to this plan as he was needed at the mission and no one could take his place there. He would have to send someone to Chicago in his stead, but who could be trusted with such a task? He had a teacher at that time who had recently joined the missionaries whom he did not name, so we can conclude that he was not much of a help to the mission. McCoy realized that it was a question of this gentleman or no one, so McCoy sent him off to Chicago with detailed instructions concerning all that he had to lay before the treaty commission. These were general plans for widening the scope of the Indian mission and particular ones for setting up a mission station and school among the Potawatomis. After rehearsing all he had to say with McCoy, the teacher left, taking Abraham with him as a companion-interpreter, and made for Chicago on August 2nd. McCoy had, however, not been forgotten by the Government who had counted on his help and he must have been overjoyed when on August 9th, Colonel Trimble, a United States Senator, called on him personally to discuss the treaty. The kind Senator asked him to write down all his plans and suggestions for the future of the Indians and give him a detailed written account of the work he was now doing. The good man then promised McCoy that he would do all in his powers to represent his wishes to the Government. McCoy must have given a real deep sigh of relief as he wrote, "Through the favour of a kind Providence, our propositions at the treaty of Chicago were successful, notwithstanding that matters were not arranged precisely in the manner that we had marked out in our plans."[5]

At the treaty meeting, not only had the Government spoken up for McCoy's plans but the Potawatomis themselves. McCoy's good work and friendship with them secured his future work among them. This had not been easy as the Potawatomis were opposed by Roman Catholic priests who had been watching McCoy's progress with dismay. When the Government at the meeting decided to finance a teacher and a blacksmith among the Indians, the Roman Catholics put in a claim saying that the Indians preferred their teachers. This was strongly denied by the Indians, and the Potawatomis presented the Government with a square mile of land to be used by the Baptist Mission and insisted that McCoy should be the teacher appointed to undertake the work. The Government representatives agreed and $1,000 per annum for 15 years was promised to cover McCoy's expenses and those of the blacksmith. When this news reached McCoy, he was overjoyed but decided to settle the matter of how the money should be used straight away to avoid any possible criticism concerning its misuse. He stated that he would accept $400 per year which should be put into a common missionary fund and be administrated by the Board. $365 per year were to finance the blacksmith's work, the rest of the money being used to buy iron and steel for the blacksmith's shop. This shows how selfless McCoy was and how he had no intention of gaining earthly riches for himself. One might say

---

[5] *History of Baptist Indian Missions,* p. 113.

that he erred too far in the opposite direction as he was now hoping to run a new mission station manned by himself, his wife and several co-workers on almost the same wage as was usual for a single person. Furthermore, it took a year and a half before any money was eventually forwarded to McCoy. Whether this was due to the Government or the Board, McCoy does not say. This was not, however, the only dream come true for McCoy. On drawing up the treaty, the Government had also promised grants of $1,500 to finance a teacher and a farmer among the Ottawas and appointed McCoy to superintend the persons thus employed. The Government made it clear that in financing these projects, they were wishing to support the work of the Baptist Mission. McCoy had hitherto only made concrete plans for one more mission station. Now he was able to plan for two. All that he needed now was the missionary staff to fill the posts appointed, and some subsidiary workers. This, McCoy felt, was where the Board ought to come in.

Treachery from a co-worker

Meanwhile, the temporary teacher, a non-Baptist whom McCoy had sent to Chicago, became greatly tempted by the salary offered for a teacher to the Ottawas and applied for the post without consulting either McCoy or the Board. After borrowing McCoy's horse on a pretext to visit Ohio, he even obtained papers from an Indian Agent to be laid before the Governor of Michigan, saying that he was authorized to supplant McCoy. When McCoy discovered what was happening, he remonstrated with the man, informing him that his behavior was highly fraudulent and the post must go to a Baptist of the Board's choice. The teacher, still nameless, threatened McCoy that if he sought to prevent him, he would do so at his peril. The person then set off, with another man who was making the same journey, to lay his forged papers before the Governor of Michigan. McCoy could not undertake anything in person as he was tied to the mission station during his wife's absence. This did not stop him from having a brilliant idea. He wrote out the true state of affairs and committed the document to a friend who was sending some communications to Detroit, the seat of the Governor. The friend then entrusted the sealed letters to the man who was accompanying the too ambitious and fraudulent teacher. Little did the man know that he was not fleeing justice but carrying his own condemnation with him. Needless to say, the man's deceit was revealed and nothing came of his action.

The search for a suitable fellow-missionary

Now McCoy made every possible effort to add to his missionary family so that they could start on the work allowed them by the Potawatomis, the Ottawas and the U. S. Government. One person wrote asking to join the mission but was obviously ill qualified for the task and McCoy had to reject him. A soldier of good education had visited Fort Wayne on several occasions and persuaded McCoy to buy him out of the army so that he could become a teacher at the mission. McCoy wrote to the soldier's commanding officer who agreed to release him on payment of $60 dollars and if a substitute were found.[6] Both conditions were duly met and the ex-soldier now started to teach. It was not long, however, before the man proved to have no idea of teaching, could not control the pupils and was often quite drunk so that McCoy had to dismiss him. In August a substitute was found but after a month or so, he, too, proved to be totally unsuitable and was quickly replaced by another person who also gave up the work very soon. McCoy was rather shocked to find that the last two would-be teachers were professing Christians and members of Baptist churches but did not appear to have any work of grace in their hearts. McCoy had better hopes of a Mr. John Sears of New York who called in at Fort Wayne while on a preaching tour of the white settlers. Sears had an initial calling to the Indians and wished to test his calling. McCoy took him on a short tour of some Indian villages and explained the work to him. Sears appeared to be the man for the job so McCoy arranged for him to appear before the Board and seek an appointment at Fort Wayne. Meanwhile, McCoy's ideas were moving on and he was in touch with the New York Indians, concerning a possible interest from their side in forming a mission. Though a representation of eight men from the tribe visited McCoy, it soon became evident that they had merely arrived to be fed and looked after for a while and their tribe had already invited another denomination to work with them. Unlike the Methodists, McCoy would not set up a missionary work where other Protestant missionaries were already working.

Criticism of the mission from misinformed Christians

McCoy did his very best to entertain strangers as if they were angels unawares, yet even this Christian characteristic brought him

---

[6] See letter from Allen to McCoy dated June 3, 1821, McCoy Papers, Reel 1.

into ill repute with those who contributed to his cause. Often rich Christians who donated poor men's mites were the first to suspect McCoy of misusing those mites. This is illustrated by an extraordinary letter from a Benjamin Archer who with great pomp wrote to McCoy saying that the mission's reputation was at stake, the reason being:

> That while you was Supported by the Publick your Table was Spred with the most Superfluous Dainties and Especially that of Liquors that the United States Could afford and that you Presided over the Company like a little God and how often you made those feasts.[7]

Since McCoy was an ardent campaigner for a total ban on the sale of alcohol and petitioned the Government continually to enforce such laws, the accusation was particularly evil. Happily, those who visited McCoy, including a group of Roman Catholics, to check the facts and fill their own tummies, found hominy on the table and a jug of water. More true to facts was the letter of John Vawter to Col. Richard Johnson which has been preserved among the McCoy Papers in the form of a newspaper cutting, though the name of the newspaper is not attached:

> Sir - On the 11th and 12th of December last I was at Fort Wayne, which place is little better than a wilderness being surrounded with numerous Indian visitors from the neighbouring tribes, but what claimed my attention mostly was the good order and harmony that appeared in a school of about 80 young Indians, who had voluntarily come under the tuition of Elder Isaac McCoy perhaps one of the most pious of his day; and who has devoted more of his time to Indian reform than any other man in the United States, considering his possessing but a small portion of this world's goods, and of an extreme feeble constitution - but when brought nearest the grave his mind seems most deeply impressed with the deplorable situation of the Indians. He lives poor, although himself and wife appear well-reconciled and consider they are working for the Lord. The Elder informed me that his greatest affliction was that of not been able to receive into his school as many as wished to come under his care, owing to his limited means to support them and could not consistently with his feelings intimate to the old Indians his poverty. He said that provisions and clothing,

---

[7] Letter dated May 3, 1821, McCoy Papers, Reel 1.

Books and paper would all be very acceptable as donations in support of said school. I thought if it were practicable to obtain part of the ten thousand dollars, put at the disposal of the President of the United States (above what has been received) it could not be better applied, not intrusted into hands more safe. The family of young Indians with the family of whites all sit at the same table and eat of the same dish and appear to take learning in all respects as readily as the whites. Could you be a means of aiding this man in his laudable undertaking, I shall consider you have added another laurel to your wreath of honour.

Accept dear sir, my best wishes,

for your future prosperity

John Vawter.[8]

McCoy again seriously ill

Shortly before Mrs. McCoy returned, the McCoy children were attacked by bilious fevers which did not appear serious. When McCoy's turn came round, he became dangerously ill, lost all sense of touch, his legs and arms became cold and he all but lost his powers of sight, speech and hearing. With no help at hand, his ministry and work had to stop and the pupils quartered out among friends. Though sick in body and unable to move, McCoy testified to having periods of sweet blessing when he felt the closeness of the Lord. His mind was calm, he tells us, and death had lost its sting. McCoy was totally prepared to meet his Maker. Then he thought of his Indians and prayed that he might be spared for their sake. Afterwards he recorded concerning the answer to that prayer, "While I apprehended that there was not a physician within one hundred miles of me, God so ordered it that that very night two physicians stepped into my room."[9] When Mrs. McCoy arrived with her new baby and the three other tiny tots who had journeyed with her, she was now well but her husband still very ill. "Mercy," McCoy recorded, "was mingled with affliction."[10]

---

[8] McCoy Papers, Reel 1.

[9] *History of Baptist Indian Missions*, p. 118.

[10] Ibid, p. 118

The Indian students' way of dealing with bad teachers

It was now four years since the McCoys were appointed by the Board of Missions and they were still without missionary support. Isaac therefore prepared another pamphlet to be distributed, outlining the present needs of the mission station for manpower and goods. He also wrote to all those individuals who had given or promised their support in the past. Though some material support came in as a result of this appeal, there were still no workers forthcoming. Meanwhile, two more would-be teachers had come and gone and just as the school was able to start up again in November, the question of good teachers became acute. On November 29th a man arrived, who had answered McCoy's written appeal to the nearest white settlement, and he was immediately employed. The trouble with the school was that the students were all keen to improve their knowledge but were very impatient and even rude to those whom they felt had not the abilities to teach them. If they thought a teacher was good, they made him their "father" as they had made Lykins. If they thought him to be useless at his job, they did not give the person long to prove otherwise but made their opposition known. In this case, the pupils found out that their new teacher was addicted to alcohol which they had come to detest for obvious reasons. They thus painted their faces, found some old tin-cans in lieu of drums and some sticks to serve as mock-weapons and did a war-dance around the teacher's house, frightening him out of his wits. McCoy's laconic comment was, "They wished to be understood that their contempt of him was in proportion to the indignity which they believed he had offered to an institution which they were bound to respect."[11]

The Board sends yet another man ill-prepared for missionary work

McCoy had given the Board a detailed report of the Chicago Treaty and was anxiously awaiting a reply. He had suggested that as he was to supervise the Government's efforts to improve the Indians' situation, he ought to meet with the Board to discuss a joint strategy. The Board wrote in November informing McCoy of their agreement and invited him to visit them in Philadelphia and Government representatives in Washington. As McCoy was again without a teacher, he hated the thought of having to leave Mrs. McCoy alone with all the

[11] Ibid, p. 121.

work. He then heard that the Board had at last reacted and were sending him a missionary couple with two small children to help in the work. The man, Peter Clyde was almost fifty years of age and was a weaver who had recently arrived from Scotland. McCoy was able to read between the lines that Clyde was not a preacher, though a good man, and had little idea of what missionary work among the Indians entailed. McCoy quickly sent a man off with horses to meet him on the way and help him through the wilderness. As the Clydes' arrival was delayed, McCoy set off for Philadelphia on December 4, 1821 and was able to meet Clyde on his way and give him some advice concerning the mission. The impression he gained of Clyde, however, was that he was a fine Christian who was thoroughly out of place in the Indian wilderness. He thus continued his journey with very mixed feelings.

McCoy's first journey for discussions with the Board

The journey to Philadelphia took 26 days, most of which time, McCoy had to ride on horseback, often swimming his horse across icy rivers and sleeping under the stars in bitter cold weather. It was the first of some twenty-odd journeys that McCoy would make to the capital on behalf of the Indians. While camping out in the highly inclement weather, he wrote to his wife saying:

> You and I my dear have been called in providence to experience much trouble, fatigue, and self-denial. Nevertheless we have always possessed the best blessings on earth. We have ever lived together in one mind, enjoying the sweetest peace and affection that conjugal ties can bind together. We are helped in relation to our children and are blessed in being called of God to suffer for his sake.[12]

On his way to Philadelphia, he called on Giles Jackson, a member of Concord Baptist Church, Ohio, with whom he had corresponded about the need for missionaries. Jackson now made a formal application to be considered a missionary, asking McCoy to present it to the Board. On reaching Philadelphia, McCoy found the Board had already moved almost en bloc to Washington to attend the opening of their latest project and fund-eater, Columbian College. This college was one of several enterprises started by the Board which gained nationwide criticism among the Baptists and put the whole

---

[12] Letter dated December 23, 1821, McCoy Papers, Reel 2.

idea of missions into disrepute. Previous to the setting up of the Triennial Convention and the Missions Board under its auspices, each local Association more or less financed its own work which was usually limited to local needs. The needs of the Western churches were greatest as they were receiving the most settlers with all the problems that attend such a large movement of people who had become little more than nomads. The Convention and Board, however, were staffed on the whole by Easterners who were not faced with the problems of the West. The Convention looked upon themselves as the only Baptist channel for the financing of Baptist work and all Associations were expected to bow to their authority when distributing funds. Many Westerners thought that this was a very one-sided form of support indeed and that when they sent hard earned funds to the Board's headquarters in Philadelphia and later Boston, that was the last they saw or heard of them. Isaac McCoy had to suffer much from this kind of centralized church government. Whenever the Board were tardy in sending McCoy sums agreed on or when they refused to honor his drafts, McCoy would make a desperate appeal directly to the churches and to individuals for help concerning the mission's immediate needs. This produced letters of protest from the Board who argued that all funds collected for the Indian Mission should be sent to them to be used at their discretion. This meant in practice that the starving McCoys and their co-workers and pupils would have to send money that they urgently needed on the long journey to Boston and then wait one to four months (according to where they were at the time) until they heard whether they were considered entitled to it or not. [13]

A second bone of contention was that funds which could have been used for evangelistic purposes and building up the new churches, were put into activities which were planned to benefit mainly the East but which became bottomless barrels and financial fiascos. One of these was the Columbian College now started, another was an expensive journal called the *Columbian Star,* the third was a Tract Society and the fourth the *Latter Day Luminary* already mentioned, all of which proved financial flops. The result was that not only did the Baptist Board members lose much of their fortunes which they had invested in these enterprises but also thousands of dollars made up

---

[13] See, for instance, letter to McCoy from Luther Rice from Columbian College dated May 11, 1824 and McCoy's reply of June 20th of that year. Also letter from McCoy to Dr. Bolles dated November 23, 1826.

from many more thousands of widows' mites[14] sent in from all parts of the Union. The state of affairs was quite scandalous. Matters became more notorious when the Baptist Board insisted on keeping the Columbian College "white," before they went bankrupt, and banning all Indians from it. The whites suffered, too, because work among the Western settlers was almost completely suspended so that the money saved could be used for the college. Yet, it was there that evangelistic work was the most necessary. There is no doubt that this highly questionable state of affairs contributed to anti-missionary feelings towards domestic and foreign missions in the Western country. The Board's agents were fleecing the homespun frontier pioneers who needed every penny they could earn, in order to enrich the work of New England's top-hat wearers. Indeed, this factor, in the long run, proved to be more counter-productive to missions than the New Light, Campbellite and Parkerite protests of the 1820s. Such a pseudo-doctrinal lobby against evangelizing Indians, whether from America or Asia, hardly lasted a decade, whereas the Board's policy carried on up to the Civil War.

McCoy's meeting with the Board proves very positive

At Philadelphia, McCoy met John Sears who had visited Fort Wayne to test his calling. Sears was still convinced that he should become a missionary to the Indians. So, weary as he was, McCoy hired a carriage and made the six days journey to Washington with Sears so that he could make his case known to the Board. McCoy met the Board on January 7, 1822 and was delighted to find they accepted his plans for establishing further missionary stations. Jackson was given the task of setting up a smithy for the Potawatomis and Sears was appointed as teacher to the Ottawas. They also invested him with the authority to select candidates and collecting agents for the Indian mission and accepted Sears as a missionary making him McCoy's personal assistant. McCoy wrote home to Christiana to tell her that the Board had invested more authority in him than he would have

---

[14] The Baptists organized "Mite Societies" to help support missions among their poorer members.

given any man if he had been a Board member.[15] The Board also advised McCoy to work closely with the Secretary of War, John C. Calhoun, who was in charge of Indian affairs, perhaps not knowing that the two men were already in correspondence. Calhoun was soon sought out and gave an audience to McCoy, Rice, Staughton, Brown and Burgiss Allison who had formed a special Indian Committee. Calhoun encouraged McCoy greatly in his work, promising to assist him as much as possible within the bounds of the treaties and laws covering the Indians. A grant of four to five hundred dollars a year was made for the appointment of a miller to serve the Miamis' mills which had already been built. This miller was to be appointed by the Baptist Board but no candidate was available. McCoy, whose wages were less than the craftsmen the mission was employing, found that the entire administration and reporting to both Board and Government rested on his shoulders but he still had no one to relieve him at Fort Wayne. However, the Board generously told McCoy that he could draw on them for $3,000 but asked him to deduct any amount from this sum which might come in the form of cash donations or goods such as clothing.[16]

A further tragic incident in the life of the McCoys

When McCoy returned to Fort Wayne, very ill after the journey, he received the frightful news that an Indian had tried to strangle his eight-year-old daughter Elizabeth (b. Aug. 17, 1813) and left her bleeding from the neck, mouth and nose, thinking her dead.[17] The child appeared to recover but the Indian responsible for the deed challenged McCoy to fight with him so that he might revenge what had happened to his daughter. McCoy, thinking of his Christian witness first and foremost, refused both to have the Indian hunted down by the law or to meet him in combat. This, according to the Indians' custom meant that McCoy was now free game for the man

---

[15] Letter dated January 8, 1821, McCoy Papers, Reel 1. The actual year was 1822. McCoy had obviously written 1821, forgetting that the new year had started.

[16] The facts revealed here are mainly gathered from McCoy's *"History"* and Reel 2 of the McCoy Papers.

[17] McCoy tells the terrible story in a letter to Staughton dated March 15, 1882, McCoy Papers, Reel 2 and in his *"History."*

who had tried to kill his child. The man, however, was killed shortly afterwards in a drunken brawl with another Indian. Elizabeth never fully recovered, dying a few months later on August 13, 1822 while McCoy was a hundred miles away trying to find food and fodder for the winter and bargaining with the Government representative for future mission sites.

Johnston Lykins returns to take over the school

To further McCoy's misery on returning home from his meeting with the Board, he again fell ill and was unable to preach for some eight days. There was much to comfort him however in this illness. News had reached them that churches on the Western frontier were about to send three missionaries to the relief of the Fort Wayne mission. This was especially encouraging as Kentucky and Indiana, from where the promised missionaries came, were commencing on a severe anti-mission period coupled with acute stagnation in growth. The Indiana brethren had also sent the missionaries a large number of pigs and the Ohio brethren had sent a number of cows. At the same time, a number of clothing parcels arrived and small money gifts. All in all, it appeared that more comfortable days were ahead for the mission. The greatest comfort of all, however, had been the reappearance of Johnston Lykins. It had been planned that the school should restart on March 4th without a permanent teacher. Much prayer was sent up and then Lykins walked in on March 11th, saying he would take over the school until missionaries were sent. This was a day of rejoicing indeed for McCoy as he loved Lykins as a son.

The Family Rules

On February 15, 1822, McCoy, acting on principles practiced by William Carey at Serampore, felt he ought to establish the mission on a firm basis of cooperation and unity of spirit. He had put together twelve rules for general missionary conduct to be accepted and signed by the missionaries and this was now forwarded to the Board for approval under the heading *General Rules for the Fort Wayne Mission Family*, which became known simply as the *Family Rules*. On March 14, 1822, the Board passed the following resolution:

The Family Rules (forwarded by Mr. McCoy) of the mission having being twice carefully read, Resolved, That the said rules meet the full and decided approbation of the board.

The full text reads:

We, whose names follow, being appointed missionaries to the Indians by the General Convention of the Baptist denomination for missions, deem it expedient for our comfort and usefulness to adopt, in the fear of the Lord, the following general rules for the regulation of the mission family, viz:

1st. We agree that our object in becoming missionaries is to meliorate the condition of the Indians, and not to serve ourselves. Therefore,

2d. We agree that our whole time, talents, and labours, shall be dedicated to the obtaining of this object, and shall all be bestowed gratis, so that the mission cannot become indebted to any missionary for his or her services.

3d. We agree that all remittances from the board of missions, amid all money and property accruing to any of us, by salaries from Government, by smith shops, by schools, by donations, or from whatever quarter it may arise, shall be thrown into the common missionary fund, and be sacredly applied to the cause of *this* mission; and that no part of the property held by us at our stations is ours, or belongs to any of us, but it belongs to the General Convention which we serve, and is held in trust by us, so long as said society shall continue us in their employment: provided that nothing herein contained shall affect the right of any to private inheritance, &c.[18]

4th. We agree to obey the instructions of our patrons, and that the superintendent shall render to them, from time to time, accounts of our plans, proceedings, prospects, receipts, and expenditures; and that the accounts of the mission, together with the mission records, shall at all times be open for the inspection of any of the missionaries.

5th. We agree that all members of the mission family have equal claims upon the mission for equal support in similar circumstances; the claims of widows and orphans not to be in the least affected by the death of the head of the family.

---

[18] This had been a moot point with Sears and a matter of dispute with several new missionaries who knew of this general agreement before they applied for a missionary post in the missions founded by McCoy and Lykins.

6th. We agree that when any missionary shall not find employment in his particular branch of business, it shall be his duty to engage in some other branch of business, as circumstances shall dictate.[19]

7th. We agree that, agreeably to their strength and ability, all the female missionaries should bear an equal part of the burden of domestic labours and cares, lest some should sink under the weight of severe and unremitted exertions; making the necessary allowances for the school mistress.[20]

8th. We agree to be industrious, frugal, amid economical, at all times, to the utmost extent of our abilities.

9th. We agree that missionaries labouring at the different stations belonging to this mission are under the same obligations to each other, as though resident in the same establishment.

10th. We agree that it is the duty of missionaries to meet statedly at their respective stations, for the purposes of preserving peace and harmony among themselves, of cherishing kindness and love for each other, love to God, and zeal in the cause of missions.

11th. We agree to feel one general concern for the success of every department of the mission, for the happiness of every member of the mission family, and to feed at one common table, except in cases of bad health, &c., in which cases the persons thus indisposed shall receive special attention, and shall be made as comfortable as our situation will admit.[21]

---

[19] No better example was shown here than that of McCoy who was Superintendent, blacksmith, gardener, farmer and even cook.

[20] This was an important item as one of the chief causes of unrest among a number of would-be missionaries was that they thought their status forbade them to do menial chores. McCoy had no such inhibitions and often worked in the kitchen for his wider family and tilled the soil. Mrs. McCoy never shunned bearing the major burden of domestic work. One of the chief weaknesses of the Board's missionaries (Evan Jones excluded) to the southern tribes were tantrums caused by class-consciousness among the various missionaries. Some of Jones' co-workers despised him, for instance, because he married a woman thought to be a mere domestic help. Eliza McCoy, Isaac's niece, came into a relatively large fortune and had enjoyed a first-class education but she always remained a humble co-worker with those from other, less affluent or learned backgrounds.

[21] As the family became too large to eat all together in the small dining-room, meals were taken in successive groups.

12th. We agree to cherish a spirit of kindness and for-bearance for each other, and, as the success of our labours depends on the good providence of God, it is our duty to live near to him in public and private devotion, and to walk before him with fear, and in the integrity of our hearts, conscious that he ever sees us, and that by him actions are weighed; realising that we are, at best, only instruments in his hand, and hoping that when we shall have finished the work given us to do, we shall dwell together in heaven, in company with fellow-labourers from other parts of the vineyard, and with those for whom we are now strangers and sufferers in this wilderness, and, to crown our happiness, shall gaze eternally on Him whose religion we are now endeavouring to propagate, to whom shall be ascribed *all* the glory of the accomplishment of our present undertaking."[22]

McCoy was to experience a number of disappointments regarding the *Family Rules* as a number of would-be missionaries who arrived at the station, refused to live by them. At first the Board was in whole-hearted agreement with McCoy but when the Board eventually came under a new leadership and was transferred from Philadelphia to Boston, their views changed. Personally, however, McCoy lived by the *Family Rules* all his life, as did the majority of the missionaries connected with McCoy and those in other areas lived similarly.

The Clydes leave the mission field after a few months greatly discouraged

The Clydes disappointed McCoy. Not because they were not decent Christian people but because they had a totally different picture of how a missionary should live. They confessed that they needed more comfort for their family life than the mission afforded them and they had begun to doubt the usefulness of the mission unless both the conditions and the numbers of missionaries were improved. The very thought that McCoy now intended to set up a new station in an area totally devoid of the white man's comforts alarmed them considerably as they could not imagine how a mere handful of people could undertake such a work. On April 15, 1822, Clyde thus penned

---

[22] *History of Baptist Indian Missions*, pp. 170-172.

the following letter of resignation to the Corresponding Secretary, Dr. Staughton at the Board:

DEAR BROTHER: The object of my becoming your missionary was, that I might thereby aid in ameliorating the condition of the Indians. My desires to be useful in this business have not abated. But, after an experience of more than five months, I have come to a settled conclusion that, owing to the present, and the prospect in relation to the future situation of my family, it would be most serviceable to the mission for me to retire from the service of the board. It is expected that the mission will shortly remove further into the wilderness. This circumstance has a discouraging effect on the mind of my wife, notwithstanding she is as desirous to be useful to her suffering fellow-beings as ever she was.

Having taken all these things into consideration, and believing it to be the duty of the servants of the board to accept of their patronage no longer than they can be useful, I humbly beg leave to tender to the board of missions this my resignation, accompanied with grateful acknowledgments for their generosity and kindness.

As preparation is making to locate the mission among the Putawatomies, and it is therefore important for brother McCoy to know who will certainly accompany him, as the season most favourable for my providing for my family will soon be past, and as the situation of my family renders a settled home indispensable, I hope it will not be considered premature for me to return to Ohio by the first conveyance.

I trust that my resignation will not be a matter of discouragement to the board, nor to any who may feel disposed to serve them, and whose circumstances will enable them to be useful. I am more and more convinced of the duty of Christians to endeavour to reform these exceedingly depraved and wretched people, and experience has taught me the pressing necessity which calls for more missionaries at the station. I am well satisfied with the qualifications of brother and sister McCoy for the stations they fill; but what can two or three missionaries do in a work like this? Nothing short of a conviction that I could not strengthen their hands could induce me to leave this brother and sister, with whom I could live on such amicable terms, or to quit a field which, with all my heart, I wish to be cultivated.

Your communications to me please to direct to brother McCoy. Trusting that the board will have the goodness to

accept my resignation, I remain their humble servant,
PETER CLYDE.[23]

A ripe harvest but few laborers

On March 26, McCoy heard from Indian Agent Johnson that the Treaty of Chicago had been ratified by the Senate and that McCoy could now draw on the Secretary of War for the funds which had been promised to him.[24] The McCoys now could go about extending their school in the hope that its future was secure. Now that some older girls had become pupils, Mrs. McCoy taught them spinning and sewing. Soon a loom was set up to weave the yarn that the girls spun. The boys were encouraged to learn to use agricultural tools so that they could help their parents settle down to a farming life. The Indian Agent, Mr. Kerchevall, encouraged the Indians in the area to use their annuities to farm their lands instead of squandering them on whiskey and soon seven Miami families settled down near the station and began farming land. Other Miamis started breeding cattle or pigs. This development encouraged the Indians to work closely with the mission station and its school. In April, McCoy was surprised by a visit from the chief of the Massinawa band who had hitherto been feared for their hostility and addiction to whiskey so that the Indian Agents had forbidden McCoy to start a mission among them for fear that they would soon kill him. Now the Miami chief told McCoy that he found the missionary's ways the best. He would settle down himself and grow corn and send his two children to the school. When he heard that McCoy was planning to establish a mission among the Potawatomis, he showed great disappointment but McCoy promised that he would now do his utmost to have a special Miami mission set up, as he had originally planned. Shortly afterwards, another Miami chief came from the Tippecanoe area, famous for the battle between General William Henry Harrison and Tecumseh's Indian Confederation in 1811 on the eve of the second war with Great Britain. The chief told McCoy of the excellent nature of his homestead and how McCoy would be greatly welcomed. McCoy sighed and exclaimed, "The fields around us appeared to be whitening for the harvest, but we could not obtain

---

[23] *History of Baptist Indian Missions*, pp. 122-123. See also document signed by the McCoys and the Clydes dated April 15, 1822 concerning the amiable separation, McCoy Papers, Reel 2.

[24] McCoy Papers, Reel 2.

labourers."[25] It seemed that the mission was not to enjoy the new recruits who were so urgently needed to man the missionary stations that McCoy was planning. The new candidate from Indiana, a Baptist minister, for instance, had shown in his letters that he had no idea of the privations he must endure as a missionary and as his expectations in no way resembled the reality at Fort Wayne, McCoy was compelled to advise him not to join the mission.

Further evidence of the Board's ignorance of the mission's situation

Though times were hard and boiled home-grown corn with no meat or vegetables was still often the only diet, McCoy was now able to work theoretically without costing the missionary board a penny due to funds sent in by the Government and friends. McCoy began to have second thoughts about turning all monies over to the ownership of the Board as they were far less adept at using funds wisely than he and Mrs. McCoy. Indeed, the bulk of the Board's money for missionary work was coming from the wages granted to McCoy and a growing number of helpers, yet the Board often insisted on using the money against the wishes of the men on the mission field. The Board could not understand that goods out in the wilds were more expensive than in so-called civilized areas and they naively spent money on foodstuffs and livestock not realizing that the food might become useless on the long and risky journey to the mission station and the livestock perish or escape. At times, the Board became most patronizing and grudgingly allowed McCoy money for basics which he could have paid for out of his own pocket had he kept his wages. The making of long reports to the Board, listing every penny that was spent under circumstances that the Board could not understand also took up much of McCoy's time which he could have spent preaching Christ.

The wretched circumstances of the Potawatomis

The Potawatomis continued to fill McCoy's mind and heart as he saw that the Miamis were improving their situation but he was hearing terrible tales of Potawatomi poverty and destitution. In April, 1822, the McCoys experienced a sight which they could not easily forget and which McCoy described in all its pathetic realism:

---

[25] *History of Baptist Indian Missions*, p. 138.

On the 14th of April, 1822, four of our Putawatomie pupils, who had been absent through the winter, returned, ragged and wretched enough. They informed me that their grandmother, an aged woman, was lying at a camp a little distance from our house, at the point of dying. In the afternoon we were informed that the old woman was dead. Two young men, who were her grandsons, intimated to me, through the medium of some of their relatives belonging to our family, a wish that I would assist in burying her, and appeared to be very thankful when I consented. My wife and I walked to their camp, where we found the corpse lying on the ground, wrapped in an old blanket. In this place and position the old woman had lain several days before her death, as we discovered by the whitish appearance of the grass underneath her. It had been raining, and sometimes snowing, for several days, and the earth was very full of water; to all which she had been exposed, without even a tent or a piece of bark to shelter her from the storm from above, or to save her from the water beneath. The few rags which had served for her clothing were filthy in the extreme, and under and about her were vermin, such as might be seen about a putrid carcass that had lain some days on the earth. The sight was shocking, and was rendered more so on account of the depravity and insensibility of her children and grand-children who were about the place. The whole company exhibited a scene of poverty, wretchedness, and wickedness, which scarcely could be found among any other people in the world besides these miserable Indians. Near the corpse were a man and two women drunk; several others were in but little better condition. A few were sober, and appeared solemn. All were destitute of any shelter, excepting a piece of a tent-cloth which partially covered two or three of them. The wind was high and cold, yet they had not more fire than would have laid upon a common fire-shovel. All their clothing, bedding, cooking vessels, and furniture of every description, would not have constituted a back load for one of them. Not a particle of food was to be seen about the camp, except a piece of a dog which they had butchered on that morning, and which was hanging on the limb of a tree. In dressing the animal they had not skinned it, but had singed off the hair in the fire. For our comfort we gathered a few sticks and kindled a fire. At my request, one showed me the place where they wished the grave to be dug. Their apology for troubling us was, that "they had no implements with which to make a hole in the ground." In order to convey the corpse to the grave, they placed on it a pole extending a little

beyond the head and the feet, and with leather strings tied
it fast to the pole in several places. A short pole was next
placed across the stomach, between the body and the first
pole. Four men then took hold, one on each end of the two
poles, and carried this wretched female to the grave. When
the corpse had been placed in the grave, one of them put a
piece of tobacco at the head, and pronounced the following
valediction:- 'Grandmother, you have lived long enough; you
have now died, and left all your children. Grandmother, I
give you a piece of tobacco to smoke that you may rest
quietly in your grave, and not disturb us who are alive. This
is all that I have to give you; we will all smoke for you. Our
father (alluding to myself) will take care of your
grandchildren.[26] Grandmother, I now bid you farewell.'

We then placed boards over the corpse, and filled the
grave, after which they built a fire at the head and another
at the foot. This done, all retired to their camp to conclude
the funeral ceremonies, by smoking and by drinking
whiskey. O, sin, what hast thou done![27]

Scoffers become helpers

Though there were few white people around Fort Wayne, most
of them were Roman Catholics who were visited from time to time by
priests who preached against the Baptist Mission Station. McCoy
answered by inviting the priests to his home and showing them the
work being done for the Indians.

Another visit at this time was by the State Marshall who was
an avowed opponent of missionary operations among the Indians and
had troubled the churches in 1818, influencing them to oppose missions. After seeing the work McCoy was doing, he wrote to Congress,
congratulating McCoy on his fine work and his letter was published in
several leading newspapers. One newspaper editor made a gift to the
Board of $60. Now McCoy could write, "Thus Providence ordered that

---

[26] The McCoys did take care of the children, one of the boys was from now
on called Isaac McCoy by the Indians after his "father".

[27] *History of Baptist Indian Missions*, pp. 131-132.

one who had been a formidable opposer, after spending a few days at the institution, should become an active helper."[28]

Jackson arrives and sets up a smithy

Now Giles Jackson and his family joined the McCoys and the news came that Mr. Sears had several friends who wanted to become missionaries to the Indians. Again, however, the Board had sent a man in Jackson who had no calling to the ministry. They felt, however, that he would be suitable to take on the tasks of a blacksmith and thus be eligible for a government grant. Jackson, however, proved to be a very sensitive man and because the Board did not treat him as a missionary and even forgot to mention him in their official reports, in spite of McCoy's urgent request, he soon became dissatisfied with his position. Another difficulty at this time was that many direct gifts came in from a number of sources. This was quite an embarrassment for the mission as they had surrendered all claim to funds and property to the Board which meant that technically they had to forward all direct gifts to themselves to the Board and await their judgement as to how they should be used.

Further signs of material and spiritual need among the Potawatomis

Throughout May of 1822 McCoy sounded out the Potawatomis concerning setting up a mission station among them. The missionary was constantly shocked at the acute poverty in which many of this tribe lived. On visiting the area in which the Potawatomis had requested him to settle, McCoy saw sights which rent his heart. One of the experiences he relates in his own words will suffice to depict the needs of a people who the romantic poets of the age were praising as "the naked savage" and depicting their lives as if they lived in eternal bliss, being one with nature. McCoy relates:

---

[28] *History of Baptist Indian Missions*, p. 134. This person was the Mr. Vawter previously mentioned. See Vawter's letter to McCoy dated April 25, 1822, McCoy Papers, 1822.

The wigwam composed of flags was circular, about ten feet in diameter, and about seven feet high in the centre. The smoke from the fire in the middle of the hut escaped through an opening above. The door was closed by a deer skin attached to the upper part. Within lay a woman on the ground, whose groans indicated extreme agony, and whose appearance presaged a speedy dissolution. Her body and arms were uncovered, excepting as she occasionally drew over them an old blanket, which, in her restlessness, she was perpetually shifting. Six days before this time she had become the mother of twin sons, one of whom had died, and the other was scarcely alive. I already supposed that I had witnessed among Indians the extreme of wretchedness; but a sight of this infant, which was brought to me that I might see it, together with the indescribable condition of its mother, surpassed any thing which I had ever beheld, and excited in me feelings both of sympathy and horror. The babe was placed on a board, as was common with those people, with pieces of an old blanket around it, to which, and to the infant, now six days old, I suppose a drop of water had never been intentionally applied. It gasped for breath; 'but why', thought I, 'should it desire to live, seeing that its life must be that of a miserable Indian! Or shall our benevolent institution, to be erected here, become a house of mercy to such, in which shall be concentrated, for their benefit, the sympathies and charities of Christians![29]

As was his custom and calling, McCoy gathered the poor villagers together and preached the gospel to them, noting that the women of the tribe had gathered with the men, which had hitherto not been the practice of the Potawatomis. The chiefs then told McCoy that they were happy to hear the gospel from his lips and wished to hear him again often. One of the chiefs pronounced a benediction on McCoy, saying, "May the Great Spirit preserve your health, and conduct you safely to your family, give success to your labors, and bring you back to us again."

Throughout these weeks of visiting the Potawatomis, McCoy found the people industrious but living on next to nothing. Apart from hominy and an occasional pigeon, they appeared to have no bread or meat and existed on roots, weeds and a few dried beans. Even these stocks, McCoy tells us, were small. On his return to Fort Wayne with a number of new pupils, McCoy heard that a murderer had slaughter-

---

[29] *History of Baptist Indian Missions*, p. 139.

ed a man near the settlement and had forced his way into the mission station in order to kill one of the pupils who had fled before him. McCoy's eldest son, still a boy, and Lykins had had great difficulty in persuading the violent man to leave them in peace. Also in McCoy's absence, a would-be missionary had turned up at the station, announcing he had obtained a life's calling. After only two or three weeks experiencing how the missionaries really lived, the once-eager candidate had changed his mind and departed. One good thing, McCoy found on his return, was that Mr. Jackson had set up his blacksmith's shop and was teaching an Indian boy the trade. Another was that various Indians had visited the station, each promising land to the missionaries if they would set up missionary work among them.

Johnston Lykins comes to faith in Christ

June 2, 1822[30] was a great day for the McCoys. Johnston Lykins professed faith in Christ and asked to be baptized, thus following in the footsteps of his predecessor Corbly Martin who was now pastor of a growing flock in Ohio. As usual when McCoy went on a longer journey, he came back ill and exhausted and now had great difficulty in conducting Lykins' baptismal service which was held on the banks of the Maumee River. McCoy preached sitting down and he was scarcely able to wade out into the river and baptize Lykins. The new convert now told the McCoys that he wished to identify himself fully with the Christian goals of the mission and presented himself as a missionary for the work of the gospel. McCoy was only too pleased to give Lykins the right hand of fellowship and promptly, using the powers the Board had recently given him, he presented the young teacher with a letter appointing him a missionary.

> Fort Wayne, June 15, 1822
>
> Agreeably to regulations of the Baptist Board of Missions for the United States, in relation to the appointment of missionaries to the Fort Wayne mission, the bearer, Mr. Johnston Lykins, at his request, and upon a full acquaintance with his character, is hereby duly appointed a missionary, in conjunction with those already labouring at this station.
>
> As Mr. Lykins has dedicated his life to this service solely for the good of the Indians, without the promise of hope of

---

[30] See brief undated note to this effect on Reel 2, McCoy Papers.

any pecuniary reward whatever, expecting nothing more
than a subsistence, it is hoped that all good people will treat
him with that respectful attention which his talents, piety,
and self-denial merit.

Isaac McCoy.[31]

From now on, Lykins' name was to be connected closely to that
of McCoy in their great 24-year partnership in bringing the gospel to
the Indians. McCoy, when writing to Staughton about Lykins,
described him as "A little over 22 years old, of respectable parents, a
man of good sense, few words, much meekness, piety and zeal. But
withal is too diffident. He manages the school well, and gives good
attention to other business, the management of which has been
committed to him."[32] Lykins always felt closely attached to the
Potawatomis and was able to translate the Gospel of Matthew and the
Acts of the Apostles into their tongue.

Peck continues to defend McCoy's work against Parker's onslaughts

Meanwhile, John Mason Peck was trying to support McCoy on
his home front. The Indian mission found its greatest supporters in
the States of Kentucky and Indiana and Daniel Parker, in his efforts
to fight missions of any kind, had decided to attack the missionary
idea at its base, which he felt was the Wabash Association of churches
supporting the Indian Mission. Peck often acted as a defensive shield
for those under Parker's attacks and wrote in his journal while staying
at New Princeton, Indiana in June, 1822:

Monday, 10th. I preached before the association on missions.
The Wabash Association, though, while Brother McCoy was
amongst them, warm friends of the mission - at least a
majority were - have in too many instances become opposed.
Prejudices have risen up, and some are, I doubt not,
influenced by selfish motives. It appears very evident that
Parker is determined not to yield, or give up the ground he
has assumed. To effect his purpose he has been engaged for
some time among a portion of the churches.

---

[31] *History of Baptist Indian Missions*, p. 143. See also McCoy's letter to
Staughton concerning Lykin's conversion, baptism and missionary appointment, McCoy Papers, Reel 2.

[32] Ibid, letter to Staughton.

After some amendments to the constitution of the association had been discussed, the subject of missions came up. This was occasioned by one church having charged another with having supported missions as constituting a grievance. This gave full scope for a discussion on the propriety of missions. Mr. Parker opposed them with all the ingenuity of his power, and Mr. Wm. Polke as ably defended them. I then obtained leave to speak, and entered on a detail of facts connected with this subject. The whole discussion lasted about five hours, and excited peculiar interest in the public mind. A large assembly seemed unwilling to stir from the place till the decision was reached. I have never before met with so determined an opposer to missions in every aspect. But the decision gave a decided victory to the cause of missions, fully sustaining the church which had contributed to their support.[33]

Dealing with white bootleggers

Parker's anti-mission campaign which dealt with every aspect of evangelism personal or corporate, was now in full force but McCoy had another problem to deal with at the time. In spite of stringent laws prohibiting the sale of alcohol to the Indians, white bootleggers were never a scarcity in the Fort Wayne area so the missionaries now thought it high time to do something about it. On June 12th, they called a meeting of all the white inhabitants of the district to see what could be done to stop illicit sales of strong liquor. It was decided to set up a watchdog society to make sure that any breach in the laws appertaining to sales of alcoholic beverages should be immediately notified to the authorities. All the citizens seemed willing to assist the courts in this way but the newly founded society discovered that the nearest court at Winchester some eighty miles away had little interest in breaches of the law at Fort Wayne. Again McCoy verbalized his feelings in one of his typical understatements, "the success of the society was not equal to the kindness of its resolutions." Realizing that the keepers of public order were few and far between in the area where McCoy worked and their capacities were limited by reason of distance and numbers, the Government gave McCoy special powers to deal with the bootleggers. When McCoy was eventually dismissed by

---

[33] Quoted from Peck's journal by Rufus Babcock, *Memoir of John Mason Peck, D. D., Edited from His Journals and Correspondence,* p. 174.

the Foreign Missions Board, heavy drinking once again became prevalent among the Potawatomis and Kansas tribes as no effort was made from the Board's side to keep the bootleggers out. When McCoy became the Corresponding Secretary of the new American Indian Mission Board, he was again able successfully to enter into consultation with the President himself concerning anti-whiskey peddling laws.[34]

---

[34] See letter from the A.I.M.A. President William C. Buck to the President of the United States dated March 15, 1844.

Chapter Five
Setting Up the Carey Mission (1822)

Implementing the Chicago Treaty of 1821

The Chicago Treaty of the previous year had been signed and sealed without any real indications of its being implemented as far as Indian missions were concerned, either from the Government in providing posts, or the Board in filling them. McCoy had long felt that it was time that he contacted the Government's representatives for Indian affairs to start things moving but he had been at first so busy and afterwards so ill that he had not managed to look into the matter. The Department of War had now placed the management of Indian treaties in the hands of Lewis Cass, Governor of Michigan with whom McCoy already enjoyed the best relations and was in close correspondence. Col. Johnston, the Indian Agent, always addressed McCoy as "your friend and servant" and showed great respect and friendship to McCoy. Even Cass always dealt personally with McCoy in spite of being in such a high position and addressed him "with much esteem." McCoy, however, was always careful to address Cass as "Your Excellency." Such facts show how accepted McCoy had become in Government circles and how much his fine Christian character, expertise and witness had opened the very doors that could be of greatest assistance to the work God had given him to do.

Hoping that Cass would now have a definite plan, McCoy decided to make the 200 mile journey to Detroit and discuss with him the Government's promised aid in setting up missionary stations among the Potawatomis and Ottawas as specified in the Chicago Treaty. Cass wrote to McCoy on July 6th to say he would have a plan ready during the next few days[1] but McCoy, anticipating that it would be so, left for Detroit on July 9th before receiving the letter. It was the height of the summer weather and he soon found that the summer

---

[1] See Cass' letter in McCoy Papers, Reel 2.

trail brought with it almost as many hardships as his winter journeys because of the flies and mosquitoes which drove the horses quite mad and caused the humans terrible irritation and pain. Governor Cass received McCoy with great cordiality and promised him that the treaty would be fulfilled to the letter. John Sears was to be made teacher to the Ottawas and McCoy was asked to name two blacksmiths for the Potawatomis and Ottawas who should enter the Government services under the auspices of the Indian mission.

Governor Cass now fitted McCoy out with an exact description of what he expected a Baptist missionary to do and in what way, they, the Government, could cooperate in this work. As McCoy was quick to tell the Board in his report sent off on July 26th, if they had exerted themselves and provided more missionaries, Government support would have been all the greater. This rather lengthy document must be reproduced here as it represented not only the will of the Government at the time but also that of McCoy and the Baptist Board who were one in their acceptance of the measures proposed. Indeed, the Board had encouraged McCoy to seek the very help which he had so successfully obtained. This is important to bear in mind as a decade later the Board had both radically altered their views of the Indian mission and changed their politics which resulted in them accusing McCoy of being more a Government agent than a Christian missionary. It also helps to explain how the Board felt free to accept Government aid through the intervention of McCoy, yet eventually strike him from their lists of missionaries because of his efforts to find a land for the Indians where they could live in peace. This view, the Whigs in the Board now thought, was Jacksonian politics and to be rejected.

Detroit. July 16, 1822

SIR; By the --- article of the treaty of Chicago, the sum of fifteen hundred dollars is appropriated for the support of a blacksmith, teacher, and a person to instruct the Ottawas in agriculture, and for the purchase of cattle, farming utensils, &c.; and the sum of one thousand dollars is appropriated for the support of a teacher and blacksmith for the Putawatomies. The establishment for the latter is to be formed on a section of land, to be located in the Indian country, south of the St. Joseph's, and, for the former, north, of the Grand river.

Having been instructed by the Secretary of War to avail myself of your services upon this subject if they can be advantageously used, and believing the interests of the United States, as well as those of the Indians, will he promoted by your employment, I have no hesitation in conferring on you the appointment of teacher for the Putawatomies, and also upon your associate, Mr. Sears, that of teacher for the Ottawas. Your duties as superintendent of the establishment, by the Baptist church, for the civilization and improvement of the Indians, will be separate from and independent of those which will be required of you under the treaty; and for the execution of the latter, agreeably to the instructions you may receive, you will be responsible to the proper officers of the United States.

As teacher, you will give such instructions to the Indians, old and young, as you may deem best suited to their capacity, habits, and condition. What portion of these instructions shall be moral and religious, must be referred to your own discretion. Schools for the education of youth will come within the sphere of your duties, so far as circumstances may require, and as the bounty of individuals or of societies may provide for the support of the scholars. But no other expenditure than your own compensation must be expected from the United States for this object.

Accompanying this I transmit you an extract of my letter to the Northern Missionary Society, which will exhibit to you my sentiments on this subject, and which render it unnecessary for me to repeat them in this letter.

But, independent of these objects, your duties, as teacher, will extend to the whole circle of Indian wants, and to all the means of Indian improvement, whether moral or physical.

1st. It will be a paramount duty to inculcate proper sentiments towards the Government and citizens of the United States, to persuade the Indians, as far as possible, to withdraw their views and affections from a foreign Power,[2] and to restrain them from any acts which would render them obnoxious to our laws, or expose them to the lawless attacks or depredations of individuals.

2d. All attempts to meliorate the condition of the Indians must prove abortive, so long as ardent spirits are freely introduced into their country. Their continued intoxication is the bane of all our efforts. Every hope,

---

[2] Here, of course, the British are meant as many Indian tribes still had loose affiliations dating back to the War of 1812 and beyond.

feeling, and consideration, are sacrificed to this over-whelming passion. It is an absolute mania, which they appear to be wholly unable to resist, and which sweeps before it every barrier of self-regard, of moral duty, and of natural affection. One fact will place this lamentable evil in a clearer point of view than the most laboured discussion. At the treaty concluded September last, at Chicago, Topenebe, principal chief of the Putawatomies, a man nearly eighty years of age, irritated at the continual refusal, on the part of the commissioners, to gratify his importunities for whiskey, exclaimed in the presence of his tribe, 'We care not for the land, the money, or the goods; it is the whiskey we want - give us the whiskey.'

Under such circumstances, your efforts must be unceasingly directed to prevent the introduction of ardent spirits Into the Indian country. Congress have done their duty on this subject, and if the laws are administered with vigilance and fidelity, the most salutary consequences may be anticipated. You must explain to the chiefs, and the more reasonable men, the misery and destruction which the indulgence of this habit will entail upon their race, and endeavour to promote the establishment of associations with the avowed object of preventing the introduction and use of ardent spirits. In fact, no terms must be made with this devastating enemy, and the final accomplishment of your object will depend, in a great degree, upon your success in this first and most important effort.

3rd. It will be necessary for you to observe the conduct of the traders, and report any infractions of the laws to the nearest agent, that proper measures may be taken to investigate the facts, and to punish the offenders, and more particularly the offence mentioned in the preceding article, of introducing into the Indian country ardent spirits, either by traders or others. The nature of the evidence and the names of the witnesses will, in all cases, accompany your report.

4th. In all this section of country, the fur-bearing animals, as well as those used for food by the Indians, are disappearing. It is impossible for the different tribes to support themselves by the product of the chase, and it is highly important that their attention should be directed to agriculture, and to the rearing of domestic animals, before their condition has become such as to render further exertions hopeless.

There is no stipulation in the Chicago treaty for the employment of any person to teach the Putawatomies agriculture, or to provide domestic animals for them. They will, of course, be deprived of the aid of any labourers, and also of any assistance in the purchase of cattle and horses. But still, the duty of recommending these subjects to their attention must be faithfully performed. The considerations proper to be urged are too obvious to require enumeration. They embrace their means of present subsistence and all their hopes for the future. Without this radical change in their habits and views, their declension must be rapid, and their final extinction near and certain. Besides, all prospect of moral improvement must depend upon a previous improvement in their physical condition. By rendering them stationary, by assigning to each a separate tract of land, and thereby teaching them the value of exclusive property, and by enabling them to furnish their food with less fatigue and more certainty by the labours of agriculture than by the chase, we shall gradually teach them the advantages of our arts and institutions, we shall prepare them for such instruction as they may be able to comprehend, and as may suit their altered condition. But to reverse this natural order of things, and to undertake to explain to them the obligations of religion and the moral duties of life, while they are naked, starving, hopeless, and helpless, is to ensure the failure of the plans which charity has devised, and zeal is now prosecuting for their melioration.

Endeavour, therefore, by precept and example, to reclaim them from the life of a hunter. Your time and services cannot be better employed, and I trust you will, ere long, realize your most ardent expectations.

5th. The cash annuities which the different tribes receive from the United States might be made very service-able to them, if judiciously expended. It will be proper, therefore, that you should advise them what articles they ought to purchase, and endeavour, as far as possible, to restrain them from procuring whiskey, or trifling and expensive ornaments, which contribute nothing to their comfort or support.

6th. It is important that their implements of agriculture, their clothing, and domestic animals, should not be sold; and as the law expressly prohibits the traffic, under a specific penalty, you will report, as in the former case, any violations of it to the nearest Indian agent, and you will also explain to the Indians the immense sacrifice which this custom occasions to them, and the little proportion there is between the value of the articles which they give and receive.

7th. The Indians gain nothing by resorting to our settlements. They exchange every necessary article in their possession for whiskey. They violate the laws, and are exposed to punishment. They commit depredations upon the property of our citizens, and the amount is deducted from their annuities, and, above all, they resort to a foreign country, where they barter immediate promises and future services for substantial presents, where an influence is acquired over them, injurious to us and destructive to them; you will endeavour to persuade them, therefore, to remain at home. Their annuities will be principally paid to them in their own country. There are traders enough to furnish them with goods, and to receive their peltries in exchange.

8th. It will be proper for you to visit, occasionally, their villages, to become acquainted with the different individuals, to examine their wants, and their modes of living, and to acquire their confidence in such a manner as to give the greatest effect to your advice and representations.

An annual compensation will be allowed you of four hundred dollars; and you can select a blacksmith, whose annual compensation will be three hundred and sixty-five dollars. These allowances will commence with the commencement of your duties upon the reservation. The balance of the appropriation, being two hundred and thirty-five dollars, will be expended in the purchase of steel, iron, &c., and in other contingent expenses.

The blacksmith will be under your direction, and will be employed in repairing guns, in making traps, spears, hoes, tomahawks, axes, and the necessary farming utensils. He will be kept faithfully employed.

You can transmit a statement of the articles and materials required, as well for the establishment upon the St. Joseph's, as for that upon Grand river, embracing tools, iron, &c., and such as will be deemed proper will be sent to Chicago.

The tools for the blacksmiths may be either furnished by them at a fair price, or sent from here upon your requisition.

Mr. Sears's compensation will be the same as yours, and he or you can select the blacksmith for Grand river. The blacksmith will be allowed three hundred and sixty-five dollars per annum.

Mr. Sears's duty will be regulated by the principles here laid down, and he will be governed by these instructions, of which you will please to furnish him a copy, as far as they apply.

But the stipulation for the Ottawas is more extensive, in its objects and amount, than that of the Putawatomies. A teacher of agriculture is to be provided, and in the execution of this stipulation I think it will be better to employ two or three native young men as labourers. They should be sent to the different villages, to split rails, to make fences, to build cabins, to plough, and to plant, and to raise corn. As the Indians will at first be averse to labour, it is expedient to consult their prejudices, and to give them as great advantages from our limited means as possible; and I think it will be much better to employ young men at low wages, as actual labourers, rather than one person at a higher rate, as a mere teacher of agriculture.

It is desirable, as these persons must live among the Indians, that they should understand their manners, and, if possible, speak their language. I think, therefore, it will be better to send Canadians from this place, and I shall accordingly pursue this course, and direct them to report to Mr. Sears for instructions. He will station them as he may think best, and direct and superintend their labours.

I shall send a few ploughs, chains, yokes, &c., to the agent at Chicago, with instructions to forward them to Grand river, to Mr. Sears, for distribution.

I expect the principal Ottawa chief here in a few days, and until his arrival I shall delay making any provisions respecting cattle and horses.

Some allowance will be made this year towards the erection of buildings for the teachers and blacksmiths; but the amount will be limited, and will be made upon the receipt of your estimate and report, after reaching the seats of the establishments.

You will exercise a general superintending power over the persons at Grand river, as well as those at St. Joseph's, and will make regular semi-annual reports to the agent at Chicago and to me; and, to enable you to do this, Mr. Sears will make regular reports to you.

These reports must exhibit the situation of the establishments, the number and occupations of the several persons employed, the quantity of labour performed, the number of persons taught, the condition of the schools, if there are any, the progress made in mechanic arts and agriculture, and prospects, by which the exertions of the several persons may be determined, and the efficacy and final result of the experiment ascertained.

Your reports will also be accompanied by an estimate of the probable expenses for the next half year, detailing, under distinct heads, the several branches of expenditure, with as much accuracy as possible.

Payments will be made to yourself and to the several persons employed, as near the beginning of January and July in each year as practicable. Forms of the proper vouchers and accounts will be hereafter transmitted to you; and on the receipt of these vouchers, signed by the several persons, money will be remitted to you for their payment.

The sites for the respective establishments upon the St. Joseph's and Grand rivers are to be located by the President of the United States. I shall despatch a competent person, in a few days, through that country, to ascertain the most eligible situation for these establishments, that I may report the facts to the Secretary of War, to be laid before the President. I will communicate to you the instructions which the Secretary of War may give upon this subject.

The same person will be authorized to apply to the proper chiefs, to ascertain their feelings and wishes, and to receive any representations they may wish to make.

The Indian agency at Chicago is nearer the St. Joseph's than this place. I am not yet satisfied whether it would be better that instructions should from time to time be given you from that place or from here. The decision, however, shall shortly be made; and in the mean time you will please to attend to any instructions which the agent at Chicago may give.

You will observe that this whole arrangement is temporary, and subject to any alterations which the Secretary of War may make. I shall report my proceedings to him, and he will approve or disapprove them, as he may think proper. Whatever instructions he may give will be carried into full effect.

> I am, sir, very respectfully,
> your obedient servant,
> Lewis CASS.[3]

---

[3] *History of Baptist Indian Missions*, pp. 145-151.

A closer look at McCoy's involvement in the 1821 treaty

A number of highly important historical documents have been preserved which give deep insight into how the treaties which formed the United States of America were made and carried out. In the days before typewriters and telephones, not to mention computers, and when even shorthand was in its infancy, everything had to be recorded in long hand. It is almost amusing to picture McCoy, sitting down at Cass' side, writing out his applications for teachers, missionaries, millers and tools and then handing them over to Cass who immediately grants the requests in writing, stating, "I have received your letter of this date, and I think it proper . . .etc. "[4] At first sight, it might seem that the tasks imposed upon McCoy and his fellow-missionaries through their connections with Government policies were much the same as their usual missionary duties. It turned out, however, that they meant a great deal of extra work. McCoy was required to make seven reports a year, two to the Indian Agent at Chicago, two to the Governor himself, one to the Secretary of War, one to the Board of Missions and one to the Government inspector who would visit the mission stations to see that all was preceding well.[5] Yet, McCoy was very pleased with this arrangement, seeing that the Government's commitments to the missionary stations brought with it the full commitment of the Board and bound them into the whole process of shared responsibility. Furthermore, the application of Government funds for the mission was committed to the Board who were bound to publish a complete financial statement regarding the mission in their various periodicals. In this way, McCoy hoped that a more regular income would be vouchsafed for the mission and the needs of the mission would become known throughout the country. As things turned out, McCoy's lengthy and detailed reports to the Board mentioning treaties, acts and bills and Government policies were never really understood by the Board and their disadvantage in not understanding these matters often led them to mistrust McCoy who understood them fully. One negative consequence of this ignorance

---

[4] See McCoy's and Cass' letters dated Detroit July 16th, McCoy Papers, Reel 2. This must have been the swiftest long-distance journey McCoy ever made as he was in Detroit and hard at work within a week of his departure from Fort Wayne.

[5] See also McCoy's list of the correspondence he had to undertake as Superintendent of the mission dated October 2, 1824, McCoy Papers, Reel 3.

was that the Board never really understood what their responsibilities and duties were in their stewardship of Government grants. Indeed, much of the money promised the mission never reached the missionaries' pockets due to the Board's failure to comprehend the situation but also due to their changing politics, their general mismanagement and the fact that the Government required of the mission a stability in organization and man power which it often could not provide. For instance, the wages due to teachers were only given after a term of probation was ended and then payments were made every six months and then to specific persons. If during this period a teacher resigned or was dismissed, the grant was not paid. Thus Mr. Sears did not stay long enough among the Ottawas to receive a teacher's grant but he still had to be kept as long as he remained in the mission by the other missionaries who pooled any income they received into the common mission purse.

The Sears family join the Indian Mission

On August 1, 1822 Mr. and Mrs. John Sears arrived. They were totally exhausted as they had been compelled to travel by night because of the heat and mosquitoes of the day and had repeatedly lost their way. Their journey had taken far longer than expected and their provisions had run out. To make matters worse, Sears' brother Benjamin, who also wished to become a missionary, and their father, a retired Baptist minister, had become separated from the rest of the family and McCoy had to go out and look for them. McCoy wasted no time in telling the newly-arrived that he felt that there were enough believers in Fort Wayne to constitute a church and that they should look upon themselves as such and continue their witness in the area as an indigenous part of it and not merely as missionaries representing churches far away. He had already made preliminary arrangements which were to take place on August 3rd. On that day, McCoy formally certified Benjamin Sears as a missionary and presented his proposed Articles of Faith and Church Constitution for the approval of his fellow missionaries and Indian and Negro representatives who were present. The Articles were accepted by all. As it was the custom of the Baptist churches to have ministers from already established churches to officiate at the founding of a new one, McCoy had written to four ministers within about a hundred mile radius, inviting them to attend the church-founding ceremony. By this time, however, the anti-mission lobby among the frontier Baptists was growing and two churches refused to offer any assistance to a church formed through missionary work. A third minister, McCoy tells us, "was prevented by proper considerations."

The establishment of the Fort Wayne Church and its Declaration of Faith

Corbly Martin, close friend of the mission, turned up for the occasion and preached from Isaiah 35:1 "The wilderness and the solitary place shall be glad for them." Thereafter, the right hand of fellowship was given by Benjamin Sears Sr. and Corbly Martin gave the charge, declaring the group of believers to be a true Christian church. *The Declaration of Faith* drawn up by the new church is one of the finest ever agreed upon by an American Baptist church and reveals elements that have quite disappeared from modern Baptist witness. It will be quoted here in full as an incentive to ponder over. Perhaps it will serve to remind the one or the other what positive doctrines we have lost in today's churches.

> We, whose names follow, being convinced of the propriety and utility of a church state, and having due knowledge of each other in respect to experimental and practical religion, by consent and with the assistance of Elder Benjamin Sears, of Meredith, New York, and Elder Corbly Martin, of Staunton, Ohio, do agree to unite in a church compact, upon the firm basis of the Scriptures of the Old and New Testament, as being of divine authority, and the only infallible rule of faith and practice. And whereas there are different opinions among professed Christians in relation to the true meaning of Scripture, therefore, in order to prevent unpleasant disputation, and to cherish harmony of senti-ment, we deem it indispensable to subjoin the following expression of the leading features of those doctrines of the Gospel most liable to be disputed, which shall always be considered as the sentiments of this church.
>
> ART. i. We believe in one only true and living God, who is infinite and unchangeable in all his divine perfections or attributes, such as wisdom, power, justice, love, &c., the Creator and Preserver of all things; and that he cannot be brought under the least obligations to any of his creatures. ART. ii. We believe that in Deity there is a Trinity, of Father, Son, and Holy Ghost, in all respects equal, and

153

unlike the subordination between father and son among men.

ART. iii. We believe that God is not liable to the least disappointment, but that eternity is at all times fully comprehended by him, so that neither the malice of hell, nor the wickedness of men on earth, can any way frustrate his eternal purposes.

ART. iv. We believe that God made man upright, but he has voluntarily fallen from his uprightness; that in his fall he lost all traces of virtue, (moral goodness,) and became wholly averse to godliness; yet he is, on that account, under no less obligations to his God.

ART. v. We believe that as there is nothing new with God, it is his eternal purpose to save those who ultimately will be received into heaven, not upon the supposition of any condition to be performed by them, but wholly in consequence of what Jesus Christ has done in their behalf.

ART. vi. We believe the Son of God united himself to humanity, and in that state fulfilled in his life the law of God, which was binding on man, and suffered in his death the penal requisitions of the same.

ART. vii. We believe, agreeably to the inevitable consequences of articles first, third, and fifth, that Christ's life, death, resurrection, and intercession, were, and are, in behalf of those, and those only, who shall enjoy the benefits thereof.

ART. viii. We believe that regeneration is effected by the operations of the Spirit of God only, and is an essential preparation for the enjoyment of God in heaven, and an assurance of title thereto.

ART. ix. We believe that, through grace, all who are regenerated will be preserved in a gracious state, and will certainly go to heaven.

ART. x. We believe it to be perfectly congenial to the Scriptures, and to the spirit of the foregoing articles, for ministers of the Gospel to command all men indiscriminately to repent, and to exhort them to believe the Gospel.

ART. xi. We believe that God hath appointed a day in which he will judge all men by Jesus Christ.

ART. xii. We believe that the joys of the righteous will be eternal, and that the sufferings of the wicked will be of endless duration

ART. xiii We believe that the suffering of the wicked is the spontaneous consequence of their own wickedness, and not the effect of any thing in or done by Deity, hostile to their happiness.

ART. xiv. We believe that none but believers in Christ ought to be baptized, and that immersion is the only scriptural mode of baptism.

ART. xv. We believe that none but baptized believers in Christ, united in Gospel order, have a right to communion at the Lord's table.

ART. xvi. We believe that God hath set apart one day in seven, for rest and religious worship, and that the first day of the week ought to be observed as such, in resting from our temporal concerns, excepting works of necessity.

And being united together upon the foregoing plan, we deem it our duty to walk in all the commandments and ordinances of the Lord blameless, which, that God may enable us to do, let every member, at all times, fervently pray.[6]

Isaac McCoy   John Sears
Christiana McCoy   Mary Sears
Giles Jackson   Johnston Lykins
Mary Jackson   Benjamin Sears, Jun.
                                Missionaries

Wiskehlaehqua, *a Delaware woman*
Ann Turner, *a Miamie woman*
Jesse Cox, *a black man.*

Seeking Associational recognition: an initial disappointment

Calling themselves the "Putawatomie Mission Church," the missionaries, white Christian workers, the Indian believers and Jesse Cox applied to the Mad River Association at Lost Creek, Miami County, Ohio for membership on August 28, 1822. Although McCoy believed firmly in the autonomy of the local church he believed that it was essential that the brethren should live in harmony with their fellow churches and strengthen that fellowship in association life. Thus, whenever McCoy or his Indian mission co-workers were able to establish a church, they immediately sought fellowship with the nearest association of Baptist churches which were usually, or at least allegedly of the "Regular" kind. Now, of course, they had to make their position on evangelism and missionary work clear as Campbellism and Parkerism were turning people's gazes away from the fields ripe unto

---

[6] *History of Baptist Indian Missions*, pp. 155-156.

harvest. The Potawatomi church thus sent in a full description of their history and policies, enclosing also a copy of their *Declaration of Faith.*[7]

Meanwhile, Corbly Martin, was seeking to rally the Miami county churches around the cause of the Indian mission in general and the Potawatomi mission church in particular, reading to the churches McCoy's reports and informing them of the new church's progress and needs but he received a big disappointment. Wilson Thompson was appointed Clerk at an Association meeting and given the task of explaining why the Miami County churches could not enter into fellowship with the mission church and help support it.[8]

> Dear Brother, in conformity to the appointment of the Miami Baptist Association, I present you with the reasons why this Association cannot cooperate with you, in the affairs of the Fort Wayne Mission, which are as follows. The fort Wayne missionary establishment is under the government of the Philadelphia board, and we believe, that the corruptions of that Board are so many, and so grate, that we cannot feal willing to have any connection either directly, or indirectly, with them in missionary affairs under there forme of government, Which we think to be dispotic in the hiest sense - The procedings of the bord also in many instances, we think to be, foreign from the christian carrecter, and very dishonarable to the Baptist cause - and we believe that in the general they have greatly departed from the simplicity of the gospel - being over anxious to please the wourld, and those of every denomination, in order to get the more money. Although we are very sensible that money is indispencible in the mission cause, yet if anchciety after it tempt a minister to despence with truth in order to gain it be his nead, or object wat it may we cannot approve of his mesurs, but look at his conduct as base; if the Lord neads Money to aid in the spred of the gosple <u>he</u> will despose the people to advance it without seling the truth for it, these with many other reasons, to newmerous to deliniate in the limits of a letter, but some of them more stuberen perhaps, than that of the bord's preventing us from ading you, unless in such awaw [a way], as shall be directly, or indirectly, ading them, and

---

[7] See microfilm copy of application on Reel 2 of the McCoy Papers. Jackson resigned on the day the application was written.

[8] Original spelling kept.

if we should give you a present, be it much or little, the board must have an a count of it and you are charged with it, thus we are prevented from doing any thing, for you unless we do it in connection with the Board. The united voice of every member that spoke on the subject, was in approbation of your conduct, object, candure and mission establishments and many expressed there grate wishes to assist you, bouth with there substance and influnce, if it were in there power to do so without having anything to do with the bord directly, or indirectly; but as the Board will not allow you to receive, nor us to give in such a way, we are deprived of giving to him that neadeth unless it be in conjunction with those, who we view as our opressors, that have taken from us the priviliges of giving as we believe duty directs. We often cast an eye to fort Wain and sympothise with you and our sister that we believe are suffering many privations, and many falce and reproachfull incinuations of the wicked, and others that would fain make the wourld believe that riches and luxury are your object, these things have no baring on our minds, for we think we know better than to hear such insinuations, without contridicting the slanderer. We believe also that we are as desirous for Indian reforme &c. as any other part of the world and we think that there is not one Minister in our Association but what would use all the influnce he has for the benifit of youre establishment they could, without having any sort of connection with the bord. These are our views and while remain to be, and the bord continues as it is, we cannot in good concience coopperate with them in giving that ade which we would feel it our duty to do were you not under the patronage and restrictions of that bord: now let our reasons apear to you to be strong, or weak, they are such as have governed our dissision on your letter.[9]

From what Thompson said at the time, no one could accuse his church of being anti-evangelistic in any way and much if not all of what he said concerning the Board must have been seen by McCoy as representing the truth. One might, however, have thought that where

---

[9] Letter to McCoy dated September 11, 1822, McCoy Papers, Reel 2. Thompson was later to join the Primitive Baptists and alter his views considerably away from McCoy's position. For an account of Thompson's further dealings with McCoy, read, *The Autobiography of Elder Wilson Thompson, Embracing a Sketch of His Life, Travels, and Ministerial Labors* (Greenfield, Indiana: D.H. Goble, 1867).

a Christian church sees need, as in the case of the Fort Wayne mission, it would feel obliged to give. As Thompson explained, the matter was not so simple. In giving to the mission, the Miami County churches would be identifying themselves with the policies and politics of the Foreign Mission Board which had indeed set itself up as a parachurch organization with its self appointed task of dictating to its member churches. The only honorable alternative for the Ohio brethren was to have nothing whatsoever to do with such a hierarchy. The privations of McCoy and his wider mission family obviously tore at the hearts of the Ohio brethren but they felt that their hands were tied and their pockets buttoned up. Why McCoy did not separate entirely from the Board at this time is a question this biographer has not been able to answer. It is very likely that McCoy was in a constant dilemma concerning the subject himself but the times when he had real doubts were often followed by true blessings at the hands of the Board. Perhaps the best attempt at an answer to the puzzle is that McCoy was so busy carrying out his calling that problems such as Board affiliation or not received a most subordinate place in his thinking.

Corbly Martin, however, wrote to say that had McCoy himself been at the Association meeting, things would have been different. We are "in the midst of a generation of crooked adversaries," was his comment on the present situation of his churches. It is obvious that Martin felt that Daniel Parker was behind the Association's attitude to McCoy and he had visited the Wabash Association churches to see what influence Parker had there. He found very many brethren completely under Parker's spell and now they were at fierce enmity with William Polke, now a State Commissioner and surveying engineer of wide reputation. Martin told McCoy that the brethren in the Wabash Association were in a lamentable position and true religion had been forced into the background. Brother was fighting brother in the most savage passions.[10] Perhaps this gives us a deeper insight into McCoy's situation. He recognized the weaknesses of the Board but saw that those who opposed their work the most were the very people such as Daniel Parker who were not worthy to throw the first or any stone. Thus a movement which had room for improvement was not to be given up merely because of the arguments of another movement of a far inferior caliber.

---

[10] Letter written November 6, 1822, McCoy Papers, Reel 2.

Making preparations for a further mission station and Elizabeth's death

The missionaries now made preparations to survey the St. Joseph's River area. McCoy was ready to set off with Sears but Elizabeth's condition worsened and it seemed that her earthly end was in sight. McCoy sent Sears ahead and told him that he would catch up with him should Elizabeth revive a little. This happened and the family pressed McCoy to be about his business whereby he hurried on to catch up with Sears on August 8th. The party had no sooner arrived at the Potawatomi encampments when the news reached McCoy from Johnston Lykins that there was now no hope that Elizabeth would ever recover and that Mrs. McCoy and her daughter Delilah and a number of the girl pupils were ill.[11] Further news reported that the Jacksons and many of the Indians were also very ill.

McCoy quickly met the commissioners and chiefs and arranged for the setting up of a missionary station and then dashed off on the 100 mile return journey to help care for his family and friends. Five miles from home, he received the news that little Elizabeth had died, never recovering from the murderous attack of the Indian--but it was the Typhoid Fever which struck the final blow.

Illness and dissatisfaction within the Fort Wayne Mission family

Soon the entire Fort Wayne church with school and pupils suffered from the fever and from lack of nourishment with no medicine to alleviate the illness. Lykins had studied Medicine but he was unable to do anything substantial against the fever because of the lack of facilities and medication. McCoy and his fellow missionaries were very distressed as the Board appeared to make very little effort to keep them supplied through the following autumn and winter and seemed to be inconsiderate of the great difficulties under which they were living. They had not been in touch with the mission for months and seemed to be quite disinterested as to how the new missionaries were getting on. This caused first the Jacksons and then the Sears to complain that they had been promised more support than they were getting and they had become disillusioned with the way the Board was managing affairs. Jackson told McCoy plainly that his family could not and would not put up with such difficult conditions and besides his

---

[11] Lykins letter of August 13 is on Reel 2 of the McCoy Papers.

wife and children, he had a mother to support. Jackson did not like living in a closely-knit community and had not the spiritual comfort which he had formerly enjoyed. On August 28th, Giles and Mary Jackson handed in their resignation. McCoy managed to persuade Jackson to stay at least a year with the mission as a hired craftsman and help them set up a blacksmith shop in the Potawatomi area according to the 1821 treaty. He was promised $200 plus board and expenses for the year and given $170 in advance. This was not a breech with the usual custom of the missionaries who held everything in common as Jackson was no longer a missionary, indeed, he had never been officially recognized as one by the Board. This deal with Jackson sadly gave the mission's Roman Catholic enemies ammunition to use against them. It was common knowledge that the Government had promised $365 per annum for a blacksmith to the Potawatomis so the rumor was spread that McCoy had been paid that amount and had given the blacksmith $200 and pocketed the remaining $165 himself. At the time of Jackson's employment as a hired worker, neither the Government nor the Board had paid McCoy a penny towards such wages and the agreement with the Government referred to an employee of the Board and not to one who had resigned from his post and was now merely privately employed. Moreover, as soon as Jackson had arranged to stay on for another year, he left the mission on a holiday for several weeks, which was an unknown luxury for the McCoys and Lykins. It must have been a great comfort to McCoy to receive a letter from William Polke, saying how he was feeling drawn to the Indian mission. He was running for Governor at the time and had asked the Lord to show him which way he had to go, into politics or into the Indian mission. In his letter, Polke, however, told McCoy that their joint enemy, Daniel Parker was rallying his followers and they were making great havoc in the Associations and had obviously focused their anger on McCoy's work.[12]

The Sears threaten to resign

Now John and Mary Sears protested that they, too, might resign as their consciences could not allow them to see their children so deprived of health and material needs. Sears had a high view of his missionary status and wished to be treated accordingly. Some donations from private givers had begun to come in but the Sears

---

[12] Letter dated August 18, 1822, McCoy Papers, Reel 2.

family, who refused to acknowledge the *Family Rules*, like the Jacksons, looked upon themselves as been employed by the Board and thus expected their full support to come from that direction. They wanted a substantial wage and not charity. The McCoys and Lykins saw the matter quite differently. They were placed where they were by the Lord and however they were maintained, either by their own efforts, that of cheerful givers or by means of an obviously reluctant Board, they took this as from the Lord and did not allow the Board to interfere with their calling. All the missionaries, however, felt that the Board ought to have made the needs of the mission known to the churches in their publications and ought to have at least kept their word regarding the support of those they had recently sent out. Sadly Sears, instead of approaching Lewis Cass through his superintendent, wrote to him directly concerning his demands and how he was not prepared to go ahead unless they were fulfilled. Indeed, Sears had decided that he should leave the mission and spend the winter at Detroit so that he could study medicine. This must have been a disappointment to the Secretary of War as he had done his very best to have the Chicago Treaty implemented as soon as possible and to the mission's advantage and other denominations would have jumped for joy at the chance which the Baptists had received.[13] Nevertheless, while McCoy examined the St. Joseph area for a possible site for his new Potawatomi outreach, Sears went up to the Grand Rapids area to view possible sites for the Ottawa mission. McCoy found a good site a hundred miles northwest of Fort Wayne, about thirty miles from where the St Joseph River flowed into Lake Michigan. Sears found a site for the Ottawas about a hundred miles from the mouth of the Grand River and a hundred and fifty miles from the Potawatomi site. However, Sears who was totally new to this kind of survey work, was not able to record his findings adequately enough for the site to be found again.

Lykins care of the sick at Fort Wayne

Towards the end of August, a Baptist minister named Phineas Nichols visited the station and found thirty seriously ill people. The surprised man had come to see whether or not missionary life held any

---

[13] See Cass' letter to McCoy speaking of Sears' unwillingness to start his work until the following spring dated August 28, 1822, McCoy Papers, Reel 2.

attraction or calling for him. When he saw all the suffering and poverty, he soon gave up any interest in becoming a missionary to the Indians. John Sears now returned from the Ottawas in extremely poor health himself and found his wife and brother even worse off. Now thirty-nine of the mission family were invalids. So many were ill, including the preachers, that church services had to be canceled and the school closed. Lykins seemed to be made of steel and even McCoy himself fared better than most. McCoy had long recognized the true value of Lykins, now his closest friend and says of this time in which he merely heard grumbles from the mouths of the newcomers:

> Mr. Lykins alone remained to me a friend, whose circumstances enabled him to be a counsellor and a comforter; and such he certainly was. Neither the performance of the most disagreeable services for the sick, whether they were missionaries, their children, or Indian children, nor their peevishness and unreasonable demands, nor the deathlike discouragements which, in various forms, hovered around our abode, moved him from his noble determination to *do right*. He never became impatient, nor formed hasty conclusions, for the sake of getting out of a scene of distress. Seldom do circumstances occur so fully to attest what a *man is*, as those under which Mr. Lykins was at the time placed. It was not his amiable disposition alone by which we profited. His soundness of judgment in administering to the sick, and in relation to missionary affairs generally, was constantly developing.[14]

On September 9th, McCoy set out for Ohio on matters of business and to obtain supplies but he was really too ill to travel as he was suffering from a high fever. His condition grew worse on the journey and after traveling 60 miles, McCoy collapsed and could go no farther. His thoughts at this time are expressed in his *History*:

> How dark are the late dealings of Providence! The very existence of the mission seems to be menaced. The sick at the establishment suffering for want of attention; the school suspended; some of the missionaries have forsaken the field, and others will probably soon follow; important

---

[14] *History of Baptist Indian Missions*, pp. 161-162. McCoy's good opinion of Lykins is echoed in the *Latter Day Luminary* for October, 1822, p. 313, where the editor says, "Mrs. McCoy is much pleased with his (Lykins) talents, his ardour for usefulness and his exemplary conduct."

business requiring my presence in the white settlements, and still more important business will demand my presence a few days hence at Fort Wayne, while I am forbidden to go to either place; my family sick yonder, and I sick here, in a place in which the thought of being confined is intolerable; some important engagements with the Miamies and Ottawas in danger of being thwarted; to which may be added many other discouragements, so that the cloud becomes gloomy and the day dark! "Yet, through the stormy cloud, I'll look once more to Thee, my God."[15]

The day after McCoy penned these lines in his journal, he managed to travel another 20 miles in an ox-cart and was then met by Captain B. Leavell who had been notified of McCoy's illness and had come to convey him to Piqua, Ohio and put him under a doctor's care. While at Piqua, two of McCoy's sons who were at school thirty miles away, traveled to visit their father and took over much of the business he had to do for the mission. John Mason of the Mad River Baptist Association also visited McCoy and the two shared deep fellowship together. McCoy wrote that it was as if an angel had visited him. Mason told McCoy that if the Board of Missions stopped their patronage of the Indian mission, the Western churches, in spite of the anti-missions movement among them, would "amply sustain" McCoy's work. McCoy commented, "This was seasonable consolation, in view of the fears we had felt on the subject of support." Mason's views, good as they were, turned out to be little more than personal as the anti-mission sentiment was at this time actually growing among the churches of the Western frontier.

Daniel Dusenbury joins the missionary family

At Piqua, McCoy was joined by Daniel Dusenbury who was progressing to Fort Wayne with a view to becoming a missionary. He had received no funds from the Board so McCoy had had to forward him enough money to complete the journey. Now, McCoy was laid on a bed in a wagon and accompanied by Dusenbury, two hired lady workers and a resident of Fort Wayne, they all started on the journey back to the mission station. On the way, one of the ladies became ill and so McCoy gave up his bed for her, though he was still very weak himself. The party moved on without McCoy who now traveled on

---

[15] p. 162. These words are taken from McCoy's *Journal.*

horseback but had to stop and rest after short periods of riding. The missionary returned home to find his family still ill, though improving, but this time Lykins had been struck down. The brave and noble man had worked night and day for many weeks, looking after up to forty patients and was now totally exhausted and suffering from a very high fever. By this time, Dusenbury had received deep insight into the trials and tribulations of the Indian mission field. This did not prevent him from signing the *Family Rules* and pledging his all to the aims of the mission.

On Sunday, September 29th, McCoy, still too ill to stand, preached sitting in a chair. It was a time of unrest as the Miamis had just received their annuities and the drinking season had arrived. Many Miamis had hoped to settle down as farmers but the United States Agent had now proved indifferent to their needs and was giving them no support. Frustration was drowned in strong drink and the drinking season was accompanied by the murdering season. Six Miamis were killed, and property, including horses were stolen. Daniel Dusenbury, quite unacquainted with these matters, had bought a new horse, rode to a neighboring house and tied it up outside. On coming out of the house, the animal had gone, stolen by two Indians who had been watching Dusenbury. McCoy sent out people who knew the area to spy out the hiding place. They soon found the horse and it was brought back to its owner. This was Dusenbury's first lesson in what missionaries call GMT i.e. General Missionary Training.

Lykins now becomes seriously ill while the Carey Mission is established

On October 8th, 1822, Lykins left the mission to journey the 280 miles to Vincennes on both mission and private business, visiting McCoy's former churches and William Polke while in the neighborhood. His return was delayed for a number of weeks owing to a serious illness which struck him down. Lykins suddenly became deaf and was plagued with thoughts that a deaf man could not engage in missionary work. Caring almost single handedly for the almost some forty sick people for so long had gradually weakened even his iron constitution. The day after Lykins left, despite illness, bad weather and many setbacks including the loss of an ox-wagon with the oxen, McCoy journeyed with several members of his family, a number of Indians, pupils and hired helpers a hundred miles into Potawatomi territory, some 180 miles from the nearest other settlement. Mrs. McCoy with four children and Benjamin Sears had to stay behind as their illness rendered them immovable. At the new site, McCoy and his party pitched camp, calling the place Carey,[16] after William Carey, the Serampore missionary. Immediately, they set about erecting domestic buildings and a school with McCoy joining the work for example's sake, though he was still far from well.

Rumors that the Board wished to shut down Fort Wayne and concentrate on Valley Towns

In the midst of all these struggles, McCoy had two letters from Staughton, the one saying that the Board had increased difficulties in finding competent missionaries for his new work. The second included a circular which stated that no less than twenty-six new missionaries had been sent to work at the Valley Towns Cherokee Mission. Allowing for the overruling Providence of God, it was still very much apparent to McCoy that human nature felt much more at home in the relatively cultivated atmosphere of the Cherokee farmlands rather than in the wilderness ways of the so-called "wild tribes." McCoy had always believed that by the time Carey and Thomson were set up as new missionary stations, the Board would have provided missionaries enough to keep Fort Wayne going. Polke wrote to say that he had heard rumors that the Board were going to drop Fort Wayne from their program but now McCoy was so committed to moving on that he could not look back, whatever the Board intended. Once settled in Carey, however, McCoy arranged with the Indian Agent Col. Johnson that the Fort Wayne land ceded to the mission should remain under its care for the next twelve years. In this way, McCoy forced the Board to keep a missionary interest in the area. Indeed, the Board sent out a printed General Circular to the churches in association with them dated May 26th, 1823, stating that the Fort Wayne Station would be maintained. Apparently, they had hoped that Sears, who refused to take up his post among the Ottawas, would continue to work at Fort Wayne but Sears made it quite clear to the Board and to the Fort Wayne Government Agent Kerchevall that he had no such plans.[17] Happily friends of the McCoys' in the Green River Missionary Society kept up a work there and the school was continued under Government patronage.

---

[16] Now Niles, Michigan.

[17] See Sears' correspondence with the Board and Kerchevall for the first half of 1823, McCoy Papers, Reel 2.

Chapter Six
The American Serampore (1822-23)

Preparing the move to Carey

It was now decided to move the entire Fort Wayne community, thirty-two persons in all over snow covered land to Carey. Before this could happen, McCoy had to journey to Ohio in the freezing cold to take care of transport arrangements. A new setback, however, attended the move as the Miamis refused to have their children tutored on Potawatomi soil. Shortly afterwards the Miamis approached McCoy, pleading with him to look after their spiritual needs and offering him land in their territory for a mission station and school as they had no dealings with the Potawatomis. The reason behind this was a blunder of the whites who at the Treaty of Greenville in 1795 allowed the Potawatomis to move into Miami territory on the Wabash. McCoy promised that he would be only too willing to set up such a work, given the required manpower. He did strive to find people interested in their spiritual welfare but sadly had to realize that, "among the hundreds of thousands of our denomination in the United States, none were ready to enter upon the arduous though delightful duties of reclaiming the Miamis."[1] It is astonishing that a man called to such hardships as McCoy could describe his predicament as "delightful."

Benjamin Sears dies

On November 11, 1822 the Board wrote to tell McCoy that they had resolved to accept Benjamin Sears as a missionary. The news brought no joy to the Fort Wayne family. Benjamin had departed for

---

[1] *History of Baptist Indian Missions*, p. 176.

a better world just a few days before. McCoy had judged him to be of an entirely different caliber to John Sears and wrote of his death:

> Mr. Benjamin Sears, who had long languished under a typhus fever, had died on the 3d of November, 1822. He was a son of the late Rev. Benjamin and Ann Sears, was born in Meredith, New-York, June 16, 1800. Was baptized in the summer of 1815. Subsequently he was led to desire, most earnestly, to dedicate his whole life to the service of God. But he discovered no opening to a sphere of usefulness until after the appointment of his brother to missionary service, when he learned the want of missionaries at this station.
>
> He had been bred a farmer, and was robust, and hoped to be useful to the natives by instructing them in agricultural pursuits, as well as in the doctrines of Christianity. He made no pretensions to the ministry. He reached our place on the first of August, 1822. His application to become united with us was cheerfully accepted, and the approbation of the board of missions applied for. But their answer was not received previous to his decease.
>
> He was permitted to labour with us only twenty-three days, before he was prostrated with the prevailing fever, which terminated his life. He was favoured with the attendance of physicians, and was made as comfortable as our distressed situation would admit. More than two months he was unable to turn himself in bed, and he became reduced to a skeleton. It was a great consolation to know that under his deep afflictions he exercised a patience and resignation to the will of God, that indicated much spiritual mindedness. His desire to be useful to the Indians seemed not to be impaired by disease. And when his prospect of being spared to labour for them was blighted, he directed that his clothing, and whatever else of small articles of which he had control, should be applied to the benefit of the mission, either among the Ottawas or the Putawatomies. In prospect of death, his hopes of a blessed eternity remained firm and unshaken: with humble confidence he rested his hopes for salvation on Christ alone. He retained his senses until the last, and appeared to be unmoved when it was intimated to him that his end was near.

He was decently interred by the side of our
Elizabeth, who had died the preceding August. There rests
his dust, while his soul, no doubt, rests in heaven.[2]

Sears demands better treatment and working conditions

Meanwhile John Sears was moping and moaning, though he
had not been struck down with illness as seriously as his brother and
father.[3] Nothing was good enough for him. He demanded better conditions, better buildings and more money. He was also not content to
share all with his brethren and looked for ways to improve his own
circumstances. When Sears heard of McCoy's building plans for the
new missionary station that he was to man, he protested that they
would not meet his personal future needs. All were aware of this but
also aware of the fact that no money was available for a more complex
building project. Sears thus decided to borrow a large sum of money to
finance what he called *his* building and *his* work. The McCoys were
alarmed as this would be tantamount to telling the Government they
were dissatisfied with their proposals. It would be declaring open
opposition to the Board and once the rumor spread that the mission
was living in debt, it would utterly destroy the Indians' trust in them.
Furthermore, Sears was unwilling to accept McCoy's authority and
leadership in these matters and refused to think of sharing any income
with the McCoys, Lykins, Dusenbury and the wider family, including
the Indian pupils. From McCoy's comments on this matter in his
History,[4] it would seem that he thought the Board might give up its
patronage of the mission at any moment and now he felt that Sears'
behavior might be the last straw to tip the scales against them.[5] To
McCoy's mortification, Sears told a Government official all he knew
about the financial state of the mission and their fears concerning
future support. This official realized that Sears was speaking without

---

[2] *History of Baptist Indian Missions*, pp. 175-176. A brief biography of and
tribute to Sears is given in McCoy's report to the Board dated December 19,
1822.

[3] Benjamin Sears, Sr. had left the mission for New York as a very sick man
and died on the way at Delaware, Ohio.

[4] p. 165.

[5] See also McCoy's letter to the Board dated December 19, 1822, McCoy
Papers, Reel 2.

discretion and advised McCoy not to trust Sears with any confidential matter. All this was clearly an affront to the more experienced missionaries and quite in opposition to the current principles of the Board.[6] McCoy and Lykins had principally drawn up the *Family Rules* to avoid such a situation developing. Looking back in 1840, McCoy had still not changed his mind and wrote:

> It will be seen that the *Family Rules*, so called, became not only an article of agreement between the missionaries themselves, but also a written contract between the missionaries of the one part, and the board of missions of the other part. These engagements placed the missionary beyond the influence of temptation to worldly mindedness; for whatever he might receive for services rendered the Government, or from individuals or societies, or directly from the board, no part of it was his own; he was charged with it, and was liable for it to the board, until he expended it according to their directions. He was entitled to nothing more than his current support. If he should become deficient in economy or usefulness, it was the business of the board to dismiss him, at which time he went out empty. This policy effectually stopped the mouths of the malicious and the ignorant, who, not having ever felt the influence of disinterested benevolence, might be disposed to attribute the toils of missionaries to a desire to accumulate property. By this agreement, every body perceived that they could not increase their property, for they held none of their own at the station, and all their receipts and expenditures were examined by their patrons, the board of missions.
>
> It may be well to remark in this place, that while the formula by which it may be done may differ in relation to other Baptist missionaries, and to missionaries of other denominations, the relation between them and their patrons, respectively, is formed upon the same principle as the above; that is, that the missionary is to receive nothing more than his current support, and is liable to be

---

[6] See McCoy's sad report to the Board, written November 1, 1822 in which he explains how his Christian brethren cause more problems than the heathen Indians and outlines all that Sears had undertaken against the cause of the mission. McCoy Papers, Reel 2. See also Sears' letter to the Board in which he says he can clear his name "from all blame or censure", dated January 22, 1823, also Reel 2.

dismissed at the pleasure of his patrons, at which time he can claim no more than his necessary clothing.[7]

Sears resigns amidst extraordinary behavior on his part

Such ideas did not impress the novice missionary Sears, who now maintained that before taking up his tasks as a missionary to the Ottawas, he would like to study medicine and would leave for Detroit where he hoped to enter a college. Again, McCoy asked who was to pay for all this and again Sears had no idea. McCoy reminded Sears that he had been commissioned by the Government to settle among the Ottawas without delay and he should drop all further plans in order to make this his objective. Sears refused to go. He also refused to keep accounts of his expenditures for the Board whom he felt were deliberately neglecting their inland missionaries. By this time, Sears would not listen to McCoy and Lykins and began to act most selfishly and even criminally. McCoy had laid out money for equipment to be taken to the Ottawa base because the Government had promised to meet such bills as soon as the mission got under way. Sears took this material, and also a horse and carriage and sold them, keeping the money for his own ends. Perhaps the sad fact of his brother's death hastened John and Mary Sears' decision to depart from the mission, seeing as they left on November 26, 1822. Before going, the Sears told the McCoys, in the presence of several others, that they had no complaint to make of the way they had been treated by them. Apparently unknown to the Fort Wayne family, Sears now made straight for Philadelphia and arrived there before McCoy's report on Sears' behavior reached its destination. Here, it appears, he lost no time in blaming the McCoys for his personal situation.

Initial difficulties at Carey soon overcome

Immediately after settling down in Carey, food began to run out. When no flour was available, and a journey to the nearest flour mill 195 miles away was out of the question, we find McCoy writing bravely, "Blessed be God, we have not yet suffered for want of food, because corn is an excellent substitute for bread. But having now eaten our last corn, we cannot avoid feeling uneasiness about the next

---

[7] *History of Baptist Indian Missions*, p. 172.

meal."[8] McCoy met up with a kind Frenchman who told him, "I got some corn, some flour; I give you half. Suppose you die, I die too." Soon McCoy, his family and some thirty pupils found that each time they ate their last meal, God provided another. McCoy wrote in his journal John Newton's lines:

> The birds without barn or storehouse are
> fed -
> From them let us learn to trust for our
> bread;
> The saints what is fitting shall ne'er be
> denied,
> So long as 'tis written 'The Lord will
> provide.'[9]

After February 13, supplies which had been delayed on the way from Fort Wayne through the loss of two oxen and the inclement weather, arrived bringing stocks of badly needed food and clothing, with the latter item being sent by friends in Massachusetts. A few days later, Mr. Lykins arrived, having been detained at Vincennes through illness, but he was now in robust health. This was a great relief for McCoy who was now reduced to a skeleton himself and had hardly the energy to walk. His journal entry for Sunday, March 2nd reads:

> Unable to preach, and scarcely able to walk, I feel something like a prisoner shut up from society and gospel privileges. The long train of successive and trying difficulties through which we have come, and in which we are still involved, has occasioned much "searching of heart." "If it be so" that we have been called of God to the work in which we have been engaged for some time, "why are we thus?" Could we at all times feel assured that we have not "run before we were sent," and that it might not be said, "who hath required this at your hand?" we could toil and suffer with more fortitude. But how are we to determine the path of duty? We ought not to conclude that we have lost the way, merely because the path is rough. Nothing with which we have met has produced greater dis-couragements than our disappointments in relation to missionaries. We, who commenced our labours five years

---

[8] Written on February 8, 1823, *History of Baptist Indian Missions*, p. 181.

[9] *History of Baptist Indian Missions*, p. 182.

ago, little expected that at this time there would be only two
or three missionaries at the station.[10]

The Sears affair awakens the Board to the mission's needs

The outcome of the whole matter concerning Sears was greatly
to the benefit of the relationship between the McCoys and the Board
as it obviously awakened the Board to the facts of the true state of the
Indian Mission. The missionaries had heard nothing of developments
until the Spring of 1823 when Dr. Staughton, the Corresponding Secretary of the Board and one who now identified himself closely with
McCoy, wrote:

> Philadelphia, April 2, 1823.
> My DEAR BROTHER McCoy: I think I
> know the heart of a missionary, and I am sure I am no
> stranger to his trials. I am happy the Lord has supported
> you under so many, and trust he will sustain you to the
> end. I never thought your selection of the Rev. John Sears,
> to be your associate in missionary service, a happy one. I
> have no reason to believe he is otherwise than a real
> Christian, but all Christians are not qualified for mis-
> sionaries.
> In January last, Mr. Sears came with his
> wife to Philadelphia. I was at that time in deep affliction,
> having lost, by death, my inestimable companion, with
> whom I had lived thirty years.
> Perceiving that Mr. Sears was privately
> prejudicing the members of the board against the Fort
> Wayne mission, I *had called* a meeting of the board on the
> 17th of January, when he was requested to be present. He
> was full of complaining. He told the board that he
> entertained as high an idea as ever of the piety, zeal, and
> devotedness of brother McCoy, and yet it came out at last
> that he complained that * * * * (Here follow twenty seven
> counts, or complaints.)
> The full confidence I have ever entertained
> in you led me to make such a reply to these charges as was
> by no means acceptable to Mr. Sears; but the evidence itself
> is, in several instances, so contradictory, that I felt it my
> duty to cover the fault-finder with the shame it appeared to
> me that he deserved. He even condescended to particulars

---

[10] *History of Baptist Indian Missions*, p. 184.

that it was no less unmanly than ungodly to have uttered. I took, on the occasion, the charges hastily from his lips, and it is *only at the direction of the board* that I copy them, and transmit them to you.

The board at this meeting passed merely the following minute :

'Brother John Sears made a verbal statement of his difficulties and dissatisfaction in relation to the Fort Wayne mission. The board suspend their judgment until they hear from brother McCoy. A draft of thirty dollars was ordered in his favour, to help him on to New York.'

At a meeting of the board, February 2d, 1823, your letter having reached me, the following minute and resolutions were passed: 'A letter was received from brother McCoy, on the subject of the Rev. John Sears's retiring from Fort Wayne, on which,-

1st. Resolved, That this board sympathize with brother Sears, under the afflictions he has sustained in the loss of his father and brother.

2d. Resolved, That the measures adopted in the whole of this case, by brother McCoy, appear to have been wise and salutary, but that the board will communicate to brother McCoy the objections raised by Mr. Sears against the economy of the mission.

3d. Resolved, That the Rev. Mr. Sears is at liberty to retire from missionary service under the board, his mind appearing disinclined to the privations which evangelical labours among the aborigines of our country essentially require.

4th. Resolved, That Mr. Sears be requested to furnish the board, as early as may be, with a full account of his receipts and expenditures while in their service.

5th. Resolved, That the corresponding secretary is instructed to communicate the preceding resolutions to brother McCoy and brother Sears.'

A special meeting of the board was held on Friday, the 14th of March, from which I have the pleasure of making the following extracts

'A letter dated St. Joseph's, January 25, 1823, was received from brother McCoy, containing his journal from February 9, 1822, to January 24, 1823. Resolved, That the board very sincerely and affectionately sympathize with their brother in all his trials and deep afflictions, and trust that the God of all consolation will continue to be his support in every work of faith and labour of love. The board, under the influence of these feelings,

173

rejoice that their brother is pleased with the situation in which he now lives, and hope that the blessings of heaven from above, as well as those from the earth beneath, may ever rest on him and all the mission family.'

Let none of the foregoing communications prevent you from drawing on the board for such sums as your necessities shall require. I believe the board are wholly satisfied with what you have done and are doing. I pray the Lord may support you. Let none of these things move. If God approve, all will be well -- forever so. My children unite in love. Let me hear soon from you. Your affectionate brother,

Wm. Staughton.[11]

The Board clearly divided on its missions policy

This was a letter to delight the McCoys' hearts and Staughton's kindness along with that of Spencer Cone was one of the several reasons why McCoy persevered with his attachment to the Board as a whole. By this time, however, there were clearly two different factions in the Board, representing two different opinions regarding Indian Missions. The way in which Isaac McCoy seemed to be one with the political opinions of the day concerning Indian resettlement was causing concern among those who were less pro-Government in their views. Perhaps it is more true to say that McCoy's Christian principles regarding a future for the Indians without threat of racist persecutions was gradually becoming the pattern for more enlightened politicians. However, these differences of opinions within the Board had become so dominant that the scene was being set for a major reshuffle among its members starting with a unilateral departure from the *Family Rules* in 1826 and the relocation of the Board to Boston that year.

Good news from the mission field

Once Lykins was back, the school blossomed and increased in numbers. Thirty pupils were now taught, clothed, fed and housed by the mission and the number continued to increase. Within weeks there were over sixty mouths to be fed at the station. Kind friends in Massachusetts sent five boxes of clothing worth $340 and a good deal

---

[11] *History of Baptist Indian Missions*, pp. 167-169. See original full length letter dated April 2, 1823 in McCoy Papers, Reel 2.

of bread had arrived via Fort Wayne. Governor Cass kindly sent several laborers to help at Carey and they were scheduled to eventually go with the missionaries to the Ottawas. Corbly Martin had not forgotten his missionary friends and had procured for them a flock of one hundred and thirteen sheep. Friends in Kentucky had fitted Martin out with $100 dollars of clothing and almost $200 dollars cash. Help came, too, from several other addresses in Kentucky and Ohio. Again, however, malicious reports were spread that the missionaries were living in affluence. Some thought that the value of the clothing sent, which were mainly castoffs, was at brand new Washington prices and should be subtracted from the amount received in cash donations. Others were anxious that the Indians might end up being more affluent than the whites. Others thought that McCoy was selling the clothing at a great profit which was put in his own pocket. This led many to inquire of McCoy how things were being managed and when they heard of the true state of affairs, they increased their giving so that good came of evil. A Mr. and Mrs. Wright arrived at the mission and pledged themselves to assist Mr. Lykins at the school. Two men also came from Ohio to help with the building arrangements. On their way, the men had tried to cross the St. Joseph's River on a block of ice which capsized and the men had to swim for their lives in the freezing water.

Dusenbury goes, Polke comes

All this good news of more supplies and more helpers was rather balanced off by the resignation of Mr. Dusenbury for whom the difficulties over the winter had been too much. The fact that there were now well over 60 mouths to be fed at the mission had quite frightened him from continuing the work as he found it just too much for the small band of missionaries to cope with. McCoy had suspected all along that Dusenbury, modest and inoffensive as he was, would not be able to make the grade and had thus not even applied to the Board for his official recognition. This news was again offset by a letter from William Polke dated June 1, 1823 in which he said that he felt he should give up all worldly occupations and join the Indian mission. Polke had long been thinking and praying on these lines but there had been much to tempt him into other spheres. He had been put up for Congress, nominated as Governor and also as Indian Agent for Fort Wayne. All these posts seem to have been well within Polke's reach, especially the first two as Polke was the only serious candidate. At first, Polke's wife had not been at all keen on the idea of exchanging her comfortable life for that of a mission station, but she gradually came round to believing that the move was God's will for her family so now both husband and wife said they were prepared to forsake all and become poor missionaries. Furthermore, Polke promised that he would use half of the money he gained on his property to pay his way in the mission's service so that no one could say that he was joining the Indian mission because of the income he might gain and the Board would be spared the expense. When Polke began to add up his worldly goods, however, he found that he could not raise the sums he was thinking of. He had been very generous to his relations and neighbors, lending them substantial sums of money and when he strove to obtain the loans back, the one said all his money had recently been stolen, the other said he was bankrupt and could not pay and a third said if he paid, he would be completely penniless, so Polke had to leave them in his debt. Other problems for Polke were how to take care of his aged father who had hoped to live with him, what to do with a Negro servant girl who had just given birth to a child from a white man in Vincennes, and how to provide an education for his children whom he would have to board out. It seemed that Polke was having great difficulty in "giving up all" and he was about to enter the mission field with many problems still unsolved. While waiting to put his house in order before joining McCoy in the autumn, Polke was asked to become the Indian mission agent of the Red River Association and was able to collect a good deal of material and several hundred dollars in cash for the Carey mission settlement.

Sears continues to criticize the Indian Mission

Meanwhile, Sears was still causing anxiety for the mission. He had challenged the system of education used, claiming that specimens of handwriting shown to illustrate the work of the school were products of other establishments, which was quite untrue. He had told the Board that the Mission was supposed to be for Indians which he took to mean full-bloods. Many of the mission's pupils, however, were of mixed blood which somehow Sears thought was against the Board's policy. Apparently Sears' idea was that if the pupils had white relations, especially white Christian relations, those relations ought to be paying for their children's education. In short, Sears who was the newest and least experienced member of the mission staff, claimed to have superior knowledge and experience in all matters. When questioned concerning Sears' allegations by the Board, McCoy had to enlighten them concerning their educational policies and curricula and about how white blood had come into Indian veins and explained that only one child, a girl, had a traceable Christian father who might be able to pay if that were the mission's policy. At the time, as McCoy reported to Governor Cass, no less than 28 of the Indian pupils, mixed-bloods included, could neither understand nor speak English at their reception into the school. As it was, the Indians in the school were all registered as such by the Government of the U.S. and accepted as such by the Indians themselves.[12] McCoy could have pointed out that at this time, the Board were pouring thousands of dollars into the Cherokee mission whose Indians had most likely the highest percentage of white blood of all the tribes and where slavery was common among those of mixed blood. But at the time, the Valley Towns Mission had no former member asking awkward or embarrassing questions, though that time was to come. Sears had made a major tactical mistake in quoting Giles Jackson as his ally in complaining that McCoy mistreated the Indians. What had happened was that the Miami Indian children had refused to move with the mission to Carey. Sears had taken this as a sign that they had supposed themselves ill-treated by McCoy and did not want anything to do with him. Sears had not understood the real reason behind the situation, i.e. that the Miamis had no dealings with the Potawatomis and would not allow their children to be boarded among Potawatomi tribesmen. Apparently, for Sears, Indians were Indians, whatever their tribal affiliations. Happily Jackson and Lykins could both testify to the accuracy of McCoy's refutation of Sears' accusations and the fallacy of Sears' own statements. What Sears had apparently not told Staughton was that the Potawatomi church had unanimously placed him under censure for spreading false rumors and thus bringing discredit to the work of the mission. Even Giles Jackson who had been most dissatisfied with his own situation, testified personally to the Board that McCoy was beyond criticism in his management of the mission's affairs.

A hazardous journey

In the spring of 1823, McCoy and the Wrights made a six weeks' journey across icy waters and snowy plains to Ohio via Fort Wayne and back, driving three wagons to secure more food and funds and collect twelve cows and a flock of sheep. The lack of roads and

---

[12] See McCoy's letter to Staughton from Carey dated June 10, 1823, McCoy Papers, Reel 2.

rapidly thawing earth made transport almost impossible and progress was very slow. Crossing the Eel, Elksheart and St. Joseph Rivers in makeshift canoes and on the backs of large logs was a perilous adventure in itself. Much food, including a precious cargo of peas, potatoes, flour, salt and seeds was lost on the way due to the party's vessels capsizing. The missionaries had to spend two days looking for seventy sheep which had wandered but all but one were found. The party arrived at Carey totally exhausted and found the Carey missionaries, workers and pupils living on short rations. McCoy entered into his Journal, "Many are thy mercies, O Lord! By thee we have run through a troop of difficulties, and by our God we have leaped over walls of obstacles."[13]

The situation at Carey

By this time, Carey Station was growing into a true community center and a settlement village in its own right. There were five log cabins, ranging in size from 16 by 18 feet to 20 by 26 feet. There was a school house which was also 20 feet by 26 feet, a blacksmith's shop, a smoke house, a milk house, and a stable 24 by 26 feet. Sixty acres of land adjacent to the station was fenced off for cultivation and the station owned 175 head of cattle, 90 hogs, 80 sheep and six horses. They were in the process of planning a mill and a school house for female Indians.[14]

McCoy felt that it was high time that he fulfilled his promises to the Ottawas and establish a mission station and school for them. It was not easy to get away as the Indians had been promised someone to teach them to plough, harrow and other farming tasks but as Dusenbury and the Sears family were no longer part of the team, the task fell on McCoy himself. Also the Indians needed McCoy at the time to help them in their transactions with Governor Cass concerning the Chicago treaty. At times, McCoy had as many as forty Indians to deal with at once. The food which was lost on the river had to be replaced and seed potatoes and other vegetable seed was needed for planting in order to provide food for the following winter. Again the canoe carrying the goods capsized and almost all was lost. Now McCoy and his friends had to tour the country for miles around with little success, trying to

---

[13] *History of Baptist Indian Missions*, pp. 189-190.

[14] "History of Fort Wayne Mission," *American Baptist Magazine*, 1823-24, pp. 330-336.

beg, borrow or buy foodstuffs for the growing number of dependents which had to be fed.

Preparation for the Thomas Mission starts in earnest

At last, McCoy began his journey to the Grand River on May 26, 1823, taking a Frenchman named Paget as his guide, an Indian pupil and one of the men sent by Cass. McCoy was loath to leave his family without bread but on the way, he met Indians who had a bushel of corn to sell so he sent them along to Carey. Once among the Ottawas, McCoy soon realized that he was among those who did not know him. No sooner was his back turned than the little food they had with them disappeared. McCoy was, however, successful in his protests and had the stolen goods returned. John Sears had reconnoitered the land but on arriving there, McCoy's party saw no similarity between what they found and Sears' description so they had to survey the country again in order to find a suitable site for a base. McCoy's authority was soon recognized by the Ottawas but this led to many embarrassing moments. The story was quickly spread that he could control the moon and the stars and cure every illness. It wasn't long before lines of "patients" visited McCoy to ask for healing and even miracles.

McCoy soon found that he had arrived at a most inopportune time. The Government had not entered into discussions with representatives of the entire Ottawa people in drawing up the Chicago Treaty concerning their future. They had merely consulted the principle Ottawa chief Kewikishkum who had signed away a good portion of his tribe's land. The tribes-people and lesser chiefs believed this to have been an illegal act as, by ancient rights, the land belonged to the entire tribe and was not the personal property of the chief. Sadly, it had been a common practice with the Government to make discussions easy for themselves and deal with the principle chief of a tribe, promise him certain personal privileges and thus coax him to sign away his tribe's lands. This was one of the causes of many a war between whites and Indians and even inter-tribal warfare. The Cherokees as a people began to react violently to any member of their tribe who signed away land in this way and made it a capital crime. Thus, when McCoy insisted on parleying with all the chiefs together, Kewikishkum refused to show his face for fear of retaliations. The other, lesser, chiefs refused to speak with McCoy until the leading chief was there and suggested that they should all start drinking whiskey until he arrived. This would have made any talks impossible, and McCoy, of course, protested strongly against this, demanding that the chief must appear. The Indians told him that they had to wait until the whites decided what to do when they were in the minority, so McCoy would now have to be patient as he was the minority. McCoy, however, was thinking of his starving family and how he must get back to them soon and go looking for food.

It soon became apparent that the Indians were hoping to regain their lost land by McCoy's intervention, which was quite an impossibility. McCoy did find that there was one fear which he could ease at once. The Indians had been led to believe that the missionary station would be financed by their annuities and that pupils would have to pay 410 dollars a head for their schooling. McCoy realized that once he convinced the Indians that his motives were pure and that he was there for their benefit alone, they would be cooperative. He was thus able to reassure the Indians that the mission station and school would not cost them anything but the land they had already offered to give the mission, which had been the general wish of the Ottawas. All in all, however, McCoy was rather disappointed at this first encounter with the Ottawas and discovered that there was still much work to be done before the Indians could feel secure under the control of the whites.

Indian hardships under the whites lead McCoy to plan an Indian State

The journey back to Carey was most strenuous as the party had completely run out of food and the mosquitoes were unbearable. After swimming their horses across the Grand River, they were able to buy a little corn and feed on a groundhog, all of which was not enough to go round. Paget's horse collapsed and both horse and rider had to be left behind, then McCoy's horse broke loose one night and the whole party had to search until ten a.m. the next day before it was found. The Indians whom the party met on the way were as starving as the missionaries who could purchase nothing from them but an occasional potato or two. At last they came to the Kallamazoo River which McCoy called the Kekenmazoo according to its Indian pronunciation. Here the starving and mosquito-bitten missionaries found hospitality at the home of an Indian named Gosa whose wife prepared meat for them but the family had no bread. McCoy had only a little tea left which he shared with the Indians. The feet of one of McCoy's party were so sore that he had to be left behind at Gosa's until they healed. Now the party moved on with McCoy pondering on what he had heard from the Ottawas. They had confessed that they trusted no treaty and it was obvious that they would be one day robbed of all their land, or at best driven elsewhere until the whites would demand even that land from them. McCoy recorded his thoughts of June 4th in the words:

> ...after all our labours to put our mission into operation, we shall in a few years be driven away, to encounter new hardships in another part of the wilderness, or if we remain here, it will be only to witness the decline and ultimate ruin of the people of our charge, for no band of Indians has ever thriven when crowded by white population. Hardly can we hope to surmount present obstacles, and do the Indian a little good, before our business here must fail, by causes which we cannot control.[15]

Such thoughts led McCoy to think in earnest of his long cherished plan to provide a home for the Indians away from white interference. Here, McCoy was thinking in completely opposite terms to missionaries to the Indians who had gone before him and very many of his brethren among both the Baptists and Presbyterians. Since the days of John Eliot (1604-90), it had been the custom of white Christians, concerned for the spiritual welfare of the Indians, to set up colonies for them in white areas so that they could come under the Christian and civilizing influence of the European settlers. Thus Eliot founded colonies of "praying Indians" at Natick, Concord and Grafton housing some 1,500, and several thousand more Indians were settled in Martha's Vineyard, Nantucket and Plymouth Colony.[16] Such an ideal was very much part of the Presbyterian Indian policy in McCoy's day and McCoy was to find that wherever he campaigned for free land for free Indians, he would find the Presbyterians, equally fine Christian men, arguing for incorporating the Indians into the white system. The Presbyterians had their lobby, too, at the Baptist Board of Missions. Even Baptist Evan Jones, great Indian missionary as he was and full contemporary with McCoy, fought hard against the formation of an Indian state in the Indian Territory which was coming into existence through McCoy's influence on the Government. Those friends of the Indians who disagreed with McCoy, however, did not

---

[15] *History of Baptist Indian Missions*, pp. 196-197.

[16] See Fiske's *The Beginning of New England*, pp. 202-205, 208-210, 237 for a discussion on Eliot's missionary aims. This author does not agree with Fiske concerning the supposed "scanty intelligence and still scantier moral sense" of the Indians as a people in relation to whites.

share his realism. It was not a question of equal rights for Indians and whites to live side by side. The question was the rights of the Indians to live at all. Jessie Page, author of great missionary biographies such as those of Henry Martyn and David Brainerd, writing on what he called "the horizon of the Twentieth Century", and referring back to the eighteenth, says:

> It will be noticed, in the foregoing, that strong drink, that curse of all nations, had already begun to produce its fatal results upon the poor Indians. Perhaps there is no more conspicuous example to be found in the history of any people, of the swift degradation of a race through drink, than in the case of the North American Indians. The fine qualities of these people, their dignity and hardihood, have rapidly disappeared by the desolating contact with what is miscalled civilisation. Since Brainerd's day they have lost their land wholesale, and are fast dying out in poverty, drink and despair. What drink has begun, the bullet is rapidly completing, and the Indians, among whose forefathers Brainerd laboured, and about whose life all New England poets have sung, will soon be a forgotten people.[17]

It was this thought that moved many Christians to give up the Indians for lost and merely strive to ease their supposed final days. Thus a time and money consuming project like the colonization of the West by the Indians was considered a cruel plan indeed and the last nail in their coffin. This feeling, sadly, came to dominate the Baptist Board. McCoy felt that the Indians would be lost if they remained under the evil influence of white bootleggers and traders and continue to be the victims of unjust treaties. He believed strongly that there was still mercy on God's side for the Indians and that they might be preserved as a people if they were removed from the forces which were destroying them and allowed to settle down and manage their own affairs. To provide such a permanent home for the Indians became McCoy's one great ambition. On June 4th, 1823, as McCoy was journeying along on horseback, he pledged himself to God to do all in his power to promote a plan to allow the Indians to colonize the free land west of the Missouri which had not yet been opened to U. S. settlers. This was to be in his own words, "the most important business of my life."

---

[17] *David Brainerd: The Apostle to the American Indians*, p. 74.

The Stephen Long Expedition visits Carey and praises McCoy's work

Once back home, McCoy was cheered by the way the Carey station had been kept in good spirits and strong faith throughout his absence, though food was scarce. Lewis Cass had sent a note to say that McCoy could draw on his department for $100 within the terms of the 1821 treaty, which was a real boon. Lykins was away looking for corn and soon came back with a bushel and a half which was all that was to be found. A new teacher, Miss Wright,[18] had come from Ohio and was looking after the girls' education. Another cheering fact was that while McCoy was absent, a five-man group of explorers on a Government sponsored expedition led by Major Stephen H. Long had visited the mission and had become deeply impressed with the work. In his first volume on the expedition, describing the journey from Fort Wayne to Chicago, one of the members, William H. Keating,[19] pays high tribute to the mission and says:

> There is in this neighbourhood an establishment, which, by the philanthropic views which have led to its establishment, and by the boundless charity with which it is administered, compensates in a manner for the insult offered to the laws of God and man by the traders. The reports which we had received of the flattering success which had attended the efforts of the Baptist missionaries on the St. Joseph's, induced us to deviate a little from our route, to visit this interesting establishment. The Carey mission house, so designated in honour or the late Mr. Carey, the indefatigable apostle of India, is situated within about a mile of the river St. Joseph's. The establishment was created by the Baptist Missionary Society in Washington, and is under the superintendence of the Rev. Mr. McCoy, a man whom, from all the reports we heard of him, we should consider as eminently qualified for the important trust committed to him. We regretted that, at the time we passed at the Carey mission house, this gentleman was absent on business connected with the establishment of another missionary settlement on the Grand river of Michigan; but we saw his wife, who received us in a very hospitable manner, and gave us every opportunity of becoming acquainted with the circumstances of the school.

---

[18] I have not been able to discover the relationship between Mr. and Mrs. Wright and Miss Wright if any.

[19] *Major Long's Expedition to the Sources of the St. Peter's River.*

The spot was covered with a very dense forest seven months before the time we visited it; but, by the great activity of the superintendent, he has succeeded in the course of this short time in building six good log houses four of which afford a comfortable residence to the inmates of the establishment, a fifth is used as a school room, and the sixth forms a commodious blacksmith's shop. In addition to this, they have cleared about fifty acres of land, which are nearly all enclosed by a substantial fence. Forty acres have already been ploughed, and planted with maize, and every step has been taken to place the establishment upon an independent footing. The school consists of from forty to sixty children. It is contemplated that the school will soon be increased to one hundred. The plan adopted appears to be a very judicious one. The plan adopted in the school purposes to unite a practical with an intellectual education. The boys are instructed in the English language, in reading, writing, and arithmetic; they are made to attend to the usual occupations of a farm, and to perform every operation connected with it, such as ploughing, planting, harrowing, &c.; in these pursuits they appear to take great delight. The system being well regulated, they find time for every thing; not only for study and labour, but also for innocent recreation, in which they are encouraged to indulge; and the hours allotted to recreation may perhaps be viewed as productive of results fully as important as those accruing from more serious pursuits. The females receive in the school the same instruction which is given to the boys; and are, in addition to this, taught spinning, weaving, and sewing, both plain and ornamental. They were just beginning to embroider; an occupation which may, by some, be considered as unsuitable to the situation which they are destined to hold in life, but which appears to us very judiciously used as a reward and stimulus. They are likewise made to attend to the pursuits of the dairy, such as milking of cows, &c. All appear to be very happy, and to make as rapid progress as white children of the same age would make. Their principal excellence rests in works of imitation; they write astonishingly well, and many display great natural talent for drawing. The institution receives the countenance of the most respectable among the Indians. There are in the school two of the grand children of Topenebe, the great hereditary chief of the Putawatomies. The Indians visit the establishment occasionally, and appear pleased with it.[20]

---

[20] *History of Baptist Indian Missions*, pp. 197-198.

Here was advertisement indeed for the mission and that from one of the highest academic sources in the country, in a volume being read by many in authority who were interested in the biological, geological, archaeological and human geography of the United States of America. The needs of the mission were also clearly stated as Keating ended his glowing report by saying, "When we visited them, they were on short allowance." Actually, it was pro-Indian missions Long who put off many friends of the Indians and Indians themselves from being attracted by the "go west" solution to their problems. Major Long had been originally delegated by the Secretary of War in June, 1819, to find the sources of the Red River, to continue the work of Lewis, Clark and Pike. In his 1820 report of their progress along the Arkansas River, Long stated, "In regard to this extensive section of the country between the Missouri River and the Rocky Mountains, we do not hesitate in giving the opinion that it is almost wholly unfit for cultivation."[21] McCoy's own journey's of exploration in order to resettle the Indians was to prove this sweeping statement wrong.

---

[21] *The American West Year by Year*, p. 53.

Chapter Seven
The Thomas Mission to the Ottawas (1823)

Laying down plans for the Indian Territory

On June 23rd, 1823, on his way back from the Ottawas, McCoy's thoughts turned again to the future of the Indians and his dreams of providing a new home for them, far from negative white influence. He thus decided to write to Governor Cass on the matter and also to several Congressmen and to his brother-in-law William Polke at Maria Creek. His idea was to form an association which had the Indians' interests at heart and which would campaign for the colonization of lands chiefly accrued by the Louisiana Purchase west of the Mississippi which had not yet become states within the Union. Obviously, McCoy did not at this time realize what his missionary colleagues in other areas and denominations might think of his plan as he cheerfully states, "It was thought that each denomination of Christians which had missions on the east of the Mississippi would be so warmly in favor of the plan, that they would severally encourage the people of their charge to emigrate."[1] McCoy also wrote to the Board, outlining his plan and received a swift and rather sobering answer which merely stated, "A committee has been appointed to consider it."[2]

It may be wondered how McCoy, who lived in such remote places, knew about the situation in the west in the area which became known as the Indian Territory and is now Oklahoma, Arkansas and part of Kansas. Several members of McCoy's family, including his brother John were Congressmen and since around 1817, McCoy had been in touch with politicians, missionaries and explorers whose in-

---

[1] *History of Baptist Indian Missions*, pp. 200-201.

[2] Ibid., p. 201.

terests lay westwards. McCoy was a frontiersman himself, having been brought up in Kentucky and Indiana and during the period of his earliest interest in the Indians, news of the spectacular discoveries of Meriwether Lewis (1774-1809) and William Clark (1770-1839) was in everyone's mouths. The two soldier-statesmen-explorers put the Mississippi and the Missouri firmly on the map of the New World and from then onwards for a hundred years, it became customary to refer to east or west of the Mississippi in describing where a place was situated.[3] These discoveries alone led to a number of reports issued by President Jefferson which inspired many easterners and even people in the Old World to "move west."[4] Now he was in touch with Major Long and his team of explorers, writers and soldiers and no doubt Mrs. McCoy and Lykins had sounded out Major Long and his men out on what they had discovered along the Mississippi, Missouri, Red and Arkansas Rivers.

The Board once again impose severe restrictions on the work at Carey

Just as the Carey community was growing and plans were being laid for the Thomas settlement,[5] on the Grand River among the Ottawas, Luther Rice, who had been one of McCoy's chief supporters, wrote on behalf of the Board to say that the Carey missionaries should no longer look to the Board for any general financing but each need must be outlined specifically and met as funds were available. In plain terms, this meant that every bag of corn and loaf of bread the missionaries needed must be applied for in writing in advance and then months of waiting would have to ensue before either the money for the item came or a negative reply was received. So resolute was the Board that they refused to honor a draft drawn for $552 some time before their new decision became official and allowed that to bounce, too.

---

[3] Formerly Easterners referred to their position relative to either east or west of the Appalachian Mountains, most Americans up to 1806 living east of these mountains. In that year the Cumberland Road project was commenced to open the way for pioneers.

[4] See *Message from the President of the United States Communicating Discoveries Made in Exploring the Missouri, Red River and Washita by Captains Lewis and Clark, Doctor Sibley and Mr. Dunbar*, February 19, 1806. Zebulon Pike was exploring the Mississippi around the same time.

[5] To be named after Dr. John Thomas, William Carey's missionary partner.

McCoy had always avoided getting into debt and had disagreed with Sears on the subject. Now the Board had forced the mission into debt and weakened its testimony. To make matters worse, the Wrights, in whom a large sum of money had been invested, decided that they were not suited to help in the school. The missionaries had long learned as the poet Cowper that the frown of Providence merely covered God's smiling face for a season and this was now the case. Happily, with the arrival of Luther Rice's letter from the Board, came the news that Congress had decided to send the mission $183 dollars for their work and Mr. William Polke of Indiana, after corresponding with McCoy, had applied directly to him to become a missionary. This time, McCoy did not refer the candidate to the Board but sent him money for his journey to Carey. Another good piece of news was that the mission's creditor said that he would keep the matter quiet about the debt, otherwise it would reflect negatively on his own business. He merely urged the mission to make it their priority to balance their accounts as soon as possible. Also twenty-one Bibles had been sent to the mission so regular Bible study work could be commenced with the Indians and a number of pupils could use Bibles for their own private devotions.

A day in the life of the station

McCoy now furnishes us with a detailed description of a day in the life of the station by writing:

> At the opening of the day, during the shorter nights of summer, and earlier during the longer nights, the sounding of a trumpet was the signal for all to rise. At sunrising in the longer days, and earlier during the shorter, the ringing of a bell summoned the family to morning prayers, after which the children were directed to their morning labours. At half past six the trumpet called to breakfast, and the ringing of a small bell directed the family to become seated at table. We all sat down together at the same table, and the native children received the same attention, there and elsewhere, that white children would have received, had we kept a boarding school for them. As our dining room would not contain all at the same time, the larger scholars ate first, and one of the teachers attended to the table until all had left. At eight o'clock in summer, and half an hour later in winter, the scholars were called together, and they were dismissed at twelve. Half past twelve dinner was called. At

two the scholars were again called in, and were dismissed at five in the longer days, and at half past six supper was called. Between sunsetting and dark in summer, and never later than eight o'clock in winter, the whole family were again called together to evening prayers. Besides singing, reading, and prayer, a portion of Scripture was usually expounded. All were required to retire to rest at an early hour, and if circumstances made it necessary for any to remain up later than the hour for retiring, they were required to be silent after nine o'clock. It was made a point to attend promptly *to time*. The moment that the hour arrived for rising, the trumpet sounded, and at the moment when the trumpet or the bells directed to any other thing in the routine of business, it was not deferred on any account.

On Saturdays the schools were suspended, and the boys were allowed part of the day for recreation. Twice in the week they were permitted to bathe in the river in summer, and to amuse themselves on the ice in winter, accompanied by the teacher, or some one else, to prevent accidents. On Sabbaths, only two meals were eaten. At half past ten the trumpet announced the approach of the hour for public worship, which commenced at the ringing of a bell half an hour later, and at half past four in the afternoon we again assembled for public worship. At this time, Mr. Lykins, Mrs. McCoy, and myself were the only missionaries at the station. Generally our business was divided between us, but we were not particular to limit ourselves to these rules, but one would take hold of the work, which belonged to the department of another, whenever it was necessary.[6]

McCoy's writings are a major source on Indian culture, religion and folklore

McCoy began making strenuous efforts to get the work among the Ottawas going. Lykins went on ahead to organize the school and McCoy visited the chiefs along the Kekenmazoo River to try and cope with the political and financial fears the Ottawas still had. He arrived at the river just as the Ottawas were preparing for a time of conferencing, feasting, dancing, singing and religious ceremonies. McCoy received no formal invitation to join but merely went along

---

[6] *History of Baptist Indian Missions*, pp. 201-202. See also McCoy's original report dated July 1, 1823, McCoy Papers, Reel 3.

with his hosts as if it were quite natural for him. What he experienced of the festivities is recorded in his *History* and this six paged narrative is one of very many detailed eyewitness accounts of the practices, customs and ceremonies of early 18th century Indians contained in McCoy's published literary remains and in the vast amount of his unpublished papers. Whether he is dealing with the more northern Potawatomis and Ottawas or the more southern, Cherokees, Choctaws or Creeks,[7] McCoy gives us deep insight into the ways of the Red Men so showing up the futility of his modern culture-context critics who strive to portray him as being totally uninterested in the Indian way of life. Typical of McCoy's traducers is Robert F. Berkhofer, Jr. of the Department of History, University of Wisconsin who, in spite of his praiseworthy task of reprinting McCoy's *History*, yet views his subject with a glaring lack of objectivity due to an obvious lack of sympathy. Speaking of "the egocentric bias" of McCoy's *History*, Berkhofer concludes that:

> the most interesting omission in the volume is any insight into Indian attitudes and customs. After twenty-three years among the Indians, McCoy seems as oblivious of their culture as when he first entered among them. In this blindness he was like most other Americans.

The fact is, there are few reports of the age, whether penned by explorers, travelers, journalists, or missionaries, that reserve so much space to portraying Indian culture. This has led, for instance, Professor William Unrau[8] of Wichita University to use McCoy as one of his main authorities when dealing with the ancient customs, religions, geographical locations, numbers and even archaeology of the

---

[7] In McCoy's day, the Baptist Board divided the Indians into two distinct groups for purposes of missionary outreach. The first was represented by the tribes along the northern and western frontiers of the United States from New York to Wisconsin. The most prominent missionary here was Isaac McCoy. The second group was represented by those tribes living in North Carolina down to Georgia and Alabama. Here the most prominent Baptist missionary was undoubtedly Evan Jones. McCoy added the Indian Territory to this rather artificial division of the tribes. Traditionally the so-called Five Civilized Tribes, representing roughly the second division, have been separated for purposes of study in the history of the Indians from the more northern tribes and the so-called Plains Indians.

[8] See Unrau's excellent book, *The Kansa Indians: A History of the Wind People*, 1673-1873.

Indians, in particular the Kansas tribe. McCoy's books, annual reports, lectures and letters all give deep insight into the lives and customs of numerous tribes including their language, religions and modes of hunting and warfare. A typical example of such accounts can be found in McCoy's 1836 *Annual Register of Indian Affairs* where he appends a 35 paged essay entitled *A Plea for the Aborigines of North America* in which he outlined his findings concerning the number of Indians, their housing, division of labor, nomadic habits, dress, horsemanship, tools, weapons, means of livelihood, boat making, kitchen utensils, cooking, alleged cannibalism, amusements, system of reckoning,[9] medicine and means of government. Whether McCoy is describing the Indians' burial rites,[10] hunting methods,[11] methods of husbandry or their ways of preparing food, he is a first class recorder of information. McCoy even describes in detail how the Osages scalp their enemies.[12] His descriptions of the Indians' way of combining religion with personal hygiene in their steam bath rites, his accounts of their attitudes toward marriage, their children's upbringing, old age, and relations between the sexes are written with the eyes of an explorer and scientist besides coming from the heart of a missionary devoted to them. His lengthy report of the Indian traditions regarding the Flood and their feast and fast days is of special interest.[13] In outlining the Indians' views of nature, their spiritual life, their blood feuds,[14] their attitudes to sickness and its cures, even their politics and ideas of law, McCoy always remains respectful. If he errs at all, it is in his humor as a number of the Indians' more theatrical practices were very funny to watch. This was by no means to McCoy's discredit as he found the Indians had a real sense of humor, too, and they were fully aware of the entertainment value of their traditions. McCoy

---

[9] See McCoy's letter to a Mr. Frist or Trist dated March 20, 1829, McCoy Papers, Reel 7.

[10] See especially McCoy's lengthy description of Indian burial practice and other customs in the *Latter Day Luminary*, October, 1822, pp. 313-343.

[11] See McCoy's description of a buffalo hunt on pp. 355-356 and passim of his *History of Baptist Indian Missions*.

[12] *History of Baptist Indian Missions*, p. 357

[13] See McCoy Papers, Reel 7. The account had been dated July 18, 1831.

[14] See also McCoy's report (January 30, 1839) as a brief to aid General Tipton for a lengthy account of how blood feuds are carried out and other tribal practices. McCoy Papers, Reel 10.

always promised the Indians that he would not laugh at their behavior unless they made it clear that their design was to produce laughter.[15] When faced with modern writers who are biased against McCoy because they can neither place themselves objectively in his age nor sympathize with his calling, nor share his sense of humor, it will perhaps not be out of place to reproduce McCoy's exact and rather lengthy description of the festivities which greeted him among the Ottawas on the banks of the Kekenmazoo River:

> Early on the morning of the third day we reached the Ottawa settlements on Kekenmazoo, and were informed that they were about to spend the day in the observance of a religious ceremony, which would be accompanied by dancing and feasting. We went immediately to the house of the chief, White Sparrow, who, with one male companion, and three women, one of whom was his wife and another his daughter, had already engaged in the exercises of the day, in the house fitted for the occasion. Without doors a man and his wife were preparing a considerable quantity of bear's meat, venison, turkey, and porcupine, for the feast. The chief's wife had the kindness to suspend her exercises long enough to set before us a little food, which we needed. The chief asked for tobacco to smoke with his people, and seemed much pleased that I added a little salt.
>
> The apartment in which the services were performed had been specially constructed for such occasions. Stakes were driven into the ground at proper distances, on which poles were tied horizontally, with bark; on the outside of these grass mats were fastened, which raised a temporary wall, about as high as a man's breast. The hall was about twenty feet wide and sixty feet long. On three sides were spread mats and skins for the company to sit upon. Through the centre three posts were erected, ranging with each other the longer way of the apartment, and extending so much higher than the sides that a temporary roof, in case of rain, might be made to rest upon poles that lay along upon their tops.
>
> On our arrival the chief was delivering to the few who were with him short speeches, to which the others occasionally responded with O-oh, in a more plaintive tone than is commonly heard among Indians. Between speeches, the chief drummed, and all sung. Two of them held in their hand a gourd, to which had been fastened a

---

[15] See, for instance, p. 362, *History of Baptist Indian Missions.*

wooden handle. Gravel or corn within the hollow of the gourd made a rattle resembling a child's toy. The drum consisted of a skin stretched over the end of a small keg, after the heading had been displaced, and was beaten with one stick only; the strokes, without changing their force, occurred regularly, at the rate of about one hundred and thirty in a minute. The gourds were shaken so as to make their rattling in unison with the strokes of the drum.

About eleven o'clock, thirty or forty persons, including men, women, and children, assembled about thirty yards from the dancing house, at which place they left most of their children and some of the women. The others formed in single file, and marched until the leader reached the door of the dancing hall, and halted, the whole maintaining their order. The leader stamped a few times with his foot, crying, Ho! ho! ho! Those within responded with their Ho; several who were on the front end of the line sung for a few minutes, and then all marched into the hall, and around the room three times, halting and singing twice each time. Invariably through the whole day, when they marched around the room, the circle was described by turning to the left, so that if a person seated near the door to the right desired to walk out, he never retraced his steps, he walked around the room, with his left hand towards the centre, until he reached the door. All took their seats with their backs against the wall.

A principal man then arose, and addressed the company in a speech of considerable length; after which one drummed, two rattled their gourds, several sung, and two women and one man danced. The musicians and dancers then passed round the hall, severally pointing a finger to each one seated as they passed, and using words which I did not understand. The person pointed at responded each time with a mournful groan, A-a-a; these took their seats; another man arose and made a speech; two men held a short private consultation in a low voice, and then mixed some powders, which they called medicine. A little tobacco, or rather the common mixture of tobacco and the leaves of other plants, which they use in smoking, made fine as if prepared for the pipe, was sprinkled at the foot of the two posts of the door, and of those planted along the centre of the building, and a small quantity put into the fire. Another man arose and delivered a lengthy speech, which was followed by drumming, singing, and dancing. A little respite ensued, which the men employed in smoking; another speech was made, and followed by the dancing of ten persons to music; another turn of smoking ensued, and the two men who had charge of the medicine allowed each person to take a little between the fingers, and put it into an otter's skin, with which each was furnished. These skins had been taken off the animals entire, including the bones of the head. The sack thus formed by a whole skin has an opening into it on the throat, which is generally the fashion of an Indian's tobacco pouch. These medicine bags are esteemed sacred, and are used for no other purposes than those belonging to this festival occasion, and to hold the sacred medicine. Artificial eyes, usually of metal that will glisten, are inserted; the teeth are disclosed by the drying of the skin, and the sides of the mouth are ornamented by soft feathers, dyed red, extending along the jaws three or four inches. The tails are ornamented with porcupine quills, dyed various colours, to the end of which, and also to the feet, small brass thimbles amid bells are suspended, which make a tinkling sound whenever the skin is moved. Each keeps his or her skin hanging on the arm at all times while in the house during the festival, excepting when seated, at which time they are hung on the wall, by the owner's seat.

Another speech being delivered, four men and two women marched out at the door of the hall, with *Ha-hos* and gesticulations which cannot be described. They formed a semicircle in front of the door, and one of the men delivered a speech, which was followed by singing. Their otter skins were held horizontally in the two hands, with a tremulous motion that rattled the trinkets suspended to them, and which made the skin assume the appearance of the living animal when about to leap forward. While thus shaking their skins they ran around, now stooping towards the earth, and then stretching upwards and hallooing; they then marched into the hall again, severally pointing a hand to each one seated as they passed, and each person pointed at uttered an awful groan, as before. They marched around the hall, until they reached the door again, when each of the four men pretended to swallow a small bullet, which apparently almost choked him, and gave him great uneasiness at the moment; but, as he did not fall to the ground, it was understood that he was wise and good, and expert in the performance.

All these fooleries were but preliminaries to the regular course of exercises on which they were now prepared to enter. Two principal men took the lead; each held in one hand a rattle, and in the other a piece of folded cloth, to defend the hand against injury when the gourd should be struck against it. The leader delivered a speech, and all became seated again, when the drummer and the gourd men on each side of him beat in unison, while the leader sung alone. Three or four persons presented themselves before the drum, and danced; when these dancers had retired to their seats, the musicians rose, and the leader delivered a brief speech. They then marched twice around the hall, with their instrumental music, stopping to sing a few minutes at the completion of each semi-circle. The drummer then, facing the door, became seated by the middle post, with one of the rattlers behind, and the other in front; the principal one delivered a speech, at the conclusion of which they both commenced singing, and then rattled, and were joined by the drummer. Now all appeared to become inspired with new life. Some rose and danced in their places, then others, until all were on their feet, and dancing to the sound of the drum and gourds. Suddenly, as if moved by supernatural impulse, one man stepped forward from his place into the space left for them to pass in single file around the room, which, as before observed, is always with the left hand towards the centre; he bends forward, whirls around, (always to the left,) appears frantic, though not mad, shakes his otter skin, crying *Ho-o-o-o*, in a quick, frightful tone. He falls into the rear of the music, now passing around the room, and somewhere in his circuit he becomes more frantic, gives a few louder *Whoh-whos*, and suddenly punches the nose of his otter skin against some one of the company, who are all standing with their backs to the wall. The person punched either drops to the earth, as if dead, like a butcher's beef, or bows and staggers back against the wall, uttering a horrid shriek of *O-ho-ho*, as if pierced to the vitals. He now kisses the nose of his otter skin, with gestures expressive of profound respect and warm affection. These fond kisses counteract the electric shock just received from the nose of his neighbour's otter skin, and in half a minute he is restored, and falls into the rear of the company as they march around with the music.

When a person fell, apparently lifeless, I noticed that he never hurt himself in falling. Each one invariably fell in the same position. In about half a minute he would recover and rise, and, as in the other case, fall into the company of the music. Each one, on recovering from the electric shock, before he went around the room once, would become frantic, and *Whoh-whoh* oftener and louder than usual, and punch his otter skin at the nose of another person; after which he danced until he came around to his proper place, where he again took his station, with his back to the wall. In this manner they continued to go around the room, usually seven or eight persons at a time, with their music, whooping and dancing, and shaking their otter skins, and punching them towards each other's faces. Sometimes a short pause is made, and again the vocal music strikes a new tune, and at the same instant many set up a hideous whoop of *Ho-ho-ho,* until the ear is stunned with almost every frightful kind of noise that can be imagined. Having proceeded in this way a sufficient length of time, the music ceased, and each took his and her proper place against the wall. The principal actor, followed by the other gourd-man, with the drummer in the rear, went twice around the hall, halting and singing twice in performing each circuit; at length, halting at the man who was designed next to use a gourd as a leader in the farce, they made an uncommon ado in hallooing, and in singular noises and gesticulations, and finally laid down their gourds, cushions, and drum, at his feet. They then continued around the hall once more, each pointing a finger at every one as they passed, groaning each time, and being answered by the person pointed at with a frightful groan.

Another now takes the lead, and the same ceremonies are acted over again; and this round of ceremonies is repeated until every male has once led in the exercises. If therefore, the company be small, the exercises will end the sooner. Sometimes the company is so large, that the services continue until late in the night, and even all night. The females follow in all the exercises, but never lead. They carry their otter skins or medicine bags, sing, dance, blow, &c., and at this meeting one went so far as to deliver two short public speeches, but this was a rare occurrence. The males having each led in a round of the regular ceremonies, all became seated to rest, and the men smoked. On coming together, each had brought a kettle or bowl; seven or eight large kettles of boiled meat were now brought into the house, and every one's small kettle or bowl was placed near the food. A man then arose and delivered a speech. Next, the man who had superintended the cookery distributed to each a portion, using a sharpened stick for a flesh-fork; and when a piece was not too hot, he took hold with his hand.

It was now between sundown and dark; they all ate, having nothing before them besides meat. Another speech was delivered, and when it was concluded, every one rose, with his vessel in hand, in which remained a considerable portion of food. They marched once around the room, and the leader halted at the door, where he performed some antic feats, attended by noises of divers kinds, and then marched out of the house, followed by all, in single file; and those who did not reside at the place marched directly off to their homes, not stopping within sight to speak to any one, or even to look back. A portion of food was sent to me.

The Indian who was with me had accepted an invitation to participate in all the ceremonies. When we were alone, at camp, on the following night, I asked him if the presentment of the nose of the otter skin did really give them pain, when they gave the horrid shriek, and staggered back, or when they fell apparently lifeless on the ground. He was embarrassed, being unwilling to tell me a lie under the circumstances attending my inquiry, and on the other hand reluctant to acknowledge the deceptions they had practised. He looked abashed, and said, falteringly, 'It hurt a little.'

At a separate fire food was prepared for a number of women and children who did not join in the ceremonies. They were not displeased at my looking on, but did not invite me into the hall. None were allowed to enter that place, except such as were prepared to engage in the exercises. Some of their orators spoke deliberately; others spoke as fast as the tongue could clatter. It is supposed that a capacity to deliver very long sentences without taking breath is a fine accomplishment. I was often reminded of our Lord's words respecting 'vain repetitions in prayer,' a favourite word being repeated once or twice in almost every breath throughout the speech.

This ceremony is called Me'ta'wuk'; that is, Medicine dance. It is considered a religious ceremony, and moral lectures are given to the audience, and addresses made to spirits, as though they were visibly present; as, for instance, when the leader of the company reached the door of the house in the morning, with the company in single file in his rear, he halted, and stamping three times with his foot, said, ' *Ho-ho-ho* - I see you now, I see you now, I see you now!' three times, affecting to see a spirit that was present to preside over the meeting. One man within responded in behalf of the spirit, and invited the company in. More privacy usually attends these festivals than was observed at this, and often many rude feats of legerdemain are performed.[16]

---

[16] *History of Baptist Indian Missions*, pp. 206-212.

The Board declares itself bankrupt

McCoy received an alarming letter from the Board, dated August 6, 1826 and signed by Luther Rice. McCoy was told that his plans for the colonization of an Indian Territory had been received by the Board and a committee had been appointed to look into the matter. A committee had also been formed to contact Lewis Cass with a view to obtaining more of the $10,000 his Department allowed charitable organizations for Indian improvement. The reason for this latter move was that the Board's funds were entirely exhausted. They were bankrupt. He thus asked McCoy, as if it would be no problem whatsoever, not to draw on the Board in any way. As the mission stations at this time must have numbered some sixty people, if not more, this information was bad news indeed. Luther Rice told McCoy that the only way out the Board had was for them to appeal to the Government. What Luther Rice was actually saying was that the things of the Lord must now be financed by Caesar. Also, Rice's news was in complete contrast to the glowing printed report to the churches that the Board had sent out on May 26 of that year. This had not mentioned any sums of money being used but had proclaimed a worldwide expenditure for a work that was blossoming.

Corbly Martin comes to the relief of the mission yet again

Happily, the mission had an invaluable friend in Corbly Martin who immediately wrote out a warm tribute to the work of the mission with a full description of its situation and needs. He then had it printed under the title *Address to the Friends of Christianity and Civilization*, adding the address of Postmaster Samuel McKay, who had offered himself as an agent for the mission, to whom donations should be sent. At the same time James McCoy wrote to say that he had been collecting for the mission and would be able to send or bring a substantial donation soon. Martin was able to collect goods, livestock and cash to a value of over $3,000, which was a great asset to the mission. One might have thought that this was yet another clear signal to McCoy to break with the Board but he refused to do so even when the Board's own *Columbian Star* made an "unhappy mistake" in its report on the matter, making it appear that the mission was reluctant to publish a financial report which they had sent in for that end. This caused the mission a good deal of embarrassment. [17]

An assistant teacher obtained

In September the mission gained the services of Solomon Mittleberger as an assistant teacher. Mittleberger had the most beautiful, consistent handwriting imaginable and as over half of his pupils were learning to write for the first time, his writing must have proved an excellent pattern for the pupils. Contrary to Sears' criticism of the school's arrangements, Mittleberger was thrilled with the work going on at Carey and wrote on December 29, 1823:

> I have uniformly experienced the most kind and generous treatment from the Rev. Isaac McCoy - whose impartial, and truly affectionate and fatherly conduct towards my person at the Establishment has been such, as to command my esteem and admiration. [18]

The Ottawas give the go-ahead for the Thomas Mission Station

On October 3, 1823, McCoy was visited by a party of around twelve leading Ottawas in order to discuss McCoy's proposals for his mission station. The Ottawas were "very much pleased" with these proposals and gave McCoy the go-ahead, fitting him out with enough food for the homeward journey.

As usual, McCoy was rather anxious about how he would find Carey as it was now two months since they had received word that the Board's funds were exhausted. On his arrival, he found that Mrs. McCoy was ill again and the whooping cough was spreading rapidly among the children and youths and had already caused two fatalities. Again, McCoy received insight into the thought processes of the Indians. A dead pupils' relations had been invited to the funeral but refused to partake of the meal that was prepared for them, saying that their deceased must be hungry where they now are and so they must fast themselves. McCoy and Lykins now examined the financial state

---

[17] See McCoy's letter to Luther Rice, dated November 3, 1823, McCoy Papers, Reel 3.

[18] McCoy Papers, Reel 3.

of the mission and were so shocked at their findings that they dare not tell Mrs. McCoy for fear that it would render her fever worse.

Brighter days for the Carey Mission

Blessings always quickly followed disappointments at Carey and towards the end of October 1823 a Government official, Charles Noble, was sent to Carey to see how the mission station was improving and whether the Board's commitment to the Chicago Treaty was being implemented. Mr. Noble was so impressed by the missionaries' work that he gave the station a glowing report which caused Governor Cass to write to McCoy personally saying, "Your report and that of Mr. Noble are entirely satisfactory. The affairs of your agency appear to be in the best condition, and, if the experiment is ever to be successful, I am satisfied you will make it so."[19] Shortly afterwards, McCoy heard from his family and friends in Kentucky and Indiana who were always busy making the needs of the Indian mission known. Now they were strengthened by Corbly Martin who was traveling along the Western frontier from time to time on behalf of Carey mission. It was thus chiefly through Martin that Miss Fanny Goodridge of Lexington, Kentucky had been won for the mission. On November 5, 1823, McCoy was overjoyed to be visited by his brother John who had accompanied Miss Goodridge on the long and dangerous route. Two weeks later, William Polke and his wife arrived and affirmed that they had come to stay and would run the Ottawa mission among the Indians that had once kept Polke with his mother and other members of the family captive for several years.[20] Now the missionary work could be expanded, more teaching and preaching could be done and Miss Goodridge wasted no time in starting up a Sabbath school for the Indian women and looking after the rather neglected female side of the school's work. Now, again, a church could be formed and the missionary band with a few Indian Christians were able to share the Lord's Supper together on November 28. The first harvest at Carey proved very successful and for the first time in the mission's history prospects of a comfortable winter seemed promising.

[19] *History of Baptist Indian Missions*, p. 218. Noble's private letter to McCoy and recommendation of the Carey Mission are to be found on Reel 3 of the McCoy Papers.

[20] Many of Polke's relations had been killed by Indians and he had fought at the famous Battle of Tippecanoe in 1811.

Life at Carey now took on a pleasant routine as the work of preaching, farming and educating progressed. To complete the happiness of the mission, Rice wrote in December to tell McCoy that his drafts were now being honored again and each missionary station could draw on the Board for a maximum of $1,000 per annum.[21]

---

[21] McCoy Papers, Reel 3.

Chapter Eight
Looking for a Permanent Home for the Indians (1824-1827)

McCoy again visits the Board and Government representatives

The Carey missionaries decided that it was the right time for McCoy to pay a visit to the Board and to the Secretary of War to discuss the future of the mission. McCoy thus wrote to the Board concerning the possibility and the Board cordially invited him to join them in Washington where they would be meeting. The most urgent topic for discussion was the Board's refusal to pay outstanding bills which would easily have been covered if the Board had kept to the allowance promised in May of 1821. The mission was now in debt to the tune of over $1,000, chiefly due to food bills that the Board had refused point blank to meet. Then, McCoy wished to hear if the Board still recognized the need for a witness to the Indians by the Baptist churches. If so, McCoy would seek their backing in laying all his plans for missionary extension and financing before Congress and also ask their further cooperation in making the mission better known to the Christian public. In particular, McCoy wanted urgently to discuss with both the Board and the Government his views for the colonization of the Indian Territory. Another matter that McCoy wished to take up with the Board was the financing of hired labor. This was proving too expensive as the missionaries had agreed to pool all resources but hired hands kept their full wages. McCoy wished to convince the Board that missionaries were actually cheaper than hired labor because they did not receive a salary and shared all they had. The best combination finance-wise was to employ missionary-teachers as the Government would pay them a salary of $400 per annum each, which would be pooled in its entirety into the buildings and schools but not used to finance the traditional preaching and evangelistic duties of the missionaries. Thus the Board must see to it that more missionaries were sent to Carey and Thomas. McCoy also decided to ask the Board to honor their promise to appoint a mission agent whose duties it would be to keep the churches up to date on the affairs of the mission and organize and coordinate material support. Such a person's expenses should be a matter for the Board rather than the pockets of the missionaries. An agent would be able to take all the responsibilities of organizing the distribution of funds to the mission from the Board's hands who would then only have to audit the books, publish financial reports and interview would-be missionaries. After outlining these latter thoughts concerning an agent in his *History*, McCoy adds sadly, "But such an one we never were able to enlist in the service."[1]

McCoy seemed to always choose the worst weather for traveling and now on December 29, he started off for Washington via Fort Wayne and Ohio, estimating that he would be away some five months. On his way to Washington, McCoy interviewed various would-be candidates for the Indian Mission. Letters from Mrs. McCoy, Lykins, Miss Goodridge and Polke are extant from this time and show how they missed the fellowship of the Carey Superintendent. Especially Lykins seemed like a child without his father when McCoy was absent.

"Our man" in the Government's employment

McCoy was very warmly received by the Board at the Capital, but he was told again frankly that he could expect no money from them because they had none and that he must provide for his own support and seek donations to pay his latest bills. This was the very opposite to what Rice had informed McCoy before he set off for Washington. It appeared that the Board considered McCoy as "Our Man in the Government's Employ" and therefore the Board need not keep him. Indeed, they had actually referred to him as such in their recent reports. The policy of the Board now seemed to be that they would approve anything that McCoy suggested because he was recognized as the best man for his job, providing he turned to the Government for help and not them. McCoy was surprised to find that the committees which had been formed to consider the colonization of the Indians and to confer with the War Department concerning further grants had merely sat to decide that they would table everything for a future meeting. The same happened when McCoy was present and all he heard was such decisions as, "Resolved that the same committee be

---

[1] *History of Baptist Indian Missions*, p. 204.

continued and that the papers now presented, be referred to them and that they be requested to confer with the President of the U.S.A. on the subject submitted to them," which was just about the same decision they had come to in the meeting before without acting on their resolutions. McCoy asked for the Board to agree that Polke should be allowed to work as a deputy surveyor in the neighborhood of the missionary settlement, but this too, was referred to a committee not yet formed. At least one positive resolution was that Polke would be suggested to Governor Cass as a fit person to be a teacher to the Ottawas which rather suggested, however, that they expected Governor Cass to finance him. It would appear so as such a wording had never been hitherto used for the appointment of missionaries by the Board. Indeed, the word "missionary" was never used in the case of Polke who was so earnestly seeking to serve in such a capacity. Yet McCoy had especially stated in his application for Polke that he wished to work "in the capacity of a missionary."[2] McCoy had obviously thrown in the suggestion of the part-time occupation for Polke to test the Board. He knew their policy was not to allow missionaries to have other means of employment on the basis that they were paid for full-time work in the spreading of the gospel. So, either they said "No" to Polke's part-time work or said "Yes" to his becoming a missionary supported by the Board. The Board's method of deferring the motion put forward to a later date helped them out of both difficulties. When the Board refused to honor their financial commitments, McCoy usually suspected the reason to be that money otherwise earmarked for the Indian mission was going to finance overseas' work. This time, it was obvious to McCoy that the Board had invested a good deal of donations for missionary work in the Columbian College, the institution which the Board had hoped would help give their denomination a more respectable name.[3] As the Columbian College had reaped so much money which was sown for the Indian harvest, McCoy explained that it was only proper that the missionaries children should be educated there. With Luther Rice's backing, McCoy was able to persuade the Board to send his two eldest sons to the college.

---

[2] See McCoy's letter to the Board dated August 20, 1823, McCoy Papers, Reel 3.

[3] See McCoy's copy of his propositions to the Board dated February 4, 1824, McCoy Papers, Reel 3.

McCoy at last authorized to raise funds directly for the Indian Mission.

Another small victory for McCoy was that hitherto the Board had not supported McCoy in applying directly to the Baptist churches for funds. Now Staughton, acting in the name of the Baptist Convention, gave McCoy a written affidavit, authorizing him to raise funds for his mission in the Convention's name. This read:

> This may certify, whom it may concern,
>
> That the Bearer of this the Reverend Isaac M'Coy, in consideration of the pecuniary necessities of the Indian Mission station, of which he is Superintendent, at Carey, on the waters of the St. Joseph; is hereby instructed to make such collections and to procure such donations and subscriptions as he may be able for attaining the assistance that is required.
> The Board of Managers of the General Convention have the satisfaction to state their conviction that Mr. M'Coy is a brother, pious, self-denying and laborious, entitled to the fullest confidence and deserving universal esteem. The Mission has prospered and is prospering under his assiduous care, and, it is hoped, the measures already in operation and others that are on the eve of being attempted, with a divine blessing will rescue many of the wretched Aboriginies of our country from the ruin which their present situation menaces.
>
> In testimony of the above, the Board have directed the seal of the Baptist General Convention to be attached to this recommendation.
>
> Mr. Staughton
> Cor. Sec.y
>
> Washington , Ca
> Feb.y 23, 1824[4]

This fine gesture was typical of the new friendship which had sprung up between McCoy and Staughton. McCoy had declared his brotherly love for Staughton shortly before his journey to Washington. Christiana had given birth to a girl whom the couple called Maria

---

[4] McCoy Papers, Reel 3.

Staughton McCoy. Sadly, when money was raised, McCoy found that the Board members had either changed their minds about how the funds were to be used or Staughton had acted without consulting his fellow board members.

McCoy gains further support from the Secretary of War but the Board questions his plans

Not wishing to wait until the Board's committee became active, McCoy now sought an interview with James Monroe the President of the U.S.A. which proved abortive so he called on John C. Calhoun, the present Secretary of War with leading members of the Board. The Indians were still considered under Calhoun's department as they were still suspected of being more sympathetic to Britain than the U.S.A.. Several members of the Board warned McCoy that if Calhoun rejected his plans for homelands for the Indians, the Board would drop the idea, too. However, after Calhoun had listened to McCoy's ideas, he agreed that they were sound and worthy of putting into practice. He advised the Board to have McCoy place his plans before Congress at once. Calhoun also made more funds available for McCoy's work. The Board showed enthusiasm at first but afterwards questioned the proposal, telling McCoy that he should seek the backing of the press first and then put the matter to Congress at a later date. It appears that the Board did not wish to become directly involved in the matter of providing the Indians with a permanent home. McCoy did not protest but was obviously disappointed. As he had obtained no definite backing from the Board, apart from their giving him their blessing to canvass where he could for support, he left Washington and traveled through a large number of cities and towns, including New York, speaking to the ordinary Baptist pastors of his work. One pastor in New York protested strongly at the idea of an Indian Mission which caused very many other ministers to look into the matter with very favorable results for McCoy. Three influential Baptist pastors, Thomas Baldwin, Daniel Sharp and Francis Wayland, Jr., threw their weight behind McCoy and opened many doors for him. Col. Johnson and his brother fitted McCoy out with a fine testimonial to give McCoy a political backing, but what they wrote seems to have come from two true Christian hearts.

McCoy's success at fund-raising criticized by the Board

Soon McCoy was promised support from churches all over the country. On visiting Governor Cass at Detroit, McCoy was told that Polke's salary would be paid according to the Treaty of Chicago and he should take over the Ottawa school, leaving Lykins free to return to his duties at Carey. When McCoy returned home to Carey on June 11, 1824, he carried with him books and clothing for the sum of $820, 30 bushels of wheat, 100 barrels of flour, 24 barrels of salt, $560 from the Government, a promise of an additional $200 a year annuities and money gifts amounting to $1,623. He also brought the news that Mr. Robert Simerwell, whom he had met in Albany, was going to join the mission. Simerwell was born in Ireland in 1796 and had emigrated to North America in 1813 when he took up residence in Philadelphia. McCoy wrote in his *History*, "From that time forward the mission did not suffer for want of bread, nor did our pecuniary wants ever again become so great as they had been." He also added, "the mission, henceforth, cost the charity funds of the board *nothing*."[5]

On May 11, Luther Rice wrote to McCoy, criticizing him strongly. It was his fault and his fault alone, Rice told him, that the Board were unable to honor outstanding drafts sent to them by Phillips. The Board was now in the embarrassing situation of having to ask Phillips for an extra 30 days respite on one draft and McCoy would have to find the $500 for the other draft himself. Actually, by this time, the Board owed Phillips $1,486.03.[6] Rice's astonishing reason given was that though the Board had told McCoy that he should find the necessary money for the support of the mission himself, this did not mean that he was free to manage it as he wished. All funds he raised were the property of the Board and should be sent to them. In other words, all that McCoy had collected on his strenuous journey to canvas funds for the mission should have been sent to Boston for the Board to administer the money as they deemed fit. The great bulk of the money McCoy had raised, however, was needed to pay off immediate debts that the Board had not honored according to previous arrangements. Furthermore, many friends of the mission had refused to have their drafts made payable to the Board because of its reputation for mismanagement. Phillips and the Board had a business arrangement whereby the Board had agreed to forward Phillips cer-

---

[5] p. 223.

[6] Letter from Joseph John, Phillip's partner, dated June 23, McCoy Papers, Reel 3.

tain amounts at regular intervals. Phillips complained to his business colleague John at this time that the Board were not keeping to this agreement.[7] When McCoy arrived home after an absence of almost six months, he found the mission in such a dire financial state that it was necessary to put the money to use immediately. Actually, if McCoy had not used the cash at once, as he told Rice, his family would have starved. They were on emergency rations and the few pounds of flour left were being fed to the small children and the sick only. Corn, too, had run out so that the mission was in a needy state indeed. McCoy was shocked to find out that the mission had been left without funding for the entire period of his absence. The manual workers had not been paid during this time and this matter needed to be settled immediately. Phillips had already sent two drafts to the Board, i.e. the two that Rice could not honor, but McCoy paid them $192 for further goods bought and left them an extra $40 or $50 for future needs. The Board had not paid a penny toward McCoy's traveling expenses to Washington and back and not covered the costs of sending the goods he had collected for the mission to Carey. These two items, alone, amounted to $300 which McCoy had paid from the money collected. Thus, in his letter to Rice dated June 14, McCoy told his rather irate friend, "You see, dear brother, that I could not have done otherwise and I assure myself that this explanation will prove entirely satisfactory to yourself and other worthy brethren."[8] Rice received McCoy's letter of explanation on July 8th and replied the same day. It was as near an apology as could be expected in the circumstances. Rice had come to an agreement with Phillips, he told McCoy, and all debts would be paid. It was obvious from the letter that Rice was hoping to have two thirds of the mission's expenses paid by the Government.[9] The financing of the Columbian College was now such that Rice said he hoped soon to be free from embarrassment. What he meant was that the Board currently owed the Government $25,000 and they were now hoping that a bill would be passed in the Senate to relieve them of their duty to pay off their scandalous debts.[10] Congress kindly came

---

[7]   Letter from John to McCoy dated June 23, McCoy Papers, Reel 3.

[8]   Reel 3, McCoy Papers.

[9]   McCoy Papers, Reel 3.

[10]   See Rice McCoy's letter to his father from Columbian College dated February 2, 1825, McCoy Papers, Reel 4. The author uses the word "scandalous" with propriety as the Board had embarked on an expensive extension program for the college which would only add great debt to great

to the relief of the college in 1833 by granting city lots to the value of $25,000, the proceeds of which were to be put in a fund for the college staff's salaries.

Rice's dilemma

Actually, it was a commonly held view among the Baptists that McCoy's old friend Luther Rice was himself the chief cause of the mission's financial embarrassment. Originally called to India as a Presbyterian missionary, he soon returned to America after becoming a Baptist in order to move his Baptist brethren to interest themselves in home and foreign missionary work. He originally intended to return to the foreign mission field but he was given so many other arduous tasks by the Board that he had to give up hope of fulfilling what he thought was his true calling. On his return to America, Rice proved to be the most powerful engine behind the growth and development of the Baptist Board of Missions as a church umbrella organization. Rice showed great skill in procuring funds for the missionary cause but his colleagues on the Board left Rice to collect the money but ignored his plans for how it should be used. Rice was all for living from hand to mouth as the Lord provided, raising money as the need arose. The Board wished to put finances on a commercial basis, relying on invested capital to provide the necessary interest which would finance their work. The time, however, was one of inflation in which invested money lost its value and buying power, so that the Board began to borrow money to supplement interest gained and soon they were in debt. As Rice was officially the Treasurer, though acting under the Board, he fell into disgrace, being blamed for the Board's mismanagement. The overwhelming evidence points to the fact that the Board had long wished to rid themselves of Luther Rice and saw in their financial misery a chance to create a scapegoat of Rice and rid themselves of him at the same time. Luther Rice never complained of the blame put upon him and remained loyal to the college all his life. It is clear, however, that the Board had not only left Rice alone with

---

debt. They were obviously gambling on the chance that the Government would relieve them of their debts.

the responsibilities of financing their enterprises, but they also left him alone with the blame when those enterprises proved failures.[11]

John Taylor, who features often in Polke's letters to McCoy, complained to those supporting the Indian mission that they must shake off the shackles of the Board as they were introducing a new form of aristocracy "with an object to sap the foundation of Baptist republican government." Whether the Baptists were influenced by Taylor, Parker or Campbell, who were quite different characters with widely different ideas of the gospel, nevertheless, all looked upon Rice as some form of popish indulgence-seller so that the Board could finance their national schemes to the detriment of the local churches.[12] Though McCoy came to suffer the most personally from Rice's alleged doings, he always remained true to his old friend, and found his replacements on the staff of the Board far less reliable. After McCoy was told that he would receive no money and the Columbian fiasco was the cause, he still could say of his old friend:

> At this time the Rev. Luther Rice, who had been instrumental in bringing into existence the Baptist General Convention, was the most efficient man in connection with its board of managers. To a liberal education and extensive personal observation of men and things in different countries, he united uncommon powers of intellect. His reliance, however, upon his own resources of judgment was too great. He undertook to perform more than any one man could do, and sunk under the weight of cares which a generous heart had induced him to assume. By attempting (in a degree alone) to establish the Columbian College for the benefit of our own, and of other countries, debts accumulated faster than he was able to collect means to pay them. He became embarrassed, and in the midst of his indefatigable career his usefulness became suddenly abridged. By a similar reversion, a man of ordi-

---

[11] This author, after scrutinizing Rice's numerous transactions of behalf of the Board and following his correspondence and that of the Board's with him and the Indian missionaries had come to realize that the blame traditionally put on Rice is unfair. Rice was indeed made a scapegoat for the Board's general incompetence. It is also true to say that the Board's debts increased after Rice's removal from office. See the appendix on Rice which handles the situation in greater depth.

[12] See correspondence from the Wabash Association and Maria Creek on Reel 2 of the McCoy Papers. See also Sweet's many references to the Baptists in his *The Story of Religion in America*, especially pp. 255-257.

nary fortitude would have been driven to despair, but Mr. Rice, after his usefulness had been reduced more than fifty per cent, struggled on, doing good to the extent of his opportunities.

At the time of my second visit to Washington, Mr. Rice's affairs were approximating a crisis. Nevertheless, with all his toils and cares, he found leisure to show himself the substantial friend of the Indians, and a sympathizing brother to missionaries. He warmly advocated the scheme for the colonization of the Indians, and kindly favoured the design of taking my sons into the Columbian College. Speaking to him of the great reluctance with which I had left the missionary station on this tour, he encouraged me to hope that all had been directed by an unerring Providence. God had, perhaps, permitted our necessities to become such as to force me to make this tour, in order that I might be instrumental, somewhat, in promoting the colonization of the tribes - a measure which he believed was fraught with more important consequences than any labours of mine could effect within the small sphere of immediate missionary operations.[13]

The Board pleads with the Baptist public to help them out of their financial miseries

In June, 1824, the Board of Foreign Missions sent out a General Circular, addressed to *The Baptist Associations throughout the United States, the numerous Mission and Education Societies, both Male and Female, and to the Institutions and Individuals who are employing the various talents committed to their charge for promoting the Empire of the Son of God*. Going through the various missions the key words were "encouraging," "gratifying" and "promising." Nothing was said specifically about how funds had been used but the readers were told that though "employing the strictest economy," "their funds are exhausted," and besought their readers, "by the mercies of God" not to let them plead for money in vain.

---

[13] *History of Baptist Indian Missions*, pp. 219-220.

Success among the Potawatomis

The schools grew in leaps and bounds and now 59 Indian children,[14] apart from several whites and Jesse Cox were eagerly doing their lessons and still more children were promised. Sadly, however, the Miami children left at Fort Wayne were without a teacher. Even so, McCoy found that he had more time to learn Potawatomi and visit the Indians and preach in their houses. A hundred Potawatomis gathered regularly at the mission to hear McCoy preach.[15] All opposition seemed to have fled and McCoy was received warmly wherever he went. At times, the McCoys entertained as many as five chiefs at once. It was, however, clear that the chief's sympathies were still with the British and McCoy had to be very diplomatic in how he treated them, especially when they came to ask him to loan them transport so that the could go to Canada for a pow-wow with the British who had promised them presents!

Sears strives to drive a wedge between McCoy and Lykins

John Sears was still causing bother between the mission, the Government and the Board, doing his utmost to cause strife. If ever two souls were united in harmony, they were those of Isaac McCoy and Johnston Lykins. Lykins continually owned McCoy as his own father and almost wilted when McCoy was absent for any length of time as he missed him so much. Now Sears spread the evil rumor that Lykins was strongly critical of the man who was to become his father-in-law and with whom he would spend 25 years in perfect harmony until McCoy's death. Lykins was deeply shocked at the news and wrote the following statement to be distributed to all who had been the recipients of Sears' slander:

> Carey, St. Joseph, April 26, 1824.
>
> Rev.d John Sears of New York having stated that I was dissatisfied with Elder I. M.Coy, and with his management of the Mission.

---

[14] McCoy's report to Cass dated June 30, 1824, McCoy Papers, Reel 3.

[15] See McCoy's lengthy letter to Wayland dated July 14 and his letter to Spencer Cone dated July 19, 1834 for glowing reports on McCoy's success among the Potawatomis, McCoy Papers, Reel 3.

> I beg leave to say to the publick that, no such dissatis-
> faction has ever existed in my breast towards Mr. M.Coy,
> nor towards his management of the Mission, and that I
> believe that he has ever discharged the various duties of his
> station with becoming zeal and economy.
>
> Johnston Lykins[16]

McCoy feared to be terminally ill

McCoy was severely ill again during the summer of 1824 and hope for his survival was almost given up by his fellow missionaries. Too weak to write himself, McCoy dictated letters to be sent to the Board and to friends of the mission such as Francis Wayland Jr. His journal entry says, "I have given direction respecting my private concerns. My sufferings this day have been considerable, nevertheless I am surrounded with mercy; I receive all the comfort that kindness can impart; and, above all, I am allowed the consolations of the Bible and the hope of heaven."[17] His thoughts went out to the Indians that he loved and prayed, "that God will mercifully save the people for whom I have considered it a great privilege to be allowed to labour."[18] He obviously thought he would soon die and was distressed by the thought that the Indians had few friends among the whites, adding in his journal, "Our mission has not been, and is not likely to be, amply supported by the society we serve; it is now supported by the personal exertions of the missionaries."[19] Believing that he was near death, McCoy wrote out a document appointing Lykins as his successor to the superintendence of the mission until the Board appointed a new Superintendent.

Lykins faithfully carried out McCoy's duties and wrote to the Board on August 24, 1824 to tell them how McCoy was "brought near to death" by his serious illness. Lykins continued:

> Do you often think of your solitary brethren at Carey? Have
> you wept over the unfortunate Indian, and asked the

---

[16] McCoy Papers, Reel 3. See Lykin's letter to McCoy dated the same day where he speaks of his shock at finding out how malicious Sears was.

[17] *History of Baptist Indian Missions,* p. 230.

[18] Ibid.

[19] Ibid.

blessed Jesus to clothe him with righteousness and humility? I ask these things, because I trust that you and many
other dear friends in the East, would willingly mingle with
us the tears of sympathy, and that you do often pray the
Lord to be merciful to this mission.

. . . . . . Let your prayers often ascend before the throne of
grace, that we may be found faithful before God, and yet be
made a blessing to the heathen.[20]

When McCoy regained a little strength, he wrote to the Board
concerning Lykins, saying, "I hope the Board will continue him in the
Superintendence. He has stood firm and faithful amidst the severest
trials."[21] In another letter, sent to Governor Cass, McCoy recommended that he should approve of Lykins as his successor. In these letters,
McCoy writes very highly of Mr. Simerwell. In like manner, McCoy
sent letters to be read among his Indian friends, promising them that
the work of the mission would continue. However, we find McCoy
writing a month or so later, "'In my distress I cried unto the Lord, and
he heard me,' and restored me to health, though it was the 5th of
September before I was able to walk to the house of worship."[22]

Columbian College debts take the Board's mind off its missionary work

Meanwhile, the Mission Board were so bogged down with the
affairs of Columbian College and the great debts they had incurred in
that project that they completely neglected to do anything for the
cause of the Indians. McCoy had written several times to Rice asking
him to make the needs of the Indian mission known to the Baptist
public in the Annual Report and also publish information concerning
how they envisaged financing the mission in the future. The report
was published without referring to Carey or the needs of the mission
in any way. McCoy wrote to both Staughton and Rice, urging them to
persuade the Board to mention the Indian mission's plans for the
Indian Territory before Congress. He also asked them how he could
possibly do his book keeping and plan ahead when the Board mentioned one sum privately and another, different, sum publicly while

---

[20] *American Baptist Magazine*, Nov. 1824, 1823-24, p. 458.

[21] Document written August 10, 1824, McCoy Papers, Reel 3.

[22] See *History of Baptist Indian Missions*, pp. 229-230.

McCoy received neither amount. Rice wrote back at the beginning of September to say that now the mission could only draw on the Board for $150 for the quarter year already past and the same amount for the following quarter.[23] On October 1st, McCoy had to remind the Board about this promise and tell them that they had not forwarded the last two quarters of Government allowances. Nothing whatsoever had been done by the Board to lobby Congress concerning the spread of Baptist missions in the Indian Territory, which McCoy had repeatedly begged them to do.

William Polke threatens to resigns as a missionary

One event at this time is passed over in the extant McCoy Papers with scarcely a mention but it must have caused McCoy much anguish. William Polke, after only a matter of months on the mission field, left for Vincennes and Maria Creek to take part in Association meetings on the grounds that he would raise funds on behalf of the mission. He returned in the late autumn but shortly afterwards he and his wife confessed that they wanted to return to their old life because of family and financial problems. Polke certainly had the hands-on skills required by a missionary but he seemed to be more in his element debating with Daniel Parker and organizing his friends rather than living the life of a missionary. Though he had told McCoy before being employed on the mission field that he had decided that a missionary must forsake all and not demand a wage, his disappointment at the Board's way of looking after those under its patronage was great and he began to see that one cannot keep a large family on fair words and promises alone. Referring to Polke, George Evans, the Home Mission Agent, told McCoy that "he may be as good a man as ever walked and yet not the man for a steward."[24] Actually, Polke's eventual resignation from the mission field was wind in the sails to Parker's arguments as he believed that anyone who put their trust in the Board of Foreign Missions was lost. After Polke's resignation, he continued to work as an Agent for the mission and helped in the relocation of the northern tribes when they journeyed to the Indian

---

[23] Letter from Rice to McCoy written September 2, 1824, McCoy Papers, Reel 3.

[24] Letter dated September 8, 1824, McCoy Papers, Reel 3.

Territory.[25] Polke's letters show how that he, too, had become highly suspicious of the Board and how churches which supported the organization were being forced out of the Associations. Rice McCoy wrote to his brother to tell him that his local fellowship of churches in the Blue River Association had withdrawn from the Board on the grounds of their bad stewardship, suspected low morals and misuse of their printing presses to promote their own fame. Rice said the brethren were most shocked at the way the Board had used Mrs. Ann Judson, who recently visited England and the States, as a propaganda agent. As a result, the anti-Board feelings had turned into anti-mission feelings. To argue with these people, Rice said, was to try and stop a surging river in its course. A further piece of news from Rice was that his wife had given birth to a son who was to be called *William Carey*. There were obviously no anti-mission feelings in Rice McCoy's home.[26]

Government approbation and baptismal blessings followed by Maria McCoy's death

Towards the end of October, 1824 a commission arrived at the mission sent by Governor Cass to report on how things were going. One of the members, an army colonel, was a Roman Catholic and the McCoys were obviously anxious as to what he would say on seeing the 63 Indian pupils at evangelical prayer. The commissioners were not merely delighted with the excellency of all they saw but confessed that they were excited and thrilled by the success of the mission among the Indians. The commissioners stated firmly that the Government must feel itself under great obligation to support the McCoys in their work. Meanwhile further blessings as well as crosses came upon the missionaries. The bulk of the white hired workers who joined the mission, approached McCoy privately, telling him of their sins and need of forgiveness and peace with God. Two men thus came to profess Christ as their Savior and were baptized shortly after. Only a matter of days later, three whites were baptized on profession of faith and one former Roman Catholic was converted but died before he could be baptized. Now Indian children began to profess conversion. As more and more

---

[25] On May 25, 1825, McCoy wrote to Francis Wayland to say that only he, Polke and Simerwell were at the station. This may have been a reference to Charles Polke who worked at Carey for a short time.

[26] Letter dated November 27, 1824, McCoy Papers, Reel 3.

Indians joined the worship, less and less English was used in the services. The missionaries felt they should exercise caution at first before baptizing the Indians but it was so apparent that four of the older pupils were now the Lord's that they were baptized before the year was out as well as the blacksmith and the German cook. One of the missionaries wrote, "It seems that a celestial atmosphere may descend to earth, and may be breathed and enjoyed even in this literal wilderness."[27] The writer felt that he had never felt the presence of God as strongly as on that baptismal day.

By January, 1825 the young church witnessed its sixth baptismal service when another four Indian youths were baptized in the river. Two further baptismal services followed in the same month. Soon news came from Thomas that a similar work of grace was going on there and both Indians and whites had professed Christ and been baptized. There was more opposition, however, at Thomas both from the Roman Catholic French and the Indians, while Polke escaped being murdered by a hair's breadth. Soon however, an old Indian chief confessed Christ and was baptized in March of 1825. To crown the happiness, on March 17th, Robert Simerwell and Miss Fannie Goodridge who had done marvelous work in evangelizing the Indians, male and female, were united in marriage. Simerwell had been working as a blacksmith up to now so McCoy put in an application for him to be made a full missionary. Around this time Corbly Martin was also joined for life to a cousin of the McCoys and hoped to settle not too far from Carey. These happy scenes were darkened by the death of Maria Staughton, the McCoy's youngest daughter who had only lived eleven months. Maria was the third of the McCoys' daughters to die after Isaac and Christiana had become missionaries.[28]

President Monroe approves of giving the Indians their own home in the West

Despairing of the Board doing anything more for the Indians, McCoy had his ideas of Indian homelands reported in the press and continued to petition Congress about settlements west of the Mississippi. On January 13, 1825, the mission received a copy of the President's Annual Address and read that President Monroe had made

---

[27] *History of Baptist Indian Missions*, p. 254.

[28] See letter from McCoy to Staughton dated November 9, 1824, McCoy Papers, Reel 3.

Indian colonization a Government policy exactly in the terms suggested by McCoy. Fort Gibson and Fort Towson in present day Oklahoma were being used as communication centers from where the relocation of the tribes was to be organized. Typical of the views of the whites concerning Indian development, the so-called "civilized tribes"[29] were to be relocated first. Congress now envisaged the dividing line between the Indian Territory and the Union as being much the same as the line drawn by the British in 1763 and included present day Oklahoma and Kansas. White settlers north of the Red River had to be moved to Texas so that the Choctaws could be relocated in that area. After the relocation of the "civilized tribes," the so-called "wild tribes" were to follow. These included the Shawnees, Potawatomis, Chippewas, Munsees, Iowas, Sacs and Foxes, Wyandots and Kick-apoos. Now McCoy was in constant correspondence with the Secretary for War, Governor Cass and the United States Indian agents, planning the necessary reforms. Though McCoy's plans for the colonization of the Indian Territory were modified somewhat over the years, in the main, they were as described in his own words in 1837:

Plan of the Indian Territory

The country which we denominate the *Indian Territory,* is bounded as follows: Beginning at the source of a small river called Puncah, after a small tribe of Indians of that name, and running down the same eastwardly to Missouri river: thence down Missouri still eastwardly, about one hundred, and fifty miles: thence down Missouri southwardly, about two hundred miles, to the western line of the State of Missouri: thence south along said western line, to the N. W. corner of the State of Arkansas: thence southwardly on the western line of Arkansas: about seventy-eight miles to Arkansas river: thence south on the line of Arkansas to Red River: thence up Red River westwardly, to a meridian two hundred miles west: thence northwardly to the beginning. The whole about equal to a tract of six hundred miles long, and two hundred miles wide.

It is proposed to limit the Territory to the distance of two hundred miles west of Arkansas and Missouri because the country farther west, for the distance of several hundred miles, is uninhabitable on account of the absence of wood.

---

[29] Choctaws, Chickasaws, Cherokees, Creeks, and Seminoles.

The above limits have not yet been fixed by the Government of the U. States, but a report favorable to those limits, and a Bill for thus establishing them, have been submitted to the consideration of Congress by the Committee of indian Affairs of the Senate; and there is little, if any doubt, that Government will decide in favor of that bill.

Upon the propriety of establishing an Indian Territory, the southern boundary of which shall be Red River, and the eastern the States of Arkansas. and Missouri and Missouri river, there appears to be great unanimity of sentiment among government men. A Bill to this effect, and similar in its provisions to that before the Senate has been before the House of Representatives for the last three sessions of Congress. The condition of the tribes within the Territory, and their relation to one another, and to the U. States, are such as daily increase the necessity of civil organization.

The outlines of the plan of organization, are briefly the following, viz: Delegates are to be chosen by the several tribes, to represent them in a general council, once a year, or oftener if necessary. The character of this council will be similar to that of the legislative council of one of our Territories. It will be competent to enact laws of a general nature for the Territory. These laws will take effect after they have been approved by the President of the U. States. Each tribe will enact laws which relate merely to its own internal concerns: similar to the action of townships, or of city corporations. The tribes thus confederated, will choose a delegate, who must be an Indian, to represent them at the seat of government of the U. States, during each session of Congress; and who will act as agent for his constituents. He will be paid by the U. States and his compensation will be equal to that of a member of Congress. All civil offices, excepting two, which shall be created in the Territory by this organization, will be filled by Indians, if such be found competent to discharge the duties. In addition to the security given the tribes of their possessions by treaty stipulations, they may hold their lands by patents from the government of the U. States.[30]

---

[30] See *Periodical Account of Baptist Missions within the Indian Territory for the Year Ending December 31, 1836,* pp.6-7, and also *Remarks on the Practicability of Indian Reform, Embracing their Colonization,* 1829.

This land was situated in territories known as "Unorganized" which had not become states within the Union. Nowadays this area would comprise the States of Oklahoma[31] and Arkansas[32] but it was widened to include much of present day Kansas, including the Kansas side of Kansas City and also the Westport, Jackson County, Missouri side of Kansas City, because McCoy made his resettlement headquarters at Westport.[33] In February, 1825, however, Monroe lost his presidency to John Quincy Adams and as the colonization of the Indian Territory had been pioneered by Monroe, many felt that the cause of Indian relocation was now lost. Happily, Calhoun was elected as Vice-President and he remained a supporter of McCoy's plans. Cass, too, was always ready to support McCoy's aims. Meanwhile, McCoy persuaded his friends among the Indian Agents and Congressmen to send in recommendations to the Secretary of War on behalf of the Board concerning Indian colonization which were also accompanied by their recommendations to the Secretary to support McCoy in his endeavors.[34]

Stop and go all the way

Now the school had sixty-seven pupils and gifts of money and clothing were coming in from friends all over the States. Spencer Cone of New York was particularly active in promoting such work. One worry for McCoy was that the Board had again changed tactics and were advising McCoy to draw on them but it was obvious that they were giving McCoy this advice only when money came in from the Government which was supposed to be used for Government projects only. Luther Rice's letters on behalf of the Board at this time must have been the most frustrating one could receive. They were stop and go all the way, one letter saying please draw on us and the next saying

---

[31] This name was proposed by the Rev. Allen Wright, principal chief of the Choctaw Nation, in 1866, and was derived from two Choctaw words, *okla*, meaning "people," and *humma*, meaning "red."

[32] From the Quapaw, meaning "Downstream People".

[33] Non-Americans usually imagine Kansas City to be in Kansas only, whereas it is situated on both sides of the Kansas river and thus in the states of Kansas and Missouri.

[34] See William McLean's and the two Johnson brothers' letter to the Secretary of War dated February 23, 1825, McCoy Papers, Reel 4.

that though McCoy had done as recommended, the Board had difficulty meeting the bill and could McCoy offset it with donations? McCoy stipulated that Government money was to be used on Government property and schooling alone but as this financing was in the hands of the Board, he had no oversight of what was happening.[35] His suspicions were deepened when the Board did not publish his financial report for 1823, in which he had laid open all his accounts. Nor did the Board publish his financial report for 1824 or 1825. This was not Luther Rice's fault as the Board were playing the same cat and mouse game with him.

The Board continues to speak with two different voices

McCoy explained to Staughton on March 8, 1825 that the public had been promised that the missions accounts would be laid before them, indeed, they demanded it. McCoy had done his duty so why should the Board not do theirs? McCoy also wanted to know why the Board hesitated in appointing agents for the Indian mission to collect funds.[36] Ironically enough, just at this time, Francis Wayland Jr., a Board member, wrote from Boston on March 9, 1825 to chide McCoy for going to the newspapers to appeal for funds and not approaching the Board to publish his reports who would do a better job of it and also reach more people with their magazines than the local newspapers. McCoy replied to Wayland on March 19th to tell him that he had been trying to persuade the Board to do just that for three years.[37] Simerwell then sent Wayland copies of all the receipts of the last year, obviously hoping that he would put pressure on the Board to publish them.[38] The pressure seems to have worked as the missionaries received a note from Luther Rice dated April 2, promising them that their three unpublished annual reports would be printed that Spring.

---

[35] See Rice's letter to McCoy dated March 26 and March 31 which illustrate this dilemma. See also Rice's letter to Carey dated May 11, 1824, McCoy Papers, Reel 3.

[36] McCoy Papers, Reel 4.

[37] Ibid.

[38] Copy of letter dated March 30, ibid, Reel 4.

Everything in the Board's garden was portrayed to the Baptist churches as being very lovely

In the next Board of Managers Circular dated June 6, 1825, the Carey Mission was referred to in the following optimistic words with no mention of the trials the missionaries were going through because, they, the authors of this glowing report, were not fulfilling their commitments:

> On the Carey mission station, in the Michigan Territory, during the past year, the dews of heaven have descended. In the waters of St. Joseph, nine white persons, attached to the mission, and eleven native Indians, have been baptized, in the name of the Lord Jesus. Other indications of the progress of the gospel of the Redeemer, have appeared, and the hearts of brother M'Coy and his associates are filled with joyous expectations.

Although the Columbian College was on its last legs financially, the following reference must have been judged by many to have been a last effort to gain interest in its development and growth. The high spiritual and moral standards the Board professed to require of the students was enough to put any humble aspirant off and the fact that the Board were going to double the college's size must have raised many a question mark in the minds of Baptist readers. In the circular, Staughton wrote:

> The number of students in the Columbian College increases. Among those devoted to the service of the ministry, such are found, whose exemplary conduct, whose ardent piety, whose assiduity in their studies, and whose devotedness to the kingdom and glory of the Lord Jesus, encourage the persuasion that they will become, in a high degree, blessings to the church. A new edifice, of the same magnitude with the existing one, is ascending."

Concerning the College Treasurer and Agent, Staughton wrote:

> Unremitted in his labours of love, brother Rice, the Agent of the Convention, continues his evangelic course. That the blessings of the Lord may succeed his endeavours, must be the prayer of all who are looking for and hastening to the coming of the day of God."

All these fine words to the churches at large seemed to be chosen to disguise the fact that the college had debts of many thousands of dollars, and its Board were blindly going into further enormous debts so as to double its size.[39] It would have paid the Board to have honestly declared to the Baptist public the precarious state they were in. Instead, the public were led to believe for another year that the college was going through a period of financial, spiritual and material growth and was in no need. This was against the wishes of Luther Rice who insisted that quarterly statements of the college's financial situation should be published. Nobody on the Board took any notice of him.[40] When, in 1826, the Board at last told the churches of their mismanagement, they washed their hands of any blame and made Luther Rice, their most faithful and loyal fundraiser, their scapegoat.

Spiritual and material blessings at Carey draw the bootleggers

The missionaries were now able to bring peace between the rival tribes at Carey and Thomas. As game had become scare in the area, the missionaries encouraged the Indians to grow corn and vegetables, plant fruit trees and keep cows and sheep and some thirty families settled down to a peaceful agricultural life. The pupils and missionaries always helped where they could and loaned implements and transport facilities. A flour mill was built so that the Indian farmers could grind their corn. More conversions and baptisms followed both among the white workers and Indians. McCoy did not mention the separate names of the newly converted but merely wrote of them as being "many young men whom we had employed at different times as labourers," and "many of our pupils and some other Indians."[41]

Hearing of the prosperous state of the Indians, evil white traders now settled on the border of the Indians' lands and started selling whiskey to the Indians. Soon the Indians were trading everything they had to purchase the "fire water," even the bedding of the pupils at school. The new Agent of Indian Affairs, John Tipton, at Fort

---

[39] See Staughton's letter to McCoy on the subject dated July 30, 1825, McCoy Papers, Reel 4.

[40] See Appendix on Luther Rice.

[41] *History of Baptist Indian Missions*, p. 264.

Wayne, wrote to McCoy asking for his help in bringing the bootleggers to bay and McCoy, because of his intimate contact with the Indians, was able to bring forward evidence concerning this illicit trade and did not hesitate to forward this to Tipton and to Lewis Cass.[42] McCoy felt powerless to protect the Indians but realized that they would listen to those of their own people who were respected.

McCoy applies to Columbian College to accept qualified Indians as students

McCoy believed that his mature pupils should now be trained for responsible positions in Indian society as ministers, businessmen and politicians. He felt that if he could persuade the Government to pay for their training at Columbian College, this would achieve many positive aims. As the Board were encumbered with much of the financing of the college, Government grants would ease their financial problems, the step would make the Board more conscious of their responsibilities to Indian Baptists and the young Indians would be fitted out to protect their own people from the evils of the whites.

Thus, on July 11, 1825, in a long letter of eight pages, McCoy wrote to Dr. Staughton, his closest friend on the Board, asking him to consider the prospects of opening the college to the Indian leaders of the future.[43] He also laid out detailed plans of how the youths might be financed, mentioning Government aid which was given other colleges in similar circumstances. McCoy suggested that the College need only advertize that the Indian students were coming and enough donations would come in to pay for the Indians' studies. McCoy gave the Board a detailed report concerning the degree of education the possible candidates had attained. Fearing that there might be difficulties at the Board, McCoy also applied to Baptist Seminaries not under the Board, yet stressing that Columbian College was first preference. The Baptist Theological Institution at Hamilton, New York, a non-Board institution, immediately offered to accept the young men.

McCoy waited month after month for a reply from Staughton and from the other Board members to whom he had applied, but although these gentlemen wrote regularly, thanking McCoy for his letters, they did not so much as mention the subject of Indian students

---

[42] See, for instance, McCoy's letters to Tipton dated March 23, and Cass, March 24, 1825, McCoy Papers, Reel 4.

[43] McCoy Papers, Reel 4.

at the Columbian College. At last, Luther Rice made a most brief and unsatisfactory response to McCoy's request on October 7, 1825, writing, "I also expect we shall get aid for the young Indians you have recommended." Unsatisfactory as this statement was, McCoy took it to indicate that his request had been accepted and he could proceed to the Columbian College with the Indian youths but, nevertheless, wrote again to Rice on October 31st asking for confirmation and more information, also hinting that he was looking for institutes of higher education for some of his promising female pupils. On November 21st, McCoy told Staughton that he was anxiously awaiting a definite reply from the Board concerning the seven boys who were designated for Columbian College and requested again the Board's help in finding a college place for two Potawatomi girls. McCoy emphasized that when the Indians received their own country, they must be in a position to administrate it well which they could only do if they had the necessary training.[44] A few days later, McCoy received a letter from Luther Rice dated October 31, 1825 saying concerning the Indian youths, "I think it desirable they should, as soon as practicable, come on - I hope you will hear from the Cor. Sec.y soon on the subject."

Rice's letter was enough for McCoy and since he had been invited by the Board to attend the Baptist Convention in New York the following Spring, he decided to combine the task of taking the boys to Columbian College and attending the Convention, so made plans to set off at once. A letter to Francis Wayland dated November 24,[45] as McCoy was just about to set off for the Columbian College, reveals that McCoy was rather frustrated that the Board had not replied in detail to his report on the qualifications of the seven Indian youths made over four months previously and that they did not seem to have consulted the Government adequately enough on how to finance the Indians' education.

Meanwhile, McCoy received a letter from his sons Josephus (b. April 13, 1808) and Rice (b. January 26, 1807), telling of resignations on the staff, expulsions and suspensions of students and of the dire financial circumstances in the Columbian College. Rice wrote that they could not understand why the college had embarked on an ambitious scheme to double its premises when it was obviously in a state of bankruptcy.[46]

---

[44] McCoy Papers, Reel 4.

[45] Ibid.

[46] Letter dated December 8, 1825, McCoy Papers, Reel 4.

McCoy continued to write to Congressmen, explaining to them the pros and cons of an Indian relocation west of the Mississippi. He seemed now to be sure that legislation would be made to that end but wished to secure the rights of missionaries to enter the Indian area and provide Christian teaching and schools for the Indians. On October 2, 1825, McCoy wrote to Senator William Hendricks of Indiana, applying for the post of Agent, to organize the relocation of the Miamis and Potawatomis from the Fort Wayne, St. Joseph River areas, saying that he would take up residence in the new country so as to continue his work among these tribes.[47]

The Polkes follow up their threat to resign

The Polkes with their very large family had done great work in the short time they were on the mission stations but now, at the beginning of July, 1825, they felt they had to resign for the sake of their growing children. The "toils and privations" which Polke mentioned in his last letter while at Carey, had been too much. Humanly speaking, McCoy must have been very upset about Polke's resignation because this jeopardized the entire Ottawa work and the "toils and privations" which Polke had experienced were the general lot of Christian workers in the Indian mission. However, there is not an iota of resentment in any of McCoy's remarks on Polke's leaving the mission and both families remained in deep Christian harmony, love and friendship over the years. McCoy answered Polke's letter of resignation by writing:

> My wife and myself beg you to accept from us in particular this sincere assurance of continued regard for you as a Christian, and friendship and respect for you as a relation. We desire sister Polke, now absent, to accept for herself the same assurance of friendship, fellowship and affection. We so pray that our gracious God may preserve, sustain and comfort you both and bless your family with good things, and that at last it may be found that you have not sustained damage by your well-meant efforts to benefit the unfortunate Indians. We pray that your lives may be happy and useful.[48]

---

[47] McCoy Papers, Reel 4.

[48] Ibid.

McCoy proceeds to the Columbian College with his seven Indian students

On December 17, 1825 McCoy wrote separate letters to Rice and Staughton saying that he could wait no longer for more details concerning the Board's acceptance of the Indian students and would set off on January 10th, bringing the seven youths who were baptized members of the church to be placed at Columbian College, and two non-Christian boys who would be placed at Princeton, New Jersey. He would travel to Ohio first where the boys would be fitted out with clothing and then proceed to Washington, trusting that the Board would not only respect his decision but welcome it. He hoped to arrive at the college towards the end of February.[49] On the same day, Rice wrote to McCoy, not mentioning the Indian boys at all but merely begging, almost ordering, McCoy to use his influence with the Government to obtain a grant for $20,000 so that they could continue to extend the college premises. "Let me ask you to do this immediately," were his final words.[50]

On January 10, Lucius Bolles wrote to McCoy, telling him that the Foreign Mission department of the Baptist Convention had come under new (his) management and he had found their treasury empty and that McCoy would understand that overseas missions had preference over the work among Indians. This alone was enough to signal "Danger!" to McCoy as up to now, the Convention had always included Indian missions under the rubric "foreign missions." Furthermore, Bolles wrote that it was "inexpedient to remove Natives from their own people, for purpose of education." Bolles had also found McCoy's suggestion that a group of Eastern Baptists, including Mr. and Mrs. Bolles could pledge themselves to support an Indian pupil "inexpedient." This was Dr. Lucius Bolles round about way of saying, "No" to McCoy's wishes concerning placing the Indian youths in the Columbian College without mentioning the subject directly. He suggested that the Government should be persuaded to set up special centers of further education for Indians where they could be among their own people. McCoy was to become used to this evasive way of being advised by the Board. But Bolles advice arrived far too late to stop McCoy's journey which he had started while Bolles was penning his letter.

---

[49] Ibid.

[50] Ibid.

To illustrate what a turmoil the Board was in, Luther Rice wrote McCoy on January 13, 1826, saying: "I am glad you are coming on with the young Indians and I have no doubt they can be accommodated and educated here." Rice does not mention Bolles but says he will consult Staughton and Brown on the matter, which rather suggests that nothing had been officially discussed concerning the Indian boys becoming students at the college at all. It seemed that Bolles was saying, "No" on his own initiative and Rice was saying, "Yes" on his.[51]

While McCoy was on the move, his brother Rice McCoy wrote from Livonia to say that there was trouble in the Wabash and White River Associations because of Daniel Parker and that the Baptist churches were now being split into pro- and anti-mission churches as a result of his campaigning. It seemed that wherever an Association meeting was held on the Western frontier, Parker would demand a hearing and not rest until he obtained one, only to set brother warring with brother. Among the churches nearer Livonia, Rice informed Isaac, Arianism seemed to be growing.

An unacceptable proposition

McCoy's party set off for Washington on their long journey in the worst of winter weather. McCoy, who bore the entire responsibility of guiding the young boys safely to their destination was struck down with the fever again. On February 22nd, the party was met by a courier with a letter from Mr. Rice ordering McCoy to take the youths to the Choctaw Academy in Kentucky, saying "this course would satisfy the board, but no other would." In another letter, however, Rice said this was providing McCoy could get a Government grant for the boys.[52] This was an unacceptable state of affairs. The Choctaw Academy was run on a private commercial basis by Senator Richard Johnson who was something of a rival to McCoy in obtaining government grants for schools. His "academy" was run on a pay-as-you-learn basis, with the Indians providing a large percentage of the finances. The school was not attached to the Baptist churches and only loosely "Christian" besides being in no way higher academically than the Carey school. On the contrary, Johnson's pupils were trained in

---

[51] Ibid.

[52] See Rice's letters of January 27 and 28, also Staughton's of January 28 to McCoy, McCoy Papers, Reel 4.

manual skills rather than academic. McCoy wanted to give his pupils a better academic training not a worse. Furthermore, the school had only twenty-one pupils, compared to the seventy in the Carey School. In spite of Johnson's personal use of a $6,000 annuity earmarked for the Choctaws themselves, he was badly in debt and his school's future was in question. There would have thus been no point whatsoever in the Indians going there.[53]

The Board's ignorance of Indian traditions, needs and aspirations

This unexpected reaction from the Board was tantamount to saying that a higher education would be denied suitable Indians who ought to merely learn to be manual workers. The Board had also not considered the fact that the Chippewa, Potawatomi and Miami youngsters would be better housed under the auspices of neutral whites than among Indians of tribes who were traditionally hostile to them. It would be putting the so-called "wild Indians" among to so-called "civilized tribes." Again, the Board had completely failed in their understanding of the customs, needs and financial circumstances of the Indians. Here, obviously, Bolles' influence could be seen. He believed Indians were better off with their "own kind," not realizing the enormous cultural and political differences which divided one tribe from another. Staughton now wrote, and by way of apologizing for the new move on the part of the Board, said that he had mislaid McCoy's initial inquiry concerning the Indian students, therefore he had not been able to deal with McCoy's questions. He told McCoy that Johnson had visited the Board and persuaded them to use their influence to have Indians sent to his school which made McCoy, now very ill, eager to press on and argue his case personally with the Board, feeling his was better than Johnson's. McCoy was on very good terms with Johnson and knew that the Senator was very skilled at gaining

---

[53] Due to enormous grants which Johnson procured from the Government and directly from the Indians, Choctaw Academy grew fast until there were around 90 pupils about a year later. Rice and Josephus McCoy visited the school in Kentucky during April, 1827 but confessed that there was little done there to improve the condition of the Indians and they did not appear to be occupied in any way but were encouraged to remain "in idleness entirely." See the McCoys' letter to their father dated April 26, 1827, McCoy Papers, Reel 5. The two students felt it wrong that Johnson had received all of the Potawatomi grant stipulated for schools among the Potawatomi but he was using the money for a Kentucky school miles away from the tribe.

opportunities for himself through his political efforts. This skill helped Johnson to become Vice-President of the United States from 1837-1841 under President Martin Van Buren. There is no doubt at all that the Board looked to Johnson, who was related to the Secretary of War, to use his influence in gaining the $20,000 grant they had applied for from the Government. They also needed Johnson's vote when Congress considered their plea to have their enormous previous debts canceled. Perhaps Staughton's final argument was the most distressing coming from a Christian missionary college. Staughton said that the white students would object to Indians being placed among them. As things developed, this argument was shown to be completely untrue and was a most shameful, artificial excuse on the part of the Board.

A President not allowed to preside over his college

Leaving most of the boys in Maryland where he had found temporary lodgings for them, McCoy sped on to Washington where he met Dr. Staughton who presently told him that he had "strenuously opposed" the measure to have McCoy and the youths sent to Kentucky. As Rice, too, had sent at least two letters to McCoy encouraging him to bring the Indians to Columbian College, all this must have been very puzzling to McCoy who must have wondered what opponents he now had on the Board and how it could come about that the President himself was not allowed to preside over the college. The new broom, alias Lucius Bolles, was now striving to sweep away the Board's debts and put the organization on a stable financial basis. The parole was now commercial ability rather than Christian, or even charitable, liability. This meant, as Evan Jones and Isaac McCoy, the Board's most successful and prominent missionaries to the Indians found out, a strong curtailing of their work.[54] There was currently a strong lobby in the Board who were campaigning to exclude Indians from the college on the grounds that they were too expensive. As it did not cost the Board more to educate their white missionaries' children than the Indians, this argument must be seen as threadbare and was used to disguise other reasons. There were those on the Board, who were certainly using this argument because of racist reasons and others who believed that it was a sheer waste of time educating a race that would die out anyway.

---

[54] Bolles even insisted on planning McCoy's and Jones' food budget for them, forbidding them even to consume bread made of flour, tea, coffee, or sugar.

The Columbian College students petition to allow the Indians to study at their college

Rice and Josephus McCoy, who had been medical students at the college since early 1825,[55] organized a petition to accept the Indian boys which was unanimously approved of by the students and presented to the faculty. Thus the Board's argument that the white students would not accept the Indian boys was shown to be totally false. The students even promised to finance several of the Indians from their own pockets. Then the truth came out. McCoy's plea to the Government concerning financing the Indian's wider education *had* been heard. A grant of $100 a year per head had been promised to each Indian pupil so that the Board's financial argument against the Carey scholars was seen to stand on a very shaky foundation. The Board and college faculty, however, remained adamant, arguing that there was no room for Indians at Columbian College. The students, however, continued to rally round their Indian brethren and gave McCoy a generous donation so that whichever college the Indians were able to visit, something was done to help them when in need. McCoy was quick to make this gesture public by writing to the *Columbian Star* and telling them of the whole story of the student's generosity and the Board's decision to reject the Indians.[56] Also, McCoy wrote to the local newspapers along the route he had taken with his Indian pupils, thanking the people for their neighborly help. In this way all those who had helped the Indian boys were thanked and the entire country heard that the American Baptist Board of Foreign Missions had a college to promote missionary work but they would not accept those who wished to be trained as indigenous missionaries and shut Native Americans out. Less polemic articles were sent to the Baptist denominational magazines. A report in the *Baptist Magazine* was read by the mother of a highly qualified doctor who wrote to say her son would be pleased to accept one of the Indian students as his trainee-assistant. Another lady read McCoy's report in the *Columbian Star* and immediately offered to assist two Indian boys finance their college education. Other letters came in from societies who had read McCoy's accounts and pledged themselves to assist the Indians in their education. The secretaries of several worthy Christian colleges wrote

---

[55] Columbian College had been given a charter to teach Medicine in 1821 and commenced giving tuition in November, 1824.

[56] See McCoy's letter to the Editor of the *Columbian Star* dated March 17, 1826.

to McCoy, offering an open door to his pupils. Thus, though things had not gone as McCoy had planned, the black cloud turned out to have a silver lining and it looked as though further education for Indians in the Union would now become an accepted proposition.

Bolles reacts by advising McCoy to remove his sons from Columbian College

Luther Rice had made it plain to McCoy in a letter dated December 26, 1825 that the Board would be grateful if McCoy could use his influence with the Government and procure grants for Columbian College. McCoy had been successful in his way but the Board had wanted to use the money as they wished and invest it in the fabric of the building rather than in the future lives of the Indians. Here was a strange situation, indeed. The work Baptists such as McCoy and Evan Jones were doing was now recognized nationwide and a real work of grace was being done among the Indians. It was chiefly through the influence of these men that the Government had began to be more humane towards the Native Americans. Indeed, it was through such work that the Government's eye had been fixed on Baptist schools and colleges and had moved them to offer a supporting hand. The Chicago Treaty of 1821 indicated that the Government even preferred to support Baptist Indian missions than those of the Roman Catholics, Presbyterians and Methodists. Yet, the Board who campaigned for worldwide evangelism on paper, in practice appeared to be too racist to take the gospel to their next door neighbors. Worse was to come. The whole Indian Mission was seen as a drain on funds that could have been applied to the more exotic and romantic foreign mission movement. Dr. Bolles therefore persuaded the Board not only to reject Indian candidates but also to refuse to finance the education of family members of their own missionaries to the Indians. On June 17, 1826, Lucius Bolles, now Corresponding Secretary of the reorganized Baptist Missions Board with its seat at Boston, wrote to McCoy, informing him that it was considered "inexpedient" to keep Rice and Josephus at the school and they must seek an education elsewhere and not at the Board's expense.[57] This move on the part of

---

[57] Soon afterwards, due to mismanagement and incompetent financial speculation, Columbian College had to be given up and was taken over by a consortium of other denominations. The Board lost credibility throughout the Baptist churches, especially in the West and South.

Bolles led to at least three resignations on the college staff, including the McCoys' tutor and guardian, Mr. Wait.[58] This is hardly surprising as, only a few months before, Dr. Staughton had written to McCoy saying:

> At our late examinations, which occurred about the middle of the current month, I have the happiness to inform you that each of your sons distinguished himself well. It imparted the most entire satisfaction to the Trustees and the Faculty. I have no hesitation in saying that we have not at the College two more meritorious students. Their diligence is uniform and their deportment exemplary. I trust, that yourself and Mrs. McCoy will find in them abundant sources of consolation.[59]

Hamilton College, New York accepts the Indian students

On being told that the Indians could under no circumstance be admitted at the college, McCoy and his students turned their weary horses towards Hamilton, New York where McCoy wrote, "Here we were welcomed by the Rev. Nathaniel Kendrick, D. D., President, and all others of the faculty, and by the students and the people of that neighborhood." Christians from far and near sent in their donations to supplement the Government's $100 dollar per pupil. We find McCoy writing years later, "No doubt, Heaven approved and will reward the kind attentions which these Indian boys received while at Hamilton. The expenses of this undertaking had not been incurred at the cost of the board."[60]

An ultimatum sent to the Board

McCoy prepared a lengthy 27 page report with some thirty-two lines to a page, outlining the history of his missions from the year

---

[58] See letter from Josephus McCoy to his father dated July 5, 1826. See also McCoy's long and passionate plea to the Board concerning the education of missionary and Indian children dated September 27, 1826, McCoy Papers, Reel 5.

[59] Written July 30, 1825, McCoy Papers, Reel 4.

[60] *History of Baptist Indian Missions*, p. 271.

The Hamilton Literary and Theological Institute located at Hamilton, New York. This stone structure was built in 1823, just three years before Isaac McCoy was there with his seven Indian students from the Carey Mission in Michigan. "They belonged to the Ottawa, Chippewa, and Potawatomie tribes and rode into the village on Indian ponies to the astonishment of townspeople and students." One man later recalled "seeing them throw tomahawks at a mark on a tree about three rods away and the bystanders' amazement at their accuracy in hitting it with the handles up or down as the audience requested." Howard D. Williams *A History of Colgate University, 1819-1969* (New York: Van Nostrand Reinhold Co., 1969), pp. 26, 47. Others noted the fondness of the Indians for singing hymns. John Tecumseh Jones, one of the seven, later became a preacher and was instrumental in founding of Ottawa University in Kansas (Ibid., p. 48).

1817 and his ideas concerning the duties of a missionary, with his views concerning the necessity of a self-ruled Indian state and the education which would be required for the Indians who would be called on to manage such a state. It is a remarkable piece of Christian zeal combined with great statesmanship. This document was presented to the Board of Foreign Missions with a view to its being laid before the Baptist Convention so that there would never be any doubt what McCoy believed, what he felt could be put into effect and what role he felt the Convention and the Board of Managers could be playing in such a plan. It was as if McCoy was sending out a challenge to the Board, "Accept this and we can work together. Reject this and we must go our various ways." As matters turned out, the Board continued to be as they had always been, they accepted McCoy's plans with one voice and rejected them with another. It was this ambivalence in the Board's nature against which McCoy was powerless and never knew how to act. Once again, with hindsight we may believe that now was the time McCoy ought to have broken with the Board and gone his own way, but somehow, in the Providence and mercies of God, McCoy still felt bound to a Mr. Facing-Both-Ways, probably merely because that figure sometimes faced his way and he was thankful for any means, however deficient, that, together with other means, might help him accomplish the work God had given him to do. This ambivalence towards McCoy is illustrated in Bolles' letter informing him that his sons were no longer welcome at the college. In the same letter, Bolles said that the Board had met and resolved:

> That Rev. Isaac McCoy one of our missionaries at Carey Station, be appointed the Agent of the Board to select a country West of Missouri and East of the Rocky mountains for a purpose of Indian Colonisation, subject to the instructions of the Board and that he proceed whenever he shall be directed by said Board.[61]

Important evidence in face of the Board's later denials

This letter is an important document in judging the Board's later criticism of McCoy that he was never appointed as a missionary of the Board to such a position and that his work in relocating the Indians was purely a government occupation which proved that he had left the Board's services and his position as a missionary. Here, McCoy

---

[61] Written at Salem, June 17, 1826.

is clearly authorized by the Corresponding Secretary of the Board as the Board's Agent and missionary to select a country for Indian colonization. Even this good news, however, was accompanied with news of developments which cannot have pleased McCoy. Bolles told him that the Board were consulting the American Board of Commissioners for Foreign missions on the Indian question. The latter Board was a consortium representing Presbyterian and Congregationalist churches which was decidedly against a relocation of the Indians, even though their three major Indian mission stations Harmony, Union and Dwight had sought to influence their patrons to support a permanent home for the Indians west of the Mississippi. The American Board of Commissioners seemed as far away from the grass roots of missionary activity as the Baptist Board so it was probably only natural that they should merge their thinking. McCoy was able to share fellowship with the Presbyterians far easier than with the Methodists but he did think that their views concerning the Indians "deserved more credit for the piety of their hearts than for the information of their heads."[62] The American Board of Commissioners were petitioning the Government to "spare the Indians," which McCoy felt meant in practice that the Indians should be left where they were until they were annihilated. It is clear that McCoy felt that the Baptist Board was consulting too much with the Presbyterians and Congregationalists and "drank so deeply" the views of the other denominations that he feared they would do nothing to save the Indians from being wiped out.[63]

McCoy seeks higher education for both sexes

Back at Carey, it was a relief for McCoy to know that the older and more intelligent boys were now at college but the school was producing female scholars of equal ability. There were now seventy pupils at the school which was conducted on coeducational lines for want of female teachers, there being forty-two males and twenty-eight females.[64] Thus McCoy wrote to the Board, though he must have had his tongue in his cheek, asking them to consider doing something

---

[62] *History of Baptist Indian Missions*, p. 379-380.

[63] Ibid, pp. 377-378.

[64] See McCoy's report to John Leib at the Department of Indian Affairs dated August 24, 1826, McCoy Papers, Reel 5.

towards the higher education of female Indians. Again, tongue in cheek, McCoy added, providing this is without cost to the Board. McCoy stated that if this was not possible at present, would the Board consider campaigning for such an institution? As McCoy ought to have realized, "the board were not much interested," but McCoy found an institution in Ohio that was willing to take on intelligent young Indian ladies for certain short-term courses.

In his endeavor to promote the education of young Indian adults of both sexes, McCoy met up with his first major co-ed problem. One of the students enrolled at Hamilton who was a baptized church member, had wished to marry one of the missions female pupils but McCoy had advised the couple to put off marriage until they were qualified. While the young man was at Hamilton, his fiancée gave birth to a still-born, premature child. McCoy was at first deeply shocked and angry that the young couple had behaved in such a way but then he was filled with remorse at the fact that he had been instrumental in causing the illegitimate birth by his advice which, by hindsight, had proved to be wrong. McCoy did not brush over this shared responsibility in his report of the sad incident to the Board and to the Hamilton College. His letter to the Hamilton student is a fine display of pastoral advice and care, informing the young man that he should return and marry his fiancée at once and that he was suspended from church membership for a time. Nevertheless ways were explained to the young Indian how he could return to the fold of the church. The young mother of the still-born child had not dared mention her pregnancy and had not sought help when complications arose. It is obvious that McCoy was thinking had he been more open to the wishes of his students, the couple might now have been happy parents.[65] Lykins visited the wayward young man who was most repentant and professed that he loved the girl deeply and wanted to marry her but also wished to continue his studies. A letter of deep repentance from this person dated June 4, 1827[66] is extant and in beautiful writing. In it, he tells McCoy how he expected to receive a letter from him full of curses because of his conduct but found that McCoy had written in deep tenderness, goodness and kindness and that he was a father indeed.

---

[65] See McCoy's letters on the subject throughout July, 1826, McCoy Papers, Reel 5.

[66] McCoy Papers, Reel 5.

The Board appoints new missionaries but reject the Family Rules

McCoy showed some anxiety concerning the continued work among the Ottawas at Thomas but Robert Simerwell had now contacted two men from Cincinnati, Jotham Meeker and W. M. Crosley who asked to be taken on as missionaries and were accepted by the missionary family and the Board towards the end of 1825. This meant that staff numbers remained constant and there was new hope for the Thomas station. Mr. Crosley stayed from November 24, 1825 and left the following May but Mr. Meeker stayed on. In 1826 a Mr. and Mrs. Leonard Slater and a Miss Lucretia Purchase were added to the list of missionaries, this time directly appointed by the Board, which was a departure from the mission's accepted practice. Furthermore, the Slaters were made directly answerable to the Board which contradicted the *Family Rules* of the mission which the Board had previously accepted as binding. Mr. Meeker, though only 21 years of age, settled down immediately in the work, at first as a teacher and preacher although he had been trained for seven years in Cincinnati as a printer, which was really the only formal education he had. Nevertheless, Meeker proved himself to be a skilled linguist and was able to master three tribal languages and reduce them to a phonetic script of his own invention. After spending two years moving between Carey and Thomas, and a relatively long period away from the mission due to domestic problems, he eventually became Superintendent of the Ottawa Mission.

Meeker's naming ceremony

The Indians usually gave a special Indian name to their own children when they had proven their worth, so the Ottawas decided to "name" Meeker according to his character. McCoy describes the naming ceremony in his *History of Baptist Indian Missions*:

> I was on the eve of setting out, when they desired me to tarry a short time, until they could bestow on Mr. Meeker a name. They conferred with me privately on the propriety of the measure, and on the suitableness of a name which they had proposed amongst themselves. We then all became seated, in a serious manner, as of a matter of great moment had been on hand, when the old chief, Blackskin, arose and shook the hand of all the whites, both male and female; then turning to me, said, 'My brother, it is nothing bad that I am now about to say. We are all pleased that you have

238

brought this young man to live with us. We are happy to hear that he is a speaker of things that are good. It is difficult for us to pronounce his English name, and we therefore desire to give him an Indian name. We have decided that his name shall be Mano-keke-toh. We have given him a good name. We hope he will remain with us, to teach us and our children good things, so that our children will be benefited, and be worthy of good names which you will give them.' He concluded by giving Mr. Meeker the hand, addressing him by his new name. I made a brief response, and also gave Mr. Meeker the hand, under address of his new name. On similar occasions of conferring a name among themselves, the recipients, or one of his friends, is expected to give a feast; we were happy that this part of the ceremony could be dispensed with upon the present occasion.[67]

The name given to Meeker shows how the Indians had understood and appreciated his ministry. It means "He that speaks good words" or "A preacher of righteousness."

McCoy turns directly to the Baptist Convention for help

From a material point of view, and because all resources available to the senior missionaries were still being shared, the mission was now in a more comfortable position. The teachers, blacksmiths and bakers were theoretically financially secure because of government grants but these were obviously being used by the Board to finance the rest of the mission's work, assisted by a few direct grants from friends of the mission. Moreover, whenever the Government asked for a flour mill or blacksmith's shop to be erected, the costs had to be paid by the mission on the spot which then the Board applied to the Government in order to recover such costs. This turned out to be a most impractical method. A typical example of this problem was the grist mill that the government built at Carey in the summer of 1825. The contractors demanded $850 of McCoy who was compelled to pay and then plead with the Board to meet this debt with the appropriate Government grant. Rice replied on October 7, saying that he had no capital to pay for the mill but McCoy could draw on the

---

[67] pp. 317-318. See also William G. Cutler's description of the naming ceremony in his *History of the State of Kansas, Indian History, Part 7, Ottawas.*

Board for $150 which was his usual quarterly allowance.[68] Several missionaries and a large team of hired workers were presently working at the mission stations, employed by the Mission Board whose responsibility it should have been to finance their work. But, no funds were forthcoming from the Board's missionary and charity funds. McCoy, however, had heard that friends had donated money to the Board earmarked for the Carey Mission and so we find McCoy writing regularly to the Board, asking for these funds to be used to pay off the mission's debts.[69] Because of this fact and because he had become dubious of receiving any backing from the Board regarding Indian resettlement, McCoy now turned to the Baptist General Convention for help. The Convention met in May of 1826 in New York and the following resolution was passed:

> *Resolved,* That a memorial be presented at the next session of Congress, expressive of the entire approbation of this Convention of the design of our Government to locate the aborigines of our country in the West, and of our readiness to Co-operate in such a measure, and praying Congress to increase the appropriation for Indian reform.

Under new management

There was now a general feeling among the Baptists that their Mission Board had been unwise to tie themselves down to financing the Columbian College to the detriment of missionary work. It was decided to move the Board from Washington where it was then sitting and place its permanent seat in Boston, Massachusetts, appointing a new secretary and, what was most important, a new treasurer, Heman Lincoln. Those members of the Board who were tied down to their Columbian College duties and debts were now no longer part of the managerial side of the Board or, what was called the "Acting Board." Though McCoy shared a lasting friendship with Rice, Staughton and other members of the Board, he was at first relieved to find that they no longer exercised authority over finances. Even Staughton, who had lost his position, commented, "Since the Revolution that, most provi-

---

[68] See letters between McCoy and Rice dated August 30, and October 7, 1825, McCoy Papers, Reel 4.

[69] See, for instance, McCoy's letter to Rice dated September 3, 1825, McCoy Papers, Reel 4.

dently, has taken place in our College, you will find the charges very greatly diminished. Before this every thing was unsystematic and wild. All is now reduced to order and economy." Staughton, who had not heard from Bolles on the matter, naively believed that McCoy should now be in a position to send his sons on to Columbian College at his own expense and no further hindrance would be made. He obviously did not know that his successor, Bolles, was against having Josephus and Rice at the college on principle. That principle being that missionary children need no better education than that which the mission station provides.[70] Bolles had consulted the American Board of Commissioners on this matter and found that Presbyterian and Congregationalist missionaries did not send their children to college so the Baptists ought not to either. Writing weeks after Bolles told McCoy that his sons were not welcome at the college, Rice wrote to McCoy, also thinking that the boys were leaving merely because McCoy could not afford to keep them on. Rice told McCoy that he would try and raise the necessary money for them.[71] Apparently, Bolles, who now referred to Rice disparagingly as "our late agent"[72] had not told the old Board anything about their new policies. Indeed, he wrote to McCoy to tell him not to take any notice of Rice as he had "nothing to do" with matters of financing any longer.[73] It is interesting enough here to note that Staughton called the take over by the New Englanders a "revolution." McCoy, not so much interested in revolutions as being able to continue his day to day work with the Indians, commented on the 1826 Convention's resolutions, hoping they heralded a change for the better, with the words:

> Embarrassed for want of pecuniary support for our mission, we had made great efforts to obtain it from Government, and from benevolent societies and individuals, and these efforts had been successful to a degree that excited grat-

---

[70] See Bolles' extraordinary view of missionary children's education in his letter to McCoy dated September 1, 1826, McCoy Papers, Reel 5.

[71] See Rice's letter to McCoy dated September 20, 1826, McCoy Papers, Reel 5.

[72] See opening words of Bolles letter to McCoy concerning his break with Rice dated November 28, 1826, McCoy Papers, Reel 5.

[73] Ibid. Bolles entire correspondence with McCoy appears chronologically intermixed with other correspondence in the McCoy Papers but is also copied and gathered together in 67 numbered pages on Reel 5.

itude to God. Still we had sensibly felt, from the first, the want of the zealous co-operation of the board in devising and accomplishing measures which we deemed of vital importance. The inconvenience to us was the greater, because we could not, without injury to our good cause, tell the public that we were left to contrive and manage for ourselves; and the prints emanating from the offices of the board (the Latter Day Luminary and the Columbian Star) being deficient in information respecting our missions, and in requesting help in means and missionaries, less interest was felt in our behalf than would otherwise have been the case. Persons with whom we corresponded, on reading our letters to them, often expressed astonishment that the board should not do more to inform the public of our condition and wants. We supposed that the absorbing interests of the Columbian College had diminished their attention to missionary affairs.[74]

The Board's new policies

Sadly, McCoy found that the new broom did not sweep any cleaner. Bolles decided to reject the *Family Rules* which had formally been accepted by both the missionaries and the Board. He tried to introduce salaries with each missionary receiving a wage which was expected to cover all his costs. McCoy, Lykins and Simerwell all wrote against this proposal as hitherto the missionaries were in charge of different sections of the work which were more or less demanding financially and where money had been superfluous in one section, it was well used in another. It was impossible, McCoy argued, "to distinguish between costs of these and costs of those."[75] The missionaries also felt that being paid salaries would limit their overall income because the Board would tell them when extra needs arose that they had been paid and that was that. The missionaries also pointed out that their financial needs were different according to what duties they had to perform. The 85 members of the family were all fed by two missionaries who were responsible for the material welfare of all these

---

[74] *History of Baptist Indian Missions*, p. 279.

[75] See McCoy's discussion of the impossibility of separating one missionary's costs from another when commenting on the Valley Towns Mission in a lengthy, undated report placed at the end of 1826 on Reel 5 of the McCoy Papers.

people. If they only had their salaries to rely on to cover their expenses, they would be penniless very soon and the other missionaries would still have money so that they would have to help their fellow missionaries out. Why not then have everything in common from the start? Bolles gave in for a while but worked himself out of his dilemma by engaging new missionaries himself and putting them under a salaried contract.[76]

Another departure from the *Family Rules* was that each missionary was now expected to keep a personal account of his own particular work and be able to present this to the Board whenever it was called for. This was to be a secret action between the Board and the individual missionary. Hitherto, the missionaries had planned their work together and made a joint report concerning their endeavors to the Board. Thus, nothing was undertaken without all the missionaries knowing about it and discussing the matter together. The work of the Board, too, was benefitted by this system as they could see at once what was going on in the mission and what blessings were being experienced and what trials. From now on, a kind of petty rivalry was to occur in the reports of the new missionaries as they were encouraged to criticize their older and more experienced brethren. This is very evident in the cases of Meeker and Slater and missionaries to come such as Barker and Blanchard. Each journal-keeper felt he had to keep a record of the entire work of the mission from his own point of view which included critical remarks concerning his colleagues who were not privy to those remarks. Equally dangerous for the well-being of the missionary family, the Board felt that they could enter into secret communication with each member of the missions. This led to a breaking down of the harmony and discipline among the missionaries. Time and time again, the Board would write to McCoy and Lykins, saying that complaints had been forwarded against them by younger members of staff whom the Board would not name, nor even say what those complaints were. This also made Lykins' work the more difficult. He had proved to be the most competent of the missionary staff in supervising the book-keeping, placing orders, paying bills, etc. He still had the responsibility of making sure that the mission was kept on a good financial footing but now had to enquire into how individual salaries were being used. When the missionaries had everything in common, no one minded Lykins asking for receipts

---

[76] See McCoy's, Lykins' and Simerwell's 14 pages of correspondence with Bolles on this subject dated July, 1826. Also Bolles letter to McCoy dated September 1, 1826, McCoy Papers, Reel 5.

but now wages were private, such enquiries became unwelcome. They were still necessary, however, as each missionary received monies from different sources which had to be accounted for in the general missionary budget. Again, this led to later difficulties with certain new members of the missionary family. William Polke had been one who always showed severe irritation when asked to produce documentation for monies received and expenditures made.[77] It was not everyone who could live according to the *Family Rules* but the McCoys and Lykins felt it was a far more efficient way leading to the benefit and harmony of the mission as a whole.

A Board suffering from its own blunders

Most detrimental to the Indian mission's life, however, was the Board's new policy, shown at the 1826 Convention concerning the overall necessity and importance of Indian missions. Foreign missions was now interpreted as meaning "overseas missions only." After attending the conference, McCoy summed up the Board's new attitude by writing, "I was much distressed on observing how imperfectly Indian affairs were understood, and the little probability there was that Indian missions would be zealously prosecuted."[78] The true apathy of the new Board to Indian missions was shown within a few months. On September 1st, Bolles wrote to McCoy to tell him that on no account must he finance the education of any Indian child without first consulting the Board and that the Board was unanimous in believing that a missionary school for Indian children was totally superfluous and only served to give Indian children a feeling of superiority over their fellow Indians. If any schooling took place, it must be to teach them manual work. Bolles went on to give McCoy a good dressing down as if he were an officer who had just caught a private asleep on guard duty. After telling McCoy that his school would be better shut down, Bolles went on to say that he was going to contact Governor Cass in order to renegotiate Government grants. This was no wonder as the main source of Government grants that the Board was receiving was for the mission's school. If Bolles did away with the schools under present conditions, he would also do away with the grants which was the last thing he wished to happen. As usual, the

---

[77] See Polke's criticism of Lykins in his letter to McCoy dated August 14, 1826, McCoy Papers, Reel 5.

[78] *History of Baptist Indian Missions*, p. 280.

Board's worst enemy was their own blunders. Bolles said, too, that he wanted the Government to take on all the costs of the Indian students at Hamilton. These students were not costing the Board a penny but the way Bolles was thinking soon became apparent. Baptists were paying the extra $50 a year necessary over and above what the Government was already paying towards the students' fees. For the seven students this amounted to $350 which, if it had been sent to the Board, could have been used for another purpose.

Two brilliant Indians wish to become doctors: the Board opposes them.

A further test case of the Board's new racist apathy was seen in their reaction to the situation of two further brilliant pupils at the Carey school. The young Christian Indians indicated that they wished to be trained as doctors to help their own people cope with the many diseases brought to them by the whites. This had been one of the great aims of the mission all along as McCoy believed strongly that Indian missionaries, Christian doctors, craftsmen, etc., would be able to serve the Indians far better than the whites. Indeed, McCoy argued that this was the only way to keep the Indians from certain extinction as a people. Now that Columbian College was closed to Indians, places for the boys were found in a medical school at Castleton, Vermont where they were to commence studies in January, 1827. McCoy wrote to the new Board asking for their blessing. McCoy emphasized that the Board would not have to pay a penny in support of the boys as this had been promised by friends of the mission. He did ask the board for permission to use some of the missions' funds (which the Board did not now provide but still insisted on administering) to pay for the boys journey to Vermont, "unless the board should prefer making a direct appropriation for that object."[79] After a six months' delay the Carey Mission received a letter from Bolles arguing strongly against sending the boys to medical college. In an understatement typical of McCoy when he was deeply disappointed, he said, "The reasons which were assigned for their decision were by no means satisfactory to us."[80] Seen from a more neutral standpoint and with hindsight, the reasons the Board gave were the very worst possible. The new Boston Board argued that if the Indian boys were sent to college there would be

---

[79] Ibid, p. 300.

[80] Ibid, p. 300.

what they called "mischievous consequences."[81] This "mischief," they explained would be that when the Baptists realized how successful the Indian mission had become, they would empty their purses in support of such ventures and then they would be unwilling to give money to the foreign mission.

This was too much for McCoy who, for the first time, decided that the Board was utterly and completely wrong in their estimate of Christian work and he could no longer abide by their decision. He therefore told the Board:

> We, too, felt a deep interest in foreign missions, and claimed the honour of not being second to any in our esteem for the missionaries who were labouring in foreign fields, in our admiration of their devotion and self-denial, and in the ardour of our desires for their success; but we supposed that placing some select youths from among *our heathen,* in the white settlements, to qualify them for superior usefulness among their heathen kindred, so far from producing the result apprehended by the board, would promote a spirit of benevolence favourable to missions, both foreign and on our own continent. The fear that we should monopolize public attention, and public munificence, was thought to be not well founded. Moreover, we had consecrated all the life and labour that God would allow us to the temporal and spiritual welfare of the indians. While the board justly contemplated the objects of foreign missions as being *'great,'* as they chose to designate them, we felt that the considerations involved in missions to the Indians ought not to be esteemed *small.* It was a duty which we could not dispense with, even to avoid the sacrifice of feeling which we must make in departing from the instructions of the board, to do *all that we possibly could for the benefit of the people of our charge.* We did not claim the right of adopting measures of our own, contrary to their instructions, at their cost; this had not been contemplated. We had made great exertions to obtain the means of support, and from April, 1824, up to that time - nearly three years - the board had applied to our use no other funds than properly belonged to our stations, and which could not, without our consent, be applied any where else. According to these views, and without any feeling of disrespect towards our patrons, though differing from them in judgment, Mr. Lykins, on the 25th of January, 1827, started from Carey, for Vermont, with the two candidates for a medical education. Their

---

[81] Ibid, p. 300.

English names were Francis Barrow and Thomas Baldwin.[82]

Rice and Josephus McCoy also wish to continue their medical studies

Sadly, the boys, after they had made great progress with their studies, contracted pulmonary consumption through working with their patients and quickly died. This was the very major illness from which they were striving to protect their people. At this time, Rice and Josephus, McCoy's two eldest sons, were also called to study medicine with a view to returning to the Indian mission. They found places at Lexington. Here Senator Johnson's friendship with McCoy came in very handy. Johnson, knowing that he had snapped up several Government grants which otherwise would have gone to McCoy, was anxious to make it up to his friend and suggested that he could be of service in obtaining training for McCoy's sons at Lexington in Kentucky. Johnson therefore wrote a very warm letter to the leading physicians at Lexington, outlining the excellent qualifications and characters of the boys. Of McCoy himself, Johnson says:

> I hope you will be able to take them upon such terms as will benefit both parties and in doing so you will oblige a Citizen who has great Claims upon every good man, as no man has done more than Mr. McCoy in elevating the human character. I have assured Mr. McCoy of your good disposition, and that you will converse with him frankly and free and give him the very best advice.[83]

The professors at Transylvania University, Lexington duly accepted Rice and Josephus as medical students and they qualified in early 1829. They also did courses in surveying so that they could help their father in mapping out the Indian Territory.

---

[82] Ibid, p. 301.

[83] See letter from Johnson to Drs. Dudley and Richardson dated October 30, 1826, McCoy Papers, Reel 5.

The work at Carey and Thomas goes on with ensuing blessings

Meanwhile, a work of grace was going on at Carey and Thomas and a letter from Robert Simerwell written from Carey to McCoy who was at Thomas, dated December 15, 1826, closes that year with a description of how a man named Jacob French was converted in their midst and how the whole gathering wept tears of joy. The going was hard at Carey because a number of bootleggers had settled down not far off and the Indians were often drunk. This evil trade had not yet spread as far as Thomas, and there conversions were more numerous towards the end of 1826. On December 25th, the Thomas School was opened by McCoy and five pupils arrived for tuition, another eight being added during the following weeks. On the same day, McCoy wrote to Col. Richard Johnson, Kentucky Senator, Governor William Hendricks of Indiana and Col. William McLean who had a Government appointment in Ohio, to ask for their assistance in nominating himself as Agent for the colonization of the Indian Territory by the Indians.[84] McCoy had recently taken part in a treaty between the Potawatomis, Miamis and the Government whereby the Indians had surrendered a fourth of their land to the Government in exchange for lands west of the Mississippi and McCoy was anxious to be off and secure this land for the Indians.

---

[84] These letters are to be found on Reel 5 of the McCoy Papers.

Chapter Nine
Making Ends Meet (1827-28)

_____

The missionaries defend themselves against accusations that they are living too well

The New Year started at Carey with a cheerful letter to McCoy, who was still at Thomas, from Simerwell who had now been long enough in the mission to realize that he was in his element. His attitude to the Board was one of patience and good humor. Referring to recent mail from Boston, Simerwell told McCoy:

> My prayer is that we may act so that all who speak evil against us may speak falsely. You will learn by Mr. Lykins that the Board is still making inquiry respecting us but what of that, the Lord is able to take care of his own cause and we trust it is his cause we are engaged in.[1]

What Simerwell brushed off with good humor, became a more serious matter when, on January 10, 1827, in McCoy's absence, the Simerwells, Meeker, Lykins and the Slaters, who had not yet left for Thomas on the Board's advice, prepared an answer to Bolles' latest accusation that they were induldging themselves and the Indians and even eating pork! The missionary family, described exactly what was taught in the school and referred Bolles to a previous letter from McCoy which outlined the mission's daily program. Then they wrote:

> A few days since we received your letter written at Washington, and leave a regular answer of it to Mr. McCoy, but respectfully solicit the privilege of saying that its arrival has added to our daily griefs and discouragements, the <u>deep-felt pain</u> of having to bear unmerited censure. While sitting down to partake of our daily fare, to some of us the contents of your letter have recurred and supplied the place of more than half a meal.

_____

[1] Letter dated January 3, 1827, McCoy Papers, Reel 5.

249

If tears could convince you of the integrity of our hearts, those shed while this is penned might bear an humble part, and those shed around our solitary abode, might prove more than you could ask of confirmation of this kind. We rightly maintain that we have lived poor, and that we have not indulged in the common use of Coffee and Tea. We are sure that, to bring your servants below their usual fare - heretofore, would shame the Board themselves. We forbear to enter into any explanation of our mode of living, as these things have been repeatedly told, and have as often, by the Board, been treated as suspicious and false. All of your Missionaries at Carey hold a visit to this place by a member of the Board for the purpose of examining into the situation of the Mission to be indispensably necessary, as they cannot nor will not as Missionaries rest under the censures communicated in your last letter. In this we only allude to that part of your letter which relates to our mode of living etc.

We assure you sir, that our hands are weakened and that harmony of feeling cannot exist between the Board and their Missionaries here until these things are adjusted.

Your letter will be forwarded soon to Thomas and will be fully answered by Mr. McCoy.[2]

Mealtimes at the station were also occasions when general problems were discussed and letters read out. One can imagine the missionaries quite losing their appetite while Bolles' latest attack was being read. The mission's request that a member of the Board should share in the station's life for a period of time was often repeated but never taken up by the Board. Though the Board were now trying to instil into the missionaries that they were all independently selected and controlled by the Board as equals and though they had stopped referring to McCoy as Superintendent, it is obvious that the missionary family still looked to McCoy for their leadership and expected him to be their chief defender against an over inquisitive and suspicious Board.

Bolles' reply concerning the Indian medical students

Bolles had written that he could on no account agree to the Indians being encouraged to enjoy a college education and had refused to even spend a penny on their traveling expenses. If they wanted to go to Vermont, he told the missionaries, then they should go alone and

---

[2] McCoy Papers, Reel 5.

on foot. Lykins had, however, now pledged himself to take the two medical students to their college and had formerly understood that the Board were merely against higher education for the Indians because of the costs the Board might be involved in and not because they were against higher education for Indians on principle. Lykins thus wrote on January 10th to the Board, telling them that their whole aim in their missionary work was to prepare Christian Indians to look after themselves, their tribes and their new country and for this end, they needed a good education. Lykins then told Bolles that he was taking the boys to Vermont, not because he wished to be rebellious but because he wished to do the right thing and that he would raise the money himself somehow to pay for traveling expenses. He told Bolles forthrightly that the Board were now dampening the missions hopes and doubling their discouragements and blasting all their expectations of being able to save the Indians from a certain destruction. Lykins explained to Bolles that the latest treaty with the Potawatomis and Miamis had left many of them landless and homeless and the Baptist Indian Mission's plan of establishing them as an independent people under their own educated rulers was their only hope of survival. He asked Bolles plainly if he wished to take away from the Indians their only hope. Here Lykins was arguing in the same way as McCoy who had told him that the Americans had enslaved the Africans not because they were black but because they had no religious, cultural, educational and political structure which could save them. If Africa had the churches and universities which the whites had, nobody would think that they were a people only worthy of being enslaved.[3] Lykins, realizing that many of the new moves from the side of the Board were aimed at isolating McCoy from the other missionaries, told Bolles that he need not think McCoy was following a course without consulting the other missionaries. They were, in fact, pleased to tell him that they were of one mind with McCoy.[4] What Lykins did not put in his letter to Bolles was that he had consulted the church at Carey concerning taking the two students to Vermont and they had unanimously approved of this action and resolved that he should undertake the journey.

---

[3] These thoughts are to be found in the 67 paged collection of letters between the mission and Bolles on Reel 5 of the McCoy Papers.

[4] See Lykins' letter to Bolles of January 10, 1827, McCoy Papers, Reel 5.

A case of absentee bishopism

Here was a true sign that the Board had grown into a parachurch activity similar to the British Baptist Missionary Society which had gone through the same trouble almost a generation earlier. The brethren at Serampore had formed a church with their own pastor and church officers and had drawn up a church order of their own as a true, Biblical, local church. Andrew Fuller on the home front, object-ed strongly to this move and, taking on the role of an absentee Bishop, dictated to the church, whom they should accept as members and what church order they should follow. Sadly, the Serampore church gave up its independence so as not to break with the mission Board, or as the missionaries themselves put it, they threw out the gun to preserve the ship.[5] Instead of basing his advice on the Scriptures, Fuller, com-manding a role similar to Bolles, gave them a nice piece of Grotianism to help them with problems of church discipline. He told the brethren that, "the form and order of the Christian church, much more than that of the Jewish church, are founded on *the reason and fitness of things*."[6] In the case of Carey Mission, we find Bolles in far off Boston, telling the local church that its own resolutions should be subordinate to the Board's on the grounds that they were reasonable and fitting, seen from his perspective, of course.[7]

McCoy complains again of the Board's tardiness

McCoy wrote on January 23rd but he had obviously not heard from the other missionaries and knew nothing of Bolles last letter sent to Carey as he writes he has not heard from Bolles since September 1st. He tells Bolles that the school at Thomas is growing but that he has been very ill again. He also informs Bolles that Luther Rice had written to him concerning a sum of $666.66 which had been granted the mission by the Government and which Rice had paid into the

---

[5] See E. Daniel Potts, *I Throw Away the Gun to Preserve the Ship: A Note on the Serampore Trio,* B. Q, xx, 1963-64. See also Fuller's strictures on the Serampore church in *Works,* vol III, p. 451 ff., especially p. 503 ff.

[6] Fuller's emphasis. See his letter of April, 1804 to Serampore in Principles of Church Discipline, *Works,* vol. III, p. 452.

[7] See also Brian Stanley's *C.H. Spurgeon and the Baptist Missionary Society,* B.Q, 29 (7), 1982, pp. 319-328.

Board's treasury in the early summer of the previous year. McCoy wished to know why the mission had not received that money and why they had not received the usual quarter grant for schools and buildings which had been due on October 1st. He also wished to know why the mission had only received $1,500 from the Board's own funds in three and a half years, which was contrary to all arrangements with the mission. McCoy also reminded the Board that they had sat in Washington last November to discuss Indian missions, including Indian relocation, but the missions had heard nothing concerning decisions made at that meeting.

Severe weather hits Carey and Thomas

When McCoy penned these words, Carey and Thomas were passing through the worst weather ever experienced in living memory so that many Indians were dying of cold and hunger. The missionaries were holding special meetings for prayer for the starving Indians but could not help them much without the Board paying them what was due to them from the Government and the Board's charity fund. Lykins had to postpone taking the students to Vermont because of the severe weather but was able to start off at the end of January. Lykins wrote to McCoy on January 20th to tell him that all was well at the mission. He enclosed Bolles "disheartening" and "unmanly" letter which he found "vexatious" and "insulting," and a copy of the Carey missionaries reply to it. Lykins thought it was rather odd that Bolles had criticized the missionaries for their lack of good faith and punctuality, yet he himself refused to forward donations specially earmarked for Carey of which the mission was in dire need. He said how important it was that the Board should send a delegation to inspect the mission and suspected that enemies of the mission in Cincinnati and "some who have retired from the mission" had been taking advantage of Bolles' ear. Lykins then aired with McCoy his ideas of placing a few of the pupils who were at the end of their courses in law school so that they might be in a better position to help their own people.

Slater becomes the Board's Indian Mission informer

As matters turned out, though on the surface, all the missionaries openly agreed with McCoy and Lykins and affirmed this in church meetings, one member of the missionary family obviously saw this as a mere formal process to disguise his own judgement and actions. Leonard Slater had been secretly corresponding with the Board and had criticized Lykins for "troubling the waters" in his decision to accompany the two medical students to Vermont. Slater does not appear to have understood the positive sense of the imagery he used as the angel who troubled the waters in John Chapter 5 made sick people whole but Slater was misusing the phrase to divide an otherwise healthy missionary family. Slater did write to McCoy later, telling of his letter to the Board and almost boasting of how he withstood Lykins, yet he did not enclose a copy of his letter. This action of Slater's was only the beginning of much anxiety on the missionaries' part as it turned out that the Board had no need to send a delegation of inspection to Carey and Thomas as they had placed a fifth column man, or, to use a more modern expression, a "mole" in their midst who was doing the work clandestinely for them. Slater's wife had become ill on reaching the mission and there had been no improvement for months, a fact that might have caused Slater to question their role in the mission. Meanwhile, Simerwell, not knowing that Slater was in private correspondence with the Board, wrote to McCoy, who was still gravely ill, to tell him that the missionaries thought it would be best not to enter into discussion with the Board until they sent the delegate insisted upon to examine the station. In this way, Simerwell argued, they would come "under the necessity of punishing themselves with their own rod."[8] Presumably he meant that the Board's arguments would backfire on them and they would be the ones to be ashamed of their own behavior.

Bolles' plans for a new Indian Mission

Throughout the whole of 1827, the Board continued to be very tardy in keeping to the financial arrangements they had made with the missionaries. Bolles wrote to McCoy in February[9] to tell him that the Board was faced with many thousands of dollars in bills which it could not pay. The only answer, he told McCoy, was to borrow money, cut down on expenditures, and set up more supporting societies. Because of the mismanagement before his appointment, Bolles felt that interest in missions had waned and it would most likely be a long time before they were receiving as much income as in 1817. Bolles not

---

[8] Letter dated February 2, 1827, McCoy Papers, Reel 5.

[9] Letter dated February 22, 1827, McCoy Papers, Reel 5.

only blamed his predecessors for the present situation, though he, himself, had been an influential member of the old Board, but also the Indian mission which he felt had been run badly and too much money had been spent on it. Bolles envisaged an itinerant Indian mission whereby the missionaries visited the homes of the Indians with the emphasis on prayer and conversation. He suggested that McCoy should imitate the Methodists who were good at this method. This would reap far more spiritual fruit and be less expensive than McCoy's present method of evangelizing the Indians. This time, however, Bolles was less dictatorial on the subject and merely added, "I should like your thoughts on the subject." Where good was done to the Indians, it was best, Bolles affirmed, when it was done by means available to the Indians. What he meant was that the Indians should pay for the missionaries' work out of their own annuities and then the Board would have no problems. Actually, it was the Indians' annuities and grants which were paying the Board's way but the Board's present problem was that the monies which they received from the Government for Indian improvement, which were part of the Government's annuity deal with the Indians, were being used to pay off unrelated debts which were still continually being made in spite of the new Board.

Bolles replied most cryptically to McCoy's reminder that the Board had not sent the mission money for a very long time. Apparently monies earmarked for buildings at Thomas and "another station" unspecified (Valley Towns?), had become missing. Bolles gave no information as to how the money had disappeared but merely spoke vaguely of people who should not be entrusted with benevolent enterprises. Whether this was a dig at Luther Rice or not, it is difficult to say. Rice had, however, reminded McCoy that monies for the previous summer had been paid by the Government and he had turned them over to the Board personally, so it seems that there was still a weak link in the Board's managerial chain. However, it is clear that Bolles was washing his hands in innocence to remove any suspicion from himself. Later, Bolles allowed McCoy to draw $600 of the $666.66 dollars granted by the Government for Thomas but still the Board owed the mission monies for the past nine months or so. Whether it was a wise thing to do or not, McCoy now asked Rice to use his connections with the Government to find out exactly what sums were being paid to the Board for the work at Carey and Thomas so that he would always know what claims to make on the Board.[10] Although

---

[10] See McCoy's letter to Rice dated March 13, 1827, McCoy Papers, Reel 5.

Rice was officially disgraced, McCoy could not cast him off as a friend as he had shown McCoy so many proofs of true brotherly love, therefore McCoy wrote to him:

> While I live I shall feel grateful for your particular kindness to me and to my dear family. I sorrow for your misfortunes, and no one in the world will more rejoice on that day when a merciful Providence shall restore your comforts - and your comforters.[11]

The new Board shows even greater inability concerning Christian stewardship

Bolles' tactics now seemed very ill-fitting indeed. The new Corresponding Secretary had backed a move at the last "revolutionary" Convention to have new trustees take up the task of rescuing Columbian College from its financial miseries. A professor at Columbian College, Alexis Caswell, who had taken care of Rice and Josephus McCoy for some time, now wrote to McCoy on March 22, 1827 to tell him that a number of these trustees had resigned soon after taking up office.[12] This was only after it had become apparent that instead of rescuing the college, they had "diminished the income, incurred several suits, suffered almost all the notes in Bank to be protested and lessened the prospect of filling up the subscription of $50,000."[13] No better way for Bolles could have been found to destroy the college. This forced Staughton, Wait and Rice to make almost panic-stricken tours of the country to try and raise funds to keep the college in Baptist hands. The general feeling in the college, however, was that it must come under entirely new management or be disbanded. Caswell did his duty in helping the college financially by presenting McCoy with a bill which by previous agreement with the Board, they ought to have paid. One further interesting point in Caswell's letter was the news that several students at Columbian had become Christians and had been baptized. The college was originally intended for Christian workers and missionary candidates, i.e. for Christians only. This is why McCoy planned to only send baptized

---

[11] Ibid.

[12] These were six in all, only one of them, Baron Stow being a Baptist. Circular of the Columbian College D. C., March 26, 1827.

[13] Circular of the Columbian College, D. C., March 26, 1827.

Christians to the college and the non-Christians to Princeton. Now it seemed that Columbian College was prepared to take on non-Christian white students in their financial need.[14] The college reported on March 26, 1827 that they were in debt to the tune of $95,142,18, not counting the thousands they owed the Government which they still hoped would be annulled by the Senate.

McCoy is publicly acknowledged for his work for Indian reform

Meanwhile, Lykins had visited Detroit and spoken to Governor Cass' staff concerning Indian Improvement funds. This may explain why Agent John Tipton wrote to McCoy on March 3, 1827 to say that the War Department had decided to make McCoy the sole administrator of the Miami educational grant and Tipton would be interested to know how McCoy was going to dispense it. This was a real answer to prayer for McCoy who was seeking to provide the Miamis with not only elementary but also higher education, especially for the girls who had been rather neglected up to now.[15] The unbelievable thing was to happen, however. The Board were to fight their own mission's right to the grant and have it paid to a non-Baptist cause which promised to put in a good word with the Government concerning the Board's debts.

The Tuesday, March 27th edition of the *Indiana Journal*, no mean newspaper, proclaimed to the nation that Isaac McCoy was now a man of importance in working out treaties with the Indians. A full report was given of the treaty made with the Potawatomis in the previous Autumn and McCoy's name was listed as official witness to the proceedings. The report was signed by Lewis Cass, J. Brown Ray and John Tipton, and, after his approval was obtained, also by the President, John Quincy Adams. Likewise mention was made of McCoy's schools at Carey and Thomas and the names were given of some sixty or more of McCoy's pupils who would receive land and grants from the Government. This was chiefly thanks to McCoy's strenuous work on behalf of these pupils and the result of his enormous correspondence with Government officials and visits paid to them on behalf of the Indians. Sadly, Bolles interfered with McCoy's plans to gain the bulk of the educational grant from the Government on the grounds that he taught the bulk of the Indian children who

---

[14] McCoy Papers, Reel 5.

[15] See McCoy's letter to Cass dated March 13, 1827, McCoy Papers, Reel 5.

were eligible for such grants. Bolles backed instead Col. Johnson's Choctaw Academy, arguing that all Indian children should be sent there, though only one pupil attended his school from the Potawatomi and Miami area coming under the grant. With the Board's backing, Johnson eventually secured the entire grant. McCoy was deeply distressed at this as the Board were obviously turning their backs on their own people. He wrote to Bolles on April 16th to tell the Corresponding Secretary that he was not only totally misinformed about the grants available for Indian education but also Johnson's eligibility for those grants. Rather than the Potawatomis and Miamis wanting the money to go to the Choctaw Academy as Bolles affirmed in his defense, most of these tribes had never heard of the place. Realizing that Bolles was now arranging matters with Johnson and Cass which were not to the benefit of the Indian mission, obviously because of favors the Government might give them in other financial spheres, McCoy demanded that Bolles should forward him copies of all letters from the Department of War he received and copies of all letters relating to the treaty of the previous October with the Potawatomis and Miamis. Aware that McCoy had been treated unfairly, Governor Cass wrote to him personally on May 22, 1827, inviting him to take part in a further treaty at Green Bay with the Indians that summer and requesting that they should have a meeting together about further grants and consider the prospects of a new mission at St. Marie. Cass promised McCoy that all expenses would be paid.[16] At the same time, Cass told Bolles of his move and on May 26th Bolles wrote to McCoy giving him the Board's approval.

Bolles accuses McCoy of spoiling the Indians

Though McCoy had written time and time again pleading with the Board to keep to their agreement with the Indian mission and with the Government, very little had happened to reassure the mission that they were being treated honestly and fairly by the Board. What grieved McCoy the most was that, though the Board might be receiving little money from the churches, he knew they were receiving Government grants, paid every quarter, for Carey, which were just not being passed on. Instead, Bolles had written scolding letters to McCoy, complaining that the Indian pupils were faring better at the mission than they would do when they returned home. He told McCoy the tale

---

[16] McCoy Papers, Reel 5.

of an Indian youth found weeping after having left the mission, realizing that from now on life would be harder for him. This was proof enough for Bolles that McCoy was spoiling the Indians and thus ruining their chances of later integration into their tribes. Bolles had heard that the Indian pupils had milk for breakfast and found this scandalous. He also had heard that the Indians had bread made with flour and that occasionally tea and coffee were drunk at the mission. McCoy retorted by asking Bolles if he wished them to give up the mission entirely and not treat the Indians as human beings. He also reminded Bolles that he and Lykins had raised thousands of dollars in Government grants, not to mention all that they had raised in Baptist donations and yet Bolles would not even allow them to use a little of that money for the education of children for which purpose it was intended by gracious givers.[17]

McCoy answers Bolles' complaints about the mission

In the above mentioned letter dated April 16th concerning the Board's interference in the matter of Potawatomi and Miami grants,[18] McCoy deals with some of the major accusations of Bolles against the mission and the mission's complaints against the Board. After explaining how Bolles had let the mission down in the case of Johnson and his Choctaw Academy, McCoy goes on to consider Bolles suggestion that McCoy should give up mission stations and schools, relying on itinerant work among the Indians and teaching the children in their homes. He tells Bolles that itinerant work is no substitute for a stable local church ministry and teaching. He then argues that if the Indian children are at home, few Indian parents would allow them to be taught when they could be making themselves useful with the household chores and the general work which has to be done. Besides, Indian villages are not permanent sites and they are here today and gone tomorrow, therefore a fixed pattern of visitation so that teaching and evangelizing can be built up circuit-wise on the Methodist pattern, which Bolles had recommended, was not possible -- besides not being practical. Appertaining to Bolles suggestion that Baptists should adopt the methods of Methodists among his Potawatomis, McCoy says that the Methodists have no missionaries among the "unimproved Indians"

---

[17] See the 67 pages of McCoy-Bolles correspondence on Reel 5 of the McCoy Papers.

[18] McCoy Papers, Reel 5.

and where they were laboring, they were rendering little service as they made proselytes without due regard to faith and doctrine. Allying with the Methodists became a major aspect of the Baptist Foreign Mission Board's policy and led to at least one station, run by Barker and Blanchard, losing its distinctive Baptist character and teaching. Their irregular camp meetings took the place of regular pastoral, local church-based work.

It was a different matter, conceded McCoy, with the Cherokees and Chickasaws, i.e. the so-called Civilized Tribes, since they were settled more permanently, at least at present. Thus, with the so-called Wild Tribes among whom McCoy was working, he argued, one might do good for a few on a short term basis. But this was no real substitute to having a mission station built where there is a good deal of Indian movement and having all the children together so that they can later evangelize and educate their villages themselves. Furthermore, McCoy reminds Bolles that the Board is gaining a considerable amount of money from the Government because of the Indian mission stations being stationary according to Governmental specification and that any work among the Indians must have Government approval and be carried out according to treaty specifications. This means that if it were not for treaty regulations, there would most likely be no Indian mission whatsoever. Perhaps McCoy's strongest argument against Bolles' ideas, however, was that the Corresponding Secretary's plans could not save the Indians from extinction and it was the work of the Indian mission not only to win the Indians for Christ but to preserve them as a people. And this entailed relocation to and colonization in the Indian Territory.

McCoy had already told Bolles that bread made of wheat flour was a rare luxury at the station and that they chiefly relied on corn bread. But corn had to be grown, reaped, threshed and ground so a mission station needed land and at least hand mills to do this. Otherwise, the mission would only be able to buy flour once a year when a vessel visited the nearest lake selling it for $5 per bushel.

William Polke's protest

A surprising letter now arrived from Maria Creek penned by William Polke. He protested that he had heard that the mission felt he had been too critical of them of late and he wished to defend himself from any false suspicions and explain his case. While at Carey, he had been a little critical of Lykins, suspecting that his faith was not very strong and that he was too timid in his public preaching. But now he attacked Lykins furiously, saying that if anything wrong had been said about him, it must have been Lykins who said it. He claimed that though he esteemed McCoy still, he had learned that he was "like other men liable to be mistaken and imposed upon." Suggesting that he could not go into further details so as not to wound McCoy's feelings, he believed that an official investigation should be set up. In all, the letter is most strange as Polke seemingly wished to deny that he had said anything detrimental to the missionary family yet the entire contents of his letter contained criticisms which he allegedly was not guilty of uttering. The fact was that Polke, after proclaiming to both his friends and enemies that he was ready to leave all and follow Christ into the mission field had soon decided that he was not at all cut out for such work and had retired as quickly as possible. One of the more general reasons he gave, however, for his retreat was that "we conceived ourselves not treated with that friendship which we expected." This had made him the laughing stock of his Parkerite enemies and Polke was now looking to McCoy and his friends to help him win back both his self-respect and respect in the eyes of others. Thus when it was rumored by one of Polke's critics that Lykins had told somebody that he believed Polke was not cut out to be a missionary, and hinted that Polke had merely joined when other enterprises had failed, Polke felt greatly insulted and demanded retribution. He argued that Lykins could only have criticized him because he wished to supplant him at Thomas and come into possession of his Government-sponsored salary for his own gain.

Now Polke himself had confessed to his only becoming a missionary after other ventures failed in his many letters to the Indian mission family. This may have been passed on to others but Polke obviously did not know under what circumstances and, anyway, the fact was true and commonly known. It is interesting to note, however, that though Polke had uttered similar sentiments concerning Lykins, of which the entire missionary family had been witnesses, Lykins had not made an issue of the matter or seen the incidents as a ground for strife. Nor had he written such letters as Polke was now writing. The trouble was that the churches in the Long Run, Wabash and White River areas were going through a terrible time of inner strife and Polke, who had not only his Christian character to defend but also his status as a political figure, was under great pressure from all sides and he was obviously cracking up under the strain. Furthermore, a number of his relations were still very closely attached to McCoy and the Indian mission and could neither sympathize with

Polke nor listen to his complaints. Especially McCoy's children were much loved by the entire Polke[19] family.[20]

McCoy's reply to Polke

McCoy wrote a long letter to Polke on May 28th,[21] three days after returning to Carey from Thomas. He said that he had heard no reports whatsoever that his brother-in-law had been criticizing the mission and that Polke was also highly mistaken in thinking that Lykins was guilty of misconduct. McCoy stressed that he did not merely *think* Polke was mistaken but he *knew* he was. McCoy explained that he had personally suggested that Polke should take on the task of teacher at Thomas and there was nothing there to tempt Lykins to obtain personal gain as Lykins gave all his income to the mission and none of the missionaries regarded the work Polke was doing as anything other than normal missionary work. In other words, there was nothing to Polke's job which might have tempted anyone to think that Polke was being favored in any way. Furthermore, at that time, Lykins was acting superintendent at Carey and was perfectly content with his position there and had made it quite clear that, though he was always ready to take on new tasks, he never coveted any special ones. McCoy told Polke that Lykins was a man of few words at the best of times and it was just contrary to his nature to spread tales such as Polke suggested he did. Apparently, McCoy felt that Lykins' weakness was to say too little rather than too much and that Mr. Liston, who told Polke that Lykins' opinion was that Polke had fallen in character before entering the mission, was obviously using Lykins to enforce his own opinion. McCoy then added, "We cannot alter men's opinions with regard to our popularity." It is obvious that McCoy believed that people had been aggravating Polke with tales of the mission merely as a tool in their inner disputes. They quite simply wanted to goad Polke, and they had succeeded.

McCoy, however, is very grieved with Polke's accusation that Lykins "was not a man of honourable character." To this accusation, he answered:

---

[19] Some members called themselves Polk by this time.

[20] See Polke's letter to McCoy dated April 15, 1827, McCoy Papers, Reel 5.

[21] McCoy Papers, Reel 5.

You and I, bro. Polke, know very well that from a boy he
has been remarkable for his morality and rectitude of
conduct. The State of Indiana, nor no other state ever
produced a man of a more <u>irreproachable</u> and <u>unblemished</u>
character than Johnston Lykins.

McCoy was plainly put out with the way Polke addressed his
wife in his letter of complaint as "Mrs. McCoy," instead of his sister
Christiana. He also protested at Polke's complaint that people felt he
had not been treated with kindness at the mission as nothing but
kindness was shown him by the entire missionary family. Had he not
felt this? Obviously, McCoy explained, your enemies at home are feeding you with these stories which have nothing to do with your friends
at the mission. Rather than speak of setting in motion an official
investigation, McCoy advised Polke to turn a deaf ear to his enemies'
tricks and not "stoop to listen to their pratings."

McCoy again writes to Bolles

McCoy addressed Dr. Bolles at the Board again on May 29,
1827 explaining what difficulties, even agonies, the Carey Mission was
going through because of the Board's neglect and hindrance of
funds and donations reaching them. He tells Bolles how the Board is
bringing themselves and the mission into disrepute because they are
not keeping to their arrangements made with traders on behalf of the
mission. McCoy explains by way of example, that the mission has had
to run into debt again to the sum of $460 through goods ordered from
H. G. Phillips of Ohio alone because of the Board's neglect to pay
promptly. Phillips, knowing that Government grants had been allotted
to McCoy, and after consultation with the Board, had considered
McCoy creditworthy. McCoy was closely in touch with Government
Agents such as Johnson and Tipton now and also in personal correspondence with Governor Cass, so he knew exactly what amounts of
money he could reckon with besides the Board's own financial
commitments to the mission. He also heard through Rice whether
those monies had been already forwarded to the Board or not. He
therefore writes:

We have not received one dollar from the charity fund of the
Board for one year, and nothing of the Government
allowance which became due the 1ˢᵗ of October. The first
quarter's allowance for the current year became due Jany.
1ˢᵗ, the second April 1ˢᵗ, the third will become due on July

1ˢᵗ. The two former quarters alone the Board doubtless have in possession, and this last is equally to be calculated upon.[22]

It is apparent from McCoy's letter that he is totally dissatisfied with the way the Board carries out its business, always sending money after debts have been made, if at all. McCoy wants to know why the Board cannot send money in advance for the purchase of necessary items so that the missionaries must not always live in debt, not knowing when the Board will make up its mind to pay. McCoy said that he would sell off mission property and even the shirt on his back to pay off debts but there were no buyers in the wilderness. This moves him to plead with the Board, saying:

> Why the Board should force their missionaries into the necessity of begging - begging - begging for help, without giving them mere good words, and this too when they are well acquainted with our actual necessities - and when they have, in trust, funds given by our Government for our relief, is to us exceedingly strange - unaccountable!! We have just cause of grief - we are greatly aggrieved.[23]

Then McCoy goes on to tell how the missionary work is progressing so well in both stations that he can safely say it was never better. The school at Thomas had now twenty-one pupils and Lykins was now there with Mr. and Mrs. Slater. Meeker was presently in charge of the Carey school. McCoy expresses his pleasant surprise that though the amount of whiskey-peddling had increased and with it the intoxication of the Indians, the spiritual work at both stations was blossoming and providing great blessings. However, the missionaries had to put so much labor into providing food, equipment and funds and generally making both ends meet, that they were greatly

---

[22] McCoy Papers, Reel 5.

[23] Reports concerning the new Treasurer Heman Lincoln show how he is systematically funding bills by loans. See, for instance, "Missionary Funds Must Be Replenished," *American Baptist Magazine* January, 1827, p. 30. The annual Treasury reports in the magazine show what an enormous grassroots support there was for the Indian Mission but McCoy's letters show that this money was just not getting through to its proscribed target. One can only surmise that the loans mentioned by Lincoln were taken from the funds earmarked for the Indian Mission, as the Board occasionally hinted was the case.

restricted in their preaching, teaching and visitation work. McCoy tells Bolles that there is apparently little communication between him and the treasurer Heman Lincoln, so he would now write directly to Lincoln to find out how matters stand which might save time in obtaining funds due.

News about the other missionaries

In his next letter to Bolles dated June 7, 1827,[24] McCoy reminded the Corresponding Secretary that Meeker had been working at the station for a year and both he and the missionary family had made repeated applications to the Board to have Meeker officially recognized as a missionary. All these requests had gone unanswered. McCoy explained how deeply he regretted this silence on the part of the Board as Meeker was a great asset to the mission. More pleasant was the news McCoy just received that the U. S. Agent for Indian Affairs, Ramsey D. Potts, and Lucretia Purchase, the new missionary, were married in June, 1827, thus linking the mission more strongly to the efforts of the Government to protect the Indians. McCoy performed the ceremony and asked the Board to allow Mrs. Potts to be able to leave the Board's employment without censure, because of her new duties to her husband. As the couple would be living only a mile away from the mission station, McCoy argued, they would still be of great service to the work without being officially under the Board's patronage. However, Mr. Potts received a call to the mission field and was subsequently ordained and moved to the Indian Territory where he and his wife served as missionaries. The only other piece of news in connection with these letters is that the "rheumatism in the head" which McCoy was stricken with at Thomas six months previously, still afflicted him and that often he was little better than an invalid.

McCoy hears from his mother and brother

On June 15, McCoy's mother Elizabeth sent him a lovely, deeply spiritual letter giving us an equally deep insight into the family piety in which Isaac McCoy had been brought up. She closed her letter with the words:

---

[24] McCoy Papers, Reel 5.

Remember me to all your children, and to the Indian part
of your family also. My best respects to Christiana, her
labours are so great yet she can reflect for her comfort that
she is at work in a good cause. And now my son I commend
you to the Lord, may you enjoy his blessing when you go
out, and when you come in, live religiously, be persevering,
patient and humble, trust the Lord at all times and beg his
directions in all cases, and may you see to your everlasting
satisfaction, an abundant harvest from your labours, and be
an instrument of doing much good in the cause, and at last
enter into the joy of your Lord. Don't forget your Mother.[25]

McCoy's brother Rice added a postscript referring to the
"confusion that prevails" at Columbian College, saying, "what a pity
it seems to be, that people will not do right." Rice speaks of difficulties
arising through correspondence with slave holding Baptists and that
a termination of slavery seems very doubtful. He speaks of great
revivals happening in Kentucky and Ohio and says of his Baptist
brethren in general:

I do believe that the truth is generaly preached by the
Baptists, yet conclude there is quite too much formallity in
religion, and no doubt, a gross errour in discipline, and
more in the use of it. The doctrine of Salvation by Grace,
with all its branches are most precious, and calculated to
give solid comfort to the saint, and the Idea that the love of
Jesus is 'stronger than death' is calculated to yield more
comfort, than many volumes that are written.

Slater challenges McCoy's leadership and criticizes his actions

On June 18th an Indian by the name of Noonday wrote to
McCoy from Thomas saying how he regretted that McCoy had left
them again, as it was essential that someone should teach them in
their own language which the missionaries left at Thomas could not
do. He pressed on McCoy the importance of having missionaries who
would stay permanently with the Indians and learn their language.
This letter was followed three days later by a complaining, indeed,
highly insulting one from Slater[26] who said he had seen Noonday's
letter and had difficulty gaining the Indians' friendship as he could not

---

[25] Ibid.

[26] See McCoy Papers, Reel 5 for both letters.

understand their language. He insinuated that McCoy was only popular among the Indians because he could speak their language and bribed them with gifts. He had thus spoiled the Indians with displays of friendship and indulgence, making things difficult for the missionaries who remained. Slater was also peeved that McCoy could teach without being severe but Slater had to "correct" the pupils when they were unruly, which appears to mean that he had to use the rod. Slater complains that they were not used to such "corrections" and were now prejudiced against him. All this, he maintained, was McCoy's fault. He therefore asked McCoy to make his task easier by paying a pupil's father to allow his son to leave the school at Carey and come to Thomas as his personal interpreter.

Slater was the youngest and least experienced of the missionaries but he was already covering his own deficiencies with complaints against McCoy, arguing that it was McCoy's fault that his own situation was so difficult. One might have thought that a good missionary would have followed McCoy's example so that he might have had more success rather than suggesting that his older brother had an unfair advantage over him. Slater's letters are full of the most pious utterances which are nearly always accompanied by selfish sentiments or criticisms of others, given with an air of assumed superiority. At the time of his complaints, Slater had a maximum of twenty pupils, whereas his successive Carey counterparts had seventy youths with whom they had far fewer problems than Slater. The Board constantly published Slater's letters which breathed a spirit of apparent authority and maturity and expressed his own work in glowing colors. This made Slater a favorite with the Board, who never knew what was actually going on at Thomas where Slater was moping, groaning and blaming all but himself for his loneliness and hardships.

McCoy deals with Slater's complaints

McCoy answered Slater's letter promptly, complimenting him on the good work he was doing and says kindly, "Our prayers for your success are daily offered to the father of mercies. We sympathize with all your trials, and shall ever rejoice in your happiness."[27] He informed his younger colleague that he could not force one of the boys to leave Carey, but the one suggested by Slater was willing to help out on a voluntary basis for a time, though with some reluctance, and also with

---

[27] Letter written June 27, 1827, McCoy Papers, Reel 5.

the proviso that he may return whenever he feels the time has come. McCoy stressed that the boy's father would think it wrong, even insulting, to be offered "compensation" and it would be injurious to the boy. McCoy must have known that this would not please Slater and would be taken as a further sign of McCoy's "indulgent" way of dealing with the Indians. Concerning Slater's expressed difficulties in gaining the Indians' friendship, McCoy says gently that this cannot be gained by gifts or being over-indulgent but by a "frank, open and friendly course of conduct in general, bearing in mind that you are among men of good natural understanding and of acute sensibilities." Here McCoy is expertly telling the young novice that he will get nowhere by playing the strong-armed school teacher among a people whom he thinks must be either cajoled or bullied into accepting his teaching but by a deep desire to be useful and by a knowledge and acceptance of the Indian's character and abilities. Nevertheless, McCoy tells Slater frankly that he will be of no use to the Indians unless they are given just cause to love and respect him.

Turning to Slater's accusation that McCoy had unfairly gained the friendship of the Ottawas by distributing gifts, and that he had been too lenient with the children, McCoy told Slater that the entire paragraph was based on a totally incorrect view of things and the note of censure given must be rejected. Indeed, McCoy found Slater's remarks quite astonishing. McCoy had shown Slater how to teach with a firm hand and Slater had seen just how such a method worked. Therefore those who taught at the school before Slater are not to be blamed if Slater is not able to teach with the same success. McCoy then tells Slater that there is not the slightest hope of his being successful as a teacher unless he begins to put the blame for any weakness where it belongs and that is in himself. A spirit of meekness and diffidence of one's own self is indispensable in the life of a missionary. Typical of McCoy's generous nature was that when he made his official reports to Dr. Bolles at the Board on July 2nd of that year,[28] he did not mention having any difficulties with Slater. With hindsight, one might think he ought to have done so as Slater, who received no disciplinary opposition from either his fellow-missionaries or the Board, continued to go his own way and found it next to impossible to fit himself into a missionary team.

---

[28] McCoy Papers, Reel 5.

Lincoln and Bolles respond to McCoy's questions regarding financing the mission

       McCoy's report of July 2nd was one of the most positive ever, showing real progress in the work of the missions. He had refrained from dealing with financial matters in the letter because he had chosen to address Heman Lincoln, the Board's new treasurer, directly on the subject, which he did on May 29, 1827. Lincoln replied on July 7, explaining to McCoy that he could not answer his queries fully in the absence of Dr. Bolles, who was on a fund-raising tour. He informed the missionary that "we were obliged to send five thousand dollars to Burmah" as one of the reasons for funds being so low. Lincoln also told McCoy that the Board was to receive a mere $300 from the Government that year which was half of what had been promised. The reason was that the bulk of the money due to the Board had already been paid in advance and used. Obviously McCoy would have been interested to know how the Board had spent these funds since the mission had not received them. What is plain from Lincoln's letter is that he looks to the Government in connection with the financing of the Indian mission in matters of hundreds of dollars, whereas the Burma mission was thought of in terms of thousands.[29] As matters turned out, Dr. Bolles informed McCoy on August 15[30] that the Government had now granted the Board $1,000 for the education of the Miami. McCoy was free to draw on this money, Bolles promised, but immediately after making this statement, he told McCoy that as the Miamis under McCoy's care had already profited from the Board's charity fund and as also buildings had been financed from this fund, it would be necessary for McCoy to deduct those expenses from the Government grant. In other words, Bolles, as so often, raised hopes in McCoy that money would be forthcoming, only to dampen them in the same breath. Actually, in McCoy's letter to Bolles of May 29, McCoy had emphasized that the mission had not received a dollar from the Board's missionary (i.e. charity) fund for a year, nor had it received Government grants due, so that, in reality, the Board was greatly in debt to the Indian mission but Bolles made things appear as if the shoe was on the other foot. Bolles merely scolded McCoy for always seeing things in the light of the mission and not from the point of view of the Board. He told McCoy that Luther Rice had wrongly kept back bills which he ought to have given Josephus and Rice McCoy for their

---

[29] Ibid.

[30] Ibid.

education at Columbian College so that Bolles had used the Indian mission's allotment of the charity fund to pay off those bills. Now he told McCoy this, "was just the same as if paid to your station." Obviously this was not "just the same" since McCoy knew nothing of either Luther Rice's or the Board's action and, furthermore, the old Board had promised free education for missionary children so that no valid bills could be given them. This also meant that the accusation that Rice had "held back" bills was false as no bills were forthcoming.

McCoy must have wondered about Bolles next remark. "It is an immense relief to the Board," the Corresponding Secretary declared, "to cherish the hope" that "Carey and Thomas, will under a prudent management, be sustained by what is raised there, together with the receipts from Government." In other words, Bolles wanted a self-supporting Indian mission so that further thousands could be sent to Burma. One wonders why he did not take the obvious logical step and demand of the overseas missions that they should also be self-supporting. Bolles closed his disparaging letter with a piece of real discouragement for McCoy. As the Congregationalists and Presbyterians of the American Board were not interested in the colonization of the Indian Territory, the Baptist Board felt that they could not make any progress in that matter, either. After telling McCoy throughout the letter that his ideas were quite at variance with the Board's, Bolles signed off "with lasting esteem." Negative as was Bolles' letter, there was one positive and most pleasing piece of news in it. McCoy had long campaigned for the recognition of Jotham Meeker as a missionary as he had been laboring up to this time in no official capacity and financing his own way. Bolles told McCoy that the Board had met and decided to give Meeker missionary status. Meeker was now at Thomas with Slater.

Slater receives McCoy's letter in very bad grace

On August 2, 1827, Slater replied to McCoy's letter of June 27 in which he had taken up Slater's strong criticisms. Slater's reply can only be described by the word "impudent" if not by the words "highly insulting." He tells McCoy that his letter was not intended as a reproof as he would have behaved exactly as McCoy if the means had been placed at his disposal. This is but a thinly veiled repetition of his accusation that McCoy bribed his students into submission. He rejects McCoy's evidence to show that his own criticisms had been unfounded by saying that they might have been incorrect seen from the light McCoy placed on the matter, but they were correct seen in the light he himself wished to convey. It seems that McCoy was being lectured from all quarters on the right use of light at this time. In his defense, Slater gives McCoy a list of examples where McCoy entered into friendly conversation with the Indians and was subsequently obviously well-received by them when he sang, preached and prayed. Slater told McCoy that he could not deny that he had conversed with the Indians concerning temporal matters such as finding work and had promised to help them. All this, Slater argued, showed that McCoy had gone out of his way to court the Indians' favor and had made it impossible for himself to get on equally well with them. This again, provides deep insight into McCoy's love for the Indians and his lack of any prejudice against them contrasted with the stiff patronizing position of Slater who felt that "fraternising with the natives" was not part of the white man's, nor even the missionary's, duty. What makes Slater's defense of his own questionable conduct even more difficult to understand is that, he now transfers his interpretation of William Polke's supposed indulgent behavior to his Thomas pupils on to McCoy as if he thought that what was wrong in the one must be also the behavior of the other. Polke had failed, however, in his missionary aims, but Slater was arguing that McCoy had been successful, but for the wrong motives.[31] From now on, Slater was to send McCoy most extraordinary letters, treating him as if he thought he were some errand boy who was only there to run his errands, as for example his letter of October 7, 1827 concerning McCoy's intended visit to Boston. In this letter, Slater gives McCoy a list what only can be called "orders," repeating "you will do" and "I wish you to do," as if McCoy were the junior colleague. Concerning the matter of payment for the various purchases which he told McCoy to make on his behalf, he added "some society or individual would incur the expense."[32] On the same day, Meeker wrote to Johnston Lykins[33] to say that a dark cloud was hanging over Thomas and the Indians were grumbling and claiming that McCoy had told them a great falsehood. He had said that when he left Thomas, he would be replaced by men equally as good. The Indians were now disheartened that this had not happened.[34] This was not a humble realization on Meeker's part that

---

[31] Ibid.

[32] McCoy Papers, Reel 6.

[33] McCoy was currently on his way to Boston and Lykins was in charge of the Carey Mission. McCoy arrived at Boston on November 9th.

[34] McCoy Papers, Reel 6.

he was not up to McCoy's standard but, as subsequent letters proved, a direct criticism of Slater. The two missionaries just could not get along together.

McCoy again at Boston

When McCoy arrived at Boston, he immediately took up the question of Indian colonization with the Board who now promised to petition Congress. Dr. Bolles had even been persuaded to accompany McCoy to Washington so that both men could hand over the memorial in person and thus make sure that it reached the right people.[35] McCoy and Bolles wrote:

To the Honorable the Senate and House of Representatives in Congress assembled

The memorial of the Board of Managers of the Baptist General Missionary Convention for the U. States, humbly sheweth, that, Whereas, the Indians who remain on small reservations in New England, and in the States of New York, Ohio, and Indiana, together with those bordering on the frontier white-settlements, are rapidly decreasing in numbers, and as a people perishing; and Whereas your memorialists confidently believe that locating these unfortunate people in some suitable location of country, would not only rescue them from extinction, but elevate them in social life to happiness and prosperity, they have resolved to attempt the formation of a settlement to which may be invited such of the natives as circumstances shall justify.

In June 1826, your memorialists appointed an agent to attend to the selection of a place for the settlement contemplated, and matters relating thereto, and they do now respectfully pray Congress to grant them permission to form such a settlement as the above mentioned design proposes, which shall be furnished with the necessary institution in science, morals, husbandry, and the mechanic arts, on the Elkhorn river westwardly of Council Bluffs - on the Missouri river - or elsewhere north of the territory of Arkansas, and between the state of Missouri

---

[35] See McCoy's letters to Josephus and Rice McCoy dated November 17, 1827. McCoy sent the letter to Lexington but his sons were then either at Fort Wayne or had already reached Carey.

and the Missouri river on the east and North east, and the Rocky mountains on the west. The said settlement to be under the entire control of the Government of the U. States according to common usage on the small reservations set apart for missionary establishments in Michigan territory and elsewhere.

And your memorialists further ask leave to invite to said settlement at its commencement, such of the pupils of the schools under their charge, and that of others, and such individuals and families of the Brotherton Indians, the Shawanoe, the Chippewas, the Ottawas, the Putawatomies, and the Miamies as shall be inclined to accompany the agents of your Memorialists to the proposed settlement and subsequently such as shall be willing to join them.

And your Memorialists as in duty bound will ever pray.

In behalf of the Board

Lucius Bolles Cor. Sec.

Boston, Nov.26, 1827.

McCoy's position as the Board's Agent and employee

Two days later, Dr. Bolles wrote a detailed letter from his home in Salem, Massachusetts to Hon. James Barbour, Secretary of War, outlining plans for Indian colonization and affirming that they had appointed Isaac McCoy who had already been ten years in the services of the Board as their official agent in these matters. Bolles added, "We are happy to believe that our views in relation to Indian reform are in perfect accordance with those of the Government." This letter, dated Salem, November 28, 1827[36] is further important evidence towards a correct understanding of subsequent developments in the life and work of McCoy as, when the Board radically changed their policy on the matter, due to an obvious change of politics, they denied outright that McCoy ever represented their interests and was in their service in the matter of Indian colonization. McCoy, they then argued, had acted entirely as a Government employee. Here, however, Bolles clearly recommends McCoy to Barbour as the Board's agent who will

---

[36] For this important letter and the above material see McCoy Papers, Reel 6.

carry out the Board's orders in "a union of effort" with the Government. This was the nearest McCoy came to be a Government employee, i.e. one on loan from the Board in a joint effort, yet under the Board's orders.

While at Boston, McCoy was also successful in persuading the Board to set up a station at Green Bay, having been assured in former correspondence with Governor Cass that the Government would not only agree to the venture but give them a measure of support. McCoy was already in contact with a Lemuel Stannard, who felt called to take up the task of teaching there.[37]

Home news from the missionary family

Meanwhile, McCoy heard regularly from Christiana who was quite ill with skin trouble and numbness in her arms and hands. Josephus, Rice and Lykins all wrote frequently but McCoy also received single letters from his other children, John Calvin, Sarah and Delilah. The latter was now at Carey after finishing her schooling and was helping to teach the Indian girls. Very humbly, she writes:

> I am, however, trying to do as well as I can but possessing so little capacity and having so poor a sight of imparting to others what little knowledge I have myself that I feel sometimes quite discouraged but as I have caused you so much trouble and expense it would afford me much satisfaction as well as pleasure could I in return render any service either to the mission or the poor Indians for whose interest my dear parents have been so long labouring.[38]

On December 4, 1827,[39] Johnston Lykins wrote to McCoy to tell him that Meeker had left Thomas and was now at Carey, complaining strongly about Slater's conduct. This was the sole reason for his visit. Slater, Meeker maintained, was a failure as a missionary. Lykins told McCoy that after hearing all Meeker's complaints and of the Indians' resentments against Mr. and Mrs. Slater, it would be inadvisable to keep the couple at Thomas. Slater had written to the

---

[37] See Stannard's letter to McCoy dated November 6, 1827. McCoy Papers, Reel 6.

[38] Letter written November 20, 1827, McCoy Papers, Reel 6.

[39] See McCoy Papers, Reel 6.

Carey Mission, Lykins added, to say that he felt himself to be an "obstacle in the way of doing good" at Thomas and was thinking of moving to another station among the Indians. As McCoy always gave Lykins full powers of responsibility in his absence, Lykins told McCoy that he had advised Meeker to return to Thomas and take charge of the school himself and "let Bro. & sister S. merely act as assistants in a more private way until the Indians become more reconciled or some other way offers of their being enabled to remain in the mission." Lykins, who obviously did not think much of Slater's character himself, added of the Slaters, "They are no doubt humbled much since you saw them last but I think not any too much yet." This last reference was to the fact that Slater had threatened his coworkers at Thomas to write to the Board to say that they should consider Thomas as independent of Carey and place the mission under his auspices. In other words, Slater was still blaming others for his lack of success and believed that if he were given an entirely free hand, he would do better. Indeed, Slater wrote again to Lykins and Simerwell on December 23,[40] expressing a wish to move to a station not connected with Carey but also made the audacious remark that if all those who had become his enemies were removed, he would be pleased to remain at Thomas.

Pleasant news concerning Johnston Lykins and Delilah McCoy

Christiana's fourth letter written to her husband, now at Washington, on December 16th, is of special interest. Mrs. McCoy says that Lykins is looking after things very well and that his sermons are a great blessing and that she believed he should be ordained for the ministry. She then adds, "I suppose him and D[elilah] will want to get married as soon as you return. She tells me it is her own choice and it is not to accommodate anyone's feelings." Lykins and Delilah were now a couple and Delilah was to share in Lykins' missionary endeavors until parted by death. From now on, Lykins was to address McCoy as Father and McCoy both looked upon and called Lykins his son.

McCoy wrote from Washington on December 19 to his "dear, dear brothers", Lykins and Simerwell, addressing them by their first names. He told them that as the Indians were being rapidly removed from the Great Lake areas, he had now second thoughts about estab-

---

[40] McCoy Papers, Reel 6.

lishing a mission in Green Bay or at St. Marie's. He did not refer to the troubles between Slater and his brother missionaries but merely said, "Hold on - and don't be discouraged."[41]

Positive signs from Bolles

On December 20th, Bolles wrote to McCoy at Washington, where he was still lobbying Congressmen. The Corresponding Secretary greets McCoy most amiably and enthusiastically, saying, "I have felt easier about the thing as you so understand it in all its bearing & as I trust God regards it favourably." Indeed, this is the first truly brotherly and friendly letter that McCoy had ever received from Dr. Bolles who now gives his full backing to McCoy's plans and tells him that he is assured that the Government will accept them and appoint McCoy to be their agent for the resettlement of the Indians. Bolles mentioned in this connection that he had discussed alternative views with representatives of other denominations but found them inferior to what he now calls "our views". In particular, he had discussed the matter with Jeremiah Evarts (also 'Everts'), treasurer of the Presbyterian-Congregationalist American Board of Commissioners for Foreign Missions who had advised the Government against adopting McCoy's plans. This caused Bolles to state that if anything positive were done for the Indians, it would be by the "way pursued by us."[42]

Dealing with complaints about Slater

By Christmas, 1827, McCoy had received several letters of complaint from Carey and Thomas concerning Slater's odd behavior and he decided reluctantly to inform the Board. It was a difficult step to take as he was now on very friendly terms with Bolles and knew that the Board viewed Slater highly and regarded him in a special way as "their missionary." He therefore told Dr. Bolles:

> The Indians have become so prejudiced
> against Brother Slater, that he, and all the other mission-

---

[41] For Mrs. McCoy's letter and that of her husband, see McCoy Papers, Reel 6.

[42] McCoy Papers, Reel 6.

aries at both stations unite in opinion that he can hardly be useful at Thomas, especially as now situated.

Duty now requires me to detail some facts on which I had hoped to be allowed silence. Bro. Slater entered on his work, not with an impression that he must <u>learn</u> from others, but confident of his capacity to correct supposed errors in our missionary operations. I suppose the hope of being allowed <u>to do as he pleased</u> increased his willingness to leave Carey to go to Thomas.[43] Myself, my wife & others had counselled Bro. & sister Slater fully & kindly, on the course proper for them to pursue. Unfortunately Bro. Slater's confidence in his own judgement remained. On my return from Thomas to Carey, Lykins was left superintendent of the former, by commission from government & arrangement of the Mission. Lykins, believing that they were deceiving themselves and injuring the mission, suggested at different times, the course they ought to take. Discovering, as he thought, no disposition to follow advice, he became disgusted, returned to Carey, and refused to live with bro. & sister Slater. Bro. Slater also expressed pleasure that bro. Lykins had left him. Previous to Lykins' leaving Thomas the Indians became so dissatisfied with Slater that an attempt was made by an Indian, in the darkness of the night, to kill Slater with a knife. (The particulars I gave you in Bost[on].) Lykins afterwards called the Indians together and settled the affair as well as he could.

Bro. Meeker and I went out to Thomas, Slater now supposed that the prejudices of the Indians had vanished. But I soon learnt from the Indians themselves that they still despised him. This I communicated to him, gave him advice and told him most plainly, he <u>must submit</u> to the judgment and experience of older missionaries, and that some two or three years experience would enable him to give counsel to a new naiv[e] missionary. For the first time, I now discovered Bro. S[later] somewhat humbled, and we began to hope for his success. Meeker was left superintendent.

Slater, as recorded above, could not get along with Meeker at all and refused to submit to him as the spiritual and administrative head of the mission. This McCoy outlined to Bolles and told him that

---

[43] Slater had obviously believed that on becoming a missionary, he would be put in charge of a missionary station. He found it humiliating to be ranked lower than McCoy, Lykins and Meeker in eligibility as superintendent.

Slater's main trouble was his haughtiness and unwillingness to care for the problems of the Indians and bring comfort to them. He totally refused to accommodate himself to the Indians' way of thinking and to their wants and wishes. The Indians thus regarded him as a "bad man" and believed they had been deceived by McCoy's promise that they would receive a Christian missionary like the other missionaries to the Indians they knew such as McCoy, Lykins, Meeker and Simerwell. McCoy is, however, still not prepared to say that Slater has no future among the Indians and says that he has been humbled much and wishes to continue to work among the natives, but under more favorable conditions. Slater had suggested going to the Ottawas. This was a reference to the planned establishment of a school at St Marie's[44] which, if it were to materialize, was to be under the supervision of Stannard. The Government was now pressing the Board to send a teacher there who would be adequately paid by the Government. At present plans were for a school only and no mission station. This led McCoy to suggest to Bolles that Slater should have his way and be sent to the new school. McCoy concludes:

> Not withstanding that Bro. Slater has had the misfortune to incur the dislike of everybody about him, both white and red, since he went into that country, yet we all believe that his piety, his desire to be useful to the Indians and his tact for teaching a school, justify the hope that he will become a useful and worthy missionary. He is now becoming convinced how little he knew of men and things, he desires to do good to man in obedience to his God. He has failed in an attempt - he is disappointed and discouraged. Now is the time for us to take him in our arms and hold him up.[45]

This final statement was no mock-pious platitude on the part of McCoy but represented the deep loving, pastoral nature of his own heart. When writing to his wife on the matter a day later, there is no mention of the suffering McCoy had to go through at Slater's hand but he says sincerely, "Since it is probable that Bro. and Sister Slater are in distress, I think we shall all feel like taking them in our arms and holding them up."[46] Here McCoy is clearly giving Slater the benefit of any doubt. The unpopular missionary was obviously only in distress

---

[44] Also called Sault de St. Maria.

[45] Letter dated December 25, 1827, McCoy Papers, Reel 6.

[46] Letter dated December 26, 1827, McCoy Papers, Reel 6.

because he could not enforce his will on others. He was to remain a thorn in the side of his brother missionaries for many years to come, although he managed to remain on good terms with the Board. Meanwhile, Slater wrote to those whom he thought would make suitable missionary candidates, encouraging them to apply to him for a post, as if he were not only the superintendent of the mission but the Acting Board itself. McCoy only found out about this months later when one of Slater's "candidates" wrote to him, saying that he had received no reply from Slater.[47] Much good was to come of this letter, as the subsequent history of the mission will show.

Martin and McCoy under suspicion because of the Board's inaction

On December 27, 1827, we find McCoy writing a long letter to the *Baptist Recorder* on the subject of the *Latter Day Luminary*. The latter newspaper, edited by Luther Rice, had been the mouthpiece of the old Board before the New Englanders changed their priorities. It was now defunct due to lack of funds, official support and rumors concerning its financing. In the year 1823, Corbly Martin, working as a highly successful freelance agent for the Indian Mission, with McCoy's approval, had told friends of the mission that their gifts and how they were to be used would be published in detail in the *Latter Day Luminary*. The newspaper, which had already begun to appear rather sporadically, however, had merely mentioned the total sum collected by Martin and had not gone into any detail. This had angered many a friend of the mission who wanted to know whether their personal gift had been duly received and acknowledged and to what end it was used. Both Martin and McCoy were now subjected to criticism and even suspicion. McCoy explained that Martin had kept minute accounts and handed them to him and he had added a written report in great detail of how the funds were used. This was sent to the Board for publication in the *Latter Day Luminary*. In his letter, McCoy quotes extensively from his correspondence with the Board who had praised both Martin and McCoy for the exact and detailed way in which they had kept their records. Indeed, the Board had told readers of the *Latter Day Luminary* that the report in question had come in but was so voluminous that it would be printed as a supplement "as

---

[47] See letter written by Abel Bingham to McCoy dated February 5, 1828. Bingham also mentioned that a Mr. Rollin was keen on entering missionary service, McCoy Papers, Reel 6.

early as practicable".[48] Two years had already lapsed since the collection was made and McCoy, hindered by the delay in postal correspondence, made query after query at the Board. Missionary finance had now been taken out of the hands of Luther Rice, though nominally he had retained the post of manager for a while, and placed in the care of the Committee of Outfit, called thus as they fitted missionaries out with equipment etc. By 1826, Rice had been strongly censured by the Board and replaced. The *Latter Day Luminary* was discontinued and the *American Baptist Magazine* took its place as the organ of the Board. Finally the matter was looked into and McCoy received the explanation that the editor, Luther Rice, was abroad at the time and the printer, on beginning to set the type, decided not to publish the supplement on his own responsibility but wait until the editor returned. When the editor returned, McCoy was told, all traces of his report had disappeared in his absence. Sadly, this negligent state of affairs was not reported to the public with the result that both Martin and McCoy came under suspicion of not handling donations correctly. McCoy's article to the *Recorder* was to allay such fears. Probably, McCoy sent this letter to several newspapers in several states as he tended to do in such cases.[49] Martin had collected money in Kentucky, Indiana and Ohio and probably elsewhere. McCoy closed his article with a brief look at how the mission was prospering.

Signs that things were under way concerning Indian relocation

In his letter to Bolles of December 25, McCoy mentioned that he believed he would soon be requested to travel west of the Mississippi for several months with a view to the Indians' future settlement of that area. He wrote to Christiana on December 26th to say he was now planning to return to Carey and that he had found support for his venture in the West among some Congressmen, but no details were given. A letter from Rice McCoy dated January 7, 1828 shows that McCoy was planning to take Christiana with him this time and possibly set up a temporary home at Lexington, where his sons

---

[48] *Latter Day Luminary*, vol 6, No. 5, p. 153. See also p. 147 which refers to the Carey accounts.

[49] Rice McCoy sent a published shortened version of this article to his father from Lexington on January 25, 1828 but omitted to mention the name of the newspaper. The editor's name is given as Mr. Skillman. McCoy Papers, Reel 6.

were in their final year of medical studies.[50] Rice also adds that he has read in a Washington newspaper that a Mr. Mitchell of Tennessee had introduced a resolution in Congress on lines similar to McCoy's demands, so things were indeed being set in motion. McCoy was still waiting anxiously for an official Government response to his memorial. In his letter to his wife of December 26, McCoy expresses his disappointment that Heman Lincoln has not turned up, which was delaying his departure. Bolles had promised to send Lincoln to support McCoy in discussing arrangements with the Government for the Board's outreach in the Indian Territory, with McCoy as their agent or commissioner. Bolles and Lincoln had, instead, waited until the quarterly meeting of the Board on January 2nd, before making a final decision regarding Washington. Lincoln wrote the day after to say that he was on his way to Washington from Boston as the Board's decision had been positive to McCoy's wishes.

At last, on January 7, 1828, the bill that McCoy had been waiting for was printed and, after being passed twice through the appropriate departments was to be submitted to the entire House the following day. It read:

20th Congress,   **H.R. 55.**
1st Session

January 7, 1828
Read twice, and committed to a Committee of the Whole House tomorrow.

Mr. McLean, from the Committee on Indian Affairs, to which the subject had been referred, reported the following bill:

A Bill

Making an appropriation to defray the expenses of certain Indians, who propose to emigrate.

1. Be it enacted by the Senate and House of Representatives
2. of the United States of America in Congress assembled, That,
3. to enable a deputation of the Chickasaws and other Indians,

---

[50] McCoy Papers, Reel 6.

4. to be joined by such persons as the President of the United
5. States may appoint for that purpose, to examine the country
6. west of the Mississippi, for the purpose of selecting a portion
7. of it for a permanent home, the sum of fifteen thousand dol-
8. lars be, and the same is hereby, appropriated, to be paid from
9. any moneys in the Treasury, not otherwise appropri- ated.

McCoy still felt that he could not yet return home, for as he told Christiana in his next letter dated January 12, so many people wanted now to jump on the band wagon and have the privilege of escorting the Indians to the new territory, that, though he believed he would still be the first choice, others might have an advantage over him by their very presence in Washington as soon as the bill was passed if he were not there. The bill, however, was delayed so on February 2, 1828, McCoy wrote to General James Noble, whom he knew supported his plan, stressing how important it was that the bill should be given a final hearing and passed. He also gave detailed reasons why he should be chosen to escort the Indians. So thorough was McCoy in his suggestions of how the country was to be surveyed and what reports were to be made, that he even went into great details as to how the undertaking could be financed, listing several other ways should his first suggestion fail. Finally, he gave General Noble the names of fourteen Congressmen with whom the General could safely and discretely discuss the matter. Actually, he had now contacted some thirty who professed to be in agreement with him. By now, McCoy's conscience and Christiana's pleas were urging him to leave Washington, so he wrote again to the General, begging him to write at least weekly to keep him abreast of the news. McCoy also wrote a similar letter to his old friend and rival in educational matters, Colonel Johnson.

McLean's passionate plea before the House: A partial success

At last, on February 5, 1828, just as McCoy was about to set off for home, the bill was debated before the House. Mr. William McLean of Ohio, well known to McCoy, being one of his corres- pondents, gave a passionate plea for providing a permanent home for the Indians which he saw as sacred duty of the Government. McLean's enthusiasm and passion did not hinder him from outlining sound historical, social, financial, political and moral reasons for accepting his proposals. He also stressed how it was of the utmost importance that the area west of the Mississippi should be accurately examined to consider its suitability as a permanent home for all Indians. McLean was creating the very job description that McCoy was looking for to suit his aims under God. Indeed, on reading the text of this great speech, McCoy's presence can be seen in almost every word.[51] In short, the bill was approved but in a way that left much to be desired from McCoy's side. Opposition came from the Secretary of War, Peter Porter and his anti-missionary party, from those who felt that as the Indians were a doomed race, financial investment in their fate was a waste of taxpayers money, and from those who feared that slavery would spread through slave-owning Indians moving with their slaves to former slave free areas. Most worrying for McCoy was that no names were mentioned concerning possible escorts for the Indians who wished to emigrate to the new territories. McCoy's extant mail at this time gives little insight as to what exactly happened. It appears that Lincoln arrived in Washington in time to catch McCoy and they were able to obtain President Adams' ear and discuss matters with the large number of Congressmen, so that Lincoln could report to the Board that McCoy was the most likely candidate to be sent with the Indians and reconnoiter the land.

The McCoys again ill. Johnston and Delilah marry

Not quite convinced that all was well, McCoy departed for Carey on February 11, traveling almost nonstop in the terrible winter weather, with floods hindering his path all along the route. In spite of these difficulties, he arrived home in record time, reaching Carey on February 21. As usual after a long journey, McCoy arrived home worn out and feeling very ill. As also was very usual, he found his wife, too, very ill, aggravated by the extra responsibility she had had to bear during her husband's long absence. At one point, her health had been so poor that John Calvin, still only a boy, and a hired white man had attempted to swim the St. Joseph River several times, losing their provisions and baggage while doing so and making a seven days journey through the bleak winter to find a doctor for her. They were

---

[51] The entire speech is preserved in the McCoy Papers, Reel 6.

compelled to return in a state of utter exhaustion without having found a doctor.[52] After recovering somewhat, on February 27, 1828, McCoy was able to join his daughter Delilah and his right-hand man Johnston Lykins in matrimony.

Good news from the Board

Lincoln's report appears to have been more positive than McCoy viewed the situation. In next to no time a Board meeting was called and the following resolution was duly dispatched to McCoy:

> At a meeting of the Baptist Board of Foreign Missions held at Boston on the 26th of February, It was Resolved That anticipating appointment by the Government of the U.S. of their missionary the Revd Isaac McCoy to go on a tour of survey with a view to the future location of the Indian tribes, he be authorised to accept such appointments & to submit to such instructions as may be given him in relation to the same, provided, those instructions be in accordance with the known wishes of the Board, & further, that in the execution of his appointment, no expense to the Board shall be incurred.

> Attest Lucius Bolles, Secretary
> Salem, March 3. 1828.

This was accompanied by a most encouraging letter from Bolles, outlining in full the relationship the Board expected McCoy to maintain with itself and with the Government. As this document states categorically that McCoy is being sent out in accordance with the joint and identical aims of the Government and the Board, it must be quoted in full so that the reader may bear it in mind when faced with alternative interpretations later placed on it by the Board. Bolles writes:

> My dear Brother,

> In view of your expected tour of the West, I need say but little by way of introduction. You will be the agent of the Government, as such will receive directions from them. Their general object will cover our specific one,

---

[52] See *History of Baptist Indian Missions*, p. 328.

which we are desirous you should keep in mind. It is our anxious wish to find a permanent <u>home</u> for the Indians who have been, or may be trained in schools, together with their relatives and others who may unite with them to form a settlement, persuaded that this is the best if not the only method of securing to them the blessings of which they are capable & the immunities to which they are entitled. We desire for them a situation favourable to their health, social peace & individual prosperity. Of the country, your long experience & well-known regard to the well being of Indians, will induce a better selection, than any rules we can prescribe to you. You will not of course commit this body to any engagements into which you shall enter, but leave your calculations & plans open for their consideration & final conclusion. We have no doubt you will go forth with a heart raised in supplication to heaven & we trust to follow you with the same spirit, assured that the enterprise will prosper only as far, as it is in accordance with the will of God & carried forward under his guidance. In fact, our souls rely on him & we would not willingly attempt any thing without him.

Wishing you much comfort of the Holy Spirit, I remain

Yours truly, L. Bolles, Sec.

P.S. Before leaving Carey, you will I trust make arrangements for one of the families or brethren, to occupy the new station at the Sault St. Marias, & inform us fully in relation to the same. I have written twice to Mr. Stannard, but have not yet heard from him, for which I cannot account. We will give instructions to the brother who is to go, as soon as informed of his designation & and shall be gratified by any suggestions you may offer as to best measures to be pursued there etc etc. Hope you found all well at Carey.[53]

Here several features are important to note. The Board were commissioning McCoy to go out as their missionary to serve as a Government agent with tasks congenial to both. Though McCoy was under Government orders, he was also under the Board's orders, as their missionary, in matters pertaining to their interests. Where those interests separated, McCoy's responsibility was first and foremost to the Board who would then make final decisions. Though McCoy was setting out on a very expensive tour within the scope of his missionary

---

[53] See McCoy Papers, Reel 6 for resolution and letter.

calling and direct ruling from the Board whom he served, that Board wished all to be carried out at a third party's cost.

Awaiting the voting on the Indian relocation bill with apprehension

On April 1st, Heman Lincoln wrote to McCoy, much concerned about his health and also much subdued himself concerning the Indian relocation bill which still had to go through several stages before being passed. It seemed Lincoln was having second thoughts about the bill's chances of success. Happily, when McCoy received this rather gloomy letter, he also received a letter directly from the House of Representatives[54] signed by Congressman Wilson Lumpkin containing an answer from the Committee of Indian Affairs to McCoy's and Bolles' memorial, handed in the autumn before in the name of the Baptist Convention. The Department's view, Lumpkin stressed, was favorable and they were willing to grant the aid requested according to the terms of the Indian relocation bill now waiting to be passed, Lumpkin assured McCoy that "the Bill making appropriations preparatory to Indian emigration will yet pass, altho it has & will meet with strong opposition." Another favorable letter at this time was from McCoy's new friend in New York, Spencer Cone who was a member of the Board and had become a zealous supporter of McCoy and his cause.[55]

A rose with a thorn attached

On May 6, 1828, the first signs of success for McCoy's cause appeared but there was a sharp thorn on the stem of the rose. By a treaty signed in Washington, the Cherokees were granted seven million acres of land in the Arkansas and Canadian River areas, providing they gave up their possessions and traditional lands east of Mississippi. The Indians were to move on a voluntary basis and each would receive compensation for his property lost, a gun, a blanket, five pounds of tobacco, the cost of transportation and free land on arrival in the Indian Territory. Happy as McCoy was to know that Indian relocation was now underway, he could not help thinking that the Cherokees were an unhappy choice. These were the most Europeanized of Indians and also the most well-to-do. They had also

---

[54] See McCoy Papers, Reel 6 for both letters.

[55] Letters to be found in McCoy Papers, Reel 6.

the greatest percentage of mixed bloods among them and owned the greatest percentage of Negro slaves in comparison to other tribes. McCoy had always argued that his policy was for the so-called "Wild Indians", and that the so-called Five Civilized Tribes were exceptions to this rule. The Wild Indians *must* be moved to save them from destruction, the Cherokees and Choctaws etc. who lived almost on the same terms of ownership as their European neighbors must be allowed to stay if they so willed.[56] Sadly, those Cherokees who opted to move were subjected to a great deal of hate and persecution even leading to murder by those of their people who opted to stay. McCoy's counterpart working with the Cherokees, Evan Jones of the Valley Towns Mission, took sides with those who wished to stay and made himself very unpopular with the Government. A further problem arose when the numerous white relations of the Cherokees, claimed that they were Indians and many white people married Indians so that they would receive land. Whites even went to the length of buying and adopting Indian children, then claiming land on their children's behalf. It was all quite different to what McCoy had envisaged. It was also John Quincy Adams' last stand as a President and one of his last efforts to give in to popular demand in view of the coming elections in which he would have to make way for General Andrew Jackson.

McCoy is chosen as member of an expedition to prepare Indian relocation

On May 29, General James Noble wrote to McCoy from Washington with the cryptic words which must have caused the missionary's heart to flutter, "Congress on this day has adjourned. The Bills that have passed relative to the Indians I hope will be satisfactory to you, when you see them." Noble also told McCoy that there was now a direct postal route to Carey and that he had recommended McCoy as Post Master.[57] Though it was to take another two years before the rights of the Indians were anchored in law in the Indian Territory, what McCoy read made him quickly draw up a document, saying that the mission had always regarded her stations

---

[56] See McCoy's lengthy remarks on the Cherokees in his *Remarks on the Practicability of Indian Reform*, New York, 1829.

[57] McCoy Papers, Reel 6. McCoy was made Post Master by the Post Master General on May 27, 1828. As he was about to set off to the Indian Territory, McCoy asked for the position to be given to Lykins.

as temporary settlements and now it was time for one of their body to look into the matter of a permanent Indian mission settlement in a country set aside permanently for the Indians. All those in favor should sign the document. All did, even Slater. McCoy did this so that his local mission church, his fellow missionaries and the Board, should all know that whoever went out in search of a permanent home for the Indians and the Indian mission, was doing so in full agreement with his fellow workers. The Board had already shown this agreement, now the local church and missionary fellowship followed suit.

Soon, McCoy was to receive the document of authority he had cherished and prayed for throughout the eleven years of his missionary career. It read:

To The Revd Isaac McCoy   Department of War
Supt. Indian School,
Carey, via Fort Wayne, Indiana
                                                     Off: Ind: Affairs.
                                                        10th June, 1828.

Sir,
                   The Congress having appropriated fifteen
thousand Dollars to defray the expense of an exploring
party of Indians, and you having made known the desire of
certain Potawatomies to visit the Country west of the
Mississippi, the Secretary of War directs me to inform you
that you are appointed to accompany the party, and that
you are at liberty to take with you three Potawatomies, and
if necessary an Interpreter. To you is confided the trust of
expending the means provided for the expense of the
undertaking. You will be particular therefore in the
exercise of a rigid economy and in keeping regular and
properly vouched accounts of the expenditure. Of the fifteen
thousand Dollars, I am directed to authorize you to draw for
Ten thousand on the Secretary of War, at sight, accompanying the bill with a letter of advice.
                   You will repair to St. Louis as early as
possible, and report to Genl. Wm. Clarke, Supt. Ind. Affairs,
who has instructions upon the subject, and who will name
a leader of the party, and in general give the necessary
detailed instructions for the government of your route and
movements
                   Should it be found indispensable to use
more than ten thousand Dollars, in paying the necessary
expenses of the undertaking, Genl. Clarke will arrange with
you at St. Louis for the remainder of the appropriation by
placing it within your reach, which, however it is expected

will be so managed as to cover the cost of the agents, including your own pay, and, which will be made equivalent, as far as that may be possible, to the nature and value of the services which you may render.

The Chickasaws and Choctaws are notified to be off as soon as possible. You had better drop Genl. Clarke, at St. Louis, a line saying when you will be there. <u>Move quick</u>.

> I am.
> very Respectfully
> Yr. Obt. Servt.
> Tho. L. M,Kenney"

This letter must have been beyond McCoy's wildest dreams. He had lobbied the Government to be a mere escort for the Indians and have the freedom to make his own reports both for the Government and the Board but now he was appointed not only as an escort but as the expedition's treasurer. This meant that very much of the management was in his hands and whoever the leader of the expedition was, he must consult McCoy at all times otherwise he would not know if his plans were financially feasible or not.

Congress, of course, was not without ulterior motives though they served the wishes of the Indian mission at the time. Countless European immigrants were settling the area east of the Mississippi and in the northern parts of the U. S. and making the life of the Indians most difficult. Since the Treaty of Chicago in 1821, Indians who had given up their traditional ways in their traditional territories were given an annual gratuity but as soon as the money was paid out, wicked white traders who traded in nothing but whiskey, set up "shop" immediately in the precincts of the Indians and, as a result, their money was gone in a flash. The area in which McCoy and the Government intended to settle the Indians had been left untouched by settlers because of its supposed barren nature. McCoy discovered that this was a thoroughly erroneous view as the soil was good and that all the area lacked was trees which could be up and growing in a generation. He honestly felt that the Government's decision was an answer to his prayers and, as few whites would take on the difficulties of starting a new life in what was then called The Unorganized Territories, it would belong to the Indians for ever. It is interesting to note that these territories were indeed among the last to be dominated by the whites, the Indians practicing various forms of their own statehood in present day Oklahoma, which forms the largest part of the old Indian Territory, until 1907.

McCoy's Remarks on the Practicability of Indian Reform

McCoy now felt that it was the correct time to publish his *Remarks on the Practicability of Indian Reform Embracing Their Colonization.* He had been working on this book for several years. In it, McCoy shows the methods the Europeans had used to take over Indian lands, guided by their law of acquisition by conquest alone. Previous rights of habitation and ownership meant nothing to them. The author then describes the character of the Indians, ridding the reader of many unjust prejudices, and goes on to consider the conditions under which they now had to live due to white supremacy and even tyranny. McCoy rejects totally that the Indians are a sub-civilized people on the verge of dying out because of their savage nature. He argues:

> To the concurrent testimony of all who are engaged in the labour of Indian reform, I add my own unqualified assertion, resulting from an experience of more than ten years actual residence in the Indian country, that there exists among our Indians no attachment to any pernicious manners or customs, that will not yield to sound argument, righteous example, and the offer of a better condition. I suppose that no heathen nation on the earth can be found, so easily accessible to all the customs which render civilized life blessed, and to the doctrines of the gospel, which guide to heaven, as the American Indians were, when Europeans first became acquainted with them. The entire absence of idolatry, of established forms of religion, to which all *must bend*, and their ideas of the existence of God, and I will add, of the sources of good and evil, threw the door of access to them wide open. Had they not at that time been trampled under our feet - had they been approached as men, entitled to meet their fellow men upon equitable terms - had they been greeted with the charities of our holy religion, our better things would have been received by them with open arms, and every tribe would have called us blessed.[58]

A zealous contender for freedom of thought and religion, McCoy explains that, in contrast to the practices of the whites which the Indians sadly took over, "I very much question if ever there was a man upon the continent chased out of his country, imprisoned, or whipped, for his religion, before the settlement of the whites in it."[59]

---

[58] *Remarks*, 2nd edition, p. 16.

[59] Ibid, p. 16.

He then dwells with more attention to the legal rights of the Indians to the soil on which they have lived for centuries and shows that as these legal rights have been taken from the Indians, and cannot be given back, the Government is duty bound to give them new lands with the same rights of ownership that white men are given. Such land, McCoy argues, is available and ready for settlement, namely his proposed Indian Territory. He goes on to explain how this new land can be best occupied, i.e. how the Indian Removal could take place and how the new country might be governed by the Indians under Congress but represented in it like the other states.

Had McCoy asked the Board to print his *Remarks* at their expense a mere year previously, he would have received a most certain negative answer. Now that McCoy had met Bolles, Lincoln, Cone and other members of the Board, he had managed to excite them with the prospects of success for his venture. McCoy always insisted on pleading his case, whether before the Board or the Government, in person as he had a remarkable gift of inspiring others with his own God-given ideas. Thus now the Board did not hesitate to print McCoy's *Remarks* at their own expense. McCoy made certain that each member of Congress and representatives of each State Department were sent copies, with further copies being distributed to the general public free of charge. A second edition was published in 1829 and probably a third in 1831.[60] By this time McCoy was in personal contact with at least 30 members of Congress and was invited to advise the Committee of the House of Representatives on Indian Affairs.

Although the politicians from now on gave McCoy every encouragement and backing, he realized that many of them still thought that the Indians were a doomed race and they were merely postponing their final end. Some Congressmen, however, men of honor, felt it their unbounded duty to make up to the Indians for what they had taken from them. Others who gave McCoy a measure of support believed, as he, in separating Indians from whites who should be excluded from that territory. Unlike McCoy, however, they believed that the Indians would not have American citizenship and their territory would not be part of the United States. McCoy envisaged a separate Indian State within the United States.

---

[60] My copy printed by Gray and Bunce of New York featuring the above title and an Appendix has 1829 as the date of the Second Edition but the Appendix is signed and dated Indian Territory, December 1, 1831.

Problems still facing a successful Indian removal

As a result of McCoy's and Congress' work, measures began to be taken to evacuate over a hundred thousand Indians. Both Congress and McCoy had made one slip-up, however, in their reckoning. They had not consulted the Indian tribes already living in the area west of the Mississippi. There was also the problem of slavery. The well-to-do Indians within the Muskogean tribes and their allies where McCoy had not yet worked, i.e. Cherokee, Chickasaws, Shawnee and Creeks, kept Negro slaves but the non-slave-owning states had petitioned that no new areas would be opened to slave-owning people in the South. Thus the strange state of affairs ensued that those states who campaigned for the liberty of the Negroes were against giving the Indians the chance to organize themselves as an Independent Indian State. Indeed, when the Chickasaws and Choctaws were resettled in the Indian Territory and a number, mostly of mixed blood, became very affluent, they held up to hundreds of Negro slaves, which did not improve their standing with the Northerners.[61]

Another problem was that McCoy had encouraged the Indians around Carey and Thomas to settle down and become farmers, hoping that when the inevitable move came, the Indians would be compensated well for their farms and be able to start new lives as farmers in the new territories. Yet, once the evacuation started, a number of farming Indians did not want to move and delayed things until the Government grew tired of bargaining with them. Also Congress had already moved several southern tribes to new areas where they were told they could stay for ever but now, with the Indian Territory becoming a reality, the Indians became unsettled, fearing that they would be moved again. A further handicap was that McCoy seemed to have had in mind a single Indian state split up into tribal regions but governed centrally. Once the Indians, however, went West, each tribe began to found its own nation with its own government, constitution and laws. Those tribes who had already entered the land named Indian Territory, (i.e. the Muskogean tribes), were not eager to share the land that they had staked out with newcomers from other tribes. This meant that the land must be carefully measured up and re-allotted fairly to tribes according to their size, against the protests of the earliest emigrants.

---

[61] See Arrell M. Gibson, *Oklahoma: A History of Five Centuries*, p. 170, where he gives details of Indians possessing up to 500 slaves!

Preparing to move west of the Mississippi

At last, we find McCoy speedily packing and recruiting Indians to accompany him on the journey west, though without Christiana, as he had received permission to increase the number of Indian representatives. Now Ottawas were to be added to his party. Finding suitable Indians to go with him proved a problem that he had not taken into consideration. The white whiskey traders, realizing that their trade would cease should their customers go west, strove to prevent them leaving by telling them terrible tales of intolerable heat, poisonous reptiles and fierce scalp-taking savages. The Indians approached McCoy with their fears. On being asked who told them these frightening stories, they answered, "We heard a little bird singing the news." McCoy replied that he had heard the same birds singing in the form of certain white men and explained to the Indians that the whites did not want to see their whiskey profits sink and thus were doing all in their power to persuade the Indians to stay.

New missionaries to the Indians

Meanwhile, a number of new missionaries joined the Carey and Thomas mission stations, including a group of men and their families already doing missionary work among the Indians of Tonawanta in New York. These had been initially introduced to the work at Carey and Thomas by Leonard Slater as mentioned previously. As the Department of Indian Affairs continued to press McCoy and the Board to provide them with missionaries for a station at Sault de St. Marie[62] between Lake Huron and Lake Superior, McCoy suggested to the Board that the New Yorkers could take on the task. The Board agreed and during 1828 Mr. and Mrs. Abel Bingham were transferred from New York to Fort Brady where they commenced a long service with the Chippewas. The other Tonawanta missionary, Mr. Stannard was to be sent, too, but he died before final plans were made. Johnston Lykins and Delilah McCoy, who had now joined hearts and hands in marriage, ensured that Carey received a further missionary in the form of McCoy's daughter. Two further ladies joined the missionaries but soon left because of the hardships. One lady, a Miss Karen, was sent to Burma by the Board, the other, Miss Mary

---

[62] Variously spelled St. Marie, St. Maria, St. Marias, etc.

Rice, worked among the Creeks[63] along the Arkansas River for a time but as her health did not improve and since she still felt strongly called to the Indian mission, she returned to her first post at Fort Brady. An Episcopalian minister, Mr. James Cameron, became convinced of Baptist principles and also joined the Fort Brady missionaries. The work there prospered.

Carey and Thomas still deep in debt

Meanwhile, one matter was still a nagging problem, that of finance. McCoy was under constant orders from the Board concerning Indian settlement west of the Mississippi, "but had not authorised anything in relation to this matter to be undertaken at their cost."[64] It appears, that owing to his new position as Government agent, the Board felt that they need not fund him in any way as a missionary. Yet the Carey mission was still over $1,300 in debt due to drafts not being honored by the Board and Government funds not reaching the mission. McCoy was still in correspondence with Luther Rice over a sum which Rice had paid into the Board to be forwarded to McCoy but part of which had been "lost" on the way. The Government now demanded from Rice that they should be given a written statement that the money had reached its goal and Rice, not really knowing what to do as he had received no reaction from the Board, had passed the buck to McCoy.

To make matters worse, Slater started taking the mission's affairs into his own hands and began ordering goods without coordinating his plans with the other missionaries, and with no hope of the goods being paid for.[65] McCoy told him plainly that if, in the future, he ordered goods and materials without discussing the matter with his superintendent and fellow missionaries, he would have to pay for them himself. Meeker wrote back to say that Slater had reacted as he had anticipated and taken exception to the letter saying he would

---

[63] About 1,000 Creeks were moved from the east coast to the Arkansas River by a Government treaty of 1818 but as the whites took over the area, they were then moved again around 1828.

[64] *History of Baptist Indian Missions*, p. 333.

[65] See McCoy's letter of astonishment to Slater when he heard this news, June 11, McCoy Papers, Reel 6. Further letters on this topic are to be found on this reel.

hand in his resignation and complain to the Board that he was being abused and that his opinion was not being respected.[66] McCoy promptly took the matter up with Slater who gave Meeker part of the blame for his conduct and partly McCoy, but professed he was totally innocent of blame himself. If he made decisions, the others had to respect them, was his argument. Thus, although the mission was going through a time of prosperity regarding spiritual matters, McCoy was now greatly concerned because of Slater's behavior and wondering what they could sell to pay off debts accrued which he firmly believed were the Board's debts. Thus all the missionaries at the various stations awaited the Board's financial report for 1828 with great interest. When the report was published, it was received with great disappointment. Though there was much praise in the report for the Indian missionaries, this is all they were to receive. McCoy comments:

> But in an address to the public, setting forth the wants of the missions, and soliciting pecuniary aid, the Board pleaded for Burma and Africa, and for aid to enable them to establish missions in South America, Greece, and China, and entirely overlooked their Indian stations, as though no help was needed for them; and, indeed, a pretty plain hint was given, in the proceedings of the board, that Indian stations would be amply supported by the Government.[67]

A more critical reader, on perusing the 1828 Annual Report, would find that the Board were virtually giving up the Indian Mission, or, at least, giving it up to the Government for its entire financing. The rousing, evangelical words ending the report under the heading *Address of the Board to the Churches* must have seemed like a very false piety indeed to the Carey, Thomas and Valley Towns missionaries. The anonymous Board member pleads:

> Brethren, shall it be so in the future? Will you not come up to the full measure of your duty on this subject? We call on you, in the name of Him who has redeemed us from death; we urge you by the misery of a world lying in wickedness; we entreat you, by all that is solemn in the thought of an approaching judgment, to give us your prayers, and your pecuniary aid. Let every Christian resolve that a portion of his income shall be paid into the treasury of the Lord. Let

---

[66] Letter dated June 18, 1828, McCoy Papers, Reel 6.

[67] Ibid, p. 335.

a male and female primary mission society be established in every Church and congregation. Let every one, who can afford the expense, subscribe for the American Baptist Magazine, the official publication of the Board. Let the monthly concert for prayer be punctually attended; and let every Christian, in his closet, plead with God, that he will let his way be known on earth, his saving health unto all people. Then, brethren, will your peace be like a river, while the wilderness and the solitary place will be glad for you, and the desert rejoice and blossom like the rose.[68]

Since the Board had invited McCoy to make his requests known publicly and had urged him to go to the press, he wrote an open letter under the title *To Friends of Indian Reform*,[69] outlining what the mission was called to do and what its financial needs were. In doing this, he was carrying out to the letter what the Board had suggested to him. McCoy sent the appeal for help to the Board, asking them to place it in the *Christian Watchman* and the *American Baptist Magazine*. This the Board refused to do.[70]

---

[68] *American Baptist Magazine*, 1828, p. 175.

[69] See manuscript copy (badly damaged) on Reel 6, McCoy Papers.

[70] The Board had obviously meant the secular press, not the Christian press as they wished the Christian public to finance the overseas mission.

Chapter Ten
Exploring the Indian Territory (1828-30)

Planning the expedition with Kennerly and Clarke

On July 2nd, McCoy set off on the first stage of his journey westwards to St. Louis, arriving there just over two weeks later. Here he was to meet the other commissioners. He had miscalculated the distance by a hundred miles, having to travel four hundred altogether. On his arrival, McCoy was introduced to the expedition's leader Captain George Kennerly of St. Louis and conferred personally with him as they waited for General Clarke, the Superintendent of Indian Affairs to arrive. The three men planned the journey as well as one could plan such an enterprise into unknown country. They imagined that they would be able to finish their business by October when McCoy wanted to attend an important treaty signing at St. Joseph's near the Carey mission station. He had only spent one night in St. Louis, yet we find him already writing to his "Dear Son Johnston" to tell him to contact the Government concerning the treaty and make arrangements for accommodating the delegates. McCoy had previously written to Governor Cass, asking him to delay the treaty so that he could get back in time but after a few days waiting at St. Louis, McCoy heard that the southern tribes might not arrive until the following Spring so he would never get back in time for the treaty which was originally arranged for September. Thus McCoy wrote to Cass again, informing him that he would not be able to attend.[1] Nevertheless, McCoy offered Cass the use of the Carey premises for the venue of the treaty.

Mixed news from home

While McCoy was away from home, he heard regularly from the mission, and from his sons and daughters. Lykins' letters, always

---

[1]See McCoy's letter to Cass of July 20, McCoy Papers, Reel 6.

short, exact and to the point but couched in terms of true endearment, kept him briefed. Lykins was about to send "a modest hint" to Bolles to tell him that the Board had still not given permission to draw on funds promised to the mission and of the $2,000 already due to them (probably Government funds), the Board had only sent $500. In a footnote, written on September 11, Lykins added that the treaty was to be held on September 15. Christiana wrote letter after letter, expressing her anxiety for her husband's health and safety and saying that she is longing for the time when they will become settled in their work for the Indians and have more time together as a family. Dear Christiana was as anxious for a permanent home as the Indians. Much of her letters are taken up with the oncoming treaty but she also mentions that Slater has gone to complain to the Board, otherwise all are well at Carey with not a single case of sickness there. Meeker's letter, however, reported that the missionaries at Thomas were stricken with the fever and shaking fits and two sisters were very ill indeed. The Indians there were also badly affected. In a further letter, Christiana wrote joyfully to say that their daughter Sarah had now confessed faith in Christ and had been duly baptized. Simerwell, Isaac is told, made a trip to Boston at the same time as Slater, so one cannot help thinking he had been sent to make sure the Board received a balanced view of affairs. Abel Bingham wrote from a boat named *Lady of the Lake* on Lake Erie to say that he had visited Boston where he had been ordained and he was now on his way to the St. Marie mission station assigned to him. His family would stay the winter in Washington until he had prepared a home. His letter shows him willing to take all the advice Slater had rejected and how he felt that close communication with the other stations concerning all matters appertaining to the missions was most necessary. It is obvious from these letters that something of an awakening, if not revival was going on in the Baptist churches with its epicenter in Lexington, Kentucky. Slater rather dampened the blessings contained in other letters by writing in protest to Lykins that he was fed up with the "hardness and suspicion" aimed at him and must seek redress. After writing in a most haughty fashion, he signed himself, "From unworthy Brother L. Slater."[2]

---

[2] These letters from August-October are in the McCoy Papers, Reel 6.

McCoy reconnoiters with his own men

McCoy soon found that he had major problems as keeper of the expedition's purse. The Indians were reasonable in their demands but the whites were heavy in theirs. As the Chickasaws and Choctaws they expected did not turn up, McCoy found that his team were chalking up large bills before they had even got under way. Personally, he could not stand the waiting and after several weeks of sitting around, he asked General Clarke to wave the ruling that all the parties must move together and give him permission to explore the region west of the Mississippi with his own Indians who were getting restless. General Clarke gave his permission on August 20th, adding only that McCoy should keep clear of the Pawnees who were reported to be on the war path and suggested that he take a half-blood named Mograin, who could speak Osage and Kansas, with him. McCoy's party, numbering eleven men[3] and twelve horses now embarked eagerly on a forty-nine day tour of the land west of the Mississippi which strengthened the Indians' resolution to move there and pleased McCoy enormously. The entire party were overjoyed to find an abundance of game, including buffalo, elk, deer and bear. On the way, which at times followed the Santa Fe Trail and led along the Marais des Cygnes River and across several branches of the Neosho River, McCoy was able to find out much more about his Indian friends, especially their method of burying part of an animal eaten and giving an address of thanks over the dead animal for having provided the party with food. The party soon met up with the Osage who were peaceful but lived under very poor circumstances. Wisely, when McCoy heard that the Comanches were about to pass through the country, he urged his party to be extra careful. Bells were taken from the horses harness and the party camped in silence. Once, when the party surprised a herd of elk and replenished their provisions, they were surrounded by wolves who had smelled what they had hoped would be their share. One night, the party slept peacefully while the wolves carried away their meat. They had trusted that the dog would awake them when danger approached but when the dog saw the humans sleeping peacefully, he joined them and never noticed a thing.

On August 6th, McCoy started gathering his notes, bills, receipts etc. together and began making his report under the title

---

[3] This included Mograin who joined the party a few days later and an old man whom Mograin insisted on bringing with him, though he had no horse. The party was completed by the addition of Mograin's dog.

Thoughts Respecting the Indian Territory. McCoy was well used to keeping the missionary accounts for a Board almost obsessed with detail, that is, when it came to the mission's expenditures. He thus registered every penny spent. But McCoy now started to do far more. In his report, he went into minute detail concerning the exact geographical nature of the area the party visited, its flora and fauna, its suitability for agriculture and industry and problems involving the arrival of Indians in areas where other tribes live or still claim as their hunting grounds. Actually, he had four groups of Indians to cater for and report on; the original inhabitants, mainly Pawnee, Osage and Kansa; those moved recently by treaties such as the Cherokees, Chickasaws, Choctaws and Creeks, those of the latter tribes who were to follow them but were politically opposed to them, and his Potawatomis and Ottawas who had no connection whatsoever with the Indian Territories.

While McCoy was in charge of his own company, he insisted on keeping the Sabbath as a day of worship and rest but when the various companies merged, McCoy's wishes were overruled. Even then, however, the other commissioners soon learned to respect McCoy and his Christian testimony and they asked him to conduct Sunday morning services before the company moved on.

Common opinions regarding Indians inaccurate

On the way west and back, McCoy gives his readers some fine insights into the ways of the Indians which quite contradict the common picture of the Native Americans believed by most whites. Rather than their being taciturn, proud, serious and reserved, McCoy found them chatty to the point of being noisy, lovers of entertaining conversation and tellers of amusing stories but also of tales of mystery and imagination. He was kept awake until the wee small hours of the morning by listening to one funny story after another told by the Indians even when they were completely sober. McCoy thought many of the stories worth retelling and filled a number of pages of his *History of Baptist Indian Missions* with them. Even the myth that the Indians are good trackers found McCoy's disbelief. He had constantly to correct his various pathfinders' theories as to where they were going and finally had to take over the tracking responsibilities himself. He had a particularly lengthy discussion with Mograin concerning the way they had to take and to the interpreter's chagrin, McCoy stopped following his advice.[4] However, McCoy had spent most of his life as a backwoodsman, so there would have been few whites who could have competed with him as there were perhaps few Indians.

Meeting up with the Kansas Indians

By the middle of September, the party had reached the Kansas River, called "Kansau" or "Kauzau" by McCoy, and caused an entire village of Kansas Indians a great deal of anxiety as they feared they were about to be attacked. Mograin went on ahead to assure the villagers that their visitors were harmless and soon the motley party of whites, Osage, Potawatomi and Ottawas were surrounded by the Kansas Indians who seemed to be asking questions all at once. Small gifts were distributed by McCoy's party and the Kansas provided boiled corn and buffalo horn spoons, as well as a bark roof for the night. McCoy met his first Pawnees who were staying at the camp. As they suspected that McCoy's party were Osage, they had hid themselves at first as the Osage and Pawnees were currently exchanging hostilities. McCoy insisted that the Pawnees should take part in the council which followed. The party was pleased to find that the Kansas were honest because on other occasions when meeting Indians who were strangers, various utensils, food items and small valuables began to disappear mysteriously as if by magic. On September 24, the party set off back to St. Louis, hoping the Chickasaws and Choctaws would have arrived there by now. On the way, they called at a Shawnee settlement of newly arrived Indians on the Missouri State border. McCoy decided to make Fayette his base rather than St. Louis when returning with Lykins and other Indians as planned. McCoy had hoped to return soon with the bulk of the Potawatomis around Carey, but a letter was waiting for McCoy at St. Louis from Lykins, saying that in the treaty arrangements at Carey which should have organized this, the Potawatomis had refused to sell their land.

---

[4] Roscoe Wilmeth in his *Kansas Village Locations in the Light of McCoy's 1828 Journal*, provides interesting details concerning who was right and wrong in McCoy's discussions with Mograin, coming down on the side of Mograin, p. 153.

A *further myth regarding the Indians shattered*

Although McCoy does not comment on this, it is obvious that his journey west shattered the myth of the hostile nature of the Indians. There must have been some eight or more tribes traveling together at one time but nothing of an unusual hostile nature was reported among them. Indeed, tribes who had previously been on the warpath against one another, now lived in complete harmony, sharing pipes and even old scalps! This was particularly the case with the Creeks. Some 15,000 of this tribe had quarreled with another party and separated from them, moving to the banks of the Verdigris and Canadian Rivers, but now both parties prepared a written agreement on their own initiative whereby they formally reunited as a tribe. The main aim of this first expedition was to settle the Chickasaws but McCoy was rather disappointed when they presented him with a formal letter, drawn up on the banks of the Canadian River and signed by 12 members of their delegation, stating that they must wait until they return home and await further consultation with the Government before making a final decision.

At the Harmony Mission Station

On his way back to St. Louis McCoy called at the Harmony mission station of the American Board of Commissioners for Foreign Missions. McCoy had promised to send a courier from Harmony to tell General Clarke of their coming but McCoy was also very eager to talk to the American Board's missionaries. He had been disappointed that this large, Presbyterian and Congregationalist mission had refused to back his and the Government's plans for an Indian State separate from the influence and jurisdiction of the whites. McCoy felt that the American Board had resigned themselves to the view that their work had no future and the Indians (mainly Osage) they were serving were already a lost race. McCoy thought that this pessimism was their reason for not supporting him. He had seen how the gospel could change the lives of these Indians for the better and was not without influence on the Harmony missionaries.

McCoy's report to General Clarke

McCoy had his provisional, but already Eden-like report of the tour finished by October 7, 1828, the day he arrived back at St. Louis.

He thus immediately dispatched to General Clarke the following record of events:

> On leaving the State of Missouri, I proceeded westwardly up the Osage River, generally on the north side. Passing the source of Osage, we bore south-west across the upper branches of Neosho until we intersected the main river at a point eighty miles south, and one hundred & twenty seven west, of the mouth of Kauzau river, and about twenty five miles southeast of the Sante Fe road. We then bore north-west until we reached the Santa Fe road, sixty miles from Arkansaw river & 140 due west of this state. These estimates are made according to measurement on the map, and not according to distance travelled, survey of the road, &c. We turned eastward along, & near to the Santa Fe road, to a point due south of the upper Kanzas village, then travelled north to said village on the Kansas river, one hundred & twenty five miles west of this state.
>
> I had been instructed to cross Kansas river and to return on the north side thereof. But the Indians informed me that there was not a canoe or other [vessel?]. My time was then so far consumed that I deemed it unadvisable to incur the delay that would be occasioned by crossing on rafts, I therefore proceeded eastwardly near to the Shawanoe settlement near the mouth of Kansas river, varying in our journey north and south forty miles. Thence I came, the most direct rout[e] to this place.
>
> There is a great similarity in the appearance of all parts of the country we explored. It is generally a high, rolling country, exhibiting a healthy appearance. Stone, and almost universally, limestone, sufficiently abundant for use, the soil exceedingly fertile, with scarcely the ocurrance of exception, and possessing the mellowness peculiar to limestone lands. We suppose no inconvenience from want of water, but found it happily distributed in the creeks and smaller streams all over the country, though not much running. Streams for mills and other water works are abundant, but all these would fail in the more dry season of the year. Wood is too scarce, especially beyond the distance of sixty miles west of this state, and ten miles south of Kanzas river, nevertheless, I suppose the whole country is supplied with groves and [stuaks?][5] of timber sufficient to sustain a considerable population, if judiciously located. I

---

[5] Probably "stalks".

presume myself that the scarcity of timber in this country is not so great as has been sometimes reported. The wood is chiefly along the water courses. The hills which sometimes are abrupt, though sufficiently level at the top, and other uplands formed by gentle ascent, generally rise once, twice, or three times as high as the timber in the low grounds. Travellers usually avoid crossing the water courses as much as practicable because of the unevenness of the way, the brush, and rocks and hence most of the timber is unseen by one passing hastily through the country, uninterested in the matter of wood. It would be fortunate for this country if in its settlement surveys should be so made that to each farm should be allotted so much timber only as would be necessary, and let the residue be prairie.

The Putawatomies and Ottawas whom I conducted, while they lament the scarcity of wood, and especially the almost total absense of the sugar tree, pronounce it a fine country.

On our tour we came in contact with Osage, Kanzas, Pawnees, and Shawanoes, the kind treatment received from all of whom is pleasantly acknowledged by our party. With the exception of a few very warm days at the commencement of the tour, the whole has been pleasant in all respects, and our Indians, I am happy to say, have returned with fine feelings.

With great respect Sir,

Your Obt. Servt.[6]

McCoy's duties as expedition treasurer were far from easy

Meanwhile the Creek deputation had arrived and five days later the Chickasaws and Choctaws reached St. Louis and were speedily joined by the other commissioners, two topographers and a doctor besides Captain Kennerly. McCoy was rather put off by the southern tribes appearance as they hardly behaved as he expected, i.e. as Indians, and were obviously influenced greatly by white business men. His suspicion deepened when the southerners insisted on having three whites of dubious qualification to accompany them besides their commissioners. Immediately, McCoy was handed a bill signed by a white man and marked by the Indians requesting him to hand over

---

[6] McCoy Papers, Reel 6.

$1,000 to the southerners for their free use. McCoy explained that he would make sure that their financial needs were met as they arose but refused to hand over a lump sum. The Indians agreed but their white advisors told them to ask for $500 which, again McCoy refused. General Clarke was appealed to and he then ordered McCoy to give the southerners $500. This providential move was a great relief to McCoy as he had already worked out that the money allotted to him was not sufficient to cover the costs of the expedition. However, now that General Clarke had interfered as representative of the Department of Indian Affairs, which McCoy, of course, recorded in his report, if it turned out that more money were needed, it would be a matter for the Department of Indian Affairs to clear up with the Government as they had caused the extra expenditure.

This action on the part of the southern tribes' white advisors convinced McCoy that his hopes of a Canaan for the Indians were challenged by serpents who were already entering his Eden, which led him to take a number of precautions. One of these was to present the southern Indians with an affidavit, stating the purposes of the mission, the responsibilities of the various members in general and his in particular and how he was prepared to look after and use the expedition's funding. Colonel Duncan, the Chickasaws' commissioner and his party agreed to comply. From now on, McCoy usually concluded his reports regarding Indian colonization with such words as, "if assurance can be obtained from the Government that *there* the *Indians* will be allowed to remain." Whereas the bulk of philanthropists whether Christian or otherwise, in the North and East either cared passionately for the rights of the Indians or ignored them completely, McCoy found that the whites who were influencing the southern tribes were less altruistic. He began to worry that even if the Indians were allowed to remain in the new country, they might soon be a minority among the whites. He therefore became determined to keep white supremacy and rule out of the Indian Territory. After Indian removal, McCoy realized that his next object was to see that the Indians passed laws to protect themselves, and that Congress should pass laws to avoid white interference in Indian affairs. Obviously, McCoy knew that he was open to the criticism that he was interfering in the Indian's own affairs himself, but he argued that he had been convinced of the sense of his views by the Indians and not the whites.

Now McCoy fitted his Potawatomis and Ottawas out for their return journey and found that the entire enterprise had cost $1,500 dollars. Though the expedition with the southern Indians was over approximately the same distance, taking the same time, McCoy found that their costs were $20,500. McCoy put this down to the fact that he had managed the financing of his own party completely, whereas the whites in the delegation made demands that he would only accept on Government authority but which he considered unnecessary. This fact soon became apparent in Government circles and in later expeditions, McCoy was given more authority in making sure that good economy was practiced.

Setting out with the newcomers

The new party left St. Louis on October 22nd, but immediately there was an outbreak of measles among them and a Creek died after only a few days travel. McCoy then found out the Department of Indian Affairs were wanting to place Indians north of the State of Missouri, i.e. outside of the Indian Territory outlined by McCoy. He explained the impracticability of this plan as that area was being quickly settled by whites and then the Indians would have to be moved on again. The Indians agreed with McCoy and even threatened to return home straight away. Again, General Clarke worked out a compromise. They would proceed west of the State of Missouri but not quite as far west as McCoy would have liked and further south than he had reckoned with. The next problem the party had to face was that the Choctaws suddenly decided to give up the observation tour and journey directly to the Red River where a group of Choctaws were already in residence. After making sure that he had the Chickasaws' backing, McCoy then fell into conversation one by one with the Choctaws and managed to persuade them to stay with the party. The party were actually taking McCoy's former path but in reverse, so that the Baptist missionary was on familiar ground most of the way. The Shawnees were the first settled Indians that the party encountered and friendly visits were made from both sides.

Rumors of Pawnees on the warpath

All seemed idyllic until information came from Major John Dougherty, Indian Agent at Fort Leavenworth on the southwest bank of the Missouri River[7] that 1,500 Pawnees were on the warpath and were in control of the Santa Fe Trail. McCoy heard that there was reason to thank God for deliverance as the Pawnees had struck other travelers during McCoy's September journey but his party had been spared. This time, however, McCoy was not spared injury, though he was not confronted with warring Pawnees. Galloping to catch a pack horse that had gone astray, McCoy's horse fell and landed partly on top of McCoy, crushing his leg and foot. McCoy was in great pain for the rest of the journey and never fully recovered from the accident.

Once the party reached the Osage River, they found game in plenty, McCoy once bagging two turkeys with one shot. Of all the people McCoy expected to meet on this journey, he had not reckoned with a circus director. Yet, the well-known circus proprietor Papin joined the company, having lost his way and finding he was going round in circles. McCoy jokingly mentioned in his journal that this was natural as Papin did nothing else with his horses in the circus ring under the Big Top. He had been found almost starved with hunger and quite delirious and taken to Harmony Mission and was on his way home. It appeared that he had lost his way again and would have perished if McCoy's party had not gone that way.

General Clarke hears good accounts of McCoy's work and witness

Next, the explorers met up with numerous Osage and Kansas in their villages and were able to learn a great deal about the area. McCoy also questioned the Chickasaws and Choctaws carefully and was delighted to find two or three Christians among them. One of McCoy's possessions that he found eager to lend out was his Bible and he had ample opportunities to witness to the party and preach before men who listened with great attention. General Clarke had made sure that he was kept well informed of McCoy's behavior by Captain Kennerly and was most pleased with what he heard. He thus made a formal request in writing to McCoy to go beyond his duties as expedition treasurer and keep a log-book of the expedition for the Government's later use. Since McCoy had been doing this all the time, he was pleased to have his work officially recognized. McCoy also made sure that he kept Captain Kennerly informed since he was the

---

[7] The Fort was 25 miles above the mouth of the Kansas (Kauzau) River. It was constructed in 1827 with a view to forming a base from which the relocation of Indians could be controlled and , if necessary, policed.

person who had officially appointed him.[8] McCoy was most careful to show how efficient he had been with expenditures in the case of the Potawatomis and Ottawas when he had been solely in charge.

The Government's dissatisfaction with Thomas and difficulties at Carey

Lykins wrote from Carey to say that the Government was dissatisfied with the state of affairs at Thomas, as was everybody else. He wished that the Board would appoint someone over both Carey and Thomas so that matters could be coordinated. This would not be McCoy or himself as they were now committed by the Board to Indian relocation. The only sound alternative was Meeker since Simerwell was still only officially a blacksmith, though Simerwell was fast maturing into a sound missionary worker. He was, however, going through a difficult time at Carey as no funds had come in for some time. Simerwell asked Lykins, who was also feeling the pinch, "how do you suppose we will get by this winter, we have nothing and no money to purchase any thing?[9] Before Lykins moved to Lexington in the hope of meeting McCoy there, he had raised the last income the mission had received by selling off their surplus foodstuffs to the delegates at the September St. Joseph Treaty. This had caused the Roman Catholics to write several articles in their newspapers informing their readers that the Baptist missionaries were not only living in affluence but selling off their surplus food at exorbitant prices. The missionaries soon received letters from former friends such as Horatio Pratt who reported that he had heard that the mission was a money making business and the missionaries were living in the lap of luxury.[10] Lykins felt that Carey was at an end, due to the Board's neglect and

---

[8] See Clarke's letter to McCoy dated October 17 and McCoy's letter to Captain George Kennerly dated October 19, 1828. Also his report of October 28, McCoy Papers, Reel 6. Numerous expenditure receipts for the expedition are to be found on this reel.

[9] Undated letter probably written November or December, 1828, McCoy Papers, Reel 6.

[10] This letter was sent in the latter half of 1828, see Reel 6, McCoy Papers, but it is reproduced in a more legible form at the beginning of Reel 7, dated January 3, 1829 with a question mark. Someone has written on the envelope "Pratt's foolish letter to McCoy."

the fact that the Potawatomis case for staying in the district had become "hopeless" and their only alternative was to move to the Indian Territory as quickly as possible. It was to this end that Lykins moved to Lexington to discuss matters with McCoy before going west to prepare for the Potawatomis', arrival.[11] There were signs, however, that the Board were having second thoughts on the matter and when McCoy wrote of his future plans to Spencer Cone, his New York friend and Board member merely answered by saying that the Board had been with him thus far but as to the future, it would be best if he (Cone) remained silent on the subject.[12]

More encouraging news from McCoy's friends and relations

One piece of news from Lykins was of special interest. Delilah, who had made the difficult journey to Lexington though nine months pregnant, was delivered of a son on November 29, 1828. Lykins added, underlining his words, "both are doing <u>very well</u>. We are rejoiced at this <u>favor of providence</u>." It is obvious from Lykins' letter that he had feared complications would set in because of Delilah's delicate health and the exhausting journey. Lykins also told McCoy that Meeker and a new missionary Miss Richardson were planning to be married as soon as McCoy could get to them on his return. McCoy, of course, planned to visit his own family at Lexington first.[13] Mrs. McCoy wrote several times during November to say that she had never felt so lonely as at that time and she so missed her husband's care.[14] She was now on her way to Lexington where she hoped to meet her husband. McCoy had originally planned to return to his wife at the beginning of October but he had now written to say that it would be January before they could be united. At this time McCoy received letters from two different Rice McCoys, i.e. his son who was about to enter his final year if not term, and McCoy's brother in Livonia. Rice, Sr. was able to tell his brother that their mother was doing well and had received Isaac's last letter and $20 enclosed. Unlike reports coming from Rice

---

[11] Letter dated October 19, McCoy Papers, Reel 6.

[12] Letter dated November 21, 1828, McCoy Papers, Reel 6.

[13] Letter dated November 30, 1828, McCoy Papers, Reel 6.

[14] The McCoys and the Lykins had set off from Carey, not knowing that McCoy would be delayed three months. Letters were taking months to get through and they came in batches rather than one at a time.

McCoy, Jr. at Lexington, his uncle confessed that the Baptist cause in Livonia had stagnated though the people were "at peace". Rice used the term as if he meant, they were asleep. Rice and two brethren had each four different churches to pastor as there was such a need for men to enter the ministry. On the other hand, Rice related that the Presbyterians were increasing but found as much "harm" in this as "good." However, at Silver Creek, where a number of the McCoys still lived, Campbellism was still strong and had infiltrated the Association. John McCoy, their brother, had fought against this, apparently with a measure of success. Obviously a little anxious that his brother might forget his Lord in his work for the Government, Rice tells him:

> Try, my bro[ther] to put your trust in the Keeper of Israel, for he slumbereth not, neither is weary, and remember that by humility and the *fear of the Lord*, are riches and honour and life. Be not backward to tell of Jesus and his love to the poor heathens; They may be assured that they have some white friends, who sympathise with them, and daily remember them before the Lord.[15]

A conference with the Osage

On November 18, 1828, Kennerly and McCoy gathered all the Osages together to have a conference at Chief White Hair's village and sound them out on their expectations concerning new neighbors and Government grants. While McCoy was on his way with his own Indians, the weather had changed from extremely hot to mild. Winter had now set in, snow lay on the ground and the Indians suffered so much from the cold that it was difficult to collect them together. A large fire was built and eventually no less than twenty Osage chiefs and their retinues arrived. After the usual ceremonies of shaking hands, smoking and speech making, the conference was started but postponed at nightfall because the Indians believed that one could not talk about peace in the dark. The council continued at the home of Chief Belle Ouizo the next morning and boiled buffalo meat was served to warm up the freezing delegates. Kennerly and McCoy had been anxious that the southern tribes should find out how the Osages and Kansas lived so that they could obtain some idea of how they would manage themselves. They went so far as to present the Plains

---

[15] Rice Jr.'s letter is dated November 2, Rice Sr.'s letter, November 4, 1828, McCoy Papers, Reel 6.

Indians with signs of peace such as strings of white porcelain beads and the Osage returned the compliment by presenting the Chickasaws and Choctaws with a Pawnee scalp! The Osage chiefs now made speeches to show that as the southern tribes had received the scalp of an enemy of the Osage, they were now brothers together and allies in war. This was an unwelcome turn of events for the commissioners and the southerners made no reply. The ice was broken when the Choctaws asked the Osage to show them their dances and soon all the Indians were merry together. McCoy noticed how much more eloquent in speech-making the Osage were in comparison to the southerners and how much of their Indian nature the Chickasaws and Choctaws had lost. The latter appeared awkward in council. This is quite a surprising statement coming from McCoy who held the Choctaws to be skilled orators. On the whole, however, the southern delegates were not at all impressed with the Plains Indians way of life and begged the commissioners to take them to the Canadian Fork in the hope of finding better conditions. Perhaps this was inevitable as the Potawatomis and Ottawas had found in the Osage and Kansas people of a kindred spirit who lived in a way similar to themselves. They thus felt there would be no difficulty in settling down alongside these allies. The Chickasaws and the Choctaws, however, were used to living almost as white farmers and they were faced with giving up property of a high value so they obviously were anxious to obtain similar privileges in the Indian Territory.[16]

McCoy's thoughts on Osage religion

McCoy had many heart to heart talks with the Osage and spent hours listening to their stories, learning about their legends and religion. Contrary to modern criticism that McCoy was not interested in such features, he fills some nine pages[17] of his *History* with tales he heard from the Osage and descriptions of their methods of hunting. Of the Osage view of God and their views of death, McCoy writes:

> It had been reported that the Osages did not believe in the existence of the Great Spirit. I was astonished that any one who had ever been two days among

---

[16] See McCoy's letter to Lykins via Harmony Mission, November 18, 1828, McCoy Papers, Reel 6.

[17] pp. 355-365.

them, or the Kauzaus, who are in all respects similar, should be so deceived. I had never before seen Indians who gave more undoubted evidence of their belief in God. In their speeches they make the references and appeals to the Great Spirit, common to all Indians on such occasions; and a devotional exercise is observed among them, which I have never heard existed among any others. At the opening of day, the devotee retires a little from his camp or company, and utters a prayer aloud. This may or may not have some allusion to a deceased relative or friend. The voice is usually elevated so as to be heard sometimes half a mile, and their words are uttered in a kind of plaintive, piteous tone, accompanied with, weeping, either affected or real, I suppose commonly the former. To English ears, the sound is uncouth, and we would denominate it a kind of howling. Their word for God is, Wóh-kon'-da, (Father of Life.) Their prayer runs in some such words as the following: "Wóh-kon'-da, pity me; I am very poor; give me what I need ; give me success against mine enemies, that I may avenge the death of my friends. May I be able to take scalps, and to take horses," &c. These services are performed by the women, also, with language appropriate. Some omit them; but a large portion of the middle aged and older are punctual in their observance every morning, and with less punctuality in the evening also.

  I discovered that they frequently deposited their dead on or near the surface of the earth, and raised over the corpse a heap of stones. In this heap, I saw in a few places a pole planted, to the top of which, was suspended a scalp of an enemy. Their notion was, that by taking an enemy, and suspending his scalp over the grave of a deceased friend, the spirit of the former became subjected as a slave to the spirit of the latter, in the world of spirits. Hence, the last and best service that can be performed for a deceased relative is to take the life of an enemy, and apply his scalp as above. This sentiment, it is believed, is among their strongest inducements to take human life. What a happy change upon these people, in this respect, a knowledge of the gospel would effect![18]

---

[18] *History of Baptist Indian Missions*, pp. 359-360.

The Creeks and the Choctaws respond differently to the Chickasaws

On November 2, 1828, the party, following the wishes of the Chickasaws, moved to the mouth of the Verdigris River on the Arkansas. Here, the Creek delegation met up with some 1,500 of their tribe who had moved there recently. Though the Creek delegates were formerly hostile to the party they met, after some consultation the two sides smoked the peace pipe and the Creeks already in the Indian Territory invited the other bands to join them. This invitation was committed to writing, to be read before the eastern bands. The Creek delegates then declared that their mission was accomplished and they would be pleased to return to their home east of the Mississippi and report to their people. McCoy gave them enough funds to keep them comfortable until they reached their destination. Next the party journeyed on to the Canadian River where the Indians tried their hand at buffalo hunting and killed two animals. Then on December 7 the Choctaws made their way to their brethren on the Red River before returning home. They, too, seemed to be satisfied. McCoy's problem was the Chickasaws. They had seemed most disinterested throughout the journey and as the principle design of the undertaking had been especially to satisfy the Chickasaws, McCoy was obviously disappointed when the delegation gave him a written statement saying:

Friend and Brother: In reply to your request, we have to say to you that, from the situation of affairs at home, we are not able to give you any account of the present tour. When we return home, and find our affairs settled with the General Government satisfactorily to us, we will then make our report to our Great Father, the President of the United States.

We are, with great respect, your friends and brothers,

Levi Colbert,
Ish-te-ma-tah-ka,
Emmubba,
Im-ma-tah-ish-to,
Ah-to-co-wah,
Bah-kah-tubba,
Thos. Sealy,
Isaac Love,

313

Elapa-umba,
C. Colbert,
J. McLish.[19]

The tasks of the expedition are accomplished and McCoy is reunited with his family

The remainder of the party returned to St. Louis via Harmony Mission. McCoy was sad to hear that the Presbyterians felt the cause of the Indians was hopeless and they had no intention of supporting him in establishing the northern and eastern tribes in the Indian Territory. McCoy reached St. Louis on December 24 and at first, he was mortified to find no mail but Dr. Todson, the party's physician had collected it for him and, after some difficulty, McCoy located Todson and now read for the first time that his wife and family were waiting for him at Lexington. McCoy set off for that town at once, reaching his family on January 1, 1829 after being absent from them for six months.

McCoy feels deserted by both the Board and the Government

At Lexington, McCoy heard from Lykins that he had managed to persuade Governor Cass at the September treaty to allocate the Board $1,000 per year for educational purposes. The mission never saw a penny of this money. McCoy is very cautious as to where he lays the blame for this, merely saying, "these funds, through an influence of which I did not hesitate to complain, were applied elsewhere."[20] As he says this in the same breath as he mentions how Lykins had been paying off debts which were really the Board's, the reader cannot but believe that somehow the Board was mixed up in this affair. To make matters worse, previous annuities which the mission had been promised for educating the Potawatomis and Miamis were now stopped, so McCoy felt deserted by both the Board and the Government. McCoy and Lykins thus decided that Carey should be abandoned and the mission reestablished in the Indian Territory. Both did what they could to end the financial misery of the mission speedily, especially when they heard that it would take another year before the Govern-

---

[19] *History of Baptist Indian Missions*, p. 367.

[20] *History of Baptist Indian Missions*, p. 370.

ment could work out the value of the mission and reimburse the Board so that they could set up a new mission in the Indian Territory. As McCoy now received money from the Government for his services as commissioner and teacher, he gave all the money he had received in teaching salaries to Simerwell and Meeker who were not in receipt of any funds from the Board and had no Government function at the time.[21] Lykins also gave up his teaching salary on behalf of his missionary friends. This was all in keeping with their *Family Rules*, which McCoy and Lykins still followed. McCoy also wrote to Cass, asking him to earmark subsequent teaching salaries for Simerwell and Meeker. McCoy had been paid an extra wage for his services as treasurer to the Indian Territory expedition and now his large family and the Lykins were living on that money. The Board had, however, not given permission for the missionaries to move from Carey, they had merely made it impossible for them to stay, and had not recognized the fact that they must move as soon all the Indians would be also moving west. The Government was soon selling off all the land around Carey where the Indians had lived. Thus McCoy wrote:

> We had been taught, by the experience of many years, that it devolved on the missionaries to devise measures, and to procure the means of accomplishing them. The attention of the board being chiefly engrossed by their missions in other countries, which were prosecuted with discretion, zeal, and success, they could not be expected to feel that interest in the establishment of missions among the tribes in the West that we did. We did not believe that they would grant us permission, at that time, to go west, and we therefore did not ask it; for it would have been more painful to go contrary to direct orders, than go without orders; and from the views we had taken, we felt that we had already too long delayed to remove.[22]

McCoy travels once again to Washington to meet the Government and the Board

Now the mission was in open rebellion against the Board but somehow Mr. Lykins caught the broadside of arguments that they now

---

[21] See McCoy's letter to Governor Cass on the subject dated June 27, 1829, also his letter of September 11, 1829 to Cass, McCoy Papers, Reel 7.

[22] *History of Baptist Indian Missions*, p. 370-371.

fired at the mission's policy. McCoy wrote to leading Baptists in support of Lykins, knowing that they would use their influence with the Board.[23] He returned to Carey and Thomas to see to their affairs and to speak with a young white, Daniel French, who had come to know the Lord and wished to be baptized and join the church.[24] It had become evident that the Board itself was against the plans of the mission, the Government and now the Indians to go West. It was also clear that the Board had again listened to the Presbyterians and Congregationalists rather than their own people. McCoy quickly answered the Board on behalf of the mission and, after only a short stay with his family, dashed off on yet another long journey to Washington to make his report to the Department of Indian Affairs, after which, he planned to visit the Board. His experience was that once the Board listened to him personally, they would become sympathetic to the cause of the Indians but the longer they had no dealings with him, the more they listened to other advisors. McCoy arrived in Washington totally exhausted and very ill so that he had to remain in bed for several days.

McCoy reports to Congress on the expedition into the Indian Territory

Originally, Captain Kennerly was to report on the route followed and character of the country and McCoy on the settlement of accounts. McCoy felt that this division would rule out most of the main arguments necessary for an understanding of the situation so he prepared a full report taking up all aspects not covered specifically by Kennerly. By this time, McCoy had a measure of influence with the Government because of his good name and his success in management, so McCoy, taking advantage of this, insisted successfully that his report should be considered by Congress. He also wrote to the Secretary of War, the Hon. P. B. Porter, who was an anti-mission man, giving him a long report that emphasized the need for Indian relocation, being careful to mention that the President himself approved and recommended this course.[25] Then McCoy prepared a paper for

---

[23] See Wilson Lumpkin's letter to Lykins dated January 5, 1829, McCoy Papers, Reel 7.

[24] See French's letter to McCoy dated December 27, 1828, McCoy Papers, Reel 6.

[25] *History of Baptist Indian Missions*, pp. 372-376.

Congress, outlining his main reasons for giving the Indians independence in their own country. When the official report was given by the Chairman of the Committee on Indian Affairs to the House of Representatives, it contained, in the main, all of McCoy's proposals. To make sure that his report was given wider publicity, McCoy had a thousand copies printed, above those which Congress ordered for its own use, and distributed them at his own expense.

The Board allies with the Presbyterians against the Indians' wishes

Next the Indians connected with the missions sent McCoy a formal application to the U. S. President to be moved west, asking him to forward the document. McCoy wasted no time in fulfilling the Indians' wishes and asked the Government to make good its promise to compensate them for the improvements they had made to the land which they had occupied for missionary usage. McCoy asked for Charles Noble who had examined the mission at the outset and had become a friend of the mission, to evaluate the Indians' and the missionaries' property with a view to selling the land to white settlers. The Board's move to block and complicate these transactions were now ignored by the missionaries as not being in the interest of any party, besides being financially detrimental to the Board who could not even manage their own affairs. Congress, however, also began to have second thoughts and delayed collocating the tribes to send them West. To his horror, McCoy found out that the American Board of Commissioners for Foreign Missions were now lobbying Congress to stop the action and had had a measure of success. Worse still, it was now revealed to the Baptist public at large that the Presbyterian Board was influencing the Baptist Board in denying the Indians an existence and government of their own. This led to a split between a good number of Baptist Associations, mostly Southern and Western, and the active members of the Board who were mostly New Englanders. The Parkerites and the Campbellites now believed that they had gained a major success in their anti-missions campaign and the Board received fewer funds than at any other time since their commencement.

Spencer Cone and the Home Mission back McCoy

Now Spencer H. Cone of New York came down strongly on the side of McCoy and strove to persuade the Baptist Missions Board to be influenced by their own people rather than those in a different denomination. The Home Missions also backed McCoy. Immediately on hearing of the Government's new doubts, McCoy asked the Secretary of War for official permission to lead a new tour of inspection and examine the points of uncertainty still remaining. This request was given a very sympathetic ear and eventually granted, providing that McCoy raised the necessary funds himself. McCoy accepted the challenge.

A new edition of McCoy's Remarks

Before undertaking anything on his own initiative, McCoy left Washington for Boston and conferred with the Board on April 4, 1829. First he asked the Board to print a second edition of his *Remarks on the Practicability of Indian Reform* with an added Appendix outlining the character of Indian missions, the relationship between missionary societies and their missionaries, advice to candidates for missionary service and advice to missionaries. His conclusion was a passionate appeal to the American people in general and Christians in particular to allow right and liberty to be applied to the Indians:

> The preceding remarks lead us to the following conclusion. We have within our control the means of rescuing from destruction the aborigines of our country, and of elevating them to an equality with their neighbours, in the scale of being and the enjoyments of life. The points which vitally affect their condition are involved in the policy, and consequently are under the control, of our government. Our rulers are the representatives of the people, of whom they form a part, and are acting agreeably to their directions. Hence, *when the people get right on the subject of Indian improvement,* GOVERNMENT WILL BE RIGHT.
>
> The menacing attitude assumed by opposing obstacles admonishes us that, to the strong arm of government must be united sacrifices which benevolence alone can be expected to make. No sacrifices on the part of government, as such, is required in the case, for the whole process may go on to the positive advantage of our nation. Were it otherwise, our government would not withhold the necessary aid. It would not pause to reckon dollars and cents, in an enterprize of such magnitude. The sacrifices which are necessary require us to enter into the midst of

their poverty, sorrows, and sins, to unite our efforts with theirs, in applying to their relief the comforts of life; gently to wipe the tear of grief, kindly to whisper the voice of hope, and lead them in the paths of virtue. Some of us must consent to live with them upon the principle of disinterested benevolence, that our attention being undivided, we may devote our entire selves to the work; may enter freely and fully into the *little* and *disagreeable* affairs of their condition; matters which cannot be made subjects of national legislation, except upon very general principles, and which nevertheless vitally affect the health of the nation.

While some must consecrate their lives to the object, others must contribute of their property, all that the case demands above the provisions of government. In the language of Deborah in Israel, let me ask, have we among us a competent number of persons who, like *"the people of Zebulon and Naphtali, will come to the help of the Lord against the mighty, and jeopard their comforts and their lives in the desert places of the earth, and ask no gain of money?"* Again, in the language of Ezra, will *" the people offer freely, according to their ability, for the accomplishment of this work?"* The beneficent spirit of the age responds; *we have the men; the means; and the disposition to use them.* Justice and humanity prepare to sound the trump of Jubilee, *and call the wandering outcasts to their kindred, their country,* and their HOME.[26]

This time, the Board refused to cooperate. They said they had nothing against republishing the main part but the Appendix now contrasted with their views as to how a mission should be run. McCoy felt that the Board should form their views in conjunction with the missionaries who were better informed about what was happening. Moreover, the Appendix contained McCoy's reasons for having the whole thing printed in the first place. If there were no presentation of the lot of the Indians to the public, he argued, there could be no appeal to ameliorate that lot, both factors being outlined in the Appendix. McCoy therefore decided he must again differ from the view of the Board to preserve the Board's own Indian mission, so he had the essay published with the Appendix at his own expense. Spencer Cone, himself a Board member, supported McCoy in this enterprise and supervised the printing and publication. Indeed, there were a number

---

[26] *Remarks on the Practicability of Indian Reform, Embracing Their Colonization.* New York: Gray and Bunce, 1829, p. 72.

of Board members who were in entire agreement with McCoy and had become his close friends. These gave him all the support they could under the circumstances. McCoy was far from being alone.[27]

The Board put Slater in charge of Thomas

Now the missionaries, who had all complained about Slater's behavior, received a further shock, as did Governor Cass. Against the wishes of the missionaries, apart from Slater, the Board had decided to make Thomas an independent station from Carey and put Slater in joint charge of it with Meeker. This was like trying to dilute oil with water and showed that the Board were completely void of understanding concerning the situation. The Board made this move without consulting the Government who had the official guardianship of the school. As Governor Cass refused to appoint Slater as teacher,[28] this resulted in a loss of income for the Board. Simerwell was put in charge of Carey which, McCoy and Lykins believed, was a good move. Simerwell, however, could not carry on the blacksmith's shop because the Board would not allow him to draw on them for iron, thus reducing Carey's income as Simerwell had always taken on outside work to make ends meet. Typical of McCoy's benevolent nature, when he heard that Slater was to remain at Thomas, he generously shared his remaining Government salary with him. It was always McCoy's policy to return good for evil. Nevertheless, such events prompted Christiana to complain to her husband about "a perplexing letter from Dr. boaules [Bolles]" and that, "the board is determined to ruin our reputations as missionaryes it is hard after labering so long and obtaining so much for the mission to be thus reproached so ungenerously i say it is extreamly hard."[29]

---

[27] See McCoy's letter to Cone on the subject dated May 10, 1829, McCoy Papers, Reel 7.

[28] See *History of Baptist Indian Missions*, p. 396.

[29] Letter written to McCoy from Lexington, January 29, 1829, McCoy Papers, Reel 7.

The Board misinforms the public

Meanwhile, the Board was giving the Christian public an entirely wrong view of their dealings with the Indian Mission, informing them of the many thousands of dollars they were investing into Carey and Thomas alone. From 1826 to 1829, they boasted, the Board had spent $8,568,17 on the mission Stations. The impression was given that half came from the Charity Fund and half from private Baptist donations earmarked for the Indian mission. McCoy patiently told the Board that this was completely misleading the Baptist churches. Actually, the Indian missions at Carey and Thomas had only received $450 such charity from the Board during the three years referred to. He emphasized that apart from the small sum mentioned, both missionary stations have had to sustain themselves for no less than five years from other sources.[30]

McCoy was particularly sensitive on this issue because such publications as the Board's led many a critic to believe, as S. B. Walling wrote in the *Western Times*, that the missionaries were living on "ill-gotten wealth" by duping the brethren to give them what they themselves could ill-afford. Walling complained that McCoy was a particularly "grasping missionary." Walling explained to McCoy privately that his letter was published without his permission but he stood by his opinion, although he now had doubts about at least one of his sources.[31] As he cited a talk with McCoy as his major source, the missionary can hardly be suspected of telling Walling that he enjoyed any kind of wealth in the sense that Walling understood the term.

McCoy makes sure that Indian missions were placed on the 1829 Convention's agenda

The General Missionary (Triennial) Convention was held in Philadelphia from April 29 to May 7, 1829 but though the needs of foreign missions were outlined, the needs of the Indians were completely omitted. McCoy was present and protested with such effect that the Convention took up his plea. It became very obvious that the church leaders felt that the Indians were as good as extinct so that

---

[30] See McCoy's note of April 30, 1829, and the Board's printed *Abstract of Expenditures and Receipts*, McCoy Papers, Reel 7.

[31] Letter from Walling to McCoy dated July 6, 1829, McCoy Papers, Reel 7.

efforts and funds must be channeled to where they had a greater chance of success. One learned Doctor of Divinity, the Rev. W. T. Brantley, a member of the Convention and editor of an important Christian magazine, even suggested that the Convention should pass a motion declaring that the reformation of the Indians was impractical! McCoy blamed the Board for not standing up for the Indian mission and advised those at the Convention to support the Indians. Otherwise, he argued, the missionaries must separate themselves from the Board. They were called by God to serve the Indians and even if that race were doomed, a theory which they did not accept, then they must still serve them to the last. McCoy then declared that if the Board would not support Indian missions then the missionaries had decided to form a Board for the Promotion of Indian Missions. This action of McCoy's and the interest he raised among the delegates at the Convention moved the Convention Committee to draw up three resolutions to be presented before the Acting Managers of the Board of Foreign Missions, recommending McCoy's and Lykins' plans for the colonization of the West by the Indians and the continuation of the missions to the Indians in the Indian Territory and wherever else the Indians were allowed to remain. Realizing what dire financial straits the mission was in, a resolution was added, with Heman Lincoln's approval, that McCoy and Lykins should be able to draw a thousand dollars from the Board for the coming year.[32]

McCoy's courage and skill reap fruit

This turn of events is some indication of the sheer courage and energy of McCoy in combating the Board and the Convention and his great skill in argument and, of course, his catching enthusiasm for the Indians. Once, however, McCoy raised his voice in protest at the Convention, he found solid backing from a number of influential ministers including Dr. John Leadley Dagg, pastor of Fifth Baptist church in Philadelphia, still well-known today for his *Manual of Church Order* and *Manual of Theology*[33] and one of the foremost Calvinistic Baptists of his day. Spencer H. Cone, pastor of the Oliver Street Baptist church in the city of New York, joint friend of both McCoy and Dagg, also supported the Convention's resolution. How-

---

[32] See Cone's letter to McCoy dated January 20, 1830 on the subject, McCoy Papers, Reel 7.

[33] My copies reprinted by Gano Books, 1990.

ever, not content with mere resolutions to the Board, the Convention appointed a committee consisting of McCoy, Dagg, Cone, Lincoln and Bolles to present a petition to the President of the United States. It was as if the Baptist Board had made another about-turn. This petition was an answer to years of faithful and even tearful prayers on McCoy's part as the Baptist Convention gave him not only their full support but asked the President (now Andrew Jackson) to honor the Convention with the task of helping to put Government plans into action which were, in reality, McCoy's plans. Its presentation, supported by the Board's Corresponding Secretary and Treasurer, showed that McCoy's charisma had again won the day and things were developing according to his plan. The Board's new petition to the Government read:

Washington, May 9, 1829.

SIR: By treaties with the Osage and Kauzau tribes of Indians, lands have been reserved for education purposes, to be applied under the direction of the President of the United States. The Baptist Convention for the United States have authorized me to inform you, that in the application of those lands to their object, they would be glad to be honoured with the trust.

Their views relative to the collocation of the tribes west of the State of Missouri and Territory of Arkansas perfectly agree with those of the Government, an expression of which they made to Congress, in a memorial, in 1827-'8. Mr. McCoy, who accompanied the late exploring expedition, has, in conjunction with another agent, been appointed by them to revisit that country, to select a suitable situation for the settlement of the fruit of their schools, and for education establishments, and to procure such information relative to the country as may be of service to the next Congress.

They beg leave respectfully to submit to your consideration the propriety of establishing within the Indian territory, so called, a superintendency that may tend to the judicious location of the tribes which may be settled there.

They would further suggest, with due respect, the probability that, should an expedition be sent the next spring to the Camanches, and others in the West at present at war with the Osages, menacing to emigrating Indians, and mischievous on the Santa Fe road, they would be rendered peaceable.

For reasons for the above suggestions rela-
tive to a superintendency, and to the expedition, they would
respectfully refer to pages 19, 20, 21, and 22, of the report
to the Secretary of War, of Mr. McCoy, herewith submitted.
With the highest respect,
I am, sir, your obedient servant,
Lucius Bolles, Cor. Sec'y.

Andrew Jackson, President of the United States.

This was a real breakthrough for McCoy. The Board had once
again directly identified themselves with Indian relocation and now,
indeed, wished to be given a major role in that enterprise. They also
once again established McCoy as acting under the Board's appointment. Now McCoy and Lykins were free to start up a work in the Indian Territory as planned.

A *separate Board for Indian Missions proposed*

Nevertheless, McCoy continued to develop ideas concerning a
Baptist Board of Indian Missions. This Board would not necessitate a
break with the Board of Foreign Missions but be a sister organization
under the auspices of the Baptist General Convention. As the Board
itself would not consider McCoy's plans on the grounds that a specific
Board for Indian Missions would draw funds from foreign missions,
the missionary eventually published his own proposals in 1836 in his
Periodical Account of Baptist Missions within the Indian Territory. As
this pamphlet was printed on the mission's press with the permission
of the Board, there must have been a measure of approval in their
tolerance. These proposals were in full:

Board For Indian Missions
We shall not at this time, trouble our
readers with the principal reasons, which point out the
necessity of this measure, but shall content ourselves by
reference to a few admitted facts which apply to the case, in
the hope that the plausibility of the measure will appear too
plain for its adoption to be long delayed.
It is not believed that one society could
manage the diversified benevolent operations, in which the
Baptist denomination is engaged. Such a course would be
requiring too much of one set of men. Hence, while our
benevolent labors are all designed for the glory of God, and
the benefit of man, we have them divided under different

heads; and the management of them severally, is assigned to different societies, or Boards. By this distinct action of each society, the distinguishing features, of the branch of business entrusted to its management, become more prominent, and are more fully recognized by a benevolent public; and by this judicious division of labor among the societies, an increased amount of interest and effort is elicited.

If there exists a necessity for a Bible society, or for a Home mission society, which facts are established beyond doubt, there exists equal necessity for a Society or Board, specially for the management of Indian missions. There is not so great a dissimilarity between missions of the Baptist Board in foreign countries, and Domestic missions under the management of the Home missionary society, as there is between the former and Indian missions.

Here we leave this matter for the present, respectfully soliciting for this subject, the consideration of the existing Board of Managers of the General Convention, and of the Baptist denomination, to whose judgment and zeal, it is respectfully and prayerfully submitted.[34]

Good reports from Carey . . .

Still, everything in the garden was far from lovely. The problem of finance had not been solved and in the latest official report published by the Board, though Carey and Thomas were mentioned, nothing whatsoever was reported as to how they were faring and what progress was being made. McCoy's next move was to return to Lexington and be reunited with his family, including his two eldest sons, Josephus and Rice, now freshly qualified doctors who wished to dedicate their lives to the Indian mission. Mrs. McCoy had been in very poor health but was now in good spirits and looking forward to the journey west. Leaving their families on the western border of Indiana, McCoy and Lykins journeyed to Michigan on June 19 to see that all was well at Carey and Thomas. Simerwell impressed McCoy with the way he had carried on at Carey and McCoy was able to baptize Daniel French and another young man who had recently been converted. French confessed that he had received a call to be a missionary to the Indians.

---

[34] p. 49.

. . . but bad ones from Thomas

On reaching Thomas, they found that the station was very run down, the school disbanded and the farm deserted. Slater had adopted the views of the Board who had promised him Lykins' senior post, without consulting Lykins about it and taken over the management by proxy. Meeker was nowhere to be seen and McCoy was told that he was in Ohio on business. It was obvious that Meeker could not stomach working with Slater. The poor man must have been terribly disappointed to have been so unequally yoked with his major critic who always insisted on doing as he pleased. When Meeker turned up, he made a most dejected impression. The new Board's policy at Thomas, as elsewhere, was to abandon boarding schools[35] for day schools with no financial provisions for food, accommodation and clothing. This ruling had emptied the Thomas school as day lessons were quite impractical for the kind of life the Indians still lived. McCoy and Lykins had always regretted that in all the years of the missions, the Board had never sent a single representative to inspect them, in spite of numerous requests, and thus had no first hand experience of running a mission. This need had been seen from the start of the Fort Wayne settlement and thus anchored as Article IV in the *Family Rules* which stated that the affairs of the mission should always be kept transparent so that whenever an inspection came (from the Board) they would be prepared to give a full report on all matters pertaining to their work. The Board's inability to handle missionary matters was now only too evident. They had striven to run the mission via Slater without spending a penny on it. The matter was especially sad for McCoy and Lykins as they had petitioned the Government for permission to move the Carey and Thomas pupils to the Indian Territory and thus receive a continuation of Government grants. Now that no pupils were in the school, no grant would be forthcoming. As usual, the Board had shown that they were their own worst enemy.

Parallels at Valley Towns

This attitude of the Board was not restricted to McCoy and his friends but was typical of their lax attitude to Indian missions in general. Evan Jones had started on forty years of service to the Cherokees in 1824 and was now having exactly the same trouble with

---

[35] Schools with living accommodation for the pupils.

the Board. Jones did, however, manage to persuade the Board to authorize Iveson L. Brooks of South Carolina to inspect his work and report on his progress and needs. Then, in 1833 the Board sent their treasurer Heman Lincoln to inspect Jones' Valley Towns Mission but this was planned as a visit to criticize rather than learn. Actually, when Lincoln arrived at the mission, he found more than he bargained for. He became caught up in court and church actions against Jones for allegedly murdering a woman mission worker and her newborn child.[36] Apparently whites who had married Indian women had designs on the mission property so that they could take it over and then be recompensed for their "improvements" when the Cherokees were moved to the Indian Territory. They had thus brought up the charges so that the mission would have to close down. Lincoln found himself having to take on the role of scribe during the church court proceedings. Jones was freed from any suspicion of murder by both the legal (secular) and church courts. Whatever Brooks and Lincoln reported, the subsequent action of the Board showed that they still had no idea of conditions on the mission field and expected missionaries to live on next to nothing merely because they were missionaries. They informed Jones, as they had informed the Carey and Thomas missionaries that no funds would be forthcoming for the board, lodgings and clothing of the pupils and that the Indians' parents should cover these costs. This would have emptied the mission schools of pupils as it had already done when applied to several Mission Board schools both among the southern and northern tribes. Many Indians could not afford such costs and of those who could, many refused to carry the costs. The missionaries believed that the children ought not to suffer because of such decisions. They also felt that in providing for the children's education as well as bringing them up in the nurture and admonition of the Lord, they were doing the work of evangelists to which they were called. The Board thought otherwise. Their new idea was that educating the Indians was a hindrance to evangelism because, instead of going out and preaching, the missionaries were teaching. They thus told the missionaries that they must only set up day schools and accept female students. These would be taught by the missionaries' wives, leaving the men to do evangelistic work. This suggestion shows how the Board was incapable of doing the simplest sums. The male teachers were not financed by the Board but by the Government. This had been encouraged by the Board so as to relieve them of financial burdens and

---

[36] The whole sordid story is told in great detail by William McLoughlin in his *Champions of the Cherokees*, chapter 4, *Trial for Murder*.

help pay their other debts. In the case of the Fort Wayne, Carey and Thomas stations, this money was used to finance the entire work as the Board paid little and, for a number of years, nothing. If the male teachers were not allowed to teach, the Government would not pay them wages and the mission would be bankrupt.

Further examples of the Board's ignorance concerning missionary work

Another very wrong thing in the mismanagement of the Mission Board was their strange notion that missionaries must live on starvation diets and live a life of self-denial that not a single Board member would have tolerated for himself. The Board loved to take sugar with their tea but they were horrified at the thought that this might reflect the taste of the missionaries, so they forbade them to buy both sugar and tea. Sugar, however, was one of the Indians' most cherished foodstuffs and was a sign of friendship to them. Whenever McCoy visited the Indians, he was given sugar as a token of respect. When the Indians visited McCoy, he had often no sugar to give them. This was, as far as the Indians were concerned, like refusing to shake hands. The Board members had servants to do their household chores but begrudged the missionaries household helps, often when this meant that the men had to do the cooking for the school children. But the Board asked the missionaries by what right they were giving the pupils food. Their parents must cater for that! The missionaries clothed the Indians when such clothing was available but the Board also frowned on this. Indeed, when clothing was collected for the mission by the churches and sent off, the Board deducted what they thought was the value of the clothing from the money they had promised the mission from the charity fund which was supposed to finance the mission's needs. The Board employed paid labor to build their houses and attend to their farms. When the missionaries requested that they should be sent paid hands to look after the farms, the Board members were shocked and they informed the missionaries that the students must do the farm work for free. But this would make the pupils unpaid farm-hands and thus slaves and they would have little time for tuition. Besides, how could unskilled children run a farm? This was a most sensitive issue with the Indians who naturally disliked any sign that they might be regarded as a lower class. Practical farm work, under the supervision of skilled farmers, when they could be found, was part of the school curriculum.

The Mission farms, however, were also motes in the eye of the Board. The missionaries relied on agriculture to save the expense of food transportation, to train the Indians in agriculture and to prepare the Indians for the future when, because of white settlers, they would no longer be able to live from hunting. Missionaries ought merely to preach, the Board argued. Thus they had let the farm at Thomas go to ruins. McCoy and his fellow missionaries, however, looked to Paul as their example and realized that as so little financial backing was coming from the Board, they must finance themselves. Evan Jones was persuaded by the Board to give up his model farm in order to do itinerant evangelism, leaving his wife to teach a reduced number of Indian girls. Jones was a great evangelist, perhaps the greatest the Baptists, or any denomination, had at the time. But problems arose. The mission was now neglecting to educate boys at the expense of the girls, causing social and family problems among the Cherokees. A maximum of twenty children were being taught whereas many other children would have profited from such an education. The Cherokees were urged by the Government to settle down as a farming nation but nothing now was being done to this end. The tribe was not at all pleased with the Board's decision and looked on them as word-breakers. This caused them initially to oppose Jones' work. The Board also found that they had not only to finance Jones' work but also pay an interpreter to accompany him on his preaching tours as Jones had not learned Cherokee. Rather than gain on the roundabouts what they had lost on the swings in financial terms, the Board found themselves getting deeper in debt. Though Jones led many to Christ on his travels, there was no proof that he would not have done the same in his teaching and pastoral capacity at the mission station. Indeed, it was always the mundane complaint of the Board that costs were too high in proportion to souls saved. Nor did the Board finance Jones adequately as an itinerant missionary. If it had not been for the Sarepta Baptist Missionary Society in Georgia, and private support-ers, Jones would hardly have been in a position to do his work.[37]

McCoy's second tour of exploration

On September 17, 1829, McCoy set off on his private four weeks tour of exploration so as to inform the next Congressional session of further possibilities of Indian colonization. During this tour, he wrote letter after letter to the Board and Government officials

---

[37] See William G. McLoughlin's excellent book *Cherokees and Missionaries 1789-1839*, especially the chapter *The Baptists and the Methodists*.

keeping them closely informed of his steps. McCoy's principle aim, however, was to find a site suitable for the Indian seat of government. McCoy's son Dr. Rice McCoy was to travel as his assistant as also General M. G. Clark and the Kauzau chief, White Plume. Immediately after being assured that his aims had been achieved, McCoy made for Washington to report, taking with him the requests of several tribes who wished to move west as soon as possible.[38] At Washington, McCoy was warmly received by the President and the Secretary of War but found, to his dismay that the Board were again changing their minds. They had responded most half-heartedly to the Convention's wishes regarding a further memorial in favor of giving the Indians a permanent home and had retreated from the view they had presented in their memorial to the Government in November of 1827.[39] Instead of handing in a memorial favoring an Indian settlement of the West, they merely requested that in event of a removal, Congress should provide for the Indian's future. Again, they were obviously only interested in not having to foot any bills themselves.

Support from Cone and Congress

Cone wrote to McCoy, admitting that he could not understand his own Board's action. He protested that, in effect, they had prepared two different contradictory memorials, showing that they were a house divided against itself.[40] Notwithstanding McCoy's own Board's reluctance to follow him, the President now directly engaged McCoy to advise Congress, who gave him a ready ear. In this move, the President was strongly supported by Secretary of War, J. H. Eaton and a number of leading Senators, including Lumpkin, McLean and Hen-

---

[38] McCoy's official report to the Senate and House of Representatives, dated December 5, is preserved in the McCoy Papers, Reel 7, and, unlike many of the papers in this collection at this time, shows no signs of wear and tear and is perfectly legible.

[39] See the 1829-30 memorial in a printed letter to McCoy dated March 2, 1830. The memorial itself is undated. McCoy Papers, Reel 7. The letter is signed by the Vice President of the Board, Daniel Sharp and Bolles and indicates clearly a backing down from previously held views. The writers tell McCoy that they had consulted Lincoln on the matter but the treasurer had already told McCoy that he was not privy to the change.

[40] See Cone's letter to McCoy dated December 29, 1829, McCoy Papers, Reel 7.

dricks. It was McCoy's great privilege to be invited by Chairman the Hon. John Bell to stand before and address the assembled Committee on Indian Affairs of the House of Representatives.

McCoy severely injured in a coach accident

McCoy's work, however, was curbed for several months by a very serious accident. McCoy quickly sent off reports of his meetings with the Government to various Baptist Associations and missionary bodies and traveled to Philadelphia where he conferred for ten days with alternately the entire Board or their individual members and agents. On February 13, 1830, McCoy left Philadelphia for New York where he was to confer with Spencer Cone. Just a few miles outside of Philadelphia, McCoy's coach was overturned and he was thrown out and trapped beneath the overturned carriage. His injuries were terrible and included a crushed chest, a twisted spine and broken bones which left McCoy deformed for life. McCoy brushes over the accident in a few words in his *History of Baptist Indian Missions* but his ordeal must have been horrific.[41] How McCoy was able to continue his journey is still a mystery but merely proves the strong will and courage of this amazing servant of God. His narrative continues when, though seriously injured and hindered by the severest of winter weathers, he was eventually able to drag his body to Spencer Cone's house in far off New York. As McCoy had not been expected, his friend was out on business but a servant let him in, not realizing how ill McCoy was and not being told. After an agonizing wait of over an hour, the Cones arrived. After greeting one another, McCoy merely said, "We have had an accident coming from Philadelphia, and I fear I am seriously injured. I believe, Brother Cone, some of my ribs are broken." McCoy was immediately put to bed and it was discovered that so many bones were broken that for the fifth or sixth time in his life, McCoy was told that his state would probably prove fatal. Each day for six weeks, Spencer Cone looked after McCoy, turning him carefully so that he would not receive bed sores. Happily Cone was a man of tremendous strength and yet onlookers say he cared for McCoy with the sweet tenderness of a woman. Eight weeks after the accident McCoy was still only able to move with great difficulty and could not

---

[41] This accident is also referred to in Edward W. Cone's *Some Account of the Life of Spencer Houghton Cone: A Baptist Preacher in America*. New York, London, 1856, pp. 292 ff.

bear even to wear a coat as his body was still so sore. The first thing he did on being able to walk was to attend church, thank the Lord for his recovery, and preach the gospel to hearers who were as thankful as he. Edward and Wallace, the Cones' sons became as devoted to their patient as their parents and wrote 26 years later:

> Isaac McCoy was one of the most loveable men we ever had the happiness of being acquainted with. Living his whole life amongst wild Indian tribes, and wilder frontiers-men; living a life of exposure, vicissitude, and hardships scarcely to be described; always in the saddle or the camp, and every day risking life and limb to preach the Gospel amongst those whom all the rest of the world seemed to conspire to destroy or forget - his mind and manners, instead of becoming rude or hard in these rough uses and associations, grew, all the while, softer, holier, and more loving. Nothing could be finer than his manners. Never familiar, and carrying in his quiet eye an indescribable something, which prevented any one from ever being familiar with him, he never repelled. On the contrary, he attracted; children loved him. Men were compelled to feel, in his company, that they were near something, good, kind, and noble. The warm colouring of the heart tinged his words and manner, quiet as they were in everything he did or said. If you had done anything true or good, you knew he loved you for it. When he looked at you, you felt that there was no selfish thought or scheme working in his mind; but he was thinking what he could do for your benefit, or happiness, or for the benefit of some poor soul that was in need of others' help and kindness.[42]

The Indian missionaries threaten en bloc to resign

Meanwhile, McCoy and his friends Lykins, Simerwell and Meeker became convinced that their relationship to the Board must end as the Board was not acting in the interest of the Indian Missions which they represented. While still on his sick bed, McCoy sent in his resignation to the Board, also including Lykins', saying that further resignations would follow. The reason given was that the missionaries had pledged their lives to the service of the Indians and the Board was

---

[42] Ibid, p. 283.

not acting to this end.[43] The only alternative was to establish a missionary society with the specific end of promoting Indian missions or, if the missionaries remained under the Baptist Board of Foreign Missions, they must be allowed to bring their cause to the public's attention in their own way. Cone and other friends, including William Colgate, advised McCoy to go first to the Board and give them a last chance. Thus McCoy, accompanied by Cone and Colgate journeyed to Boston and after a three-day debate on fundamentals, the Board said that they would reconsider their former conduct if the missionaries would stay in fellowship with them. McCoy followed their advice and the other missionaries followed McCoy.

Baptist influence in American 19th century politics

Shortly afterwards, on April 7, 1830, we find McCoy again in Washington for further discussions with the Government, again having to take an opposite stand to the American Board of Commissioners for Foreign Missions who were against moving the Indians, especially the Cherokees. McCoy felt that the Presbyterians had allowed themselves to be influenced by the whites rather than the Indians and, "the truth was, the matter was agitated for the purpose of attaining other ends than the welfare of the Indians."[44] McCoy, however was soon to experience that the politicians, representing the people of the United States, had listened to the Baptists rather than the Presbyterians and other religious bodies.

The bill for Indian colonization presented by William McLean,[45] now a close friend of McCoy's, on February 18, 1829 was, with some great delay, debated and passed the Senate by a vote of twenty-eight to twenty, the House of Representatives being equally divided. On May 26, 1830, the bill passed the House by a vote of one hundred and two to ninety-seven. This bill authorized the colonization of land

---

[43] Other basic reasons were as mentioned elsewhere concerning finance; the Board's hard handling of Lykins; Simerwell's being fully recognized as a missionary but not being backed by funds; the difficulties between Meeker and Slater and the Board's ever changing policies concerning schools and Indian relocation.

[44] *History of Baptist Indian Missions*, pp. 399-400.

[45] A copy of McLean's bill, H.R. 449, is photographed in McCoy Papers, Reel 7.

west of the Mississippi and stated that "the United States would forever secure and guarantee to them [the Indians], and their heirs and successors, the country so exchanged with them; and if they preferred it, the United States would cause a patent to be executed to them for the same."[46] $500,000 were allocated to put the bill into practice and President Jackson pledged himself as the security.

The President confers high honors on McCoy which he refuses

Immediately after the passing of the Indian colonization bill, the President personally appointed McCoy to the high office of Commissioner of Indian Affairs. This McCoy turned down as it was contrary to his missionary calling. The President then informed McCoy that he was putting $10,000 per year into his care for the establishing and running of schools and other areas of reform in the land west of the Mississippi. This was tantamount to giving the refused post again but without the high sounding title. To everyone's amazement McCoy declined this offer, too. Both would have meant fixed high salaries, a settled way of life, authority and comfort. McCoy told the President that there was more important work to be done and he was not prepared to put his feet up and become a mere administrator and pen-pusher. It was far more important that the Indians should be relocated first and that the land west of the Mississippi should be thoroughly explored, surveyed and plots allotted to the Indians. This had priority before whatever was to be built on those plots later.

McCoy had an extraordinary knack of getting his own way with the highest authorities and even the President now held McCoy in high respect. It was McCoy's selfless, wholehearted passion for serving the Indians that made him so useful to the Government at this time and his competence to perform the duties he suggested needed doing could not be questioned. While on his first journey of exploration, McCoy had officially been the bursar but had done a good deal of surveying and map-making. His skills were now officially recognized and McCoy was given the task of surveying and allocating lands for the relocation of the tribes. He was to start with the Delawares.

---

[46] *History of Baptist Indian Missions*, p. 400.

The death of Josephus McCoy

The McCoys set up their headquarters in Fayette, Missouri, but tragedy again struck the family. Freshly graduated as a doctor and, along with his brother Rice, McCoy's closest helper and passionate lover of the Indians, Josephus McCoy was attacked by a bilious fever while traveling to Michigan on the Mission's business. Lykins and Rice McCoy made the long journey to bring him down to Fayette under many hardships and arrived there on June 24, 1830. The family was reunited for less than a week. Josephus died on June 30. Of this sad event, McCoy wrote:

> . . . . on the 30th our dear Josephus breathed his last. This was another severe stroke, the weight of which was increased by our peculiar circumstances; but we wiped the tear of grief, in the confident belief that our son had gone to heaven. Our hopes for his future usefulness in a work to which we had devoted our poor lives, had been sanguine, but wisdom had directed otherwise.[47]

Josephus was the fifth McCoy child to die. Indeed of their fourteen children who seemed fitted out to be of great use to mankind in general and the Indians in particular, eleven died in their childhood to late youth. All of them died through malaria and other illnesses contracted in their arduous wandering through the inclement wilderness. Josephus had offered up all chances of making a career and even settling down with a family and had worked faithfully for a Mission Board who refused to pay him a penny. He truly gave his life for the Indians.

---

[47] Ibid, pp. 402-403.

Chapter Eleven
Colonizing the Indian Territory (1830-1832)

The Mission Board receives $5,721 for the abandoned Carey property

Good news for the mission came in September of 1830. Charles Noble of Michigan and a Mr. Simonson of Indiana, had carefully evaluated the property at Carey during the summer which was now to be given up. It amounted to a few cents over $5,721. By general agreement, this money was to be paid to the Mission Board for usage in establishing the new Indian mission in the reallocated Western lands. The Government had worked closely with the missionaries, especially with Johnston Lykins who acted on behalf of the Board, feeling it fitted their own ends to strengthen both the status and the work of the missionaries and even the Board itself. The Board had done nothing whatsoever to promote the sale of mission property, which had been fully the work of Lykins. He had also enlarged that property by 30 acres through his bargaining at the St. Joseph treaty. The Board had just not understood what was going on and had criticized Lykins so severely while he was striving to have the property valued that he had offered his resignation. Now, when all was completed and thousands of dollars were coming into the Board's treasury, Dr. Bolles was full of praise for Lykins' work and expressed full agreement with what Lykins had undertaken. He also assured McCoy that the Board was in favor of endorsing plans for mission stations in the Indian Territory supplied by McCoy. Bolles closed his letter by saying that he would be writing to the Secretary of War concerning further assistance, but assured McCoy in a P. S. "I believe you may rest assured that there is no want of disposition in the Board to act efficiently, provided they can ascertain in what way they can best promote the salvation of the Indians."[1]

---

[1] See Bolles' letter to McCoy dated October 26, 1830, McCoy Papers, Reel 7.

Lykins' and McCoy's views on new Board proposals for a salaried mission staff

Lykins, whose task was now to close up the Carey Mission and take the Potawatomis to the Indian Territory, had discussed the financing of their work with McCoy in view of the Board's suggestion that they might now be in a position to pay the missionaries a set wage. This seemed a real change of outlook on the Board's part as they had otherwise almost stopped funding the mission. He thus wrote to the Board in July, 1830 saying:

> Without expressing any opinion as to the amount which would be really requisite for the support of my family, it would be inexpedient for me to accept a salary less than at the rate of $500 per an[num] which is the usual compensation of a Sub Agent of Indian Affairs. As I have not taxed the Charity, or common funds of the Board for any portion of my support for a number of years I would rather not do so now, but were I to receive a salary from the Board, I should prefer, that agreeably to the proposition of Mr. McCoy it be understood that it should be paid out of some of the Government moneys which pass thro[ugh] the hands of the Board specially for the Carey mission.[2]

McCoy withstood a salaried missionary service for three further years but eventually accepted the idea as it formally bound the Board to some system of support which, though not ideal, was better than an arbitrary support where the Board felt themselves bound to nothing. Nevertheless, McCoy still refrained from using the word "salary,"[3] referring to payment to missionaries as "compensation."

The Board fails miserably to keep up with its promises and responsibilities

The Board were now committed to supporting not only the reallocation of land in the West but also to financing missionary work there among the Indians. Sadly the way the Board handled this re-

---

[2] *American Baptist Foreign Mission Societies Missionary Correspondence 1817-1959*, (ABFMS), Reel No. 99.

[3] Letter from McCoy to Bolles dated January 24, 1833. McCoy Papers, Reel 8.

sponsibility led ten years later to a final break between the missionaries and the Board as evidence was forthcoming which proved that
the Board had channeled much of the money allotted to the Indians
into other activities. Indeed, Lykins did not see much fruit for his
labors at all in the form of funds which rightfully belonged to the
mission. When, two years later, Lykins had wound up the work at
Carey and arrived at the planned missionary station in the Indian
Territory, he found that the Board had left him to buy a plot of land
from his own pocket, raise buildings without any promise of financial
help, refused to answer his letters concerning material aid for the
Indians and when they heard that Lykins was giving the Indian pupils
a meal a day, they wrote telling him that it was not necessary to feed
the Indian children.[4]

The situation at Thomas

Those, however, were problems to come. Meanwhile, things
ought to have been looking rather better at Thomas, as Jotham
Meeker had married the new missionary Miss Eleanor Richardson,
(who had been very ill), in September of 1830 in Cincinnati. Though
the general mission funds at Thomas were low, Spencer Cone had
loaned the mission family a "considerable sum" out of his own pocket,
trusting that the Board would pay him back from the Government
grants for the mission. This was one of Cone's many methods to remind his fellow Board members of their responsibilities to the Indian
mission. Another method devised by McCoy's influential friends was
to buy up the drafts the missionaries wished to draw on the Board and
then by coercion of various kinds, force the Board to pay their debts.
Sadly, however, Mr. and Mrs. Meeker gave up the Indian work for a
time. Presumably Meeker's having to share responsibility over
Thomas with Slater, plus his wife's illness had not helped matters at
Thomas.

McCoy and his two sons meet up with the famous Tenskwatawa

Though Dr. Rice McCoy had also received what his father
called "flattering" offers of employment, he chose to remain in the

---

[4] Ibid. See correspondence between Lykins and Bolles dating from May 24,
1832.

mission and support his father as assistant surveyor. Calvin, hardly more than a boy, joined them. Father and sons now journeyed a hundred and three days through the wilderness, ninety-six nights of which were spent without a roof over their heads.[5] The McCoys soon encountered Tecumseh's Shawnee tribe and discussed with them the possibility of setting up a mission and school in their area. One party was most keen on the idea, but another was "opposed to every thing like education or religion." One of the chief Shawnee delegates and one who did not wish to make a decision too quickly was Tens-Qua-Ta-Wa (Tenskwatawa) Tecumseh's brother who was variously called a shaman or The Shawnee Prophet. Tenskwatawa claimed to be in constant touch with the spirit world and taught that the Indians should go back to their own spiritual roots. He had long dreamed of a united Woodlands Indian nation so much of McCoy's arguments would have appealed to him. The Shawnees, however, because of their former pledges to the British, were still very suspicious of anything authorized from Washington.

McCoy held further meetings with Tenskwatawa and the chiefs and eventually the Shawnee nation asked for a school to be set up for their children. After McCoy had done all the preparatory work with the Shawnees, the Methodists stepped in and were asked to set up the school. This was a great discouragement to McCoy who felt the Methodists blurred the distinctions between the Indian's spirituality and their own and were far too lax in their "sprinkling" new members. He was again to encounter this kind of mass baptism in 1833 and wrote against it. Nevertheless, a door was opened for a Baptist missionary to be sent and missions among the Otoes, Omahas and Pawnees were arranged with the United States Indian Agent, Major Dougherty. McCoy asked Mr. Cone to bring this matter before the Board. Though McCoy had worked for the Board since 1817 and was obviously their most successful and most prominent missionary, he had never been invited nor appointed to any official position on the Board. His ideas were always considered as coming from a private man and thus must first be considered and debated by the Board who had little idea of what was happening on the Western mission frontier. Happily for McCoy, Cone had become the most devoted of friends with the missionary and understood McCoy's views and aims better than any other man. He also agreed fully with them.

---

[5] See Reel 7 of the McCoy Papers for Isaac and Dr. Rice McCoy's letters during this journey.

McCoy meets the Pawnees in council: The Delawares apply for land patents

Now McCoy was working in a full governmental capacity and was given a small military escort when passing through lands thought to be inhabited by hostile Indians such as the Pawnee territory. McCoy wasted no time in meeting the Pawnees in council and discussed both Government and missionary plans with a delegation of 100 Pawnees in whose area he needed to carry out a survey. One difficulty McCoy had was that Fort Leavenworth, which garrisoned a large troop of soldiers, was right in the middle of Delaware country so he had to tread warily on both sides. He therefore presented the government with proposals for a new site for the garrison which were readily accepted. McCoy was actually making history and seeing his dreams come true all in one. The Delawares appointed a chief named John Quick as their commissioner to accompany McCoy in his surveying of their future territory. Quick was convinced that his people would be happy in their new home and so he applied through McCoy as the first Indian representative ever, for a patent, proclaiming the land the property of the Delawares for ever. The granting of such a land patent had been the general practice of the Government and white settlers for years and now Indians, in this method at least, were granted equal rights with the whites.

Climatic, wildlife, geographical, archeological and geological discoveries

The autumn storms now came upon the surveyors, bringing dark clouds of dust which rolled along the ground, shutting out the light completely when they met any wayfarer and covering all with a thick coating of dirt. McCoy's party could not read their compass even when placed immediately before their eyes in the middle of the day. Soon the cold north winds grew so violent that no tent could be pitched or cooking done. Once the clouds had deposited all the sand they were carrying and the skies cleared, the McCoys observed the most interesting countryside of their travels, passing many old burial sites, places of archaeological interest and signs of big game such as buffaloes. During the cold, adverse conditions, with not a square meal to be had, McCoy and his sons cheered each other up by talking of their family back home and especially about Christiana's good cooking. Isaac dreamed of waffles and coffee and Rice of plate after plate of

340

cabbage and bacon.[6] Looking on the bright side, Rice commented that one good thing about the icy weather was that it forced the lice that were plaguing them to draw in their horns.

Dr. Bryant of Fort Leavenworth had joined them and studied with great interest the geological and mineral formations in the district. The party discovered prairie lands covered in salt and a gigantic salt water spring pouring into the Solomon River which is called Nephaholla or Water-On-the-Hill by the natives. Here, among the Kansas, comparing their words and ways with the Potawatomis he knew so well, McCoy deepened his belief that all Indian languages stemmed from one original tongue and all their customs from one source.

Meetings with the President, the Secretary of War and the Board

McCoy's party then moved on to Missouri where they considered the possibilities of establishing a mission among the Kansas Indians with General Clark. They reached Fayette on November 28th, where McCoy and his son Rice were united to their family. McCoy was only able to spend four weeks there before starting on the month-long journey of up to seven hundred miles to Washington to make his report.[7] Again, McCoy had chosen the worst of weather in which to travel and he again arrived in Washington a very sick man. Once more, McCoy was able to discuss Indian relocation personally with the President and with the Secretary of War. He then informed the Board of the openings now present in the Indian Territory where Indian Agents such as Major Dougherty[8] were urging the establishment of missions. The Board, he assured them, were faced with nothing but open doors. At the Treaty of Prairie Du Chien in 1830, large sums of money were offered to those mission Boards who would be prepared to do pioneer work in the area. McCoy was sure that he could obtain much of this money for the Baptist Board would they only put in an early claim and immediately start work. Bolles

---

[6] See Rice's letter to his sister Sarah dated October 3, 1830.

[7] McCoy's report, dated January 31, 1831 is to be found on Reel 7 of the McCoy Papers.

[8] See McCoy's letter to Bolles dated February 5, 1831. Doughtery had discussed establishing missions among the Osage, Kansas and Shawnees on several occasions and urged McCoy to move the Board to agree with them.

replied on February 11th, but the Board's attitude to the Indian mission had obviously changed again. Bolles did not take up any of McCoy's points at all regarding missions save for his recommendation of a Mr. Alexander Evans as a new missionary, a matter the Board was now looking into. Of further interest in Bolles letter is the fact that a Mr. Browning had made similar complaints about Lykins to those made by Mr. Walling about McCoy. Browning, however, had not published his complaints but addressed the Board personally about the matter and McCoy had asked for the Board to give Lykins a full report. Bolles told McCoy that they had sent all details to Lykins but knew of no evidence whatsoever that could possibly speak against him.[9]

McCoy urges the Board to take advantage of the Prairie Du Chien Treaty

Bolles' reply did not satisfy McCoy at all regarding his questions on the future of the mission, so he wrote back on February 21st urging Bolles to give him an answer.[10] Did the Board wish to take advantage of the Prairie Du Chien Treaty funds or not? Did the Board intend to open missionary stations with schools or not? McCoy pressed Bolles to consider the fact that if the Board wished to have an itinerant preaching ministry in the Indian Territory alone as he had heard discussed, then it would be wrong to expect the Government to fund such a ministry. That is the church's duty and not the Government's. McCoy would be very happy with such a situation but then the Board would be responsible for all funding from private donations alone. If, however, the Board wished to establish schools and assist the Indians in agriculture and other means of livelihood, then they must strike while the iron is hot. To be on the safe side, McCoy sent a copy of his letter to Cone, hoping that if Bolles was tempted to delay the exact and explicit answer McCoy demanded, Cone would jog his memory and conscience. On February 28th, a Government treaty was made with the Seneca Indians, granting them four hundred acres of land west of the Mississippi on fee simple terms which would put their ownership on a par with white settlers outside the Indian Territory. The colonization of the Indian Territory was under way but the Board had not even begun to establish missions apart from sending Lykins

---

[9] McCoy Papers, Reel 7.

[10] Ibid, Reel 7.

to the Shawnee settlement with a view to establishing a base there, yet with no guarantees of support. McCoy had to send Bolles two reminders before hearing from him again. Meanwhile, McCoy was busy discussing the transport of tribes to the Indian Territory with the Secretary of War and in particular, striving to sort out the mess the Potawatomis had got themselves into by some wishing to move and others demanding the right to stay, even though their lands were now taken from them.[11]

The death of yet another of the McCoys' children

While McCoy was in Washington, Christiana, Rice and Sarah had written continuously, emphasizing that all was well with the family but this was soon to change. When McCoy returned home on April 8, Christiana went into labor and gave birth to a son who died in McCoy's arms. McCoy wrote in the Family Records, "April 9th, 1831. Died our infant son who had lived only about five hours. He is buried beside our son last deceased (Josephus), in the public burying ground at Fayette, Howard County, Missouri. He was a well proportioned & pretty babe, and died from a cause not perceivable."

Belts again tightened

McCoy's funds were now exhausted. He had been using his own income for the needs of the entire Indian mission and for printing his reports which were distributed free of charge. Lykins, now back at Carey, having shown the same benevolence with his earnings, was also without money and the salary promised by the Board had not materialized. As the one always depended on the other in their family fund-sharing, all the Carey and Thomas missionaries had, once more, to tighten their belts. The new missionaries such as Abel Bingham at Green Bay did not feel the pinch so much as they followed the Board's wish in charging for tuition which the Carey and Thomas missionaries found not only impractical but impossible. Soon prayers were graciously heard and Lykins received the following resolution from the Board:

---

[11] See, for instance, McCoy's letter to John Eaton dated March 2, 1831, McCoy Papers, Reel 7.

> Voted, that Mr. Lykins be appointed as a
> Missionary to the Shawnoetown with instructions to preach
> & otherwise promote the spiritual welfare of the Indians at
> & near that place, & that he be allowed a salary of five hun-
> dred dollars per Ann[um], with his necessary travelling
> expenses.[12]

This document is as important in the history of Baptist missions as those letters from Boston during the past four years affirming that McCoy was a missionary employed by the Board which the Board later denied they had issued. Ten years later, the Board were to tell Lykins that he had not been appointed as a missionary by the Board in 1831 but that he was appointed as a Government teacher so that his salary was due from the Government through the Board. As, however, Lykins was not teaching, but doing missionary work, as specified by the Board in the above resolution, and doing medical work approved by the Board, this gave the Board an excuse not to pay him i.e. because he was not working as a teacher. This is sadly the incredibly deceitful way that the Board wormed themselves out of their own responsibilities. Lykins' reaction would be to resign and he would join his father-in-law in further missionary work among the Indians, independently of the Board.

Good as the news from the Board appeared to be at the time, there was no such good news for McCoy. He had refused to be paid a salary, arguing that this was against known missionary rules, but he did expect the Board to offer to pay his expenses when no Government money was forthcoming. He did receive a wage from the Government but this was merely per commission. When McCoy had no tasks to perform for the Government, he received no pay from them, nor expenses from the Board.

The Board give Lykins the task of moving the Carey station to the West

The Board now formally resolved to add to Lykins' tasks that of moving the Carey station to the West, ordering Simerwell to stay with those Potawatomis who were undecided until further moves were necessary. McCoy and Lykins therefore decided to divide the work. Lykins would see to the relocation of the northern tribes and McCoy would take care of the southern tribes. This at once caused complications because in the earlier resolution of April 6th, Bolles had

---

[12] Letter from Dr. Bolles dated April 6, 1831, McCoy Papers, Reel 7.

told Lykins to hire premises in the Shawnee settlement and not build - though the Board had been given Government money for such new buildings. There were, however, no buildings in the village (or town, as the Board called it) which were remotely suitable for a missionary station, let alone a boarding school. The Board had simply forgotten that the Carey family still contained a school with some 70 pupils who were also to be moved. Furthermore, in advising Lykins to hire premises rather than build, Bolles said that he was following McCoy's good advice, which was, to put the best interpretation on the matter, a total misunderstanding. McCoy's position was that there was no building suitable for a school at Shawnee and that one had to be built. Indeed, McCoy had promised the Shawnees that one would be built. McCoy, however, advised Lykins to wait for the Board's approval before building a school or mission house. It was obvious that McCoy thought such an approval would be automatically forthcoming once the situation was understood. He thus discussed the erection of such buildings with Lykins. He added in a letter to Lykins, "The Board are very good-humoured, now a days, and will hear attentively your suggestions." McCoy advised Lykins to keep a journal and report regularly to the Board, promising him full backing both regarding the Board and the Government.[13]

McCoy once again appointed as surveyor of the Indian Territory

After receiving news that Lykins would be financially on a good footing, McCoy received another commission from the government with a good salary affixed. Bolles wrote immediately to congratulate McCoy and give him the Board's full approval.[14] McCoy was commissioned by the Government to survey the country west of the state of Missouri and the Arkansas Territory and adjust the boundaries of some of the tribes already there in view of locating others. He was given a completely free hand and authorized to appoint two assistant surveyors to share the work. McCoy heard that the Secretary of War had approved of his site for the government of the Indian Territory and measures were in progress to set up the Indian legislature there. McCoy asked Lykins to look into the possibility of

---

[13] See McCoy's undated letter to Lykins with April 30, 1831? added later, McCoy Papers, Reel 7.

[14] Told to Lykins by Bolles in letter of April 6, 1831.

settling his Indians in the northern part of the Indian Territory while he surveyed the southern area.

Another lucrative post refused

As preparations were being made, the Secretary of War offered McCoy a most lucrative post whereby he could work out his own framework of service and as good as name his own terms for a salary. He was asked to supervise the Choctaw annuities and the appointment of teachers who were to receive twice as much as they had been hitherto paid. Again, McCoy respectfully turned the offer down on the grounds that it would interfere with his calling. He commented:

> This situation would have afforded me a quiet home in the Indian country, at which I could have enjoyed the society of my family, and have employed all my time in labours comparatively light, and congenial to the desires of a Christian missionary; nevertheless, I felt it to be my duty to decline the appointment. The *first* and *most important* of all matters in relation to Indian reform, at that time, appeared to be the judicious location and permanent settlement of all the tribes, where they could, "sit under their own vine and fig tree without fear." Without this, the success of future missionary labours would be rendered precarious; and to promote this permanent location had been a prominent object of our labours for the preceding eight or nine years. I saw none among the benevolent of any denomination willing to take hold of this part of the work of Indian reform; and under these circumstances I could not innocently abandon it. Yet my labours in this department were not in accordance with my natural temperament, nor congenial to my feelings as a Christian. They were, moreover, arduous, and attended with great privation; and withal my appointments were merely temporary, so that I had no *certain* income for support. But I supposed that strength would be proportioned to the work, and that He who fed the fowls of heaven would give us bread. Though I deemed it not expedient to locate in the Choctaw country myself, I made efforts to introduce others. The subject was without delay brought to the consideration of the board, and this was the origin of Baptist missions to that tribe.[15]

---

[15] *History of Baptist Indian Missions*, p. 414.

Baptist leadership in Indian Missions thanks to McCoy's work

McCoy had put his hand on the plow and would not turn back. His great pioneer work and the way he opened doors for others had given the Baptists the leadership in Indian missions. Fifty years later, on May 22, 1880, in a memorial talk on the history of the Carey Indian Mission given by Dr. Gilbert S. Bailey, the speaker said of McCoy's work:

> In that Indian Territory, the establishment of which he secured, there are now civilized tribes, with their written laws, their own legislatures, their judges and courts, their schools, their churches, and newspapers and post-offices. The Choctaws and Cherokees have far advanced in civilization. In the Indian Territory, with a population of some 80,000 there are now about 200 schools with 5,000 pupils. There are about 8,000 church members, nearly 6,000 of them are Baptists. Books and newspapers are printed in their own language.[16]

These are quite amazing statistics for a denomination that until this time was considered very small and never grew to the huge proportions it has done in North America in other countries. Furthermore, at the beginning of the Indian relocation, the Presbyterians were backed by their denomination far more than McCoy in evangelizing the Indians. When McCoy started relocation work among the Indians, he found that the Presbyterians had four mission stations among the Cherokees, two among the Osages and one among the Creeks. The Presbyterians, however, did not take advantage of the opportunities presented by the relocation as McCoy and his Baptist brethren did. Indeed, when McCoy found a tribe wishing to have a school and no one from his own mission was available, he did not hesitate to support suitable Presbyterian candidates, even when the Government were against the move. In turn, the Presbyterians offered their pulpits to McCoy when he visited them concerning Indian resettlement. Not all Baptists, however, by a long way, agreed with McCoy. Professor John F. Cady of Franklin College relates how a correspondent from Ohio wrote in the *Western Predestinarian Baptist* on June 1, 1843, "In my humble opinion, every individual who con-

---

[16] Gilbert Stephen Bailey, *The Carey Indian Mission, at Niles, Michigan, and Rev. Isaac McCoy, Its Founder. A Sermon Preached by Request to the St. Joseph River Baptist Association, at Detroit.* 1880, p. 16.

tributes to the missionary operations is ignorantly contributing to the downfall of the American Republic."[17]

McCoy refuses an offer to settle down as a Choctaw pastor for $800 a year

McCoy's faithful support of the mission Board must be emphasized here as the Secretary of War told him that if he settled down among the Choctaws as their pastor and maintained a regular preaching ministry, the Government would pay him $800 dollars a year, providing they could call on his services when needed with higher pay accordingly. This was one hundred dollars more than Dr. Bolles was receiving as his salary from the Board. When McCoy told Bolles about this offer, he explained that he had turned it down, though it would have meant he could have settled down with his family and also lived in relative luxury. His reasons given were his duties to the Board and to the wider cause of the Indians.[18] Bolles must have felt truly humbled on receiving such a letter.

Further discussions on the future of the Indians with the Presbyterians

McCoy set off on June 6, 1831 to survey an area 300 miles south of Fayette, taking his son Rice as his assistant. Rice, after his adventures with his father the year before in the Indian Territory, was very ill for several periods lasting a number of weeks but now felt fully recovered. He gave up the offer of a "flattering practice" to assist his father.[19] Lykins started out on his work to build a missionary settlement at about the same time. Mrs. McCoy and the children traveled some way with their father and were caught in heavy rains, making camping out a hazardous business. The party had to cross the unfordable Grand River by swimming across swift currents with all their stock and cattle which they had taken with them for the settlement of the Indians. Crossing only one river like this was a twenty-four hour torture. After traveling nine days, the party arrived at Harmony

---

[17] *Origin and Development of the Missionary Baptist Church in Indiana*, p. 41n.

[18] Letter written May 12, 1831, McCoy Papers, Reel 7.

[19] Letter from McCoy to Bolles, May 12, 1831, McCoy Papers, Reel 7.

Mission which was run by the Presbyterians who were still opposing Indian colonization. Discussions were carried out in a very amiable and brotherly way but the Presbyterian missionaries stood by the decision of their American Board of Commissioners for Foreign Missions to block all attempts to give the Indians their own country. McCoy also visited the Union Mission run by the Presbyterians after a further journey of about thirteen days and was given the opportunity of preaching there. A house was rented at the mission station for Mrs. McCoy and the children. Throughout the entire enterprise, McCoy kept the Government and the Board minutely informed of all the details of his work.

McCoy meets up with John Davis, a Creek Christian

It was while McCoy was in Creek country in 1831 that he met John Davis, a man who ought to be far better known by lovers of Oklahoma history. Davis was a full blood Creek Indian, or to use the ethnically correct name, a Muscogee (also Muskogee or Muskogean), who had been one of the first Creeks to "go West" from Alabama and Georgia in 1828. He settled in the Fort Gibson area known as the Three Forks. Davis had gone to a Baptist school in the Withington Mission at Tucheebachee, Alabama, near the Chattahooche River. He had been taught by the Rev. Lee Compere who described his pupil as "intelligent and sober-minded." Compere was able to lead Davis to Christ in 1827 along with an Indian girl and a Negro woman. Compere was partly supported by the Mission Board for nine years but the Board withdrew that support in 1829. At this time the Creeks were highly hostile to the gospel. The Creeks' Negro slaves were receiving Christ in substantial numbers which angered their owners so much that they took their slaves to the missionaries' homes and whipped them in front of those who had led them to Christ. Dr. Carl Rister in his *Baptist Missions Among the American Indians* says that, "this form of Creek opposition discouraged the Board from continuing the mission work."[20] Compere then moved to Montgomery, Alabama, with his remaining Creek pupils to continue his work privately. Davis felt called to be a preacher and when he was moved to the Three Forks, he began to witness to his own people and their Negro slaves, succeeding in leading several of the latter to Christ. This was brought to the

---

[20]   p. 68.

Board's notice and influential friends persuaded them to grant Davis a small salary of $200 per year to assist Davis in his evangelistic work.

McCoy takes his own denomination to task on Indian missions

As soon as McCoy and Davis met, they became the best of friends. McCoy recognized Davis at once as a man of stable character and strong determination to serve the Lord. However, Davis who was a Baptist, was working with the Presbyterians and Methodists as the Baptist denomination had not considered providing the Creeks with native pastors who would form churches. This led McCoy, an ardent Baptist himself, to take his own denomination severely to task for this neglect and for not taking advantage of the many opportunities offered among the Indians. He told Bolles:

> Here I have had the pleasure of the company of your missionary John Davis.[21] He is a man of excellent character and is likely to be the instrument of much good among the Creeks. He is modest and unassuming in his manners, remarkable for his integrity in telling of things as they are, without colouring either for the better or for the worse. He appears genuinely pious, and much devoted to the work of an evangelist.
>
> He has lately married a Creek girl, of good report, and a member of this Presbyterian Mission Church. His wife is here. He is erecting a small cabin (only 13 feet square), in the Creek settlement, whither he will take his wife in the course of two months.
>
> There is at present a serious attention to religion in the Creek settlements. A considerable number have joined the Presbyterian church, lately constituted among them, composed of Methodists, Presbyterians, and a few Baptists who were black people. A majority of the church, I understand, are blacks, (slaves).
>
> Our hearts are greatly rejoiced at the prospect of an immediate harvest of precious souls among the Creeks. I have requested Brother Davis to consider me as his brother missionary and I have also requested him to give himself wholly to the work of preaching, teaching, visiting, &c. and should he find any believers who desire

---

[21] The Board had not yet given Davis missionary status but this was McCoy's way of showing Davis' potential value to the Board.

baptism, I will obey his call when practicable and Baptize them

From what I learn, it was very desirable to many that a <u>Baptist</u> Church should have been formed instead of a Presbyterian. But no Baptist minister was there to organize them. Bro. Davis not being ordained, some Methodists among them as well as Brother Davis exhorted. A religious awakening commenced, and destitute of any other shepherd, they invited these missionaries to organize them into a Church. I feel not a little ashamed of the baptist denomination and I am grieved to the heart. Is there not in this circumstance a call to our denomination to come forward to the work, too plain to be misunderstood, and too loud and imperative to be resisted? About three hundred thousand Baptists in the U States, and none do much regarding the wretched Indians as to come and collect them into a fold and administer to them the ordinances!! O, tell it not in Gath! Brethren, in our denomination there is something <u>wrong</u> in relation to the Indians."

McCoy goes on to explain how men can be still found in the denomination who will visit the most way-off white settlements but few indeed who will establish churches in the Indian settlements. "Who will come and help us?" he pleads in his letter to Bolles, "Lord forgive the past, and help us do better for time to come!" Then McCoy returns to Davis, saying:

Brother Davis desires to give himself wholly to the ministry. The whitening fields around him demand it, and I have (instructed?) him to do so. The salary which at present he receives from the Board is not adequate to his daily wants, and to the procurement of a small amount of furniture for house keeping. I have enquired into his case, of others as well as himself. I do respectfully and most earnestly recommend to the Board to add another Hundred Dollars a year to his salary.[22]

Bolles replied on October 20 to McCoy's letter, saying that "the board are disposed to be kind & so soon as opportunity presents will send him a few good books, but think it inexpedient to increase his salary at present."[23] McCoy pressed on in his aim to have Davis estab-

---

[22] Letter to Bolles dated July 4, 1831, McCoy Papers, Reel 7.

[23] McCoy Papers, Reel 7.

lished as a missionary and pastor but by February of the following year he had only managed to gain $75 from the Board to buy Davis a horse. Finally, in 1832, Davis received full status as a missionary and pastor and received a salary of $250 which was still only half of that of his white coworkers at that time. This should not be construed as anti-Indian policy on behalf of the Board as the next white missionaries who were employed were promised only $200 per year salary! In the following year McCoy and Davis were to found the first Baptist church in the Indian Territory, i.e. in present day Oklahoma.

A perilous journey: Rice McCoy becomes seriously ill

On continuing their journey, the surveyors found that the storms would not abate and river after river had to be crossed so that for days they had to wear soaking wet clothes and boots full of water. When the rain fell, it brought with it such a drop in temperature and such fierce winds that the travelers became numb with cold and could hardly mount their horses or dismount when once they had mounted. To make matters worse, there was an abundance of scorpions, McCoy was bitten twice and lost the use of his lower limbs for several days. A Negro boy who was accompanying his Cherokee master was bitten by a rattlesnake but recovered after several hours treatment by McCoy. The missionary confessed that he had found the stories of horses being killed by flies hard to believe but now he experiences how swarms of horseflies could truly slaughter a horse. The poor animals had to be covered in leaves to protect them and their riders were compelled to travel by night so as to avoid the worst plagues. The party met twenty-five Cherokee chiefs and their spokesmen to define and secure the boundaries of their land before going on to confer with fifty Creeks and their agent on July 8th. As McCoy prepared for the next lap of the journey with Mr. Donelson who was assisting him and Dr. Rice McCoy, the latter became very ill and had to leave for Union mission so that his mother could care for him. He arrived there in a most exhausted state.

The surveyors fought on through the worst of conditions to the home of an American Board missionary called Dodge who introduced McCoy to a group of forty Osage to whom McCoy preached twice on the Lord's Day through his half-Indian interpreter Stephen van Rensselaer. Fort Gibson had sent McCoy an escort of twenty-five soldiers who came in handy at once when two hundred Osage warriors stormed the camp, thinking they were a Pawnee war party. McCoy writes, "when they discovered who we were, they ran to us at full speed, hallooing at the highest pitch of the voice, and seemed overjoyed that they had an opportunity of shaking hands instead of scalping."[24] The travelers' relief was great but it was rather diminished by the fact that as soon as the Osage mixed with them, belongings began to disappear at a tremendous rate so that the eyes of McCoy's party did not notice them disappear. McCoy had to beg the chiefs to control their people and, to his relief, a number of very needy items were returned.

The death of Charles McCoy: Rice still extremely ill

The surveying party reached Fort Gibson on August 6th and parleyed in an Osage village with Indians who had been under French influence and bore French names. McCoy then journeyed back to his family, reaching them at midnight on August 12. He was greeted by the news that his four-year-old son Charles (b. February 2, 1828) had just passed away. McCoy's next sad entry in his Family Records reads:

> Charles McCoy
>
> Was attacked with fever July 7th. Medicine could not be made to affect his disease. He died at midnight of the 21st July, 1831, in our rented house at Union Missionary Station, on Neosho River 25 miles from Fort Gibson. He is buried in the burying ground of that establishment.

To add to Isaac and Christiana's sorrows, their son Rice still lay very ill in bed. McCoy's brief words concerning his wife speak volumes, "Of Mrs. McCoy's trials, none can so well judge as a bereaved mother; and then the peculiar circumstances under which those bereavements occurred should be considered."[25]

Lykins waits in vain for promised funds

Lykins had now returned to the Shawnees to set up a mission station near their settlement but, as had so often happened in the past, the funds promised him from the Board and indeed which had

---

[24] *History of Baptist Indian Missions*, p. 420.

[25] Ibid., pp. 421-422.

been given the Board by the Government for this purpose did not arrive.[26] Nothing was available for hire so that, after waiting in vain for a reply from the Board after repeated pleas, Lykins was forced to buy a plot of land some seven miles south of the Missouri River and three miles west of the state of Missouri[27] and put up buildings at his own cost. He also bought a plot of land with a view to farming it to help support his family. As the small pox was raging in the Shawnee settlement, Lykins also set up a vaccination clinic to protect the Indians - all without the assistance of the Mission Board. McCoy was appalled at the Board's reaction, or rather total indifference, as he had thought they had recently manifested a renewed interest for Indian missions and the opportunities for service were never better. Supporting Lykins fully in his difficult situation, McCoy commented:

> It appeared to us, at this time, that uncommonly favourable opportunities were offered to the Baptist denomination to extend its usefulness, by missionary operations among the Indians; but the subject did not attract the notice, or elicit the interest, that we had a right to expect. *Indian* missions were invariably thrown into the shade, in all benevolent operations. It was a favourable time, because, by a kind of common consent, a home was about being given to the Indians, where the labours of the missionary would not be interrupted by the scattering of his flock. They who from office were required to take part in the affairs of Government, felt that the policy of the whites bore hard upon the natives, and had denied them the rights to which the original inhabitants of our country had been entitled. The Indians had a right to complain of the past, from the time of their first acquaintance with white men - to feel that their removal to the West was a great hardship, and to distrust the propositions of the Government in future. On these accounts, Government would have favoured any plans of benevolence by which the feelings of these unfortunate people would have been soothed, and that which was painful to them rendered easy. The Baptists had been placed prominently and favourably before the Government, in relation to the colonizing of the Indians; so that, for the sake of carrying out its plans, the Government

---

[26] See Lykin's letters to McCoy from the Shawnee Agency and Maj. Campbell's dated July 14, 1831 which will give some indication of the missionary's dilemma. McCoy Papers, Reel 7.

[27] Missouri had become a state within the Union in 1821.

would have given them a full share of its patronage in support of benevolent operations. The board, it was true, had been prevailed upon to propose to the Government the establishment of a mission among every tribe then within what we denominated the Indian territory; but this they had done more through acquiescence to the wishes of others, than from the impulse of their own desires. There appeared favourable openings for doing good in most of the tribes, and, in relation to many of them, we could have obtained from the Government all, or nearly all, the support needed for the missionaries; so that, in support of missions, which we desired to multiply, the benevolence of individuals and societies would have been but lightly taxed. But so little was said by the board, respecting those points which would produce effect on the public mind, that comparatively little was known and felt in favour of Indian missions, within the sphere of the influence of the board, and few candidates for missionary labours came forward and offered for this service. Of this backwardness of the board, some of us often complained. The answers of influential members of the acting board were, in substance, that "they were unwilling to commit themselves upon the great and disputed subject of Indian emigration." They were told that they had already committed themselves, and that some of us had, from the first, been avowed *advocates* of the measure; but we could more easily get the better of the argument, than produce a different practice, and one favourable to the cause of Indian reform. The board did not hesitate to publish general remarks about the Indians, or the story of a missionary relative to his local operations in teaching, &c.; but the points which would have borne with weight upon the minds of such as desired to enter a missionary field were not prominently stated.

The impression was lamentably extensive, that a mal-administration of public affairs had introduced some new system of cruelty towards the Indians, and that, while the latter were greatly to be pitied, they could not be helped; "their council fires were expiring" and the people perishing; hence, candidates for missionary labours were inclined to seek fields which promised a more fruitful harvest.[28]

---

[28] *History of Baptist Indian Missions*, pp. 422-423.

The Mormons declare Jackson County to be God's Zion for their inhabitancy

Delilah Lykins wrote from the Campbell's house on July 29th to her mother, telling her that the:

> Mormonites are about to take the country. They are preaching and baptising through the country, are trying to proceed west to find the New Jerusalem which they say is toward the rocky mountains the Agent has driven them off this side of the line and forbids their crossing it. Smith who is their leader came on a few days ago he is a very illiterate man has hardly common sense but by looking thro a transparent stone he has the prophesies revealed to him and all go according [to his] directions. He can neither read nor write.
>
> I think that they will take in Shanes family, they gave Betsey Wells one of their Bibles last sabbath, it is said not to be even a good imitation of the Bible.

Four days after Delilah penned the above words, Joseph Smith, speaking very near where the Lykins family were staying, declared all the surrounding country to be "land upon which the Zion of God shall stand" and decided to found a perfect community there of perfect people. Indeed, Smith appeared to believe that he had found his New Jerusalem in Jackson County and Delilah wrote on September 6:

> A fresh cargo of Mormonites arrived in our neighbourhood yesterday, between seventy and 100. I think that they will take possession of this country for a while, they are crowding in as near the state line as they can get, they say that (they?) can work miracles, and one woman in this last crew professes to speak all languages but when Mr. Blanchard spoke to her in ottowa, (which he speaks very well) she said that she had never been with[29] them in the spirit, that there was a few tribes that she had not been with in the spirit. I do think that they ought to be punished

---

[29] Word defaced. Context suggests "with".

and I also think - (as Mr. Lykins says) that Alex Campbell[30] ought to claim them as his grand children for they preach very much like him. they are starving here at present. I know of a widow with eight children who it is said threw three thousand into the common stock and who is now living on boiled wheat.[31]

McCoy in Mormon mythology

As the Mormon's trek route continued to pass through the Shawnee area and as the Baptist Indian mission made its head-quarters there, the Baptists encountered the militant Mormons time and time again during the next few years. Warren Jennings, in his Missouri State Historical Society article *Isaac McCoy and the Mormons*, shows how McCoy has become part of the Mormons' mythology as "the sectarian preacher by the name of M'Coy" who was a "mean and cowardly villain"[32] who strove to hinder with weapons the Mormon progress to their Promised Land. Actually, as Jennings shows, McCoy strove hard to stop a war between the enraged white settlers and Indians and the trespassing Mormons by going unarmed into the Mormon camp to try and reason with the inhabitants.

Ira Blanchard enters the Indian mission privately

Lykins wrote to McCoy concerning Ira Blanchard on the same day that Delilah wrote to her mother. He was puzzled what to make of him. The man had turned up from nowhere without either the approval of the Board or the missionaries and showed obvious interest in serving the Indians and learning their languages. He was not a Christian but showed great interest in the faith. He lived on his private income and was prepared to go to considerable expense in reaching his aims. Lykins says that there seemed to be "something

---

[30] Alexander Campbell, the leader of the Campbellites who held to a doctrine of baptismal regeneration. Campbellism must surely be regarded as one of the sources of present day Mormonism.

[31] Both letters are to be found in the McCoy Papers, Reel 7. See also letter from Rice McCoy, Isaac's brother, dated December 26, 1832 for his impression of the Mormons. McCoy Papers, Reel 8.

[32] Jennings' article, pp. 67-68.

wrong" about him, yet he could not put his finger on what and realized that Blanchard was most keen to do good. Yet, Lykins preferred to wait awhile and see how Blanchard developed before giving him any kind of recommendation at the Board as a teacher. As in his former letters, Lykins emphasizes how welcome the Baptist missionaries were made by the Delawares and the Shawnees and other tribes, yet complains that he can do nothing until the Board answers his letters. Lykins was marking time waiting for orders and getting restless because there was so much to be done.

Cass takes over from Eaton as Secretary of War

A further setback to the mission at this time was that the Secretary of War, John H. Eaton resigned his post. Eaton had always been a friend of the Baptist Indian Mission and had given them every encouragement and support within his powers. His secretaryship was taken over by Lewis Cass who had been of great service to the Indian mission when he was Governor of Michigan Territory but he was not made of the same caliber as Eaton. McCoy said, "He had a kind heart in relation to Indian reform but a doubting head." Eaton was really sure that something could be and ought to be done to preserve the Indian race but Cass, though eager to offer the Indians benevolence, thought they were a perishing race. However, Mrs. Cass was closely related to Spencer Cone and this caused the Cass family to be very interested in the affairs of the Baptist Board and through Cone and their personal connections with McCoy, they showed a continual interest in the Indian mission.[33] McCoy suggested that the Board should delegate Cone, Lincoln and himself to talk with Cass about the needs of the mission. On the same day, McCoy wrote to Cone, telling him of what he had advised Bolles to do and asking him to have an article which he had written on Indian missions and improvement printed in the *Christian Index* and *Washington Globe*.[34]

---

[33] See McCoy's letter to Bolles dated September 23, 1831 in which McCoy informs Bolles of the connections between Cass and themselves. McCoy Papers, Reel 7.

[34] McCoy Papers.

McCoy inspects the Cherokee boundaries

In September, 1831, McCoy set off on an inspection of the Cherokee boundary lines with his son, John Calvin. Donelson again served as assistant and Little John, a Cherokee, went along as the Cherokee commissioner. After only six days of traveling, Little John fell ill and died five days later and had to be buried in the wilderness. McCoy received news that Rice was a little better and was moving to Missouri three hundred miles away by coach to help in the surveying work and his youngest son, Isaac, had fallen from a tree and broken an arm, which never set correctly. He heard, too, of William and Walter Requa, two Presbyterians from the Union Mission who wished to work among the Osages in a practical way, teaching them agriculture. McCoy wrote to the new Secretary of War on their behalf. However, the two men did not seem equal to the task and gave up the idea themselves. Another Presbyterian, Mr. Redfield was asked by the Creeks to become their school teacher but the Creek agent had refused their request because of Mr. Redfield's Union Mission affiliation. As Union and Harmony were so hostile to Indian reallocation of land, this might have influenced the agent's decision. McCoy argued that you cannot force a man to give up his church in such a way, so Mr. Redfield was appointed. He soon gave up the task as did his two successors so that in 1833 Union finally gave up the station while Harmony closed down its school three years later and severed its contacts with the American Board.[35] Here were promising opportunities for the Baptist Board to step in, but they proved to be uninterested in the openings offered.

McCoy surveys Arkansas[36]

In October, 1831, escorted by eight soldiers under the command of Lieutenant Dawson, McCoy started on a new exploration and surveying tour of Arkansas where he was promptly faced with the news that the Pawnees were on the war path and had attacked and killed a number of Delawares. Dr. McCoy was still in Missouri and had again become so ill that he could not be moved. McCoy therefore

---

[35] See Daniel H. Austin's sad letter to McCoy dated June 19, 1836, telling him of Harmony's end and requesting McCoy to help him find further employment. McCoy Papers, Reel 9.

[36] Arkansas in those days included part of present day Oklahoma.

journeyed to Missouri in November, 1831 to take his son to his family to be cared for. He had to ride all the way wrapped up in four blankets because of the cold. Dr. McCoy could not be transported far, so his father left him with the Lykins in the Shawnees' camp where Rice was joined by his two sisters who had left their school at Lexington to look after their brother. McCoy reached his Arkansas destination on December 2, where he had planned to gather his entire family, his wife being already there. Letters were waiting from the Board for McCoy but, though very friendly, they avoided the issue of setting up the Shawnee mission station and all problems of finance except to say that they did not agree with McCoy's plans for paying Davis at least $300 per year, which was still far less than the pay the Board had theoretically awarded the other missionaries.[37] They also rejected McCoy's plans to send a delegation composed of Lincoln, Cone and McCoy to Cass, saying that McCoy should manage alone. This was especially a disappointment to Cone who was very willing to go to Washington on McCoy's behalf but Bolles ordered him strictly not to travel.[38]

More news regarding Thomas

As news concerning Rice's health was very bad and as McCoy was called to Washington, he arranged for all his family to gather at the Lykins' station. Before his departure to Washington, McCoy was visited by Jotham Meeker who had retired from his missionary work at Thomas and wished to set up a printing business in Cincinnati, Ohio and wanted McCoy to give him a letter of transfer to a Baptist church there. Meeker's mother lived in Cincinnati, was old and infirm, without an income and had otherwise no one to care for her. Meeker received no letter of transfer from McCoy but something of a telling off as McCoy saw the real reasons for his fellow-missionary's dissatisfaction, knowing the situation at Thomas. Meeker just could not get along with Slater. This was scarcely Meeker's fault, however, as the Board, knowing the circumstances, ought to have removed Slater from Thomas at once, instead of strengthening his position and virtually giving him all he wanted. Slater had closed the school down the previous May and McCoy recorded in a *Mem. respecting Thomas Station*, thought to have been written in December, 1831, that:

---

[37] See Bolles' letter to McCoy dated October 20, McCoy Papers, Reel 7.

[38] See Cone's letter to McCoy dated March 7, 1832, McCoy Papers, Reel 7.

>   The blacksmith has been absent much. In
> his absence Mr. Slater one time signed vouchers with the
> name of a person not there but in Worcester, Mass. to
> enable him (Slater) to draw the quarterly allowance. Some
> other times & some other persons in the employ of the
> Mission signed as tho. they were the blacksmith.[39]

Apart from this quite criminal state of affairs, McCoy noted that someone at Thomas had been allowed to draw on the Board recently for between $500 and $700. As work there had as good as ceased under the Board's mismanagement, obviously McCoy wondered who had received the money and for what ends.

McCoy's kindness to Meeker not requited

After showing Meeker the need of missionary work in Arkansas and of alternative means of providing for his mother, he was soon persuaded by McCoy to give up his home in Cincinnati and bring his family to Arkansas. Selfless as McCoy always was, he promised Meeker that he would share his income with him and arranged for Meeker to work with Davis until he had arranged something permanently for him.[40] McCoy was already thinking in terms of persuading Washington to set up a printing press in Arkansas and persuading the Board to bring out a Christian magazine in the Cherokee language. He had Meeker in mind when thinking on these lines. Nothing came of these plans as the Board set themselves up vehemently against such a move. It was the old problem, the Board did not want an inland missionary paper which would call for support of an inland mission and therefore vie for monies which would go to foreign missions. Instead, the Board persuaded Meeker to work outside of the Indian Territory and not in printing. Sadly, in later years, when the Board withdrew their connections with McCoy, Meeker sided with them and became critical of McCoy, forgetting, or rather misinterpreting, the enormous efforts McCoy had made to help him.

---

[39] McCoy Papers, Reel 7.

[40] See McCoy's letter to Alexander Evans dated February 12, 1832, McCoy Papers, Reel 7.

Blanchard turns to Slater in an effort to gain more recognition from the Board

Meanwhile, Blanchard had allied himself with Slater and hoped to gain support from him in his dealings with the Board. This availed him little, judging by a letter from Simerwell, who wrote to McCoy on January 4, 1832 to tell him, "Mr. Blanchard of whom you have heard visited the Board but from some reports the Board had heard respecting his character, saw fit to reject him. I understand from Slater (who received a letter from him) that he still intends to go among the Delawares."[41]

All the McCoys ill but the work must go on

Shortly before Christmas, 1831, McCoy proceeded from Arkansas with his wife and several children to the Shawnee mission station, a journey of 300 miles. Two assistant surveyors and a dozen other hired workers joined the party. Isaac and Christiana called on their son Rice but found him ill again. McCoy had to speed on to Washington where he arrived on March 2, 1832. He left reluctantly because all his family and all the Lykins family were very ill and he himself was most unwell but he felt it his duty to get to Washington as soon as possible.[42] He also needed to talk to the Board as the Delawares, Weas and Peorias[43] who had been moved to the territory all wanted missionaries and schools. McCoy also wanted to lay before the Government, the Board and the public his latest publication *Address to philanthropists in the United States generally, and to Christians in particular, on the condition and prospects of the American Indians*. The work is a passionate appeal to the hearts and the finances of the people to support Indian colonization or see a people utterly perish. As soon as McCoy reached Washington, a copy of the

---

[41] McCoy Papers, Reel 7.

[42] It is on such occasions that the truth of Cathcart's tribute to McCoy prefixed to this work is realized, e.g. "men who could rise to this plane of devotion to the work that he believed God had given him can see his loyalty to the Master was superior even to parental affection. No man loved his wife and children more than he."

[43] The latter two tribes were part of the Miami people whom McCoy knew at Fort Wayne.

work with a large map of the area under discussion was presented to members of Congress and heads of departments and a "large edition" printed for free circulation. When Congress read McCoy's official report to the Secretary of War, they ordered this to be printed at Government cost but McCoy had seven hundred extra copies printed for his own private circulation. The good news was now being circulated nationwide, though the Board that had originally called McCoy to his task had done nothing to support it. In his official report, McCoy had put forward suggestions indicating how to overcome the barrier of having one central Indian government to rule all the different tribes, there being now fourteen in the Indian Territory with more to follow. While McCoy was in Washington, a Creek delegation from east of the Mississippi were petitioning the Government to allow them to move west and join their Arkansas brethren.

McCoy writes to the President

A letter to the President, Andrew Jackson, with a copy sent to the Secretary of War, written at this time on the topic shows McCoy's skill in diplomacy but also in promoting both the Indians' and the Baptists' cause. He writes:

> Sir: I know that the McIntosh party of the Creeks now in Arkansas are anxious to have schools established among them, as stated in my last report. No Government provision has been made to help them in the matter; they need encouragement. While other tribes have been assisted in matters of education, they have hoped that some arrangements would also be made for extending to them the hand of help. They have looked forward to the time when the portion of the tribe on the east would negotiate for removal, as favourable for the adoption of such regulations.
>
> May I be allowed respectfully to request, which I do sincerely and most fervently, that the subject receive your favourable notice. It is not an ordinary case. Schools could be located advantageously in many settlements. There is a full Creek, who is a Baptist minister, now preaching to them, a man of unblemished character, who receives a small salary from the Baptist Board of Missions, who desires to connect a school with his labours. The Baptists have resolved to extend their missionary operations among them, and among the whole tribe, when those on the east of the Mississippi shall have arrived.

We earnestly hope that the subject of providing for the education of the Creek youth, embracing
those of both sides of the Mississippi, will receive the countenance of those who may negotiate with the eastern party
for their removal.

Respectfully, your humble servant,
Isaac McCoy[44]

The result of the matter was that the Creeks received the
promise of $3,000 per year for twenty years so that schools could be set
up in the Indian Territory. However, the year 1831 closed with
McCoy's receipt of a letter from Bolles saying that though they had
authorized Lykins to establish a mission station at Shawnee, "It
certainly will not be advisable to put up buildings or incur any other
expenses belonging to a permanent establishment."[45] Once again, the
will of the Board was diametrically opposed to the will of the mission
and to the Board's own former promises and commitments.

---

[44] *History of Baptist Indian Missions*, pp. 440-441. See McCoy Papers, Reel
7 for the entire letter.

[45] There is a hole in the letter where the month of the date had been written
but it is thought to have been written on December 6, 1831.

Chapter Twelve
The Struggle for Survival (1832-1836)

Diabolical methods of exterminating the Indians

The methods practiced by the enemies of the Indians to cause their downfall were as imaginative as they were diabolical. Some strove to divide them among themselves, suggesting that each tribe should make a nation of itself with its own nationality, borders and central government. This was not out of concern for the various tribe's welfare as such a statehood might have worked. It was because these enemies believed that united the Indians would stand but divided they would fall. The most cunning and devilish of all efforts to destroy the Red Man, however, was to deliberately introduce the small pox among them so that the terrible plague would kill them off. Soon the Pawnees were dying in their hundreds so that John Dougherty the Indian Agent reported to the Superintendent of Indian Affairs, General Clark, that he estimated that half of the Pawnees would lose their lives. The epidemic spread quickly to the Omahas, Otoes and Puncahs. McCoy heard about the dreadful crime from Lykins and immediately wrote to the Secretary of War, telling him that the small pox was now moving north to the Sioux.[1] He asked that all the Indians in the threatened area should be vaccinated. Only four days later, McCoy was writing to tell Cass that the small pox was now raging along the Mississippi and way up to Lake Michigan. To McCoy's chagrin, however, a sporadic program of vaccination was introduced for arbitrarily chosen individuals in all the tribes but not all the Indians in a given threatened area. Many thousands of Indians died.

This initial smallpox plague was to be repeated among the Indians almost yearly. Its first victims were among those tribes who had least contact with the missionaries and therefore with people who cared for their total welfare. The Pawnees, a relatively large tribe of

---

[1] See McCoy's urgent letters to Lewis Cass dated March 23, and March 27, 1832, McCoy Papers, Reel 7.

about 10,000 people, settled along the Great Platte River and since 1824 efforts had been made to establish missionary work among them, first by the Presbyterians and then in 1827 by the Baptists. Fifteen years later, McCoy had to admit that neither the Baptists not the Presbyterians had been able to make any headway whatsoever, though they were "an inviting field for missionary labors."

The Omahas were a much smaller tribe of 1,500 people who settled on the Missouri river. As they were often abused and defrauded by white traders, they remained very wary of any whites, whatever their motives. Traditionally, they were buffalo hunters but also grew vegetables. When hunting for meat, the braves spent an average of two months away from home which became longer as game became scarcer. A married couple by the name of Curtis, contrary to the wishes of the Baptist Missions Board and unknown to the senior missionaries, attempted to evangelize the Omahas as late as 1837. They used the $1,000, given by the Board for other purposes, to build a mission station which they gave up after a few months. Oddly enough, the couple made their home some distance away from the Omaha settlement, in the middle of the wilderness without any contact with either Indians or whites and without any known means of income. In spite of this negative background, McCoy could still write years later, "The prospect of doing much good there, with little cost to benevolent societies, has always been and still is good, provided energetic and devoted missionaries could be found willing to labour there."[2]

The Otoes lived on the Great Platte River near the Missouri junction and numbered some 1,600 people. They had learned to till the soil as an alternative to hunting and Mr. and Mrs. Moses Merrill were working among them, using the Otoe language, with a fair measure of success. Some thirty-six young Otoes were learning to read and write their own language by the end of the thirties. The Puncahs were a small tribe of only eight hundred people who lived near the Missouri River and had never heard the Christian gospel up to McCoy's mention of his being among them in his *History of Baptist Indian Missions* around 1839. McCoy explains how these tribes had not known strong drink in 1824 when missionaries first encountered them but in 1839, large cargoes of whiskey were being transported by steamboats up the Missouri River to be sold to the Indians. McCoy complained that those who speak of the Indians being destroyed by war speak well but the sale of alcohol to the Indians is widely encouraged and this kills off far more than the tomahawk and the bullet.

---

[2] Ibid, p. 561-562.

The Shawnee Station

The next issue was to see that Lykins was able to build the necessary school and living premises for the Shawnee children which he had been promised by the Board, money for which the Board had received in 1830. By April, 1832, there was still no sign of a penny being forwarded from the Board and Lykins had bought a plot of land privately on which he could erect a house and do some farming to help pay his way. McCoy took this matter in hand and also addressed the Board concerning the Rev. Alexander Evans[3] and Mr. Daniel French who wished to serve as missionaries. On April 16th, McCoy received a letter from treasurer Heman Lincoln, saying that the missionaries were authorized to start work and the buildings should be erected. "On this subject", Lincoln stated, "the uttermost harmony prevailed."[4] Again, the Board had made a U-turn. Indeed, Lincoln told McCoy that the Board had never been as zealous for missions as they were at present. No mention was made of financing the project, however, and McCoy's suspicions were raised when Bolles wrote to him shortly afterwards to say that he hoped McCoy would be able to persuade the Government to appoint a teacher for the Choctaws and the Board would then supply a minister to fill that post.[5]

What was happening to massive Government grants to the Board for Indian reform?

It seemed very much as if the Board were continuing their old practice of expecting the Government to pay for their missionary outreach. This seemed to be their policy especially in the Indian Territories and they were receiving thousands from the Government for Indian improvement. It is no wonder that the missionaries began again to ask what the Board was doing with all the money earmarked for the Indian mission. This suspicion grew when the Baptist Triennial Convention was held from April 24 to May 4, 1832. For the second year running, the Board of Missions left the Indian Territory com-

---

[3] See McCoy's letter to Evans dated February 12, 1832, McCoy Papers, Reel 7.

[4] McCoy Papers, Reel 7.

[5] *History of Baptist Indian Missions*, p. 446.

pletely out of their annual report. It was as if they had been left out of the Board's missionary policy.

This omission moved those with a concern for the welfare of the Indians such as the newly-elected President of the Convention, Spencer Cone, and John Leadly Dagg to present the case of the Indian Territories and the need for missionary work among them to the Convention. Cone was pastor of the Oliver Street Baptist Church in New York (1823-1841) and Dagg, a Virginian, pastored the Fifth Baptist Church of Philadelphia (1825-1834). Both pastors were in the Mid-Atlantic States of New York and Pennsylvania, which reflected a different doctrinal and practical theology from their New England brethren who tended to be more influenced by the New England Divinity of Edwards Jr., Bellamy and Hopkins and its English counterpart, Fullerism-Hallism.[6] This is one of the basic reasons why McCoy, a Regular Baptist, had more backing from the Calvinist side than those who favored Hall's universal atonement theory. Cone assembled a committee to submit a report of the needs of the Indian mission for the acceptance or rejection of the Convention. McCoy says that the facts were given "in a clearer light than anything of that kind which had previously appeared." The report was rejected by the Boston Board, reflecting New England politics concerning the Indians rather than Christian love of one's neighbor. Indeed the Board allowed themselves to be influenced by a minority who were opponents of the Indian Territory and, according to McCoy, had persuaded the Board to leave the Indian problem alone as this would mean the Board was engaged in politics. J. L. Dagg spoke passionately for the Indians and it must have been a real delight for McCoy to hear once again Luther Rice speaking in favor of missionary work in the Indian Territories. Finally, the Board agreed that missionaries could be sent to the Indian Territories, but only if they could be financed by Government funds provided for educational purposes.

---

[6] See the comparisons made between these two groups of States by English Baptists Cox and Hoby in their book *The Baptists in America*. The two Englishmen point out how the New Englanders are less particular about their Calvinism and follow the newer teaching of not only Fuller but even Robert Hall, whereas the 700-800 New York churches adhere to a "more highly Calvinistic" faith. See Chapter XIV, "Summary View of the Baptist Denomination in the United States," especially pp. 449 and 453.

McCoy's friends persuade him not to break with the Board

In this way, the Board could still maintain, in the face of criticism, that they supported Indian missions. This, of course, was a most hypocritical position to be held by an organization which was supported by the churches as their administrative body in organizing and financing the missionary cause. For the third time in his missionary career, McCoy felt he must sever all connections with the Board of Missions whose nature so obviously contradicted its name. There needed to be a Board of Indian Missions with the sole aim of looking after the spiritual, moral and physical welfare of the Indians. McCoy prepared a resolution to this effect for the Convention but again, McCoy's friends begged him not to break with the Board, so McCoy withdrew the motion.

The death of Rice McCoy

In May, 1832, McCoy received new marching orders from the Government. He again chose John Donelson to be his assistant. Things had been complicated, however. Formerly McCoy corresponded directly with the Secretary of War but now the Indian Territories were placed under three commissioners to whom McCoy had to report. Leaving Washington on May 21, he quickly sped along to Lykins' settlement hoping he would see his son Rice alive. At Cincinnati, Ohio, McCoy received a letter from his wife saying that their dear son, Rice, had died five days previously. He reached his family on June 8th and described the scene and the state of their hearts in the following words:

> This was a meeting never to be forgotten. For some time scarcely a word was spoken, while every face was suffused with tears, and every bosom heaved with sighs. O, what distress sin has introduced into the world! This was the seventh child of which we had been bereaved, all of whom died after we had become missionaries, the decease of five of whom my wife had attended in my absence. This circumstance added poignancy to the pain of bereavement. My pain was greatly augmented in this last case, by the great anxiety which our son had expressed to see me before he died. Moreover, I was not quite satisfied that I had done right in leaving my wife to bear alone this additional affliction. True, I had not left home on any of those afflictive occasions, without her approbation; and we

369

had concluded that when the interests of our missions demanded my separation from my family, it would be most safe to go, and leave the result with God, trusting that that which seemed mysterious in Providence now, would be joyously revealed in a better world. We felt these afflictions the more keenly, too, because we had long been separated very much from society, and we often felt that our circumstances, in regard to the friendship of others, too nearly resembled those of the people to whose relief we had consecrated our lives, and whose *sympathizing friends were few*. But God had ever been with us in our deepest afflictions. He was present when our late son died. As he took his leave of his sisters and brothers, and mother, the latter exclaimed, 'O, that his father were present!'. He calmly replied, for her consolation, 'My *heavenly Father* will take care of me.' Such had been the state of his mind for some time, that no room was left to doubt that his soul went to heaven, and we recorded on our hearts and in our journal, 'This is worth ten thousand worlds; O death where is thy sting! O grave where is thy victory!' How often infinite wisdom sees fit to disappoint us! Now, two sons, from whom we had hoped to obtain much assistance in the arduous work of Indian reform, and whose qualifications were doubtless of superior order, were gone.[7]

The Baptist press paid tribute to Dr. McCoy in the words:

Death of Dr. McCoy

Died on the evening of May 26, at the residence of Mr. J. Lykins, near Shawnee agency, Mo. In the 26th year of his age, Rice McCoy, M. D., son of Isaac McCoy, Missionary to the Indians.

Doctor McCoy was a graduate of Transylvania University, Lex. Ky., and was eminently qualified for the duties of his profession. His amiable disposition and scientific acquirements had secured for him the affection and respect of a large circle of friends, who, besides his relatives, deeply mourn his early departure to another world. Though well qualified to arrest disease in others, and to alleviate the sufferings of his fellow beings, he could not effectually prescribe for his own relief. This was a disease of the heart, the symptoms of which early indicated that it was incurable.

---

[7] *History of Baptist Indian Missions*, pp. 449-450.

The comparative serenity which attended a few of the latter weeks of the life of Doctor McCoy was attributed by his attendants to the solid support which he derived from vital religion.

This was the fourth son of which his afflicted parents had been bereaved in less than two years. And since they have been missionaries they have buried seven children. Yet it is true that Christians may be cast down and not destroyed. While the surviving members of the family notice with pain the empty places, filled as it were but yesterday, by four of their number, they find substantial consolation in the hope that those who have departed are in heaven. They could not desire them to be back again. More appropriate for them to say, "We shall go to them and let us prepare."[8]

The Board at last promise to release Government funds for Indian improvement

One positive outcome of McCoy's recent protests to the Board was that they finally promised to release the money provided by the Government for Indian relocation so that the Shawnee buildings could now be erected. Indeed, Bolles had written a most positive letter to Lykins a few days before the Convention apparently airing quite a different opinion to the one expressed by the Convention's resolutions. The Corresponding Secretary told Lykins that the Board had decided:

That $1,000 be appropriated to be expended under the direction of Mr. McCoy & Mr. Lykins among the Shawanoes, in erecting log houses, for the residence of the missionaries, for a school house & for a preaching place, & that they be instructed to furnish the Board with a minute statement of the items of expenditure.[9]

Lykins duly commenced building, keeping meticulous accounts of his expenditures, and forwarded the bill of $1,500 to the Board. Though Shawnee was seen as the continuation of Carey, which was to

---

[8] *American Baptist Magazine*, 1832, pp. 293-294.

[9] McCoy Papers, Reel 7.

be abandoned the following Spring, [10] and the Board had received well over $5,000 for the Carey property so that Shawnee Station could be built, Lykins was left to foot the bill alone. The Board never paid him a single penny towards settling these debts.

McCoy makes his permanent base near the Shawnee Station

One improvement was that, a teacher, Mr. Evans, recommended initially by Lykins, was now sent by the Board, at the Government's expense, to teach at the school Lykins was building and soon after Charles E. Wilson[11] arrived who was directly appointed at the Board's initiative. Evans was unhappy at Shawnee and the climate did not appeal to him so he asked McCoy in December, 1832 to have him removed to the Choctaws.[12] As the friendship between the Lykins family and the McCoys was so strong and the Shawnee station was strategically placed for McCoy's journey's both east and west of the Mississippi, the McCoys decided to erect a permanent residence adjoining Shawnee. Living first in tents, with the help of hired labor, they had a solid roof over their heads within four weeks, after which McCoy had to start on a new tour in order to select lands for the Ottawas and then move on 300 miles to Arkansas, sharing fellowship with the Presbyterians on the way. McCoy paid for his property out of his own pocket as Lykins did his plantation. The Board made no comment on this matter at the time but ten years later, they scolded both Lykins and McCoy for owning private property, though this was being used by their children and had been willed to them for their security when Lykins and McCoy had passed away. Both men had bought land as a necessity, hoping that they could sell it when the Board bought property where they could be housed. This resale was complicated by the fact that land taxes were as high as any financial gains through having the property and they could find no buyers when they tried to sell the land in 1834 onwards. Eventually, John Calvin took over the property and set up a trading station and ferry service on his land which bordered on the Kansas River and which eventually became

---

[10] Simerwell was to travel to the Indian Territory bringing the pupils and the rest of the Potawatomis with him. The Merrills and Meekers were also told to move west.

[11] See Wilson's letter to McCoy dated May 15, McCoy Papers, Reel 8.

[12] See letter written December 8, 1832, McCoy Papers, Reel 8.

part of Kansas City.[13] The Mormons accused McCoy of land speculation but he could not possibly have known that years after his death such a large city would be built on a relatively small patch of wilderness which he had bought because there was no alternative.[14]

David Lewis sent to the Indian Territory as a missionary – without funds

Now the Board asked for McCoy's advice in placing a Mr. David Lewis of New York in the Indian Territories as a teacher, suggesting perhaps the Choctaws could use him. Typical of the Board, they had not provided Lewis with funds of any kind.[15] With his usual generosity, McCoy gave Lewis money out of his own pocket to take care of his initial needs until the Board came round to supporting him with Government funds. McCoy had been much impressed by the work of John Davis among the Creeks and their Negro slaves and felt that work had priority at the time over starting a similar work among the Choctaws. The Creeks had withstood the gospel more fiercely than perhaps any other tribe but now they were proving most open to the message of salvation. Furthermore, it was high time that churches should be formed in the Indian Territory and full blood Creek John Davis would make an ideal pastor, and Mr. Lewis an ideal assistant as he was more designed for evangelistic work than a teaching ministry.

A report of the ordination service of Lewis to the Indian ministry has been preserved in the pages of the *American Baptist Magazine* and reads:

---

[13] Westport. John Calvin McCoy became Westport's first Postmaster on May 7, 1834.

[14] McCoy, with a remaining brother and sister inherited some property from his parents but much of this money was either given for missionary and other benevolent purposes or passed on to the next generation. Eliza McCoy, for instance donated some $9,125.00 of her inherited money to Franklin College alone and generously supported other charities. See McCormick's *Eliza McCoy*, pp. 102-106.

[15] See Cone's letter to McCoy dated May 9, 1832, McCoy Papers, Reel 8. The routine in employing new missionaries was to ordain him, then 'name him to the Government' to fill a post appointed by them.

Baptist Home Mission: Ordination of Mr. Lewis
On Monday evening, May 17th, in the
McDougal Street Meeting House, New York, Mr. David
Lewis was set apart to the work of the gospel ministry with
special reference to missionary labor among Indians. The
exercises of the evening were unusually solemn and interesting, the congregation large and attentive, and an anxiety awakened for the heathen in the bosoms of many persons who had previously felt but little interest in the cause
of missions.
He is expected to settle among the Choc-
taws west of the Mississippi, in the employ of the Baptist
General Convention, and with his wife and child left New
York for the place of destination, May 25th. They will be
followed, we trust, by the prayers of Christians, that the
Lord will make them a great blessing to the aborigines of
our country.[16]

The Three Forks Baptist Church constituted

After prayerful discussions with Davis, Lewis and several
Negro slaves, on September 9, 1832 McCoy constituted the Muscogee
Baptist Church, Ebenezer Station, situated three miles north of the
Arkansas River and fifteen miles west of Fort Gibson, which was the
first Baptist church to be formed in the Indian Territory and the first
Baptist church to be founded in the present state of Oklahoma. The
founding members were Davis, Lewis and three slaves, these being the
only baptized Christians in the locality. This church, as well as the
next two churches constituted in the Indian Territory and now part of
Oklahoma, were of the Regular (Calvinistic) Baptist faith and order.
Under the heading Arkansas, - Creek Nation, reminding historians
that eastern Oklahoma used to belong to Arkansas before the separate
State of Oklahoma came into being, McCoy writes at the beginning of
his report to the Baptist Board:

> I enjoyed a blessed season in Arkansas
> with our excellent missionary brethren, Davis and Lewis.
> They are both men of good sense, and ardent piety; and are
> devoted to their labours of love, in teaching sinners the way
> to heaven. I had written Mr. Lewis twice, but neither of my
> communications had reached him. He was in a land of
> strangers, and pennyless, without knowing when I would

---

[16] *American Baptist Magazine*, 1832, p. 185.

arrive to afford him relief. Nevertheless, he went to work with Mr. Davis. They preached amongst the Creeks, and visited from house to house; and before I reached them, they had fixed up on a day for the constitution of a Baptist church. In this constitution, I had the happiness of assisting, on the 9th inst.. The church consisted of Rev. Mr. Lewis and wife, missionaries, John Davis, Creek Indian, and missionary, and three black men, (Quash, Bob, and Ned,) slaves to the Creeks, who had been baptised on the east of Mississippi. The church took the name of the Muscogee Baptist Church. Mr. Lewis preached in the forenoon, and I preached at another place in the afternoon; and bro. Davis, besides interpreting, prayed, and exhorted, in both Indian and English. This was a good day to us all. We had no artifice employed to occasion excitement of feelings; nevertheless, we retired from our meeting place, not only with solemn countenances, but many faces, both black and red, were suffused with tears, and every heart seemed to be filled. For myself, I felt like seeking a place to weep tears of gratitude to God, for allowing me to witness a gospel-church formed, under such auspicious circumstances, in the *Indian Territory*, towards which we have so long directed our chief attention with deep solicitude.[17]

Progress at Ebenezer

At first, Davis was merely given a written license as a preacher which McCoy drew up but McCoy was soon able to persuade the Board and the Denomination to grant Davis full status as pastor. Sadly, the Board did not make this fact known to the Baptist public and always referred to Davis in the *American Baptist Magazine* and official reports as a "native assistant," or "native preacher."[18]

On September 16th two Creek Indians were baptized and the first Lord's Supper celebrated. From then on, new converts were added to the church every Sunday so that on October 14, 1832, ten Indians, twenty-six Negroes and one white man were baptized by Davis and by June, 1833 there were 60 members to erect a church building and also a school house. A year later, there were 80 members and Pastor Davis had translated John's Gospel and part of Matthew into the Creek lan-

---

[17] *American Baptist Magazine*, 1832, pp. 396-397.

[18] See "Report of the Board," *American Baptist Magazine*, 1834, p. 232; also "Missionary Register," *American Baptist Magazine*, 1835, p. 35.

guage. He was now ministering to a congregation of three hundred and had a Sunday School of seventy-five.

Methodist influence among the Indians

Davis and McCoy were anxious that their new church should be kept as removed from the world as possible and as close to a New Testament church as could be achieved. Very often missionaries had more lenient standards for the Indians than they had for their own people. McCoy was particularly critical of the Methodists in this respect. A Kickapoo Indian named Kenekuk but known as "The Prophet" had founded a religion composed of elements gathered from both the Roman Catholic and the Indian religions. On the more positive side, Kenekuk was an avid opponent of alcohol trading among the Indians and taught respect for the Sabbath. On the negative side, he taught flagellation to the body as a means of spiritual discipline, allowed bigamy and appeared to encourage gambling. Soon, he had not only gathered four hundred Indian adherents around him but also caught the interest of the Baptists and the Methodists. Kenekuk's adherents were mostly Potawatomis from the Carey area where McCoy had first met up with them. Kenekuk had now brought his followers to the Indian Territory and visited McCoy, who was ill at the time. McCoy himself felt that the sect had encouraging marks of wishing to progress towards a more Christian testimony but would not accept them as Christians until they professed Christ in word and deed. Then the Methodists, who were already working among the Shawnees through the invitation of another "prophet", Tenskawatawa, met Kenekuk and decided not only that he was a true Christian but that he should be licensed to preach and four hundred of his followers were baptized within two or three days. Later, McCoy was to tell the story of a "missionary" who asked hundreds of Indians to make two lines, those who wanted to serve Christ were asked to form one line and those who did not, another. The enthusiastic minister then went down the long line of those who had answered in the affirmative, sprinkling them all with water and at the end of the task pronounced all the sprinkled ones "christian". One cannot help thinking that McCoy is referring to how Kenekuk and four hundred of his followers were "christianized." Always willing to see positive signs in the work of other denominations, McCoy concludes that from then on the Prophet's people became more industrious and were now "getting into circumstances more favorable for receiving religious instruction." Relations with the Methodists at the Shawnee Station could never be too cordial. The Baptists always helped with the building and farming work themselves while the Methodists, led by Thomas Johnson who had set up a base at the station in 1830, used slave labor. [19]

Evan Jones' trouble with the Methodists

Evan Jones found himself harassed by the Methodists' methods even more so than McCoy. He was operating a teaching and itinerant ministry on a wide scale, looking upon both the seekers and Christians in the area as his parish and his flock. He thus had the spiritual oversight of several groups of Indians who were very close to a profession of faith and whom he was catechizing. He was shocked to discover that the Methodists were visiting those under his care, persuading them that as they had sought Christ, they were already his and ought to be baptized at once and become members of the Methodist church. When the Indians protested that their spiritual father was a Baptist, the Methodists said that Baptists and Methodists were all one church and so Jones would have nothing against their becoming Methodists. Once the Indians had become "Christians" in this way, however, pressure was put on them to have nothing to do with the Baptists. When the Indians objected to being sprinkled instead of immersed at their baptism, the Methodists said that this was no hindrance as they would immerse the Indians if they so wished. Jones, of course, was horrified at this sheep-stealing and protested to the Methodists concerning their ways of increasing their flocks. Such Methodist strategy must be born in mind when comparing the statistics which the Methodists gave concerning their success among the Indians. Invariably their figures were up to five times higher than any other denomination. Such comparisons, however, were entirely misleading. First, they had a lower entry threshold into their churches than the Baptists who demanded sure signs of faith, spiritual understanding and growth of their converts. Secondly, they considered all the family of those Baptized as members which meant that they included very many unbelievers in their membership. Thirdly, because many of those who joined them were not really committed Christians, as could be expected, they returned to their old traditional native religions.

---

[19] See *The Kansas City Star,* 08/04/97, "Missionaries saw opportunity to evangelize, capitalize" etc., internet.

David Lewis allows himself to be influenced by Methodist strategy

Sadly, on seeing the success of the Methodists' ministry in bringing numbers into their churches, David Lewis soon began to be more lax in testing the faith of those seeking baptism and church membership. Even while McCoy was still at Muscogee, he had to advise Lewis not to accept ten people who desired to be immersed but could give no profession of faith. These were mainly black slaves who, seeing many of their fellow slaves soundly converted, wished to join them in church membership because of family ties and reasons of friendship. McCoy remarked:

> On all suitable occasions I entreated Mr. Lewis and Mr. Davis not to admit to fellowship in the Baptist church any who could not give satisfactory evidence of their conversion to God. This was enforced by arguments based upon the *awful responsibility* that rested upon us when dealing with matters relating to the souls of our fellow-men, especially the souls of the heathen, who acknowledged their ignorance and placed confidence in our judgment. I urged these considerations until I was ashamed to repeat them. Notwithstanding all which, I had too much reason to fear that Mr. Lewis indulged this awful error.[20]

McCoy's further dealings with the Government

Now the Government began to take active note of McCoy's pamphlet *Remarks on Indian Reform* in which McCoy had presented an alternative to the Government's way of handling land purchase from the Indians. The former practice had been to give the Indians annual cash payments for land taken from them which were well under the market value. These relatively small amounts of money disappeared quickly as the Indians bought whiskey to celebrate the occasion. McCoy had argued that the Indians should be paid the value of their land exactly as in transactions with whites and that this money should be invested in new land and stock on behalf of the Indians from whom the Government had bought up old land. McCoy's suggestions were now being implemented in the case of the Chickasaws and gradually being applied to other tribes so that the Indians

---

[20] *History of Baptist Indian Missions*, p. 453.

were now becoming wealthy. In fact, McCoy says the Chickasaws became "immensely wealthy."

McCoy gave his report to the three Commissioners of Indian Affairs in the autumn of 1832 but was told that his services were no longer needed. He was now left as an unpaid missionary with no hopes of income from any other source. McCoy had received a great deal of money from the Government but he had put almost every penny of it into the Indian Mission. Edward and Wallace Cone tell how McCoy could have become very rich through Government wages and Indian generosity, saying:

> What men of the world would think a foolish honesty prevented McCoy from being a very rich man. At almost every cession of their lands to the United States by the Indian tribes, they insisted upon making it one of the conditions of the cession that he should receive a part of the land conveyed, and the expression of their desire would have ensured the prompt acquiescence of the government. But he invariably and peremptorily forbade it. His desire was for the soul of the Indian, not his lands; and his knowledge of human nature taught him that the least appearance even of a selfish care of his own interests would destroy his usefulness amongst them as a missionary.[21]

The Indians' generosity in giving land or part of their annuities to the missionaries who had helped them became one of the major criticisms against the missionaries as it was sadly true that some missionaries took advantage of it.[22] The Baptist missionaries did not take advantage of this means of increasing their income. The Indians, however, had good memories for good deeds and when a missionary died, they would donate land or money to the remaining children. Thus after Jotham Meeker died on January 11, 1854 and Mrs. Meeker on March 15, 1856, the Ottawas gave their surviving children, Element and Elias eighty acres of land each.[23]

---

[21] *Some Account of the Life of Spencer Houghton Cone*, p. 290.

[22] See op. cit. *Kansas City Star*, 08/04/97.

[23] See William G. Cutler's *History of the State of Kansas*, "Indian History, Part 7," Ottawas, p. 3, internet.

McCoy's poverty for the Gospel's sake

Edward and Wallace Cone who had access to McCoy's private correspondence with their father, after clearing McCoy's name of any suspicion of enriching himself via the Indians, quoted the following words from a letter at this time showing how McCoy was pursuing his selfless work among the Indians, irrespective of his poverty:

> Do not imagine, my dear friend, that because I am earning nothing for the support of my family, I am doing nothing in Indian business. I am busily employed in labours for the benefit of these poor people, and hope to continue busy until about the time that the last loaf comes to the table.[24]

As he had done so often in the past, McCoy could not help but think of the Mission Board which he had served for so many years and which had benefitted enormously from his work spiritually and materially without being greatly disappointed at their conduct. Writing in 1840 of this time of great poverty, McCoy says:

> In respect to pecuniary matters, I was then barely even with the world. I was constantly employed in missionary affairs, but had no income to meet the expenses of my family. During eight months I realized not a little anxiety; I durst not indulge a thought of entering upon any business unconnected with the welfare of the Indians, and, by attention to them without income, a debt was accumulating upon me that was well calculated to occasion uneasiness. Having applied all my extra earnings from the Government, which had been considerable, to the support of a cause ostensibly under the patronage of the board of missions, and as I was employing all my time in support of the same cause still, I might have preferred a just claim upon the board for support; but this I declined. My necessities, however, became so great, that I took measures to remind them of our wants, and I did it in the hope that some relief would be offered to us; but the result was not what we had hoped for. Our embarrassed circumstances occasioned more toil than we were well able to bear, and we had to labour some times with our own hands harder than our strength justified. It also added to our difficulties, that,

---

[24] Ibid, p. 289.

within the period of anxiety of which I write, I was twice
confined for a considerable time to my bed by sickness.[25]

McCoy's reference to the Board's reaction to his plea for help
in the words, "but the result was not what we had hoped for," is one of
his many stoic understatements when faced with grave difficulties.
What proved an even greater disappointment to McCoy than the
Board's attitude was that of his co-missionaries with the exception of
Lykins. McCoy had financed several of the Board's missionaries out of
his own pocket for some time, arguing that his income was the
mission's. When he made known his financial difficulties to the Indian
missionary family, none save Lykins thought of sharing their wages
with him.

A new letter from Bolles

McCoy heard less from Bolles at this time, though Lincoln and
Cone wrote regularly. Bolles now wrote on January 3, 1833[26] concerning McCoy's letter referring to Lewis of September 28th of the
previous year. McCoy had suggested that the Board should pay Lewis
$500-600 to help him settle down. McCoy had already drawn on the
Board for $250[27] dollars on behalf of Lewis and Bolles now told him
that he had liberty to draw on the Board for the rest. Bolles agreed
that Lewis should be paid a wage but suggested that this financial
responsibility should be shared by the Indians who, he reasoned,
would thus have a greater interest in the mission if they were paying
for its work. To back up what he was saying, Bolles informed McCoy
that he knew of a teacher in an American Board school who was
receiving $400 per annum from the Indians who were thus learning to
be dependent on themselves and not others. Bolles then goes on to
lecture to McCoy how much better the American Board managed their
finances. Bolles failed to mention that in striving to put American
Board practices among more affluent Indians to the test in Thomas
and the Big Lake stations, they had failed. Also, a number of American

---

[25]   p. 459.

[26]   McCoy Papers, Reel 8.

[27]   Actually McCoy had only drawn on the Board for $135. Bolles had
thought McCoy was asking for more than he had recently requested, and
gave him a light reproof, but McCoy was asking for $115 less.

Board schools had to close down because the Indians either could not or would not finance the Presbyterian-Congregationalist work.

More missionaries to the Indian Territory and further correspondence with the Board

While Bolles' letter was on its way, McCoy was writing to the *Baptist Weekly Journal*,[28] informing the newspaper of the needs of the various Indian tribes and the missions working among them. He appealed to the Baptist public for at least another twelve missionaries to go out into a fertile harvest field among the Indians. McCoy stressed that he was talking about missionaries to the Indian Territory, explaining just what this was as the Board had left out references to the territory in their annual reports of recent years. In his covering letter to the editor, McCoy outlined his plans for an Indian Mission printing press and newspaper, and asked for advice concerning staffing such an enterprise. McCoy wrote to Bolles on January 24th, saying that he was sure the Board would make ample provisions for David Lewis. Daniel French had impressed McCoy greatly with his Christian spirit and McCoy told Bolles how he was already esteemed and respected by all. He assured the Board that Lykins was striving to keep building costs at Shawnee below $1,000 but as furniture, bedding etc. must be purchased, the final cost would need the full $1,000 to cover it. A further letter from Bolles was sent on February 19, 1833, informing McCoy that the Simerwells, Meekers and Merrills would soon be moving west from their northern stations. Bolles, however, was full of criticism concerning Lewis. Instead of keeping to the amount of money McCoy had gained for him from the Board, he had gone into debt for three times the amount.[29] Quite surprisingly, Bolles told McCoy that he had heard that McCoy had forwarded $30 to Meeker the previous year and he could draw on the Board for that amount.[30] McCoy told Bolles to credit the sum to the Baptist treasurer as what he had given, he had given.[31]

---

[28] See McCoy's article thought to be written January 18, 1833, McCoy Papers, Reel 8.

[29] McCoy Papers, Reel 8.

[30] Ibid.

[31] Letter to Bolles written May 10, 1833, McCoy Papers, Reel 8.

New opposition from the Roman Catholics

McCoy was now awaiting the final move of the Carey Indians to the Indian Territory and wondered at their delay. He found out that as soon as the Baptist missionaries had left Carey, a Roman Catholic priest and several nuns had settled in the area and striven with some success to persuade the remaining Potawatomis and Ottawas to stay on the small areas of land they had not yet given up. The missionaries, however, hardly expected the papists to go so far as they did in March, 1833. *The Catholic Telegraph* produced an edition containing a year old letter and attacking the "barefaced villainy" and "redemptionless scoundrelism" of non-Roman Catholic missions, picking out Isaac McCoy as their main target. Seldom has the mean slander of popish envy at the progress of the work of the gospel been so vicious as in the letter quoted as "proof" of the immorality of the Baptist missionaries, which was so obviously written according to the motto, "If lies must be told, make sure they are big ones."

> Newburyport, Michigan, July 17, 1832
> Dear Sir, - I received your letter per mail, 15ᵗʰ inst[ant]., and am very glad to learn that you are pleased with the country. In relation to the conduct of the mission-aries at Carey, I am perfectly willing to state before the public what I know from actual observation, during the time I have resided on this river, (St. Joseph's) which is upwards of six years, and some part of the time near the missionary station. Mr. McCoy, the Principal, was, for the most part of the time, travelling through some part of the United States, soliciting charity for the poor Indians, (as he termed it,) and vessels arrived at this place in many instances, principally laden for this station with articles of clothing, brandy, wine, tea, coffee, dried fruits, &c., also medicines of all kinds; and by land, were sent cattle, hogs, sheep, &c. all of which for more or less, were disposed of to emigrants, neighbors, &c. for *cash only*, at a very handsome profit. Congress, as I was told by Mr. McCoy, appropriated $1200 yearly, in the following manner, to wit: $400 to Mr. McCoy, as superintendent and preacher, $1000 to the school-master, and $400 to the blacksmith, of which the two latter were hired for $16 per month by the superintendent. Iron and steel were furnished the Indians by the United States for the purpose of making axes, traps, knives, repairing of guns, &c. but a great part of it was made use of for the whites, which caused the Indians to murmur in many instances, but to no effect. Cattle, hogs, grain, &c.

were sold to the whites at a high price and for *cash only*.
The Indians granted to this station one section of land, for
the benefit of their children's education, of which they had
about one hundred acres under fence, and the greater part
in a good cultivation. Corn they sold at $1 per bushel, pota-
toes at 75 cents, wheat at $1.50, &c. The quality raised
could not, in my opinion, be less, yearly, than two thousand
bushels. They had some men hired by the month, at $10 per
month, but the greater part of the labor was done by those
young Indians belonging to the missionary establishment.
As soon as the whites began to settle around this station,
and began to discover the impositions practised, Mr. McCoy
made application to the Board of Missions to remove to the
Missouri country, and prayed Congress to pay him for the
improvements which he had made at this place; Congress
appointed appraisers to value the improvements made by
the missionaries; and who reported that they were worth
$5000, for which government paid them, as I have been
informed, this last winter. The improvements might have
been worth $500 possibly, but not more. Mr. McCoy left this
country for the West, between two and three years since;
some remnant of them remained until this year. The
Indians both male and female, have returned again to the
woods, practising every vice that comes in their way - they
are ten times worse than those that never saw a missionary
establishment in their lives. The above statements can be
substantially proved by men of respectability now residing
in this section of Michigan Territory. One sheet of paper
will scarcely begin to give a fair development of the history
of the manifold enormities that have been committed at this
station under the cloak of religion. I intend, during this
summer, to fit for the press, in pamphlet form, a concise
detail of the whole affair, as far as my knowledge of the
facts extends.

The reasons for Mr. McCoy's leaving this
were, in the first place, because the whites, as well as the
most enlightened Indians discovered his mal-practices; and,
in the second, because he was ordered off the Indians lands
by the chiefs. I think it will not be worth while to give any
thing in this in relation to whoredoms &c. &c. that were
practised at this station, and, no doubt, more or less, by
those pretended christians. Yours, very respectfully,

T. S. S.

This evil letter is symptomatic of McCoy's critics who just
could not get their facts right. To argue that the Government were so
careless as to estimate $500 of improvements at $5,000 is an unfound-

ed criticism of the Government rather than the Baptist Mission. The critic's argument that McCoy sold wheat for $1 a bushel is even more revealing as, if this were true, McCoy would have sold the wheat at half its market value.[32] Actually, McCoy had often paid up to $5 a bushel to obtain wheat for Carey. The author's unprincipled attack on his presumed "pretended christians," merely reflects the low personal morals of that servant of Rome. Simerwell told the author of the letter that McCoy would defend himself in print and Daniel French even prepared a written answer for publication but McCoy said this was not necessary as the man's accusations were not worth the effort and replying to him would increase the man's own self-conceit instead of making him humble. McCoy and Lykins felt that the accusations were so self-evidently wrong as all could see how frugally they lived, that it would be a foolish waste of time to write against such mean-spirited critics.

McCoy recommends that the Government continue to pay grants directly to the Board

A letter to the Commissioner for Indian Affairs, Elbert Herring, dated May 22, 1833,[33] shows how careful McCoy was to make sure that Government monies were not to be paid through him to the Indians but through the Baptist Board. The Kickapoos had received a grant of $500 per year for their education and the Commissioner had approached McCoy to make some form of direct payment. McCoy advised Herring to pay the money to the Board. No doubt McCoy felt that the more money was given the Board for the Indians' use, the more they would feel honor bound to extend their missionary and educational work among the Indians. Also, McCoy was only too aware of evil tongues that suggested Government funds went into his own pocket and never came out. The Board provided a useful ally in proving that he was far above such base actions. McCoy was also careful to make sure that Bolles received a copy of this letter.

---

[32] Indeed, a previous critic of McCoy's had priced wheat correctly at $2 a bushel but argued that McCoy was charging $1 a bushel for milling wheat. Cf. McCoy Papers, Reel 7, dated January 3, 1829 with a question mark. Someone has written on the envelope "Pratt's foolish letter to McCoy."

[33] McCoy Papers, Reel 8.

Ira Blanchard professes Christ

On June 9, 1833, McCoy wrote to Bolles concerning Ira Blanchard. He explained how Blanchard had been serving the Indians for two years at his own expense and had now professed Christ and McCoy had baptized him. McCoy emphasized that Christians ought to follow the example of their Lord in forgiving what was past and suggested that the Board employ Blanchard as a teacher. McCoy emphasizes however in his letter that the Board's recognition should end there as once the public knew about Blanchard's past, which was a secret kept by McCoy and Lykins, the Board could always say that Blanchard was employed as a teacher, not a missionary. McCoy suggested that the Board pay Blanchard $175-$200 per annum for his assistance to the mission. In the same letter, McCoy informed the Board that Alexander Evans who had recently started out on his missionary calling had changed his mind and had handed in his resignation.

The Board publicly denies that McCoy is in their service

The June, 1833 issue of the *American Baptist Magazine*, featuring the Baptist Board of Missions' Annual Report brought with it the biggest shock of McCoy's missionary life. He was thankfully reading the Board's report of the good things that were happening at the Shawnee Station which the Board had at last been persuaded to publish, when to his sheer amazement, he read that Isaac McCoy was "not in the service of the board." Apparently, he had been fired without anyone bothering to tell him about it! This blow hurt McCoy far more than the lack of money in his pocket. He had dedicated his life to the work of the mission and gone through trials and sufferings of an immense nature in order to bring the gospel to the Indians. He had also provided for the financing of a number of missionaries and mission buildings and had popularized the work of the mission nationwide, though the Board had hardly lifted a finger in this respect after Luther Rice's removal from office. Over a period of three years and more when not a penny was provided by the Board for the mission, McCoy's leadership had prevented the missionaries from giving up and disbanding. Without Isaac McCoy, there could scarcely have been an Indian Mission as he was God's certain choice for its foundation and construction. His *Family Rules* had not only kept many an Indian from starvation and exclusion from the gospel but many a mission worker, too. Now he was merely written off, without consultation and could no longer be officially called a missionary in his own denomination. McCoy quickly wrote to Dr. Bolles, the Corresponding Secretary, on July 23rd, airing his complaint and saying:

> It was with great astonishment that I noticed last night in the June[34] Number of the Magazine a statement that I was not engaged in the service of the Board. This is <u>news</u> to me. If the statement is correct please inform me when my services for the Board terminated and the reasons why they terminated, and how it happened to be published to the whole world, before any intimation of such a design had been given me.

He told Bolles that charity required him to think it must be a mistake and if so, could he place an announcement to this effect in the *American Baptist Magazine* and in the *Watchman* so that those who were told that McCoy was not one of the Board's missionaries might know that he was indeed in the Board's service. Eventually such an acknowledgment was made by the Board without adequate explanation as to how the "mistake" had been made. William G. McLoughlin in his book *Cherokees and Missionaries 1789-1839*, had looked into the matter and discovered that McCoy's expulsion from the list of the Board's missionaries was far from being a mere slip of the pen. Bolles had written to Heman Lincoln as early as December 22, 1829 stating that the Board was thinking of dissolving their connections with McCoy because of his publications outlining the plight of the Indians. In the letter, Bolles assures Lincoln that he could reckon with his support should Lincoln take measures against McCoy, encouraging him to betray their most industrious worker with the words, "Do not let your heart fail you my brother, in this day of trial."[35] However, Lincoln had come to regard McCoy highly as a friend and even Bolles gradually began to drop his initial patronizing attitude to McCoy and learned to treat him with deep respect, if not friendship.

---

[34] The issue is given as April in *History of Baptist Indian Missions*, p. 460 where McCoy also airs his complaints.

[35] Lucius Bolles to Heman Lincoln, December 22, 1829, Baptist Foreign Mission Board Papers. See pp. 267-284 in McLoughlin's book. McLoughlin is at times highly critical of McCoy, judging his actions to be often selfish, not understanding McCoy's faith. McLoughlin believes that the conflict between McCoy and the Board was, on the whole, political, McCoy being pro-Jackson and the Board anti-Jackson. This is a very simplified picture of the political, social and theological problems involved.

McCoy reminded the Board that they were doing harm not only to the Indian Mission but to themselves as they were in receipt of monies from the Government to pay for McCoy's work as an Indian Agent, doing tasks in keeping with his calling as a missionary and if the Board no longer accepted him as a missionary, the Board could not expect the Government to finance their work in any way. McCoy also pointed out that at present he was negotiating with the Government to have mission stations run by Baptists and Presbyterians set up among the Cherokees, Creeks, Osage, Kansas, Weas, Peorias and Piankashas. Besides which, he was in discussions with the Commissioners for Indian Affairs concerning the future outreach of the Board among the Otoes, Omahas, Pawnees, Kickapoos, Delawares and Choctaws and did the Board now wish to jeopardize this progress? McCoy concluded by writing:

> While I am earnestly improving every opportunity of promoting the interests of missions, and your missions in particular from the Platte to the Red River it is very unfortunate that the public should be told that I am 'not engaged in the service of the Board.'
> The whole subject and the details of it are within your reach, and to your good sense, and zeal in the cause of missions the subject is at present cheerfully submitted, in the expectation that the error in the Magazine will [be] speedily corrected.
>
>
>
> I am respectfully
> Your Obt. Servt
> Isaac McCoy[36]
>
>

This was neither the first time nor the last time such "accidents" were to occur. Indeed, ever since 1830 McCoy and Lykins[37] had been hearing rumors that the Board was in possession of material which would cast a dark shadow on their testimony as missionaries but every time they wrote and asked to see the alleged evidence, they were assured that they were as highly respected as ever and no one had ever seriously challenged their characters.

---

[36] McCoy Papers, Reel 8.

[37] See letter from Lykins' to Bolles, July 15, 1830, American Baptist Home Mission Society, Microfilm Records File, Reel No. 99.

The case of Sampson Burch

For several months, though Isaac was receiving no money from the Board, the McCoys shared their rapidly dwindling financial reserves with a Christian Choctaw by the name of Sampson Burch who had recently arrived from Kentucky. He had been educated in that State and also converted and baptized there. His church had separated him for the ministry to his own people alongside the Arkansas and Red rivers. On his way to Arkansas, he called on McCoy for fellowship and support. At the time, McCoy was writing, preaching and doing odd-jobs for the white settlers and workers, the latter bringing in a little money. Mrs. McCoy took in several paying lodgers to supplement the family income. During the time Burch stayed at the McCoys' home, the Board was appealed to as the Indian obviously needed permanent help. The McCoys were now penniless themselves, in spite of a little income, because they had to pay off the Mission's debts. Happily, the Board replied speedily, promising to take over the patronage of the Indian. Burch settled down among the Choctaws and became engaged to a Delaware Christian, all the time maintaining a good witness, but the Choctaws told Lykins that Burch was already married and had a family and had been previously guilty of violence. No proof, however, was forthcoming but this put the missionaries in something of a dilemma.[38]

The Board takes further action to consolidate work in the Indian Territory

Now it became clear that the Board was changing tactics, if not their minds, concerning supporting missions in the Indian Territory. By 1833, they had realized that it would be a far easier task for them to support a mission in a settled area than bother with straggling remnants of Indians scattered about the country. They thus began to order their missionaries from the Great Lakes area to proceed to the Indian Territory. Mr. and Mrs. Moses Merrill, newly appointed to the Chippewas, and Mr. and Mrs. Jotham Meeker, who had been working at Thomas and Sault de St Marie for some time and also Cynthia Brown of Sault de St Marie, were asked to report to the Shawnee Mission house. These missionaries reached the Shawnee

---

[38] See Lykins' letter to McCoy dated February 17, 1834, McCoy Papers, Reel 8.

settlement on July 13th. Three days later, McCoy received a further commission from the Government to survey new parts of the Indian Territory. His financial troubles were allayed for the time being. McCoy's own comment was, "Left as we had been to provide for our own support, and in the midst of great necessity, He who feeds the sparrows responded to his own gracious inquiry - 'Children, have you any food?' and relieved us for the present from painful anxieties, which had brooded over us eight months."[39]

The Meekers back again doing missionary work

The Meekers' presence at the Shawnee Baptist Mission was a major help in their evangelistic work. Meeker had been terribly disappointed by the lack of support from the Board and his dealings with Slater had had the character of a nightmare. This and the fact that he was physically incapacitated and often ill, had prompted him to give up his missionary work for a time and return to his printer's occupation in Cincinnati. Now, through McCoy's efforts, he was officially appointed by the Board as printer to the Shawnee tribe and was able to procure printing apparatus through Government grants to the sum of $468 including transport and paper and ink worth $35. By March of the following year, Meeker was printing a primer of the Delaware language and producing a newspaper entitled *Shau-wau-nowe Kesauthwau* or *The Shawnee Sun*. This was succeeded by some sixty-five works on Christian subjects, written in no less than ten different Indian languages. Meeker founded his own mission station to the Ottawas in 1837 under the Board's supervision. He moved the Shawnee printing equipment twelve years later when he recommenced publishing works in Indian languages including a bilingual codex of Ottawa tribal laws.

Carey now fully re-established at Shawnee

Now most of the Carey church had reassembled at the Shawnee Mission and a number of Delawares were baptized and given church membership. The Baptists had been content to see the Methodists run the school but became increasingly dubious about their methods of education and means of evangelization. They thus founded

---

[39] *History of Baptist Indian Missions*, p. 463.

a school of their own, entirely supported by the mission itself. The Michigan Indians were able to settle down easier after their long trek from the north as they found the same spiritual company and support as they had enjoyed in their original home. McCoy really missed the fine fellowship he had been enjoying when he went on his next surveying tour in the autumn. He was now mapping the very western boundary of the Indian Territory which was the home of very warlike Indians. Wolves, however, became more of a menace than human enemies.

The mission to the Indian Territory opens up new fields

Now that McCoy was fully in charge of the survey team, he insisted on resting on the Sabbath and that his team should gather around the Word of God. In his absence, McCoy heard that the Mission's plans of three years ago to take the gospel to the Otoes, Pawnees and Omahas, two hundred miles from the Shawnee station, had now been honored by the Board and the Merrills were starting out on the approximately 24 day journey there. Their destination was the Great Platte River on whose banks they had decided to establish the new mission. McCoy applied to the Government to appoint Moses Merrill as a paid teacher according to the terms of the treaty with the Indians and the mission were pleased to hear that the Government had decided to appoint Merrill and grant him $500 per annum. One major Godsend for the missionaries was that when they reached Otoe territory, they found suitable buildings for their work already erected as a former French trading post had been recently deserted there. A small school, a Sunday School and Bible class were soon begun and the Merrills were able to baptize their first convert in April, 1834. The Merrills were very well received by the Otoes who invited them into their large, circular earthen houses. In the Summer of 1835 the Merrills were able to build and open a school for 35 young adults but this proved a most sporadic undertaking as the students were away for at least half the year hunting buffaloes. Soon Moses Merrill could preach fluently in Otoe and gave the Indians Bible portions in their own language.

By this time, the Baptist Board of Missions was working so closely with the Government that one scarcely knew from which side various initiatives originally came. This is illustrated by a letter which came from Lewis Cass, the Secretary of War, who wrote:

Permission is hereby granted to Mr. John-
ston Lykins to visit the Indian country west of Mississippi,
under the authority of the Baptist Board of Missions, with
a view to collect and report information interesting to that
board in carrying into effect their views in the selection of
sites for missionary establishments and schools in that
region. He is recommended to the attention of all officers of
the Government, and they are desired to communicate to
him such information as may be useful in the discharge of
his trust.

Given under my hand and the seal of the
War Department, at Washington, this tenth day of September, A.D. 1833.

Lewis Cass.[40]

Now the Baptist Mission was socially and politically acceptable and the effect of its ministry was clearly in no way belittled
by the Government. It will seem strange and ironic, if not down right
extraordinary, to the modern Christian mind to imagine the peace loving Baptist denomination working under the auspices and within the
jurisdiction of the United States War Department.

Simerwell's good work offset by the failures of the new missionaries

During November, 1833, the last of the Michigan Indians,
accompanied by the Simerwells, arrived at the Shawnee station after
a most adventurous and health-risking trek. Then the evangelization
of the Choctaws in Arkansas was undertaken but Mr. Wilson, the missionary chosen for the work, lost his courage and calling. Mr. Evans
had made the three hundred mile journey to Arkansas against the
wishes of the Board and his brother missionaries and had become
completely discouraged and left the mission. When he returned to the
Shawnee settlement, Lykins appealed to the Board to reinstate him,
which they did.[41] Evans, however, became so eccentric and difficult to
manage that the Board had to dismiss him from their services. Shortly
afterwards, Mr. French who had commenced being a missionary with
Mr. Evans, handed in his resignation. McCoy concluded:

---

[40] *History of Baptist Indian Missions,* p. 467.

[41] Ibid., p. 462.

> Missions to the Indians are unpopular things, and he who does not possess resources within himself to work alone, or with few associates, to sow much and reap little, to work hard without the reward of worldly honour or money, to remain poor all his life for the sake of making the almost friendless Indian rich, and to wait for his pay until he shall get to heaven, had better not enter upon a mission to the Indians.[42]

The situation at Three Forks

Mr. Lewis, who had been working with Pastor Davis also complained that he would have to give up his work. He had looked to the Board to honor his debts, but their extraordinary patience shown to Lewis was now at an end. This time, however, McCoy defended the Board strongly, saying that Lewis had been "exceedingly imprudent" in secular matters and his debts were "foolishly created." Although McCoy had long warned Lewis that he was getting himself into grave difficulties, Lewis approached him again, asking if he could use his influence with the Board to persuade them to pay off his debts so that he could leave the Indian Territory. McCoy was always better at campaigning for other people before the Board than he was for himself. He persuaded Lewis that he was doing a good job, that the Creeks were getting on fine and Davis' ministry was also growing. He promised to get in touch with the Board on Lewis' behalf but would recommend that he continue as a missionary. Happily for Lewis - and McCoy - the Board, to use McCoy's phrase, "generously extended to him its indulgence." Lewis was not only plagued by financial difficulties. John Davis had written to McCoy on June 18, 1833 to tell him that Lewis was getting on very well with the Indians and that he enjoyed working with him but Lewis' wife had no interest in the mission and seemed to have no interest in Christian things. This must have been a great burden on Lewis.

Support from the Board for Lykins

Lykins now went to visit Wilson who had also been threatening to resign, to try and persuade him to stay but was unsuccessful and Wilson, who had been laboring as the only white man for miles

---

[42] *History of Baptist Indian Missions*, p. 480.

around, left the Territory and gave up missionary work completely.[43] McCoy tells us, however, that such dark clouds were brightened by the fact that one Delaware after another was confessing Christ and being baptized.

Now the Board took a very encouraging step in relation to Lykins in the form of a letter to the President of the U. S. A. which read:

Boston, Sept. 2, 1833

To Andrew Jackson
President of the U. S.

Sir,
I am instructed by the Board of the Baptist General Convention most respectfully to state, that in their solicitude to do what is practicable for the civilisation & improvement of Indians, in the Indian Territory west of the Mississippi River, they have appointed Mr. Johnston Lykins their Agent, to go through the said Territory & select in the several Tribes with their consent locations for schools & missionary establishments. Mr. Lykins is a gentleman already well known to many of the Indians, having laboured for years in conjunction with the Rev. Isaac McCoy for their benefit, but to travel among them, with the proposed object in view the countenance of the Executive of the Nation is highly desirable. The design of this communication therefore is with all respect, to solicit in his behalf a letter to the superintendent at St Louis & to Agents generally throughout the Territory counselling them as your wisdom shall direct, to promote the ends of his agency. Should you favor us as requested, the letter may be forwarded either directly to Mr. Lykins, Shawanoe Arkansas Territory or to the subscriber.

I am Sir with great respect
Your Obt. St.
L. Bolles

This letter provides a milestone in the work of the Board. It commits them fully to accepting the goals of the Indian Territory and to opening the same for the gospel and for education. It also establishes Lykins as acting in the services of the Board in their missionary endeavors in the Indian Territory as a man highly recom-

---

[43] See Wilson's letter of resignation to McCoy dated August 15, 1833, McCoy Papers, Reel 8.

mended by the Board and one in whom they have so much trust and respect that they can recommend his services to the President himself. All this must be borne in mind when considering the Board's re-interpretation of these events at a later date. Bolles sent a copy of his letter to Lykins, authorizing him to visit Lewis and the Creeks, Wilson and the Choctaws (Wilson had not yet left) and O'Bryant and the Cherokees, assessing their needs. Cautiously, Bolles adds, "We cannot contract for any enlargement at either station or for fresh expend-itures, unless there is a certainty of our being sustained in the dis-bursement by Government." It appears that the Baptist Board now regarded their own missionary work as being primarily an extension of Government policy to be funded by the Government. The Govern-ment reacted speedily to Bolles request and on September 13th, Bolles forwarded Lykins the necessary passport and letter of recommen-dation which he had received from Secretary of War, Lewis Cass.[44]

Further threats from the Mormons

The month of November, 1833 brought with it great anxiety on the eastern border of the Indian Territory as the Mormons were gathering in large, well-armed numbers. The alarm was spread that they were going to attack with a view to taking over townships such as Independence and Shawnee. Several inhabitants of these set-tlements wrote to McCoy, asking for his assistance in organizing some system of defense. The subscribers recommended forming a defense committee, disarming the Mormons and policing them. Those Mor-mons who had land in the district, should sell it through a disinter-ested party to make sure they got value for money but then they must leave the area. Those who were to guard the settlers should be re-imbursed for their time and effort by those whom they guard. Also those Mormons plotting to attack and rob must be prosecuted accord-ing to law.

McCoy requested by the Board to represent them before the Government

McCoy spent part of December 1833 and the following Jan-uary in temperatures as low as 25° below freezing mapping out further

---

[44] Cass' letter dated September 10, 1833 is found next to Bolles' of Sep-tember 13, on Reel 8 of the McCoy Papers.

territories but received a most unexpected letter from the Board which reached him on January 9, 1834 and was signed "Most affectionately, yours, L. Bolles." The letter was to inform McCoy that Spencer Cone had suggested he should represent the Board at Washington that winter and strive to influence the Government on their Indian policy. All expenses were to be paid by the Board! Once back home, McCoy made for Washington on February 11, 1834 and was a month on the journey. As usual, he arrived sick and exhausted and needed several days to win back his strength. The three commissioners were to report to Congress after their two-year term of office and McCoy had already given them a full report of his work and was anxious to know if he had been of any influence on the commissioners' plans for the future. The commissioners failed to meet, though Lewis Cass in his annual report had spoken in favor of McCoy's plans. This was an encouraging thing indeed for the missionaries as Cass had previously declared that "the tribes never would be colonized." Tired of waiting for the three commissioners to appear, McCoy dashed to New York to meet Cone and Dagg so that they could interview would-be missionaries and discuss the future of the Indian mission. A Mr. Smedley was felt suitable. While back at Washington, several Presbyterians who had difficulty establishing a mission among the Iowas approached McCoy to put in a good word for them at the Government. McCoy had a word with Mr. Herring, the Commissioner for Indian Affairs and the Presbyterians were given permission to start their work among the Iowas. In 1840, McCoy reported:

> The Iowas number about one thousand souls; they reside on the Missouri river. Their condition and habits are slightly improved. Government, by virtue of treaty stipulations, is affording them some assistance in the erection of dwellings and mills, the fencing and ploughing of land, in live stock, schools, etc.. A Presbyterian mission has been established among them, under the patronage of the Western Foreign Missionary Society, the good effects of which have been felt by the tribe, though in a small degree. From this mission, two excellent missionaries, Mr. and Mrs. Ballard have lately retired, and it is at present in charge of the Rev. Mr. Hamilton, Mr. Irving, Mr. Bradley, and their wives.[45]

---

[45] *History of Baptist Indian Missions*, p. 564.

Meeker's successful work as a printer

By the time McCoy reached home in May, Mr. Meeker had set up his printing press and had already produced a book in Shawnee and one in Delaware. McCoy was amazed how quickly the Indians learned to read. Meeker had not used the "Guess 80" syllable system which was excellent for the Cherokee language but not for the other Indian languages which would have needed far too many open and closed syllables to be practical. Meeker, at first, modified Guess' system but went on to develop an entirely phonetic system that could be used for all Indian languages. This meant that the Indians had not to learn separate letters and then build them into sounds which had no direct relation to the letters that composed them. Anyone who has tried to teach English speaking children to write such words as "cough," "bough," "indict," "time" and "winding" will realize the enormous disadvantages of an alphabet written language. By using a phonetic system, the missionaries were able to read texts to the Indians after a fashion even if they did not know the language. English-speaking people with a spoken knowledge of the Indian language, if given texts with a key to pronunciation, could, according to McCoy, begin to read after an hour's study. Meeker did not imagine his system being used by people who had a written language already but he did sincerely believe that it would simplify the tasks of missionaries all over the world who were faced with a language that had no available written form. Modern linguistics as shown in the work of the Wycliffe Bible Translators now use methods only differing in degrees to Meeker's phonetic writing.

The Baptist missionaries encountered nothing but enthusiasm from the Indians who were learning to read and write in days rather than weeks. The first opposition came from the Presbyterian missionaries. After years of study, a Presbyterian missionary named Cyrus Byington, assisted by Cyrus Kingsbury, Loring S. Williams and Alfred Wright, had invented a Choctaw alphabet. It was a clumsy system of letters based on the English principles of spelling and the Presbyterians had gone to enormous expense to have special printing type made for them. A grammar of Choctaw was produced by this press in 1834. This was followed by a Choctaw-English dictionary and translations of Scripture portions including the entire books of Joshua, Judges and Ruth. One must wonder at the Presbyterians preference of Old Testament books for their evangelistic work but they obviously thought that such books reflected the position of the Indians at the time and were therefore culturally more acceptable than, say, the gospels or Pauline epistles.

The Baptists, however, merely used their old English type for their translation work, arguing that as the sounds were phonetic, it did not matter how they were signified. English would be as good as Greek or invented signs. The advantage of Meeker's system was that it was easier to learn than the Presbyterian system, it was much shorter and thus also much cheaper paper-wise and printing presses were already in existence. Meeker and his friends explained to the Presbyterians that the letters they had invented might be all very well for Choctaw (which they, nevertheless, doubted) but not for Shawnee and Delaware, so many more letters must be invented, whereas the Meeker system was already up and running in several languages with fewer signs. The Presbyterians remained unconvinced, however, arguing that theirs was a first, (which it was not), and that the missionaries should follow them so that only one system would be used by all. The next surprise for the Baptists was that the Methodists took the side of the Presbyterians. This was most strange as they had been using the Meeker system with success. They now said that they had only used it because they had been pressurized by the Indians to do so. One would of thought this to be a good reason for adopting the method.

The missionaries fail to win the Board's enthusiasm concerning the Indian alphabet

The Baptists were not too discouraged by the objections of the Presbyterians and Methodists, but what took them completely aback was the attitude of the Board. They showed no interest in the tremendous fact that Indians were now reading portions of the Scriptures in their own language and not one of the Board even bothered to examine the suitability of Meeker's work. The Shawnee Mission Baptists had, in their enthusiasm, believed that the Board would be thrilled and make sure that the news was spread around, yet nothing favorable in any way to the missionaries' efforts appeared in any official Baptist publication. McCoy believed that if they had been university professors and the news of Meeker's phonetic reading system had been proclaimed from some college with a fine name, the Board would have made much of the matter. Now, however, the fact that hundreds of Indians were excited about their "talking paper," failed to impress them. With his mind ever in the future, McCoy wrote confidently, "The system, however, will, we are confident, outlive its misfortunes; and many good men, both white and red, in our own country, and good men in some others, will regret that its introduction among unlettered nations had not received earlier attention."[46] Failing to obtain backing from the Board, McCoy turned to the Secretary of War combining with his plea for teaching the Indians to read their own language a further request for the Government to employ native teachers. McCoy addressed Cass on June 10, 1836, saying:

Hon. Lewis Cass
Sec. War

Sir, I beg leave respectfully to solicit your attention to the circumstances of teaching the Indians to read in their several mother tongues and upon what we term the New System. This system is found to be so exceedingly simple that even adults, unaccustomed to the study of letters, can learn to read in their own language in the course of a few weeks.

Upon the New System books have been printed in the Choctaw, Creek, Shawanoe, Delaware, Putawatomie, and Otoe Languages, and to the Shawanoes is issued a small monthly periodical.

Many of the natives could be hired for twelve or fifteen dollars a month as assistant teachers to instruct classes of adults as well as youths which could be convened at appointed places and times, and who under the superintendence of a missionary might doubtless be rendered extremely useful.

I would respectfully suggest the enquiry whether a portion of the funds of the government applicable to the education and civilization of the Indians might not be advantageously applied in hiring Indian teachers as above mentioned.

Should this suggestion receive your favourable consideration, I would respectfully request that such missionaries as have been engaged in teaching upon the New System be allowed through your agents or sub-agents as the case may be, such sums as you may deem expedient, to be employed in hiring native assistant teachers to teach upon the new system, and that the missionaries be required to account for the sums which they shall severally receive by reporting to the agts. or sub. agts. severally the manner in which the same has been applied, and the results of the application for the purpose of making the experiment, I would respectfully recommend, that allow-

---

[46] *History of Baptist Indian Missions*, pp. 477-478.

ance be made for the Shawanoes, the Delawares, the Put-awatomie emigrants, and for the Creeks of Arkansas.

Most Resptfy Sir & Obt. Servt.

Isaac McCoy[47]

Here, McCoy's zeal and diplomacy go hand in hand. He invites the Government not only to support the new system which was a Baptist invention, but also to rule out alternative methods of reading and writing the Indian Languages practiced by other denominational missionaries. Furthermore, he suggests that the entire financing of the system be placed initially in the hands of the Baptist missionaries who were the only ones using the new system. Finally, he argued for the missionaries receiving the money directly from Government agents and not through the medium of the Board.

McCoy plans the Indian Advocate and Annual Register

Realizing the power of the printed word and the Board's reluctance to cooperate, McCoy decided to print his own semi-monthly periodical which he named *The Indian Advocate*. As his conscience could not allow the mission's printing press to be used for this purpose because of the many needy books it was turning out for the Indians, McCoy wrote to a number of printers, soliciting estimates and strove to set up a list of subscribers. He had hoped that he would find a printer ready to allow the missionaries favorable terms but no such kindness was forthcoming. Indeed, though some of the leading men in the country gave him their names, few other subscribers appeared to be interested in such a publication. McCoy then thought of producing at least an annual bulletin of missionary affairs so that a broader public would know about the mission. This would be called *The Annual Register of Indian Affairs within the Indian Territory*.

Further deaths in the McCoy family

The first issue of the *Annual Register* was printed in January, 1835 at McCoy's own cost and was written under agonizing conditions. His newly-married daughter, Mrs. Given, who was in his care, was

---

[47] McCoy Papers, Reel 9.

dying of consumption and needed continual attention. She died on March 2nd, McCoy's eighth child to die prematurely. Mr. Given was well at the time of her death but suddenly took ill and died a few months later.

Another major loss for McCoy was his younger brother Rice, who died at the age of forty-five. John McCoy wrote to inform his brother of Rice's illness on September 9, 1834 and told him, "Brother, Rice has been a number of years past a faithfull Minister of the Gospel, indefatigable in his labours, and I think the most Meek and humble Christian I ever saw."[48] John told his son, William, who was helping Isaac McCoy at the time, that his uncle's religion which he:

> had long professed appeared to be his support, and only comfort, while all earthly comforts and objects seemed to fail and prove delusive, he is now out of reach of persecution and calumny. His zeal for the promotion of practical godliness and the promotion of all the Benevolent institutions made him many enemies among the advocates of old Daniel Parker.[49]

A grave stone was set up on Rice's grave in Livonia Cemetery bearing the words, "A kind husband, an affectionate parent, a consistent Christian, an evangelical preacher, and an example worthy of imitation in all the relations of society."

David Lewis' scandalous departure

David Lewis continued to be a problem for both the missionaries and the Board. He kept on borrowing money which he could not possibly pay back. The Board showed him extraordinary patience and generosity and settled many a bill for him but when protests at Lewis' behavior poured in and Lewis wrote out a check for $500 dollars to be paid by the Board, the latter decided to help Lewis no more. The missionary was showing signs of mental derailment and visited friends of the mission to borrow money, explaining that the Board would make it up. One person, a Mr. Miller, loaned him $500 for himself and gave him another $500 when Lewis said that Davis was also

---

[48] Letter to Isaac McCoy dated September 10, 1834.

[49] Letter to William McCoy dated September 17, 1834. Both these letters were shown to Elizabeth Hayward by a Mrs. W. E. Davis of Piqua. See *John McCoy*, pp. 76, 131.

in need. When the deceit was discovered, Lewis was traced to New Orleans but he managed to dodge his creditors and went into hiding. In a letter written to McCoy by Spencer Cone, informing his friend about Lewis' ordination as a "missionary to the Heathen," he emphasized how careful they must be as "one wrong-headed or quail-hearted missionary who abandons the field of labor, does incalculable mischief."[50] Now Davis was in most difficult circumstances but soon received help from a married couple, the Rollins and two unmarried ladies named Rice and Colborn who were sent by the Board to assist at the Creek station. The Rollins had been missionaries to the Indians of the New York area and now followed their former colleague Abel Bingham to work for the Baptist Board. The Choctaws received Dr. and Mrs. Alanson Allen and also Mr. and Mrs. Eber Tucker as missionaries and teachers, both men being salaried by the Government.

Davis, another Creek Indian and Lykins work together in translating gospel portions

Meanwhile, arrangements were been made with John Davis to have the new reading and writing system introduced among the Choctaw. Davis started out on the three hundred mile journey to the Shawnee Mission but had to break his journey because of the severe winter weather of 1834-35. Davis was able to make the journey successfully in the following spring, accompanied by a Choctaw who was to assist in translating John's Gospel. The two men worked with Lykins for three months, during which time John's Gospel was put into Choctaw and initial proofs were printed, using the new system, to be tested among the Indians prior to mass printing. The Indian reception was most positive but a missionary from another denomination, whom McCoy does not name, protested strongly against the Meeker system rivaling his own. It was then rumored that the Choctaw translator whom Davis had brought with him was a man of dubious moral character, so the Baptist missionaries postponed the printing and looked into the matter. Though they found nothing which would make the man unsuitable as a translator, indeed, nothing that suggested he was blameable in any way, the Choctaw suddenly died with

---

[50] Letter written May 15, 1832, McCoy Papers, Reel 8.

the rumors still circling, so the missionaries decided to abandon the project for the present to protect the honor of the gospel.[51]

Laboring for the meat which perishes

McCoy was now once again without a source of income so Mr. and Mrs. McCoy had again to turn to growing a little wheat for bread, taking on odd jobs and taking in lodgers to make ends meet. McCoy believed that the work they were doing now needed at least 20 more full-time missionaries but the missionaries that were employed were having to labor for the meat which perishes rather than laboring in the missionary harvest field. Once again, McCoy was more than worried about the way the Board was handling its affairs. The Board, after years of hesitation, had acknowledged the need for an Indian Mission in the new territories and had prevented McCoy, once again, from handing in his resignation. It was obvious, however, that the Board still did not envisage their missionaries doing any residential work at all but they expected the men at least to perform an itinerant ministry, leaving the Indians, materially speaking, to look after themselves and, spiritually speaking, to take care of their own church life. McCoy, however, saw that this was, at the present time, an impossible plan as the bulk of the Indians were materially very poor, they were still not firmly settled in the Indian Territory and the danger that the whites would take from them their newly given rights was still great. Furthermore, it appeared that the Mormons were keen on settling in the Indian Territory because of their religious views concerning the Indians as the alleged lost tribes of Israel. A permanent and secure missionary presence was thus necessary as a bulwark against adverse influences of all kinds. Quite simply, McCoy felt that his call was to gather the sheep into a protective fold and then feed them, rather than go out into the wilderness and feed the sheep one by one as he came across them. The latter method would be far more time-consuming and expensive in the end and the Indians would have learned nothing to better their social position and make them able to stand up for themselves against the wiles of the white opportunists. This is why McCoy and his friends ran mission schools, helped the Indians to read and write, taught them how to garden, farm and work

---

[51] This Choctaw appears to have been Burch. Lykins looked into the rumors spread about him but found no evidence whatsoever which could support them.

in trades so that they may be preserved as a nation in an environment that had already made a hunting, fishing and trading way of life impossible.

The Board look for a cheaper way to run the Indian Mission

A further problem with the Board was their present attitude to financing a mission which was rather like the cuckoo's egg. They placed missionaries in areas where they trusted that the government and the Indians would look after them and often felt that they had then done enough. Indeed, when they heard that the missionaries were appealing for help within the denomination, they often asked them not to do so for fear that the donors would then not contribute to their priority missions which were abroad. Repeatedly, the Board told the missionaries to apply to them for help and rely on them to make their cause known, yet the Board hardly ever utilized the means available, especially the Baptist press, to this end. In these matters the Board were willing to compromise with the missionaries' will and allow day schools to be set up with the children eating and being clothed at home. This would be far cheaper and more practical, they argued. They somehow imagined the Indians all living under circumstances similar to their own Boston background. Often the children were very badly fed at home and had hardly any clothes to put on. In their own family environment their whole young lives were caught up in the fight for sheer survival. Though the Indians were happy to have their children educated, clothed and fed, they could not do this themselves adequately. McCoy had seen this with the Sunday Schools which were day schools. Children just did not turn up because they had nothing to wear, could not bring a decent meal with them which would nourish them for the day and they were needed at home to earn their keep. McCoy saw how the Methodists were looking after their Indians with as much fervor as any foreign mission organization and yet the Baptist Board was being "delinquent" (McCoy's word) and even grudging the Indian children a meal a day. McCoy writes, "In two or three instances, very small sums were allowed by the board for this object, but enough could not be obtained to admit of any systematic or regular course."[52] The missionaries to the Indians provided the Board with regular reports and statements, hoping that these would be passed on to the Baptist membership in some way so that their full

---

[52] *History of Baptist Indian Missions*, p. 490.

needs may be known. Yet the Board had in essence shut the doors to any kind of communication with the Baptist churches at large from both sides. They would not be moved by the missionaries' appeals and demanded that all gifts to the Indian mission should be sent via themselves and not directly to the missionaries. Even when gifts were made by the friends of the mission, earmarked for the Indian work, the Board said that such gifts ought not to be sent in for any particular cause but merely sent in as gifts to the Board who would then decide how they should be used in their worldwide missionary program. McCoy complains, "The consequence was, that our missions became more and more shut out from the view of the Christian public. The amount of donations in clothing, books, cash, &c., for the Indians, diminished until scarcely any thing was thus received."[53]

The Board withholds permission for the Indian Mission to solicit funds

By the summer of 1835, those working in the Indian mission, decided that their situation was so bad that a joint appeal must be made to the Board for food, funds and clothing. Lykins, Simerwell and Meeker then made a formal application to the Board to allow McCoy to travel through the country, informing the churches of the mission and needs of the Indians and also strive to enroll new missionaries. At the bottom of the application, the missionaries placed a piece of bait which they felt the Board would snap up. All this work on the part of McCoy, they affirmed, would not cost the Board a penny and all they asked for was the Board's approbation. "To our grief," McCoy writes, "This was withheld. The cause we well understood to be the groundless fear which they had long indulged, that Indian missions would be made to attract so much attention, that a proper share of public munificence would not be left for foreign missions."[54] The Corresponding Secretary, Dr. Bolles, added that if "the interests of the Indians require it," McCoy was welcome to put their case before the Government and the Board would cover the expenses of the journey. This seemed as if the Board were really saying, "We do not mind you canvassing for the Indians but the proper place for that is the Government at Washington and not the Baptist churches represented at Boston."

---

[53] Ibid, p. 491.

[54] Ibid, p. 492.

A further journey to Washington under most difficult circumstances becomes necessary

Perhaps the Board had second thoughts about their attitude because in December 1835, they told McCoy that they would carry the costs of McCoy's second issue of his *Annual Register of Indian Affairs*. However, a further journey to the capital was indeed necessary as the Government had hardly done anything for Indian settlement for two years. So on January 8, 1836, McCoy set out again for Washington in the worst of weather, thinking, "When realising fatigue, hunger, and cold, I have endeavoured to bear in mind that I was labouring for the benefit of people in far worse condition. I have reflected on the awful responsibilities which devolved upon me, in relation to them, commending my family to the mercy of God, and praying for success on our poor yet best efforts to promote the welfare of an afflicted and almost friendless people."[55] As he was crossing over the ice on the Ohio River, McCoy fell badly and his right shoulder was crushed. He never fully recovered from the accident and a permanent shoulder injury was added to McCoy's other marks of his dangerous life in the wilderness. McCoy was now over fifty years of age. He was a brilliant man, recognized nationwide as a leader who could have made a fortune as a Government agent and commissioner. Yet McCoy was ruined both financially and physically. He had become a physical wreck with a permanently crushed side, chest and shoulder. He had a twisted leg and foot and could only walk in a stooping position and often in great pain and his left hand was severely maimed. He had lost eight children to the savage climate and conditions through which his family had labored but was still driven on by the inner force of his high calling to defy all the ills that had come upon him for Christ's sake and the sake of the gospel. This strong calling compelled him to serve the Indian people and share his last penny and last morsel of bread with them and with his fellow missionaries. Truly, Isaac McCoy must be ranked with the very greatest in the history of evangelism and missions.

The Creeks and Cherokees appeal to McCoy for help before Congress

McCoy had not yet met up with his greatest trials. The white people of Arkansas had entered into a treaty in 1828 to allow the

---

[55] *History of Baptist Indian Missions*, p. 493.

Creeks and Cherokees to inhabit a forty mile broad strip on their western side. Now they campaigned to have the Indian territory absorbed into their State and sought for backing in Congress. The missionaries and Indians feared that if Congress backed the people of Arkansas, there would soon be no place for the Indians in the whole of the United States including the Indian Territory. On reading of the Arkansas proposals, McCoy contacted all his friends in Congress and was happy to hear that the Arkansas measures had been defeated. No sooner was this problem solved than McCoy heard that the Ottawas who were still in the Michigan area were being encouraged to give up their land but stay in the area, living on annuities, which everyone knew would disappear soon because of the whiskey peddlers that turned up in droves every time they heard of annuities being paid out to the Indians.

Slater again prefers to go his own way

Slater, who was still at Thomas, though the school had long closed down, was asked by the authorities to represent the Michigan Indians but promptly he was offered several thousands of dollars by white opportunists to influence the Indians to sell up and settle down near the whites. Slater, who had nearly always been of another mind than McCoy and was chiefly responsible with the Board for the running down of Thomas, now turned to his senior colleague and asked for his advice. As Slater used the opportunity to borrow $15 from McCoy, it must have been difficult for McCoy to take Slater's plea for advice seriously. McCoy warned Slater against the evil of allowing himself to be influenced against the interests of the people to whom he was called. McCoy told Slater to appeal to the President. At this suggestion, Slater wavered but asked McCoy to write a fitting appeal for him. This McCoy was only too pleased to do. It was now too late for McCoy to undertake anything further himself but he relied on Slater to work for the Indians' interests. Great was his dismay when he heard that Slater had not only neglected to submit the appeal but had also publicly agreed to and signed the treaty which he was supposed to have prevented. This led to the Indians under Slater's care being removed from their land. The missionary had played into the hands of the opportunists who sought to reward him. Slater now managed to persuade the Government to grant the Indians $6,400 to buy small farm lots of about 20 acres each within white settlements. About 140 families took up the offer but McCoy feared that the surrounding whites would soon gather "like buzzards about a carcass, [and] would pick them bare."[56] This was, of course, what the white opportunists had hoped would come to pass. Twenty acres was hardly enough to produce a balanced food diet for a large family and gain enough profit to buy clothing and equipment, so McCoy envisaged the whites buying out the Indians in no time and then the Indians would have nothing. Even now, the white settlers were forbidding the Indians to hunt on public land, though they had no legal jurisdiction to back them up. Again, McCoy gives his readers one of his typical understatements. He writes of Slater, "His missionary brethren think that he has erred so as to require them, for the present, to suspend the usual attachments of their fraternity."[57] To be fair to Slater, McCoy believed he would use the thousands of dollars he was given for signing the treaty to the benefit of the Indians. The problem was that Slater's ideas of what was beneficial for them differed radically from the McCoys, the Lykins, the Simerwells and other missionaries to the Indians.

McCoy tries to save something of ground lost through Slater's unwise action

McCoy, certain that the Ottawa Indians had no chance of survival within a white environment and without adequate lands, visited the Secretary of War and wrote to the Commissioner, demanding a treaty which would still give the Ottawas the right to settle down in the Indian Territory with the rest of their tribe after a trial period of five years to see if the Indians and the whites could live together. The Government consented and the treaty was signed.[58] This work of McCoy's alone shows what an enormous influence McCoy had on the Government and how high they held him in esteem; but McCoy was not yet done. He now turned his selfless energies to the question of compensation for his own Mission Board who had invested a limited amount of funds in Thomas and the Lakes area. McCoy argued that the bare investments of the Board in buildings and land should not be taken into consideration but, instead, their present market value. He pointed out that the land where the mission had stood was now sur-

---

[56] *History of Baptist Indian Missions*, p. 498.

[57] Ibid., p. 496.

[58] See McCoy's letter to Commissioner Schoolcraft dated March 27, 1836, and the Commissioner's positive reply dated March 28, 1836, McCoy Papers, Reel 8.

rounded by expanding white settlements and was therefore of great value. By this means, the Board came into possession of the net proceeds on the sale of one hundred and sixty acres of land which was, to use McCoy's words, "very considerable." McCoy, through selfless determination, rarely did anything of a financial nature that was not directed to the work of caring for and evangelizing the Indians. After working out the treaty with the Government, he bargained hard with the Board, which resulted in their promise to use the money for the benefit of the Ottawas in particular, who were later put under Meeker's care, and for general missionary purposes, including education. Now the Board could not argue that they had no money to board the Indian children and provide food and clothing for them. A few months later, the proceeds of the land were put into a trust for the benefit of the Ottawas to be administrated by Mr. Lykins. This time, McCoy was making certain that the monies he had gained for the Indians would indeed be used for them.

McCoy commissioned to survey the new Cherokee territory

May 23, 1836 heralded the movement of the Cherokees, one of the largest and most cultured of the Indian tribes, to the Indian Territory. There was a great public protest at this transportation as the poor Indians, it was argued, were being forced away from the graves of their fathers. According to Cherokee tradition, it was explained, resettlement would mean that they would be forever homeless. McCoy's view was that reallocation of land was the better of two evils. Most of the Cherokee burial grounds had been taken over by the whites in ways which McCoy said had subjected the Indians to a servility and degradation more hurtful to man than African slavery. To demonstrate that the Indians' present lot was worse than the Negro slaves, he showed how enslaved Negroes had many children and multiplied as a people whereas Indians among whites succumbed to all their evils and rapidly diminished in numbers. Also, former governments had failed to protect the Indians from their white neighbors until it was too late to put the clock back, or rather, return to the right path. Any effort on the Government's side to give the Indians their land back would have ended in political and legal turmoil. There were also now far more whites in former Indian areas than Indians. Furthermore, many of the Cherokees were for moving themselves, confessing that in their centuries of wandering, they had no idea of where their fathers were buried. Indeed, McCoy felt that this last point had been used by capricious whites to awaken public sympathy of the wrong kind so that pressure would be put on the Government to leave the Cherokees among the whites. This would have led to a complete degradation of the Indians and, most likely, to their extinction as a people. The situation, however, had become more precarious as the Seminole and Creek Indians, near relations to the Cherokees, were at war with the Government, which had been caused by the encroachments of the whites on their land. Furthermore, the Cherokees insisted that they remain a self governing body as a tribe. On July 5, 1836, Commissioner C. A. Harris wrote to McCoy on behalf of the War Department,[59] placing McCoy at the head of a surveying team to make sure that the Cherokee borders were well mapped-out. He was to receive eight dollars a day payment but was also given his now usual post of Expedition Treasurer.

McCoy appointed to help the Cherokee's obtain land patents

These affairs and others of a similar nature soon found McCoy back in New York to confer with Spencer Cone and then he was off to Washington to plead for more treaties to ease the Indians' burdens and arrange for Mr. Simerwell to be sent to the Potawatomis. He also asked the Department of Indian Affairs to give permission for a new recruit, Mr. David Rollin, to be sent as a missionary to the Creek Indians. This permission was granted. McCoy had been offered another lucrative appointment by the Government regarding the re-allocation of the Indians but he had passed it on to another, though retaining responsibility of supervision, so that he could lobby the Indian Department and Congress. Needless to say, McCoy had given his substitute his entire wage. He was thus completely without funds again but in June, 1836, he was also asked by the Secretary of War to deal with the matter of the Cherokees' wish to receive a binding patent for their land as normally given in land transactions with the whites. This was very fertile land on the banks of the Canadian, Arkansas and Verdigris Rivers. McCoy was to be well paid for this work, too. McCoy was overjoyed at the thought of the Indians taking out patents as treaties could be revised, as the Indians knew to their cost, and each tribe had entered into a different treaty which left the Indians with no united legal status for bargaining with the Government. Patents, on the other hand, were there forever and could never be argued away. McCoy thus wrote, "We therefore hailed this event as the appearance

---

[59] McCoy Papers, Reel 9.

of another star, indicating the dispersion of the clouds which had obscured the Indian's atmosphere."[60] After a period of sickness, McCoy made the long journey back to Westport and was reunited with his family on July 26, 1836 after an absence of seven months.

---

[60] *History of Baptist Indian Missions*, p. 504.

Chapter Thirteen
Consolidating the Work (1836-38)

Lykins exceedingly ill – Skigget put on probation as a minister

McCoy was shocked to find on his homecoming that Lykins, his right hand man, closest friend and son-in-law, had been extremely ill, with bleeding on the brain and was reduced to an invalid state from which he never fully recovered. Meeker, too, was in such poor health that he could do no printing nor any other work and the Shawnee Mission was, as McCoy records, "in a deplorable condition." McCoy had hoped that a Delaware named Henry Skigget who had become a church member, would be set aside for the ministry and the Shawnee missionaries supported him so that he could preach to his own people. The Board was applied to so that Skigget could be formally accepted as a missionary and they gave him a year's probation. The missionaries were highly pleased with their new colleague's work but McCoy was eventually forced to write in his *History of Baptist Indian Missions*, "For reasons, not distinctly understood, he was not reappointed by the board - a circumstance which we regretted - though a hope is still indulged that his services may be obtained."[1]

Odd ideas practiced by some missionaries

Another problem McCoy had to contend with was strife among the Delawares caused by missionaries from other denominations. These rather impractical people, who had yet to realize the significance of 1 Corinthians 5: 10[2], believed that Christians should isolate

---

[1] Ibid, p. 506.

[2] "I wrote unto you in an epistle not to company with fornicators: Yet not altogether with the fornicators of this world, or with the covetous, or extortioners, or with idolaters; for then must ye needs go out of the world."

themselves from the world not only spiritually and morally but also physically. They thus divided the Indians they sought to serve into two separate parties whom they called the "Christian Indians" and the "Heathen Indians." When McCoy met both parties, he found that the Christian spirit was as weak in the one as the other and marveled that the white missionaries were attempting to divide an ethnic and socially well-knit society into two separate peoples. The Delawares, too, were insulted at the attempts of the missionaries to separate husband from wife, parents from their children and one friend from another and had forbidden them to preach in their settlement. The ban was then imposed on all missionaries because the Delawares imagined that they all worked on the same principles. When McCoy said that his missionaries compelled no one to listen to preaching and that the Bible supports social ties such as in families and tribes, the Indians felt more at ease. McCoy then explained that he always encouraged the Indians to be good neighbors and associate sociably with one another. After working hard to promote peace among the Delawares and keep a door open to missions, McCoy recorded the results with his usual masterly touch of the understatement, saying, "We were happy to find that they imbibed juster notions of the duties of missionaries than those which had lately given them uneasiness, and that they were apparently much gratified to discover their mistake."[3]

Methodist misbehavior causes the Creek Baptist Mission to be closed

Further difficulties caused by missionaries from other denominations threatened to prevent work among the Creeks. It was alleged that a Methodist missionary had conducted himself improperly towards a "most respectable woman" among the Creeks and she was now pregnant.[4] It was also affirmed that the Methodist had told the Creek's Negro slaves that they were entitled to their freedom. This was neither the policy of the Baptists nor the Presbyterians and the Creeks informed the white traders that these missionaries had caused them no trouble. McCoy explained the standpoint of the Baptists: "Although the missionaries regretted the existence of slavery in the Indian country, they had prudently forborne to meddle with the subject. Mr. Rollin had been so scrupulously precise upon this point,

---

[3] *History of Baptist Indian Missions*, p. 506.

[4] See Roustio's *A History of the Life of Isaac McCoy* for the background of this story.

that he had refused to teach the slaves to read in his Sunday School, notwithstanding they had often entreated him to instruct them."[5] McCoy was to come under increasing criticism because of his policy of taking the gospel to all the Indians, irrespective of their attitude towards slavery.[6] One of the reasons why the Boston Board disassociated itself with the southern Brethren in the eighteen-forties on the subject of Indian missions was that the latter were eager to evangelize even the slave-holding Indians. The Indians who were able to keep slaves did so on the basis of law which they had learned from the whites that they must honor. When slavery was abolished, Indian slave owners, on the whole, showed far greater toleration to their former slaves than the whites. They were not only freed but taken up into their tribes to share their property and given full hereditary rights with the Indians' own children.[7]

The Methodist was removed from his post at once but this story was seized upon by white traders to persuade the Creeks to rid themselves of all missionaries.[8] With this aim in view, the traders drew up a petition to the commanding officer at Fort Gibson, Brigadier General Matthew Arbuckle, demanding the withdrawal of all the missionaries and, by means more foul than fair, induced the Creek chiefs to sign the document. The result was that the commander, or possibly an officer standing in for him,[9] advised the missionaries to leave the Creek settlement for their own safety. His letter, however, was sent to Rolly McIntosh, the head chief of the Creeks and it was some time before the missionaries became aware of the letter's content. On hearing the commander's advice, the white missionaries left the Creek

---

[5] *History of Baptist Indian Missions*, pp. 507-508.

[6] See letter from McCoy to Rev. Sydney Dyer dated February 23, 1844. McCoy Papers, Reel 11.

[7] See Wright's *The Missionary Work of the Southern Baptist Convention*, p. 349.

[8] Creek Indian Pastor John Davis wrote to McCoy on February 26, 1836, to inform him that whites had put pressure on the Creek chiefs to ban the missionaries and that the chiefs had told him that Rollin carried no blame whatsoever.

[9] The documents reveal something of a mix-up here as to who was responsible at the Fort for what.

settlement.[10] McIntosh, due to his mixed blood, was as much a fiery
Scotsman as an Indian and on official occasions wore a mixture of
Indian and Scots finery. He delighted in giving any Christians he
found among his people thirty-five lashes and would administer fifty
to those found preaching. By God's good providence, McIntosh's sons
became Christians and, at last, the fierce warrior chief himself was
converted and baptized.

*McCoy strives to have Rollin reinstated but the missionary decides not
to return to the Creeks*

David Rollin left, though the Creeks in council declared that
he was innocent of the general charges against the missionaries. Thus
on November 4, 1836, Rollin and his family arrived at Westport, Missouri, but McCoy was not at all pleased. He told Rollin that he should
have reported to the commander stating that he was the representative of a respectable society and had peacefully discharged his duties
under the authority of the Government and that nothing had been
undertaken to look into the matter at hand and that the missionaries
had not been given the chance to clear their name. McCoy raised the
matter with the Board and several times with C. A. Harris, Commissioner at the Department of Indian Affairs, informing the latter
that Rollin had Government authority to be in the Creek settlement
and that he had done nothing to abuse that authority. McCoy further
explained that Rollin had been instrumental in establishing a large
church which was now without an adequate teaching ministry and
that Rollin was missed by the Indians. He concluded by writing:

> We have no doubt that it is the design of our Government,
> that all under its control should be allowed to worship God
> according to the dictates of their conscience, and under this
> impression I appeal to your goodness, sir, to give the subject
> your favourable consideration. I make this appeal with the
> more satisfaction because of my firm belief that there will

---

[10] See Acting Superintendent William Armstrong's letter to the Creek
missionaries outlining the reasons for his action dated September 9, 1836,
and also the letter of the Western Creek Nation chiefs, presenting their
views on August 3, 1836. McCoy kept detailed notes of the affair under the
heading, "Notes respecting the difficulties on account of which the missionaries had left the Creek nation in Ark.[ansas]" McCoy Papers, Reel 9.

be found no obstacle to prevent the board of missions from reoccupying their missionary station.[11]

Harris looked into the matter and decided in favor of the Baptist missionaries. He then wrote to the Fort Gibson commander, requesting that he should reconsider the matter. Harris' letter is a specimen of excellent diplomacy and common sense and shows how keen the Government was to profit from the good work of the missionaries. McCoy gives the following extract:

> War Department, Office of Indian Affairs,
> May 12, 1837
>
> Sir: The recommendation given by you to the missionaries in the Creek country to withdraw from it, in consequence of the excitement existing against them in the minds of the Indians, was approved at the time, from the obvious consideration that they could render but little service while that excitement lasted. But as a specific charge has been made against only one of the number, it seems unreasonable to persist in the exclusion of the others, out of regard to an undefined feeling of dislike entertained by the Indians. The great duty of the Government is to apply, in the most beneficial manner, the means placed at its disposal, by treaties or otherwise, for the advancement of the Indians; and I regard the permanent establishment of schools, and the residence of competent teachers among them, as the most important of these means. You will impress these views on the minds of the chiefs, and also the unreasonableness of depriving their people of all instruction because one of the instructors had behaved improperly. You will inquire particularly into the causes of their aversion to the settlement of teachers in their country, and if you find that there is no specific allegation, you will say to them, distinctly, that the teachers will be invited to return and resume their labours, under the protection of the Government.
>
> Very, &c.,
> C. A. HARRIS, Commissioner

(Directed to the Acting Superintendent.)[12]

---

[11] *History of Baptist Indian Missions*, pp. 510-511.

[12] Ibid., p. 512.

McCoy was requested by the Board to journey to Arkansas and look into the matter, whereupon the Creeks confirmed that Rollin had done nothing personally to deserve his withdrawal from the Creek Mission.[13] Rollin, however, had now settled down at Westport among the Shawnees and did not feel free to leave the work he had built up there. A new missionary, Charles Kellam was appointed by the Board in his stead and the Acting Superintendent gave Kellam the status of United States school teacher.

The Indian Mission under further shadows

Due to several deaths, the enmity of certain whites and the troubles between the Muscogee tribes and the Government, the mission to the Indians was going through a rough time. Moreover, key missionaries such as Mr. Lykins and Mr. Meeker were unable to carry on their duties because of illness. All this had greatly handicapped the work among the Cherokees, Creeks and Choctaws and the Government's delay in relocating the Potawatomis had also curbed the missions' work in that tribe. The missionaries were further disheartened by communications from the Board suggesting that it was doubtful whether the missionaries would ever be able to do the Indians any permanent good. McCoy responded with a note in his journal:

> Shall we give up all for lost, and sit down in despair? No! Lord help us to hold on to the work of Indian reform with both hands; and should they by adverse matters become tied so that we cannot use them, let us cling to the subject in any way by which it can be reached; and should we be forced from it beyond the reach of efficient effort, let us die with eyes directed towards this wretched race, and hearts praying to thee to show them mercy.[14]

---

[13] Such incidences have moved authors like William G. McLoughlin to build up a case maintaining that McCoy supported slavery and eventually founded a pro-slavery mission. See *Champions of the Cherokees*, p. 236. This supposition is not justifiable as McCoy dealt tactfully with the situation as in the case of the Apostles themselves. It would be ridiculous to accuse Paul of being pro-slavery because he sent Onesimus, a converted runaway slave, back to Philemon his owner.

[14] Ibid, p. 514.

Fort Gibson continued to be a thorn in the flesh to Indian-White relationships. Not so much because of the presence of the military as the fact that white traders always felt they could appeal to the Fort's commander to represent their interests before the Indians and even put pressure on them to enter into dubious trade and land agreements. The Government wisely limited the Fort's influence in the area but it was not until 1857 that the Fort was abandoned as a military site and given over to the Cherokees. This act, however, according to historians such as Arrell Gibson, was purely out of economical interests.[15]

Death of the McCoys' daughter Christiana

McCoy was frequently called to Washington in the most inclement winter weather. On eight occasions, he had been compelled to leave home though a member of the family lay at death's door. Equally often, he had to leave a missionary friend on his death bed. Now the Board had requested McCoy to travel the 1,600 miles to Washington again on their behalf but he had postponed the journey because his terminally ill daughter, Mrs. Christiana Ward,[16] had come home to her parents to die. Mrs. Ward assured her father that she had recently come to trust in the Savior and would die in the sure hope of eternal life. She then told him that he must be about his Father's business and not delay his journey. McCoy left home on December 17, 1836; his daughter died in great pain on February 10 of the following year due to violent bleeding from the lungs. McCoy commented in his *Family Records*, "She was much emaciated, and lingered on the brink of eternity longer than could have been hoped for." Christiana left a year-old son, Thomas and an ailing husband who died the following year.

McCoy makes yet another wintry journey to Washington

After more than five harrowing weeks of battling with snow and ice, McCoy reached Washington and entered into talks at once

---

[15] See *Oklahoma: A History of Five Centuries*, p. 184 ff. for the subsequent history of Fort Gibson.

[16] Born October 18, 1816, married to William Ward May 2, 1833. William died on September 2, 1838.

with Senator Tipton on the future of the Potawatomis who, through McCoy's skilled presentation of their case, were granted land patents. It was also arranged that Simerwell, whom McCoy thought had not been pulling his weight sufficiently, should be encouraged to work among the tribe. McCoy was disappointed to find that bills which would have put the Indian territory on a more stable and well-organized footing, were not passed. On his way back home, McCoy became seriously ill again and had to be brought back by his wife and son who had managed to find a carriage to transport him. His sufferings were eased by the news that three Shawnees and a Delaware had been baptized and thirty new pupils had learned to read and write using the "new system." On the whole, the general missionary situation among the various tribes had improved.

Fixing the seat of the Indian government

After recuperating for a few days only, McCoy was on the move again in order to fix the exact location for the seat of Indian Government and surveying an area that might be suitable for relocating the Potawatomis. He was accompanied by Simerwell and a U. S. Indian Agent named A. L. Davis. John Calvin McCoy, now an official government surveyor, was sent off to mark out the boundaries of the Cherokee country. The thirteen days' journey was undertaken without danger and on arriving home, McCoy was greeted by the news that the Board had sent them two new missionaries, Mr. and Mrs. John Gill Pratt, who would take over the printing works as Mr. Meeker was going on to serve the Ottawas. The Lykins were now found to be in rather better health, though Mr. Lykins was still doing poorly. Conditions under the Delawares were far from good because white people were enticing them to lease out land to white settlers which would have eventually meant the end of the Indian Territories. Again, McCoy's selfless generosity showed what a truly great and Christian man he was. The Delaware delegation who journeyed to Washington to claim rights of leasing to whites arrived to hear that their tribe was of a different opinion and that the Department of Indian Affairs could not accept their petition. Worse for the delegates was that the whites who had promised to pay the Indians' expenses, on seeing their plans ruined, would not pay for their home journey. Feeling sorry for the Indians who had again been duped by whites, McCoy had them brought home at his own expense. The Delawares, however, refunded McCoy at a later date. On May 20, 1837 McCoy attended council with the Delawares and was able to show them that if they leased land to the whites, they soon would not be masters in their own country.

McCoy publishes his first Periodic Account of Baptist Missions in the Indian Territory

At the beginning of June, 1837, McCoy thought it was imperative that a fresh report should be sent out to make the deeds and the needs of the Indian mission known. He was now able to publish at his own expense his long planned 52 page pamphlet entitled *Periodical Account of Baptist Missions in the Indian Territory for the Year Ending December 31, 1836* which was distributed at no charge to the public. McCoy's "Introduction" to the *Periodical Account* shows his frustration at the state of affairs regarding the mission but also his diplomacy on not treading too heavily on the Board of Mission's toes. He writes in the opening paragraphs:

> This work has not been undertaken to gratify a fondness for writing, but because such a work was obviously needed. The American Baptist Magazine, is the chief vehicle of missionary intelligence of the Board of Managers of the Baptist General Convention. In it there is little room for matter relating to missions among the aboriginal inhabitants of our country. The operations of the Board in Asia, Africa and Europe, have become so extensive, that a monthly pamphlet of twenty-four pages, is scarcely sufficient to keep before the eyes of the public the conditions and prospects of missions in those countries, exclusive of accounts of missions among the Indians.
>
> It is true, the Magazine does not wholly overlook Indian missions; and some extra publications are also issued, embracing reports of the proceedings of the General Convention and of its Board. But still, there has not been room in the publications which have heretofore appeared, for such an exhibition of Indian missions as was necessary to a just understanding of their condition.
>
> We believe that we may safely state as a fact, that the condition, wants and prospects of Baptist missions among the Indians have not, at any time since their commencement in 1817, been fully held up to public view. This was necessary for eliciting energetic efforts in

support of them, and for the want of it, they have not been liberally sustained.[17]

McCoy explained that apart from three or four active members of the Mission Board, who were well informed about the situation of the Indians, there was little general knowledge among the Baptists concerning the Indians' plight. He put this down to the greater interest in foreign missions but admitted that the Board had every right to have such a preference and he himself would not wish to see fewer articles on Asia, Africa and Europe. Next, McCoy made a passionate plea for more laborers in the Indian vineyard, outlining the terrible situation of some four million Indians living in the United States and areas under her control. McCoy concluded by saying that he had told the story of the Indian mission in his own way and in the way that most faithfully exhibits the true facts about the Indians. Any member of the Board reading McCoy's account must have thought of Matthew 11:15 etc. concerning he who has ears to hear, let him hear. A few weeks later, on July 1, McCoy published the third number of the *Annual Register of Indian Affairs*, showing the difference between the actual state of the Indians and the picture given in literature, providing "an air of romance, for the sake of pleasing the fancy, and not for the instruction of the mind." He suggested that scientific research must be done on the state and circumstances of the Indians as a whole, believing that the published reports of this research and journeys of discovery into the Indian Territory would go a long way to financing the work. Respectable scientific periodicals could support the action and report on the research.

Keeping up to date with overseas missionary work

In all his communications with the Board and his publications concerning the Indian mission, McCoy was most careful to stress the value of missionary work whether it was on one's own doorstep or in lands far away. Thus Robert Drury is being too hard on McCoy when he writes in his article *Isaac McCoy and the Baptist Board of Missions*:

McCoy was so concerned and zealous for his work with the Indians that he overemphasised the needs of his work in relation to other mission work sup-

---

[17] *Periodical Account of Baptist Missions*, p. 1.

ported by the Board. He thought Indian missionary work was the most important, because he was chosen to it, and he was not in a position to know the needs of outposts in foreign countries.[18]

This view fails to acknowledge McCoy's deep interest in missionary developments abroad as witnessed, for instance, by his naming his own son after Luther Rice,[19] his daughter Nancy Judson (b. February 26, 1819) after Ann "Nancy" Judson, wife of Adoniram Judson and the northern mission bases Carey and Thomas after the two English Particular Baptist missionaries to India, William Carey and Dr. John Thomas. McCoy made his position clear in 1836 when he wrote:

> *We do not think* that too much attention has been bestowed on Foreign missions; and we should write with a trembling hand, if we thought that by praying for more assistance to Indian missions, the amount of support to the former would be diminished. *We do think*[20] that too little has been done for the Indians. Of this, we feel so well assured, that we cannot suppose any one will undertake to say that we are mistaken. We are equally confident, that increased efforts in favour of Indian missions, so far from injuring, will promote those in foreign lands, as certainly as the latter are promoted by the Home missionary cause, or by the Bible Societies, both of which, it is well known, promote the cause of Foreign Missions.[21]

The difference between McCoy and the Board on this point was that the latter felt that the pinnacle of support for missionary work of any kind had been reached and no further demands could be made on the Baptist public. If more were given to the Indian mission,

---

[18] *Baptist History and Heritage*, vol. 2, no. 1, 1967, p. 11.

[19] This is taking for granted that McCoy knew Rice in 1807 when his son was born. There are several by the name of Rice in McCoy's family, the spelling being an alternative for "Royce." McCoy's daughter Maria Staughton (b. November 29, 1823), was named after the Board member, William Staughton.

[20] My emphasis.

[21] *Periodical Account of Baptist Missions*, p. 3, also *History of Baptist Indian Missions*, pp. 521-522.

less would be available for foreign missions. McCoy's position was that the giving public was ill-informed about missions in general and needed to be educated by the Christian press as to the overall needs of missionary workers. Above all, first hand reports from within the mission fields were necessary. Indeed, McCoy felt that the general interest in missionary work was less in 1836 when he wrote these words that in 1817 when he was called to be a missionary. In those days, the Baptists, McCoy concluded, were inspired by the idea of Christian missions through Baptist Carey[22] of Britain and America's own Adoniram Judson and Luther Rice, who became Baptists in 1813[23] and chief instigators of the American Baptists' interest in foreign missions. Dr. Cady writes:

> The major impetus for projecting an organization comprehending the whole of the Baptist denomination came in 1813-1814, as a result of the appeals of Adoniram Judson and Luther Rice for support of their work in Burma. In response to this challenge, a General Missionary Convention of Baptists assembled at Philadelphia in May of 1814. Thirty-three delegates from eleven states were present. The Constitution which they adopted provided for a general Convention to meet every three years, the delegates to come from societies contributing one hundred dollars or more per year to the enterprise. A Board of Commissioners of twenty-one members would act as the executive staff during the interim between meetings. Luther Rice himself returned from Burma to take over the active direction of the affairs of the Triennial Convention.[24]

The initial enthusiasm had, however, worn off. Prof. Cady in the work from which the above quote is taken, sees the reason for the general decline in Christian interest concerning what was happening abroad as being found in the end of the conflict with Britain in 1815 and the cessation of the Napoleonic Wars. He feels that then the American attention became riveted on what was going on in their own country "west of the mountains" where the area had been cleared of Indians during the war of 1812. This would underscore what McCoy

---

[22] The Massachusetts Baptist Missionary Society was founded in 1802, following the example of William Carey.

[23] Baptized by William Ward of Serampore.

[24] *The Origin and Development of the Missionary Baptist Church in Indiana,* p. 32.

always affirmed after 1817. For the new Baptist Board "domestic missions" as they were called, were first and foremost missions to the white population moving westwards.

The counter productivity of the Baptist Foreign Missions Board

Organizations such as the Baptist Foreign Missions Board, McCoy believed, did not realize that they were becoming counter-productive. The Board's fear that Baptist support was limited, was moving them to give limited attention to missions in general. The result was doubly negative. The faithful band of givers who supported the Board did not have their interests encouraged and widened by the Board's small twenty-odd-paged missionary magazine. This must have had some influence on their giving. Possible new supporters and friends of the Indians were put off by the Board's obvious lack of interest in the Indians and thus their gifts were not forthcoming. Furthermore, the Board always advised against earmarking special gifts for special needs. They suggested that they knew best how to spend such monies. This took away the individual Christian's responsibility and discouraged many who had a prayer burden for one particular area from supporting the Board financially. They were simply afraid that their money would go to other causes.

There was also another, more sinister reason why the Board was becoming more and more unpopular and failing to rally the Baptists around the cause of missions whether at home or abroad. Many churches had begun to suspect the Board as viewing the churches as a cow to be milked for the benefit of the Board alone. This was a most serious accusation but the evidence to back it up was far from weak. The Board insisted that each church who wished to send a representative to its Conventions must pay a fee of at least $100 otherwise they would have no say in the Convention's or Board's decisions. This step alone alienated many churches, chiefly because $100 was half an average pastor's annual income. The Board, however, still felt it had a right to act as spokesman for such churches. Soon, those churches who paid the money became equally disheartened. They found that they had no visible returns for their investment in spiritual or material things, nor did their lone voice ever seem to penetrate through to the Board. The opposite seemed to be the case. The Board seemed to be an empty bottomless barrel. The more money came in, and thousands came in from Government grants for the civilization of the Indians alone, besides church giving, the more the Board complained that they were in financial difficulties. Their debts caused by borrowing from the Government irrespective of the large grants they were receiving ran into many thousands of dollars. They were forced to confess to the Government that they could not pay them and to petition the Government to cancel them. Of the few Indian missionaries the Board had, Isaac McCoy was not the only one who queried the Board's financial strategy. Peck and Welch had complained and the Board had merely shut down their work on the needy Western frontier. Evan Jones who ran the Valley Towns Mission among the Cherokees had seen this large mission go bankrupt by a Board who just did not seem to care. Jones hung on alone after several missionaries had given up but the only thanks he received from the Board was their telling him that he must not buy tea, coffee or sugar and make sure that he reported exactly what the Indians were eating for breakfast, dinner and supper and always send in proforma bills so that the Board would be able to judge whether they could meet them or not. This meant that Jones had to plan his expenses at least half a year in advance to give time for communications with the Board to reach Philadelphia or Boston and back and then make the sometimes long journeys to buy provisions. Meanwhile, the mission family had either grown or shrunk and many other needs had arisen before any money came in at all. In other words, the Board made it quite impossible for Jones to run his mission on a cost effective basis. Yet the Board emphasized to Jones that the mission could not be run on mere philanthropic grounds but it must be organized as a business. Obviously the Board felt that this should be a state run business as they told Evans to send a bill for the $2,864 he had spent on the mission's work to the War Department for reimbursement. The War Department turned Jones' request down. At this time, however, the Board were widely reported to be living in luxury on the monies coming in and setting up businesses for their own profit with the mission's funds. No wonder that Jones gave up such resident work to become an itinerant preacher among the Indians, in the hope of costing the Board far less. Yet even then he was plagued by the Board's criticism for using paid blacksmiths to shoe his horses, for hiring interpreters and for entering politics. The latter criticism was a piece of irony indeed as the Board itself dabbled strongly in politics and Jones only entered the political field to protect the Indians.[25]

---

[25] See McLoughlin's excellent and balanced account of Evan's trouble with the Baptist Board of Missions in his *Champions of the Cherokees*.

A gradual awareness among the Baptists that all was not well with their Board

Gradually the Baptist churches came to realize what the missionaries had long known--all was not well with the Board's management. Most had some idea of funds going in and of the disproportionate amounts coming out. Some members of the Board began to check the books of the others and it soon became plain that dubious activities were going on within the Board and that those who set themselves up as the churches' spokesmen were guilty of highly questionable conduct. The initial blame was placed on Luther Rice. This first Baptist missionary to India and Burma, who soon gave up his calling, was one of the cofounders of the Board and of the Columbian College, the *Latter Day Luminary* and other enterprising bubbles which all burst. He thus allegedly brought not only the Board into financial difficulties but it was rumored, he used $1,300 given to the Board by the War Department from their Civilization Fund, i.e. for the improvement of the Indians, to pay off the debts he had accrued. It is only fair to say that Rice put the blame on the business consortium that the Board appointed to look into the matter and run the Board's finances for a while. Rice claimed these businessmen were also the cause of the Columbian College getting into financial difficulties.[26] Rice would receive money from the Government and pay it into the Board's funds who would, in turn, send it, or should have sent it, to the mission. Often the mission either never saw the funds, received them only in part or were only able to draw on them many months later. The missionaries then had to send a receipt to the Board, who gave it to Rice who then gave it to the Government. As the receipts the missionaries signed and what the Board received through Rice for Indian improvement were often at great variance, Rice inevitably received the blame. Obviously not wishing to cause a scandal in the country and shut off all sources of income and have legal prosecution on their hands, the Board merely removed Rice from his office of treasurer and gave it to another. They had learned that it was to their advantage to sweep all their own dirt under their own carpets. No matter how much the Board blamed Rice, however, for any initial debt, their biggest debts made when doubling the size of the Columbian College buildings on borrowed capital had nothing whatsoever to do with Rice. He had

---

[26] See McLoughlin's study of the Board's questionable financial dealings in his *Champions of the Cherokees*, pp. 47-50. McLoughlin is far too hard on Rice.

protested all along at such an ambitious scheme, made by the very Committee of Outfit and business men who had censored him for getting the Board into debt.[27] However, in 1839, Solomon Peck, then Foreign Secretary to the Board, commissioned a report, summing up Rice's part in the bankruptcy of the Columbian College, using this supposed incident as a reason for the eastern Baptists to take control of the Board's activities.

> The zeal of Mr. Rice not being accompanied with good judgment in the management of pecuniary affairs, the college soon became involved in debt. The difficulties to which the trustees and the Convention were subjected, were extremely embarrassing, and the energies which should have been put forth for the elevation of the course of study, and the completion of the whole plan, were exhausted in struggling for existence. The affairs of the college operated unfavorably upon the primary object of the Convention; and, in 1826, that body, by a unanimous vote, withdrew from all responsibility concerning it, except the nomination, triennially, of fifty individuals, from whom the electors of the college were to choose 31 trustees. This year, Rev. Robert Semple, D.D., of Virginia, was appointed successor of Mr. Rice, who resigned his agency for the institution, but continued, gratuitously, to solicit subscriptions for the college until his death, in 1836.[28]

McCoy knew about these events, but was too busy following his calling to bother much about them. There are merely brief references in his journals and letters to Rice's dismissal which in no way affected McCoy's respect for his friend. He kept to his pragmatic view that the greater the interest aroused in missions and the scope provided, the greater would be the giving. This thought filled his mind and controlled his actions at the time. McCoy believed that the greater the information given concerning missionary work, whether foreign or home, the greater its instrumentality would be in the Lord's hands in calling new recruits to the mission field. Thus his efforts would also serve to keep the Board busy in doing the job for which the churches had set it up.

---

[27] Letter dated December 8, 1825, McCoy Papers, Reel 4.

[28] Rice died in Edgefield District, South Carolina on September 25, 1836, aged 54 years. See *History of American Missions to the Heathen*, p. 380.

McCoy did not distinguish between home and foreign missions

Another difference between McCoy's view of the mission field and the Board's was that the latter distinguished radically between foreign missions and home missions, whereas McCoy believed that a mission was a mission wherever it was carried out in obedience to the Great Commission. Thus, we find McCoy constantly addressing himself to friends of missionary activity wherever that may be. He also wrote out principles of conduct between Missionary Societies and their missionaries which were valid whatever the various fields they might represent. McCoy did however note that witnessing to the Indians appeared to be thought a tougher job than witnessing to pagan whites or people in distant countries.[29] Indeed, this was one of the principle causes of dissatisfaction with McCoy in respect of the Board. It was obvious to him that the Baptist Board of Missions put foreign missions first, followed by home missions to whites leaving Indian missions to the last, thus artificially dividing the unevangelized fields.[30] This fact motivated McCoy to campaign from 1836 on for an Indian Missions Board, staffed by people who were exclusively called to bring Christ to the Native Americans.

More news about the Pratts and the Meekers

In June 1837, while McCoy's printed plea for support of his mission was being circulated, a further new development occurred. The Meekers, having acquired a working knowledge of the Ottawa language, now left the Shawnee Mission Station to work among that people. Mr. Meeker was replaced by John Gill Pratt of Hingham, Massachusetts, who arrived on May 14 in time for Meeker to familiarize him with the printing press. Pratt worked hard at the Indian languages and was able to translate a number of books for distribution among the Indians. Sadly, he had to leave the mission after a few years when his wife became seriously ill with tuberculosis of the lungs. This compelled them to return to New England. Pratt eventually became Superintendent of the Delaware Mission and a trusted Indian Agent. As the main part of the Potawatomis had now left the Carey

---

[29] See *Remarks on the Practicability of Indian Reform Embracing Their Colonization*, 1829, Appendix II, III, and IV.

[30] See *Periodical Account of Baptist Missions Within the Indian Territory*, p. 49.

Mission area, Mr. and Mrs. Simerwell now took up permanent duties among the Potawatomis who had entered the Indian Territory. Mr. Simerwell made a final journey back to Michigan to persuade the last small groups of Potawatomis to return with him but his mission was unsuccessful. Meanwhile the Meekers, though only receiving $100 per year each from the board and a grant of $25 dollars for their children under sixteen years of age, settled down five miles north east of what is now Ottawa, Franklin County, Kansas and started a mission farm with a small school. After a few years, Meeker was able to come into possession once again of the Shawnee printing press and published many a Bible portion. Conversions among the Indians came slowly but by the forties, he was able to gather a small church around him which was pastored by one of his converts, a half-breed Ottawa named J. T. Jones who had been educated at Hamilton, the Calvinistic Seminary in New York. The Government assisted the Meekers in building a two-roomed log house in 1842 and eventually a church building was erected. The Meekers stayed at their Ottawa Mission until their deaths, Mr. Meeker dying on January 11, 1854 and his wife on March 15, 1856. They had done their work well and full-blooded Ottawas were able to continue their ministry which had been the major aim of their mission.

Problems concerning treaties with half-breeds

McCoy's next difficulty revolved around an area of 13,300 acres in the midst of the Indian Territory which had been promised to half-breeds via a treaty drawn up in 1830 but, as yet, no settlement had ensued. This area was under particular suspicion by the missionaries as the half-breeds tended to have more dealings with the whites than the Indians and thus if they settled in the Indian Territory, a door for white settlement would remain open in land set aside for Indians only. McCoy was appointed by the Commissioner of Indian Affairs, Mr. Harris, to look into the matter and discern who might be rightful claimants for land patents. As it turned out, the treaty had been drawn up on an extremely weak legal basis and with people not directly eligible for the land so that it could not be ratified. McCoy, of course, was quick to point out that two treaties could not be made with two different parties for the same land and since the Indian Territory had been reserved en bloc for Indians integrated in tribes, it would be best to let the matter of mixed-blood Indians in the area drop. The result was that nothing was ratified and the problem reserved for a future solution.

Commissioned to settle the Potawatomis, Ottawas and Chippewas

McCoy was then commissioned by the Indian Department to organize the settlement of the Potawatomis, Ottawas and Chippewas who were now entering the country from the north and east. He also located a site for the Osage subagency and measured up a seven square mile area in the middle of the territory where the seat of government was to be placed. A bill for the organization and government of the tribes was now drawn up and McCoy received the task of sounding out the different tribes on the matter. This was no easy matter as tribes such as the Delawares had never organized themselves under any formal rules and regulations and had not even a word for "law" in their language. McCoy resolved to paraphrase the proposed bill in a way that the Indians could understand, which would then be appended to the bill. The chiefs of the Delawares, Shawnees, Kickapoos, Potawatomis, Kansas, Sauks, Iowas, Weas, Piankashas, Peorias, Kaskaskias and Ottawas all signed the document.

Agitators among the white people, however, contacted the tribes and told them that McCoy was forcing them to sign documents which would give their land to the missionary and have them removed from the territory. Once the chiefs heard McCoy's own explanation, however, they were pacified. A further problem was the relocation of the Potawatomis, old friends of McCoy from his Carey days. The Indian subagent, Dr. James, insisted on placing the tribe in a far less fertile area than McCoy had chosen for them. James' sole reason seemed to be that the Indians would soon perish whatever land they received so why give them the best? Though James was an upright, godly man, his plan met the approval of the designing whites who felt that if the Potawatomis were given barren land and isolated from the rest of the Indians, the white traders could move in and trade them out of their annuities. When the Potawatomis objected to being given inferior land, the whites spread the rumor that the Potawatomis (a very small tribe of about a thousand in number, including women and children) were preparing for war with the Government. Sadly, the Potawatomis were moved to the unfavorable area in Missouri before the consent of the Indian Department was given. Indeed, Harris had stipulated that the Potawatomis were only to be moved up the Missouri if they agreed. A number of Potawatomis had refused to go and this was considered within their right. As members of the tribe continually trickled in from Michigan, Indiana and Illinois, soon the Potawatomis were as divided as ever, though the bulk of the tribe had still to arrive. McCoy, however, managed to gain concessions from the Government on the Potawatomis behalf which eased their situation.

Notwithstanding, this tribe remained split up and many members refused to move from the Michigan area, while others crossed the border to Canada, putting themselves under British jurisdiction.

Spiritual blessings attend the move to the Indian Territory

Now McCoy was busy showing the various incoming tribes the land that was allotted to them. This did not mean that McCoy was neglecting his missionary duties for he continually ministered among the incoming Indians and arranged to have missionaries sent to them. Especially at this time, there are constant reports from McCoy's pen of Indians professing faith in Christ, baptisms, church formation and church growth. Indians representing numerous small tribes were soon coming in from Detroit, Lake Huron and New York, apart from new arrivals to the tribes which were already well-established in the Indian Territory. The Government recommended that these newcomers should be immediately taught the new Baptist system of reading and writing which meant that they were giving official recognition of the system over and against that developed by the Presbyterians.

Arrell M. Gibson, in his *Oklahoma: A History of Five Centuries*, though emphasizing the nineteenth century trials of the so-called Five Civilized Tribes i.e. the Cherokees, the Chickasaws, the Choctaws, the Creeks and the Seminoles, describes this period of initial settlement as a time of relief, saying:

> On the whole, the nineteenth century for the Five Civilized Tribes was a time of sorrow, travail, and disintegration. The one bright period in this dreadful hundred years was the interval between removal, around 1830, and the outbreak of the Civil War in 1861. These were the Golden Years for the Five Civilized Tribes, a time of respite from the demands of the settlers for their lands, years during which the Indians made remarkable progress in taming the Oklahoma wilderness. They organized constitutional government, established towns, farms, ranches, and plantations. They developed and published newspapers, magazines, and books. Through a school system which exceeded anything available in the states and territories adjacent to Indian Territory, they pushed back the shades of ignorance, superstition, and illiteracy.
>
> During the Golden Years, this extensive system of education, sustained by the tribal governments and certain missionary societies, provided unlimited ed-

ucational opportunities for the Indian youth. In most of the Indian nations, it was possible for every child to attend school from kindergarten through the academy level (the equivalent of high school) and in some cases the first two years of college. From the academies, many bright young men were sent to the eastern colleges to complete their studies. After 1850, many business, social, and political leaders of the tribes were college graduates. As an example, William P. Ross, nephew of Chief John Ross, a Princeton graduate, returned to Indian Territory to edit the *Cherokee Advocate* and later to become principal chief of the Cherokee Nation.

The curriculum of Indian Territory schools was diversified. The students were taught a variety of vocational subjects in addition to the traditional subjects of spelling, biology, history, astronomy, Latin, Greek, and English, arithmetic, philosophy, and in the mission schools, Bible studies. The boys were trained in animal husbandry, agriculture, the mechanical arts, and carpentry, while the girls were instructed in child care, cooking, and other domestic arts. So-called special education is not new in Oklahoma, for the Indian Territory school systems included schools for orphans and children from broken homes, and instruction for the deaf, blind, and mentally ill.

Support varied for the schools of Indian Territory. In 1819 Congress began appropriating an annual sum of $10,000 for the Indian Civilization Fund, which was administered by the missionary groups working among the tribes. But there were many tribes to be served and there was heavy competition for this fund. Missionary societies of the various religious denominations raised money from private sources to build schools and churches in the Indian Territory and furnished teachers, ministers, physicians, and instructors in farming and the mechanical and domestic arts. The tribes appropriated funds through their tribal councils too, for the support of public school systems operating in their nations, and to subsidize schools established by the missionary societies. Tribal revenues came from several sources, but in no case from taxes on Indian citizens, for there were no taxes in Oklahoma in those times. Land, a universal basis for taxation, was held in common by each tribe, and thus could produce no revenue. Income from fees, licenses, franchises, and fines collected by the Indian governments were reserved for the support of schools. Most of the money the Five Civilized Tribes poured into their educational systems came from the annuities earned on the invested proceeds of the sale of their eastern lands. Other sources of education for the youth of Indian Territory were the private boarding schools and academies in the eastern states. Many of the more sophisticated Indian families educated their children through these agencies.[31]

Gibson defends McCoy's policy

Gibson testifies to the work of Isaac McCoy and his son John Calvin McCoy in drawing up the boundaries for the tribes[32] and shows how critics who believed that the Indians were being forced into an overcrowded piece of barren land where they could do nothing but perish argued outside of the facts. The land annexed for the use of approximately 100,000 Five Tribes Indians was 70,000 square miles which meant that there were less than two people per square mile. This compares very favorably with similar free nomadic peoples who lived in other parts of the world. The Lapps of northern Europe, a people so akin to the American Indians that ethnically and culturally they must be considered close relations, at this time had a similar ratio of population per square mile though they were still nomadic.[33]

The lot of the Osage Indian

At this juncture, McCoy found the time to take more notice of the Osage Indians, whom he felt had been the most neglected and most abused of the Indian tribes. McCoy did not criticize the Government alone for this but also the Presbyterian missionaries who had

---

[31]See Chapter Seven: "The Golden Years," pp. 141-143.

[32]Ibid, p. 183.

[33]The author spent several years doing mission work among the Lapps of Sweden and Norway and was able to draw many parallels, even linguistically, between the two peoples. There is much to show that Lapps and Indians were one nomadic people, some of whom moved east over the Bering Strait and some of whom moved west to the Kola Peninsula and Scandinavia. It is interesting to note that both broad language groups show many affinities to Semitic languages rather than Indo-European languages which gave rise to the far-fetched theory that the Lapps and the Indians were the supposed "lost tribes" of Israel. Pioneer linguists such as Baptist John Gill (1697-1771) showed affinities between the Semitic and Indo-Germanic languages, also.

started up a work among the Osage but soon abandoned the project as hopeless. The Osage Indians still lived by hunting but the buffalo had become so scarce that they had to travel many miles to find them, which often brought them into conflict with other tribes and whites on the way. They had been promised help by the Government so that they could become stationary and take up agriculture but the treaties had not been kept by the whites. To make matters worse, though the Osage received government annuities as compensation for the loss of their hunting grounds, white traders robbed them of this money by advancing them cheap goods which they claimed were equivalent in value to their annuities. The Indians had no idea of the true value of the powder and shot they received from the traders and innocently gave them their annuities of thousands of dollars in return. McCoy relates:

> They were reduced to protracted sufferings under the pressure of extreme poverty, the burden of which increased with each successive year, while they were incapable of foreseeing the end of their wretchedness; and without a friend, either among the white or red men, whose sympathies they could share, and from whom they could hear a consoling word, or receive profitable advice. If anxieties, bordering on despair, or pinching want, induced them to seek either the countenance or the helping hand of a friend among neighbouring tribes, either on their north or south, they were repulsed as troublesome visitants; and if they entered the sparse white settlements within the State of Missouri or Arkansas, in quest of food, where, from time immemorial, they had been accustomed to take the quadruped and fowl, they were flogged and forced away.[34]

McCoy had begun to visit the Osage with the gospel and material support in 1828 and had been surprised to find them completely different to their reputation of being fierce, warlike and brutal savages. He resolved to continue where the Presbyterians had left off and made the needs of the Osage known in his *Annual Register of Indian Affairs*. This step moved friends of the Indian mission to forward money so that a work among the Osage could be started. McCoy saw the work among the Osage as a new opening for Henry Skigget, the Delaware Indian, whom McCoy had long sought to employ within the mission. Skigget had worked for the Presbyterians among the Osage and acquired their language and assisted Lykins in producing

---

[34] *History of Baptist Indian Missions*, p. 536.

literature for the tribe. There were two problems in employing Skigget, however. The Board refused to accept him as one of their missionaries and Skigget had taken over the Presbyterian bias that it was hopeless to try and evangelize the Osage. McCoy decided to hire Skigget for $15 per month and invited him to start work among the Quapaw tribe, relations of the Osage, at first. This was because a posse of some 500 white Missouri citizens were at that time fighting the Osage who had become scattered and their situation more desperate. Knowing Skigget's attitude towards the Osage, McCoy had wished to wean Skigget to them by having him work among a related but more settled people. McCoy quartered Skigget with a government employee who was a committed Christian and a Presbyterian before leaving the area for a time on other business. On his return after a few weeks, he found that Skigget now shared the common feeling of despair that the Osage were beyond help. McCoy was shocked to see the Osage being "hunted like partridges". McCoy was with a former missionary at the time and exclaimed to him, "Oh that I had bread to give them!" McCoy's "Christian" friend rebuked him sharply, telling him that the Osage had rejected the kindness of the missionaries who had previously worked among them and any kindness shown them would only prolong their suffering and their sin. From now on, McCoy persistently petitioned the Government with pleas on behalf of the Osage until he had both the Department of Indian Affairs and Congress itself on his side. Then aid was promised, but the agent sent by the Government collaborated with the Osages' white antagonists and misused the Government's money. McCoy kept up his lobby, however, and by 1837 practical aid was given the Osages which saved them from certain extinction.

The good and lasting work of Ramsey Potts commences

During October, 1837, McCoy was sent by Congress to report to the southern tribes concerning a bill which had been passed to their advantage. On arriving at Fort Gibson, McCoy found that news of the bill had gone before him so he decided to turn to other, urgent tasks. At Fort Gibson, he discovered that John Davis' wife had died, a matter which was a great blow to the mission. Mrs. Davis was a Creek woman and there was no one of her tribe to replace her in the work she had done. Davis was so downcast at the loss of his wife that he could do no preaching for some time. He had also been told by the Board to give up his home because of Creek antagonism towards the missionaries so he had moved to the North Fork where another Baptist Indian church was soon constituted. Needless to say, it was the missionaries' white enemies who took over the buildings Davis had erected. Ramsey Potts, who had married Lucretia Purchase, was praying about leaving his Government work and taking up the ministry and McCoy asked Davis to go over and encourage him to be ordained. Meanwhile, Potts had become certain of his calling. Not knowing that McCoy and Davis were hoping to ordain him, Potts left for a white settlement in Arkansas and was duly ordained, to McCoy's "great satisfaction."[35] Potts and his wife took up work some 150 miles from Davis and, with the help of a Miss Lucy Taylor, started a school for girls. Miss Taylor had to retire after only a year's service on account of ill health but the Potts family were very successful in their ministry, though Mrs. Potts became ill some years later.

The Board refuses to support half-blood teachers

McCoy starts his account for January, 1838 with encouraging news of Mr. Simerwell's work among the Potawatomis where he was serving the tribe alone. An application was made to the Board to finance a half-Indian who was to help in teaching the Indians the new system of reading and writing. With characteristic generosity, McCoy shared his own income with the man for a few months, hoping the Board would work out a financial program with the Government. The Board, however, refused to back the missionaries and pay Mr. Simerwell for any teaching assistance, so the teaching project had to be dropped. This showed how certain members of the Board still harbored their old prejudice. They could not reconcile themselves to the idea that Indians could become teachers or academics in any profession.

A further visit to the Department of Indian Affairs

In the following February, McCoy again made the long trek to Washington in the severest of weather. This time his principle mode of transport was a road wagon without seats. McCoy found himself the sole traveler for several days because it was just too cold for the less hardy to make the journey. Though McCoy had winter clothing and was wrapped up in several blankets, he suffered from frostbite and his eyes became terribly inflamed. On reaching Washington, McCoy pre-

---

[35] See *History of Baptist Indian Missions*, p. 540.

sented the Department for Indian Affairs with a large map of the Indian Territory which was eventually published and thus the general public learned more concerning the settlement of the Indians and their needs. McCoy also presented the Department with a request from the Potawatomis regarding the subdivision of their land so that individuals could farm their own plots. The missionary was upset to find that though the Secretary of War approved of the plan, the Committee for Indian Affairs maintained that the Potawatomis should pay for such surveying and marking themselves. McCoy thought that this was nipping good fruit in the bud as his whole design in campaigning for the Indian Territory was to see the Indians settled in their own country under similar circumstances to the whites while having the same chances to procure property and land. The Potawatomis, he argued, want to feel that the house they lived in and the soil they tilled really belonged to them and would become the property of their children and children's children. McCoy campaigned stubbornly on and by April the Senate passed a bill in favor of the Potawatomis' wish but it was not presented before the House. The Government's reluctance to give the Potawatomis individual land rights and patents had dire consequences for their resettlement. Those still in their original homes in Indiana and Michigan now refused to move. Lykins was sent by the Government to persuade them but he came back without the Indians. Some were intent on staying; some were too ill to move and some of the more disillusioned were considering crossing the border to British Canada where they hoped to obtain a better deal. This was a sad blow for the Baptist missionaries but a greater was to come. McCoy was too busy in Washington to attend the Triennial Baptist Convention which was held in New York that year. Instead, he sent proposals with friends to be placed before the Convention, requesting that they should consider founding a separate Baptist Indian Mission with its own board and its own administration. McCoy's proposition was merely noted at the Convention but was not put to the vote. He thus felt that the clock was ticking backwards.

The Office of Indian Affairs acknowledges McCoy as instigating the Indian Territory

During the late summer of 1838, McCoy and the Choctaw Agent, Captain William Armstrong, received the following letter from the Office of Indian Affairs at the War Department:

Gentlemen: I have the honour to inclose a printed copy of a bill that passed the Senate at the last session of Congress, for the organisation of a Government for the Indian territory. An effort will be made at the next session to secure its passage through both Houses. It is believed that this will be more likely to succeed, if the assent to its provision of the principle tribes can be first obtained. It is important, therefore, that an attempt should be made to gain this. You have been associated together for this purpose, it being desirable to have the benefit of your joint influence, and of the knowledge each possesses of the subject; the one, (Captain Armstrong,) from his official position and intercourse with the tribes, the other, (Mr. McCoy,) from his agency in originating the measures, and thus far prosecuting it to a successful issue. The assemblies convened for the payment of the annuities will, probably, afford the best occasions for attending to this business. You will please to forward your reports, so as to reach this office on or before the first day of November next.

Very respectfully, your most obedient servant,
C.A. Harris, Commissioner.[36]

This letter is quite revealing and certainly reflects the high view the Government had of McCoy. Obviously Armstrong was included in the team because of his official title and McCoy, who had always rejected official Government offices, was chosen not only for his know-how and experience but because the Government willingly acknowledged that he was the instigator par excellence of the resettlement of the Indians in their own territory. Armstrong, however, was ill at the time so on September 18th, McCoy set off on a six weeks tour of the Southern Tribes, reaching the Choctaws on October 4th, in time to see them in council.

William McLoughlin misjudges McCoy

What McCoy has to write concerning the Southern Tribes ought to be scrutinized carefully by any modern reader who has been influenced by William G. McLoughlin's pen portrait of the missionary. McLoughlin writes:

Though sincere in his dedication to the welfare of the Indians, McCoy had little respect for their abilities and

---

[36] *History of Baptist Indian Missions*, p. 547.

little regard for their treaty rights or tribal integrity. His approach was thoroughly paternalistic; the Indians were 'wards of the state' and should be told by experts like himself to do what was best for them.[37]

If such a view had ever been McCoy's, which this writer doubts because of McCoy's clear testimony given in the pages of this biography, there was certainly no trace of such an attitude in McCoy during his visit to the Southern Tribes. Indeed, one can safely say that McCoy was awestruck at what he experienced. Almost everything the Choctaws did found his admiring praise. The laws they had made, the administration they had set up and their sheer respect shown for one another was almost breathtaking for McCoy. When he saw their delegates speaking in conference, he could hardly believe his eyes and ears as they showed such a grace, such a courtesy and such elocution in their delivery. McCoy soon found himself comparing debates in Congress very negatively with those that he experienced in the General Council of the Choctaw Nation. Indeed, so impressed was McCoy with the way the Indians ruled themselves that it was obvious that he regarded the alternative which he had in his pocket as hardly appropriate. When the Choctaws agreed to defer a final decision regarding the Senate's proposals for an Indian seat of government on the grounds that they lacked confidence in the United States Government, McCoy was not in the least disappointed and commented, "Notwithstanding we did not obtain such an answer as was desired, this was a very interesting interview, from which we not only derived personal satisfaction, but hoped for an impression upon the public mind beneficial to the Indians generally. Here was developed a career of improvement recently commenced, and truly auspicious."[38] On reading McCoy's full report, one gains the impression that this is another of his great understatements. McCoy was simply thrilled with what he experienced among the Choctaws.

Several speeches of Choctaw leaders are extant from this period and Thomas McKenney has reproduced a speech given to the Indian Agent which was very similar to the words McCoy heard when bargaining with the Choctaws. Col. Cobb, Head Mingo of the Choctaws who remained East of the Mississippi is speaking:

---

[37] *Cherokees & Missionaries, 1789-1839*, p. 268.

[38] *History of Baptist Indian Missions*, p. 548.

Brother -We have heard you talk as from the lips of our father, the great white chief at Washington, and my people have called upon me to speak to you. The red man has no books, and when he wishes to make known his views, like his father before him, he speaks from his mouth. He is afraid of writing. When he speaks he knows what he says: the Great Spirit hears him. Writing is the invention of the pale-faces; it gives birth to error and to feuds. The Great Spirit talks - we hear him in the thunder - in the rushing winds and the mighty waters - but he never writes.

Brother - When you were young we were strong; we fought by your side; but our arms are now broken. You have grown large: my people have become small.

Brother - My voice is weak; you can scarcely hear me; it is not the shout of a warrior, but the wail of an infant. I have lost it in wailing over the misfortunes of my people. These are their graves and in those aged pines you hear the ghosts of the departed. Their ashes are here, and we have been left to protect them. Our warriors are nearly all gone to the far country west; but here are our dead. Shall we go, too, and give their bones to the wolves?

Brother - Two sleeps have passed since we heard you talk, and we have thought upon it. You ask us to leave our country, and tell us it is our father's wish. We would not desire to displease our father. We respect him, and you his child. But the Choctaw always thinks. We want time to answer.

Brother - Our hearts are full. Twelve winters ago our chiefs sold our country. Every warrior that you see here was opposed to the treaty. If the dead could have been counted, it could never have been made; but, alas! Though they stood around, they could not be seen or heard. Their tears came in the rain-drops, and their voices in the wailing wind, but the pale faces knew it not, and our land was taken away.

Brother - We do not complain. The Choctaw suffers, but never weeps. You have the strong arm, and we cannot resist; but the pale-face worships the Great Spirit. So does the red man. The Great Spirit loves truth. When you took our country you promised us land. There is your promise in the book. Twelve times have the trees dropped their leaves, yet we have received no land. Our houses have been taken from us. The white man's plough turns up the bones of our fathers. We dare not kindle our fires; and yet you said we might remain, and you would give us land.

        Brother - Is this *truth?* But we believe now that our great father knows our condition, he will listen to us. We are as mourning orphans in our country; but our father will take us by the hand. When he fulfills his promise, we will answer his talk. He means well. We know it. But we cannot think now. Grief has made children of us. When our business is settled, we shall be men again, and talk to our great father about what he has proposed.

        Brother - You stand in the moccasins of a great chief; you speak the words of a mighty nation, and your talk was long. My people are small, their shadow scarcely reaches to your knee; they are scattered and gone; when I shout, I hear my voice in the depth of the woods, but no answering shout comes back. My words, therefore, are few. I have nothing more to say, but to request you to tell what I have said to the tall chief of the pale-faces, whose brother stands by your side.[39]

The Cherokees and Creeks suspicious of Government plans

        McCoy soon found out on interviewing the Cherokees and Creeks that they were suspicious of the Government's plan to foist a form of government on them, arguing that such a government should originate from the Indians themselves and not the whites. Sympathetic as McCoy was with this idea, he realized that the Cherokees were saying, in effect, "We are the leaders of the Indian tribes which means that we must dictate what form of government should rule all Indians." Again, rather than reject the Cherokees' wishes, McCoy confessed that they had a right to distrust the United States Government, who had made treaty after treaty with the Cherokees. They, in turn, had to continually experience that the Government made promises which it could not keep. McCoy realized that he must move the Government to do everything in its power to make up for past wrongs and give ample evidence that they would not be repeated.

---

[39] Taken from *Memoirs official and personal, of Thos. L. McKenney, late Chief of the Bureau of Indian Affairs, author of the History of the Indian Tribes of North America &c.* Reprinted in *Western Baptist Review*, vol. ii, Frankfort, Kentucky, 1846-1847, pp. 118-119.

Intemperance combated among the Delawares

When McCoy returned home on October 30, he found a delegation of Delaware Indians waiting for him with a request that he should help them draw up laws for the approval of the Government which would curb the drinking of strong spirits among them. They had already approached their Agent on the subject but he had refused to cooperate. McCoy told them not to be discouraged and that he would draw up an appropriate document for them. They found, however, a minority of the people would not agree to laws being passed, which the Agent apparently took as an excuse for not forwarding the Delawares' request to the Government. Sensibly, the Delaware majority resolved to practice temperance on a voluntarily level, even if they had to wait until it could be enforced by law. As a result of their endeavors, intemperance reduced radically in the tribe.

Chapter Fourteen
Caesar and the Lord (1838-40)

A Government post which causes the Board embarrassment

The problem of what is Caesar's and what is the Lord's in fund raising and missionary endeavors now became a major issue in McCoy's relationship with the Baptist Board of Foreign Missions. In early 1838, the Government asked McCoy to organize and supervise the distribution of the $10,000 which they reserved annually for Indian improvement. This money was chiefly made available to the various Indian mission stations and the schools they ran, and, in the case of the Baptist missions it was credited to the Board. McCoy asked the Government to provide him with a detailed account of how the money had been spent in previous years and also wrote to the Board, saying, "allow me respectfully to request permission to look on your books regularly for this purpose."[1] Though the Government readily supplied McCoy with the necessary information, even after repeated requests, the Board remained silent. McCoy refused to be satisfied with this state of affairs and told the Board that he required to know exactly what sums they had received from the Government in recent years for Indian improvement and how they had distributed them. He explained that he would have to see that each denomination who was engaged in Indian improvement should receive the correct percentage of the money but that his own denomination should not come too short.[2] As the Corresponding Secretary, Dr. Bolles, did not reply, McCoy turned to Heman Lincoln, the Board's treasurer, for information but Lincoln remained as silent as Bolles on the matter. The more the missionaries looked into the issue, the more they realized that the official annual printed report of the Board's income and expenses did

---

[1] See McCoy's letter to Dr. Bolles, July 29, 1839, American Baptist Foreign Mission Societies, Reel No. 100.

[2] See McCoy's letter to Dr. Bolles , May 8, 1838, American Baptist Foreign Mission Societies, Reel No. 100.

not tally with either the sums actually coming from the government or the sums being forwarded to the Baptist missionaries. In particular, very large sums of money earmarked for "schools" had certainly never been paid to any of the Baptist mission schools the missionaries knew of. This could mean either that the printed statements were not comprehensive and detailed enough or that grave mismanagement was being practiced. On March 1, 1839, McCoy demanded to see Lincoln's books going back as far as 1824 and insisted on being given every single entry with amount and date attached. On July 29, 1839 he wrote to Bolles, complaining that the information which was his right to demand had not been given him and he "most earnestly" urged Bolles to become active in the matter.

It was not that the missionaries were accusing the Board of embezzlement for personal gain, but that they were suspected of using Government funds to finance the upkeep of missionaries, preachers and pastors i.e. they were using secular, Government funding in order to finance the work of evangelizing and not to educate children which was a Government prerogative. This might seem like splitting hairs but the missionaries, and especially McCoy and Lykins, believed very strongly in the separation of Church and State. McCoy had previously written to Bolles on February 21, 1831 on this very matter:

> With regard to the desireableness of missionaries giving themselves wholly to evangelical labours, there is not now, nor has there been really a difference of opinion between the Board and myself. The course which we have heretofore pursued has been one dictated by necessity, and was not the result of choice. One ground of necessity is noticed below.
>
> I beg leave respectfully to remind the Board that no government aid has ever been provided for the support of a preacher, or of a teacher of religion among the Indians. It would be at variance with the spirit of our republican government to do so. If the President should direct a portion of the $10,000 annual appropriation to be given for the support of a preacher he would transcend his authority and would be called to account. They cannot hire a Chaplain to the army without constituting him an officer of the army, as much so as the surgeon is. The Chaplain to Congress is an appendage of that body, as much so as the Sargeant at Arms, or a Messenger. I state this for the purpose of settling this fact - that government never has

allowed and never can allow support to one whose business among the Indians is exclusively of a religious nature.[3]

The ground of necessity mentioned above was the matter of schools. McCoy explained to Bolles that all he had said and done in relation to establishing missions in the past was with a view to receiving Government aid for a most obvious reason. According to Government legislation published in 1819 and 1820, such missions were expected to run schools and such schools, the Government promised, would receive Government grants. It was as simple as that. Obviously McCoy was as pleased as the Board over this state of affairs as it left them able to concentrate their fund raising and giving on the essentials of a Christian ministry and the humanitarian duties of a Christian. McCoy made it clear that he made no personal claims on these Government grants but that they should be placed in the Board's treasury, entirely subject to their control. Yet, he was careful to add, "application, however, must necessarily be according to the regulations prescribed by the government, the spirit of which, I have given above." The Board did take over the responsibility of financing schools but as so little money was forthcoming from them, it was feared that neither the "render to Caesar the things that are Caesar" spirit of the Government's nor missionaries' advice was heeded. Furthermore, the missionaries felt that the Board was not doing enough to encourage Christian giving for the Indian Mission, but were relying on Government aid to accomplish that end. Consequently, by the late thirties, the missionaries were also seriously wondering whether or not all funds due to the Indian Mission, whether secular or sacred, were being diverted elsewhere.

McCoy reports on his survey work on the Cherokee borders

McCoy was now asked to report to the Government on his work regarding the establishment of the Cherokee borders. Thinking of the Cherokees' distrust of the Government because of their lax way of recognizing treaty responsibilities, McCoy added the suggestion to his report that the Department of Indian Affairs might grant the Cherokees land patents which ruled out the possibility of a takeover by whites. The Department replied, inviting McCoy to draw up a proposal for such a patent and forward it to the Attorney General for

---

[3] American Baptist Foreign Mission Societies, Reel No. 100.

consideration. The Attorney General, backed by T. Hartley Crawford, the new Commissioner for Indian Affairs, decided to grant a patent for the Cherokees. When McCoy received a copy, however, he was extremely disappointed to find that his clause, ruling out possible white infiltration into the Indian Territory, had been omitted. The reason given was that the Government agreed that the territory should remain in the hands of the Indians for ever but the former treaties with the Cherokees had not stipulated an all-time ban imposed on white settlers in their lands. This was a most unsatisfactory excuse as the old treaties had floundered on this very point. Wherever the Cherokees had been sent by treaty to supposedly dwell in the area for ever, whites had come in and forced them out. McCoy ends Chapter XXI of his *History of Baptist Indian Missions* by stating: "I regret to say, that the most serious difficulties attending the proper adjustment of Indian affairs, and placing them on the highway of national prosperity, appear to be laid in the blundering forms of their treaties."[4] H. C. Vedder in his *A Short History of Baptist Missions*, writes on this subject:

> It is stated on good authority that no fewer than 370 treaties have been made with the Indians, most of which have been violated by force or fraud. Every time the Indians made a treaty they lost something; and virtually every pledge made to them by the white man's government sooner or later was violated.[5]

McCoy comes to Evan Jones' support

It was while dealing with the Cherokees that McCoy became alarmed at the fate of Evan Jones, his counterpart at the Valley Towns Mission and now an itinerant preacher to the Cherokees. McCoy had met John Ross, the Cherokee chief during his last visit to Washington and received a good deal of information from him regarding Jones' work and the difficulties that he had. McCoy heard that the Department of Indian Affairs, with the cooperation of the Board, had relieved Jones of his duties, but no explanation for this had been given to the other Indian missionaries. At the time, McCoy was writing his *History of Baptist Indian Missions* and had approached the Board for detailed

---

[4] p. 554.

[5] *A Short History of Baptist Missions*, p. 455.

material on Jones' work among the Cherokees. The Board, however, had not provided him with the material, and McCoy now thought he knew the reason why. Jones was no longer regarded in respect by the Board. After being shown copies of letters from the Indian Agent and the Cherokee Council which were strongly in favor of retaining Jones as a missionary, whether in the East or after relocation in the West, McCoy felt he must put in a good word for his fellow-laborer in the gospel. He therefore wrote to Dr. Bolles on July 4, 1840 from Washington, explaining all that he had heard from Ross, saying:

> I am about publishing a history of Baptist Indian missions, and had hoped to find something from Mr. Jones on my arrival, to enable me to write out the article on the Cherokee mission. I would be much obliged if you would find time to furnish me with all the information you possess relative to the existing case of difficulty, and the present condition of the Church among the Cherokees, together with such historical statements relative to the past as you may find it convenient to make. Please to send me the last annual report of the Board.
>
> Mr. John Ross speaks highly in praise of Mr. Jones, and in favor of his continuance among them. I hope the Board has entered on measures to reinstate him, and if they have not, I would respectfully suggest whether the reputation of the Board, justice to Mr. Jones, the honour of religion, and the welfare of the Cherokees, do not require an immediate effort of this kind.[6]

Apparently such information as McCoy wished was not forthcoming as he provides little historical information in his *History* concerning work among the Cherokees. McCoy does, however, emphasize, in the face of the Board's now open criticism that Jones was working as a politician rather than a missionary, how Jones has persevered in the difficult work and has had the happiness of reaping a rich religious harvest. He refers to the success Jones enjoyed as a religious instructor and how he has founded two Cherokee churches. He emphasizes that in the political turmoils present among the Cherokees which led to the murder of John Ridge Jr., John Ridge Sr. and Elias Boudinot,[7] Jones and one of his converts, Chief Jesse

---

[6] American Baptist Foreign Mission Societies, Reel No. 100.

[7] These chiefs had entered into treaties with the Government to sign away their land.

Bushyhead, were blessed with success and church attendance improved with the power of their preaching. McCoy adds, with his gaze turned for a moment towards Boston and the Board, "But his loss to that people would be great, and it is hoped that they will be favoured with a continuation of his useful ministry."[8]

The smallpox breaks out again

The Cherokees and other Muskogean tribes were now threatened with an even worse enemy than the countless treaties which had often rendered them homeless. The smallpox had almost wiped out a few of the smaller tribes such as the Mandans during 1837, but the Muskogean Indians who had been able to resist the disease up to this time because of their more hygienic way of life. Now they too were being scourged by this terrible plague and evil whites were again hoping that it would prove their end. Previous efforts of the Government to implement widespread vaccination among the Indians had proved highly inadequate and now McCoy busied himself with lobbying for a more comprehensive system to protect the Cherokees, Choctaws, Chickasaws, Creeks and Seminoles.

The McCoys' daughter Eleanor dies

December, 1838 brought with it a doubly sad scene with which the McCoys were now all too familiar. Eleanor Donohoe (b. July 29, 1821), the McCoys' youngest daughter, lay dying, though only seventeen years of age. Eleanor had been married to William Smith Donohoe on August 22, 1837, though she was already in declining health. McCoy had been called again to Washington and had to start on the long winter journey knowing that he would not see his child again this side of Heaven. His one comfort was that Eleanor stood firm and faithful in the Lord, having come to a saving knowledge of Him some six months after her marriage. She died on January 11, 1839, before McCoy reached the capital. Lykins had written on January 8th to tell McCoy that there was very little hope for Eleanor's recovery and wrote to him again a few hours before her death, addressing him as "Father" in his usual way. He told his father-in-law that Eleanor was perfectly composed and even expressed happiness at being called

---

[8] *History of Baptist Indian Missions*, p. 573.

home, but he did not believe she would survive the day. On January 15, Lykins wrote again on behalf of the whole family, telling McCoy of her death and explaining the nature of her illness, why she lingered so long and why it proved fatal. The account of the suffering that Eleanor had undergone must have torn at her father's heart but the way Lykins described the actions and words of the family as they surrendered their loved one into the everlasting arms of the Lord must have been a great comfort to McCoy. Lykins signed himself, "most affectionately" and any one reading this long letter will realize what strong ties of a family nature but also of a sound and sure trust in the Lord of the Resurrection bound the two men. McCoy commented:

> The sad intelligence followed closely upon my heels; but the bitter blow contained a cordial too. Death had lost its sting, and the grave had been disrobed of its horrors. She was religiously cheerful to the last moment of her existence, and, apparently without anxiety or dread, she endeavoured to inspire others around her with similar sentiments. With lips which faltered more and more, she said, 'I am going home - Jesus - joy Jesus - great joy,' and ceased to breathe! *She was the tenth child of whom we* had been bereaved, and all since we had been missionaries.[9]

As soon as Spencer Cone heard the news, he wrote from New York to Washington on January 22nd in his beautiful bold flowing hand, expressing his sympathy and love, signing himself "Yours, as ever, thine most truly." On the same day, Mrs. McCoy wrote to her husband. This brave, noble woman wrote of yet another beloved member of the family who had been called home, now leaving only four of their fourteen children in this dark and sinful world. "If their end be like that of our departed children," Christiana writes, "then the remaining members of the family need not fear to follow them." Mrs. McCoy's heart goes out to young Mr. Donohoe who had taken Eleanor's death the hardest. As his sister had died almost at the same time, the blow had been greater. William Donohoe, who was in very poor health himself, wrote to McCoy on January 25th, addressing him, too, as "Father" and expressing his joy at the happiness and blessings he had experienced with the McCoy family. In particular, Donohoe stressed the great blessings they shared in their relationship to Eleanor, he as her husband and McCoy as her father. Then Donohoe, after expressing a wish that his end should be like Eleanor's, confessed that he could

---

[9] *History of Baptist Indian Missions*, p. 555.

scarcely call himself a Christian but added, "Yet I am resolved to lie at the feet of my Saviour in the humble hope that my sins will be forgiven, to which end - I do earnestly solicit your prayers."

Further work at Washington

While in Washington, McCoy heard of many setbacks for the mission which he had to attend to with all his energies. Charles Kellam who had replaced Rollin as the Board's missionary to the Creeks had been given full government status as a teacher but now, without consulting the missionaries, the Government had replaced him with another teacher who had taken over Kellam's house and home during his absence. Heman Lincoln, the Board's treasurer, was also in Washington at the time so he and McCoy lobbied the Government together for the reinstating of Kellam. The Commissioner for Indian Affairs granted their request without further ado. Next, McCoy worked hard behind the scenes in a renewed effort to have his plans for the organization of the Indian Territory passed by Congress. At first, things looked bright as the bill passed the Senate by a very great majority. However, it was not placed high enough on the list to be debated by the House of Representatives during their sitting and, once again, McCoy experienced nigh despair. He had been waiting sixteen years for his dream to come true and every year he had seen great possibilities that it would happen only to have his hopes subsequently dashed to the ground. McCoy thought that Congress just did not know the seriousness of the situation. Ninety-five thousand Indians were now gathered in their territory, representing twenty-three tribes but nothing was being done to make them a federal nation legally within their own state. The only comfort McCoy had was that the Indians were proving themselves able to form their own councils and laws and fractions between them were becoming less. Drunkenness was disappearing from several tribes and the Indians were careful that white whiskey peddlers should have no access to their lands. Some of the tribes had introduced severe punishments should their tribesmen be caught peddling ardent spirits. McCoy was happy to see that the Sabbath was being respected among the Indians and almost everywhere the gospel was being preached without hindrance. Before leaving Washington, McCoy had his fourth *Annual Register* printed at his own expense and distributed freely. This action was a thorn in the flesh to the Board but it gained many friends for the Indian Mission.

Rollin's death

When McCoy returned home on March 21, 1839 to hear the sad details of his child's death, he also heard that Rollin's health was failing rapidly. After leaving the Creeks, Rollin had never been able to make much headway among the Shawnees and McCoy was thinking of persuading him to work among the Choctaws. However, because of advanced tuberculosis, he had to retire from his missionary labors in April, and died on May 12th. McCoy commented:

> His life had been religious and his death was happy. His confidence in the Redeemer remained unshaken. In the time of trial, when he knew he must leave his amiable wife a widow, and his dear children fatherless, and when he was himself about to give an account of his stewardship, he derived substantial consolation from the Gospel which he had laboured to make known to the Indians. In endeavouring to secure to those poor people 'durable riches and righteousness', he, with the disinterestedness of a faithful missionary, had omitted to provide for the future support of his family. He now left them poor, but left them in the charge of the Father of the fatherless and the widow's God. He had been 'faithful unto death', and has, no doubt, received a 'crown of life'; and at the time of harvest, it is believed, he will not be destitute of sheaves gathered from the sterile regions of Indian lands.[10]

Encouraging signs as the Indian Mission continues

The year 1839 saw several new missionaries arrive at the Shawnee settlement, including Miss Elizabeth Churchill and Frances Barker. The latter had been doing school work connected to the mission on the Western frontier and had been assisted by Lykins to receive full missionary status. Lykins had also written to McCoy, arguing that Barker ought to receive a higher salary.[11] In May, the Simerwell's eldest son, a boy of thirteen, who had recently come to know the

---

[10] *History of Baptist Indian Missions*, p. 557.

[11] See Lykins' letter to McCoy dated March 8, 1838 in which he states that unless Barker receives a higher salary, he will leave the school and asks McCoy to mention this to the Board on his oncoming visit to the Convention. McCoy Papers, Reel 9.

Lord, was baptized, along with an ailing Ottawa squaw. She wished to testify to her faith in this way before being called home. On July 4th, Independence Day, Mr. Simerwell held temperance meetings which were well attended by the Indians and speeches were made by the Indian Agent A. L. Davis and Noaquett, alias Luther Rice, a full-blood Indian. On August 18th, a notable Potawatomi chief professed faith in Christ and was baptized along with a fellow tribesman. McCoy became seriously ill again but was able to bring peace to the Delawares and Otoes on his sick bed. The two tribes had begun to quarrel, so McCoy invited their chiefs to meet with him and was able to persuade them to live in peace. Once on his feet again, McCoy directed the location of incoming Chippewas from Michigan and planned a permanent location for the Winnebagoes, Stockbridge Indians and Wyandots.

Tribal quarrels occupied McCoy's mind almost constantly at this time. He realized that although the colonization of the Indian Territory was progressing well, many tribes who were now relocated and those such as the Pawnees and the Kansas who remained in their ancient territories must have new legislation to protect them from the revival of old traditional quarrels. The Pawnees and Kansas had still not buried the hatchet. In 1835, a party of Pawnees had stolen some Kansas horses. Not wishing to go back to the laws of retaliation, the Kansas had asked their Indian Subagent, Marston Clark, for legal help to gain compensation for the theft but they were told that there were no laws in the Indian Territory to cover such a crime.[12] In August, 1838, the Kansas, despairing of receiving help from the Government, persuaded the Osages to help them gain revenge against the Pawnees. They formed a posse of eighty men and attacked a Pawnee hunting party on the Arkansas. Eleven Pawnees were killed and scalped but the Kansas and Osages also suffered four casualties.[13] McCoy approached General Tipton, the U. S. Senator, concerning the problem and, at the General's request, wrote out fifteen pages of proposals for a universal law covering all the Indian tribes. McCoy's plea was for the setting up of a General Indian Council which would regulate intertribal affairs and legal responsibilities. Such an experimental council

---

[12] As much Indian criminality was caused by their drinking habits, McCoy proposed laws to curb whiskey peddling among the Indians. In a letter to Hon. John C. Spencer dated May 17, 1842, McCoy outlined most sensible laws for curbing the free sale of alcohol. McCoy Papers, Reel 10.

[13] This information is obtained from Unrau's chapter "The Failure of the Missionaries," in his book *The Kansa Indians*.

had been formed around 1833-4 and had proved highly successful. It was high time, McCoy argues, that a permanent council be set up.

The need for a pan-Indian law

McCoy explained to Tipton that the indigenous tribes, i.e. the Osage, Kansas, Otoes, Omahas and Pawnees, had long been at war with one another and with several of the eastern tribes now in the Indian Territory and that the only law that they had in common, if it could be called a law, was the law of retaliation. The only punishment the Indians knew was to take the offenders life or steal his property. Horse stealing, McCoy explained, was very prevalent and recently the Kansas had brought back to their villages at least thirty horses, stolen from other tribes whereas the Osage had rustled an even greater number of the very finest horses from the property of U. S. citizens. Shortly afterwards, however, the Osage reported that a huge number of their own horses had been stolen. This was probably a retaliation from other tribes who had been the victims of Osage raids. Indeed, the Indians had the open sympathy of Marston Clark, the Kansas Sub-agent in this matter. Clark, realizing that the Indians could not be considered lawless where no law existed, maintained that it would be wrong to take away from the Indians their right of retaliation as it was for them "the only road left to honor and promotion" since the whites had taken away all other methods. These views caused the Presbyterians and the Methodists to disagree violently with Clark and call him the most dishonoring names. This merely gained his antagonism to their church policies, whereas McCoy came up with positive suggestions rather than stubborn criticism and gained the Subagent's sympathy. McCoy had thus been able to work cordially with Clark from 1829 onwards.[14]

There was not much problem with the Choctaws, Chickasaws, Cherokees, Creeks and Seminoles who were used to living by parliamentary laws and the Delawares and Potawatomis were now also adopting a similar legal system. The other tribes had no system of laws at all whether governing inner-tribal affairs or relations with other tribes. Just imagine, McCoy argued, what a chaos would occur in a white state, divided into twenty-four districts with each district merely depending on retaliation to afford them protection against the others. They would become a terror to themselves and to the sur-

---

[14] Ibid, pp. 122-147.

rounding states. Now, because of the lawless Osage raids on the cattle of the southern tribes who lived by law, even the latter were threatening to retaliate unless the Government exercised its powers. Actually, the Government had no powers to exercise, strictly speaking, as the Indians were not U. S. citizens and the Indian Territory was not a U. S. State. While the Indians were in the East, they had stood under U. S. state laws but no such laws existed outside of the Union.[15]

McCoy went on to describe similar petty wars and raids featuring other tribes such as the Cheyennes, Kiowas, Cherokees and Otoes. It makes very depressing reading and gives the impression that the Indian Territory was far from the Canaan McCoy had wished to set up. While the General Council had been in existence, however, it had worked very well and the Indians had shown themselves to be governable and able to govern. Relative peace had reigned. Apparently Tipton was of the opinion that the Indians did not want a General Inter-Tribal Council but McCoy emphasized that he knew as much of the Indian mind as any man because of his years of experience traveling among the tribes. He therefore assured the Senator that objections to such a plan did not come from the Indians but from the whites who were trying to manipulate the Indians to their own advantage. McCoy then argued that the whites were becoming more and more numerous in the Indian Territory and thus endangering the entire idea of an Indian confederacy of nations. Here McCoy saw the fault in the Government's attitude to the southern tribes. Treaties were being made with their supposed Indian representatives who were as little as an eighth Indian and often thought more in terms of white land speculators. Many white men had married Cherokees merely to obtain their lands and annuities. Poor Indians were being persuaded by whites to give them their children for adoption. These whites then fought for and often won compensation and annuities for their young wards and then invested or used the money for their own advantage. McCoy describes these white designs on the Indians' property as being "dark as death."

Finally, McCoy presented the example of the Council of the Choctaws to show how a General Council should work. He had seen the Choctaws in action and believed that what they had achieved could be repeated throughout the Territory. Actually, the Choctaws

---

[15] See McCoy's *Address to Philanthropists in the United States, Generally, and to Christians in Particular* appended to his *Remarks on the Practicability of Indian Reform Embracing Their Colonization* for a detailed discussion of the legal problems surrounding the Indian Territory.

had invited all the tribes to take part in their parliament but the smaller tribes were worried that this would mean the end of their independence as tribes. If the Choctaw model could be used without the Choctaw name, McCoy felt that the ideal form of government for the Indians would have been found. His closing words show not only fine statesmanship but his saintly determination on behalf of the Indians and his great trust in the mercies of God:

> In our well grounded anticipation of the improvement of the Indians we are relieved of the painful reflection which has haunted us for more than half a century - that the original inhabitants of a quarter of the Globe will be driven out of the world by a second race of men and that too, not for want of room, but for want of care. Hitherto the history of our intercourse has been written in blood. Changed and better will be the Story hereafter. Pleasant indeed is the anticipation that the races of red and white men mutually enjoying peace, and alike accessible to the resources with which a bountiful providence has enriched our common country, shall be alike prosperous and happy!

The Wyandots and Stockbridges settle in the Indian Territory

In 1839, the incoming Wyandots were short of land so they approached the Shawnees who ceded 56,000 acres of land to them. The Shawnees were paid for their generosity by the Government. The Stockbridge Indians arrived without provisions being made for their relocation but the Delawares, who were near relations, said that the Stockbridges could live with their tribe if the Government would grant them a little more land. There were a number of Christian believers among the Stockbridge Indians so Lykins and his fellow-helpers were soon able to start up church work among them. Henry Skigget, the Delaware missionary, was able to help greatly with this work as he was the nephew of the principle Stockbridge chief.

Good news from the mission front

Skigget was a sure asset to the mission and McCoy had never understood why he was not accepted by the Board as a permanent missionary, in spite of his great zeal and success. He had journeyed to Wisconsin to meet some of his relations and McCoy had been anxious that his testimony might be put under too much duress once among his people. McCoy need not have worried. He wrote to Bolles on April 25, 1840 from Washington,

> Henry Skiggett who was patronised by you as a missionary one year, afterwards visited some of his relations in Wiskonsin Territory, known as the Stockbridge Indians. These he united with J. W. Newcom, another member of that tribe who was a baptist, in holding religious meetings. Last autumn a portion of that band emigrated to, and located within the Delaware country. Prayer and other religious exercises were duly observed on all suitable occasions as they journeyed. On their arrival several desired to be baptised, and on the eighth of March eleven were immersed.

This was not the only good news in the letter. McCoy went on to report:

> I have just received a letter from Mr. Lykins dated the 2nd inst. in which he says, "I returned yesterday from a visit to the Putawatomie and Ottawa Stations. On the last Sabbath there were baptised at the latter place, one white woman, four Ottawas and one Chippewa. At that place there is a great religious excitement. Before I left an other asked for baptism, and two others, all Indians, give evidence of conversion. Many are serious, and things appear promising for a general revival. This I know will be pleasant news to you. Sabbath before last I was with the Stockbridges, and I expect to leave tomorrow for that place again, taking the Delaware Station in my way. It seems that the Lord is visiting red people as well as the white, and missionaries should feel encouraged."[16]

---

[16] ABFMS, Reel No. 100.

Chapter Fifteen
The Break with the Board (1840-42)

A matter of great shame

Skigget and the Delaware believers were to suffer from the misconduct and ambitions of a white man who was appointed by the Board as a missionary and pastor, against the expressed opinions of McCoy, Lykins and Skigget regarding his usefulness and reputation. This matter was to bring great shame on the entire Indian Mission and cause many to leave the Indian churches on both sides of the Kansas River. It set off a scandalous chain of reactions which was to prove the end of the Foreign Mission Board's oversight of Indian missions sponsored by the Baptist churches. Ira D. Blanchard, known to have had a criminal record and to be of a most dubious character, professed Christ at the mission and was baptized. McCoy and Lykins persuaded the Board to give him a limited employment but stressed that this should not be widened to regular missionary work because of his character and reputation which only time and Christian living could change. Around 1831, after Blanchard had spent all his savings to finance the teaching work the Board gave him, McCoy and Lykins urged the Board to compensate Blanchard financially for his services. Both men over a period of ten years sent letter after letter to the Board requesting more support for Blanchard who, with Barker, was making great personal sacrifices to keep their schools running. Indeed, in a letter written January 22, 1841, McCoy accused the Board of malpractice in relation to Blanchard and Barker because they had received Government funds for the two men but had compelled them to sell off their personal assets in order to do their work, while the Board had applied the money "to other objects."[1] This must be born in mind when analyzing both Blanchard's and Barker's later negative

---

[1] Memorandum for the Board, dated January 22, 1841, McCoy Papers, Reel 10.

criticism of McCoy and Lykins, as the younger missionaries argued that McCoy and Lykins had always been against them.

Blanchard received board and lodgings at Skigget's home but soon the Indian suspected Blanchard of being too familiar with his wife. One day, he set out for a distant settlement on business for the mission and Blanchard and his wife believed he would be away for the night because of the time involved in such a journey. Skigget, however, finished his business quickly and returned back shortly after nightfall. On entering his house, he found Blanchard in a most compromising position with his wife. Blanchard was advised by friends to bring the matter quickly before the church before Skigget could undertake anything. The church listened to the would-be missionary's version of the incident and said they could find no obvious guilt. Lykins believed their verdict should have been no evidence of innocence but because of the church's findings, he did not report the matter to the Board. In his notes on the incident, Lykins adds "In this I erred."[2] Mrs. Skigget continued to be unfaithful to her husband and eventually left him to live with a white man whom neither McCoy, Lykins or anyone else names in their extant correspondence.

Blanchard finds support from Barker and Meeker

Soon afterwards, Blanchard was demanding full recognition as a missionary and even a status as pastor and preacher and strove to form a church of his own among the Delawares, splitting the church formed by Lykins and Skigget. This alienated him from the senior missionaries and many Shawnee, Potawatomi and Stockbridge Indians. However Meeker, who had been dissatisfied with the way McCoy and Lykins managed the mission's affairs, supported him. Meeker ran the Ottawa Mission but took it upon himself to monitor what was going on at Shawnee and Westport and report this to the Board. On December 3, 1841, he says he is of one mind with Barker and argued that if Blanchard were not given what he wanted, the mission could well lose him. Meeker mentions nothing of a controversial nature but also nothing that added new facts to Blanchard's case. His personal opinion voiced is that he would have opposed the motion to split the church if he had known the full facts but because the church was

---

[2] See Lykins' 37 paged account of Blanchard's misdemeanors and those missionaries who connived with him in "Undated Statements concerning a Controversy over the Shawnee Baptist Church," McCoy Papers, Reel 12.

already constituted, it would be folly to put the clock back. He gives a warm-hearted, brotherly recommendation of Blanchard as a hard working Christian and not a man with ideas of his own aggrandizement.

Meeker's unwarranted interference

Meeker ran the Ottawa Mission and was rarely present at Shawnee. Yet, in spite of his constant confession afterwards that he was not aware of the case against Blanchard or of the discord the new church had created, the overwhelming evidence shows that he took sides most strongly and strove to influence opinion against the McCoys, the Lykins family, including Johnston's brother David, and the Potawatomis and other Indians loyal to McCoy.[3] Meeker had been critical of McCoy since reading the proofs of his *History of Baptist Indian Missions*. Though he told McCoy that he heartily approved of the work and that it went out with his prayers, and signed a statement to this effect, along with Simerwell and Lykins, which was placed at the beginning of McCoy's work,[4] he withheld mention of his strong reservations. On July 25, 1837, he wrote secretly to the Board warning them that the work contained information which the Board would not like to see published. From now on, Meeker also became highly critical of Lykins' qualifications as a translator into Potawatomi and as a missionary, and gave the Board his gossipy opinions as if he were giving an official, authorized report. These are some of the factors which probably moved Meeker to ally with Blanchard against McCoy and Lykins. The fact is that Blanchard's action not only split the church and the missionary family, but it also split the once united tribes in the Shawnee vicinity and though McCoy, Lykins and their Indian friends strove for years to mend the breach caused, it proved a most difficult task indeed.[5] It was thus with great anticipation that

---

[3] The full case against Meeker, Pratt, Barker and Blanchard is presented in "Undated Statements concerning a Controversy over the Shawnee Baptist Church," McCoy Papers, Reel 12.

[4] See "Testimonials" (not paginated) as a prefix to McCoy's *History of Baptist Indian Missions*, Washington, 1840.

[5] See letter from David Lykins to Johnston Lykins dated Westport, June 2, 1844, McCoy Papers, Reel 11.

McCoy and Lykins awaited the Board's reaction to the quite scandalous events.

When the cats are away the mice will play

Meanwhile, McCoy was hardly in a position to influence the
Board at this time. He lived on the other side of the Kansas River and
was away in Washington during much of the time that Blanchard
campaigned for missionary status and for ordination. This did not
make it impossible for McCoy to mediate in these matters but by this
time the younger missionaries had rebelled against his authority and
towards the end of the controversy, he was dismissed from the Board's
services himself, a fact which will be commented on at length below.
McCoy did strive to mediate but neither the Board nor Meeker,
Blanchard, Pratt and Barker took any notice of him. Nor was Lykins
informed of what his younger missionary colleagues were planning
against him. He, too, was absent for some time, on behalf of the Board,
to secure for them a good price for property and land on the Great
Lakes which was gradually being abandoned as the Indians moved
west. The scenario was typical of the proverb, "When the cat is away,
the mice will play." Sadly, the Board now encouraged Blanchard by
referring to him as their missionary in their reports. Things came to
a head when Blanchard, supported by Barker and Meeker, in the
absence of both McCoy and Lykins, called a meeting to dismiss certain
members from the mission church so that a new church could be
formed under Blanchard as pastor. Blanchard believed that this move
would compel the Board to both accept him formally as a missionary
and give him a licence to preach. Never one to exaggerate and always
one to tone down reports of scandalous behavior, McCoy presented his
view of the matter in writing to the Board:

> When about to locate in this neighborhood
> in 1831 or 2, I found here Mr. Blanchard, who, as I was
> informed, had expressed a wish to labor in the service of the
> board, and whose services, I understood, the board had
> declined accepting, because his reputation had been de-
> stroyed by a violation of the laws of Ohio, of such a nature,
> and attended with such circumstances that it was believed
> he could not be appointed a missionary without inflicting an
> injury on the reputation of the Board and its missionaries.
> Mr. Blanchard located among the Delawares, and appeared
> pious and calculated to be useful. Mr. Lykins and I, for I
> believe there were at that time no other missionaries here,

proposed to the board the establishment of a school, etc. among the Delawares, and that Mr. Blanchard be employed as school teacher, for a given sum as compensation for his services. Not as a missionary. To this I understood the board consented. He was employed, and was baptized, the matter of his misfortune being kept in this country, as was supposed, within a confidential circle.

While I have been second to none in endeavoring to promote the happiness and the usefulness of bro. B. and in feeling great sympathy for him, and while I have conferred with him freely in endeavoring to make him useful, I have never deemed it expedient to acknowledge him as a fellow missionary, because I believed he had not survived the wreck of his reputation. We cannot, by personal favors, force public opinion out of its ordinary channels in such cases. I could not consent that my reputation as a man, as a christian, and as a missionary should suffer by its being said among the whites and among the Indians, that I had identified myself as a missionary with a man who, for the crime under consideration had served in a states prison; nor would such a sacrifice on my part have been of a particle of benefit to him. I believed that a modest unassuming manner was the only way by which he could improve his reputation, and that every step towards rendering himself conspicuous, unless it were an act of his esteemed meritorious by all would be sure to injure him. Brother Blanchard himself and some of our brethren have taken a different view of the matter. In my absence, and without my knowledge he was licenced to preach. This added nothing to his opportunities for doing good, for all of us who labor among the Indians impart religious instruction each in the way most easy to himself. The Licence was not yet written, and I entreated the clerk not to write it until positively required by the Church, & I entreated other brethren, and bro. Blanchard not to urge the writing of the Licence, assigning reasons which may be inferred from the above.

Our church, for convenience, held quarterly meetings on Mr. Blanchard's side of the Kansas river, and called church meetings there as often as was deemed necessary. On the 4th of July 1840 at Mr. Blanchard's, house, none being present, I believe, but those living on that side of the river, the church resolved that it should be requested to dismiss those who lived on that side of the river, to form a distinct church. Mr. Lykins and Mr. Barker arrived on Saturday, about the close of church business, and remained till after worship on Sunday. Mr. Barker was informed of what had taken place in regard to this matter,

461

but <u>Mr.</u> Lykins was not, and remained wholly ignorant of it. Subsequently, at a church meeting among the Ottowas when neither Mr. Lykins nor I was present, an order was taken for the dismission, etc. A few days afterwards an Indian brother accidently mentioned the fact to me. It was strange that the matter had not been mentioned to either Mr. Lykins or me, though several weeks had elapsed, and frequent opportunities had occurred for doing so both with Mr. Blanchard and Mr. Barker. Astonished at this information, and believing that Mr. Blanchard with a few Indian converts, were by no means competent to manage the affairs of an independent church, I wrote to the Indian converts requesting them to put off their constitution for a while. My most weighty reasons for delay, I chose not to state to them. I hastened to brother Blanchard and to br. Barker, and told each of them my reasons in full. <u>The Indians we all know, will agree to any thing we propose</u>, I supposed, therefore, that there was an undue desire on the part of bro. Blanchard to be independent in the management of a church, and that his ordination was designed, and I entreated bro. Barker and Bro. Blanchard for the reasons alluded to above, to defer the constitution for a while. So the matter rested until the 4th April, 1841, when, in my absence, brethren Barker & Meeker constituted them into a church.[6]

The Board must take some of the blame for this state of affairs

To be fair to Blanchard, the Board was partly to blame for this trouble in the churches. McCoy and Lykins had long complained to the Board that Blanchard was in financial difficulties, having received little from the Board and having had to spend his private fortune which had been considerable, in the service of the mission. Blanchard had been kept hard at work for little pay. On January 21, 1837, Jotham Meeker wrote to Dr. Bolles on Blanchard's behalf, explaining that Merrill, Simerwell, Rollin and himself believed that Blanchard should be made a missionary, the only reason given was that he would then receive a higher salary than the $250 dollars per annum which was his current wage. As Blanchard was officially a U. S. school teacher, the Board should have been giving him at least $350 yearly.

A higher salary, however, does not make a man either a missionary or a pastor and Lykins refused to write a letter of dismissal

---

[6] Letter from McCoy to Bolles dated August 5, 1841.

and assist in forming the new church with such a view in mind. His reasons were that the matter had been arranged contrary to Baptist practice and the wish of the whole church. Furthermore, the decision to separate was not taken before the entire church but at a branch meeting on the Osage River which had already brought strife and division among the brethren. Not only were a number of older members of the Church not present but a number of those dismissed to form a new church had strongly objected against the proceedings and were dismissed against their will. Moreover, Lykins had been appointed Supervising Agent of the Board in the entire Indian Territory under condition that he conferred with McCoy on all matters.[7] In this crucial situation, however, Lykins' advice in his capacity of Superintendent was not asked for but when it was dutifully given, it was not followed. Both parties appealed to the Board. McCoy and Lykins argued that the move would destroy the mission and injure the cause of religion. Simerwell, realizing that he was not in possession of all the details, wisely refused to take sides.

Blanchard continued to demand missionary status and insisted on being ordained in spite of the unrest he was causing. He obviously hoped that in forming his own church, he could speed up the process. In November, 1841, the Board responded to Blanchard's pleas in a letter addressed "To the Baptist Missionaries at Shawnee and vicinity." In the letter, Dr. Bolles, on behalf of the Board, refused Blanchard his wish, saying that he was doing useful work as a teacher and his previous record still stood in his way. Concerning the schismatic church he wished to bring to birth, the Board argued that there was no reason for its founding and it would cut off the Indians from their former pastors and teachers on whom they were still dependable and added "We have no hesitation in saying, that with such a church we cannot be identified."[8] Dr. Bolles went on to write, "The prospective ordination of Mr. Blanchard as an act authorised or encouraged by this board we object to." Blanchard's disabilities, Bolles continues, have always prevented the Board from approving of his becoming a missionary and pastor. In a P.S. the Corresponding Secretary of the Board states that though there is nothing which speaks against Blanchard's presence at conference meetings because of his relationship to the mission school, he must not be allowed to vote. It is clear

---

[7] McCoy Papers, letter from Dr. Bolles to Lykins dated April 6, 1831. Reel 7.

[8] Copy of letter from Bolles to the Baptist Missionaries at Shawnee dated November 4, 1841. McCoy Papers, Reel 10.

from this letter that Bolles and the Board were obviously and rightly afraid that until Blanchard gave a clear testimony that he had left his former ways, he could bring the Board into disrepute for associating with him in this way. So, that, one might have thought, was that.

The Board makes an inexplicable U-turn

It is now that the real mystery begins. After the Board had turned down Blanchard's application to be accepted as a missionary and be ordained in no uncertain terms, certain persons, who remained unnamed from the side of the Board, corresponded with them concerning McCoy and Lykins, and without their knowledge, brought accusations against the two men which again were never voiced openly. Strange as it now seems, the Board chose to accept the complaints made, whatever they might have been, and took the information offered as a justification for changing their mind and approving of Blanchard's appointment as a missionary and pastor. They neither confronted McCoy and Lykins with the charges made against them, nor even informed them concerning who their critics were.[9]

A few written primary and secondary documents containing complaints have come to light in God's providence, both from Lykins and those who testified against him. The letters which came directly from Blanchard and Barker have not been preserved but many a conversation with them was reported by others and they were quoted in several church meetings recorded in the McCoy Manuscripts, Reel 12. Nothing which one might think could have produced such a U-turn on the part of the Board is on record anywhere but a great deal which ought to have spoken against it. It would be astonishing indeed if the Board had been willing to accept the unfounded and often ridiculous complaints against McCoy and Lykins which are preserved in the Board's files and in the McCoy Papers.[10] It would be a more astonishing thought to believe that the Board accepted them without question

---

[9] ABFMS, Reel No. 100. Memorandum for the Board, dated January 22, 1841 McCoy Collection, Reel 10. Letter from McCoy to Bolles dated August 5, 1841, McCoy Collection, Reel 10. Letter from Bolles to the Baptist Missionaries at Shawnee dated November 4, 1841, McCoy Collection, Reel 10. There were "sentiments" expressed in the work which the Board would not wish to see made public. See ABFMS, Reel 100.

[10] See especially Reel 12's section on the "Undated Statements concerning a Controversy over the Shawnee Baptist Church."

and never gave McCoy and Lykins an opportunity to defend themselves. This, however, is what appears to have happened. The Board's obvious practice of accepting the criticism of younger men who clearly wished to take over the authority and even the houses of the older missionaries and ignoring the experienced opinion of the senior missionaries is also open to serious question. A direct parallel is found in the case of Evan Jones, missionary to the Cherokees, when the Board aided and abetted younger missionary colleagues who wished to take over Jones' responsibilities.[11]

The McCoys are dismissed from the Board's service

The fact that the Board felt they no longer had a duty to listen to their senior missionary and one of their earliest promoters and supporters was because of a most extraordinary move on their part. At the height of the differences caused by Blanchard's action, the Board decided to dismiss both Mr. and Mrs. McCoy in the most deceitful manner imaginable. They were given no notice to leave, nor advice to resign and the fact that they were dismissed was not communicated to them personally. Instead, they read in the *American Baptist Magazine* for June 1841 that, although they had been missionaries previous to 1830, since that year they had been in the employment of the U. S. Government and were not missionaries under the Board's patronage. The gist of the article was that though McCoy still had the welfare of the Indians at heart, it was a purely the secular feeling of one holding a civil office and one who performed Government duties. The Board had thus not only fired McCoy, they had back-dated his dismissal to over a decade earlier.

Immediately on reading the article McCoy wrote to the Board asking if this was a "mistake" as it had been in the similar report of 1833. Four months later the Corresponding Secretary wrote to say it was not a mistake and there had been a "virtual and silent agreement" all along between the two parties recognizing that McCoy was not under the Board's patronage. Explaining matters to David Benedict on February 11, 1842, McCoy told him that in the Board's reply he was told that measures were being taken to prevent him associating with the few missionaries left in the mission. He confessed that the Board's

---

[11] See William McLoughlin's masterly handling of this situation in his *Champions of the Cherokees: Evan and John B. Jones,* especially the chapter "Evan Jones in Defeat."

public dismissal of him had caused him "a good deal of trouble."[12] He was referring to the fact that as the Board had not only publicly disowned McCoy but also maintained that he had not been in the Boards service for over a decade, the Government were now asking themselves why they had been dealing with him as the Board's agent and entrusting almost the whole business of Indian improvement into his hands. Thus McCoy was to receive the inevitable letter signed by Hartley Crawford at the Office of Indian Affairs, Department of War, saying:

> Sir,
>
> I am directed by the Secretary of War to inform you that the reasons which induced his predecessor to confide certain special duties to you have ceased - and that on the receipt hereof you will consider that your further services are dispensed with.[13]

McCoy asks the Board to justify their action

McCoy knew that he was called to serve the Indians as a Christian, a minister and a missionary and he asks the Board in a further extremely long letter how they could possibly justify such a reputation-ruining accusation. McCoy wanted to know why the Board, if they had considered him dismissed from their services as a missionary for eleven years, had addressed him as such and treated him as being under their patronage all that time? When did they actually dismiss him and for what reasons? He explained that the fact that he had canvassed so much support for the Board via the Government was hardly a cause for the Board to dismiss him, especially as he had been appointed by the Board as their agent not only to the Indians but also to the Government. McCoy quoted from letters dating back to the late twenties in which the Board had authorized him in their name to work closely with the Government, especially in relation to the settling of Indians west of the Mississippi.

The Board, too, knew that McCoy had rejected very lucrative Government posts because they would have interfered with his

---

[12] McCoy Papers, Reel 10. McCoy underlined the word "few".

[13] McCoy Papers, Reel 10.

missionary work. They also knew that McCoy's work for the Government, within the bounds authorized by the Board, had enabled the Board to build up and finance a large part of their work. Also, lands and property which had come the mission's way through McCoy's intervention had been signed over to the Board at no profit whatsoever to McCoy. Furthermore, McCoy had been the founder and often the sole money-raiser of every single Baptist mission station under the patronage of the Board except O'Bryant's and Valley Towns missions. Even the way the Board described McCoy's present association in the *American Baptist Magazine* article was totally incorrect. The reason given for the McCoys' dismissal was that they had been working with the Government in "recent years." Actually, Mrs. McCoy had never held Government responsibilities at any time and McCoy had less connection now with the Government than he had before 1830, during the time the Board said they had considered him a missionary. "Astonishment is still further heightened," says McCoy, "when we reflect that in accepting the business for which we are excluded from your connection, I acted under your express authority!" Furthermore, McCoy asks the Board why they had authorized him to work with the Government, and repeatedly consented to and approved of this move, without telling him they were considering this to be his dismissal? As they had also stressed that his duties for the Government were "compatible with the character and designs of the mission," this was even more of a puzzle. To cap his argument, McCoy referred to the fact that he had expressly written to the Board in 1833 on reading then that he was no longer considered a missionary and the Corresponding Secretary, Dr. Bolles had apologized "promptly and affectionately" for the mistake, saying that it was "an oversight" for which he "could not account" and he put the matter right in the September issue of the *American Baptist Magazine*. Spencer Cone, a member of the Board and close friend of McCoy's, had also written to McCoy, informing him that the reference to his not being a missionary was a mistake. If McCoy were thus so affectionately declared to be a missionary in 1833 by the Corresponding Secretary of the Board, it was most strange, McCoy argued, that he was now supposed not to have been a missionary since 1830. Then McCoy goes on to quote references from the Board in subsequent years which refer to him as being a missionary in the employment of the Board. Such we will remain, says McCoy of himself and his wife, as long as their tongues can pronounce the name of Jesus to an Indian. McCoy closes by saying:

Brethren, I respectfully appeal to you to rectify whatever appears wrong by a prayerful examination of
the foregoing remarks. If the connexion between us is undesirable, you have had abundant evidence of my wishes in
that respect - let us part - But it is due to Christian candor
to inform you that I shall not be driven from my work and
the field of my labor until an appeal to the justice, the kindness, and the benevolence of our denomination has been
rejected - Then, when we can do no more to prevent it, we
must leave these dear people, by whom for twenty three
years we have been usually addressed by the affectionate
appellations of 'father' and 'Mother,' and who have occupied a place in our affections and solicitude by the side of
our own dear offspring. The greater part of the latter have
been taken to Heaven. O that we could indulge hopes of
similar blessedness for a larger portion of our red children!
But I predict that these gloomy apprehen-
sions will not be realised. I trust that your own goodness
and prudence will produce a happier result; if in this I
should be mistaken, I feel confident that the views of the
General Board will.
May the Lord direct you, & take care of us! Amen.
Isaac McCoy.[14]

Board members Cone and Lincoln had no part in the dismissal

The day after McCoy penned these words, Spencer Cone dispatched a letter to him expressing his surprise and grief on hearing
the news that McCoy had been "dropped from the list of missionaries."
Though Cone was a member of the Board, he had known nothing of
such a decision, nor who had made it. He explained to McCoy that on
hearing the news, he had immediately written to Heman Lincoln and
the two Secretaries[15] requesting an explanation but, though time
enough had elapsed, he had received no reply. Obviously greatly embarrassed at what was going on, Cone said that the Board were doing
nothing more for the Indians because of lack of funds.[16] They had

---

[14] McCoy to Bolles dated January 6, 1842, ABFMS, Reel 100.

[15] The Board had recently moved the Indian mission from the concern of the
Corresponding Secretary and Home Secretary to that of the Foreign Secretary, so Cone wrote to the latter two for information concerning McCoy's
past and present relation to the Board.

[16] Letter dated January 7, 1842, McCoy Papers, Reel 10.

recently asked him to cover debts for them which they had accrued to the tune of $20,000, requesting that he should use his own personal savings to help them. A month later, Heman Lincoln, the Board's treasurer wrote to McCoy from Washington, without mentioning that Cone had written to him without his replying. Professing to have had no part in McCoy's dismissal he confessed mysteriously that he could not give McCoy further details.[17] It appears that the Board's ruling to dismiss McCoy was far from a majority decision which, again, was quite contrary to usual sound Baptist procedure. Wishing to show solidarity with McCoy, Lincoln signed himself off with the words, "With kindest regards to Mrs. McCoy and our other *missionary friends*." Yet these words merely pressed home the fact to McCoy that the Board whom Lincoln represented had removed that status from both him and his wife.

The sheer hypocrisy of the Baptist Board

In view of the Board's quite scandalous negligence in keeping the mission's books, it was sheer hypocrisy on their part to set a question mark against his missionary calling in this way. Indeed, the Board's behavior was totally counter-productive to the missionary call. They were rapidly bringing the entire Shawnee Mission work to a standstill and had created confusion and disorder in the Indian missions as a whole. The work of the mission which McCoy had started in 1817 and which had been staunchly supported by Lykins for 20 years now lay in ruins. It seemed, indeed, as if the Board were truly intent on making an end of McCoy's life's work.

Arguments against McCoy and Lykins reviewed

A brief look at the arguments against McCoy and Lykins in the Blanchard affair reveals nothing that resembles the true situation at the Shawnee Mission in any way. Lykins wrote in his journal at this time how a white man who lived among the Delawares told him that it was rumored that he (Lykins) had turned against the mission, that he had handed over all management of it to others and that Mrs. McCoy had become anti-Indian and anti-missions and was striving to sell off the Shawnee Station for personal profit. A Mr. B. (Blanchard?)

---

[17] Letter dated February 10, 1842, McCoy Papers, Reel 10.

was allegedly telling tales of McCoy's supposed negative attitude to Barker. Some Shawnees came to Lykins in astonishment on hearing a rumor spread that the Board had dismissed McCoy for "unfaithfulness" and that Lykins had been ordered by the Board to leave the station but he refused to do so. McCoy was supposedly forming an organization to oppose the Board. It became usual for Lykins' critics at this time to also refer negatively to McCoy, knowing that Lykins was his closest friend and McCoy's son-in-law. The rumors concerning Lykins' removal from the district were probably based on a twisting of the fact that his wife, Delilah, showed all the symptoms of the illness that had brought on the death of ten of her brothers and sisters and Lykins was wondering whether they should seek out an area to live in more suitable to Mrs. McCoy's impaired health.

A letter from two Delaware Indians written to the Board[18] has been preserved which is typical of the kind of vague accusations which were leveled against Lykins. The entire first page is full of pious utterances which have nothing to do with the topic at hand, yet the second page is full of gossip about something not being "quite right" with Lykins because of his relationships with Blanchard with not a shred of solid evidence being given. Under the two signatures, the writers placed a bold P. S. with a note that, "the majority of the native brethren are of the same opinion with us in the above statement of facts." Actually, the majority of the Indian brethren were voting to complain about Blanchard and his new church at the time as witnessed below. On the third page the letters P. S. occur again, this time in a greatly exaggerated size as if introducing something of great importance. The note states, rather contradicting what has already been said about Lykins alienating the Indians, that Lykins is fraternizing too closely with the Stockbridge brethren (i.e. Skigget's tribe).[19] This is followed again by the two signatures. At some distance under these there is an N.B. giving information which might have indicated, for the first time in the document, a just ground for criticism. The two Delawares write: "We must further inform you, our Fathers of the Board, that the said Lykins generally sustains the performance of slave labour in his house." Here would have been room for the Board's criticism, if true, as they were now taking an anti-slavery position, but they never looked into this matter and no alleged proof for this

---

[18] Dated June 15, 1842, ABFMS, Reel 99.

[19] The Stockbridge Indians refused to continue fellowship with Blanchard, Meeker, Pratt and Barker. See "Undated Statements concerning a Controversy over the Shawnee Baptist Church," McCoy Papers, Reel 12.

statement was ever given. Actually, the reference could only be to Jesse Cox who was a freed slave and a student and to the Indian members of the wider mission family who helped with the catering and feeding of the needy.

The constitution of Blanchard's Delaware church was quite contrary to Baptist principles

Obviously the founding of the Delaware church was entirely irregular from a Baptist point of view. It was arranged in a private meeting between the younger missionaries with no Indians present or even invited. Immediately after its constitution serious troubles started. The Methodists had excommunicated a number of members for the gravest of sins yet Blanchard accepted them with open arms and immediately gave them full membership in his new church in order to build up the membership. Thus good living Indian Christians who strove to live pleasing to the Lord, were now flanked by liars, drunkards, extortioners, thieves, fornicators, adulterers and sexual perverts. A relatively large number thus began to leave Blanchard's and the sister churches. The Potawatomi church was now so shocked at what was going on in the new church that they recorded their disapproval in a church meeting, saying:

> Resolved, that this branch of the Potawatomie Baptist Mission Church, composed of Stockbridge brethren who have resolved to abide by the original constitution of the said church cannot be affected by any act of the so called church at Delaware, or by the acts of that part of the church, which meet at the Shawnee Baptist Mission Station.
>
> Resolved, that brethren Barker, Pratt[20] and others, in receiving members for baptism in the face of objections on the part of other brethren were in gross disorder and being in disorder, <u>cannot</u> be recognised by us as members in good standing.

---

[20] Pratt had further angered the Indians by taking advantage of Lykins' absence on the Board's business to change the time of the traditional Saturday evening meeting to a morning one without informing them. From the mission post at this time, it appears that changing times and venues became a mark of the younger missionaries aim at reforming the station. It caused, however, much confusion and bad feeling. See Delilah Lykins' letter to her husband dated March 21, 1842, McCoy Papers, Reel 10.

> Resolved, that until disorders of which we complain, in the so called church at Delaware, and among brethren implicated at Shawnee are settled properly, that we cannot recognise any committee sent by either of them to labour with us.[21]

The Potawatomi church thwarted the Board's wishes by electing David Lykins, who stood in no relationship of employment to the Board, as their new Moderator and Henry Skigget, whom the Board had dismissed from their services, as their Clerk.[22]

Blanchard's scandalous methods of obtaining new members reaps Methodist protests

The interchurch disciplinary measures taken against Blanchard's separatist action, resulted sadly in the innocent members of the Shawnee and Delaware churches being punished with the guilty and there was a marked decline in the mission work in the entire Westport-Shawnee area. McCoy and Lykins had always maintained that the Methodists were too lax in admitting new members. Now the Methodists and the Quakers were protesting strongly against the Baptists having no standards at all. Holding Lykins responsible for the state of affairs, William Johnson the Methodist Mission Superintendent and Luther Carter who was Secretary of the Methodist Conference, wrote letters of protest to him, saying that unless the Baptists ceased to baptize Methodists who were under discipline for lying, theft, drunkenness etc., they would take the matter to "the proper authorities for redress."[23]

Simerwell organizes a church disciplinary council

Church after church and denomination after denomination

---

[21] McCoy Papers, "Undated Statements," Reel 12.

[22] See also letter thought to be written January 13, 1844 which records Meeker, Barker and Pratt being reprimanded by the Potawatomi church. See also letter dated January 13, 1844 signed by David Lykins, McCoy Papers, Reel 11.

[23] Letter from Delilah Lykins to her husband dated March 21, 1842. McCoy Papers, Reel 10.

began to condemn Blanchard and his separatists. Finally, Simerwell intervened and organized a council of sister Baptist churches, calling upon all parties in the controversy to submit themselves to the ruling of the churches.[24] This was in the interest of Simerwell almost as much as Lykins because Blanchard, Barker, Meeker and Pratt had slighted him by not taking him into their confidence or seeking his help in sending off their various complaints to the Board. Some had thus associated him with the rebel missionaries. Sadly, while Simerwell sought peace, Meeker interfered, passing on gossip concerning the two parties that Simerwell was trying to draw together. Indeed, Meeker became such a gossip-monger, pitting the two sides against each other but never grasping the roots of the matter, that he caused far more difficulties for himself and others than if he had remained quiet.[25] Simerwell obviously thought that it would be best to have Lykins and Barker speaking to one another and clearing the matter up before the churches but Meeker wanted certain matters cleared up before the council of churches sat. Meeker was a good man but something of a busy body and this was one of several occasions where his interference worsened a bad situation. Perhaps Meeker was annoyed that the Potawatomi church had asked David Lykins and Henry Skigget to organize the council and sent Indian delegates to the Ottawas and the Osages, inviting them to send delegates which Meeker may well have interpreted as going behind his authority. Meeker had, however received a formal, personal invitation from Simerwell.[26]

Blanchard and his allies condemned by the church council

The churches met and condemned Blanchard's move, though the council maintained that the church could not now be disbanded. The missionaries who had written the secret letter of complaint against Lykins to the Board were censured, as was their act in neglecting to invite Simerwell to discuss the letter with them. The fact that Blanchard baptized and shared the Lord's Supper with people

---

[24] See Simerwell's letter to Barker dated October 14, 1843, McCoy Papers, Reel 11.

[25] See Simerwell's letter to Meeker dated October 9, 1843, McCoy Papers, Reel 11.

[26] See letter from David Lykins and Henry Skigget to McCoy, dated November 13, 1843, McCoy Papers, Reel 11.

who had been objected to by church members before baptism was also condemned.[27] Barker, Meeker and Pratt refused both to cooperate with the council and to accept its decisions. But now Lykins was clearly exonerated. Indirectly, the council also exonerated Simerwell by showing that he had not collaborated with the dissidents. Meeker's situation was now most embarrassing for him as he realized that he had acted in support of Blanchard without due consideration of the facts involved. He continued to work hard among the Ottawas but the work among the Potawatomis, Shawnees and Stockbridges was carried out almost entirely by Simerwell and Skigget for some time, in the face of the Board's obvious displeasure but the work had to be kept up. It was not long before the Board dismissed Simerwell too. Skigget, they merely ignored.

The Board ignore evidence in McCoy's and Lykins' defense

All this reflected very negatively on the Board as they had known very well all along what was happening and had, indeed, orchestrated it to a large extent. Apart from Lykins' explanatory letters, they had received report after report from other churches on Lykins' behalf and also pleas for fairness to be shown to Lykins from the other denominations who were engaged in Indian missions. As early as September 5, 1842 they had received a lengthy letter from Shawnee Baptist Christians through an interpreter with a statement by Chief George William annexed to it. William explained that he was a Quaker but knew the writers of the letter to be good men and Christians and that what they said in defense of Lykins was true. The writers stated that because they had hoped that their present troubles would quickly disappear, they had not approached the Board, but the situation was still so bad that they thought they must give the Board information which was obviously not yet in their possession. After outlining what Lykins had done for the Indians and how the Shawnees would not think of parting with him as their missionary and friend, they requested that everything possible must be done to keep Lykins at the mission. In particular, the Indians praised Lykins' pastoral work and the fact that he had given them the Scriptures in their own language. The men emphasized that in actual fact, their church had been increasing swiftly through Lykins' ministry and that he was

---

[27] An undated copy of these findings (copied November 8, 1845) can be found on Reel 11 of the McCoy Papers.

always on call when they were ill and went to great trouble to care for them.

The Indians go on to remind the Board that when they moved to the Indian Territory, Lykins had gone before them and worked alone under incredible difficulties to prepare for their arrival. This needed to be brought again to the Board's memory as they had received huge sums of money from the Government when Carey and Thomas were disbanded so that they could buy land and erect buildings in the Indian Territory. In 1831, Lykins was left totally unsupported by the Board who refused to provide him with a penny to buy land for the mission. He thus had to pay $175 for the 140 acres of land out of his own pocket. Lykins soon found out that the Board would not even part with the money entrusted to them by the Government for buildings either, and he had to erect those at his own expense and through personal loans and money he was able to raise through friends. From this period alone, the Board still owed Lykins some $1,500.[28]

The Indians explained that Mr. Pratt refused at times to take part in their worship, instancing one meeting when Lykins baptized six believers. Sadly, it was Pratt who refused to give Lykins access to the printing machine so that he could print and distribute his translations on which the Indian Christians were dependent for their worship.[29] The Shawnees also told how they had met regularly for

---

[28] See Lykins' Memorandum of December 10, 1842 for full details of Lykins' expenses at the Shawnee Mission Station.

[29] Meeker's expressed versions of Lykins' relationship with Pratt changed over the years. Though he formerly made neutral comments about them both, after McCoy's dismissal and Lykins' resignation, he became more critical of Lykins especially in relationship to printing Lykins' Potawatomi translation. After first accepting it, he later said that he had examined it with an Indian and found it full of mistakes. However, Meeker knew far less of the Potawatomi language than Lykins but, comparing it with similar Indian languages, concluded that it was full of typographical errors. Meeker, however, used a proof sheet that Lykins himself had rejected and Lykins used several letter signs in his Potawatomi that Meeker did not use in his translations for the Ottawas. This was not a comparison based on sound linguistic principles, to say the least. See letter written by Meeker to Allen, January 22, 1845. There is a modern defense (Autumn, 1998) of Johnston Lykins' system which the author downloaded from the Internet under pbp_ortho_lykins.html. Potawatomi Prairie Band Home Page. The Potawatomi Prairie Band are, at the time of writing, offering language courses

worship at Lykins' house but Barker had told them that these meetings were now to be held in his home. On arriving for the meeting at Barker's, the Indians were disappointed to find that Lykins was not there. On making enquiries, they discovered that the whole idea had been Barker's to force people away from Lykins' ministry. They stated that Lykins had told Barker it was wrong of him to set up a rival meeting at the same time for the same group but Barker had ignored him and had led the Indians to believe that Lykins' meetings had been put under his leadership. A further cause for concern was that Barker held church meetings without the knowledge of the members, yet at which non-members were present. These were later baptized against the express will of the church members, thus going against the church constitution. According to the Indians, it was apparent that Barker felt he had the Board's backing for such practices. They also said that a bone of contention was Barker's paying a man $50 to persuade people to join his side.

Another cause for alarm was that the interpreter whom Lykins had used successfully for many years had left because Barker and his friends were causing too much disharmony. They were unable to understand the interpreter whom Barker had engaged and the missionary had printed papers translated by the new interpreter that were incomprehensible.[30] The signatories of the letter then demanded that the Board take disciplinary measures against Pratt and Barker and insisted that if they would not, the church would see that justice was done as the present confusion and bad state of affairs could not be allowed to continue.

Arguments such as these apparently left the Board cold. The negative reasons which they felt outweighed all the positive ones were given in a letter written by the Blanchard-Barker-Pratt faction which was never disclosed to Lykins and neither laid before the church, nor the council of churches. Therefore, Lykins, the Shawnee church members and the council were completely in their right to judge the action of their critics to be illegal, non-Christian and totally against Baptist practice. Yet, when the Board at last sent an investigator, Joel S. Bacone, to the mission to look into the matter Lykins was not invited to

---

(cont.) based on Lykins' system, which they hold to be the best. See also McCoy's notes on liberties Pratt took with Lykins' work, March 2, 1842 and also Pratt's treatment of Lykins outlined in Lykins' letter to McCoy of December 8, 1842, McCoy Papers, Reel 10.

[30] This is one of the reasons why Pratt and Barker refused Lykins access to the printing press.

take part in the meeting and was not given the slightest chance to defend himself. Bacone merely consulted with the informers against McCoy and Lykins.

The Board's extraordinary conduct against Lykins

It is against such a background that one can understand how suspicious the Shawnee Christians were of the Board's policy at a time when it would have been to the benefit of the Baptist denomination to remain on very good terms with them. Shortly before these difficulties commenced, and the tempers of the Methodists were raised at the scandalous practices going on in the new Delaware church, the Wyandots, who were backed by the Methodists, had approached the Shawnees with a view to buying up a three mile wide strip of land for their own settlement. Lykins, after making enquiries, had found that the Shawnees had agreed to sell land which included the Shawnee Mission. This could have meant the end of the Baptist witness in the area when the sale took place in 1839. If the Baptists had not been shown the door then, the Methodists would certainly have found good reason to expel the Baptists now because of their anger at what was going on. Lykins, however, had made such an action almost impossible. When he heard of the transaction in the winter of 1838-9, he had quickly contacted Richard W. Cummins of the Northern Agency of the Western Territory at Fort Leavenworth and the Secretary of War, requesting them to protect the legal rights of the Baptist Mission, whatever the outcome of the sale, and had been successful in his endeavors. Thanks chiefly to Lykins' intervention[31] the Shawnee Mission was saved from a Methodist takeover. Yet, now the Board, instead of viewing Lykins with a thankful heart, were treating him as a leper. Furthermore, the Shawnees had finalized their business with the Wyandots, in keeping with the Government's wish, on the basis that the Baptist Board would keep its rights to the mission, which was now, one could say, in Methodist country. The Board was thus greatly in the debt of the Shawnees. This action alone should have caused the Board to lend a sympathetic ear to the Shawnee grievances but instead, they turned a deaf ear to them.

Thus only three months after stating dogmatically that

---

[31] See Lykin's letter dated January 28, 1839 in which he explains the proposed sale of land to McCoy and tells of his action to protect the mission. McCoy Papers, Reel 10.

Blanchard should neither be ordained nor be made a missionary, the Board not only made him a missionary and gave him a license to preach but gave their blessing to the new church that he had formed.[32] This was an act totally contrary to Baptist practice as the Board had no church jurisdiction over the Shawnee Station churches. Furthermore, Lykins, the Mission's General Superintendent, pastor and clerk of the church which was to be split, had refused to dismiss those seeking separation as no satisfactory grounds were given. Also the highly irregular move meant constituting a church consisting solely of relatively new converts and the unbaptized, all Indians, under the care of a white man whose reputation was far from good and who preached through an interpreter of dubious skills.

Further extraordinary behavior by the Board

At the same time as their resolutions concerning Blanchard as a missionary and pastor, the Board did a further extraordinary thing. In their annual report for 1842, they stated that Lykins, Meeker and Barker were teachers and not missionaries. This resulted in the strange situation of a teacher, Blanchard, of dubious morals, being "promoted" to missionary status and experienced missionaries such as the McCoys, Lykins and Meeker being either dismissed or "demoted" to being merely teachers. The Board had not only made a U-turn, they were now striving to turn the whole missionary station upside down! This meant, of course, that as they were no longer considered missionaries, the Board no longer considered themselves responsible for supporting the McCoys, the Lykins, the Meekers or the Barkers. As the Board stated that Simerwell had resigned his post - although Simerwell knew nothing of his alleged resignation - it seemed that the Board were washing their hands of any responsibility to him, too. They were, in fact, closing the Indian Mission down.

This new move of the Board illustrates the almost unbelievable state of the organizational chaos and low spiritual condition that dominated their policies. There was no doubt whatsoever that Lykins had been formally accepted as a missionary by the Board as is witnessed by Lykins' official appointment signed by Dr. Lucius Bolles on April 6, 1831 which states:

---

[32] See letter from Peck to the Shawnee missionaries, February 1, 1842. See also Delilah Lykins' comments on the U-turn in her letter to her husband dated March 21, 1842, McCoy Papers, Reel 10.

> Voted, That Mr. Lykins be appointed as a missionary to Shawanoe town with instructions to preach and otherwise promote the spiritual welfare of the Indians at and near that place.[33]

The fact was that the Board was in such confusion over the status and financing of their missionaries that they were obviously prepared to call them missionaries one day, and teachers another, according to how they envisaged funds might be raised to finance them. The Board was now under new management and letters sent by McCoy and Lykins to Bolles were answered by a new Corresponding Secretary named Solomon Peck who turned out to be a hardliner indeed. Early in 1842, Peck wrote to Lykins demanding more detailed reports from him as if indicating that Lykins was not being conscientious enough.[34] However, Peck revealed his own negligence in saying that he had misplaced Lykins last report on Potawatomi improvement and that he was "obliged to request a duplicate copy." Lykins responded by sending in several excellent hour by hour reports of his missionary activities among the Indians, including his work in translating the Scriptures. The reports show that a real work of God was going on and a dedicated and skilled missionary was at work. On June 14, of that year, however, Lykins received a further bossy letter from Solomon Peck telling him that he had been neglecting his duties as "a school teacher under the U. S. government" and could no longer be considered such. Lykins, quite shocked and surprised, pointed out in his reply that he was employed by the Board as a missionary, not as a teacher, and that he had not served as "a school teacher under the U. S. Government" since moving west over ten years previously. Lykins also defended Simerwell, whom the possibly misinformed Peck alleged had resigned from his post as a U. S. school teacher, explaining that Simerwell had not held such an appointment since entering the Indian Territory either and that his colleague had certainly not resigned from a post that he did not hold.[35]

Peck confessed that his reasons for believing that Lykins had not been fulfilling his duties adequately were based solely on reports made by Lykins' fellow missionaries. No missionary at Shawnee and the dependent stations had the authority to make such reports con-

---

[33] McCoy Papers, Reel 7.

[34] Letter dated March 5, 1842, McCoy Papers, Reel 10.

[35] See Lykins letter to Peck dated August 3, 1842 (given as August 5 in Roustio, p. 105), ABFMS, Reel 99.

cerning their senior missionary. Obviously, if Peck had received formal complaints from the mission stations, he should have brought them not only before Lykins for comment ,but also placed them before the entire missionary family and the church elders or disciplinary committee. The least he could have done was to write to Lykins, stating the charges made against him and giving him a chance to defend himself before the Board made any final judgement. Peck took none of these steps, acting again contrary to normal Baptist policy, and one could also say, normal Christian practice. Thus we find Lykins asking Peck to inform him precisely about who had said what about him. Protesting that colleagues should not tell tales in secret about one another, Lykins tells Peck, "No disqualification of a missionary can exceed that of a disposition to employ secret communications, for the purpose of destroying older missionaries to make room for themselves."

The extraordinary state of affairs which now dominated the Shawnee Mission scene was that the only missionaries accepted by the Board uncritically on both sides of the Kansas River were Blanchard and Pratt, both of whom had now personal axes to grind with Lykins merely because of his superior position as founder and superintendent of the mission.

McCoy admonishes the Board

Meanwhile, McCoy's relationship with the Board was really reaching a breaking point. He felt their procrastination and unwillingness to play a major role in saving the Indians from extinction and saving their souls was counter productive to the cause of the gospel. His words in his journal for July 4, 1837 summed up his thoughts which he had had since he entered into missionary service as a co-worker with the Board. "The Board have scarcely ever moved a step in Indian missions only as they have been either dragged, coaxed, or scared along." McCoy had long realized that the Board was no longer, if ever, committed whole-heartedly to Indian missions. There had been a marked improvement in their outreach, between 1825 to 1832 but now it seemed as if the Board had turned its back fully on the work McCoy, Posey and Jones had brought into existence. Indeed, the more the Board received money for the support of the mission land, buildings, schools and other so called "Indian improvements," chiefly through Government aid, the more the Board began to reduce their financing of Indian missions. By 1836-7 the work had been reduced by half and a number of mission stations had closed down. Facts relating to these events had not been disclosed by the Board. Looking back, McCoy summed up the situation in a letter to Dr. Bolles dated January 6, 1842:

You are aware that ever since a short time after the Actg. Board became located in Boston in 1826, I have supposed that there was a great want of efficiency on the part of the Board in this department of their labours. For a while after, we began to work within the Indian Territory west of the States of Missouri and Arkansas, especially after about 1831, the management of the Board appeared to be more encouraging than before. Missionaries and stations multiplied. But since about 1837 or 1838 there has been a diminishing of about one half. This decrease is so alarming as to induce apprehensions that, unless the retrogression in missionary operations can be arrested, our denomination will soon scarcely be known in this mission field. Five missionaries were labouring among the Choctaws at as many places. *Viz.* Rev. R. D. Potts at Providence Station and near him Rev. Mr. Hatch, who though perhaps engaged only by Mr. Potts was esteemed by others as well as himself, a coadjutor in missionary labours; Dr. A. Allen at Bethel Station, Rev. C. Tucker at Bethlehem Station, and Rev. Joseph Smedley at Choctaw Agency. At this time we have only one missionary amongst Choctaws. Among the Creeks we have two stations and a church of nearly one hundred members; at this time we have not one missionary in the Creek nation, and the church is destitute of pastoral help. Rev. D. O'Bryant removed with a church from the east of the Mississippi to those on the west This station and church was abandoned in about 1825-6. This catastrophe is now less felt than some others because other missionaries among the Cherokee have, with their flock, been transferred from the east to the west side of the Mississippi. The station among the Omaha has been abandoned. The station among the Otoes is unoccupied. A little over a year ago you appointed a missionary to this station, but up to the last advices from him, he had not yet occupied the mission premises, and if I am rightly informed, he stated to the Board not long since, in substance, that without some further action of the Board to sustain him, he could do nothing. If he should persevere under existing circumstances be happily disappointed.

We discover therefore the following places at which our missionaries have been labouring now destitute, viz. four places amongst the Choctaws, two among the Creeks, one among the Cherokees, one among the Omahas, and one among the Otoes, in all nine, unless one except that among the Cherokees, and the one among the Otoes.[36]

The Board dismisses their only Indian pastor

McCoy was particularly upset about the state of the Creek church which he had assisted in founding in 1832. John Davis had proved a most valuable asset to the Indian Mission and he had stood firm against much persecution from his own tribe who still practiced torture and whipping of those who professed the Christian faith. McCoy had just learned to his utter dismay that Davis had been first abandoned, then dismissed as a pastor-missionary by the Board two years previously. Rumors reached McCoy that Davis was now the laughing stock of the Creeks and very distressed. One Indian source told McCoy that Davis had even turned to strong drink. On hearing the news, McCoy demanded the facts from the Board and also that they should restore and continue to support such a valuable and gifted Christian worker.[37]

Further accusations against the Board from McCoy's pen

Continuing throughout the thirty-seven pages of the letter, McCoy goes through the history of the Indian Mission, showing how, through efforts of those such as himself, land had been bought, buildings set up and hired labor paid without any cost to the Board apart from their basic rates for the upkeep of missionaries. Yet it was the Board who received the title to this property. He reminded the Board that though they had not invested any money in the Carey property, $5,721.50 was paid to them when the station as transferred

---

[36] McCoy Papers, Reel 10.

[37] A hint of what probably happened to Davis is found in Solomon Peck's superintended account of the Indian Mission in *History of American Missions to the Heathen*, p. 552. Writing 1839-40 he refers to Davis in one short sentence, "Mr. Davis is now government teacher at the North Fork station." It was custom for the Board, whenever they felt that they could not support a missionary, to redefine that person as a teacher and thus dismiss him unilaterally from their service on the grounds that teachers were a Government responsibility. Nearly all the Indian missionaries had to suffer at one time or other with this stratagem of the Board's.

west and that the value of the Thomas property to which the Board was given the title, was vastly more than that of Carey because of the rise in land prices after the treaty with the Ottawas of 1836. He reminds the Board that these are not the only sums which have been placed in the hands of the Board through the work of the missionaries but that the Board received further grants of no less than $4,000 per annum for educational purposes related to Indian improvement. Yet McCoy and his fellow missionaries could not establish schools for the Potawatomis and Delawares because they were told that no funds were available and the Shawnee school was scarcely supported. When the missionaries asked McCoy to work out the Board's sums and show them what money they must have in reserve, the Board, at first, ignored them. When put under further pressure to open their books to the missionaries, they said that the missionaries were mistaken. When the missionaries forwarded proof via McCoy that they were far from being mistaken, the Board merely replied that they had no time to consider the matter.

McCoy continually refers to the fact in his letter that the Board had left the Shawnee Mission in great debt and that the Board had not paid a penny to relieve the mission of these debts and had even forbidden the missionaries to make them public. In point of fact, they had kept their common treasury closed to the Indian Mission for many years, in spite of large amounts of money being put into that treasury. This meant that the burden of financing the mission over a long period of time had been almost entirely left in the hands of the missionaries with not only no support from the Board but with their total opposition to missionaries seeking church and public donations. Ramsey Potts, the former missionary to the Potawatomis and now missionary to the Choctaws, told McCoy in 1841 that since becoming a missionary to the Indians in 1827, he had received but $110 from his denomination and that was not from the Board but a Cincinnati church. In fact, he had written to the Board regularly for two years without receiving a single answer.[38] McCoy even accuses the Board of trying to persuade the Government to give them a free hand in using their grants which were really for Indian improvement. The Board were not only tight-fisted in money matters, though money was available, they also showed their reluctance to foster Indian missions by their attitude to missionary candidates. In recent years, a number of well-qualified men had applied to the Board to become missionaries to the Indians but they were either rejected or their applications ignored.

---

[38] Letter dated November 8, 1841, McCoy Papers, Reel 10.

Merrill badly needed help with his work among the Otoes and found a most suitable man in William Allis, who had been called to the Indian mission field through an article by Isaac McCoy. Allis wrote to McCoy:

> As ignorant as I am I feel as if I could be of some use in pointing the poor Indian to the Lamb of God that taketh away the sins of the world. I am not disposed to say to this much abused race be ye warmed and filled and do nothing for their benefit.[39]

Kind Merrill took Allis under his wing and paid for Allis' keep out of his own pocket, hoping that the Board would eventually assist him financially. The Board refused to license Allis, though he was badly needed and was doing good work. According to McCoy, even Merrill was not receiving a penny from the Board for his own support.[40]

McCoy went on to remind the Board that after their move to Boston, although they had forbidden the missionaries to solicit funds other than through the Board, the Board had refused to accept donations earmarked for the Indian Mission, arguing that they alone should decide for what purpose funds were to be used. The reason given, McCoy points out, quoting from a letter from the Corresponding Secretary dated November 28, 1826, was that sympathy for the Indian Mission was so great that it would eventually undermine the foreign outreach of the Board. In relation to this, McCoy again reminds the Board of their quite unfounded and biased argument that if Indian scholars were allowed to enter schools and colleges in white areas, they would attract so much attention that people would wish to support the Indians rather than foreign missions. This was also the reason the Board gave for not allowing a Christian Indian and coworker with the missionaries to tour the churches, canvassing public support for the Indian mission.

Another bone of contention which McCoy lists was the Board's repeated practice of waiting until the older, founding missionaries were absent from a station and then exerting their influence on younger members to completely change the work of the mission. McCoy gives Thomas as a single example here, but he was already in

---

[39] Letter from Allis to McCoy dated March 19, 1838. McCoy Papers, Reel 9.

[40] Letter from McCoy to Allis dated November 19, 1838. McCoy Papers, Reel 9.

correspondence with the Board about similar practices in four other stations.[41] As a result of these difficulties with the Board, he reminds them how he and Lykins in 1830, with the backing of the other missionaries, had suggested to the Board that a distinct Indian Mission ought to be founded, separate from the foreign work but the Board refused to alter the status quo. Again, in 1838, McCoy had aired the matter of a separate Indian Mission with the Board but this time McCoy received no answer whatsoever. Nor did he receive any response to this long letter of complaint.

McCoy defends his accusers before the Board

Though Meeker and Barker had clearly been blaming McCoy for much of the catastrophic situation existing at the Shawnee Mission, and though McCoy had been publicly snubbed by the Board, he felt it his duty to support his critics in a just cause and wrote to the Board affirming the two men's status as missionaries along with that of Lykins. McCoy saw clearly which way the wind was blowing. The Board had been challenged to state precisely what had happened to the enormous amount of money which the Government had given the Board for schools. This money had been most conspicuous by its absence. Hitherto, Lykins, Meeker and Barker had believed that any funds coming their way were sent them as missionaries and they were paid out of either the Board's missionary fund or its benevolent fund but not out of its Government funding for schools. Now, by stating that Lykins, Meeker and Barker were not missionaries but teachers, the Board could account for all funds being sent to them in the past as coming from Government sources. In other words, the missionaries had been paid Government money and it had not been missing as they supposed. In this way, the Board felt that they had rid themselves of any blame in misusing Government funds. Perhaps in dealing with Lykins, Meeker and Barker, they had not considered that McCoy still considered himself both General Superintendent of the mission and the Board's agent to the Government in distributing funds for educational, but not missionary, purposes. They had also not considered the fact that McCoy was a thoroughly honest man and had underestimated his powers to defend the Indian Mission.

To this end, McCoy, on April 28, 1842[42] presented a paper

---

[41] Shawnee, Delaware, Ebenezer and Valley Towns.

[42] ABFMS, Reel 100.

before the Baptist Convention then held in New York, challenging the Board's arbitrary decision concerning the situation of the three missionaries. He stated that they were not teachers and therefore cannot have received any Government funding to cover their needs as missionaries as this would have broken standing agreements between the missionaries, the Board and the Government. McCoy wished to make it clear that if the Board had misused Government funds in the past to finance missionaries, they could not legalize the matter by re-defining a missionary as a teacher. McCoy added that duty required him to respectfully make this error on the Board's part known to the Committee for Indian Missions. The Board must have shuddered when they received this letter, knowing that McCoy might disclose his find-ings to the Government at any time concerning their mismanagement of funds. But McCoy was not yet finished. Not having received a reply to his thirty-seven paged letter of January 6, 1842, he enclosed a copy of the long letter and asked that this, too, should be laid before the Board of Managers of the Baptist General Convention. McCoy added that he "respectfully solicited the privilege of being present during the discussion of the subjects referred to in these communications."

Then, in an addendum, McCoy laid down proposals for a bet-ter way of dealing with missions to the Indians. He wrote:

> I further respectfully request the consid-eration of the following plan for obviating existing difficult-ies referred to in the foregoing, viz. the appointment of the Board of an Agency in the Valley of the Mississippi for the management of Indian Missions within the Indian Territory west of the States of Missouri and Arkansas and south west of Missouri river.
> The Agency to consist of fifteen brethren of whom the undersigned to be one, seven of whom to be so near to each other that attendance on ordinary meetings for business would be convenient. To be authorized to employ missionaries and to provide and apply the means for their support, and to manage all missionary matters within the country specified, provided that no debts, liabilities, or responsibilities of any kind whatever, should be created by the Agency beyond what would be binding on it, and not upon the Board. The Agency to report to the Board An-nually or as often as required.
> If this plan should meet with favour, the details could be filled up in the manner most acceptable to the parties concerned.

The plan met with no favor, indeed it was quite ignored, but McCoy by no means gave up the idea of putting such a plan into action and from now on made it his chief aim and calling in life.

Sketch of Clermont, Osage Chief, by George Catlin. This likeness was drawn by Catlin in 1836 for a watercolor painted soon after. Clermont had just recently become "First Chief" or head of the Osage and is shown holding a warclub.

Chapter Sixteen
The Birth of a New Indian Outreach (1842-43)

The Board now profess to have secret knowledge which would discredit McCoy

The Board did made a weak effort at addressing a few of McCoy's complaints and suggestions but came nowhere near satisfying either him or the three missionaries who now found themselves degraded to mere Government teachers. Instead, McCoy was given the vague information that the Board were in possession of knowledge that, if made public, would be of disadvantage to his calling as a missionary. This knowledge, they had allegedly received from "some of the missionaries." In other words, the Board were using exactly the same tactics against McCoy as they had used against Lykins. Again, no details were given and McCoy was left to wonder whether the complaints had come from missionaries who had resigned from the mission, missionaries who had been dismissed by the Board or missionaries who were now classified as teachers. No details whatsoever were given.

While the Convention was still in progress, McCoy handed a written request to the Corresponding Secretary Peck, stating:

> It having been publickly intimated by a member of the Acting Board that that body possessed some information which, if made public would in some manner be to my disadvantage as a missionary, and reports having reached me from various sources that this information has been derived from some of the missionaries, I am under the necessity of respectfully requesting you to forward to me copies, directed to Care of Rev. S. H. Cone, of any communication containing such information as is here attended to.
>
> Feeling confident that a fair representation of facts cannot do me any damage, and utterly at a loss to conjecture what the purport of the information alluded to

is, it is natural for me to suppose that some mistake has arisen which it will not be difficult for me to correct.

I also respectfully request copies of such communications from some of the missionaries as induced the Board to recognise a church among the Delawares which it had a short time before said it could not be identified with, and to appoint as a missionary to the Delawares a brother whom the Board had previously been unwilling to appoint.

You will easily perceive that for the restoration of harmony, which is desirable to all, it is my duty to make these requests.[1]

More empty promises

It being generally known that McCoy was about to meet Government officials at Washington soon after the Convention, he was anxiously asked by members at the Convention, including a prominent member of the Board, if he were going to air the subject of Government funding with them and what was he going to tell them. McCoy answered that he would not discuss the Board's position with the Government if he received assurance from them that in future that they would utilize Government grants for their correct purpose. McCoy was given that unqualified assurance. A year later, McCoy was to ask the Board, "Brethren, what evidence, allow me to ask, have you given of improvement in your application of those funds, or of your fulfilment of the wishes of the Convention and of the General Board?" Obviously, as far as McCoy was concerned, this was a rhetorical question. Nothing had been done but the promise had obviously been given out of fear of what the Government might do on hearing that their funds were being misapplied. Once again, the Board had deceived McCoy to save their own face. McCoy said that the Board's action, unless corrected, would severely damage the cause of religion in general and that of missions in particular. Never was a truer word spoken.

---

[1] Letter dated New York, May 2, 1842, ABFMS, Reel 100.

The Board admit that they have no knowledge detrimental to McCoy's good reputation

After waiting in vain for a reply while a guest at Cone's house and no longer allowed to continue his work as a missionary, McCoy "retired" to Louisville, Kentucky to await further events. One of the most surprising being that the Board offered him the post of a missionary as if he were a new candidate being put under the patronage of the Board for the first time! Perhaps this had something to do with his letter of May 2ⁿᵈ to the new Corresponding Secretary, Solomon Peck, as the Board's decision to "appoint" McCoy a missionary was made on May 6ᵗʰ. However, Peck had waited well over a month before replying and, probably realizing that McCoy had left Cone's and not knowing where he was now settled, forwarded his letter to Westport, Missouri. After further delay, the letter arrived at Louisville. McCoy read that the Board had now looked into the matter concerning alleged knowledge which was detrimental to McCoy's reputation and found that no such information existed.

Peck wishes to harmonize all difficulties

Peck then spoke of "a spirit of reconciliation" and a desire to "harmonize all difficulties," offering McCoy a missionary post and apparently felt he had now restored peace. Actually all Peck had done was, for convenience sake and to save the Board's face, endeavored to sweep everything under the carpet. Furthermore, his offer of a post as "missionary" soon showed itself to be an offer of a Government teaching post, so no progress had been made and the Board were still sticking to their old ways and had learned nothing from McCoy's criticisms. Once again, the Board were dreaming of using McCoy as a magnet to attract Government grants. Yet it seemed that Peck could not even now jump over his shadow and criticized McCoy strongly for his past work as a missionary when he ought to have been teaching in the school. He seemed still intent on believing that McCoy was never the Board's missionary. Naturally, McCoy again replied that at the time to which Peck referred, he was appointed as a missionary and not a teacher and shows astonishment at Peck's remark. Even so, at any other time in the past, McCoy might have accepted Peck's proposals but he believed that there was still too much wrong to be righted. He reminded Peck of his letters of January 6ᵗʰ and April 27ᵗʰ, explaining that the problems had not been dealt with, adding, "I hope I shall be excused for declining missionary labour under the direction of the

Board, while these difficulties, of which I have complained, remain unsettled."[2] The new post offered to McCoy would have entailed a total acceptance of the Board's policy up to date and in particular an acceptance of their decision regarding Blanchard with no explanations given. McCoy knew very well that, though this might be seen as a chance to "harmonize difficulties," it was once again a question of harmonizing everything to suit the Board. It was a mere one-sided appeal to McCoy to swallow his differences with them and proceed as if there was nothing to complain about and as if he had never complained. But McCoy still wanted to know, he explained to Peck, why the Board recognized a minister and his church although they had considered the minister disorderly and said they could not be identified with the church, only to change their mind completely shortly afterwards and without consulting the senior missionaries or the churches, license the wayward minister and split an hitherto harmonious church into two. McCoy closed his letter by saying, "I beg you to be assured that my desires to spend my life in labors for the salvation of the Indians have not abated. It is my prayer that God will grant me this privilege and will guide my steps aright."

Lykins hands in his resignation

Meanwhile, Lykins was so disgusted with the way the Board was bringing ruin to the Indian Mission that he felt he must resign though he had given the best twenty years of his life selflessly for the service of the Indian Mission and under the patronage of the Board. His brother David, had also served the Board faithfully for some years without ever asking for a penny in support. Lykins' letter of resignation, sent to Dr. Joel S. Bacone,[3] was short but to the point:

> Dear Brethren,
> After serving in the capacity of your missionary to the North American Indians for the term of about twenty years, events, which I could not control, appear to me to require that the connection hitherto existing between us, should be dissolved.
> Availing myself of the presence of your

---

[2] Letter to Peck dated August 4, 1842.

[3] Bacone's surname is alternatively spelled with or without a final "e".

Agent, Revd Professor Joel S. Bacone, I respectfully tender to you, through him this my resignation.

In taking my leave of you, I cannot forbear an expression of regret, that I have been compelled to differ in opinion with the Board touching certain matters, & to take exceptions to the conduct of some of your missionaries, the details of which have been communicated to Mr. Bacone, and I assure you that my desires to do good to the Indians remain unabated, and for them I expect to continue to labor.

May the richest of heavenly influence, and blessing, attend you in the prosecution of your ardent labours of love.

> Very respectfully
> and affectionately, yours,
> in the bonds of a precious
> Redeemer
>
> J. Lykins.[4]

Lykins, however, still received criticism from the Board and Meeker gossiped about him to the Board, accusing him of having given up missionary work to practice as a doctor after his resignation. This was a most unfair criticism as Lykins had always served the Indian Mission as a doctor alongside preaching and translation engagements. He did not stop either work after his resignation. Furthermore, Lykins had a wife, who was in most delicate health and did not live long after his resignation, and a family to keep and he needed income to pay for his children's education. Brave Lykins did not cease to be an active, witnessing Christian just because he no longer bore the name of missionary. The only reaction Lykins received from Secretary Peck, who had received news of his resignation, was that the latter wrote to him saying, apparently as a bad joke, that as the Board were dissatisfied with his course they could not honor any drafts coming from him without a satisfactory explanation in future.[5] As usual, the Board thought in terms of money rather than the plight of a man they had treated badly. This letter was a great disappointment to Lykins as he felt that he had offered his resignation in a true gentleman-like way, and the Board should either formally accept his offer of resignation or formally reject it. Peck's letter merely snubbed him. It is obvious from Lykins' correspondence, that if he had received a satisfactory reply,

---

[4] December 1, 1842, ABFMS, Reel 99.

[5] Letter dated January 31, 1843. McCoy Papers, Reel 11.

and if the Board had accepted his explanation of his conduct sent to the Board in writing and given to an agent of the Board orally, then he would have remained under the patronage of the Board. But the new regime in the Board obviously did not want him. Furthermore, Lykins had sent his letter of resignation to Bacone who was serving in lieu of Bolles who had been removed from his post which was taken over by Solomon Peck. Both Bolles and Bacone had come to respect Lykins and spoke well of him but obviously Peck was of an entirely different mind.

Lykins appeals to Bolles

Writing to Bolles again, two months after his resignation, Lykins told him that Peck's letter was quite unfair due to the fact that, before his resignation he had asked the Board's permission to appear before them, to give them a thorough explanation of all his actions and invite them to question him. The Board had refused to receive him, though their agent had told Lykins that they were not dissatisfied with him.[6] In his letter to Bolles, Lykins lays down further reasons for his decision to resign:

> 1. I was opposed to the course of the brethren in constituting a church at Delaware, because the act was disorderly and was not gotten up in accordance with the rules of Baptist churches. Because it was opposed by some of the missionaries and was not acceptable to many who were constituted into this church. Because the brethren, knowingly, in pushing forward the measure violated a known and acknowledged principle of Missions viz: harmony of views and action. And because it was foreseen that the measure would carry utter confusion into the rank of the missionaries as well as set up discord and division in the church. And have not these results followed? In the course I took I confidently expected to be sustained by the Board as well as by all good men; for I could anticipate no other conclusion than that the Board would disapprove, wherein it was found to exist, of wrong.

---

[6] Both McCoy and Lykins continually heard the most contradictory stories coming from the Board. This was because the Board itself was in chaos with at least two different factions, one sympathetic to McCoy and Lykins, the other not. Sadly it was politics, commerce and financial mismanagement which had caused the breach. Peck and Bacone were now sweeping with new brooms as Bolles himself had done after the Board moved to Boston.

I was opposed to acknowledging Blanchard as a missionary until he was appointed by the B[oar]d which some persisted in doing, thereby forcing others to ab-sent themselves from the missionary conference.

I was opposed to his being identified with us because under the peculiar circumstances of the case the honor of the cause of missions forbid it. With all the facts known, I am free to abide the decision of all men on this subject.

I was opposed to their haste (some of the missionaries) in receiving and baptising members. To their lax dealing with disorderly members & to the admission to the communion table, of some accused of great and scandalous crimes. To their reception of members, thought by some to be unfit, in the face of strong remonstrances against their Baptism as well as reception. I was opposed to the reception of worthless members of the Methodist church, labouring under the censure of that church for "lying, theft, drunkeness &c."[7]

A brief look at Lykins' position before he resigned

Lykins explains how the alleged complaints from his younger brethren that he started to spread rumors against them are quite untrue. It was the repeated demand of the Indians that he should do something against the Blanchard-Barker team which forced him into action. An Indian lady whom Lykins met weeping, confessed that she could no longer remain in Blanchard's break-away church. One of the reasons being that a new member who was a known rogue and drunkard, had been admitted and baptized, yet he cohabited with and fornicated with a beast and did so after his testimony of saving faith and baptism. No church enquiry was made or discipline practiced in this case, as in other similar atrocities. No one who applied for membership was rejected. Lykins protested to Bolles that the testimony of the Indian churches was now ruined through Blanchard and Barker's laxity and lack of pastoral acumen. He was also saddened by the fact that his younger brethren had refused him permission to use the mission press to print his translations and in their printing and reprinting of his works for the Indians, they had actually removed his name from the title page. Perhaps the worst blow to Lykins was that after he had re-

---

[7] Letter dated February 24, 1843, McCoy Papers, Reel 11, and ABFMS, Reel No. 99.

tired and events had more than justified his opposition to Blanchard's ordination, the Indians, (apart from the small group already noted), appealed to him to withdraw his resignation, and begged the Board not to accept it. But the Board still accused Lykins of evil intentions which they had picked up from hearsay. They had never even bothered to check the allegations. Lykins thus goes on to say:

> 2. I was compelled to resign and retire from the service of the Acting Board, to escape a tissue of persecutions and misrepresentations unheard of in the annals of Mission. Because I could not consent to labor in connexion with persons, who were calculated to pull down faster than I could build up. Because I could not identify myself with some of the missionaries without losing the confidence of native brethren. Because I felt that in view of the past, that to attempt it would be to court indignity and to fail of doing good. Because the agent of the Board had forborne to investigate and settle the difficulties of which I had complained. Because I thought I had reason to suppose that the missionaries in writing to the B[oar]d. respecting me and by their subsequent deportment designed to drive me from the field.[8] And because the health of my wife did not admit of subjecting her to the exposure and toil consequent to a station remote from the white settlements. And because the missionaries refused to refund me monies faithfully and honestly expended by me in the employment of our interpreter. And because I could not consent to the various misdoings of the missionaries.
>
> I did not retire willingly. I did not resign in order to preoccupy another station in favor of another society or Board. My wish was to have remained at Shawnee under the direction of and sustained by the Acting Board of For. Miss. if the way could have been cleared of difficulty. During the progress of our difficulties I became aware that my course would subject me to misrepresentation to consequent loss and pecuniary embarrassment. In view of all I resolved to be faithful and discharge my duty. And now with whatever of unmerited censure my name may be loaded or how ever much I may suffer in any way I

---

[8] These men not only strove to drive McCoy and Lykins from the mission that they had founded but, while still in the employment of the Board, traveled to the places where McCoy and Lykins subsequently served, spreading evil rumors of their former superintendents. Even when McCoy held conferences for his new mission, the Blanchard faction would turn up to sow strife.

rejoice that I was enabled to stand up and do my duty. I claim to have been faithful. If I must fall in consequence of it let me suffer until history shall exhume my reputation. Towards my misguided brethren I desire to entertain no worse feeling than that of pity. Toward the Acting Board certainly no feeling but that of a Christian missionary. If they knew really my course I should have their sympathy. It could not be otherwise. They are men fearing God and loving righteousness.[9]

A very belated, cold, judgmental reply from the Board

The Board reacted very slowly to Lykins' resignation. Indeed, there is just a tiny indication that Peck might not have known of Lykins' resignation when last writing to him as he maintained that Bacone formally laid Lykins' letter before the Board a good two months after its reception. It could be that Bacone wished to give Lykins time to change his mind or perhaps he was afraid of how Peck might react. This is obviously the view Peck wished Lykins to believe when he eventually replied several months later but Lykins, now expecting only the worst from Peck, tells him that he finds his story "queer." Although Lykins had handed his resignation to Bacone, he received no reply from him. Peck's response was written on August 31, 1843 in the form of a "cold"[10] judgmental letter which was, according to Lykins, "a document calculated to screen the guilty and condemn the innocent." Also, Peck wanted to know more details of the practices going on at the Shawnee Station and vicinities which Lykins had alluded to but Lykins protested that he wished to be spared the pain of further exposing the malpractices of the missionaries to whom Peck alluded and of thereby placing the Board in an undesirable position before the public. Apparently Peck was eager to make Lykins' complaints and charges public but Lykins told him that these had only been raised when Peck, moved by the secret complaints and charges of others, had asked him for an explanation. Understandably, Lykins was upset that Peck was prepared to put all the blame on him for the disruption and none on Blanchard and the Board. Actually, the Board had already distributed minutes of a meeting which suggested just that. Furthermore, Lykins pointed out that when Professor Bacone

---

[9] Ibid.

[10] So Lykins who replied to Peck's letter on September 24, 1843. McCoy Papers, Reel 11.

visited the Shawnee Mission, he interviewed all the missionaries who were concerned in the matter but left Lykins out and never spoke to him at all on the matter. The "facts" which Peck held against him, Lykins argues, were all gathered at meetings to which he was forbidden to attend and was not present. Indeed, Bacone listened to Blanchard, Barker and Pratt and told Lykins that he did not want to listen to him unless he was prepared to "overlook the past." Here Lykins shows no bitterness as Bacone had hinted to Lykins that he was only acting, unwillingly, under Peck's orders and had reported in writing to Peck that there was nothing which spoke against Lykins' continuing as a *missionary* under the patronage of the Board. Furthermore, Lykins tells Peck that Meeker was also present at Bacone's investigations and that he (Bacone) had reproved them strongly for their attitude to Lykins and the state of affairs in their churches. "Did he reprove them at the mission but justify them before the Board?" Lykins asks rhetorically, knowing full well that Bacone had not.[11]

The embarrassment of former McCoy biographers

Most older Baptist biographers have stood between two opinions in recording McCoy's life. On the one hand, they wished, understandably, to avoid controversy with or negative comment on the denomination they loved and on the other hand, they wished to portray McCoy as the great saint he undoubtedly was. This gave rise to a compromise in which little was said about McCoy's break with the Board who professed to represent the Baptist denomination and little was said about McCoy's life after being dismissed from that Board. Reasons for the break between the missionary and his Board are left to those who are looking for historical accuracy in a academic dissertation such as Edward Roustio's or to those who are able, as this present writer, because of no national or, until very recently, denominational ties with either McCoy or the antebellum American Baptist Board of Foreign Missions, to write the story of both McCoy and the Board from a neutral, and thus perhaps more objective, perspective.

Roustio is certainly correct in saying that a chief reason for the Board's negative attitude to McCoy was the latter's insistence that Government funds be used solely as specified by the Government. The

---

[11] The most odd thing about this letter, which is obviously a rough copy of the original, is the 21 signatures under it, some of which are repeated in whole or part as if the signatories were practicing their signatures.

Board's Treasurer, Heman Lincoln, parted on amiable terms with McCoy but his main fear seemed to have been that McCoy might use his influence with the Government to cut off their generous funding.[12] Also his intimate knowledge of the Board's abuse of the Government's trust in them must have made them wish that they were not bothered by the founder of their Indian Mission.[13] Clearly, McCoy had served as a conscience prodder to the Board which they felt they were better off without. Another major factor was also certainly McCoy's insistence that the public should be informed more about the needs of the Indian Mission and that they should be allowed and encouraged to earmark their gifts for the Indians and not leave their money to be distributed elsewhere at the discretion of the Board. The fact that the Board radically changed their politics after coming into the hands of the Easterners obviously played an important part in the McCoy-Board relationship. The Baptist Board wished to work ecumenically with the Presbyterians in Indian evangelism which meant virtually leaving the Indians where they were until they died an unnatural death. There were many very dedicated Presbyterians who loved the Indians dearly but this should not disguise the fact that, on the whole, they felt they were preparing a nation to die in hope and die peacefully. McCoy did not merely wish to lead the Indians to heaven but also to save their nations for posterity on earth. Another reason was the Board's refusal to continue their agreement to accept the *Family Rules*. Up to the Board's removal to Boston, McCoy argued that there had been no such thing as "mine" and "thine" in the mission station but Dr. Bolles had introduced them into missionary work. More minor reasons were the problem of education for the missionaries' children, the Board being loath to take on this financial responsibility. The reason that must have settled the matter for McCoy was that the Board were, in effect, winding down their work among the Indians and there was literally no future for the evangelization of the Indians if left solely in the Eastern hands of the Boston Board. As McCoy said in a letter to David Benedict, dated May 16, 1841, "I must go forward in mission work whether they will or not."

---

[12] See letter from McCoy to Benedict dated May 16, 1841, McCoy Papers, Reel 10.

[13] Roustio, pp. 179-180.

A separate Indian Mission based in the West was now inevitable

It was obvious that McCoy must eventually start up his own mission based on the love, prayers and funding of a church whose heart was open to the Indians. The wonder was that McCoy had remained for so long in association with a church body which had clearly developed into a parachurch organization and had become more a fund-raising commercial enterprise rather than a spiritual and material support to needy missionaries. Close friends to McCoy such as Lykins, Cone and Dagg had seen it coming for years but had persevered with their brother in the Lord. McCoy had sought the heart of the Convention in 1838 and again in 1842 but to no avail. They did not see the necessity or use of even such an organization as a Committee for Indian Affairs. Among the first to hear of McCoy's new plans for an Indian Mission were the Indians themselves. On July 26, 1842, McCoy wrote to Thomas Hendricks, Henry Skigget and Timothy Toney whom he addressed as "Principle men of the Stockbridges." McCoy told them:

I write to you and to your people to whom I hope you will send this, to assure you and them that I have the same love for you all, and the same desire that you may all be pious and happy in this world, and well prepared for the next, when I am far from you as I have when near to you. Nearly twenty-five years ago my wife and I determined to consecrate the remainder of life to the welfare of the red people. We have struggled long and hard to help them. While we were with them, endeavouring to teach them the road to heaven, we were almost constantly calling to our white brethren in the States to send more missionaries to help us. Seventeen times I have made journies to Washington and other places in that country, to persuade the government to help the Indians, and to persuade christians to help them, and as I grew older I talked louder and stronger for the red people. I thought they ought to help them more. The red people need more preachers, some preachers who are red men ought to be kept constantly employed, in exhorting their people to become religious, and they ought to have more schools for the education of their children. Since I left home last March many of my baptised brethren from many States in the U. States, have met for the purpose of sending more missionaries to the red people, and for the purpose of employing more of those of them who are pious, to preach and to teach school. This printed circular will inform you respecting the nature of our association. Our places of meeting will be Cincinnati and

Louisville. I must stay and help them a few years, and then my wife and I desire, if the Lord will, to return and lay our bones by the side of our own dear children, and the bones of our dear Indian brothers and sisters. Thus far the Lord has smiled on my poor efforts here for the benefit of the red men. Several good missionaries are ready to go out to the Ind. Ter. as soon as one can get our Society properly organised. I hope the time is not distant, when the number of spiritual labourers in the Indian country will be very much increased. We hope also that the work will go on with zeal until all the tribes - even those furthest off, shall be blest with the bible.

I expect to visit Washington next year to ask the government to help our new Society.

Brethren and Sisters take courage. I think a brighter day is dawning on the red people than they have ever before seen. I think what a glorious time it will be when all tribes, even the poorest and wickedest, shall become industrious and happy people, and thousands and tens of thousands of them be worshippers of God in Spirit and in truth.

By my wife I received a kind letter signed by eight names. I find you have some trouble, this is not surprising. The Devil will endeavour to give you trouble, for he is ashamed for fear that the Indians are, about to all become christians. But trust in God - do right - be religious, and God will take care of you.

My wife and I will endeavour [to] see you in a hasty visit to your country in November next, if the Lord will, and then we expect again to return and work a while in this country. Give our affectionate regards to all friends, and tell all red people whom you see that we are still the same friends of them we ever have been, and their sincere friends we shall remain until death.

Brethren T. Hendricks, Skigget and Toney, the Lord help you. Be faithful - do all the good you can, and be assured I am, as ever, your unchanging friend and brother,

Isaac McCoy[14]

Kentucky and Ohio the center of interest in the Indians' future

McCoy over the years had gained much sympathy from the

---

[14] McCoy Papers, Reel 10.

Baptist churches on the Western frontier and in the new states who had recovered to a great extent from the ravages of New Light illuminations, Campbell's ritualism[15] and Parker's dualism which had threatened to stifle evangelism and church growth. There was also much sympathy shown to the mission from the Northern states and New York. Various Baptist organizations and publications began to place a stronger emphasis on their Christian duties and commitments to the red men. Kentucky and Ohio became the center of this interest and on June 18, 1842 the *Baptist Banner & Western Pioneer* published a special edition featuring the need for a Western organization which would support Indian missions. This was the circular which McCoy had sent to the Stockbridge Indians. Its leading article stated:

> The Committee appointed[16] by a conference of brethren upon the subject of originating an organization in the West for the promotion of the spiritual interests of the Indians upon our borders, present the following Report.
> The Committee have been influenced by considering the facts, that the Indians are on Western ground, in the vicinity of Western people, who are living upon the very soil lately owned and traversed by the fathers of these diminished tribes - that the West is probably the most appropriate field of any portion of our country for prominent and responsible action in their behalf - that their condition calls upon us for prompt and special effort, and is worthy of action distinct from other religious enterprises, yet operating in fraternal harmony with all, and that this branch of benevolent effort, is, in a high degree, calculated to rouse the sympathies and enlist the energies of our denomination in the West.
> The Committee have also carefully considered the fact that Indian Missions have been heretofore included in the Foreign field, and committed to the superintendence of the Board of Managers of the Baptist General Convention for Foreign Missions, in whom the committee have ever placed, and still place, the highest confidence. But they have also seen that the Board have a great responsibility and press of work, in sustaining the

---

[15] Several members of Mrs. McCoy's family had become Campbellites and were still practicing that religion. See letter to McCoy from the AIMA agent Morse, dated Fort Wayne, September 25, 1843, McCoy Papers, Reel 11.

[16] S.W. Lynd, W.C. Buck, J.L. Waller, F.A. Willard and W.M. Colgan.

missions in Asia, and other foreign countries; and that while they have conscientiously done all that they judged wise, and within their power, and, under the peculiar circumstances of the case, probably no other body of men could have done so well; yet distinct applications for Indian Missions have rarely been made by their agencies, and could not have been distinctly made without more or less embarrassing their general operations. All that they can possibly secure through the instrumentality of the same agent in any portion of our country is really needed for the purpose of carrying on their operations in foreign countries; and the committee are fully persuaded that a separate agency would contribute greatly to the advantage of the Indian tribes, and the extension of Christianity among them, while according to well known laws of the human mind, it would promote an increased amount of liberality towards other benevolent enterprises.

Many thousands of the Indians have reached the limits of their wanderings, and must now be speedily civilized and evangelized, or they must perish. The committee are deeply impressed with the idea that no time should be lost. The present appears to your committee to be a most favorable period for organizing a society to operate specially among the Indian tribes. Our brother, Eld. Isaac McCoy, so long and favorably known as the friend of the red man, who has consecrated his life to their spiritual and eternal interests, is now disengaged, and ready to act as agent in any enterprize that may gratify the long cherished desire of his heart.

The Committee are perfectly aware that the subject of establishing an agency in the West has been referred to the Acting Board of Managers of the General Convention, located in Boston, with instructions to correspond with brethren in the West, and ascertain their views; and while it would seem but christian courtesy to await their action, yet they themselves, and our brethren generally, will no doubt appreciate our motives in anticipating such action in view of the following considerations.

The proposed correspondence will fail to secure any expressions upon the part of Western Baptists to aid the Board in their decisions; because, were the whole West in favor of an agency of the Board, the brethren could not be found, at any suitable point, who would be willing to embark in such agency, without the same authority to act in the premises as the Board at Boston, and responsible for their action only to the Baptist Triennial Convention. To wait the decision of the Convention upon this point, would defer a work which ought to be commenced immediately, and probably no future occasion would furnish the same facilities for operating in the West, in behalf of the Indians, as the present.

While, therefore, it may appear to be rather a delicate matter to anticipate the action of the Board at Boston, and it is our earnest desire to cooperate with them in all the designs of the Convention, yet the delicacy is in the view of the committee only apparent; because, should the Board agree to constitute an agency in the West, it must be of such a character as to be equivalent to a distinct society in its executive operations; in which event the whole intermediate period would be an entire loss; and should the Board determine that no such agency is necessary in the West, leading brethren here and in other sections of our country would be unwilling that nothing more should be done for the Indian tribes, and a society would unquestionably be originated, in which event still further time would be lost, and without any ultimate advantage perceptible to the committee.

The Committee wish it to be distinctly understood that in these remarks no reflection is intended upon the wisdom of the Board of Missions, or upon their disposition to promote to the extent of their power the interests of the Indian tribes; but their operations in the Foreign field necessarily embarrass their operations in behalf of the Indians, so that they cannot do the things which they would.

The Committee, therefore, believe that it is the duty of the Western Baptists to unite their strength upon this point, and aid the Board at Boston, and the Baptist General Convention, in their noble enterprise.

No confrontation with the Baptist Board of Foreign Missions was sought

This article was an almost perfect example of diplomacy and public relations expertise. Instead of openly confronting the Board of Foreign Missions and thus causing strife throughout the Baptist churches within the Union, McCoy's new organization presented itself as a rescuer of the Board from its embarrassment and as a helping hand to assist the Board in doing what it really would like to do. The article shows how eager the friends of the Indians were to seek for peace among the brethren and to strengthen the united effort of Baptists to win the Indians for Christ and alleviate their material misery.

Now McCoy's former churches shook off the last relics of Campbellism and Parkerism and joined the new missionary enterprise. In this move, John McCoy, Isaac's brother, was particularly active. The churches of Lost River, Salem, New Albany, Mill Creek, Charleston and one by the odd name of Sink-Hole Elect, joined up to form the Bethel Association which resolved:

> That this Association regard with peculiar interest the claims of the Foreign Mission Society (the American Indian Mission Association), and particularly the field occupied by our Red Brethren and rejoice in the prospect of special organization in the Western Valley, that will seek their civilization and Christianization. We would recommend a more frequent remembrance of the Aborigines of our own country, in our monthly concerts of prayer, and alms deeds.[17]

McCoy's brother testifies to the former hard battle with Campbellism and Parkerism

When the battle with Cambellism and Parkerism was over, John McCoy entered into his diary for February 11, 1858:

> With humble gratitude to God I hail one more birthday in my short pilgrimage here on earth. I am now seventy-six years old - have been a professor of religion about thirty-five years, have experienced some sore trials in the world, but the hardest with false Brethren in the church. Have contended against Campbellism and Parkerism some times almost alone, but I have thought God blessed my feeble efforts. Yet very little have I done for my Blessed Master, who has done so much for me.[18]

---

[17] Hayward, *John M'Coy*, p. 70.

[18] "John M'Coy's Diary," in Hayward's *John M'Coy: His Life and His Diaries*, pp. 446-447.

The A.I.M.A. is born

The Committee appointed by the members of the Western Baptist Publication Society organized a conference at the Ninth Street Baptist Church, Cincinnati, Ohio, on October 27, 1842 with the purpose of founding a mission to the Indians as its major outreach and concern. It was here that the American Indian Mission Association, known as the A. I. M. A., was born[19] and Isaac McCoy was asked unanimously to take charge of this mission as its Corresponding Secretary. McCoy had always thought that Spencer Cone of New York would be the better man for such a post but that great friend of the Indian mission had written to McCoy on January 1842 to tell him that he was now "too old and broken down" to be of any active use in any "distinct organization." At the time, Cone was Chairman of the American Baptist Home Mission Society which had been founded in 1832 at Cone's suggestion[20] and he had quite enough work to do for a man of frail health. Soon, however, the A.I.M.A. began to work hand in hand with the Home Mission Society, thus assisting to persuade the Foreign Missions Board, who had stopped sending missionaries to the Indians, to allow the A.I.M.A. to gradually absorb their former Indian missions. In 1855, nine years after McCoy's death, the A.I.M.A. was to merge with the Home Mission Board of the Southern Baptist Convention.

---

[19] The great work done among the Indians by Baptist Christians is sadly hardly known among the churches at large and even among present day Baptists. This ignorance is illustrated by Charles Henry Robinson's 533 paged *History of Christian Missions* where neither the American Baptist Board of Foreign Missions, nor the American Indian Mission Association is mentioned. There is the briefest of references to the American Baptist Home Missionary Society and a sentence on the work of John Stewart who died in 1823 (See p. 378 of that work).

[20] It is interesting to note that Austen Kennedy de Blois in his Introduction to Dr. Charles White's *A Century of Faith*, the centenary volume of the American Baptist Home Mission, mentions the "sacrificial ministries" of McCoy and Merrill as being instrumental in the founding of the Baptist Home Mission. One cannot help speculating on what would have happened if the home organization had taken over the Indian mission rather than its "foreign" counterpart.

McCoy addresses the mission's friends

In his speech before the delegates at the Cincinnati Conference, McCoy spoke of the overwhelming response to the 400 circulars, each accompanied by a private letter, which McCoy had sent to strategically placed Baptists. There had only been one negative reply among "very many" positive and enthusiastic ones. What must have been a great blessing to McCoy and the answer to many a prayer was that he could announce that the Long Run Association had met and approved wholeheartedly of the new mission's designs and stated in a special resolution that they approved of McCoy's appointment as Corresponding Secretary. The strife of the Campbell-Parker era had passed and once again McCoy's home Association was supporting him. Daniel Parker, after causing havoc among the Western churches had become so extreme that from around 1835 on he had threatened to kill all missionaries and was finally excommunicated by his own church,[21] for holding and publishing heresy.[22] He campaigned on with his rebel church of nine members but was now classified by the Baptist churches at large as a Joseph Smith or an Alexander Campbell. As McCoy read letter after letter that had come in from twelve States of the Union, the District of Columbia and the Indian Territories to the thrilled audience, he must have felt that at last his calling was bearing fruit and the Indians were about to receive the support they deserved. Six families, he announced had pledged themselves to the Indian mission and one single man, while several others were in the process of testing their calling. The new Indian Mission Association proved a major support to the brethren who had been forced out of their churches by the Campbellites and had been struggling ever since to find sound fellowship. There are several letters among the McCoy Papers, informing McCoy how dispersed brethren were now forming churches again. One of the most pleasing to McCoy must have been a letter from Charles Scott, written probably on August 15, 1844. Scott explained how their cause had broken up because of Campbellism but now McCoy's former elder and co-pastor with his father, George Waller, had helped the church to reconstitute itself and they wished once again to share fellowship with McCoy's cause.[23] The church had now a membership of 162 and Waller was able to preach there once a

---

[21] Locust Church.

[22] This was because of his warring nature and Two Seed teaching.

[23] McCoy Papers, Reel 11.

month.[24]

The new A.I.M.A. committee

The A.I.M.A. committee was formed and contained men of the finest caliber. William Calmes Buck (1790-1872), one time editor of the *Baptist Banner & Western Pioneer* had been an officer in the War of 1812 and after returning to civilian life, he evangelized the whole Mississippi valley, drawing large crowds to hear his preaching. J. H. Spencer gives samples of his busy itinerary in his labors for the Lord and says of him:

> William Calmes Buck was one of the leaders of God's host, in Kentucky, at a period when a wise, bold leader was most needed. To him, the Baptists of this Commonwealth, and of the whole Mississippi Valley, owe, more than to any other man, their deliverance from the narrow prejudice against missionary operations, which had been chiefly fostered by Alexander Campbell, and the chilling spirit of Antinomianism, enkindled by Parker, Dudley, Nuckols and their satellites. More than any other preacher in the State, did this champion of Christian benevolence stir up and foster the spirit of missions. Possessing great physical strength and remarkable powers of endurance, he traveled on horse-back, among the churches, winter and summer, day and night, and urged upon them the solemn duty of supporting their pastors, at home, and sending the gospel to the perishing, abroad. He possessed a strong, steady nerve, a cool self-possession and a courage that did not falter. His tongue was as the pen of a ready writer, and his voice was as the roaring of a lion. Perhaps no other man ever preached, in Kentucky, that could command the attention of so large an audience, in the open air. Who will question, that God called and qualified him, for the specific work he performed![25]

Buck pastored churches in, Virginia, Union County, Kentucky,

---

[24]   Letter from Burcks Branch Baptist Church to the Long Run Association probably written around August, 1844. McCoy Papers, Reel 11.

[25] *History of Kentucky Baptists*, vol. II, pp. 171-172. Spencer is referring to Daniel Parker, Thomas P. Dudley and Andrew Nuckols, keen anti-missions enthusiasts.

Mississippi and Alabama and served in the Civil War as a chaplain to the forces. He published several theological works and a *Baptist Hymn Book*.

F. A. Willard and Thomas S. Malcolm[26] were two good friends who were instrumental in building up the Second Baptist Church in Louisville. Willard improved the church's membership from around fourteen members to ninety-six in three years (1839-1842) after which Malcolm took over the work and increased the membership to 171 within four years. Within those few years, Malcolm baptized 124 of his converts. The Long Run Association owes its recorded history up to 1842 to Malcolm's pen. Sadly for Louisville, and the new Indian Mission Association, both men left the town for further services around 1845, Willard probably moved south, whereas Malcolm accepted a pastorate in Philadelphia.

Dr. John Lightfoot Waller (1809-1854), son of George Waller, who became President of the Bible Revision Association[27] in 1851 seems to have sat on the board of most Christian evangelistic and charity organizations in the Kentucky area. He became well-known among Baptists as an opposer of Campbellism although still in his teens and not yet a professing Christian. After conversion, he became editor of the *Baptist Banner* and the *Western Pioneer* which he merged before handing over the paper to Buck in 1841. Waller served as clerk to the General Association of Kentucky Baptists and Corresponding Secretary of the Executive Board and became the board's General Agent in 1841. He entered the ministry in 1840, taking over his father's church and five years later founded the *Western Baptist Review*. Waller became a delegate to the Kentucky Convention for Woodford County, winning his seat by a good majority. Waller was about to start work on a history of the Kentucky Baptists when he was called home in 1854, having lived only forty-five years.

---

[26]   Malcolm was the first secretary of the new missionary association.

[27]   S. W. Lynd, a further committee member of the Indian Missionary Association also worked for the Bible Revision Association. Lynd was William Staughton's son-in-law and biographer. McCoy was able to befriend him and win him to the A.I.M.A. after Staughton's death and after he wrote up Staughton's life.

Southern and Western Conventions pledge support for McCoy's missionary outreach

Soon association after association began to link up with the new organization. McCoy visited convention after convention, relentlessly seeking to interest his brethren in his work for the Indians. The Union Association of Indiana pledged its support from the start. The Georgia Baptist Convention met in May, 1843 and resolved:

> That we heartily approve the American Indian Missionary Association, and recommend to our brethren and churches that they do the same; also that a committee be appointed to recommend to this body the best way by which the Convention may aid the object.

The Convention voted to become an auxiliary of the Indian Association and promptly donated $200 towards its support. Humphrey Posey, who had commenced as a missionary to the Indians only months after McCoy and who had founded the Valley Towns Mission among the Cherokees was sent as a delegate to the General Association meeting on behalf of the Indian Mission as also the less well-known E. Dyer. Exactly a year after its foundation, the Kentucky Baptists drew up the following Preamble and Resolutions at their General Association meeting in Georgetown:

> Whereas, in view of injuries which the Indian tribes have sustained in consequence of the settlement of white men in their country, they have a stronger claim upon American christians than other nations who have not been thus injured, and whereas very favourable openings for doing them good present themselves, therefore,

> Resolved, That the information afforded this Association of the success and future prospects of the Indian Mission Association is especially cheering, and calls for devout praise to God; and that we hail the indications of divine Providence in favour of that society as a pledge that the wilderness shall soon be made to flourish as the garden of God; and we earnestly commend it to the favour of the churches and blessing of the God of Missions."

At last the long planned Indian Advocate is published

McCoy's long wish to have a journal regularly printed to inform the Christian public of the needs and progress of Indian missions was fulfilled in the founding of the *Indian Advocate*, published monthly in Louisville, which now became the seat of the mission's headquarters.

Now efforts were made to discuss whether the American Baptist Foreign Mission Board were willing or not to allow the A.I.M.A. to take over their work. It had become clear to the Foreign Mission Board that their first love was indeed the foreign mission and that they had neither the interest or could spare the funding to keep up their Indian missionary stations which now needed re-manning to a large extent. Spencer Cone and John Mason Peck, who had also started on his evangelistic work around the same time as McCoy, put forward motions to the Foreign Mission Board to, at least, work closely with the A.I.M.A.. Among the Board members, Solomon Peck and a small group of his friends protested at such an action but the denomination at large was for the Indian Missions being run by those who gave it their entire interest. Among the missionaries themselves, Meeker, whom McCoy would have loved to have at his side, remained aloof and even critical of the new missionary association.

Chapter Seventeen
The Crowning Work (1843-46)

McCoy puts all his energies into the new work

Now at fifty-eight years of age, McCoy found that he needed to dash around the countryside, organizing the work, with the energy of a young man. Within just a few months, he had traveled 1,000 miles, preaching, lecturing and attending association meetings. He tells his son Isaac:

> I am hard at work writing to many in different parts of the U. States in reference to our missionary affairs, and in visiting preachers and others on the same subject. So far as I have ascertained the views of leading members of our denomination, either by letter or orally, and from those on the east, as well as those on the west of the mountains, they are almost all in favor of our proposed "American Indian Mission Association."[1]

News from the supporters

It is a delight to read the numerous letters, from "ordinary" Christians to the most influential, who wrote to McCoy, offering support. Those already working among the Indians were, on the whole, very supportive of the new association. Charles Kellam wrote from the Creek Mission Station, very interested in cooperating with McCoy in his new work and invited him to come to his assistance. Kellam explained that there had been a spiritual breakthrough among the Creeks and a continuous revival had been going on for twelve months. During this time, he had baptized one hundred people and a co-worker, Mr. Tucker had recently baptized thirty-three more. Kellam

---

[1] Letter dated August 1, 1842, McCoy Papers, Reel 10.

related how he needed another missionary to help him and said that now a revival was going on, the Presbyterians have become interested in the Creek work and were thinking of setting up a work there, too. Kellam thought they would have difficulties as the Creek Indians on becoming Christians obviously preferred to become Baptists. Kellam hoped that McCoy would be able to help him.

Other missionaries such as B. C. Morse were not able to give such glowing reports, nonetheless, their letters show that they were reaping small harvests here and there as the Indian Mission moved into new areas such as Georgia and South Carolina. Actually Morse's work was more as an agent to sound out the area than to evangelize it, though he did not neglect to preach the gospel wherever he went. He was also authorized to collect funds from the various supporting churches and bodies and seek out those who were called to the Indian mission field.[2] Morse led a lonely life traveling through Indiana, Illinois, Ohio, Georgia, South Carolina, New York and New Jersey on behalf of the Indian Mission. His letters, written in beautiful hand-writing, reveal how he felt himself unsuited to the task and how dejected he became at times through homesickness, but also how he bravely carried out his work. McCoy fitted Morse out with testimonials to be presented to the various churches Morse visited and they provide us with a fine testimony of this humble child of God.[3] It is very moving to read with what love and respect Morse always addressed McCoy, calling him "Father" and signing himself as McCoy's son in the faith. Though Morse was now employed by the Indian Mission, he had been sent out by the Baptist church at New Albany, which he had formerly pastored and some time later East Baptist Church, Louisville supported him. This was in keeping with McCoy's sound practice of having churches support their own missionaries where possible. Morse's letters, especially his of January 1, 1844, from Society Hill, South Carolina, give deep insight into the problems that divided both the Union and the Baptist denomination. It was a great trial for Morse to give up meeting his fiancée for many months on end because of his travels and on being given a unanimous call to a church at Sing Sing, New York, he married and settled down there as a Baptist pastor towards the end of 1844. Morse's work as agent for the A.I.M.A. was

---

[2] See McCoy's letter to Morse, dated November 4, 1843, outlining his duties. McCoy Papers, Reel 11.

[3] Letter of Recommendation, dated November 1, 1843 signed by McCoy. McCoy Papers, Reel 11. There are several letters from Morse's pen on this reel.

taken over by G. B. Davis, who had worked for years as an agent for the American Bible Society. His testimonials and letters of recommendation, which have been preserved in the McCoy Papers, describe Davis as "extremely efficient" and "faithful" as a Christian worker. His first task was to work in Alabama for the Association.[4]

"Old" missionaries appointed anew

On March 4, 1843, McCoy wrote privately to Dr. Robert E. Pattison of the Foreign Missions Board, telling him of the advancement made. He explained how the A.I.M.A. had officially appointed Johnston Lykins a missionary on February 2nd,[5] trusting he would accept. The new Association were hoping that he would now continue his present work as an evangelist and physician under their auspices and support. McCoy had not heard Lykins' answer yet, but when it came, it was in the affirmative. It appears from this letter that McCoy had advised Lykins not to resign from the Board "provided the settlement of difficulties existing there would, in his estimation, justify it" and he was pleased that he was still working among the Potawatomis. As Lykins had resigned, McCoy did not need to poach him from his former patrons. McCoy had probably hoped that Lykins might have been a positive link with the Board in winning them over to the realization that a separate work for the Indians was necessary. The Indian Mission Association had also asked Lykins' brother David to consider becoming an A.I.M.A. missionary and on his acceptance, he was appointed missionary to the Weas on March 11, 1843.[6] Johnston Lykins' faithful interpreter, De Shane, had also accepted an appointment as missionary under the patronage of the Association. Brave, faithful Henry Skigget, who had been slighted in more ways that one by the Foreign Mission Board, was now also appointed an A.I.M.A. missionary and he was joined by Shawnee Chief Blackfeather who had supported McCoy so staunchly against the Board and the younger

---

[4] See McCoy's letter to Davis dated December 5, 1845, McCoy Papers, Reel 11.

[5] This date is not given in McCoy's letter but is taken from McCormick's *The Memoir of Eliza McCoy*, p. 45.

[6] David Lykins stayed there until the summer of 1845 and was then replaced by a Mr. Adams. He then continued his work at Shawnee.

missionaries, especially Barker.[7] In reality, it was Skigget who really founded the church among the Stockbridge and Delaware Indians. Thus Blanchard had not only robbed Skigget of his wife but also robbed him of his church. McCoy, who did not share the racism of his former patrons, was eager to appoint Christian Indians as fellow missionaries.

The Potts join the A.I.M.A.

What must have been a real joy to McCoy was the fact that Mr. and Mrs. Ramsey Potts decided to join the new mission. Potts had founded the first Baptist church in the Choctaw Territory, which he named Providence. This was situated ten miles west of Fort Towson and five miles north of the Red River. Starting with only four members, Potts commenced a blessed ministry and his faithful preaching brought in many repentant sinners. During one baptismal service, those watching were so moved that eighteen of them were convicted and professed faith in Christ. Shortly afterwards, Potts was able to baptize twenty-one new converts. Soon Potts had set up a daughter church across the Texas border and had to travel many miles on horseback to take the gospel to his two flocks. As he always preached along the routes he took, people came to faith in Christ on the way, so Potts soon found himself with four churches to pastor. Potts' wife was now an invalid and could not assist him in the work. Though he applied constantly to the Board, who were theoretically employing him, for support and missionaries to pastor his churches, they more or less ignored him and, indeed showed disapproval of his work. Finally Potts told the Board that they should make up their minds whether he was indeed in their employment or not and act accordingly. Wyeth writes in his *Poor Lo!* of how the Board refused to grant Potts all requests for aid so he turned to Isaac McCoy. Wyeth adds, "By unanimity on the part of all concerned, he and Mrs. Potts were commissioned at once by the new Association." This would suggest that the Board of Foreign Missions were only too pleased to be relieved of having Potts dependent on them.

Such appointments virtually meant that the work of the gospel was not only spreading southwards but it was continuing on both sides of the Kansas River. Many Stockbridge, Delaware, Potawa-

---

[7] See letter from David Lykins dated Wednesday night, February 8 (no year) in the undated collection of the McCoy Papers, Reel 12.

tomi and Shawnee Indians, as McCoy explained to Pattison, had previously forsaken the churches run by the remaining Foreign Mission Board staff and could be now gathered into churches again.

The Baptist Board had now virtually closed down their Indian mission

The American Baptist Board of Foreign Missions had now virtually given up their work among the Indians but their leading men, oddly enough, still strove to put obstacles in the way of the A.I.M.A. especially regarding McCoy and Lykins. The latter had more or less finished his translation of Acts into Potawatomi and other smaller portions of the Scriptures which were in the hands of Pratt when the break with the Board came. Pratt also had in his possession the proofs of Lykins' Matthew translation. Now McCoy asked the Board respectfully to return the manuscripts and the proofs to their owner and author. This the Board refused to do, although they added that they had no intention at present of going ahead with the printing. Their decision may have been based either on sheer animosity towards Lykins who held the copyright, or the fact that the Board had frozen work among the Indians and wanted nothing more to do with them, or because they had no staff to implement the checking of the manuscripts and proofs. The only man they had who would have been able to do this work was the Potawatomi Indian, John Jones,[8] Meeker's friend, who was now quite critical of Lykins and had showed that he was not sympathetic to Lykins' work. Whatever their reason for not going ahead with the printing, it would have been a fair and honorable move on their part to allow the manuscripts to be returned to those who were willing to put the translations into printed circulation. Instead, they hinted that if they saw money, they might change their minds.[9]

---

[8] The correspondence extant relating to the behavior of the Indians throughout these troubled times shows them moving backwards and forwards in their allegiance to various Christian leaders. The only reason for this is probably that they showed full trust in whoever happened to be placed over them in their churches at a particular time and rarely criticized what they were told. This fact was often abused by the whites. This might also explain why Blanchard wished to have the Delawares on their own with only himself to guide them.

[9] See letter from McCoy to Lykins dated February 22, 1844, McCoy Papers, Reel 11.

Delilah Lykins dies

Lykins and his wife continued to work faithfully among the Potawatomis but Delilah, who had been in delicate health some years, died on September 23, 1844. She was the eleventh of the McCoys' children to die on the Indian mission field. Lykins himself had been in poor health for some time and was heavily affected by his wife's death. McCoy then made him General Missionary-In-Charge of the Kansas River Territory. Speaking of Mrs. Lykins' death and the fact that the Lykins were one of God's first gifts to the A. I. M. A., Wyeth says:

> Mrs. Lykins was also the first of the Association's missionaries to be released from earth. The Master received from her renewed evidence of fidelity to the cause of the lowly, in one more year of consecration, then bade her enter into His rest. She went to Louisville, seeking recuperation in the arms of her parents and by the aid of physicians, and when it became apparent that she was uncurable, nothing could deter her from hastening back to the Indian country, that she might make her grave with those for whom she had cherished a pitying interest from her childhood.[10]

The Simerwells also join the A.I.M.A.

Happily the Simerwells, who had joined the A.I.M.A. on August 19, 1844, were able to labor among the Potawatomis. Simerwell had been finally dismissed from the Foreign Mission Boards' ever dwindling list of missionaries for reasons which were mere trumped up charges. It was obvious to most people outside of the Board and many people in the Board that Simerwell's high integrity was not in the least damaged. The final reasons the Board gave Simerwell for his dismissal was that he was carrying out the work of a blacksmith, and was not handing in his wages to the common missionary fund. This showed that the Board's left hand did not know what its right hand was doing in a most negative sense. Concerning Simerwell's occupation, Dr.Bolles had backed him in 1840 to carry on with that profession and concerning his wages, the Board knew very well that if they had kept them for use in the general missionary fund, this would mean that they would be breaking their arrangement with the Government

---

[10] *Poor Lo!*, pp. 73-74.

516

and with the missionaries. The missionaries were to be funded by direct donations from their Baptist brethren not the Government. Again, the Board were obviously wanting government salaries to finance their missionary work. Furthermore, Simerwell had never received a penny out of the common missionary fund as a result of his missionary activities and lived on a mere 450 dollars a year which was hardly sufficient to keep body and soul together, never mind finance his work and pay for his children's education in addition. The latter payments had been promised by the Board but never materialized. If he had given up his salary to the Board, he would have been penniless. However, Simerwell had told the Board that should they send a missionary to pastor the Potawatomi church, he was prepared to share his wage with him, knowing that such a missionary would not be adequately funded by the Board who appointed him. In April, 1844, Solomon Peck informed Simerwell that the Board were closing down their work among the Potawatomis. On August 21, 1844, the A. I. M. A. Board appointed Simerwell as their missionary to the Potawatamis.[11]

Eliza McCoy becomes a missionary to the Indians

Sad as it was for McCoy to lose his daughter to the hardships of the mission field, he was overjoyed to see his niece, Eliza McCoy (1813-1891), follow in her footsteps. Eliza was the daughter of his brother John McCoy and Jane McCoy, née Collins, of Silver Creek, Clark County, Indiana. She was born, the seventh of ten children, on April 1, 1813 and brought up in a large area of wilderness that her father was gradually turning into farm land. John was apparently converted when Eliza was eleven years of age and he then became a member of the Silver Creek Church, serving as a trustee, clerk and deacon. Eliza was the first of John and Jane's children to profess faith in Christ. She was baptized in 1829 and joined the Silver Creek Church which was then pastored by Isaac Worrell. Eliza was happy to see seven of her eight surviving brothers and sisters come to faith in Christ but sad to see the decline in the spiritual welfare of her church as Campbellism tore through its ranks. Soon after Eliza's conversion and baptism, the McCoys with a number of fellow believers separated

---

[11] See *The Contribution of Mr. Johnston Lykins and Robert Simerwell to the Preservation, Advancement and Evangelization of the American Indians*, esp. pp. 113-115 for a detailed account of these proceedings.

from the majority of the church, and re-founded the Silver Creek Baptist Church on its former principles and statutes, believing rightly that the Campbellites had perverted the faith of the church. The Association accepted the move but as they became influenced in their turn by Campbellism, they eventually ousted the McCoys and their friends in 1834 because of their Calvinistic and evangelical principles. A Christian, the Association now maintained, could not believe in missions, Sunday schools, tract societies and temperance which were of the devil and his work. In 1834, John McCoy assisted in the founding of Franklin College and remained on its board until his death twenty-five years later.

By this time, through hard work, John and Jane McCoy had become relatively prosperous so they could send Eliza to good schools where she maintained her Christian witness but also assisted in her home church, now Salem Baptist Church, as a Sunday school teacher. At the age of twenty, Eliza was sent for three years to the County Seminary at Wilmington, Indiana under the management of her brother Isaac. Here Eliza met Sarah Ann Osgood (1819-1852) who was called to serve the Indians with her. After Wilmington, Eliza studied at the Charlestown Seminary nearer home. Eliza's mother had died in 1835 and now she found that her father was managing badly on his own so she felt she must stay at home and manage his household. The fact that her brother John who lived with her and their father, had still not professed Christ had also prevented Eliza from having thoughts of marriage and leaving home. She believed that it was her duty to share Christ with John and provide a home for him.[12] Eliza followed the work of her Uncle Isaac very closely and when the A.I.M.A. was founded so near her home, all that she heard daily from her wider family gave her a deep longing to help the Indians herself. She finally applied to be accepted as a missionary to the Indians at the beginning of July 1844, now thirty-one years of age. Her uncle was, of course, thrilled and in his capacity of Corresponding Secretary wrote to his niece, officially welcoming her to the work of the mission and outlining her future duties:

LOUISVILLE, Ky., July 22, 1844.

Miss Eliza McCoy.

DEAR SISTER: On the seventeenth day of

---

[12] See Eliza McCoy's letter to her uncle outlining her humble fears and desires, dated July 1(?), 1844, McCoy Papers, Reel 11.

June last the Board of Managers of the American Indian Mission Association appointed you a missionary, to labor among the Putawatomie Indians within the Indian Territory. You will be expected to teach a school, and in every way in which you may have opportunity to impart religious instruction, by means of Sabbath schools, religious visits, and conversations, prayers, etc. The people to whom you go are susceptible of high mental improvement, and you will, as far as practicable, contribute to the elevation of their character. The history of the world shows that in all ages the improvement of females has been too much neglected. Your labors to instruct the females of the red race in domestic virtues and all useful knowledge, and especially in the duties and doctrines of Christianity, will be bringing salutary influences not only to bear upon the more obdurate sex, but it will be introducing those influences into the nursery, where the mouldings of mind and character are begun. Neither the Indians nor any other race of people can be elevated to the blessings of wholesome laws, intelligence in arts and in science, humanity and happiness, while the female half are degraded in a condition below their proper sphere; and especially if we would hope for a community to become religious we should promote piety among the females. The Board have been deeply affected with the meek distrust in yourself and the humble hopes you indulge of usefulness manifested by you in your communications on this subject; nor would they say aught to cause you to depart from the feet of Jesus, where others have meekly sat before you. Yet, be assured your calling is high, honorable, and involving great responsibilities. Your success, like that of the most eminently useful on earth, depends on the blessing of God. The two following sentences may form an appropriate motto. "I am of myself less than nothing and vanity," but "I can do all things through Christ who strengtheneth me." Remember, too, that in this world you will have tribulation. Could you correctly anticipate the character of your trials you would be better prepared to meet them. But they will commonly be of a nature unexpected; and if not so fully understood by us as to enable us to feel appropriate sympathy, they will all be known to God. Let the people with whom you shall mingle see that Christ and His religion is the burden of your thoughts, and the pattern from which you borrow the example that you furnish to others. We will contribute to your comfort as far as practicable. The sum of one hundred dollars in cash per annum has been voted for your support after reaching the field of your labors. This will probably be inadequate; but it is hoped that the deficiency can be supplied by donations in clothing or other articles which are not cash. Please to keep a journal, from which forward to us, frequently, such extracts as you may suppose will be interesting, and write us in such manner as you may deem proper. They who contribute to the support of missions are gratified with knowing their condition.

You will find among the people to whom you go some who are pious, and by all you will, we doubt not, be received with kindness. The brethren Lykins will assist in introducing you to the people, and it will be their duty and their pleasure to afford you counsel and assistance in all your affairs. In every matter of doubt or serious difficulty, or emergency of any kind, you are requested to appeal to one or both of them. While we feel confident that no restrictions unpleasant to you will embarrass your own views in regard to operations, we desire you to pay due respect to the views of the elder brother Lykins, who has had much experience in missionary matters, and who is an agent of the Board in the management of the affairs of our stations. May the nature of your employment and the appreciation of God cheer you, and Heaven's blessings be richly enjoyed by you. Signed by order and in behalf of the Board.

Isaac McCoy,
Cor. Sec., etc.

LOUISVILLE, KY., July 22, 1844.

To whom it may concern:

This is to certify that the bearer, Miss Eliza McCoy, was on the seventeenth day of June, 1844, appointed a missionary to the Indians by the Board of Managers of the American Indian Mission Association in Louisville, Ky. She has been instructed to labor as a school teacher among the Putawatomies, on the Osage River, within the Indian Territory, and in various ways to impart religious instruction to the extent of her opportunities. This appointment has been made upon testimonials full, clear, and unequivocal in favor of her talents and piety and devotedness to the interests of religion and the welfare of fellow beings. She leaves relatives and acquaintances to whom she is exceedingly dear, and to tear away from whom is like disturbing the strings about her heart and theirs, to make her residence with strangers of another race of people. She exchanges the comforts, refinements, and prospects of this land of civilization and religion for whatever may be experienced of a different character in the Indian's land. And all this self-denial is without the hope of any pecuniary reward beyond what is barely sufficient for her support for the time being. She goes to assist in elevating the degraded Indian female to the sphere in mental culture, domestic virtues, and Christianity for which the sex has been designed by the Author of our existence. She works on earth upon a thorny spot, but will not receive her reward in full until she gets to heaven.

Fervent prayers for her comfort and usefulness follow her, and she is most affectionately commended to favor and esteem wherever she may be. Especially is she commended to the Putawatomies, to whom we trust she will be the instrument of communicating lasting blessings.

> Signed by order and in behalf of the Board.
> Isaac McCoy,
> Cor. Sec., etc.

Meeker opposes the new mission

It was at this time that Jotham Meeker became most critical of the A.I.M.A.. On May 6, 1845, he wrote to Solomon Peck at the Baptist Foreign Mission Board requesting permission to work on behalf of the Board among the Potawatomis, which had become one of the A.I.M.A.'s main centers of service, and that John Jones[13] be appointed his assistant at $250 per annum. He knew that Johnston Lykins, who had just lost his wife, was already working among the Potawatomis and that the Simerwells were to continue to work with the A.I.M.A. there. He also knew that Eliza McCoy had started a school for Potawatomi children on the Osage River some fifty miles from the Westport settlement. In spite of this, and relying on some gossip he had picked up via Jones who was a member of the Ottawa

---

[13] Jones was one of the Indian boys McCoy had hoped would be allowed to study at the Columbian College. He received his higher education at Hamilton College, New York. Jones had been a member of the Ottawa church for seven years.

Mission Church and not the Potawatomi,[14] Meeker told Peck that the Simerwells were not and did not wish to be missionaries, that Lykins was not doing any visiting and was known as a physician and not as a missionary and that Eliza McCoy had no regular school hours and only taught three or four Indians when they chanced to visit her. Meeker adds that "Mr. Jones has always felt that no real good could be hoped for from the labours of Messrs. Lykins and Simerwell" and thus concluded that the A.I.M.A.'s presence among the Potawatomis was in name only. Here, it is clear, that the quarrels which had attended McCoy's dismissal, the Lykins' resignation and later the Simerwells' dismissal and the strong support these missionaries received from the Shawnee and Potawatomi Christians were still influencing opinions among both whites and Indians. That Meeker's information concerning the Simerwells was entirely wrong is witnessed by the A.I.M.A.'s December 1845 *Monthly Report* which described Simerwell's (and Lykins') missionary activities in glowing terms.

Lykins now General Missionary-In-Charge

If Meeker were as well-informed as he professed to be, he would have sympathized with Lykins in his loss and realized that he had been especially appointed as a physician by the A.I.M.A. which in no way indicated that he was not a missionary. Furthermore, Lykins had just been relieved of the work at Potawatomi for wider duties as General Missionary-In-Charge[15] and was organizing the establishment of a trade school for the Potawatomis. The Simerwells, who later worked closely with Eliza, had been appointed to succeed him in August, 1844. We know from Lykins' mail at this time how seriously he still looked upon his missionary duties.[16] He was now putting the finishing touches to his Potawatomi translation of Matthew and the Acts of the Apostles which had been put into book form at Meeker's and Pratt's printing press without Lykins having the opportunity to correct the proofs. Now Meeker, in criticism of Lykins' action in performing the translation, strongly opposed it because of the typo-

[14] Jones was, however, a Potawatomi Indian.

[15] Lykins had taken over much of the administration, organizing conferences, examining candidates etc. He still, however, felt himself very much a missionary.

[16] See his letter to McCoy dated October 17, 1843, McCoy Papers, Reel 11.

graphical errors and the scarcity of Potawatomis who could read. Again, Meeker's sole informant regarding alleged weaknesses in the translation was Jones. His sole evidence was a page or so of Lykins' translation which the missionary had discarded as being not good enough to be used and had done a better translation, which Meeker obviously knew nothing about or did not feel was worthy of mention. Meeker did not speak Potawatomi himself though he was highly critical of Lykins' knowledge of the language which his fellow-missionary had obtained after studies of many years.[17] Also, in his criticism of Lykins Sr. and the Simerwells, Meeker had completely forgotten David Lykins and his wife who were working strenuously for the A.I.M.A. among the Potawatomis. In his letter, Meeker gives the Board the impression that it was his idea alone to serve the Potawatomis, one of his reasons being that Simerwell was doing nothing. Actually, according to Simerwell, he had informed Meeker of the need for a further missionary at Potawatomi but Simerwell and Pratt had both recommended a Mr. Braybrook who appeared willing to take on the work, and not Meeker. Simerwell had also asked Lykins to find help for him in his work among the Potawatomis as the Board of Foreign Missions had officially closed down their work there so there were none of the Board's missionaries to share the burden.[18]

Meeker's criticism of Eliza McCoy totally unfounded

Meeker's strong criticism of Eliza McCoy was also totally unfounded. She had been assigned to do pioneer work among the Potawatomis on the Osage River, fifty miles from Westport where she was to start up a day school and Sunday school. Miss Osgood was given a similar task among the Weas which was a new opening for the A.I.M.A..[19] Such work took time to establish and it was hoped that the

---

[17] See Meeker's letter to Rev. Ira Allen dated January 22, 1845.

[18] Letter to Johnston Lykins from Andrew Fuller (the Indian not the famous British Baptist of that name) and Robert Simerwell dated August 19, 1844.

[19] See McCoy's letter to Harvey of the Department of Indian Affairs, dated August 5, 1844 concerning permission to open up a mission among the Weas. McCoy Papers, Reel 11. The Methodist Indian Mission Conference protested in writing to McCoy on September 2, 1844 as they were planning a similar move. A letter from the Department of Indian Affairs at St. Louis written October 11, 1844 confirmed official approval for the A.I.M.A. to go ahead.

day schools would grow into boarding schools as day school pupils tended to visit the schools erratically according to whether their parents needed them for household chores or not. During the hunting season, it was difficult to keep any Indian pupils at any kind of school. By the time Meeker was making his report concerning Eliza, she had already increased her three or four initial pupils to twelve and her class grew so quickly that she had twenty-eight in a very short time. Meeker's gossip was thus most obviously unbalanced and biased. He was also measuring with different measures. For instance, Meeker, signing himself "Moderator," had joined Pratt in petitioning the Foreign Mission Board exactly three years earlier, during their tiff with McCoy and Lykins, to grant Blanchard $225 per annum to set up a school among the Delawares, saying "the number of scholars proposed being eight." In the same letter, the two men asked for Barker to be paid $225 for teaching a proposed number of ten pupils at the Shawnee Mission.[20] Eliza was, unlike Blanchard and Baker, a qualified teacher and graduate of two colleges and received $100 per annum paid by the ladies of the Baptist church at Talladega, Alabama. She also received a possible $50 extra provided through common funding.[21] Eliza, however, gave twenty-five percent of her salary to finance poor children of whatever color who would otherwise have received no education.[22] It is also clear from Meeker's letter that even the low numbers "proposed" in the Board's school were based on future hopes rather than present facts, yet Miss McCoy was in active operation at the time of Meeker's criticism with pupils of flesh and blood, and not imaginary statistics. Indeed, the Westport pupils whom Miss McCoy taught before moving to found a work of her own, and whom Isaac McCoy, Jr. later taught, numbered twenty-six in 1845, with the numbers "increasing steadily."[23]

Meeker was also guilty of concealing information from the Board which would have thrown new light on Eliza McCoy's situation and probably won the Board's sympathy rather than their criticism. On October 23, 1844, a fierce tornado swept through Westport and Independence, tearing people and buildings along with it, causing much

---

[20] Letter to the Board dated May 4, 1841, ABFMS, Reel No. 100.

[21] Out of this money, Miss McCoy also purchased Bibles, including French ones, for distribution.

[22] See, for instance, Hayward's *John McCoy*, p. 134.

[23] See Isaac's letter to his father dated Westport, November 23, 1845, McCoy Papers, Reel 11.

suffering and many deaths. Eliza McCoy was teaching in the sturdily built, two-storied school-house at Westport. Suddenly the sky turned red and then yellow and was full of fire and a terrible howling noise was heard. The windows all crashed in at once and the whole building collapsed like a stack of cards and was swept off from the foundations. Eliza McCoy was left among the rubble with her head cut deeply in several places and her body grazed and bruised. It was a miracle that she was not swept away with the building as afterwards its timber and furniture was found scattered over a mile-long track and the bedding, linen and clothing were found hanging from the tops of trees. One of the ten people killed was a woman with a six-week-old baby. The infant child was blown into the air but was later found some distance away in the woods quite unhurt. In spite of this terrible ordeal, Miss McCoy and Miss Osgood were on their way two or three days later to take the gospel to the Wea people, spending their first night without sleep due to of the howling of the wolves around them. [24]

It took twelve days for the news of the natural catastrophe to reach Jeffersonville, Indiana where John McCoy, Eliza's father, was hoping to receive mail from his daughter. On Monday, November 4, he entered into his diary:

> Purchased a pair of Shoes at $1.25 of Beach & King, for Eliza - then crossed over to the City, when I heard the distressing intelligence of the dreadful tornado at Westport, Mo., but have not learned what individuals of our friends have suffered in this calamity, I wait in awful Suspence untill I receive further intelligence.

Two days later, John McCoy entered into his diary the words:

> Assisted my Brother (Isaac) in boxing up goods to send our Missionaries among the Indians. at dark two letters are recd. from Westport giving information of the Providential escape of our friends in the dreadful Tornado which passed them the 25th. ult.[imate] rending houses in which our friends were at the time, all to atoms, while a Merciful Providence miraculously preserved the inmates. how manifest is the controlling hand of a merciful

---

[24] While checking through this manuscript in Enid, Oklahoma, no less than fourteen tornadoes are sweeping through the State and even large sturdy buildings are being sucked up and destroyed as if they were made of flimsy paper. We Europeans can hardly imagine the awesome devastation they cause.

God in the awful scene above mentioned. how can I be sufficiently thankful for Eliza's preservation who was in the midst of the tornado. O! Lord help me to praise thee.[25]

It was on this initial period of Eliza McCoy's missionary life that Meeker based his criticism on what she was doing. On the very same day that Meeker wrote his gossipy, busybody letter to the Board, Eliza wrote to John McCoy from her new Potawatomi base, explaining that she was giving lessons in her room as the school building (destroyed by the tornado) was still being rebuilt. She assured her father that despite the difficult situation all were now in and which had led to the Indians drinking excessively for five or six weeks, she still trusted that her work among the Potawatomis would be useful, saying:

> At present our prospects are gloomy, but I suppose we must expect dark as well as bright seasons, and walk by faith. I don't despair, nor feel the least inclined to abandon the field. We must expect to go slowly, and meet with many blasted hopes and trials, which come in a way we do not expect.[26]

Meeker's criticism reflected the growing differences between Southern and Northern mentality

There was yet another reason behind Meeker's suspicion of his former superintendents and colleagues. Lines were already being drawn which culturally and politically separated the North and California from the South and what was the Western frontier before the opening up of the Indian Territory. The Board of Foreign Missions had identified themselves, apart from two or three objectors such as Spencer Cone and John Mason Peck, with Northern and Eastern politics. In the more southern states, the Baptists were consolidating into their own associations and conventions entirely separated from the north. In 1845 the Southern Baptist Convention was formed which immediately identified itself with the work of the A.I.M.A. and recommended to its churches in a formal resolution, that they should sustain the Indian Mission with zeal and liberty. Thus the union

---

[25] John did not receive Eliza's report of the incident, written on October 28, until November 12 when he first heard of her injuries.

[26] This is clear from a letter Eliza sent to John McCoy on May 6, 1845. See McCormick's *Eliza McCoy*, p. 60.

among the nation's and Indian Territory's Baptist churches was dissolved some fifteen years before political union was severed. Meeker believed his allegiance should be with the Northern Board.

Eliza writes to her uncle

Eliza McCoy's saintly, selfless life has been sympathetically recorded by her nephew, Calvin McCormick. She had experienced a relatively well-to-do childhood and early adulthood and her new life brought with it many hardships, including constant fevers which accompanied most of the missionaries' lives in the Kansas, Osage and Ohio river districts. A letter is extant dated Pottawatomi Baptist Mission, January 29, 1846 in which she writes to her uncle, Isaac McCoy after recovering from a period of illness and at a time when the Potawatomis were away hunting, taking their children with them:

Very Dear Uncle:

For nearly two weeks I have had no chills and fever, and I begin to hope that I am well. Various circumstances in connection with the little value these people place on education, prevent the children from coming long or regular enough to school to derive much benefit. Under these discouragements I have labored ever since I have been at Putawatomie, and now, while looking over all that I have done it appears almost nothing. I do not write in this way from a desire to leave. No, I do not know how I could bear the thought of leaving the field of labor while there remains a gleam of hope of usefulness. When we ask the Indians to send their children to school, they almost invariably say they would if we would keep them in our family all the time, as is done among the Shawanoes. Some have told us that for many years they have had the promise of a boarding school, but for as many years they have been disappointed, and now know not what to depend upon. If affairs could be managed so as to open a boarding school I think we might labor successfully, and then I should be cheerful and happy in the hope of benefiting the poor, unfortunate children of the Western prairies.

A few weeks since, a man was so anxious to send his little daughter to school that Mr. and Mrs. Simerwell agreed to take her into the family, as he lived too far for her to attend from home. Yesterday he came and pleaded so hard that they could not refuse to take the sister also. He said he did not like to send her to the Catholic

527

school. Brother Simerwell told him that if she came to our house he must allow us to teach her to read the Bible. He said that was what he desired. He said that he had a Bible that you gave him many years ago, and in which he reads and discovers that it condemns many things allowed among the Catholics. (This man when a boy was a pupil at Carey, Michigan, and was there taught to read at the Baptist school.) O! if we only had the means, we could work. I ask nothing on my own account, but for those who are really perishing for want of the bread of life. Would that I could speak with a voice and emphasis that would fasten upon the hearts and sympathies of all who live in your happy, happy Christian land.

Pray for your unworthy niece,

Eliza McCoy.[27]

The letter moved McCoy to set in motion plans for boarding schools.

Meeker's criticism played him into the hands of the Jesuits

It was truly a pity that Meeker was so openly outspoken in his criticism of Lykins as the Potawatomi Mission under Lykins' leadership was not only being criticized by a few of Lykins' former fellow-missionaries but by the Roman Catholics. The Papists were jealous of the fact that the Baptists had been able to enjoy a huge slice of Government funds for educational purposes and they were campaigning hard to persuade the Government to allow them to channel off a good deal of that money. Where the Baptist Foreign Mission Board closed down their work, the Roman Catholics moved in with the Board apparently happy to do business with them. Miss McCoy told her father:

The Jesuits can not give up the idea of monopolizing all the school fund. You remember the efforts made by them a year ago to get both schools. When they failed they said, "Never mind, we will watch Dr. Lykins and find some fault, and get him out of the country, and then we can succeed." But after watching with a hawk's eye they can find none, and now have persuaded their own party, with some others, to say they do not want a physician; that

---

[27] This letter shows, too, that Simerwell is still at the station and working in harmony with the McCoys in spite of Meeker's hints to the board recorded above.

the money expended for his salary had better be appropriated to some other person, thinking by this means to get rid of him. They are holding councils in various places for that purpose; and also to take possession of our buildings and farm. But how far they will succeed time will tell. I hope that Providence will not permit so many years of toil and labour to be entirely lost; yet if some speedy efforts are not made to prevent, much, very much will be lost. And I believe that the only remedy will be spiritual means. You know when popery reigned over the world, all carnal weapons were too weak. It was not until the Sword of the Spirit was raised that the beast was wounded, and now that alone can give the fatal stroke.[28]

The Jesuits had found out that Lykins had come off best in his differences with the Foreign Missions Board and now was at the head of a band of faithful workers who were determined to live for Christ alone. Though the A.I.M.A. had initial difficulties caused by the Board of Foreign Missions' determination to hold on to funds granted by the Government for Indian improvement, the matter had been cleared up with the Government and important people such as Lewis Cass and Wilson Lumpkin supporting them in the face of growing Roman Catholic claims. The latter were now striving hard to reverse this Baptist success even if it meant jeopardizing their own work.[29] Lykins' accreditation as physician to the Potawatomis was suddenly withdrawn by the War Department on May 31, 1844.[30] Politicians friendly towards the A.I.M.A. contacted Hartley Crawford for an explanation, suspecting that the Jesuits had been exerting their influence. Crawford denied this but his explanation proved that his denial was merely formal. The Roman Catholics, the enquirer was told, had complained about Protestant "interference" in general and Lykins in particular so that the Department had appointed a committee to look into the

---

[28] Letter dated August 31, 1849, McCormick, pp. 72-73. This letter shows, too, that Lykins is still an integral part of the A.I.M.A.'s staff.

[29] On one occasion, indeed, Lykins was told that he could expect no further money for that period as the Roman Catholics had succeeded in persuading the Government that he was a person of bad reputation and had been given the entire grant.

[30] Lykins had not been paid for his services to the Government for a year and five months but on May 31, 1844, he received a statement from the War Department saying he was to receive back payment from January 1, 1843. McCoy Papers, Reel 11. The sum was fixed at $1416.66 2/3 (two thirds).

matter. If the "sects" as Crawford called the various church bodies, could not agree among themselves, he would see that they were all thrown out of the Indian Territory. "Under these circumstances," Crawford argued, "it would be impolitic and unwise to appoint Doct. Lykins to any office among the Potawatomies."[31] Any criticism of Lykins from Meeker's or Jones' side was thus, in effect, an encouragement for the Jesuits and a step towards ending their work. Happily, Crawford's indifference towards Lykins changed quickly, or perhaps other Potawatomis had made themselves heard in favor of Lykins because he soon received further Government appointments as a physician to the Potawatomis.[32] In the spring of 1846, Lykins was even asked to consider a nomination as Government Indian Agent himself.[33]

Sadly, Hartley Crawford was all too quick to act on negative reports against the Baptist missionaries as shown in his action against Evan Jones in 1839. He had been told that Jones was guilty of the most atrocious crimes and thus, without checking the facts, gullibly wrote to Lucius Bolles to inform him that Jones was undesirable as a missionary to the Indians.[34] Lewis Cass had shown himself to be a far greater friend of the Indian Mission.

Skigget writes to Lykins

Johnston Lykins received a warm letter from his old friend Henry Skigget dated April 29, 1845 which contained much interesting though rather mystifying information. Skigget had suffered much from the Blanchard-Barker scandals and had been excluded from the Delaware Church, obviously because of his protests at what was going on. He was now worshiping with the Methodists, though he was a staunch Baptist by persuasion. Referring to the recent difficulties, Skigget addressed Lykins as "a fellow-sufferer in this unfriendly world" but gave a hint that things were about to be better at his and Lykins' former church, saying:

---

[31] Letter dated March 15, 1844, McCoy Papers, Reel 11.

[32] See statements from the United States to Johnston Lykins concerning payment for services rendered throughout 1844 and 1845 etc. on Reel 11, McCoy Papers.

[33] Letter from Lykins to McCoy dated March 27, 1846, McCoy Papers, Reel 11.

[34] See McLoughlin's *Champions of the Cherokees*, p. 193-197.

> I thought that I would write a few lines
> But I have not much but I can say the troubles that have
> Been hanging around us seems to be at a stand yet we dont
> Realy feel our selves safte [safe? in safety?]. The great ty-
> rants has at last Been put Down in publick they took their
> final fall the 11 of this month, the Delawares had to put
> them Down and it was not done in a corner.
>   The enemy has Been in our rank the mat-
> ter will be explained whenever I can see you.[35]

The findings of the church council concerning Blanchard reach the A.I.M.A.

Skigget was obviously referring to information he had heard concerning the much delayed church council meeting to look into the action of Blanchard, Barker, Pratt, Meeker and the Board which had led to Lykins' resignation. A council at which Lykins' name, at last, as Lykins foretold, would be cleared. This council, however, did not sit until August. As Skigget obviously had difficulties spelling "April" in his letter, it might just be possible that he had meant to write "August."

McCoy, who had been ill for several months, wrote to his son-in-law on September 10, 1845 and told him then that the findings of the church council had been placed before the A.I.M.A. Board and that they were gratified to see how "creditable" Lykins and their party had come out of the battle.[36] David Lykins was rather more explicit when he wrote to his brother on September 26th, as he had spoken to various representatives at the church council and they had shown that Barker and his associates had behaved wrongly. David Lykins, however, wrote that Barker was trying to make the best of things by now claiming that both sides had been in the wrong. Indeed, there were still no signs whatsoever that the guilty members showed any remorse. Meeker who, in his journal, had referred on several occasions to the troubles with Lykins and hinted that Simerwell was also implicated, recorded on August 1, 1845, "Delegates from several churches meet to investigate charges preferred against Br[ethre]'n Blan-

---

[35] Letter written from Fort Leavenworth, Kansas, McCoy Papers, Reel 11.

[36] McCoy Papers, Reel 11.

chard, Pratt, Barker and myself"[37] but he neither recorded the verdict of the council nor his own views of it. Dr. Lykins' brother commented:

> The whole decision is This, and This <u>alone</u> will the council support: = Barker & co. out of <u>order</u>, in error, The greatest of which is in <u>supporting a man</u>[38] of notoriously <u>bad character</u>."

David Lykins added that now and for ever ministers and Baptist associations must accept the findings of the council, and he advised his brother to have them published.

The Blanchard party hit back

Perhaps this was because, on August 21, a friend of Blanchard, Barker, Pratt and Meeker, signing himself "Lesli"[39] had written a most glowing report to the editor of the *Christian Watchman* concerning how these men were "greatly beloved" by all the Shawnees, Potawatomis, Ottawas, Stockbridges and Delawares and how evident was the unity of love and trust among them. He explained how devoted all were to one another and how successful were the enterprises of the three men, yet how terrible tribulations had come upon the churches through one man who had disguised himself as a sheep.[40] This is obvious a reference to Lykins and was engineered to counteract the findings of the council of churches which showed that the truth was quite different. It is interesting to note that the article, which was published, was written under a pseudonym, the author being in reality a Mr. Ellis. No sooner had this article appeared than a Mrs. Eliza Fuller wrote from Shawnee to tell McCoy that the situation there was in

---

[37] See Extracts from Meeker's journal in *Jotham Meeker: Pioneer Printer of Kansas* compiled by McMurtrie and Allen, pp. 98-99, 105-106.

[38] The words "order" and "supporting" are underlined three times in David Lykins' letter.

[39] Other MS give "Leslie." See Lykins' undated refutation of this article in McCoy Papers, Reel 12, "Undated Statements concerning a Controversy over the Shawnee Baptist Church." Here, the "certain individual" referred to as causing "the sea of tribulations" at Shawnee is obviously Blanchard.

[40] McCoy Papers, Reel 11. Referring to Br. B. and his wife (Blanchard? Barker?) the writer underlines the words, "greatly beloved by the church."

a most hopeless state with few meetings being held. She reported that Mr. Ellis had not attended normal worship, which had almost ceased to exist, but a special two day joint-fellowship meeting of the Baptists and the Methodists[41] to which the Indians had been encouraged to attend by means of a promised feast. The report was totally misrepresentative of the week by week life of the church. Yet Mr. Ellis had spoken of the way the missionaries fed the Indians and how they were overwhelmed with work in doing so as if this was their daily occupation. Mrs. Fuller comes very near to saying that the whole affair was orchestrated to give a totally wrong impression to outsiders of what was really happening. She goes on to write:

> Happy would it be for these people and this mission were the indians as he represents but the reverse is the case - such incorrect statements can do no good. They give the Christian community a false impression - excite hopes not to be realised under the present state of things - whereas if a true representation were made it might call forth the prayers and sympathies of the christian church - and be attended by a divine blessing.[42]

Mrs. Fuller was full of complaints concerning the lack of church discipline practiced which indicated that the Barker-Blanchard team had not changed their views for the better. One can understand the low spirits Mrs. Fuller was in as she describes the days of God's mercies when McCoy was there and compares them with the doldrums the Barker-Blanchard team has caused where church life had become "unsanctified by grace."

Ellis' totally exaggerated article is also difficult to accept because at the time of its writing the Baptist Foreign Missions Board was debating whether they should disband themselves, turn themselves into a lay organization, close down their Indian missions, hand them over to the A.I.M.A., form a new Indian mission association for the Northern States only, or establish a new foreign missions board on a more limited scale.[43] Some brethren were even proposing a union of

---

[41] The Methodist Superintendent, William Johnson, who had protested against the Barker-Blanchard-Pratt team had died.

[42] Letter written October 17, 1845, McCoy Papers, Reel 11.

[43] See letter from J. M. Peck from the Board's meeting at the Philadelphia Convention to McCoy dated September 27, 1845. It seems that at last the Board had come to the general conclusion that clergymen were not the best

the Board's work with that of the A.I.M.A.. Although this was almost a declaration of bankruptcy on the part of the Foreign Missions Board, there was obviously no hard feelings against the A.I.M.A., indeed, the Board had stressed, according to J. M. Peck, now its Chairman on Indian Affairs, that they sought cooperation and harmony with the missions McCoy and his friends had brought into being. Lykins had been exonerated by the church council and now, in reality, the Board's feelings amounted to an exoneration for Isaac McCoy. Two months later, McCoy heard from J. M. Peck that the Foreign Mission Board at the Baptist Convention were finding their Indian work declining and wished now to enter into brotherly negotiations with the A.I.M.A..[44] Oddly enough, now that Blanchard's true character was common parlance, the Board took no disciplinary action against him and made no apology to McCoy and Lykins for their unbrotherly conduct towards them based on their support for Blanchard.

McCoy advises against publishing the council's minutes

Johnston Lykins referred the matter of publishing the council minutes which exonerated him to his father-in-law, but McCoy advised against such action. He felt that readers who obviously would not know the background to the council meeting might believe that what the minutes revealed was characteristic to missionary work among the Indians and that all missionaries were "backbiters." He thus concluded, referring to Blanchard and Barker, "I am aware that the council found them guilty, but they have not spoken of it in a way to be of any use to the public." McCoy and Lykins had received justice. They did not need revenge.[45] McCoy was now in deep correspondence with the Board of Foreign Missions who were rapidly turning once again to McCoy's advice, if not leadership. Conscientiously, McCoy did not want to rock the boat that was so peacefully gliding into the correct harbor by publishing anything that would disturb that course.

(*cont.*) people to handle fiscal matters.

[44] Letter from Peck dated November 20, 1845.

[45] McCoy to Lykins probably written November 10, 1845 or shortly before (date on second part of page), McCoy Manuscripts, Reel 11.

The work among the Creeks and Choctaws is strengthened

McCoy had long been troubled that the flock he had establish-ed at the Muscogee Church at Ebenezer, Three Forks (Oklahoma) had been allowed to go without a pastor by the Foreign Missions Board so long and he had striven to find a person competent, and indeed, brave enough to take John Davis' place. The Creeks were still fiercely opposed to missionary work among them, apart from the provision of free education, and they still practiced their old law of applying thirty-nine whiplashes to the backs of any of their tribesmen who became "me-ko-sa-pulke" or "praying people." Happily two Creek brethren, Joseph and William Islands had been shepherding flocks in North Fork since around 1840, assisted by Negro preachers, one of whom, known as Old Billy, had led Joseph Islands to Christ. It was not long before the Island brothers turned to McCoy for assistance and the A.I.M.A. Board was pleased to make Joseph Islands one of their missionary pastors. The following is just a sample of the difficulties of being an ambassador for Christ in the Indian Territory of those days. Joseph Islands relates:

> We have had great persecution here, which Brother Smedley has informed you. Brother Jesse received fifty stripes, and Brother Bitly received the same; and Brother O-Sah-he-na-hah, a native, received fifty stripes. These three brothers belong to our Church. One coloured man, a member of the Methodist Church, has received fifty stripes, and one native sister, of the same, received fifty stripes, and it was supposed that she would die, for they whipped her until she fainted, but she recovered. They commenced with the intention to whip all we leading ones, saying that would stop all the rest of them. They said we were the ones that's causing all the people to pray. They want to whip me and my brother Harry; and on one Saturday the opposing chief sent out and gathered his people to come to our meetinghouse on the Sabbath to whip us; but God restrained their wrath, and some feared to come upon us; and from that time they never whipped any more.[46]

The Association promised Joseph Islands financial support for his work and forwarded him an initial draft of $50 but Islands refused to accept the money, arguing that it would be a poor testimony to his

---

[46] *Poor Lo!*, pp. 77-78.

unconverted fellow Indians if they heard he was receiving money. Instead, he asked for books which would "bring me [him] to the knowledge of the gospel."

McCoy had also long wanted to send a missionary to the Choctaws whom he admired so much. They were now living near the South Canadian River in the southeastern area of what is now Oklahoma. McCoy had thought that Morse, who was used to a wide itinerant ministry, would be the man for the task of combining a work among the Choctaws with keeping an eye on the Muscogee Church, but he felt unequal to the task. On May 23, 1844, the Board was pleased to appoint Sidney Dyer and his wife to this work and the choice proved a remarkably good one. In his letter of appointment, McCoy wrote the solemn and sober words:

> You go to people, who in more than three hundred years' acquaintance with men from Europe, have discovered little to convince them that the Bible teaches good will towards man, or that they had a friend upon earth. You go to assure them by your example and instructions that they <u>have</u> friends on earth - that they have a <u>friend</u> in heaven. Long as has been the period of missionary efforts for the Salvation of the red men, yet so feeble have those efforts been that missionaries at present in the field and you who are on your way there may be esteemed only <u>pioneers</u> in this great work. So live then brother and sister, and so labor, and so die, that they who succeed you, will be benefitted by your example - "Be faithful unto death."[47]

The unction of being "faithful unto death" was probably suggested to McCoy by Joseph Islands who had asked him to send his people an evangelist "who is not afraid to die for Christ's sake." Dyer showed this faithfulness and under threat of losing life and limb did a great work among the Indians of the Canadian River and Fort Gibson area. He soon found worthy companions in the Islands brothers and their faithful Negro helpers, and held camp meetings in the Three Forks and North Fork districts which drew hundreds of hearers. Indeed, Walter Wyeth says that there was a "great awakening" at North Fork, and as many as twenty-two were baptized after Dyer preached on the memorable day of the Green Corn Dance when the whole party had to cross over into Choctaw territory so as not to raise

---

[47] Letter from the A.I.M.A. Board to Dyer, thought to have been written on May 23, 1844.

the passions of the Creeks.[48] Soon afterwards, Dyer was able to baptize forty-four more new converts. Dr. J. M. Gaskin and Louise Haddock in their gem of a book *Baptist Heroes in Oklahoma*, say that at Dyer's camp meetings, one could count 500 to 600 horses tied to the trees there awaiting their riders who were learning of the Indians' heavenly friend. Joseph Islands died as a young man in 1848 after establishing a sound New Testament church with 170 members, all who had been gathered in just a very few years. By 1854 Gaskin and Haddock tell us, the Three Forks Church had 450 members and the North Fork Church 375 members.

Dyer, who published several volumes of poetry, wrote of the Indians:

> The Indian tribes, scarce known to History's page, -
> And where so soon alas! Alone we'll find them!
> For, hurled from earth, as with a tempest's rage,
> Their names and graves will be wrecks behind them -
>
> To these poor wanderers in their native land,
> Bespoiled of home, oppressed, and sorrow driven,
> We give the warm and sympathetic hand,
> And lead the way to brighter homes in Heaven.
>
> Where once was heard the wild exultant shout,
> With ghastly trophies at the war-belt clinging,
> The red-man kneels in worship most devout,
> In Christ-like love his soul's redemption singing.[49]

J. M. Peck supports McCoy on behalf of the old Board

Two months after being told that the Foreign Missions Board were willing to cooperate with McCoy, he heard most welcome news again from his old friend J. M. Peck. McCoy had approached the Foreign Mission Board with his proposals and Peck now confessed that their Indian missions were disintegrating and that resolutions had been proposed at the Baptist Convention that the Board should formally enter into brotherly negotiations with the A.I.M.A..[50] A report

---

[48] *Poor Lo!*, pp. 74-75.

[49] *Baptist Home Missions in America*, p. 280.

[50] Letter from Peck dated November 20, 1845.

was published which must be quoted in full as it was one of the crowning victories of McCoy's missionary calling:

> Report of the Committee on the Communication from the
> American Indian Mission Association.
>
> Your Committee to whom was referred the communication
> from the American Indian Mission Association ask leave to
> exhibit the following Report.
>
> The proximity of the Indian Mission
> Association to the Indian Territory; - the interest manifestly
> felt in the churches in the Western Valley to rally around
> that Association as a center of action;- the confidence
> reposed by this Convention in the ability and willingness of
> that body to sustain and carry forward the work of Indian
> Missions;- the wider fields opening and the pressing calls
> made in foreign lands, demanding the undivided energies
> and means of this Convention;- and the deficiency for sev-
> eral years past in our resources to carry forward the vast
> work to which God has called us in our eastern fields;- are
> circumstances favourable to having Indian Missions
> brought under the care of the Indian Mission Association.-
>
> Therefore, Resolved, That it be
> recommended to the Board to give special and persevering
> attention to this object;- to renew correspondence with the
> Board of the Indian Mission Association on the subject, and
> to take such other measures as may be deemed advisable to
> bring the subject before the Missionaries in the Indian Ter-
> ritory, that their views may be consulted and the whole
> business be finally disposed of as may be satisfactory to
> each party concerned.-
> All which is respectfully submitted.
> J. M. Peck, Chairman

Interesting enough was that Solomon Peck, who had been the
most critical of the so-called Acting Board's men against McCoy and
Lykins, signed this document.

There were obviously mixed feelings about John Mason Peck's
support of McCoy and some Board members began to play down Peck's
role in supporting his friend, claiming that he acted more out of pity
for McCoy rather than for reasons of missionary strategy. This is the
attitude Board Member, Rufus Babcock, takes to Peck. Babcock was
the last individual to see Peck's fifty-three volumes of journals and
letters when he gave them over to the Mercantile Library in St Louis.

The story goes that he sent them to a paper mill to be turned into wrapping paper. Babcock, in his work *Memoir of John M. Peck,* allegedly bases all he says on Peck's own words but obviously interprets them in a manner quite foreign to Peck's character as revealed in his extant writings. Paul M. Harrison does an excellent job of explaining this phenomenon in his 1965 "Introduction" to the Southern Illinois University Press reprint of Babcock's *Memoir.* Thus Babcock says of Peck's attitude to McCoy and his work:

> He [Peck] pushed forward to meet the Western Association in Cincinnati. He reached the city the 27th [Oct. 1842], after the meetings had commenced. Here he participated in all the important deliberations. The formation of the Indian Missionary Association was one of the chief of these; and though he did not expect much benefit from it, further than to gratify and sustain the veteran McCoy and his family, and to gratify some local feeling in the West, which was scarcely satisfied with having a mission so peculiarly Western in its scope, managed exclusively by an Eastern Board, he thought it better on the whole to gratify this demand [rather] than to resist it.[51]

From 1842 to 1846, i.e. during the four years after Babcock closes his account of the relationship between McCoy and Peck, the two men were in most brotherly correspondence concerning the American Indian Missionary Association, as witnessed also by the above quoted letter. These records were readily available to Babcock, and would have most likely altered his view of the relationship between McCoy and Peck, had he consulted them and used them.

McCoy against attacking the Blanchard group in the press

Lykins now prepared a refutation of Ellis' article for publication and was supported by W. C. Buck, then President of the A.I.M.A., and David Lykins. Naturally, Lykins was most upset at being described as a wolf in sheep's clothing by Ellis but here, again, his father-in-law intervened. He told Lykins that Ellis had not named him in person so that they could not be attacked on that point. Obviously, Lykins was intended, but this could not be proved. If Lykins were to object, McCoy argued, the Blanchard-Barker group would suggest that

---

[51] Babcock, p. 314.

this showed that Lykins had a guilty conscience or say that a Methodist was meant and not Lykins. In this way they would gain an advantage over him and anger him the more. McCoy also pointed out that of the thousand of the *Watchman's* readers, not one in a hundred would associate the offensive reference with Lykins. Obviously, McCoy felt that the morals of Barker-Blanchard and co., as he called them, would permit any lie but for the sake of Lykins' own testimony and the future of the Indian Mission, he advised again against refuting them in print. McCoy told Lykins that the Report of the Baptist Convention concerning a probable hand-over of the Foreign Mission Board's work among the Indians to the A. I.M.A. had been published in almost all of the Baptist periodicals in the North, South, East and West of the United States so that the position of himself and Lykins had been clearly vindicated without them having to go to the press against their enemies. McCoy added that the Foreign Mission Board had itself testified to the public's confidence in the A.I.M.A.'s position and that Lykins himself was again highly respected by Government, Board and Association alike. Knowing this, McCoy advised Lykins, he should not bother about the petty article of one who had not the courage to sign his own name nor mention Lykins'. McCoy then told his son-in-law that he should read the current issue of the *Monthly Report* where he and Simerwell were held up to public view as examples of patience, and fidelity in missionary labors. As a further soother, McCoy spoke of plans for his new venture with the *Indian Advocate* and promised Lykins that, "the designs of those mischievous men to injure you will not be overlooked. Well may they come out like Satan 'with great wrath' for they have reason to suppose that their time is short." Lykins, as usual, was pleased to follow the advice of his devoted father-in-law. [52]

Seeking reconciliation

Instead of nursing his grudges, Lykins and his brother strove to be reconciled to Barker, Meeker and Pratt. A reconciliation with Barker proved impossible. He refused to recognize the new Potawatomi Church under David Lykins' pastorate and refused to acknowledge the findings of the council of churches and the Blue River Asso-

---

[52] See letter dated December 7, 1845, McCoy Papers, Reel 11. In this letter, most encouraging concrete plans, already partly materialized, for a number of new missionaries and agents are laid, showing how the work is growing.

ciation which had condemned his action. A reconciliation with Meeker was most improbable but Lykins was able to write to McCoy at the beginning of 1846 to tell him that he and Pratt were in fellowship again.

The situation had been very difficult for Pratt. As a young, keen missionary, he was immediately seized upon by the Board to be their "informant" on the characters and activities of his fellow missionaries. One of his tasks was to spy on the senior missionaries and report to the Board about what he had seen or heard. This, no doubt, caused him to suffer from a bad conscience and, at times, he rebelled and told his fellow missionaries what the Board demanded of him. We have a letter extant which was written by Pratt to Lykins on the subject, in which Pratt says:

> I have had interviews with Dr.Bolles and intend to have more. They have requested me to be within call for a while so as to enable them to inquire, as often as things present themselves to their minds in regard to the condition of their missions in your vicinity. I find them peculiarly inquisitive, and no part of man is left unexplored. So that sometimes I have to answer questions which in other cases,[53] I had rather not have had asked.[54]

Pratt had now come to regret and condemn Barker's and Blanchard's irregular and divisive actions and confessed in his own excuse that he had been "carried away with excitement." Since the end of 1845, Pratt had striven to mediate between the Lykins on one side and Barker and Meeker on the other and was supported by the Potawatomis and Weas. Johnston Lykins wrote to McCoy on April 13, 1846 explaining how things had turned out:

> By some action of the church yesterday we are entirely separated from Barker and Meeker. We voted that they had by their course excluded themselves, that all connected with them should be separate from us, but will not affect the standing of native converts.[55] Pratt made acknowledgements and settled the affair in that way. We feel relieved of a long standing trouble and have voted to

---

[53] Word unclear in MS.

[54] Dated November, 1834, Reel 8.

[55] A lengthier version found at the end of Reel 11 of the McCoy Papers makes it clear that though Barker and Meeker are excluded from fellowship, the Indian brethren in their churches are not.

send delegates to ask admittance into Blue River Association.[56]

The Board waited six years before annulling Blanchard's ordination on grounds of adultery

These events had obviously transpired some months earlier and Lykins had not previously mentioned them to his father-in-law, perhaps fearing that the information would cause him some anxiety in view of his transactions with the old American Baptist Foreign Missions Board. It is strange to relate that Blanchard drops fully out of the missionaries' correspondence at this time and one wonders whether it was because a reconciliation with him was thought not possible or was even undesirable or that he was no longer at the Delaware Church. On January 7, 1848, some six years after the Board had received positive evidence that "there was something wrong" with Blanchard, and a year and half after McCoy's home-call, the Board who had connived with Blanchard all the way against McCoy and Lykins finally annulled Blanchard's ordination and dismissed him from their services on the grounds of his adulterous character.[57] No attempt was ever made by the Board to justify their former support of Blanchard nor were apologies forthcoming to Skigget, McCoy's widow, and widower Lykins for the ignoble treatment they had received from the Board. No apologies were made by the Board to the Potawatomi, Shawnee, Delaware, Ottawa and Stockbridge churches for the terrible tensions and destruction of fellowship which the Board had imposed upon the Indians through their mismanagement, worldly action and lack of spiritual and moral discipline.

The Government move the Potawatomis again

Just as McCoy thought that all was well with his work, he received news from Lykins that the Government were planning to resettle the various Potawatomi bands who were somewhat scattered along the eastern edge of the Indian Territory. Further rumors arrived, saying that the Senecas, Shawnees, Quapaws and other tribes on the Osage River were about to be moved and a treaty to that effect

---

[56] McCoy Papers, Reel 11.

[57] Meeker's journal, McMurtrie and Allan, p. 108.

was being prepared. McCoy replied to Lykins on January 30, 1846, shocked beyond measure, saying, "I am very much opposed to it. As soon as they begin to move the tribes about, the whole policy will be unsettled. The next thing after their removal will be the settling of white people on the lands they leave." This, too, for McCoy, meant that the Indian Territory for which he had campaigned for so long and so successfully was now in danger of being broken up, with the result that the Indians would be rendered homeless once more. It was, to him, a sign that certain parties in the Government wished to have the Act of 1834 setting aside a "permanent" home for the Indians repealed. McCoy was also aware that the Indians had been promised their own territory as a Christian gesture and their possession of this country was, to them as to McCoy, a sign that the Christian God was with them. Once the territory was broken up, McCoy felt that it would be most difficult to rally the Indians again for Christ. Though he had been very ill for a long period the year before and was still very weak, McCoy felt he must once again journey to Washington and plead the cause of the Indians against the "abominable measures" which were now being discussed by the Union's politicians. It was to be his last strenuous journey to the capital.

Isaac McCoy returned from Washington much the worse in health, suffering from what he called inflammatory rheumatism and loss of appetite, but he refused to take to his bed as there were such urgent matters to attend to. He was in high hopes that a law would now be passed securing the external boundaries of the Indian Territory and letters from Washington now assured him that such a law was inevitable. Even so, he continued to campaign for the retention of the external borders to the Indian Territory. On April 16 at a conference of the A.I.M.A. at Columbus, Mississippi, the Association Board wrote a long letter to the President of the United States, arguing for a retention of the external borders of the Indian Territory as they were defined at the time of the passing of the 1834 Act. It appears from this letter that McCoy was in possession of information showing that certain politicians were striving for an amendment to laws passed before the 1834 Act which made it possible for whites to give the Indians an alternative piece of land should the Indians' land be required for white settlers.

Consolidating the old work and starting new ventures

McCoy was now impatient to have the entire work among the Indians, neglected by the Board of Foreign Missions, up and running again without further delay. First, he made sure that the old stations were fitted out with buildings and schools, as in the case of the Potawatomis and the Weas. He then planned new work among the Chickasaws, Creeks, Senecas and Mohawks, employing a number of new missionaries and agents, all of whom had extremely good testimonials. Next, he introduced a system of funding the A.I.M.A. missionaries in advance each quarter so that the A.I.M.A. missionaries should not go through the torments of never having cash in hand to meet requirements and thus have to go into debt. Relying heavily on Lykins to organize the reforms, McCoy was very strong in his praise of his son-in-law. McCoy was also liberal in his praise for Simerwell. The latter had just written to McCoy who told Lykins, "I like the letter and love the man."[58]

Some Eastern Baptists still claimed authority over the West

Though the Board of Foreign Missions were gradually phasing out their work among the Indians, there were those among them who would not tolerate any other body doing work among the Native Americans in the name of the Baptist churches. John McCoy attended the General Association of Baptists held at Franklin in 1843 and was most upset at the anti-Indian Mission sentiments expressed there and the "expressions of abuse" used by the Easterners against their Western brethren. Attacks against the A.I.M.A. were so fierce that John tells how Isaac had to repel them with energy and force:

> leaving no room for a doubt but that they are both engaged to injure as far as in their power, the interest of this organisation in the west, and also the good character and influence of some of its worthy patrons, and it is manifest our eastern Brethren are determined to crush every organisation or institution in the west which is not subservient to their caprice, and peculiar notions, or rather their immediate control.[59]

The A.I.M.A. missionaries could not understand why Meeker was visiting conferences at which A.I.M.A. delegates were attending, apparently with the sole idea of opposing them though he had re-

---

[58] Letter written March 27, 1846, McCoy Papers, Reel 11.

[59] John McCoy's journal entry for August 11, 1843, taken from *John M'Coy: His Life and His Diaries*, pp. 80, 132.

ceived nothing but kindness from their hands in the past. Solomon Peck was still something of a problem. Although he had signed the document recommending full cooperation with the A.I.M.A., he too, along with Professor Stevens who had so angered John at the Franklin Convention,[60] still hung on to visions of an American Baptist Foreign Mission Board which would dominate over and represent American Baptist policies and thus serve as the spokesman, if not chief executive of the national Baptist denomination. McCoy wrote to Lykins:

> Solomon Peck and his Clique are too ambitious to consent to a transfer of their missions to us. But almost the whole denomination is in favor of it. Necessity will drive them to the measure, not only because of the overwhelming opinion against them, but abolition will compel them, so far as Cherokees, Shawanoes, and Delawares are concerned. Solomon told me they did not intend to appoint any more missionaries to the Indians. We must not hurry matters too fast, all will soon be right - I wish Meeker was out of their scrape - He would do well if placed in good company.[61]

Meeker makes off with the Potawatomi Church Book

There was another reason why the A.I.M.A. people wanted to contact Meeker. After the Potawatomi Church had recovered somewhat from the Blanchard affair, they elected David Lykins as pastor. This ought to have been recorded in the Church Book but it had disappeared. Pratt told the church that he had caught Meeker wrapping it up to take home with him, which he had no business to do as he had no function whatsoever within the Potawatomi Church. Pratt had not hindered Meeker in his suspicious undertaking and that was the last ever seen of the Church Book. Could it be that Meeker was wanting to obliterate any negative allusions to himself and his friends which might be open to public view? If so, he must have been greatly disappointed at the outcome because the new Church Book recorded both the disappearance of the old book at his hands and the fact that

---

[60] Professor Stevens had criticized the *Baptist Banner and Western Pioneer* which favored Indian missions.

[61] Ibid.

Meeker had refused to cooperate in the church councils and conferences.[62]

The Foreign Missions Board turn to McCoy for advice and help

There was one further matter which was to McCoy's advantage. The Foreign Missions Board, in winding up their work with the Indians, were eager to sell any former mission land which could be legally proved to be theirs and also cash in on the improvements made to Governmental property in their care. As such property had been obtained mostly through McCoy's intimate connection with the Government, they needed McCoy to help them sort out matters of ownership and rights. This was a most delicate situation for the Board as it was their misuse of Government provided facilities and compensation gained through improving them which had led to their quarrels with their missionaries.[63] A further problem involved in these transactions, which must have saddened McCoy's heart, was that the Baptist Board was actually aiming to sell former Indian Mission territory to the Roman Catholics. The McCoy family had endangered life and limb and used all their energies and prayers to obtain that land for their missionary work. The irony of the situation was that the Board could not do without McCoy's help in this their last disgrace. McCoy had come to the Board's help while he was at Washington and had clinched a property deal for them, but once he left, the Board began to play for more time and, most likely, more money and then turned again to McCoy to help them out of another mess they were getting themselves into. It was just like old times! McCoy's comment here is typical of the way he strove to live at peace with all, including those who had made themselves his enemies. He told Spencer Cone on May 15, 1846:

> The conduct of the Board towards me has long been such that I felt under no obligation to aid in their affairs in any way excepting upon the christian principle of rendering good for evil which I have had an opportunity of doing, and have done often.

---

[62] There are many Church Book entries appertaining to the Potawatomi church at the end of Reel 11 of the McCoy Papers.

[63] See, for instance, Heman Lincoln's letter to McCoy dated April 24, 1846, McCoy Papers, Reel 11.

"Good and glorious" news

McCoy's theme in these last letters of his earthly existence is the "good and glorious" news that many Indians were coming to know the Lord among the Shawnees, the Potawatomis and the Creeks and that backsliders were returning to their former churches. McCoy explains to his old friends such as Cone and his new correspondents such as Agents Helm and Pitts how Joseph Islands has been ordained and that thirteen new converts were baptized on that occasion with twelve more soon following. This latter news was good news indeed as the Creeks still exercised their wicked law of whipping anyone who professed to becoming a Christian. It was not unknown for an entire worshiping congregation of thirty Creek Christians or more to have their worship stopped by the Creek's own police force who were often merciless in applying the lash. Islands used to hold meetings in secret in the woods and Mary Wright relates how Islands would then pray for his people, his persecutors, the police and their spies who he would call by name before the Lord. Those spies were invariably listening, hidden in the woods and one particular man was so convicted when he heard his name called out as one who betrayed the Church of Christ that he was convicted of his sin and joined the Christian band. Wright, too, tells of Indians ordered to whip their fellow tribesmen and women but the courage and testimony of their victims made them helpless to strike them.

McCoy had a great love for the Creeks ever since meeting John Davis and setting him up as pastor of the Ebenezer Church. Then, around 1831, with great joy, he had found many Creeks who longed for the gospel and he had written to Dr. Bolles on September 23, 1831 to say:

> The Creeks are exceedingly anxious for schools, as well as for preaching. They have requested a missionary from this station to live among them and teach &c. They have agreed to supply him and his family with bread and meat, and school house. The pupils will be fed and clothed at their home.[64]

McCoy was staying at the time in Cherokee country at Union Mission Station on the Neosho River, which was run by the Presbyterians. He was in hopeful expectation that the Board would take his letter as a hint for the Baptists to show more enthusiasm for the

---

[64] McCoy Papers, Reel 7.

Creeks. McCoy was not successful in gaining the Board's backing in this endeavor and even Harmony gave up its work. Shortly before writing this letter, McCoy had entered into his Journal:

> The most favourable, and inviting openings for missions now present themselves in many different places in this Territory, and yet our Board (old Foreign Mission Board) seem afraid to even tell the public of these favourable openings, 'lest they should commit themselves upon the Great (and disputed) subject of Indian emigration.' I am grieved with our denomination, and am truly ashamed of them.[65]

Now, McCoy was in a favorable position to mobilize the Baptists so that what they had failed to do in the past might be done enthusiastically in the present under sounder leadership.

Lykins wrote to his father-in-law on the same day that McCoy wrote the above mentioned letter. He informed McCoy of the advice he had received to accept a nomination as Indian Agent and told his father-in-law of the opposition growing against a new Potawatomi removal among businessmen. Lykins added that this was, "a feeling which I have cherished among them to the greatest possible extent." He reported that he had just been preaching among the Wea and met up with Simerwell, who was drawing far more Potawatomis than previously by his preaching. Lykins could also report that the new school building and other material improvements at the Wea station were coming on well, but that Miss Osgood had been ill since the previous summer. Apart from the latter news, the A.I.M.A. stations seemed to be going from strength to strength. Miss Osgood continued in poor health but kept on with her missionary work among the Weas bravely until 1852 when she was called home, Abby Lykins, David's wife, following her to their eternal rest a week later. The Government Indian Agent gave a speech in honor of the two ladies saying:

> To a singleness of purpose and devotion to the interests committed to their charge they united a high order of capacity and intellectual fitness for their peculiar and most delicate and difficult duties. And I fear there must be a long lapse of time before their places may be filled.

---

[65] Entry for August 31, 1831.

Their memory should be cherished, and treasured by all the friends of Indian Missions.[66]

Eliza McCoy moved to the Wea station after Miss Osgood's death to continue her work.

Advising young missionaries

On May 19, McCoy sent a long and enthusiastic letter to S.R. Mason who had applied to be accepted as a missionary. McCoy seemed to be in great form and was rejoicing in the rapidly expanding work of the Indian Mission. This was followed three days later by a joint letter to Lykins and Simerwell, announcing that he had finally sent the *Indian Advocate* to the press and that they would find "much that will be gratifying" in it. He advised them, as "old missionaries" to keep an eye on their younger brother Adams at the Wea Station and told them that the Government's Committee for Indian Affairs had promised him that they would set up "a bill in favour of establishing by an Act of Congress the exterior boundaries of the Indian Territory, and making all the Indians within secure." Enclosed was a copy of a letter to Adams in response to Adams' query concerning allowing in visitors who wished to report on the state of the mission. McCoy's answer shows that he had not moved one wavering inch from his original missionary views laid down in his *Family Rules* at Fort Wayne. He advised Adams:

> Upon the subject of brethren from the churches within the States visiting your institution, and making reports to us, the Board think that incidental visits and communications from good brethren in the white settlements, would be gratifying to us, But the Board and the public have entire confidence in the missionaries. The best and most zealous friends of the Indians within the States, do not feel half the interest in Indian missions that the missionaries do, and the latter are ten times better prepared to make useful reports and statements than the former. Our missionaries are a fraternity of brethren and sisters, <u>forming one family</u>. Their objects and interests are the same. The success of one, is the success of the whole. All that is dear to them is involved in their undertaking. Hence they seek to sustain each others' labors.

---

[66] Taken from McCormick's *Memoir of Eliza McCoy*, pp. 76-77.

Then McCoy tells Adams that he is not expected to be able to show the experience of one who has been at the same work for ten years or more, but that he should seek contact with Lykins and Simerwell should he need advice. Wea had become one of the Indian Mission's most important sites and McCoy was a little anxious that young Adams might find the going hard and be influenced by the comments of non-missionary visitors who were there today and gone tomorrow. Perhaps also, McCoy was thinking of the report Ellis, alias Leslie, published as a temporary visitor to an Indian Mission station, though not knowing what he was talking about. It is, however, obvious that Adams had told visitors to his station that they should report on what they found to the Association because he felt himself too pressed for time to make a report himself. McCoy thus gently rebukes him saying that they would have appreciated his written reports for publication and they trusted that they would soon be forthcoming. Adams was also asked to send in receipts for goods received and also answer other mail which had been sent.

As long as the grass shall grow

By June of 1846, the alarming news had reached McCoy that the Government were about to move the Potawatomis, Chippewas and Ottawas in spite of major protests on the grounds that the tribes were now divided because of their various settlements at Council Bluffs on the Missouri and Osage rivers. To make matters worse, the Government were persuading the Kansas to sell them a huge area of their "promised land" to accommodate the other tribes, thus causing a widespread disturbance among the Indians who had been told that the land they now occupied would be theirs "as long as the grass shall grow." Naturally the missionaries and staff of the A. I. M. A. were engaged in obtaining the best deal possible for the Indians and the result actually brought the various tribes, with the exception of the Kansas, a larger area of freedom and now the Potawatomis were once more united after many years of being dispersed in various bands due to Government policies. The Kansas were richly reimbursed for their sacrifice. The Indians were given two years in which to move as from July, 1846.

The new home of the Potawatomis and their allies extended over 576,000 acres making it thirty miles square. The area was situated on its eastern boundary two miles west of Topeka and sixty-two miles west of the Missouri River. It was thus to the north of the Sac and Foxes and west of the Delawares and Shawnees. The Potawatomis had received $850,000 for their former lands in Iowa and Kansas and the Government required them to pay $87,000 for the new land, which they were well able to do. The Government was to pay all removal costs and also reimburse the Indians for any costs arising when they built their new homes at Council Buffs and along the Osage River. Johnston Lykins, Eliza McCoy and the Simerwells were directed to follow the Potawatomis to their new homes which meant building another missionary station and schools.

The Baptists, however, were not alone in seeking to build schools in the Potawatomis' new tribal area and all the major denominations put in bids. Soon all but the Baptists and Roman Catholics had dropped out of the competition and these two denominations were given permission to start educational work. Lykins planned the Pottawotomie Baptist Manual Labor Training School whose subsequent history has been masterfully portrayed by Thomas P. Barr in the fifty-seven paged booklet of that name. Opposition from the general public to the Roman Catholic work was strong as they were considered not "strictly American." Whereas the Baptists, Methodists and Presbyterians were indigenous organizations, the Roman Catholic clergy still received their marching orders from abroad.

A life well lived and a brave task well done

Isaac McCoy had withstood many hardships as a missionary and won many battles but the wounds incurred were manifold. As a result of his sufferings, his chest was crushed, his spine was twisted, a thigh-joint was deformed, a leg and foot twisted and his left hand seriously maimed. He had lost eleven of his fourteen children through illnesses closely related to the hardships the McCoys had endured on the mission field and his remaining daughter Nancy Judson was a mental and physical wreck because of those same hardships and the constant fevers she had endured.[67] Though McCoy was always a handsome man, as a result of his injuries, he walked with a very pronounced stoop and limped badly, often in great pain. He was given up for dead at least half a dozen times because of high fevers and his extremities had suffered frostbite on numerous occasions while em-

---

[67] In his will written in 1835, Isaac left most of his property to his wife so that she might be able to continue to care for Nancy who "is mentally and physically incapable of taking care of herself." See Hayward's *John M'Coy*, p. 138.

barking on winter journeys of a thousand miles and more on behalf of the Indians. Sleeping on wet or frozen ground in the same soaking clothing for weeks on end is hardly designed to make a man fit and healthy. By 1846, Isaac McCoy's duties on earth were at an end. After a life of struggles, he had accomplished all that his heavenly Father had required of him. The Indians had their own Eden, the A.I.M.A. was on a sturdy footing and McCoy was everywhere respected as the faithful and successful man of God that he was. It was now simply time for him to reap the eternal benefits of his work. McCoy traveled to Jeffersonville to preach on June 1, 1846 and on returning to his home in Louisville caught a cold which brought on the old complaint which he called "putrid fever." After an illness of three weeks, McCoy died in his sixty-third year, his work being done. His last words were, "Tell the brethren to never let the Indian mission decline." He was spared the further pain of seeing the Union, and with it the Baptist churches, split down the middle by the slavery question and the Civil War. His work was gradually absorbed into the domestic mission of the Southern Baptist Convention. He was buried in Louisville's Western Cemetery in a very humble grave and nobody seems to have noticed until long afterwards that the dates on the tomb stone were wrong by ten years. The inscription, however, was fitting and this reads:

Rev. Isaac McCoy,

Born June 13, 1784.
Died June 21, 1836.

For near thirty years his entire time and energies were devoted to the civil and religious improvement of the aboriginal tribes of this country. He projected and founded the plan of their colonisation, their only hope, and the imperishable monument of his wisdom and benevolence.

The Indians' friend - for them he toiled through life;
For them in death he breathed his final prayer.
Now from his toil he rests - the care, the strife.
He waits in heaven, his work to follow there.

It took some time to send the news of McCoy's homegoing to his family who were spread all over the States at the time. Dr. Lykins wrote from Potawatomi to McCoy's widow:

My Dear Mother,

I have just read the letter of my dear Sarah which gives the mournful news of Father's death. . . . . . Sad news!! Melancholy in the extreme!! But why should we repine at what the Lord has done; since it is right, and since the same lot so soon awaits us all.

I think I need not tell you that I sympathize with you under this great trial and bereavement, for this is known to you; and that I should be deeply affected by this bereavement is understandable for next to my own father, he certainly shared the largest in my affections and attachments. Perhaps his own sons[68] affectionate as they are could not love him more than I have done; but in this strain I will not now indulge.

This melancholy stroke has fallen with dreadful forebodings on us all but we are trying to console ourselves that tho, God has taken away our Head, yet the strength of his own arm is not diminished; The missionaries will this evening try to express their feelings on this mournful occasion and their doings will be forwarded to the Board by our (word illegible). My fears and anxieties for the welfare and success of the Ind. Mission cause must be great, but will endeavor to adopt the dying remark of the good Dr. Edwards, "Trust in the Lord and you will have nothing to fear."[69]

David Lykins also wrote to Mrs. McCoy, addressing her as "Mother" and telling her that her husband was looked on not only as a leader but as "the moving spirit in every effort, intended for the amelioration of the condition of the suffering Indian." He enclosed the resolutions of the missionaries who met at Potawatomi in the evening of July 6:

Whereas the missionaries of the Board of the A.I. Miss. Association, in the Northern section, have heard with unfeigned grief of the death of their friend, and brother, the beloved Elder McCoy, late Corresponding Sec. of the Board, and for more than thirty years, the untiring friend of the suffering Indian, as well as the efficient promotor of every effort having for its end the amelioration of the condition of that neglected race.

---

[68] John Calvin and Isaac were the only sons still alive.

[69] Letter dated July 6, 1846, McCoy Papers, Reel 11.

Therefore, Resolved 1st. That while we mourn the loss we have sustained as fellow laborers in the great work of evangelizing [the][70] Indians, we will cherish the cause which was near[est][71] his heart in life, and elicited his last prayer in death.

2ond. Believing the cause in which we are engaged to be of God, and not dependent on the instrumentality of any one individual, however great, or good; we will not yield to discouragement, or relax our efforts for the salvation of the Indians, but rather feel called upon to increase them.

3rd. That the brethren, and sisters of this missionary connection tender to our beloved, and venerable Sister McCoy, assurances of our deepest sympathy in her afflictions, and also to the Board in the loss they have sustained.

4th. That we all unite with the Board in the observance of the day set apart by them, for special prayer, in seeking direction from on high, and that an address be delivered on the subject of our late bereavement, as a tribute of respect to the departed, and with a view to the benefiting of our souls.

5th. That a copy of the foregoing be forwarded to the Chairman of the Board, and also to sister McCoy, by the Clerk of the Missionary Conference.[72]

McCoy's death came at a time when many had hoped that he would live to enjoy the pleasures of seeing his mission prosper for many years to come. Perhaps none of the numerous letters of condolence to Kitty expressed an understanding of McCoy's death as did that written by her niece Eliza McCoy. Eliza had already faced death on numerous occasions in her young life and knew full well the folly of anchoring oneself to earthly joys when to depart and be with the Lord would be far better. She also had been given the gift of comforting those suffering from grief and agony, seeing clearly the hand of the Lord in these matters. Eliza wrote the following letter to her aunt, upon learning of the death of her uncle. It is a fitting closure to this life and testimony of Isaac McCoy:

---

[70] Hole in letter here.

[71] Hole in letter.

[72] Signed by David Lykins, Clerk, July 6, 1846, McCoy Papers, Reel 11.

PUTAWATOMIE BAPTIST MISSION, June 9, 1846.

MY DEAREST AUNT:

More than once I have attempted to address you this evening, but fearing the sorrow of my own heart would lead me involuntarily into a train of remarks which would add to your grief rather than soothe, I have as often laid down my pen without forming a letter. I this evening, for the first time since hearing the heart-rending news, fully realize that my beloved uncle, the long-tried and faithful friend of the almost friendless, is gone - no more to plead their suffering cause before the churches, before the inattentive, and the rulers of our country. That face so often bedewed with sympathy's tear is now cold and pale beneath the sod of the valley, and that heart so often swollen with pity for others' woes is now stilled in death, amid friends and kindred who will no more hear his kind advice, nor see that peculiar cheering smile which characterized his countenance when meeting them.

. . . And if sorrow and suffering here will be gems in the crown of rejoicing of the Redeemer, you, dear aunt, will have many, for many and bitter have been the tears you have shed, while long and severe have been your oft repeated trials. And now the king of terrors, not satisfied with bereaving you of almost all of your dear children, has again entered your peaceful dwelling, and with a more than ever relentless hand, torn from you your last earthly support. Ah! He has shaken your fortitude to the very *center*. But, O happy reflection! tho smitten and stricken to the most secret recesses of the heart, you still have an inexhaustible source of comfort, a heavenly refuge to which you can ever fly, however dark the clouds or loud the winds or raging the sea.

. . . He whose ear is ever open to the afflicted, He who when on earth wept with the weeping, will hear and readily administer the healing balm. I do rejoice, and would even feel the deepest gratitude, that uncle was so mercifully spared to us and to the poor Indians as long as he was, although I may feel, with others, that it is a mysterious Providence, and inquire why one so universally useful was taken. But his work was done. . . . I have reflected much upon the infinite happiness with which his soul is now filled. By an eye of faith I have followed him to the heavenly city. At the entrance stood his parents, all of his brothers but one, with eleven of his children, to welcome him through the gates. Nor were these all; for near by there stood a group arrayed in robes of victory with harps of gold in their hands. And as they raised the notes of praise to their loftiest strain, they said, 'We are those from the red man's land, to whom you carried the news of salvation. We listened to your story of a Savior's dying love; we believed, cast ourselves at the feet of that Savior, sought and obtained His mercy. We have, some of us, long since been called home. Now, with heavenly rapture, we hail you as you enter upon eternal rest from all your earthly toils.' But even this is not all. He was introduced into the very immediate presence of the Savior in whose cause it was his meat and his drink to labor when on earth.

. . . I fancy I now see you standing on Jordan's bank, gazing beyond its floods to the Canaan of rest, until the waves at your feet, heretofore frightful, now appear gentle undulations which will but assist in wafting you across; where you will have the oil of joy for mourning, and the garment of praise for the spirit of heaviness.

Your affectionate niece,

Eliza McCoy

Chapter Eighteen
McCoy's Indians

The following brief descriptions refer to the history and characteristics of the various tribes among whom McCoy carried out his missionary activities. The fact that these tribes exist today is, to a very great extent, because of the love Isaac McCoy felt towards them and the life he offered in his Lord's service so that they might live.

Cherokees

Muriel Wright in her *Indian Tribes of Oklahoma* tells us that there are almost fifty different ways of spelling the term "Cherokee" whose origin is merely speculative, "Rock People," "Cave People" and "Tobacco People" being only a few of the many suggestions given. Hodge's *Handbook of American Indians* suggests that the name "may have been" originally chiluk-ki. Significant enough is the fact that the Cherokee often call themselves Ani'-Yun' wiya,' meaning "The Principle People."

The Cherokees' oldest known place of habitation is along the Tuckasegee River in present North Carolina and the language now spoken among the Cherokee is that of the former mountain bands known as Atali which has also become the Cherokees' standard written language. Nowadays, most Cherokees live in the area known from 1839-1906 as the Cherokee Nation in northeastern Oklahoma but some Cherokees never moved west and their descendants are still to be found in North Carolina.

The Cherokee Nation established their own written law in a Council held in 1808 through the agency of Charles Hicks, friend of Sequoyah (George Guess) who first reduced the Cherokee language to writing. It was most likely that Hicks and Sequoyah moved their tribe to allow Christian missionaries to build churches and schools among them. In his 1835 *Annual Register*, McCoy outlined the area of land set apart for the Cherokees in the Indian Territory, describing it as:

557

The Cherokee country is bounded as follows; beginning on the north bank of Arkansas river, where the western line of Arkansas territory crosses the river; thence northwardly along the line of Arkansas territory, to the S. W. corner of the state of Missouri; thence north along the line of Missouri, 8 miles, to Seneca river, thence west along the south boundary of the Senecas, to Neosho river, thence up said river to the Osage lands; thence west with the southern boundary of Osage lands as far as the country is habitable; thence south to the Creek lands; and east along the northern line of the Creeks to a point about 43 miles west of the territory of Arkansas, and 25 miles north of Arkansas river; thence to Verdigris river, and down Arkansas river, to the mouth of Neosho river; thence southwardly to the junction of the North fork and Canadian rivers; and thence down Canadian and Arkansas rivers to the beginning.

The treaty of 1828 secures to the Cherokees, 7,000,000 of acres, and then in the same article adds, lands westward as far as the U. S. territories extend.

They own numerous salt springs, four of which are worked by Cherokees. The amount of salt manufactured at the whole, is probably about 100 bushels per day.

They also own two lead mines. Their salt works and their lead mines are in an eastern portion of their country, and all the settlements yet formed are within this eastern portion, which embraces about two and a half millions of acres.

Politically, this eastern portion of their country embraces four districts, viz :- Lee's creek Dist. Flint Dist. Illinois Dist. and Neosho Dist.

Principal Chiefs are Maj. John Jolly, and Black Coat. Col. Walter Webber was another, but he died within the last year. It may properly be said that the Cherokees have adopted the habits of civilized man. There is not one village in their country; they are, generally, agriculturalists; a few are mechanics and salt manufacturers. The late Col. Webber was a merchant who was doing a respectable business. At present, John Drew, John Brown, and Ellis F. Phillips, are merchants in good business. It is supposed that the Cherokees own 2,500 horses, 10,000 horned cattle, 10,000 hogs and 300 sheep; 100 waggons; a plow, and often several plows to each farm; several hundred spinning wheels and 100 looms.

They raise corn, beans, peas, pumpkins, cabbage, turnips and potatoes, in great abundance, and some have commenced the growing of wheat.

Their fields are enclosed with rail fences. They have, generally, good log dwellings, (for a new country) many of which have stone chimneys to them, with plank floors; all erected by themselves. Their houses are furnished with plain tables, chairs, bed-steads, and with table and kitchen furniture, nearly or quite equal to the dwellings of white people in new countries.

They have one grist mill and two saw mills, erected at their own cost.

Their form of civil government resembles that of one of our states.

Their Legislature consists of upper and lower house. Each of which has a President and a Secretary; meets annually in autumn, and may be convened at other times by order of the principal Chiefs.

Each district has two Judges, and also two light horse-men, (sheriffs) who are prompt in the discharge of the duties of their trust.

Baptist work among the western Cherokees was pioneered by William Standige, followed by Duncan O'Bryant who pastored the Liberty Baptist Church which he established at Tinsawatee in Georgia with seven native, six Negro and ten white founder members. The church moved west in 1831. After O'Bryant's death around 1834, Mc-Coy's good friend, David Rollin took over the work under the patronage of the Board of Foreign Missions. Rollin set up a school which averaged 40 pupils in 1835, but the Board supplied no money towards their support, though free tuition was given. Rollin experienced a great adding to the church in the Indian Territory. Humphrey Posey founded a mission station among the Cherokees at Valley Towns, North Carolina in 1819[1] which was then led by Evan Jones and Indian chief Jesse Bushyhead assisted by Indians John Wickliffe, Oganaya, Dsusawala, Doyanungheeskee and Oledastee. Sadly the Baptist churches were split by the political turmoils of the times. O'Bryant and his church decided to move west to the Indian Territory as the situation of the Indians in Tinsawatee became intolerable. Jones backed by Chief Bushyhead, one of his converts, decided to campaign for the right of the Cherokees to stay in North Carolina. Fierce political unrest now ensued among the tribe which even led to the murder of

---

[1] Posey had done itinerant work among the Cherokees since 1817.

chiefs who recommended the colonization of the Indian Territory. In this time of political unrest, however, true blessings came to the Baptists. In 1840, McCoy wrote:

> The aversion of the party to removal being so great that they (the Bushyhead party) made no preparation to depart until compelled by the presence of United States' troops, there was reason to fear that in the vexations and calamities of this world they would think little about preparing for the next, and that even Christians might lose much of their spiritual-mindedness. But it was not so. Up to the time of their assemblage for removal, the labours of Mr. Jones and Mr. Bushyhead were blest with improving success. Attendance on preaching improved, Christians became more zealous and united, and conversions and baptisms more frequent; and after they were assembled in encampments, necessarily under many sufferings of body, rich blessings continued to descend on their souls, considerable numbers were baptised, and comfortable communion seasons enjoyed.[2]

By 1840, McCoy estimated that there were between five hundred and a thousand Christians among the twenty-two thousand Cherokees of the Indian Territory, most of them being members of Baptist churches.

Chippewas and Ottawas

The Chippewas or Ojibways trace their name back to an Algonquian word which means "to roast until puckered up," which is a reference to the way in which they pucker up the leather on the seams of their moccasins. The earliest home known of the Chippewas is around the Great Lakes where many still live, both in the U.S.A. and Canada. They merged more or less with the Potawatomi in Kansas and, much earlier, with the Ottawas so that McCoy treated the Chippewas and Ottawas as one tribe. When the tribes moved west, many Chippewas and Ottawas settled in what is now Ottawa County, Oklahoma. Others of the Chippewas merged with the Munsee[3] and

---

[2] See *History of Baptist Indian Missions*, pp. 571-573.

[3] The so-called "Christian Indians".

Wáh-pe-say "The White," Wea. By George Catlin.
He holds a pipe - tomahawk and wears large medallions in his ears. The Weas had consolidated with the Piankashaws in 1820, when these two small tribes removed from Indiana to Illinois and Missouri and then to Kansas.

Wah-pón-jee-a "The Swan," Wea. By George Catlin.
Painted in 1834, Catlin depicted The Swan as a "distinguished" warrior.
The streaks of red paint on the face were common for Indians of this
period and appear in many of Catlin's portraits.

Kee-mo-rá-nia "No English," Peoria,
shown here holding a "looking glass" or mirror. The Peorias were closely
associated with the Weas and Piankashaws, and formally united with
them in 1854.

On-sáw-kie "The Sac," Potawatomie.
In this portrait he holds a "prayer-stick" indicating he was a disciple of
the Kickapoo prophet "Foremost Man." Catlin described his subject as
"using his prayers most devoutly."

Ni-a-có-mo "To Fix With the Foot," Piankashaw.
He wears a combination of native and European clothing, with "a black coat and vest and a white shirt as well as strings of beads and feathers in his hair." He has also applied red paint to his jaws, neck and ears.

Tchong-tas-sáb-bee "The Black Dog," Osage Chief.
Painted by Catlin in 1836, he is dressed in "a huge mackinaw blanket." It
was a common practice among Osage men to shave their heads except for
a small ridge on the crown, but their chief shown here apparently didn't
follow this custom.

Meach-o-shín-gaw "Little White Bear," Kansas.
Painted by Catlin in the early 1840's, and described by him as "spirited
and distinguished brave, with a scalping-knife grasped in his hand."

Ni-có-man "The Answer," Delaware Chief.
The Delawares, like the Creeks, favored headgear consisting of "vari-
coloured handkerchiefs or shawls, which were tastefully put on like a
Turkish turban." Catlin noted that among the Delawares he encountered
"some renowned chiefs," one of whom was The Answer.

Potawatomis in Kansas and eventually moved to present day Potawatomi County in Oklahoma.

Like the Chippewas, the Ottawas are still spread around the Great Lakes and also on Manitoulin and Cockburn Islands, Georgian Bay, Canada. The two tribes who moved from Ohio to Kansas had already merged by 1840 and entered the Indian Territory as one people. This was perhaps because the Chippewas in this area had been reduced to very few families by the middle of the nineteenth century and thus virtually ceased to exist as a separate tribe. In 1854, 8,329 acres of land in what is now Franklin County were granted to the last independent survivors of the Swan Creek and Black River Chippewas, which they eventually were able to own by fee simple. The name "Ottawa," or its variant "Ottoway," comes from an Algonquin word for "to trade." The Ottawas received their name from the French. The first U. S. treaty was made with them in 1785 at Fort McIntosh along with the Wyandots, Delawares, and Chippewas. This was followed by treaties in 1789 (Fort Harmar), in 1795 (Greenville) and in 1807 (Detroit), the latter including transactions with the Potawatomis. These treaties were the means of ceding thousands of square miles from the Indians. After the treaty of Detroit, the Ottawas were settled in the Miami River, Lake Erie and Roche de Boef areas but were told they would have to give up even that land after ten years. The Ottawas were compelled to give up this area, apart from a few fee simple plots, in 1831 and received fifty square miles of the Indian Territory bordering on the Shawnee settlement along the Kansas River. Other Ottawas were removed from the Ohio River to a 12 mile patch in the Maria des Cygnes area, now part of Franklin County. McCoy describes the condition of the Ottawas in 1840 in the words:

> The Ottawa settlements commence about thirty miles west of the State of Missouri. Only three hundred and fifty have yet reached this country. They receive help in improvement from the Government of the United States; they are not quite so far advanced in civilization as the Delawares and Shawnees, but the indications of increasing industry and economy among them presage a rapid rise to a prosperous condition. Mr. Meeker has a small school, in which, instruction is imparted in the English language, and he receives pretty good attention to preaching. David Green, an Ottawa, who has been baptized within the last two years, takes a part in the performance of public religious exercises and acquits himself much to the satisfaction of the missionaries. To enable him to employ a portion of his time in religious labours, some of the nearer

missionaries made a contribution of money from their means of support, respectively. In the mean time, the case of David was brought to the consideration of the board of missions by Mr. Meeker. The board resolved to patronise him, but its funds being low, an amount sufficient only to enable him to employ one-third of his time in missionary labours has as yet been allowed him. It is hoped that this circumstance will not be long known by a benevolent public, before it will furnish the means to enable this promising young man to employ all his time in preaching Christ to his countrymen.

Part of a small band denominated Chippewas, but scarcely distinguishable from Ottawas, arrived in the autumn of this year, and have located adjoining the Ottawas.[4]

Choctaws

The Choctaws belong to the Muscogee tribes and are closely related to the Chickasaws. They were found by the earliest European explorers in the Mississippi region and in present day Alabama. The Choctaws' real tribal name is "Chahta" or "Chäh'ta," though this is not of ancient origin. The name is thought to be related to the color "red" used as a symbol for war, just as "white" was used as a symbol for peace before the white men came on the scene. Others believe that the name derives from a Spanish word "chato," meaning "flat," referring to the Choctaw custom of flattening the foreheads of male infants. A bag of sand was strapped to the child's forehead at birth and then the child was laid for a time on his back in a wooden mold or frame to keep him from moving. Since the days of McCoy and prior to the founding of Oklahoma as a State within the Union in 1907, the Choctaws had governed themselves on a par with the parliaments of Europeans, their laws having been written down since 1822. Grant Foreman argues in his *The Five Civilized Tribes* that these laws came through Christian influence. Their necessity certainly also came through white threats to their well-being, as illustrated by the example Foreman gives from Chief Hoolatohooma's laws which reads:

> Brothers: The first law I have made is, that when my warriors go over the line among the white people and buy whiskey, and bring it into the nation to buy

---

[4] *History of Baptist Indian Missions*, p. 568.

up the blankets and guns and horses of the red people and get them drunk, the whiskey is to be destroyed. The whiskey drinking is wholly cast among my warriors. The Choctaw women have long been in the habit of destroying their infants, when they did not like to provide for them. I have made a law to have them punished, that no more innocent children be destroyed. The Choctaws formerly stole hogs and cattle and killed them. I have appointed a company of faithful warriors, to take every man who steals, and tie him to a tree, and give him thirty-nine lashes.[5]

The tribe founded the Choctaw Nation in 1866 in the area bordered by the Arkansas, Canadian and Red Rivers, below the Cherokee Nation, in southeastern Oklahoma. Indeed, McCoy, found their parliamentary methods and skill in debate and public speaking second to none. Some Choctaws did not move west of the Mississippi River and are still to be found in the state of Mississippi, most notably in Neshoba County. The Choctaws were among the very first Indian tribes to move west to the Indian Territory.

McCoy relates in his *History of Baptist Indian Missions*:

The Choctaws are estimated at fifteen thousand, and are the most southern tribe; they adjoin the State of Arkansas on the east and Texas on the south and west.[6] The Chickasaw tribe, numbering five thousand five hundred, is merged with the Choctaw, making the whole number twenty thousand five hundred. These are justly entitled to the appellation of a civilized people. Before the late difficulties, the Choctaws having had time, since their settlement in their permanent home, to organize their civil government judiciously, must be said to be, at this time, in advance of every other tribe. We say more: No Indian tribe, since the discovery of America by white men, except the Choctaw, has fully exchanged the savage customs for the institutions of civil government. Their existence, as a civilized community, is in its incipient stages. Nevertheless, the foundation appears to be permanently laid, for the promotion of civilization, to the entire exclusion of the customs peculiar to savage life in the management of public affairs.

---

[5] Foreman, pp.20-21.

[6] Oklahoma was not yet a separate state.

The United States Government is bound to afford considerable assistance to the Choctaws and Chickasaws, in making them comfortable, in schools, &c. The Methodists have missionaries among them. According to the discipline of that church, their missionaries frequently change places, so that new missionaries may be introduced into the Indian country this year (1840), in lieu of those who served in the preceding year. The Presbyterians have several stations, occupied by Rev. Messrs. Kingsbury, Byington, Wright, Woods, and Hotchkin, and their wives, and Mrs. Barnes, Miss Clough, and Miss Burnham. Mr. Kingsbury and Mr. Byington are veterans in missionary labours.

The Baptists have four missionaries among them, who occupy as many stations, viz. Rev. Messrs. Smedley, Potts, Hatch, and Dr. Allen, all of whom have wives, excepting the first. Each holds an appointment under the United States' Government, as teacher of a school, for which he receives a salary which supports him without cost to the Board of missions. A small church has been organised at Mr. Pott's station, which is the only Baptist church in the nation. Very favourable openings for preaching the Gospel successfully and for teaching schools appear in many places.[7]

Creeks

The name "Creek," like most of the present day names of Indian tribes, is a relative young appellation, thought to have been given this tribe by the British in the colony of Carolina as used in a report dated 1720. Formerly, the Ocmulgee River was called Ochese Creek and the Indians living on the banks of the river were called Ochese Creek Indians which was shortened to "Creek." The tribe was later divided into Upper Creek and Lower Creek, representing the western and eastern bands, for administrative purposes. The Creeks are also called "Muscogee," a name which carries as many theories of its derivation as letters in it, and the Red Stick people, as in the 1813-14 Red Stick war. "Red" is a term widely used among the Indians as a war-sign and sticks were used to mark out the days of a war. In time, the Muscogee word for "stick" has come to mean "tribe." It is the term "Muscogee" which has been chosen by linguists to describe the Muscogean languages which unite a number of Indian tribes.

---

[7] pp. 573-574.

The Creeks were traditionally divided into Kasihta, Coweta, Abihki and Coosa and other bands who were known as the Wakokai, Eufaula, Hilabia, Atasi, Kolomi, Tukabahchee, Pakana and Okchai, which may indicate that these were formerly separate tribes which merged. These divisions, as well as other special characteristics of Lower and Upper Creeks, have all but disappeared. The Creeks are now situated throughout Oklahoma where they formed the Creek Nation in 1866. The Lower Creeks settled in the Indian Territory in 1828, colonizing the area north of the Arkansas River and west of the Verdigris River. The Upper Creeks settled around 1836 between the Canadian River, the North Fork River and the mouth of Little River and up the Deep Fork valley.

There are stories that the Creeks formerly had a written language before the white settlers came and a specimen of this language is said to have been framed and hung in the Georgian Office in Westminster, England in the eighteenth century, but no trace of it exists today. The *Handbook of American Indians* not only refers to tales of pictographic records on soft stone and copper etc. but features illustrations of them, though these are thought to be fakes.

Writing in 1840 on the subject of the Creeks, McCoy says:

> The Creeks and Seminoles have become blended; their whole number is computed to be twenty-four thousand one hundred. Their country commences about forty-five miles west of the state of Arkansas. Many of these may properly be denominated civilized, though a majority fall below that appellation. They have not yet recovered from the damage sustained by emigration; nevertheless, their prospects of becoming comfortable, and of improving in industry and virtue, are very good. Considered as a tribe, they are in these respects a little in the rear of the Cherokees and Choctaws. By treaty provisions, the United States' Government is bound to afford them assistance in improvement, schools, &c. The Presbyterians and Methodists have had missions among them, but have relinquished them.
>
> No mission within the territory has been more favoured, at times, with animating prospects, than the Baptist mission among these people, and none has been equally subject to unexpected and sudden repulses. Our narrative on the preceding pages left Mr. Kellam and Mr. Mason, and their wives, on their way to resume the labours of this station, as formerly pursued; but new difficulties were met, and neither of them resumed the occupancy of the mission buildings of the first station. Mr. Kellam took

up his residence near Mr. Davis's which is an eligible situation for usefulness, and Mr. Mason remained for the present within the State of Arkansas. The former retained his commission as United States' school teacher, and collected a school, which he instructed in English, at his new residence. Within the summer of this year, he yielded to an invitation of the United States' agent for the Creeks, and returned to his former residence in the mission house at the first station, and left his school on Canadian river in the charge of Mr. Davis, who was appointed United States' school teacher. Thus both stations were again put into successful operation. Mr. Davis has married a second wife, which circumstance, it is hoped, will relieve him from many domestic cares which lately were a great hinderance to his usefulness; and with his school in English, and some instruction imparted also in the Creek language, there is reason to hope that attention to his preaching will be improved. In reference to this mission, we are reminded of what has elsewhere been stated, that the formidable difficulties which attend the management of Indian affairs, or the management of missions, do not originate with the Indians; it is the influence of white men about them that occasions the serious troubles. Painful as it may be, the reader is not permitted to take leave of this mission without being told that it is again under a cloud. Mr. Kellam had not long occupied the mission buildings, to which he returned from the vicinity of Mr. Davis, before new disturbances arose between him and one of his white neighbours, and he retired to the white settlements in the State of Arkansas. An effort will be made to occupy the station by Mr. and Mrs. Mason.[8]

Delawares

The Delawares were an Algonquin tribe who settled the lower parts of what is now Pennsylvania and along the Delaware River and its tributaries, from whence the tribe obtained its name. The river was named after the British nobleman, de la Warr. One of the tribe's several names is Lenni Lenape, which means "original man"[9] as the Delawares claim superiority over other tribes by their direct family descent from the First Man. Pride comes before a fall, however, so that

---

[8] *History of Baptist Indian Missions*, pp. 570-571.

[9] Wright maintains that the name means "men of our nation."

when the Delawares were conquered by the Iroquois, they were given the name of "Woman." The French changed the name "Lenape" to "Loupe," calling the tribe "wolves." By 1778, when the Government began to envisage a united Indian state within a white state but under its control, overtures were made to the Delawares to become the new state's leading tribe. The 1804 treaty at Vincennes, however, rather than make the Delawares supreme, robbed them of much of their land and gave them land in return on the White, Ohio and Kentucky Rivers which was already claimed by others, both Indian and white, and partly even granted to others by treaties. Indeed, the Delawares were hounded from place to place by treaty after treaty until they moved to the Indian Territory after 1829, and were given lands for their sole inhabitation surveyed and organized by Isaac McCoy. The U.S. insisted, however, on maintaining a military base at Fort Leavenworth in spite of an agreement with McCoy to remove all white presence and control. The Baptists had early connections with the Delawares through the colonization process but a mission proper was not established until 1832 and a school built in 1833. John Gill Pratt, McCoy's co-missionary, became Superintendent of a special Delaware Mission in the late thirties. McCoy wrote of the Delawares in 1840:

> The Delawares are in the upper angle formed by the junction of the Missouri and Kauzau rivers. Their number is stated at nine hundred and twenty-one. Many of the tribe are scattered in other sections of country. These are considerably advanced in civilization, and are advancing with an increasing ratio of improvement. They are pretty well supplied with cattle, horses, and swine; generally live in neatly hewn log houses, though small, and without much furniture within; have farms enclosed with good rail fences, and enjoy a comfortable supply of subsistence throughout the year. Their minds and morals are also improving. Government has assisted them, and will continue to do so for many years, in improving their circumstances. The Methodists have had a mission among them several years, and the United Brethren (Moravians) have recently transplanted a mission of theirs among them from Canada to this place. The Baptist station may he said to be prosperous. On the 7th of July, 1839, two intelligent Delawares of influence were baptized. Religious worship is usually pretty well attended; and also instruction in reading, to a limited extent, both in English and Indian, is im-

parted by Mr. and Mrs. Blanchard, and Miss Case. Here, also, missionaries are needed.[10]

Iowas

The name of this tribe is often spelt "Ioway" which is the way "Iowa" was formerly pronounced. This is thought to be derived from the Siouan word "Ai'yuwe" which means "marrow." The *Handbook of American Indians*, however, suggests that the word "iowa" means "sleepy ones." The Iowas call themselves Pahodje (of unsure meaning) and are thought to be closely related to the Otoes and Winnebagos. The tribe settled down in Kansas as agriculturists very early and lived with the Sauk and Fox from around 1811 with whom they practiced lead mining. There are still a good number of Iowas living on the Kansas-Nebraska boundary, others settled in Payne County, Oklahoma after leaving northeastern Kansas. McCoy reports in his *History of Baptist Indian Missions*:

> The Iowas number about one thousand souls; they reside on the Missouri river. Their condition and habits are slightly improved. Government, by virtue of treaty stipulations, is affording then some assistance in the erection of dwellings and mills, the fencing and ploughing of land, in live stock, schools, &c. A Presbyterian mission has been established among them, under the patronage of the Western Foreign Mission Society, the good effects of which have been felt by the tribe, though in a small degree. From this mission, two excellent missionaries, Mr. and Mrs. Ballard, have lately retired, and it is at present in charge of the Rev. Mr. Hamilton, Mr. Irving, Mr. Bradley, and their wives.[11]

Kansas

The Kansas Indians are known under a variety of names. McCoy called them Kanzaus but other writers refer to them as Can, Kan, Caw, Kaw, Kay (the last two are Oklahoma names), Ka-anzou, Kansies, Kantha and even Excansaquex (from the Spanish). The

---

[10] *History of Baptist Indian Missions*, pp. 565-566.

[11] p. 546.

Kansas are one of the five Dhegiha tribes which belong to the Siouan language family and share the same language with the Osage Indians with whom they allied from time to time in their joint histories, especially in times of war. They also have close ties with the Omahas. The name is supposed to be derived either from Siouan words meaning "south wind" and "swift." Both derivations are probably related, the Kansas being also described as the "Wind People" because of their agility and speed. The tribe have given their name to the Kansas River and the State of Kansas as they formerly lived in the area where the Kansas River joins the Missouri. According to modern censuses, the Kansas have diminished vastly in numbers since McCoy's day and are now numbered in hundreds rather than upwards to two thousand. The Kansas emigrated to the Indian Territory in their entirety in 1873, long after McCoy had died. McCoy describes briefly the state of the tribe in 1840 but mentions them on numerous occasions in his journals and reports. Of the tribe, he says:

> The Kanzaus are estimated at seventeen hundred and fifty souls. The villages are on the Kanzau river, about one hundred miles from its junction with the Missouri. By treaty stipulations, the United States Government has promised to afford them assistance in agriculture, schools etc. From these provisions, they have derived some, though not much benefit. Their condition, until very lately, was similar to that of the Pawnees and Omahas. Recently, a few have made some hopeful efforts at agriculture. The Methodists have a mission among them, recently established, and upon a small scale; the Rev. W. Johnson, missionary. Here is a favourable opening for more missionary efforts.[12]

Professor Unrau refers to McCoy's work among the Kansas tribe on numerous occasions in his book *The Kansa Indians: A History of the Wind People*,[13] showing how he reported their poverty to the authorities and lobbied the Government for immediate improvement grants for them.[14] Unrau explains how, "Unlike the Catholics, certain Protestant denominations were more aggressive and not so easily discouraged in their plans to bring salvation to the Kansa. 'The day for

---

[12] *History of Baptist Indian Missions*, p. 565.

[13] Far more often than in the ten pages recorded in the index.

[14] Op. cit. p. 40.

cold speculations, and tedious theories, respecting the fate of the aborigines of America, has gone by', asserted the Reverend Isaac McCoy from his surveyor's camp in Indian Territory in 1831. 'Are we what we profess to be, THE FRIENDS OF THE INDIANS? Then let us manifest our faith by our works.' By the time these forceful words had been directed to philanthropists and Christians throughout the nation, McCoy had done much to establish himself as a leader of the Protestant cause among the Indians west of Missouri."[15] Unrau also points out that McCoy's co-worker John Gill Pratt at the Shawnee station, assisted by his fellow missionaries, had produced the first ever book written in the Kansas language, allegedly containing some 7,200 words. Sadly no copies of this twenty-four paged pamphlet are extant.[16]

Kaskaskias

There is a Kaskaskian word "kaskaskahamwa," which means "he scrapes it off by means of a tool." As the Kaskaskias were skilled hide-dressers and makers of clothing from the skins of animals, it is thought that this occupation has given the tribe their name. Though less well-known today, the Kaskaskias were once the leading tribe of the Illinois Confederacy of Algonquian speaking Indians.

Most of the tribe now belong to the Peorian Confederacy and are to be found in Ottawa County, Oklahoma. They are greatly reduced in number in comparison with former times. It is thought that this is not so much because of early conquests with the whites but the fact that in 1769, a Kaskaskian murdered the great Ottawa chief Pontiac at Cahokia, Illinois and thus his tribe became the sworn enemies of the Ottawa, Sauk, Fox, Kickapoo, Potawatomi and several other northern tribes. In 1803, the year of McCoy's marriage when he and Christiana were preparing themselves to move to Vincennes, a treaty in that town compelled the Kaskaskias to cede all their land in the Illinois Territory[17] to the United States.

After 1803, the Kaskaskias gradually merged with the Peorias and McCoy said of them in 1840:

---

[15] Op. cit. p. 122.

[16] Op. cit. p. 10.

[17] Illinois was first constituted the Union's twenty-first state in 1818.

The Peorias and Kaskaskias make one small band of one hundred and forty-two souls, who reside on the east of the Ottawas (in the Indian Territory). Their condition is similar to that of the Ottawas, and is improving, in which they receive help from the Government of the United States. The Methodists have a mission among them.[18]

Kickapoos

The Kickapoos belong to the Algonquian language family and the name derives from the word Kiwigapawa which means "he moves about, standing now here, now there." The tribe is closely related to the Sauk and Fox. The Kickapoos farmed land throughout their known history and lived in villages of bark-covered houses. They covered a vast area of land in Wisconsin, Illinois and Texas and even moved to Mexico in 1850 with the Seminoles for a time. Though most of the Mexico Kickapoos moved to the Indian Territory (Oklahoma and Kansas) in 1871, a number are still to be found there. McCoy encountered the Kickapoos often and their prophet Kenekuk, who is still spoken of among the tribe, consulted McCoy on the future of his people. Referring to the Kickapoos settled in the Indian Territory in 1840, McCoy says:

The Kickapoos are about forty miles lower down the Missouri river, and number about four hundred souls. Their circumstances are more comfortable and their habits more improved than those of the Iowas and Sauks. It may be said that many of them are becoming agriculturists; they keep live-stock, and apply horses and oxen to draught. Government has assisted them materially in these improvements, and is still assisting them. The Methodists have a mission among them upon a small scale, under the management of the Rev. Mr. Berryman; and the Catholics, also, have a small establishment.[19]

---

[18] *History of Baptist Indian Missions*, p. 568.

[19] Ibid, p. 565.

Miamis

The name Miami, which means "the people who live on the peninsula" was given to the tribe by the Chippewas but the Miami call themselves Twa^nh twa^nh, which means, "the cry of the crane." This gave rise to the name Twightwees which was formerly used of the tribe. The Miamis are of the Algonquian language family and were first encountered by Europeans near the Great Lakes. The Miami moved by degrees to the Indian Territory, the largest number entering the area in 1846, but there were later emigrations to Indiana where they had formerly lived and where McCoy first met the tribe. Present day Miamis in Oklahoma have been merged with the Peoria and are known as the United Peorias and Miamis. Others still live in Kansas and Indiana. McCoy had commenced missionary work among the Miamis in 1817 but the Board's promise to extend the work did not materialize. McCoy relates that "a once powerful tribe has been brought to the brink of destruction." The Piankashas and Weas whom McCoy encountered were Miami bands (s.b.)

Omaha

The name Omaha is thought to mean "those going against the wind or current." They are members of the Dhegiha group of the Siouan family with the Kansas, Quapaws, Osage and Poncas. Their traditional enemy appears to have been the Sioux. The tribe was reduced to some 300 members by the small pox in 1802 but, according to the *Handbook of American Indians*, had increased to 1,600 by 1843 which agrees roughly with McCoy's 1840 estimate. McCoy writes of this tribe:

> The Omaha tribe consists of about fourteen hundred souls. Their settlement is on the Missouri river, about eighty miles above where it receives the Great Platte river. Like all rude tribes in the wilderness, they have received from the whites some guns, iron tools, cooking vessels, and clothing. Nevertheless, their minds and their habits may be said to be unimproved. Their intercourse with traders has, no doubt, rendered obstacles to their improvement more formidable than they were before their acquaintance with white men. They cultivate a small amount of vegetables, but rely chiefly upon the chase for subsistence. A hunting tour of about two months is made by them, in quest of buffalo, in the early part of the warm

season of the year, and another in the latter part. At these times, few, and frequently, none, are left remaining in the villages. To avoid surprise by an enemy, they proceed with great caution and some order, usually in two or three lines, fifty or one hundred yards apart. Spies are kept in advance, to look out for a lurking foe, and to descry the buffalo before the animal becomes affrighted.

Their houses are constructed of earth, circular, and in form of a cone, the wall of which is about two feet in thickness, and is sustained by wooden pillars within. The floor is the earth, and is usually sunk about two feet below the surrounding surface ; the smoke escapes through an aperture in the centre, which answers the double purpose of chimney and window. The door is low and narrow, and closed by suspending in it the skin of an animal. An enclosed entry, extending from the door proper six or eight feet, is sometimes made, which adds much to the warmth of the dwelling within. These houses are destitute of chair, table, or bedstead. The inmates coil about a fire, on mats of flags, or skins of animals. Regularity of time is not observed in preparing and participating of food. They manufacture no cloth, do not enclose cultivated lands with fences, keep no other live stock than horses, which are not applied to draught. There are treaty stipulations, by which the United States' Government is required to afford them some assistance in relation to agriculture, smithery, education, &c., by which they have not yet profited.

Mr. Curtis, who went among the Omahas in 1837, contrary to what had been requested and expected, and for reasons not known to us, made his location about twelve miles from the people of his charge. He remained at his station a few months, and left it without having accomplished any thing. The buildings, which cost the board of missions a thousand dollars, have been left without an occupant, in an uninhabited desert. This is the unpleasant condition of this station, after nine years' effort of some of the missionaries to put it into operation. The prospect of doing much good there, with little cost to benevolent societies, has always been and still is good, provided energetic and devoted missionaries could be found willing to labour there. Mr. Curtis, and Mrs. Curtis, who is an amiable woman, and a devout Christian, are still residing in those remote regions, near the junction of the Missouri and the Great Platte rivers, but not in an Indian settlement, and receiving no support either from the board of missions or from the

Government. He is not exerting any influence upon matters beneficial to the Indians.[20]

Osage

The Osage belong to the Dhegiha group of the Siouan language family, their name being a corruption of the French pronunciation of Wa-zha-zhe, a name whose meaning is now lost. This Southern Sioux tribe is related to the Kanzaus, Omahas, Quapaws and Poncas and also belong to those tribes known as the "Plains Indians" and were indigenous to the Indian Territory. The Osage were settled on land rich in oil deposits which brought them great wealth. McCoy wrote in 1840:

> The country of the Osages commences twenty-five miles west of the State of Missouri. They number five thousand five hundred and ten souls, and in regard to improvement are similar to the Otoes. No tribe has been so much neglected by the Government of the United States, so much imposed upon by rapacious traders, or so grossly traduced by both white and red men, as this wretched people, who have been incapable of pleading their own cause, or of telling their own story of sufferings. During the last eleven years, they have presented an inviting field for missionary effort, which might be entered with the prospect of imparting much benefit. Government has at different times made liberal provisions for the assistance of these people in improving their condition, but hitherto, for want of regard for their interests, on the part of those who have mingled with them for the purpose of applying the means of relief, no benefit of consequence has been afforded them. The Baptists have made an effort to establish a mission among them, and are hindered only by a want of missionaries. The Presbyterians had missions among them, but they have been abandoned.[21]

---

[20] Ibid, pp. 560-562.

[21] Ibid, p. 569.

Otoes

The Otoes are related to the Missouri tribe, or at least they speak the same language. Perhaps the Otoes were called Missouri when they settled on the banks of that river. The name Otoe or Oto is thought to mean "lecher," so it would be understandable if members of the tribe preferred to be called Missouri. The Otoes form the Chiwere group of Sioux Indians along with the Iowas. Like most of the Indian tribes, they were first heard of in the Great Lakes area and they gradually wandered south and west because of pressure from white settlers and Government troops. McCoy related in his *History*:

> The Otoes number about sixteen hundred souls. They reside on the Great Platte river, and a few miles only from its junction with the Missouri. Until lately, their condition did not differ from that of the Omahas and Pawnees. Since the establishment of the Otoe mission, some indications of a spirit of improvement have been seen among them. By treaty stipulations, the United States have provided for their assistance in agriculture, smithery, schools, &c.; these have been partially applied, and not without success. Some of the Otoes have been encouraged to use more industry in agriculture than formerly. It would be difficult to repress a smile at the awkwardness of rude man, even while the tear of pity and good will would steal over the cheek, to see the Otoe chief holding the handles of his plough, while his wife or child led the horse.
>
> Mr. and Mrs. Merrill have both acquired a pretty thorough knowledge of the Otoe language, and they impart religious instructions without an interpreter. The Indians give pleasing attention to preaching when they are in their villages, which unfortunately, as it happens with all uncultivated tribes, is but a small portion of the year. Little has yet been done in relation to instruction in the English language. About thirty-six, chiefly young men, receive instruction in reading in the Otoe language, while they are within the reach of the place, to whom boarding in part is furnished by the mission.
>
> A temperance society has been formed among the Otoes, of which thirty-six of that tribe became members. We fear that the history of the society will testify more honourably to the zeal of the missionaries than to the fidelity of the members. Nevertheless, as missionaries to the Indians never find water in which they can lie upon their oars, but are accustomed to row against strong cur-

rents and contrary winds, zeal in this case, with the blessing of God, may accomplish much.

Humanly speaking, nothing seems to be
wanting to ensure a good degree of success, but the addition
of more missionaries of zeal equal to that of Mr. and Mrs.
Merrill. Both of these missionaries have suffered not a little
from ill health, and there is too much reason to fear that
Mr. Merrill's declining health will soon bring him to the
grave.[22]

Pawnees

The Pawnee tribe, who belong to the Caddoan family, were
formerly called "Chahiksi-chahiks" which means "Men of Men" but
this appellation has dropped out of use. The present name has very
many variations such as Pani, Pana and Panamaha and was perhaps
given the tribe by the French. Most of the many theories concerning
the origin of the word, relate to the particular hairdress of the Pawnees. The name is thought to be derived from paríki, which means "a
horn" referring most likely to the Pawnee scalp-lock. The oldest maps
made by whites around 1673 locate the Pawnees along the Arkansas
and Missouri Rivers. Though the Pawnee always had a reputation for
being warlike, they never carried out a war with U. S. troops. McCoy
relates:

The Pawnee tribe is on the Great Platte
river, about one hundred miles from its Junction with the
Missouri river. Their number is usually estimated at ten
thousand souls, and their condition is similar to that of the
Omahas. By treaty with the United States, they are entitled to smitheries, and agriculturists to aid them, live stock,
mills, &c., and some provision is also made for educational
purposes.

It was in 1827 that the Baptists made the
first effort with the Government of the United States to
make an arrangement for establishing a mission in the
vicinity of the Pawnees, and which was designed for their
benefit, and that of other tribes near. The commencement
of the stations among the Otoes amid Omahas was in accordance with this design. For the Pawnees, with twelve
years' effort, we have found no Baptist missionary willing
to labour. Two Presbyterian missionaries, viz: Messrs. Dun-

---

[22] Ibid, pp. 562-563.

bar and Allis, with their wives, have undertaken a mission for this tribe, under the patronage of the American Board of Commissioners for Foreign Missions. In 1824, the male missionaries mingled with the people of their charge, but subsequently they took temporary residences on the bank of the Missouri river, one hundred miles from them. The missionaries have qualified themselves for future usefulness by the acquisition of the Pawnee language, but have not been able to impart any benefits to the tribe. This, for the last fifteen years, has been an inviting field for missionary labours.[23]

Peorias

Again, the French are probably responsible for the name "Peoria," which is supposed to be derived from the native word "piwares," meaning "he comes carrying a pack on his back." The tribe belongs to the Illinois Confederacy of Algonquian origin and is known to have lived at the mouth of the Wisconsin River in ancient times. Most Peorias live nowadays in Ottawa County, Oklahoma. McCoy mentions the Peorias in conjunction with the Kaskaskias (s.a.).

Piankashas

The name of this tribe is derived from a Miami word "payungg sh'ah," meaning "those who separated and formed a tribe," indicating that the Piankashas were once part of the Miami tribe. In McCoy's early ministry, the Piankashas were settled on the present Indiana - Illinois boundary, along the Wabash River, but they were compelled to cede their land to the U. S. Government at the Vincennes Treaty of 1805. McCoy refers briefly to the Piankashas in conjunction with the Weas (s.b.).

Poncas

The Ponca is one of the five Dhegiha tribes with the Omaha, Osage, Kansas and Quapaw. Linguistically, the Ponca language is Siouan and identical with that of the Omaha's. The name is thought

---

[23] Ibid, p. 562.

to have originated from a Siouan word meaning "leading head." The tribe is traced back to a permanent village structure in Dakota, where they practiced agriculture apart from seasonal hunting expeditions. The majority of the Poncas now live in Oklahoma but there are bands in Nebraska. McCoy relates:

> The Puncah is a small tribe of about eight hundred souls, of the Omaha family, residing near the Missouri river, on the northern extremity of the Indian territory. Their condition is similar to that of the Omahas, and is unimproved. They have never enjoyed the benefit of a missionary, and have been too long neglected.[24]

Potawatomis

The Potawatomis, also called Potawatomies, Putawatomies or Pattawatimas, looked upon themselves as a most ancient nation, calling themselves "The Brave Men." The word Potawatomi is supposed to be derived from a word meaning "people of the place of the fire." The tribe is closely related to the Ottawas and Chippewas in language and customs. They were divided into two so-called bands, these being the Woodland Indians of the Wisconsin and Michigan areas and the Prairie Indians of Illinois and Indiana. Their territory once stretched from Lake Superior to the Illinois River. The Potawatomis were partakers of the Fort Harmar Treaty of 1789, followed by the Greenville Treaty of 1795 and the Fort Wayne Treaty of 1803. As usual much land was given up in return for annuities, the Potawatomis receiving promises of $1,000 per year. A relatively large number of the Potawatomis allied with Great Britain in her wars with the Americans but eventually signed "perpetual peace and friendship" pacts with the U. S. Government in 1815 and 1816. At the 1821 and 1833 Treaties of Chicago which ended the Potawatomis' days as a mighty nation, the tribe gave up millions of acres of land in exchange for a so-called "permanent home" in the Indian Territory. It must be emphasized that hitherto the usual preamble in white treaties with the Indians was that the treaty would last "as long as grass grows and water runs." It became one of McCoy's main callings in life to see that such phrases did not become mere empty words. These pre Civil War treaties also secured for the Baptist Board of Missions 320 acres to be used as a base for missionary work among the Potawatomis. A

---

[24] Ibid, p. 560.

measure of permanency was obtained, chiefly through McCoy's endeavors but the resettlement of the Potawatomis was characterized by one blunder after another. Initially, the first 1,000-1,500 members of the tribe were wrongly directed to an area outside of the Indian Territory and some 240 miles from the land allocated to them. These Indians were reluctant to move again and further treaties were made with them in the thirties, forties, fifties and up to the outbreak of the Civil War which caused a great deal of uncertainty and obvious suspicion of the Union's intentions. One evil characteristic of these treaties which was entirely the Government's fault, was that whiskey was freely given the Indians as a "reward" for their cooperation. McCoy tells about such an incident, when to celebrate the 1821 Chicago Treaty, seven barrels of whiskey were distributed among the Indians for immediate consumption which resulted in such drunken revelries and quarrels that ten Indians were murdered on the spot and another five shortly afterwards.[25]

The first missionaries to the Potawatomis in the Indian Territory were Isaac McCoy, Johnston Lykins and especially Mr. and Mrs. Robert Simerwell who had served the tribe in the north since the early twenties.[26] McCoy reported in 1840:

> The Putawatomies adjoin the bands last mentioned (the Weas, Piankashas, Ottawas, Peorias etc.); only about sixteen hundred and fifty have yet emigrated to this place. They have but recently arrived, and have not had time to make themselves as comfortable as the Ottawas, and others of their neighbours. As a whole, they are, perhaps, a little in the rear of their neighbours in civilization, but they have among them more men of talents, education, and enterprise, in proportion to numbers, than either of the five bands last mentioned. Assistance to a considerable extent, in the common improvements of civilization and education, has been secured to them by treaty, from the Government of the United States. The Methodists have a mission among them, on a small scale, and. the Catholics have a mission in which two priests are employed.
>
> The Baptist station, transplanted from Michigan, is going into operation here, under auspicious circumstances. A small school in English is taught a portion of the time, and some instruction is imparted in the Indian language. The missionaries from the nearer stations assist

---

[25] *History of Baptist Indian Missions*, p. 116.

[26] Ibid, p. 569.

Mr. Simerwell, and attention to religious instruction is very encouraging. A temperance society has been formed, the Indian members of which have increased to about sixty, a few of whom are Ottawas. Permanent and comfortable mission buildings are now going up, under the superintendence of Mr. Lykins. Missionary associates are very much needed by Mr. and Mrs. Simerwell in their arduous labours. They have suffered considerably by sickness.[27]

Quapaws

The Quapaw or Kwapa derive their name from "Ugakhpa," which means "downstream people." They belong to the southern Dhegihas and are thought to have moved to the James and Savannah River area on the Atlantic Coast in prehistoric times and then gradually migrated back westwards. The Quapaw are thought to have separated from the Omaha to move down the Arkansas River, the former becoming the "downstream people" and the latter the "upstream people." Indeed, the French called the Quapaw the "Arkansea" from which the name of the Arkansas River is supposed to have derived. The name "Arkansas" is similar to a Siouan term for "South Wind," a name often applied to the Quapaw and Kansas Indians. McCoy wrote in his 1840 *History*:

> The Quapaws, southeast of the Osages, are about six hundred in number, and are a branch of the latter, separated from the body many years since. They have made some advances in civilization, and are assisted by the Government of the United States. They have never been favoured with a missionary; the field, though small, would be found "white for harvest".[28]

There was some difficulty and misunderstanding regarding the 96,000 acres where the Quapaws were to settle in the Indian Territory. By mistake, they settled on lands reserved for the Senecas and Shawnee and had subsequently to move northwards leaving the Senecas and Shawnees to their south with the Osages to their northwest and the Neosho River to their west.

---

[27] Ibid, p. 569.

[28] Ibid, p. 570.

Sac and Fox

The Saukeek, Sauks or Sacs were originally a separate tribe from the Fox Indians but had already merged with them before the time of white settlement when they populated the western shores of Lake Michigan and the Chicago River. The word "chicago" is a Sauk word meaning "onion" as wild onions grew on the banks of the river named after them. The tribes moved to the Wisconsin area and Rock River Valley and were compelled to give up their lands east of the Mississippi in 1804 by a treaty which granted them a mere $1,000. As a result of the opposition of Chief Black Hawk against giving up traditional lands, the Black Hawk War ensued in 1832 with dire consequences for the tribe, who then retreated to Iowa. The defeat of Black Hawk on land which had been given him only a few years previously in exchange for other lands is a black mark indeed on the history of the U.S.A.. The major battle took place on the Bad Axe River in Wisconsin where the Sauks were fully overpowered by U.S. and Sioux troops. Black Hawk saw that his situation was hopeless so he had a white flag raised where it could be seen by the enemy. The U.S. forces chose to ignore the life-saving flag and proceeded to massacre the tribe, including the aged, women and small children. Sinister enough, the land which formerly belonged to the Sauks on the west bank of the Mississippi River but was taken from them by brute force, was sold to white settlers in 1833 under the euphemistic heading "Black Hawk Purchase." A tiny remnant of the tribe moved to the Indian Territory in the late eighteen thirties but it was not until 1867 that the bulk of the remaining Sauks left Kansas and Iowa and moved to what is now Oklahoma. While the tribe was situated in present day Kansas, they were evangelized by Isaac McCoy. One piece of evidence showing connections with McCoy is the name of one of their most famous native preachers, Isaac McCoy, who was named after the missionary whom he knew as a child and was ordained to preach by the Ottawa Baptist Church in the northeast of the Indian Territory before returning to his own tribe. One of his first converts among the Sauk was Chief Keokuk (1780-1848). As there was still no constituted Baptist church among the tribe, McCoy sent the chief to the Ottawa church, which was 140 miles away, to be baptized. The pastor, however, refused to baptize Keokuk because he had two wives. The chief returned sadly back home and met McCoy just as he was about to leave for a meeting and told him his news. The two men prayed together about the problem and then went to the meeting. The younger of Keokuk's wives was converted at this meeting. She had wished to become a Christian for some time but the fact that she was the second wife of a man had caused her to believe she was ineligible. She had thus made up her mind that it was wrong to be the chief's second wife and that she must give up the chief if she wished to receive Christ. The problem was now solved and both the chief and his once second wife were baptized. Several more were converted and in 1874, a church was constituted with McCoy as its pastor. He pastored the church for eight years before taking up a new work. In all, McCoy served as a preacher and pastor for fifty years.[29]

The original Isaac McCoy, mentions his contact with the Sauks in his journals and reports from time to time and wrote briefly in his *History of Baptist Indian Missions* in 1840:

> The Sauks are about five hundred in number, being only a branch of the Sauk nation. They are located within a mile of the Ioways, and are in a similar condition. They are also deriving some benefit from the United States' Government, by virtue of treaty stipulations for assistance in improving lands, schools, &c.[30]

The name Sauk or Sac is derived from the Algonquian word "Osa'kiwug" which means "people of the outlet," or, "people of the yellow earth." This was most likely to distinguish them from the Fox who were called "Meshkwa kihug" or "the red earth people." The spelling and pronunciation "sac" and "fox" is from French attempts to pronounce the tribes' own names. Both tribes were noted for being formidable in war. The color red, in the name of "Red Fox," also given to the Fox, indicates this, "red" being the color symbol for war. The Sac and Fox now live in two communities in Oklahoma, a few live in Kansas and a larger band live in Iowa.

Senecas and Shawnee

The name Seneca is a Dutch derivation from an Iroquoian word Oneniute'ron'non meaning "people of the projecting rock." Muriel Wright expresses doubt whether the Seneca Indians who live today in Oklahoma are indeed of Seneca stock.[31] After been forced to

---

[29] Robert Hamilton provides a photograph of the elderly Indian McCoy on page 38 of his book *The Gospel Among the Red Men.*

[30] Ibid, p. 565.

[31] *Indian Tribes of Oklahoma*, p. 238.

cede 40,000 acres of their traditional land in Ohio to the U.S. Government in 1831, the tribe dwelling in Ohio moved to the Indian Territory. The Shawanoe or Shawnee derive their name from the Algonquian word "shawun," which means "south," which is probably a reference to their position in relation to the other tribes when they migrated from the Atlantic Coast westwards. McCoy writes of the two tribes:

> The two bands denominated Senecas, and Senecas and Shawnees (Shawanoes), have become partly blended in one. Their number is four hundred and sixty-one. They are considerably advanced in civilization, and Government helps them in improving their condition. The Methodists undertook a mission among them, but relinquished it. Here, also, a missionary would find encouragement to labour, though his sphere, unless extended to others immediately adjoining, would be small.
>
> The Shawanoes in the territory are reckoned at eight hundred and twenty-three. Some of the nation are in other countries. They live on the south side of the Kauzau river. My wife and I hail from the Baptist station in this tribe, though our business relates to every tribe. Our connection with the General (Missionary) Convention has never been changed from the first, excepting that within the last ten years we have been at liberty to act, in many matters, upon our own responsibility, in which cases the board is not accountable, either in regard to the propriety of the measure, or the cost that may be occasioned. We support ourselves, but should our resources (which are our earnings in the service of the Government) fail, as they probably will, our claims upon the board for support will be similar to those of other missionaries.
>
> The condition of the Indians is so closely connected with the affairs of the Government, that, in order to procure facilities essential to a successful prosecution of missions, it has appeared necessary for some one to approach a little nearer to political matters, than was strictly proper for a missionary society; and in making these advances beyond the proper sphere of the society, prudence suggested that the latter should not become liable to either cost or blame. All the advantages, however, which these efforts produce, are secured to the board's missions. We act in concert with other missionaries, and in harmony with the views and designs of the board.
>
> The station has suffered much on account of the poor health of the missionaries. Mr. and Mrs. Pratt

laboured under difficulties of this character, especially the latter, whose symptoms of diseased lungs became so alarming, that they deemed it expedient to return to her kindred in New England, respecting the propriety of which measure their nearer neighbouring missionary brethren concurred in opinion. We feel sensibly the loss of these young missionaries, especially in the printing department, in which Mr. Pratt's place has not yet been supplied, and follow them with our prayers that they may yet be spared to promote the interests of the Indians, to which they had ardently devoted themselves at the commencement of their career in useful life. All deeply regret the suspension of the operations of the press, and the board have resolved to furnish another printer as early as possible. The general health of Mr. and Mrs. Lykins is not good - hers, especially, is poor. In the latter part of May, the scarlet fever made its appearance in the neighbourhood, and each of them and their children suffered so severely, that they could scarcely leave their house for five months. Mr. Barker and Miss Churchill have also suffered by sickness. On these accounts, little has been done among the Shawanoes during many months. On the 23d of October, Mr. Barker and Miss Churchill were united in marriage. They are now collecting a school, with the prospect of success ; and the operations of the station, excepting the printing department, are evidently improving. In my own family some one was suffering with fevers, mostly of alarming type, from the middle of July until about the first of December. At one time, Mrs. McCoy's recovery could scarcely be hoped for, and mine, during many weeks, was almost despaired of.

By means of the press, the Shawanoe station has possessed advantages superior to any other, in imparting substantial benefits to the Indians. There have been printed in the Delaware language four books, three of which were small, and one large; the latter being a *Harmony of the Gospels*, originally compiled by the Rev. Mr. Zeisberger, of the Moravian church, now revised by Mr. Blanchard. In Shawanoe, three books have been printed, and part of the Gospel by Matthew. A second edition of one of these books has been printed; also, one book in Shawanoe, for the Methodists. In Putawatomie, four books have been printed; in Otoe three, all small, one of which has been reprinted for the use of the Presbyterians among the Ioways; in Choctaw, one book; in Muscogee, (Creek,) one school book, and the Gospel by John; in Osage, one; in Kauzau, one for the Methodists, and in Wea, one for the Presbyterians; in Ottawa, two; besides a considerable number of hymns in different languages, not included in the above list. All of the above were upon the new system. Also, three numbers of the Annual Register of Indian Affairs, and one number of Periodical Account of Baptist Missions; besides which, there was issued, until late difficulties occasioned a suspension, a small monthly paper, of only a quarter sheet, edited by Mr. Lykins, entitled 'Shawanowe Kesauthwau' - Shawanoe Sun.

These people, like the Delawares, are advancing in civilization, and are in similar circumstances, possibly a little in advance of their neighbours. They also receive help from the Government, by virtue of treaty provisions. The Methodists and Friends (Quakers) have each a mission among them; the former under the superintendence of the Rev. Thomas Johnson, and the latter under the management of Friend Moses Pearson.[32]

Stockbridge

The Stockbridge Indians are named after a village by that name which was built near their Massachusetts tribal settlement. Earlier, they were known as the Housatonic, occupying the Housatonic Valley to the south of present day Berkshire County, Massachusetts. They later settled in the New York area and it was from there that a small group moved to the Kansas area in 1839. These subsequently settled in the Indian Territory and later became citizens of the Cherokee Nation. Other Stockbridge Indians merged with the Quapaw, and the Delaware.

When Henry Skigget visited some Stockbridge Indians in Wisconsin, he found several Christians among them and was able to lead a number of others to Christ. It was actually Skigget who brought the Stockbridge Indians to the Indian Territory. When the party reached the Shawnee Mission, the new converts were baptized and the Stockbridge Indians joined the Delaware Church. The Delawares, however, tended to distrust the Stockbridges and feared "lest the Stockbridges become too wise, and outwit their great-grandfather, the Delaware chief."[33]

---

[32] *History of Baptist Indian Missions*, pp. 566-568.

[33] *Poor Lo!*, p. 120.

Weas

The name of the Wea tribe is thought to be derived from "Wawiaq-tennang," which means "place of the curved channel" and probably gave rise to the name "Eddy People." The Weas speak an Algonquian language and are related to the Miamis. Earliest encounters with Europeans place the Wea on the banks of the Wabash where they lived in numerous villages. Others lived in Illinois and on the Indiana boundary to Michigan. They are now situated in Ottawa County, Oklahoma. Of the Weas and Piankashas, McCoy says in his *History*:

> The Weas and Piankashas constitute one band, computed at three hundred and sixty-three souls, resident on the east of the Peorias, and adjoining the line of the State of Missouri. They are also aided by the Government of the United States., and are in circumstances similar to the Peorias and Ottawas. The Presbyterians had a mission among them, but abandoned it at a time when its usefulness was improving. A missionary, who could consent to locate within a tribe so small as this, would here find an inviting situation for usefulness. These four bands last named are of the Miami family, and the main body of that tribe is expected soon to locate by the side of these bands. This event will enlarge the field of labour.[34]

These two tribes received an area of land in the Indian Territory south of the Shawnees, north of the Potawatomis and east of Missouri extending over 160,000 acres.

Wyandots

The Wyandots are descended from the Hurons but were driven from the Lake Huron region by the Iroquois and settled in the Detroit area, spreading out to Lake Erie and the area of Sandusky Bay. The U. S. Government made a treaty with the Wyandots, the Delawares, the Chippewas and the Ottawas at Fort McIntosh in 1785. In this treaty, the Government granted lands to the Wyandots that belonged to the Shawnees and encroached on Miami territory so that the inevitable future strife was formally programed. Such treaties were considered permanent but in 1817, the year McCoy started his mis-

---

[34] Ibid, pp. 568-569.

sionary career, Commissioners Lewis Cass and Duncan McArthur annexed a large portion of land south of Lake Erie which had been promised to the Wyandots by treaty for permanent possession, now promising to pay the tribe $4,000 annually for ever in lieu of the land. Some smaller patches of land were given to the Indians by patent. Most of these treaties seemed to have been written in invisible ink and were not worth the paper they were written on. The Wyandots moved initially to the Indian Territory in 1839 but did not start colonizing land in the fork of the Kansas and Missouri Rivers in earnest until 1842 when they sold up their Ohio possessions. An area of 23,000 acres was allotted the tribe but they had to pay the Delawares $185,000 for the land. Some ten years later, the land was split up so that separate Wyandot owners could take out a fee simple patent for each plot which became their property with rights attached similarly to those given to the whites. Early missionary work among the Wyandots was done by the Methodists in the Lakes and Ohio area but the Baptists assisted the Wyandots in their activities of colonization and served them in the Indian Territories.

The bootlegging of whiskey to the Indians, with all its attendant woes, was perhaps the greatest evil that McCoy encountered in his missionary life. In 1840, over a decade after commencing his great work in the Indian Territory, McCoy wrote:

> When I first came to this country, in 1828, the Puncahs, Omahas, Pawnees, and Otoes, were almost strangers to the use of intoxicating drink. At this time, vast quantities of whiskey are consumed among them. In the summer of this year, 1839, fifty barrels of alcohol were rolled off a steamboat at one time, and deposited in a cellar at a trading house on the northwest bank of the Missouri, above the mouth of the Great Platte river. Spirits are commonly transported to the remote tribes, in the form of alcohol, in order to save cost, and is afterwards diluted for use. Taking the above instance of deposite, as a sample of the *many* which occur in those regions, what floods of this destroying liquor are those wretched savages drenched with in the course of a twelve month! The extent of the evils thus produced could only be learned from a history of the infernal regions. Where are the laws forbidding the introduction of ardent spirits into the Indian country? Where are the officers of Government who have been stationed in the Indian country for the purpose of preventing infractions of law? Where are the bonds which traders give, with sureties and heavy penalties, by which they bind themselves to obey the laws of the United States? Such mockery of law and

587

justice might well produce a blush on the cheek of every citizen of the United States. Of this murderous traffic, one cannot think without horror, nor speak without indignation, tempting him to transcend the bounds of moderation. We talk of indians being distressed and destroyed by war; but we destroy them much *faster in times of peace* than in times of war. If the bloody history of the Spaniards in the West Indies and Mexico, in the sixteenth century, is revolting to the feelings of the reader, what must we say of our own countrymen, in this *nineteenth century*? They murdered by slavery in the mines, or by cross-bows and bloodhounds; but we murder by poison, which, if more slow in its effects, is more insidious, and certain, and dreadful. And can no remedy be found? If the laws of Congress cannot reach the case, and arrest the destroyer, cannot Christians come and arm the sufferers with the doctrines and influences of the Bible, by which they will be rendered invulnerable to these satanic assaults? There can be no other remedy than this. Laws cannot effect a cure of the evil, because they cannot be executed. By the introduction of civil institutions, the Indians must be taught to love life, and respect themselves, and by an acquaintance with the Bible be made to love holiness and practise it; until the salutary influence of these principles shall predominate, they will be exposed to their fell destroyer. Here, then, upon Christians rests an awful responsibility. Can they withhold their help and be innocent? Were it practicable, this interrogatory should be extended to every Christian, of every denomination, in the United States, and urged with the ardour which the contemplation of eternal things inspires.[35]

McCoy was always eager to awaken the consciences of his brethren with heartfelt appeals for help and support, even if it meant, as in the following, indicting his own dearly beloved denomination, as a whole, for their apathy towards the mission field present at their doorstep.

On account of erroneous opinions of Indian character, bad measures of Government, and criminal neglect of Christians, the condition of these people has hitherto appeared less hopeful than that of any other upon the earth; while, at the same time, their vigour of intellect, and the absence of established forms of worship, placed them in a condition more susceptible of favourable im-

---

[35] Ibid, pp. 563-564.

pressions, tending to improvement, than any other heathen nation.

The apathy of Christians upon this subject has been unaccountable. Of our own denomination we may speak with more freedom than of others. The Baptists connect with their churches none who are not supposed to be genuinely pious. Their number, within the United States, is over five hundred thousand, and yet they are, comparatively, doing nothing for the Indians. In regard to the propagation of the gospel in Asia, Africa, and Europe, the denomination is liberal and enterprising; but for the conversion of the aborigines of our own country it is but little inclined to labour. It will be seen, by our history that their efforts have been few and feeble. Very favourable opportunities for doing good have frequently passed away without improvement, for want of missionaries, and the few who have been in the field have not been amply sustained in their labours. *During the last ten or twelve years, scarcely any thing has been contributed for the promotion of Indian missions. They have been sustained almost wholly by means obtained from the Government of the United States. This is a startling fact, of which, it is probable, the denomination is not fully aware.*[36]

Can we, whose souls are lighted
With wisdom from on high, -
Can we to men benighted
The lamp of life deny?
Salvation! O Salvation!
The joyful sound proclaim
Till each remotest nation
Has learned Messiah's Name.

---

[36] p. 575. Emphasis is McCoy's.

The only known portrait of Luther Rice is
this silhouette, cut by the daughter of
Samuel Redd of Cedar Vale, Virginia sometime before his death. The original is in the
collections of the Virginia Baptist Historical
Society , Richmond.

Very sincerely yours

Luther Rice

Below In 1873 Columbian College, located in Washington, D. C., was re-
named Columbian University, and is shown here as it appeared in the late
nineteenth century. In 1904 the name was again changed to its present
designation as George Washington University.

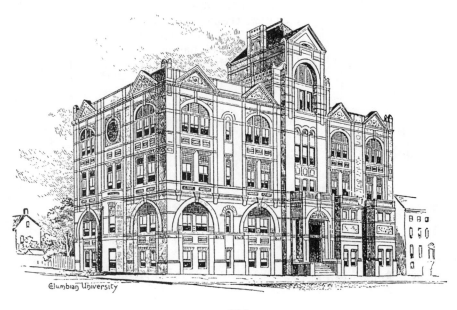

Columbian University

590

Appendix 1
Luther Rice and the Columbian College Fiasco: A Vindication

The Baptist Board of Foreign Mission's Scapegoat

Luther Rice has been given due praise for his work in helping to set up the American Baptist Board of Foreign Missions and for his great success in his preaching ministry. Yet Rice's reputation has been seriously damaged because of his allegedly running Columbian College into enormous, even breathtaking, debts. These debts served as fuel for the anti-mission fires which Alexander Campbell, Daniel Parker and John Taylor were lighting. Of modern commentators, William McLoughlin, giving Lucius Bolles as his source, is particularly outspoken in accusing Rice of grave negligence and misappropriation of funds.[1] On reading numerous works, including Rice's own accounts and the accounts of others listed in the Bibliography and also reports in the *American Baptist Magazine* from 1819 onwards, I have become convinced that it is high time that Luther Rice was vindicated of the many charges raised against him. A detailed examination of Rice's involvement in the financing of various projects such as the Baptist Triennial Convention, the Columbian College, the *Latter Day Luminary* and the *Columbian Star* is not possible in a brief appendix to a biography of another Christian leader, but the following arguments may assist future writers in attempting a more thorough study.

---

[1] "Luther Rice had taken $1,300 sent by the War Department from the Civilization Fund and appropriated it to pay off his private debts." See *Champions of the Cherokees*, p. 50.

Luther Rice's Fine Christian Character

Before going on to consider the immediate reasons behind the Board's disciplinary measures against Rice, it will be profitable to pay some attention to Rice's character and attitude to personal responsibility and loyalty to his denomination. On examining Rice's life and testimony, it becomes at once obvious that Rice was a very meek man who was very conscious of his own failings and tended, because of this, to put his trust in others unflinchingly and accept their criticisms of him without question. This is seen in Rice's youth in his attitude to his father, who scorned his son's religion and abilities, yet Rice never flinched in his devotion to him. This highly positive characteristic stayed with Rice throughout his entire life. This explains why the Convention, Baptist Board and Columbian College trustees all felt they could load Rice with any burden whatsoever and he would not only carry it but also humbly bear his fellow Christian's criticisms when things went wrong. Throughout all his writings, we find Rice, burdened with great problems which were mostly not of his making, yet emphasizing the way of meekness, love, benignity and inoffensiveness in his dealings with his critics. His advice was always:

> Let us very earnestly strive that these beauties may be woven into the very web and texture of our whole deportment. Let us give the most heedful and persevering diligence to gain the ornament of a meek and quiet spirit, which is in the sight of God of great price. This is the amiableness, which free from selfish ostentation, it may be truly said, that it
>
> "Needs not the foreign aid of ornament
> But is, when unadorned, adorned the most."[2]

Around 1817, William Staughton said of Rice, "He knows how to bear indignity without resentment, and fatigue without complaining."[3] Luther Rice had many an opportunity to testify to these characteristics in himself while working on the Board of Trustees.

---

[2] *Memoir of Luther Rice*, p. 42.

[3] See Moore's *Baptist Mission Portraits*, p. 122.

The Bearer of Other People's Burdens

My second argument in Rice's favor is that, from the start of his Christian walk, Rice was taken advantage of by others who exploited him and pressed his meekness to limits totally unattainable by most other men. It seems, that because of an abundance of this excellent characteristic, Rice had to bear burdens which should have been borne by others, but for convenience's sake and because of their own inabilities and lack of enthusiasm for hard work, they placed on Rice's shoulders. In short, if there was any "donkey work" to be done, Rice was chosen to do it. Examples are numerous but it will suffice here to say that the thirty other trustees of Columbian College not only conferred on Rice all the administrative duties of Treasurer but also made him one of three Board Members appointed to canvass for and solicit funds. However, the other two agents, Dr.Alvah Woods and Rev. Elon Galusha, though they were especially appointed as Rice's advisors and agents in financial affairs, appear to have viewed their post as a mere honorary title. This meant that Rice had to cover all the states of the Union himself and even go outside of it in his efforts to raise money for the college. He was also burdened with much of the administrative work of the college, leaving little else for the other trustees to do. During this time, Rice did not receive any salary whatsoever from the Convention, the Board of Managers or the Board of Trustees. However, his far more affluent and educationally better qualified, salaried brethren on the Board of Trustees were content to let him do the work with occasional complaints when Rice arrived unpunctually at a meeting after making one of his many thousand mile journeys through the wilderness. Furthermore, the other trustees, as also the Board of Foreign Missions, expected Rice to be their spokesman in the *Latter Day Luminary* and *Columbian Star* and take on the entire editorial work. He was also expected to keep up a continual correspondence with all the missionaries supported by the Convention. Rice, however, was seldom given an independent say in Convention or Columbian College affairs. His calling was to have brilliant ideas and then hand them over to the Board of Managers who insisted that they knew better. The Convention and Board would then modify Rice's plans in a most impractical way, have Rice put them into action and then blame him when things went wrong.

A *Fund Raiser Without Parallel*

My third argument in Rice's defense is that he had been entangled in financial struggles all of his Christian life and yet had mastered them all, including problems relating to Columbian College. Rice's ability to raise funds under adverse conditions is well illustrated by Rice's call to the Indian (Asian) mission field. Although the London Missionary Society and the American Board of Commissioners for Foreign Missions financed a European tour for Adoniram Judson when he was still only a missionary candidate and covered all costs relating to the voyage and equipment for the four other candidates and their families, yet it was determined that Rice should raise the money himself for his passage and equipment. It took him a mere nine days.

Rice's sufferings to preserve the good name of the Baptist Convention, the Board of Managers and the College Trustees led him into many deprivations. His long and hazardous journeys were hardly fewer than those McCoy was compelled to undertake and Rice was equally familiar with the American outback as was his missionary friend. Rice put every penny he gained into the work of the Board and College and even when friends offered to buy him clothing when his clothes were reduced to rags, he would tell them to give the money to the college instead. Rice received a patrimony of some $2,000 but turned it all over to the college. After an initial courtship with a young lady who was not prepared to share his calling, and because he was always on the move, Rice remained unmarried. All in all, Luther Rice raised many hundreds of thousands of dollars for the Baptist Convention and the Columbian College.[4]

No Equal as a Minister of the Gospel in All the States

Luther Rice was not only a genius at fund raising, he was a brilliant and most devoted preacher who could be used of the Holy Spirit to move the most hardened heart to melt in repentance. As an evangelist in the West and South, he equaled, if not excelled, the work of Peck, Welch and McCoy. He preached the whole Gospel to the whole man, empowered by a strong belief that he was to preach the full doc-

---

[4] This will be seen to be true if only the published records of Rice's fund-raising are studied. However, Rice is known to have sent in numerous payments to various Boards which, owing to intrigues and negligence in these Boards, were never publicly acknowledged.

trines of grace as taught by the old Particular Baptists, emphasizing the experimental nature of living under the everlasting love of God for His elect. This is one of the many factors which drew him to William Staughton, one of America's earliest preachers of sovereign grace, commonly known as "Gillites."[5] William F. Broaddus writes:

> As a minister of the gospel, I doubt whether brother Rice had an equal in all these United States. I have had the privilege of listening to the pulpit exhibitions of many to whom common fame had awarded a place in the very first rank of preachers, and I am free to confess, that I have never heard so *complete a gospel* from the lips of any man, as I have heard from him. I do not mean to say, that he excelled in what are generally considered as indispensable to an accomplished pulpit orator, such as gesticultation, rhetorical precision, etc. He was by no means deficient in these particulars; but it was in real strength, as an expounder of the Bible, as a teacher of the way of salvation to perishing sinners, that he excelled. His ordinary mode of variety of objects named, and great simplicity of language, but a fervency and unction of soul seldom equalled. He seemed to draw very near the mercy seat, and to speak as one who was familiar with the employ. It has been often observed by the pious, that they have derived more spiritual profit from his prayers, than from any laboured discourses. He scarcely ever prayed in public, without uttering the most humiliating confessions of the exceeding sinfulness of sin, while he gloried in the freeness and sovereignty of that grace, which is treasured in Christ Jesus, and which is made effectual unto salvation by the

---

[5] Staughton produced the first American edition of Gill's *Body of Divinity* by means of a concise, one volume abbreviation which he edited. This fact needs to be emphasized as modern Southern Baptists, on the whole, adopted later New England Presbyterian-Congregationalist forms of Fullerism which eventually led them into Arminianism. The Founders' Conferences are making a brave and highly successful effort to turn Southern Baptists back to the faith of earlier fathers such as Dagg, Boyce, Staughton and Rice. One of the main reasons for the founding of the Southern Baptist Convention was to gain freedom from New England *doctrinal* as well as political domination. Now, over a hundred and fifty years later, this freedom has not yet been fully accomplished. The mouse which frightens the elephant is still with them.

indwelling of the Holy Spirit. Among the topics which he never omitted to mention in his petitions, were the interests of missions and education. In connection with the latter subject, the Columbian College was usually mentioned by name.[6]

Looking at the Facts

The facts show that Rice was continually hampered in fund-raising by the authority of the Triennial Convention and his fellow trustees. Rice initially suggested financing the college by subscription but was overruled by the Board and Convention who believed in "an expenditure more rapid than the influx of funds," which meant that instead of planning and building as funds came available, the college borrowed money with no guarantee of being able to pay it back. They started off with a debt of $30,000, which was thus not of Rice's making. Indeed, Rice had raised almost single handedly some $40,000 dollars for the college at a time when that amount was considered a fair sum with which to build an academic establishment. Furthermore, as seen by Rice's letter to the Board dated April 30, 1824, he was greatly perturbed by the laxity with which the Board dealt with funds. Rice had insisted that he should make regular quarterly payments of amounts received. An official report would then be sent to the Board for publication in the various Baptist circulars and magazines and the monies paid into the treasury. These regular payments, however, after being sent to the Board, were not confirmed by the Board and Rice's financial reports were often not printed by the Publishing Committee in the Board's Annual Report. Thus Rice, in the above mentioned letter, very meekly and politely, asks the Board what has happened to the quarterly payments he has sent for the last year amounting to $5,962.77 "for the various purposes of the Convention," and what had happened to the $9,426.58 he had sent specifically towards the costs of the college? Such questions will be familiar to the reader who has followed Isaac McCoy's odyssey with the Board of Foreign Missions. Rice, as McCoy, was never to know what had happened to many of the financial fruits of his labor.

Furthermore, Rice questioned the propriety of the Board's practice of not using legacies for the purpose they were intended, i.e. to be used directly to pay for running costs, but investing them in order to gain interest. Such investments must be redeemed, Rice ar-

---

[6] Taken from Taylor's *Memoir of Rev. Luther Rice*, pp. 244-245.

gued, as soon as debts occur. This was not happening. Investing falsely was ever a weakness of the Convention's and College's Board but Rice's policy was obviously to offset debts immediately by money in hand. In this connection, Rice gently criticized the Board for going into debt over and above what was in the treasury but allowing this to be seen as if he, Rice, were the one guilty of mismanagement. In the case in question, Rice testifies that he was in North Carolina at the time and the Board acted against his will. Even so, Rice points out, it was his efforts that rectified the ensuing deficit. In this long letter, written most probably because the Board had officially said they were neither in receipt of Rice's accounts, nor his reports, Rice emphasizes that he has most definitely sent in not only the accounts and the money but that his reports were there to be examined by the Board at any time.[7]

Dealing with Dubious Practices

Another cause of concern in Rice's dealings with the Board was the fact that he would receive sums from the Government to pay for the Indian Mission's schools which he forwarded to the Board yet the full amount never reached the Mission's teachers. The practice of the Board was apparently that if they received a sum of, say, $666.66 for McCoy, the sum would be rounded down to the next lowest round figure, in this case, $600. The loss of $66.66 was, however, most serious in McCoy's strained financial situation. This figure reflects an actual case which caused a long drawn out correspondence between McCoy, Rice and the Board which was never resolved. Rice was always open about the monies he received, but McCoy found to his constant dismay that a like openness was hardly a characteristic of the Board.[8]

Rice was also most keen on keeping the college in the hands of the Baptists and out of the hands of the commercial world but soon the Convention began to put the college into the hands of non-Baptists. At first, they stipulated that only a third of the trustees should be from other denominations but when Lucius Bolles took over as Corresponding Secretary of the Board, at least half of the trustees were recruited from non-Baptists and a consortium of business people were called in to put the college on a good financial footing. This consortium of business experts soon made matters much worse be-

---

[7] Letter written from College Hill, D. C., April 30, 1824.

[8] See letter of McCoy to Rice dated March 13, 1827. This correspondence has been referred to in the body of the biography, giving further sources.

cause they had no contact or even dealings with the giving public. Baptists just did not look upon missionary and educational enterprises as commercial projects. Columbian College was thus ceasing to be a Baptist college. It was also ceasing to be a *Christian* college. Rice had envisaged a college to train missionaries for the foreign field with the emphasis on language work and exposition. Soon, however, the college was taking in non-Christians, indeed, anyone who could pay the fees. They were also offering a wide selection of academic studies and paying highly qualified men high wages to obtain them as professors. Coupled to this was the extraordinary fact that the Baptist Convention were begging large sums as loans from non-Baptists. Even President Adams did not escape their solicitings and he was moved to lend the Convention $10,000. The Convention's extraordinary method of paying back this debt to the detriment of Columbian College's financial stability is explained in detail by David Benedict who initiated the transaction:

> For the payment of this sum, at my instance, while I was a member of the Board, a mortgage was given on the college premises. My argument was, that as Mr. Adams loaned this large sum in good faith, to a denomination with which he had no connection, in the crippled state of the institution, he ought to have as good security as could be given him. This fact I had the pleasure of stating to the President in his own house in Washington. This business was finally settled to the satisfaction of the distinguished benefactor.

This was only one of many financial manipulations with which Rice had no direct dealings. Indeed, the fund-raising scenario at the Board, which Benedict describes, is bizarre to say the least. The Board member and historian relates how he and his colleagues took part in heated "cross-firing" concerning the financing of the Convention's speculative aims and balanced their accounts by borrowing money from one department to loan to another in which the Columbian College was invariably the sufferer. It was quite obvious that the Board of Managers, instead of looking forward to the day when all the Columbian College debts would be paid off, saw the money coming into the college as a means of financing other enterprises. The Board comforted their consciences by saying that all their debts would soon be "repaid by the commanding eloquence and herculean efforts of a hitherto most successful solicitor," alias - Luther Rice![9]

The Convention and Board of Managers Exercise Authority without Responsibility

A further point which must be considered in conjunction with this is that the Triennial Convention who had purchased the 1,000 year lease on the land where the college property stood, took over the fee simple of the college in May, 1824. This meant that the college was entirely the property of the Convention and the Convention was thus responsible for its finance and maintenance, not an individual member of the Board of Trustees named Luther Rice, who they soon demoted to a mere Agent. Incidentally, when Rice was removed from his position of Treasurer, the new man on the Board was paid a substantial salary though Rice's full-time position had been honorary. The paying of salaries to Board members as also members of the Convention's Board of Managers, though honorable in itself, was a substantial financial burden to the Baptists at large. Much of the money that Rice canvassed served merely to support officials and Board members though Rice himself was denied that support. Added to this is the extraordinary fact that though Rice gave personal property to the Convention worth many thousands of dollars,[10] the Convention gratefully accepted that property but bound Rice legally to pay for its upkeep. More extraordinary still is that though the *Latter Day Luminary* and the *Columbian Star* were Rice's personal property, the Board demanded that they should be viewed as the true, legal proprietors and gradually elbowed Rice out. They yet expected Rice to continue to finance the projects in spite of their taking over the management which proved a mismanagement. This would all seem to be a great display of naivety on Rice's part but the saint was so willing to relieve others of any burden which he thought he had imposed upon them that he overloaded himself unduly in helping what he believed strongly was the cause of God. Rice was always ready to submit his will to others in Christian authority.

---

[9] *Fifty Years Among the Baptists*, p. 119 ff.

[10] As did also Obadiah Brown and Spencer Cone.

Missing Opportunities - On Purpose!

It is interesting to note that enough money for educational purposes was available to the Convention and Board at the time but the Convention ruled that it should be used to build other educational establishments. Indeed, though they were in great debt concerning their first college, they were already planning no less than ten others. Baptist expansion through education had become the new fashion but instead of consolidating what resources they had and going on from there, the Convention was "stepping out in faith" and starting new project after project, feeling that the sorely tried Baptist public would foot the bills. A further euphemism the Board of Managers used for such speculative action, which carried them into enormous debts, was following "their duty to widen the scope of their exertions as much as in their power;" and "by such arguments and measures, as their wisdom and piety may suggest." The Convention, however, had been left $30,000 by a kind benefactor for educational purposes, so this would have exactly covered the $30,000 which the Columbian College needed. However, Dr. William Staughton, the President of Columbian College, took no steps to have this and other donations used for his own work but actually proposed the setting up of a new rival institution, to be called Hope College, which Staughton suggested should be given to Brown University. This motion was carried in Rice's absence as the Treasurer was risking his life at the time in the wilderness, soliciting widows' mites.

Shifting the Blame

In 1826, under the auspices of Lucius Bolles, the new Corresponding Secretary, who was also a member of the college Board of Trustees, a committee was set up to look into the reasons behind the college's financial difficulties. A document was produced, signed by Bolles, which must have been the most extraordinary piece of passing the buck ever initiated by such a committee. Though Bolles continually stresses that Rice always acted under the authorization of the Board of Trustees and with their sanction, and that it was impossible to find particular actions of Rice which could be censured, the Board gave Rice the full blame, finding him "too loose in all his dealings" which resulted in his "thus abusing their high confidence in him." Rice, though practically speaking, a founder of the Baptist Board of Foreign Missions and its main protagonist, was, as a result of Bolles' and his committee's "findings," discharged from his services on the

Board of Foreign Missions. No blame whatsoever was placed on Staughton, the President of the college. No blame was placed on Woods or Galusha, either, though they were Rice's financial agents. Indeed, Woods had caused tumult in the college by absenting himself for a full year in England when he was being paid as Professor of Mathematics and Natural Philosophy to teach at Columbian College. After three years in this office, he became Professor in the same Faculty at Brown University. Galusha, whom Cathcart calls "one of the best known men in the State of New York," was nominally agent for numerous local and national institutions, including the Columbian College, so it would have been physically impossible for him to have carried out all the duties associated with such agencies other than in an honorary, non-active capacity. One can only suspect that Galusha and Woods were not included in the general criticisms leveled at Rice because they were two of the most well-known, respected and influential American Baptists of the day. As if to assure Elon Galusha that no suspicion was attached to him, the college Board elected him to Rice's office of Treasurer and paid him a substantial salary, relying on demoted Rice to raise the money for his unsuccessful successor's wage. Anyone else would have viewed this as the final insult but Rice humbly bowed to those who said it was all in the interest of the college.

The True Culprits Make Yet More Debts

While the Convention were groaning under the burden of their enormous debts, yet planning a spending spree of building new colleges and even doubling the size of Columbian College, they had another money consuming vision. They would finance a new Home Mission and build a gigantic headquarters with spacious accommodation for its office staff and Board members. Naturally, the organizers, supported by the Convention, imagined how eager the Baptist churches would be to send them the thousands of dollars necessary. They therefore sent out appeals to this effect to touch the consciences of churches and Associations and remind them that it was on their behalf that the Convention was acting. Thus new "steps in faith" were taken in full knowledge that the old steps in faith had not been backed up by appropriate works. This project, which was thought out after Rice's dismissal, was thus none of his making but made his fund raising trips to pay off the college's debt all the more difficult. Opposition among the churches, especially in the South and West where Rice had had the most backing, was now growing rapidly because of the Convention's constant demands. There was already a movement in the frontier states to break from their New England bondage. It certainly was not slavery alone that separated the South from the North as the writing was on the wall long before the slavery question was raised and even when it was raised, Heman Lincoln assured the South that slavery was no issue with them. It is this writer's firm opinion based on a wide reading of nineteenth century records that the main reason for the breach between Baptists in the South and the North was that the North insisted that the South and West should be remote-controlled from Boston. It is thus only proper and right that the South and (the then) West should withdraw from such tyranny.

Rice, a Victim of "The Great Reversal"

No suspicion was placed by history on the Board's treatment of Rice nor was Rice's culpability questioned. The Baptist public were merely given the 1826 report without being informed that the condemnation of Rice had not found unanimous backing on the Board.[11] Pondering on these matters, I was overjoyed to see an unpublished work, written in 1960, which went a long way to rehabilitating Rice's worthy name. In May of that year, Raymond H. Taylor handed in his doctoral thesis on *The Triennial Convention, 1814-1845. A Study in Baptist Cooperation and Conflict.* In this work, Taylor shows how the new Baptist Board of Foreign Missions which came to power in 1826 had one aim in mind. They were intent on a total reforming and re-shaping of the Convention with all its aims, Taylor calls it a "dismantling." They wished also to start up an entirely new form of management of Baptist affairs, which ruled out education. Thus, not only the Columbian College had to go, but also Rice, who was seen as the staunchest defender of the old system.[12] All missionary management

---

[11] One version of the report had a note affixed saying "I certify that the foregoing report was not unanimously accepted. O.B.B., President." This was O.B. Brown who was actually Vice-President of the Board of Managers in 1826 but seems to have presided over the various disciplinary committees formed to examine Rice and may have served in lieu of President Staughton. See Benedict's *Fifty Years Among the Baptists*, pp. 121, 186.

[12] This was certainly a further misjudgement on the part of the Board as Rice had suggested many of the changes which actually took place. The simple story is that Rice was not liked so Rice had to go, whatever his views were.

was to be centralized in Boston with the total emphasis on overseas missions.

Taylor calls this move on the part of the new Board, "The Great Reversal."[13] Concerning the new Board of New Yorkers and New Englanders and their relation to Rice, Taylor says:

> While it may be difficult to suppose that Christian brethren would seek deliberately to besmirch the character of one of their own, it is equally difficult to read the Proceedings of the Convention in 1826 without arriving at this conclusion with regard to the attack on Rice.[14]

William Staughton's Role in the Affair Examined

It is interesting to note that Taylor lists Staughton as being censured by the new Board, too, although this fact is nowhere revealed in other works on this subject, nor, for that matter, in the documents Taylor quotes.[15] There is sufficient evidence, however, to compel an unbiased historian to raise certain questions concerning the placing of blame on Rice's broad shoulders while allowing Staughton to get off scot-free. Staughton was co-editor of the *Latter Day Luminary* with Rice, yet he apparently received no blame, or, at least, no official censure when the magazine became a financial liability. More extraordinary still, when debts began to increase at Columbian College, Staughton resigned with most of the trustees and several professors, leaving Rice more or less alone to foot all the bills himself. Of course, Rice had no legal obligation to do so as the new Corresponding Secretary had removed him from office, but the Board still relied on his loyalty and money-raising skills.

Staughton's resignation forced the Board to close the college down until it could be reorganized. This resulted in further enormous debts. This move apparently caused no eyebrows to be raised or suspicions that Staughton was running away from his responsibilities. Nor did Staughton's next move, which, with hindsight, appears more puzzling still. A new Baptist college was being set up in Georgetown,

---

[13] See Chapter IV, "The Great Reversal, 1826," *The Triennial Convention 1814-1845*, p. 94 ff.

[14] Ibid, p. 101.

[15] Ibid, p. 118.

Kentucky. Its Board hoped, speculatively, that the Kentucky Baptists would finance the scheme. Even before the buildings were completed, this college asked Staughton to become its President and Staughton accepted the call. The financing of the building and the building work itself took longer than planned and four months later, Staughton was still awaiting his inauguration to the presidency of a college set up basically with the same inherent problems as the one he had so recently left. The Lord spared him the experience of possibly jumping out of the frying pan into the fire. Staughton suddenly died before he could take on his new office. He was fifty-nine years of age.

As much as Rice was open to criticism throughout his work for the Convention by the Convention, as sheltered was Staughton from any form of internal censure. Indeed, his very presence at the Convention, not to mention his position on the Board of Managers, reflects high favoritism and Staughton always enjoyed exceptional treatment shown to few others. One typical example of special treatment was that only those churches, Associations or states who sent $100 dollars per annum towards the support of the Convention could send delegates to the Convention. These delegates could be then considered as office-bearers. If the states sent more money, they could send more delegates. Staughton was a citizen of Philadelphia and later Washington, D. C., but the money supplied by these states did not suffice to allow Staughton to become a delegate and thus an office-bearer. As the Convention wanted Staughton to be of their ranks, whether normal rulings were applied or not, they hit upon the idea of having Staughton represent any state which had sent in proportionately more money than delegates. Thus Staughton found himself representing states in which he did not reside. At the time of the disciplinary meeting which removed Rice from his office, Staughton, along with Bolles, was representing Massachusetts. Benedict explains that this practice was conformed to the constitution of the Convention but it meant that people were put in power despite the fact that their home churches had not sent them to the Convention as delegates. No doubt the reason for the high regard the New Englanders, at least, had for Staughton was based on the fact that in the England days of his early adulthood, he had been part of the movement among British Baptists to support William Carey in his missionary enterprises.

Be this as it may, Staughton, as President of Columbian College and President of the Board of Managers must surely take a good portion of the blame because of the high offices he held during the years that both the Convention and Columbian College fell into serious debts. He had, or ought to have had, full oversight of what was going on and, indeed, carried full, official responsibility. Yet Staughton's biographer and son-in-law, S.W. Lynd, lays a protecting hand on his father-in-law and writes:

> The subsequent embarrassments of the college are well known. It is equally well known, that pecuniary affairs were the least that ever occupied the mind of Dr. Staughton. He appeared to be entirely satisfied with the statements of those to whom the management of the college was trusted. He was assured, in his own mind, that the pecuniary difficulties of the college were trifling: and he was sanguine of its success.[16]

According to Lynd, Staughton's head was too taken up with heavenly visions to think about how those visions were to be funded on earth. This is a nice pious way of ridding Staughton of any of his earthly responsibilities but this picture does not agree with the down-to-earth scenes which the history of the Convention and further accounts in Lynd's work reveal to us. As early as August, 1818 the Baptist Board had unanimously decided to invite Staughton to take over the Presidency of the college. With this Presidency came full responsibility for running the college. Indeed, in the lengthy description of the founding of the college quoted by Lynd, including long quotes from the Convention's Board of Managers and the college's Board of Trustees, Rice does not play even a secondary part. The fact is that Rice is not once mentioned as carrying any primary responsibility whatsoever. Lynd stresses that his father-in-law was chosen to lead the college because of his possessing a mind prepared for any emergency, a profound judgement, and an ability to discern problems quickly and work out a solution. Lynd writes of Staughton, "Action was his motto."

Staughton Failed to Act on Knowledge He Most Certainly Had

Rice was Staughton's closest friend with whom he kept in constant fellowship. Rice supported Staughton at all times, indeed, Barnes and Stephenson say, "Rice and Staughton were a wonderful team."[17] When Staughton's brave and godly wife was dying and talk was of a family reunion in glory, Rice's was the very first name they mentioned among friends whom they wished to meet again. Because

---

[16] *Memoir of Dr. Staughton*, pp. 263-264.

[17] *Pioneers of Light*, p. 281.

of this closeness to Rice, however, if Rice were guilty of the great neglect attributed to him, Staughton, with his keen mind would have easily recognized what was going wrong, especially as Rice always discussed the college's finances with almost any Christian he met. If anything were wrong, Staughton, with all his astuteness, would not only have known it, he would have recognized his responsibility to act. Indeed, the evidence points to the fact that influential Baptists had turned to Staughton first as the one bearing the major responsibility in complaining about the way the Columbian College and the *Latter Day Luminary* were being financed and only subsequently to Rice. Such documents as have been preserved would seem to indicate that after appealing to the person holding the most authority and not receiving a satisfactory answer, they appealed to Rice to rectify any mismanagement of funds and use his amazing energies and faith to do something to put matters straight. David Benedict, who was on the Board when Rice was "disciplined," quotes a letter from influential Boston Baptist Dr. Thomas Baldwin, dated as early as November 22, 1819, in which the writer addresses Rice on the issue after having approached Staughton. It is obvious from this letter that Baldwin feels that his initial contact with Staughton had not altered matters for the better.[18] For years, Staughton did not act and yet presided over a college faced with bankruptcy, afterwards pleading that he had had no idea!

Staughton Turns His Face to the Wall

When Staughton woke up very late to the fact that his college was in financial ruin, he made a determined last-ditch effort to raise funds which sadly ended in panic. Quite simply, he ran away. However, according to his son-in-law, whenever a finger of suspicion was pointed at him, Staughton washed his hands in innocence, feeling himself "personally aggrieved"[19] at his just critics' behavior, claiming that "enemies of unrighteousness"[20] were attacking him. His letters are full of self-pity as he proclaims that God only knows what he has suffered and he refers to his constant mental affliction[21] because of the

---

[18] *Fifty Years Among the Baptists*, pp. 121-122.

[19] Ibid, p. 264.

[20] Ibid, p. 270.

[21] Ibid, p. 270.

college's financial difficulties. There seemed to be no sense at all present in him, that he was part responsible for the dilemma. Indeed, Staughton, according to Lynd, had blandly planned and organized the curriculum and teaching staff without giving a thought to how it would be financed. If the picture given us of Staughton is true, and Lynd knew his father-in-law very well, it is difficult to imagine such naivety, especially as Lynd otherwise depicts Staughton as one who notices everything. Furthermore, Lynd presents Staughton as not even mentioning Rice's troubles, and in Staughton's letters referring to the Columbian controversy, not a word of accusation is uttered against Rice, but oddly enough, for such a close friend, not a word is said in Rice's defense.[22] Here we see the enormous differences in the characters of Staughton and Rice. When Staughton was placed with his back to the wall, he succumbed to self-pity, rejected accusations against himself and turned his face to the same wall. Rice was of far more manly stuff and, looking his accusers in the face, he, because of his love for his denomination and the responsibilities the Convention had placed most selfishly on him, shouldered the whole blame vicariously. This is true Christ-like heroism and ought to be at last recognized as such by American Baptists at large.

Taylor Lays the Blame for Rice's Unfair Dismissal at Wayland's Feet

Another surprise is that Taylor names his version of the true leader behind the dismantling of the Board as Francis Wayland, a person never mentioned before in this connection. Indeed, Wayland, Taylor points out, was Chairman of the committee which censored Rice for his alleged lack of financial acumen in running the *Luminary* and the *Star*. According to Taylor, Wayland did not even consult Rice's annual reports which he had punctually sent to the Board from 1820 to 1826, though it was the lack of such detailed reports that was complained of.[23] Thus Rice was condemned without the known documents being examined, which would have easily cleared his name. Finally, as if to make the farce more perfect, Taylor's detailed assessment of the financial reports made to discredit Rice, showed that they all displayed a most negligent lack of care and competence, with Rice's

---

[22] Ibid, pp. 215-228; 262-279.

[23] Ibid, pp. 106-107.

judges drawing up "puzzling documents"[24] based on "a curious piece of reasoning,"[25] which led them, at times, to ignore totally the transactions under criticism which had been minutely documented by Rice and which would most likely have freed him from blame. Truly this action must go down in history as "The Columbian College Fiasco."

Rice's Last Great Work for the College and Convention

Meanwhile Rice was busy touring the country, working hard to collect money to cover the remaining debts. He was paying off the debts at the rate of at least $20,000 a year, apart from raising thousands for other educational and missionary projects. J.B. Taylor[26] tells us that "the labours he (Rice) performed were sufficient to wear out five men of vigorous minds and iron constitutions."[27] Yet the new Board seemed to be bent on increasing their debts by thousands still, thus adding to Rice's terrible burden. Indeed, throughout his office as the Convention's Treasurer, Heman Lincoln's policy was to borrow one dollar in three that he spent. Benedict records how, as late as 1838, the Convention were still borrowing $25,000 per year.[28] In May, 1829, three years after his discharge from the Mission and Columbian College Boards, Rice, still working slavishly to finance the college, wrote to the trustees to tell them that he was, at last, close to balancing their books for them:

> Toiling as I have done for the Institution without any compensation and even providing for my personal expenses of late by special means, I am without home and utterly destitute of property. However, after having laboured for the benefit of this college nearly ten years it is a source of no small consolation to me that it has now the prospects of realizing complete relief, ultimate enlargement.

---

[24] Ibid, p. 106.

[25] Ibid, p. 107.

[26] Not to be confused with R. H. Taylor.

[27] *Memoir of Rev. Luther Rice*, p. 185.

[28] *Fifty Years Among the Baptists*, p. 189.

After penning these words, Luther Rice was pleased to enclose a letter of resignation to the Board of Trustees. Rice was now a free man as nobody could possibly charge him with dishonorable conduct or of leaving the Board in debt. His work, he imagined, must now be done and he could turn to other important things. The trustees, however, began to make further debts and Rice, though having no responsibility whatsoever for the college's mismanagement and having no commitments to the Board, started raising further funds to pay off the debts. He also canvassed $15,000 for an instructor and strove to raise thousands of dollars for scholarships for the support of young ministers.

Rice had always hoped to marry, settle down and pastor a church but the college still made new debts and Rice found himself having to give up all his plans again. He felt duty bound to set off on the road, begging for money with no rest in sight. Even after suffering a stroke, he still marched on sending a seemingly never-ending stream of money to Columbian College. However, he grew weaker and weaker because of his hard and dangerous life and developed abscesses on his liver, though some say it was appendicitis, then inoperable. Rice passed away peacefully on September 25, 1836, knowing that his labors had not been in vain because the Columbian College was once more almost free from debt and by the turn of the next decade was not only out of the red but decidedly in the black. All Luther Rice possessed at his death was an old horse whom he named Columbus, which was the nearest he could get to a name sounding like Columbian, an old cart and a tiny piece of land just inherited. These three he bequeathed to the college.

A Prophet, Worthy of Great Respect, Not Honored in His Own Country

From 1844 onwards, the Columbian College began to sell off the forty-six and a half acres of land on College Hill that Rice had donated to the college around 1818. By 1873 the land altogether had fetched no less than $200,000. Rice had made the college rich. Yet the myth persists that Rice was the sole culprit who brought Columbian College financially to its knees. Winfred Hervey says of Rice, "he died as he had lived, among comparative strangers, and no tear of kindred affection bedewed his grave."[29] Rice was a prophet who was not honored in his own Baptist country. Yet others honored him. In 1904

---

[29] *The Story of Baptist Missions*, p. 179.

the college passed completely into the hands of non-Baptists and became the George Washington University. The new Board of Trustees paid full tributes due to the blessed memory of Luther Rice and declared of him, "We salute him today as our Founder."

The successors of the Triennial Convention and the Baptist Board of Foreign Missions have still to write a full official vindication of this brave, self-offering man of God to whom they are so much in debt. Furthermore, Luther Rice must be viewed with Isaac McCoy as one of the greatest Baptists and Christians that the New World has ever produced.[30]

---

[30] The information on which this appendix is based is found in the *American Baptist Magazine*, 1823-24, pp. 137, 139-140, 143, 159, 161-164 and the American Baptist histories and Rice biographies listed in the Bibliography besides the works mentioned above.

Appendix 2
McCoy's Reconnaissance Tour with the Potawatomies and Ottawas 1828

Sept. -1

Set off from Harmony Mission at 9 o'clock - Our company consisting of six Indians, two interpreters (who also are part Indian) and two hired white men, with 13 horses.

We have now left the State of Missouri and entered the Indian Territory, It therefore becomes my duty to describe the country through which we pass. Thus far it is a beautiful rolling, prairie country - happily diversified with streaks of woodlands - Limestone appears on the sides of hills, and in the riverlets [?].

Sept. 5

An Osage whom we had taken for a guide deserted us. At half past ten reached a large creek which being muddy detained us an hour & a half in crossing. At 3 crossed another creek near its junction with Osage river - encamped on the former.

We have this day passed thro a fine limestone country. In a few instances sandstone appear. Timber on the river appears to be about one mile in width, and that along each large creek half a mile, on smaller branches less, and consisting chiefly of oak and hickory, with some walnut, ash, etc.

The prairie bottom lands are usually covered with a beautiful grass for hay - We seldom find a quagmire.

We ascended a high natural mound from which we saw the country on both sides of the river stocked with timber sufficient to support a tolerably dense population

The nature of the soil may be compared with that of the praries of Illinois in the western parts generally. Hills rise to considerable height - round - oblong, etc. etc., exhibiting a singular appearance because in general they are destitute of timber- These hills are heaps of stone, which appear on the sides - not in large masses, and sometimes on the summits.

611

Saturday, Sept. 6

By high rocky bluffs, I was several times prevented from crossing Osage river. At half past 5 succeeded, and encamped on the south bank.

Wood today has been more abundant than heretofore. High lands come in nearer to the river and creeks, and the timber often stretching out on to the hills. The hills more abrupt than formerly, from the tops of which spreads out a beautiful rolling country. Slopes that wash, steep side hills, and all water courses disclose a bed of limestone. The condition of the stone may be compared with that of the middle counties of Kentucky. The soil is almost universally rich – darker than the timber high lands of Kentucky, and possesses the mellowness peculiar to limestone lands.

The river and creeks here, though still too sluggish, are stony and more clear than those below. Along the river and creeks are fertile bottoms of timbered land, sometimes subject to inundation, covered with oak, ash, hickory, walnut, hackberry, honey locust, etc.

Sept. 12

We have now left Osage river. The water in it and its tributaries is too stagnant. Streams for miles are abundant but all these would fail in the more dry season of the year, the same as those farther east in the State of Missouri. From our Saturdays encampment to the sources of the river - a distance of more than 70 miles there can be no want of water for common use of man and beast - Farther down spring water appeared scarce. The country promises health except immediately on the banks of the larger streams, where as in most similar cases in the western country, it will be subject to Agues & fevers. The soil is almost universally fertile - and the whole abundantly supplied with limestone. It is the most sightly country I ever saw.

Sept.17

This day's journey lying across the lands dividing Neosho & Osage from Kanzas river, I had expected to find the country almost wholly destitute of timber, in this I have been happily disappointed. Timber is more scarce than formerly yet the country will admit a tolerable settlement the whole way. It rises to the dividing lands - then descends towards Kanzas - Continuing high, rich and abounding in limestone.

We have left Neosho waters, which country requires no other description than to say, it resembles that on the Osage - rather less timber, and perhaps better watered. It may justly be pronounced an excellent country so far as I have seen it.

Sept.19

Timber on the Kanzas is sufficient to allow a dense population for four, five, or more miles on each side. It appears to be well watered. Small creeks and [word missing, probably 'rivers'] are numerous, and wooded and watered.

Sept.20

The country continues the same in appearance, except that the lands, though rich, are not quite so fertile as on the Neosho.

Sept.24

I am ready to pronounce the country I have explored excellent. Timber is too scarce, but by a judicious arrangement in settlement a vast population can be conveniently situated - lands should be so laid out that to each farm should be allotted so much timber only as would be sufficient, and let the residue be prarie.

There is scarcely a quagmire in all the country. I saw only one pond of water, and that covering almost an acre of land. Notwithstanding there is so little wet land, yet grass for hay is abundant, especially on Neosho.

Hogs will thrive in any country while it is new. This country is too high & dry and open to be well adapted to the growth of that animal after it becomes thickly settled. it will always be remarkably well adapted to the growth of cattle and sheep. Attention to these will be the principal business of farmers. The extensive grazing and the abundance of hay of the praries will supercede the necessity pasturage & meadows on farms. I extended my tour west of the State of Missouri 140 miles on a direct line as measured on the map say, 160 miles, the nearest way that could be travelled, and within 60 miles of the place where the Santa Fe road crosses Arkansaw river. I have been enabled to form a pretty just estimate of the country 80 miles in width and 150 from east to west, making 12,000 square miles, or 7,680,000 acres.. How much further west the country is inhabitable I am not able, from observation, to say.

Bibliography

Specific Works Dealing with McCoy, His Family and Associates

Bailey, Gilbert S. *The Carey Indian Mission at Niles, Michigan and Rev. Isaac McCoy, Its Founder, A Sermon Preached by Request to the St. Joseph River Baptist Association at Detroit*: Christian Herald Print, 1880.

Bartee, Wayne. *John Mason Peck: A Pioneer in Advancing the Gospel* Missouri Baptist Heritage Series (Brochure), William Jewell College, Liberty, Missouri, undated.

Berkhofer, Robert F. "A New Introduction" to Isaac McCoy's *History of Baptist Indian Missions* New York and London, Johnson Reprint Corporation, 1970.

Brackney, W. H. (Ed.) *Dispensations of Providence: The Journal and Selected Letters of Luther Rice 1803-1830* Rochester, NY: American Baptist Historical Society, 1984.

Cone, Edward and Cone, Wallace. *Some Account of the Life of Spencer Houghton Cone, A Baptist Preacher in America* New York: Livermore & Rudd, 1856.

DeGolier, Florence. *Ta-Pooth-Ka and His Descendants: The Story of Moses and Eliza Merrill* 1967 Centennial Observance: Omaha, NE: Nebraska Baptist State Convention, c. 1967.

Hayne, Coe. *Vanguard of the Caravans: The Life Story of John Mason Peck.* Philadelphia: Judson Press, 1931.

Hayward, Elizabeth. *John M'Coy: His Life and His Diaries.* New York The American Historical Company, Inc., 1948.

Guide to the Microfilm Edition of the Isaac McCoy Papers 1808-1874. Topeka:Kansas State Historical Society

Lynd, Samuel W. *Memoir of the Rev. William Staughton, D. D.* Boston: Lincoln, Edmunds & Co., 1834.

Lyons, Emory J. *Isaac McCoy: His Plan of and Work for Indian Colonization.* History Series No. 1., ed. F. B. Streeter, Fort Hays Kansas State College Studies, 1945.

Malone, Dumas, ed. *Isaac McCoy,* (signed E.E.D.), *Dictionary of American Biography,* vol. vi New York: Charles Scribners & Sons, 1933.

McCormick, Calvin. *The Memoir of Miss Eliza McCoy.* Dallas, TX: the author, 1892.

McCoy, Isaac. *Annual Register of Indian Affairs, 1835-38.* Reprinted, Enid, OK: Regular Baptist Publishing, Inc., 1998; Springfield, MO: Particular Baptist Press, 2000.

_____. *A Periodical Account of Baptist Missions Within the In-dian Territory For the Year Ending December 31, 1836.* Indian Territory: Shawanoe Baptist Mission House, 1837.

_____. *Address to Philanthropists in the United States, Gen-erally, and to Christians in Particular, on the Condition and Prospects of the American Indians.* n.p., n.d.[1831?].

_____. *History of Baptist Indian Missions.* Washington, D.C. William M. Morrison, 1840.

_____. *Remarks on the Practicability of Indian Reform, Em-bracing their Colonization.* New York: Gray and Bunce, 1829.

_____. "Report on Conditions of the Indian Territory to the War Department." *Executive Documents of the House of Rep-resentatives,* Doc. No. 172, pp. 1-15. Washington, D.C.: Dudd Green, 1832.

McCoy, William H. *Notes on the McCoy Family,* (Ed. Elizabeth Hayward) Rutland, VT: The Tuttle Publishing Company, Inc., 1939.

McMurtrie, Douglas C. and Allen, Albert H., *Jotham Meeker: Pioneer Printer of Kansas.* Chicago: Eyncourt Press, 1930.

Roustio, Edward R. *A History of the Life of Isaac McCoy in Relation-ship to Early Indian Migrations and Missions as Revealed in*

His Unpublished Manuscripts, A Dissertation Presented to the Faculty of the Central Baptist Theological Seminary, Kansas City, May 1954. [Since published as *Early Indian Missions, as Reflected in the Unpublished Manuscripts of Isaac McCoy*. Springfield, MO: Particular Baptist Press, 2000].

Schulz, George A. *An Indian Canaan: Isaac McCoy and the Vision of an Indian State*. Norman: University of Oklahoma Press, 1972.

Stewart, Walter S., *Early Baptist Missionaries and Pioneers*, Vol. 1, "Isaac McCoy," viii, pp.189-228. Philadelphia: Judson Press, 1925.

Taylor, James B. *Memoir of Rev. Luther Rice*. (1840) Nashville: Broadman Press, 1937.

Thompson, Evelyn Wingo. *Luther Rice: Believer in Tomorrow*. Nashville: Broadman Press, 1967.

Wyeth, Walter N., *Isaac McCoy - Christiana McCoy, A Memorial*. Philadelphia: W. N. Wyeth, 1895.

General Works on Baptist Missions Featuring McCoy and the Indian Mission

Baptist Home Missions in North America, 1832-1882, New York: American Baptist Home Mission Society, 1883.

Barnes, Lemuel C. et al, *Pioneers of Light*. Philadelphia: American Baptist Publication Society, 1924.

Barr, Thomas P. *The Pottawatomi Baptist Manual Labor Training School*. Topeka: Kansas State Historical Society, undated, (Reprint from the Kansas Historical Quarterly, 43, Winter, 1977), pp. 377-431.

Eaton, W. H. *Historical Sketch of the Massachusetts Baptist Missionary Society and Convention 1802-1902*. Boston: Massachusetts Baptist Convention, 1903.

Gammell, William. *A History of American Baptist Missions in Asia, Africa, Europe and North America*, Boston: Gould, Kendall & Lincoln, 1849.

Gardner, Robert G. *Cherokees and Baptists in Georgia*. Washington, GA: Georgia Baptist Historical Society, 1989.

Hamilton, Robert. *The Gospel Among the Red Men: The History of Southern Baptist Indian Missions*. Nashville: Broadman, 1930.

Hervey, G. Winfred. *The Story of Baptist Missions in Foreign Lands from the Time of Carey to the Present Date*. St Louis: Chancy R. Barns, 1885.

McLoughlin, William G. *Champions of the Cherokees: Evan and John B. Jones*. Princeton University Press, 1989

McLoughlin, William G. *Cherokees & Missionaries, 1789-1837*. Norman: University of Oklahoma Press, 1994.

Moore, John Allen. *Baptist Mission Portraits*. Macon, GA: Smyth & Helwys Publishing, Inc., 1994.

O'Beirne, H. F. *Leaders and Leading Men of the Indian Territory*. American Publishers' Association, 1891.

Parker, Daniel. *A Public Address to the Baptist Society, And Friends of Religion in General, on the Principle and Practice of the Baptist Board of Foreign Missions for the United States of America*. Stout & Osborn, 1820; reprinted by Hamilton Press Inc., 1988.

Peck, Solomon (Ed.). "History of the Missions of the Baptist General Convention," in Joseph Tracy, comp., *History of American Missions to the Heathen, From Their Commencement to the Present Time*. Worcester, MA: Spooner & Howland, 1840. Reprinted, New York: Johnson Reprint Corporation, 1970.

Rister, Carl Coke. *Baptist Missions among the American Indians*. Atlanta: Home Mission Board, S. B. C., 1944.

Vedder, Henry C. *A Short History of Baptist Missions*. Philadelphia: Judson Press, 1927.

Walker, Robert Sparks. *Torchlights to the Cherokees: The Brainerd Mission*. New York: Macmillan, 1931.

White, Charles L. *A Century of Faith, The American Baptist Home Mission Society*. Philadelphia: Judson Press, 1932.

White, Mary Emily. *The Missionary Work of the Southern Baptist Convention*. Philadelphia: American Baptist Publication Society, 1902.

Wyeth, Walter. *Poor Lo!: Early Indian Missions, A Memorial*. Philadelphia: W. N. Wyeth, 1896.

Histories of American Baptists with References to McCoy's Life and Times

Benedict, David. *Fifty Years Among the Baptists*. New York: Sheldon & Co., 1860. Reprinted, Little Rock: American Baptist Association, 1977.

Brackney, W. H. and Eltscher, S. M., *A Guide to Manuscript Collections in the American Baptist Historical Society*. Valley Forge, PA: A. B. H. S., 1986.

Brackney, W. H. *A Traveler's Guide to American Baptist Historical Sights*. Cooperative Publications of American Baptist Board of National Ministries and the American Baptist Historical Society, 1982.

Cady, John F. *The Origin and Development of the Missionary Baptist Church in Indiana*. Franklin, IN: Franklin College, 1942.

Cathcart, William. *The Baptist Encyclopaedia*. 2 vols, Philadelphia: Louis H. Everts, 1881.

Cox, F. A. and Hoby, J. *The Baptists in America: A Narrative of the Deputation from the Baptist Union in England to the United States and Canada*. New York: Leavitt, Lord, & Co., 1836.

Dillow, Myron D. *Harvesttime on the Prairie: A History of Baptists in Illinois, 1796-1996.* Franklin, TN: Providence House Publishers, 1996.

Gardner, Robert G. *A Decade of Debate and Division: Georgia Baptists and the Formation of the Southern Baptist Convention.* Macon, GA: Mercer University Press, 1995.

Gaskin, J. M.. *Baptist Women in Oklahoma.* Oklahoma City: Messenger Press, 1985.

Haddcock, Louise and Gaskin, J. M. *Baptist Heroes in Oklahoma.* Oklahoma City: Messenger Press, 1976.

Lambert, Cecil Byron. *The Rise of the Anti-Mission Baptists: Sources and Leaders, 1800-1840.* (1957) New York: Arno Press, 1980.

Leonard, Bill J. *Dictionary of Baptists in America.* Downers Grove, IL: Intervarsity Press, 1994.

Mercer, Jesse. *A History of the Georgia Baptist Association.* Washington, GA, 1838. Reprinted, Washington, GA: Wilkes Publishing Co., 1980.

Routh, E. C. *The Story of Oklahoma Baptists.* Oklahoma City: Baptist General Convention, 1932.

Sharp, W. A. Seward. *History of Kansas Baptists.* Kansas City, KS: Kansas City Seminary Press, 1940.

Spencer, J. H. *A History of the Kentucky Baptists.* 2 vols. Cincinnati, OH: J. R. Baumes, 1885, 1886. Reprinted, Lafayette, Tennessee: Church History Research & Archives, 1984.

Sprague, William B. *Annals of the American Pulpit.* vol. vi, Baptist. New York: Robert Carter & Bros., 1865. Reprinted, New York: Arno Press, 1969.

Torbet, Robert G. *A History of the Baptists.* Philadelphia: Judson Press, 1955.

Specific Secular Works on the North American Indians

Billard, Jules B. (Ed.). *The World of the American Indian*. Washington, D.C.: National Geographic Society, 1979.

Catlin, George. *Letters and Notes on the North American Indians*. (Ed.) Mooney, Michael MacDonald. Engelhard, NJ: Gramercy Books, 1995.

Curtis, Edward S. *Die Indianer Nord-Amerikas*, Taschen, 1997.

Debo, Angie. *And Still the Waters Run: The Betrayal of the Five Civilized Tribes*. Norman: University of Oklahoma Press, 1989.

Eaton, Rachel. *John Ross and the Cherokee Indians*. University of Chicago, 1921.

Ehle, John. *Trail of Tears: The Rise and Fall of the Cherokee Nation*. New York: Anchor Books, 1989.

Foreman, Grant. *The Five Civilized Tribes*. Norman: University of Oklahoma Press, undated reprint of 1934 edition, vol. 8 in The Civilization of the American Indian Series.

Hodge, Frederick W. (Ed.). *Handbook of American Indians North of Mexico*. 2 vols. Smithsonian Institution, Bureau of American Ethnology, Bulletin 30, 1910.

Lyons, Grant. *The Creek Indians*. New York, 1978.

Taylor, Colin F. *The Plains Indians*. Salamander Books, 1994.

Troccoli, Joan Carpenter. *First Artist of the West: George Catlin*. Tulsa, OK: Thomas Gilcrease Museum Association, 1993.

Unrau, William E. *The Kansa Indians: A History of the Wind People, 1673-1873*. Norman: University of Oklahoma Press, 1971.

Wright, Muriel H. *A Guide to the Indian Tribes of Oklahoma*. Norman: University of Oklahoma Press, 1986.

Dissertations and Unpublished Documents

Black, Charles Herman. *One Hundred Years of Baptist Missionary Administration in Oklahoma*, A Dissertation Presented to the Faculty of the Central Baptist Theological Seminary, Kansas City, 1950.

Cloyd, A. D. and Curtis, H. F. *A Memorial for Rev. Moses Merrill and His Wife Eliza (Wilcox) Merrill: Missionaries of the American Baptist Missionary Union to the Otoes*. Courtesy of the American Baptist Historical Society.

Clarke, Arthur M. *First Protestant Work in Nebraska: The Moses Merrill Story*. A paper read by Dr.Arthur M. Clarke for the Greater Omaha Historical Society at the site of the Merrill home near Bellevue, October 12, 1958.

Dane, John Preston. *A History of Baptist Missions Among the Plains Indians of Oklahoma*. A Dissertation Presented to the Faculty of the Central Baptist Seminary, Kansas City, 1955.

Gibson, L. T. *Luther Rice's Contribution to Baptist History*. A Dissertation submitted in partial fulfilment of the requirements for the degree of Doctor of Sacred Theology in the School of Theology, Temple University, 1944.

Hutcherson, Curtis A. *The Contributions of Dr.Johnston Lykins and Robert Simerwell to the Preservation, Advancement and Evangelization of the American Indians*. A Dissertation Presented to the Faculty of the Central Baptist Theological Seminary, Kansas City, Kansas, May 1952.

Taylor, Raymond Hargus. *The Triennial Convention, 1814-1845: A Study in Baptist Cooperation and Conflict*. A Dissertation Presented to the Faculty of the Graduate School, The Southern Baptist Theological Seminary, May, 1960.

Yeager, Randolph O. *Indian Enterprises of Isaac McCoy, 1817-1846*. A Dissertation Presented to the Faculty of the University of Oklahoma, Norman, 1954.

History of Indian Missions and Territories Before Isaac McCoy

Adair, John. *Founding Fathers: The Puritans in England and America*. Grand Rapids, MI: Baker Book House, 1986.

Bartlett, W. H. *The Pilgrim Fathers of New England*. Nelson & Sons, 1866.

Bremer, Francis. *The Puritan Experiment*. Detroit: St James Press, 1977.

Campbell, Douglas. *The Puritan in Holland, England, and America: An Introduction to American History*. New York: Harper, 2 vols, 1893

Cockshott, Winnifred. *The Pilgrim Fathers*. Methuen & Co, 1909.

Cutler, William G. *History of the State of Kansas*. A. T. Andreas, 1883, as reproduced in the Kansas Collection Books in the various Indian Nations Home Pages, Kansas City Public Library and the Kansas State Historical Society.

Douglas, James. *New England and New France*. Toronto, 1913.

Edwards, Jonathan, (Ed.). *The Life and Diary of David Brainerd*. Chicago: Moody Press, 1949.

Fagan, Brian M. *Kingdoms of Gold, Kingdoms of Jade: The Americas Before Columbus*. New York: Thames and Hudson, 1991.

Fiske, John. *The Beginnings of New England, Or the Puritan Theocracy in Its Relation to Civil and Religious Liberty*. New York: Macmillan, 1889.

Gaustad, Edwin S. *Liberty of Conscience: Roger Williams in America*. Grand Rapids, MI: W. B. Eerdmans, 1991.

Houghton, S. M. (Ed.). *Five Pioneer Missionaries* (incl. Brainerd and Eliot). Edinburgh, Scotland: Banner of Truth Trust, 1987.

Mather, Cotton. *The Great Works of Christ in America*. 2 vols. Edinburgh, Scotland: Banner of Truth Trust, 1979.

Krickeberg, Walter. et al, *Die Religionen des alten Amerika*. W. Kohl-
hammer Verlag, 1961.

Page, Jesse. *David Brainerd: The Apostle to the North American Indians*. S. W. Partridge, undated.

Robinson, Charles Henry. *History of Christian Missions*. Glascow,
Scotland: T. & T. Clark, 1915.

Rowse, A. L. *The Elizabethans and America*. New York: Macmillan,
1959.

Schreiber, Hermann. *Die Neue Welt: Die Geschichte der Entdeckung
Amerikas*. Casimir Katz Verlag, 1991.

Slocum, Charles E. *History of the Maumee River Basin*. Defiance, OH:
C. E. Slocum 1904.

Sweet, William W. *The Story of Religion in America*. Grand Rapids,
MI: Baker Book House, 1979.

Willison, George F. *Saints and Strangers*. Reynal & Hitchcock, 1945.

Zierer, Otto. *Geschichte Amerikas: Asyl der Freiheit (1600-1800)*.
Sebastian Lux Verlag, undated.

Journals, Quarterlies and other Periodicals

Anonymous, "Memoir of the Rev. William Staughton, D.D." (Review of
Lynd's book and the author's (editor's?) personal recol-
lections), *American Baptist Magazine*, 1834, pp. 266-274.

Anonymous, "Ordination of Mr.[David] Lewis," *American Baptist Magazine*. 1832, p. 185.

Barnes, Lela. "Isaac McCoy and the Treaty of 1821," *Kansas Historical
Quarterly*. Topeka: The Kansas State Historical Society,
1936, vol. v, pp. 122-142.

_____."Journal of Isaac McCoy for the Exploring Expedition of
1828," *Kansas Historical Quarterly*. Topeka: Kansas State
Historical Society, 1936, vol. v, pp.227-277.

————— . "Journal of Isaac McCoy for the Exploring Expedition of 1830," *Kansas Historical Quarterly*. Topeka: Kansas State Historical Society, 1936, vol. v, pp. 339-377.

Brackney, William H. "Triumph of the National Spirit: The Baptist Triennial Conventions, 1814-1844," *American Baptist Quarterly*, vol. iv, June, 1985, Number 2, pp. 165-183.

Drury, Robert M. "Isaac McCoy and the Baptist Board of Missions," *Baptist History and Heritage*, vol. ii, No. 1, Jan. 1967, pp. 9-14.

————— ."The Life of Isaac McCoy: Minister, Missionary, Explorer, Surveyor, Lobbyist, Administrator and 'Apostle to the Indians'," *The Trail Guide*, vol. x, June 1965, No. 2., pp. 1-16.

Edmunds, R. David. "Potawatomis in the Platte Country: An Indian Removal Incomplete," *Missouri Historical Review*, lxvii:4, Columbia, Missouri, 1974, pp. 375-392.

Haykin, Michael. *The Apostle of the Indians of the West: The Life and Ministry of David Zeisberger (1721-1808).*

Jennings, Warren A. "Isaac McCoy and the Mormons," *Missouri Historical Review*, vol. lxi, Oct. 1966, No. 1, pp. 62-82.

McCoy, Isaac. "Letter from, Arkansas, - Creek Nation," *The American Baptist Magazine*, vol. xii, Dec. 1832, No. 12, pp. 496-497. Articles and letters from the pen of Isaac McCoy in the *American Baptist Magazine* which I have used widely are so numerous that they would require a large bibliography of their own. Readers are requested to study the indices of this magazine for every year from McCoy's appointment by the Board until his death, i.e. 1817 to 1846. Otherwise almost all these documents are contained in the microfilm copies mentioned below.

————— . "Isaac McCoy's Second Exploring Trip in 1826," ed. John Francis McDermont, *Kansas Historical Quarterly*, Vol. XIII, 1944-1945, The Kansas State Historical Society, pp. 400-462.

————— . "From Mr. McKoy to the Corresponding Secretary," *The Latter Day Luminary*, vol. i, March, 1818, pp. 43-44.

McCoy, Isaac. "From the Same to the Agent of the Board," *The Latter Day Luminary*, vol. i, March, 1818, p. 44.

_____. "From Mr. McCoy, near Vincennes," *The Latter Day Luminary*, vol. i, May, 1818, pp. 90-91.

_____. "From Mr. McCoy, near Vincennes," *The Latter Day Luminary*, vol. i, July, 1818, pp. 182-185.

_____. "Miami and Other Indians," *The Latter Day Luminary*, vol. i, May, 1819, p. 412.

_____. "Indians of Illinois," *The Latter Day Luminary*, vol. i, August, 1819, pp. 450-452.

_____. "Indians of Illinois," *The Latter Day Luminary*, vol. i, October, 1819, pp. 503-505.

_____. "Station at Fort Wayne," *The Latter Day Luminary*, vol. ii, August, 1820, pp. 189-190.

_____. "Station at Fort Wayne," *The Latter Day Luminary*, vol. ii, February, 1821, p. 298.

_____. "Fort Wayne Indian Mission," *The Latter Day Luminary*, vol. ii, May, 1821. pp. 386-387.

_____. "Fort Wayne Mission," *The Latter Day Luminary*, vol. ii, May, 1821, pp. 401, 478-488.

_____. "Fort Wayne Mission, Extracts from the Journal of the Reverend Mr. McCoy," *The Latter Day Luminary*, vol. ii, October, 1822, pp. 313-343

Potts, E. Daniel. "I Throw Away the Gun to Preserve the Ship: A Note on the Serampore Trio," *Baptist Quarterly*, XX, 1963-64.

Shoup, Earl Leon. "Indian Missions in Kansas," Kansas State Historical Society *Collections*, XII, Topeka, 1912, pp. 65-69.

Stanley, Brian. "C. H. Spurgeon and the Baptist Missionary Society," *Baptist Quarterly*, 29 (7), 1982, pp. 319-328.

Taylor, Jeffrey Wayne. "Daniel Parker (1781-1844): Frontier Baptist Warrior for the Old Way," *Baptist History and Heritage*, vol. xxxii, April 1997, No. 2, pp. 54-64.

Thompson, Evelyn. "Isaac McCoy and His Work Among the Great Lake Indians," *Baptist History and Heritage*, vol. ii, No. 1, January 1967, pp. 3-8.

Wilmeth, Roscoe. "Kansas Village Locations in the Light of McCoy's 1828 Journal," *Kansas Historical Quarterly*, XXVI, 2, 1960, Topeka, Kansas, pp. 152-157.

Microfilms

Isaac McCoy Papers (microfilm edition) manuscript division, Kansas State Historical Society, Topeka. Web Site (Web-Page) downloads.

Isaac McCoy Papers (microfilm edition) manuscript division, Kansas State Historical Society, Topeka, Reels 1-13, 1808-1874.

Correspondence: Reel 1, Calendar of Correspondence, 1808-June 1821; Reel 2, July 1821-June 1823; Reel 3, July 1823-1824; Reel 4, 1825-June 1826; Reel 5, July 1826-August 1827; Reel 6, September 1827-1828; Reel 7, 1829-April 1832; Reel 8, May 1832-May 1836; Reel 9, June 1836-1838; Reel 10, 1839-1842; Reel 11, 1843-1874; Reel 12, Undated Fragments, McCoy's Autobiography, Survey Notes, Maps, *History of the Origin of the Ottawa Indians*, Notes on Indian reform, Undated statements concerning a controversy over the Shawnee Baptist Mission, Works by Rice and Sarah McCoy, MS of a hymn book; Reel 13, *History of Baptist Indian Missions*.

American Baptist Foreign Mission Societies. Records, 1817-1959. (Includes records of predecessor organizations) Originals at American Baptist Archives Center, Valley Forge, PA., Microfilmed by ABFMS. Distributed by American Baptist Historical Society, 1106 S. Goodman St., Rochester, NY 14620. Reel No. 99. Evan Jones (Cherokee), 1843-1865; John Jones (Cherokee), 1852-1861; Charles Kellam (Creek), 1836-1842; Jane Kelly (Shawnee), 1843-1845; David Lewis (Creek), 1832-1835; Johnston Lykins (Putawatomie), 1827-1843; Eleanor

Macomber (Qjibwa), 1830-1834; Isaac McCoy (Putawatomie), 1825-1826; Reel No. 100, Isaac McCoy (Putawatomie), 1827-1843; James Mason (Creek), 1838-1840; Jotham Meeker (Shawnee), 1829-1853, (Ottawa), 1837-1855; Moses Merrill (Shawnee), 1832-1835, (Otoe), 1836-1840; Elizabeth Morse (Cherokee, Shawnee), 1843-1865; Harriet Morse (Ojibwa, Cherokee), 1842-1844, 1856-1859; Duncan O'Bryant (Cherokee), 1830-1834; John Pratt (Shawnee), 1836-1848; Reel No. 101, John Pratt (Shawnee), 1848-1865; Ramsay Potts (Putawatomie), 1827-1830, (Choctaw), 1835-1848; Lucretia Purchase (Putawatomie), 1826-1827; Mary Rice (Ojibwa, Creek), 1831-1836; David Rollin (Creek), 1834-1836, (Shawnee), 1837-1839; Robert Simerwell (Putawatomie), 1827-1844; Leonard Slater (Ottawa), 1826-1856; Joseph Smedley (Choctaw), 1837; Amanda Stannard (Ottawa), 1830; Columbus Sturgis (Cherokee), 1834-1835; Lucy Taylor (Choctaw), 1838; Susan Thompson (Delaware), 1827-1828; Eber Tucker (Choctaw), 1835-1836, (Creek), 1843-1845; Harvey Upham (Cherokee), 1844-1852; Willard Upham (Cherokee), 1843-1861; Mary Walton (Delaware), 1829; Abigail Webster (Shawnee), 1840; Erastus Willard (Ottawa), 1857-1860; Charles Wilson (Choctaw), 1832-1835.

Miscellaneous

Brown, William Adams. *The Church in America*. New York: Macmillan, 1922.

Conant, Hannah C. *The Earnest Man: A Memoir of Adoniram Judson, D.D.* Boston: Phillips, Sampson & Co., 1856.

Davis, Horton. *The Worship of the American Puritans 1629-1730*. Peter Lang, 1990.

Fuller, Andrew. *The Complete Works of Andrew Fuller*, ed. Joseph Belcher. Harrisonburg, VA: Sprinkle Publications, 1988.

Garraty, John A. *American History*. New York: Harcourt, Brace, Jovanovich, 1982.

Gibson, Arrell M. *Oklahoma: A History of Five Centuries*. Harlow Publishing Corporation and University of Oklahoma Press, 1965 and 1981 editions.

Josephy Jr, Alvin M. *The American West Year By Year*. Crescent Books, 1995.

Morehouse, Henry L. (Prepared by), *Schools of the American Baptist Home Mission Society*. n.p., 1892.

Murray, Iain H. *Revival & Revivalism: The Making and Marring of American Evangelicalism 1750-1858*. Edinburgh, Scotland: Banner of Truth Trust, 1994.

Noll, Mark A. *A History of Christianity in the United States and Canada*. London: SPCK, 1992.

Waller, John L. ed. "Baron W. Stone and the Kentucky 'New Light Stir'," *Western Baptist Review*, vol. ii, 1846-47, pp. 346-353; 361-371; 421-428; 462-466.

Há-tchoo-túc-knee "The Snapping Turtle" (Peter Pitchlynn, 1806-1881), Choctaw, by George Catlin. Charles Dickens met Peter Pitchlynn in 1842 while both men were traveling by steamboat from Cincinnati to Louisville, and was impressed by Pitchlynn's command of the English language and his wide reading, adding that he was "as stately and complete a gentleman of Nature's making, as ever I beheld." This portrait was executed during Catlin's stay at Fort Gibson, Oklahoma.

Index

Index of Names

A

Adams, Mr. - 513, 549-550
Adams, John Quincy (U. S. President) - 220, 257, 283, 287
Ah-to-co-wah - 313
Alexander, Mrs. - 90
Allen, Dr. and Mrs. Alanson - 402, 475, 481, 564
Allen, Ira M. - 523
Allis, William - 484
Allison, Burgiss - 127
Anderson, Captain (Delaware chief) - 73
Archer, Benjamin - 121
Armstrong, Captain William (Superintendent and Choctaw Agent) - 415, 437-438

B

Babcock, Rufus - 25, 64, 141, 538-539
Bacon[e], Joel S. - 476-477, 491-493, 496-497
Bah-kah-tubba - 313
Bailey, Gilbert S. - 25, 347
Ballard, Mr. and Mrs. Aurey - 396
Baldwin, Thomas (pastor) - 60, 206, 606
Baldwin, Thomas (Indian medical student) - 247
Barbour, James (Secretary of War) - 273
Barker, Frances - 243, 260, 457-462, 470-474, 476, 478, 485, 494, 497, 514, 530-534, 540-541, 584
Barnes, Lela - 6-7,
Barr, Thomas P. - 551
Barrow, Francis (Indian medical student) - 247

Bell, John - 331
Bellamy, Joseph - 368
Belle Ouizo (Osage Chief) - 310
Benedict, David - 465, 498, 598, 602, 606
Berkhofer, Robert F. - 33, 190
Berryman, J. C. - 571
Bingham, Abel - 13, 279, 293, 298, 343, 402
Black Coat (Cherokee Chief) - 558
Blackfeather (Shawnee Chief and missionary) - 513
Black Hawk (Sac Chief) - 581
Blackskin (Ottawa chief) - 238
Blanchard, Ira D. - 243, 356-358, 362, 386, 457-465, 469-470, 472-474, 478, 480, 491, 494-497, 514-515, 524, 530-534, 539, 541, 545, 568, 584
Bolles, Lucius - 13, 103, 116, 125, 227, 230, 232-233, 235, 241-244, 249-253, 255-260, 263, 265, 268-269, 272-273, 276, 278, 280-281, 284-286, 291, 298, 323, 324, 330, 336, 338, 342-345, 348, 350, 358, 360, 364, 367, 371, 381-382, 386-388, 394-396, 405, 443, 447, 456, 462-464, 467, 478-479, 481, 493-494, 497, 530, 541, 591, 597, 600, 604
Boudinot, Elias (Cherokee Chief) - 447
Bradley, Mr. - 396, 568
Brainerd, David - 9, 182
Brantley, William T. - 322
Braybrook, Mr - 523
Broaddus, William F. - 595
Brooks, Iveson L. - 327
Brown, Cynthia - 389
Brown, John (Cherokee merchant) - 558
Brown, Obadiah B. - 127, 228, 599, 602
Browning, Mr. - 342

631

Index

Index

Index

Index

Index

Index

Index

Index

Index

Index

Index

Index

Index

Index

Index

Index

Index

Index

Index

U

Union County, KY - 507
Union Presbyterian Mission Station - 236, 349, 352, 359, 547
Union Town, PA - 10, 41-42
Unorganized Territories - 286

V

Valley Towns Mission, NC - 89, 97, 99, 100, 117, 165, 177, 242, 287, 326, 425, 467, 485, 509, 599
Verdigris River - 302, 410, 558
Vermont - 12, 245-246, 250- 251, 253-254
Vincennes, IN - 10, 39, 46, 48, 53, 61-62, 72, 74, 83, 85, 95-96, 98, 164, 171, 176, 215
Virginia - 43, 75, 427, 507

W

Wabash Baptist Church - 50
Wabash District Baptist Association - 49, 53, 63-64, 140, 158, 210, 228
Wabash River area - 46, 48, 62, 68, 78, 83-85, 103, 166, 261, 577, 586
Washington City (D. C.) - 6-7, 9, 13, 28, 91, 94, 113, 124, 126, 183, 202-203, 205-206, 208, 211, 227-228, 249, 272, 275-276, 281-283, 286-287, 298, 315- 316, 318, 330, 333, 341, 343, 360-363, 369, 396, 405-406, 410, 418, 436-437, 440, 447- 450, 456, 469, 489, 499-500, 543, 546, 598, 604
Western Cemetery, Louisville, KY - 552
Western Foreign Missionary Society - 396

Westport, MO - 52, 220, 373, 411, 415, 458, 490, 521, 523-525
Wichita University - 190
White River area - 48, 50, 62, 261, 567
White River Baptist Association - 228
Wilmington, IN - 518
Wisconsin - 33, 46, 190, 455- 456, 571, 578, 581, 585
Wisconsin River - 477
Withington Mission, Tucheebachee, AL - 349
Worcester, MA - 361

Index of Topics

A

African-Indian comparison - 251
African repatriation - 22, 88
A "mole" at work - 253-254
Anti-mission movement (see also Parkerism, Campbellism) - 52- 56, 316
Arianism - 228
Arminianism - 595

B

Baptist General Convention (Triennial) - 10, 12, 59-60, 205, 210, 222, 235, 239-240, 244, 256, 286, 321-324-325, 367, 374, 394, 420, 423-424, 437, 451, 486, 488-489, 499, 501- 503, 591-593, 596, 598- 599, 601, 604, 610
Battle of Fallen Timbers - 85
Battle of Tippecanoe - 1811, 133, 200
Black Hawk Purchase - 581
Black Hawk War of 1832 - 581
Bootleggers (Whiskey peddlers) -

651

Index

Index

Index

Roman Catholic - 100-101
Roman Catholic activities and opposition, 13, 65, 68, 91, 118, 121, 136, 160, 216-217, 232, 308, 376, 383-385, 528- 530, 546, 551, 569, 571, 579

S

Shakers' Millennial Church - 58
Slavery question - 22-23, 287, 292, 409, 413-414, 417, 470, 552
Small pox - 354, 365
Southern Baptist Convention - 552
Stephen Long Expedition - 183-185
Sunday (Sabbath) Schools - 28, 107, 404, 414, 519

T

Transcribing and translating Indian languages - 140, 373, 397-398, 399, 402-403, 459, 515, 522, 557, 565, 584-585
Treaties of Chicago 1821; 1823 - 11, 104, 117-119, 133, 143-152, 161, 179, 200, 207, 232, 289, 578-579
Treaties of Fort MacIntosh 1785-1787 - 561
Treaty of Fort Harmar, 1789 - 561, 578
Treaty of Fort Wayne, 1803 - 578
Treaty of Detroit, 1807 - 561
Treaty of 1828 (Cherokees) - 558
Treaty of 1836 (Ottawas) - 483
Treaty of Green Bay - 258
Treaty of Greenville, 1795 - 166, 561, 578
Treaty of Prairie Du Chien - 341-342
Treaty of St. Joseph - 308, 336
Treaties of Vincennes, 1803-5 - 567
Two-Seed teaching - 27, 506

W

War of 1812 - 10, 56, 85, 112, 133, 145, 507
Wheeler-Howard Act - 36
Wycliffe Bible Translators - 397

Index of Native American Nations, Tribes and Bands

Brothertown Indians - 69, 273
Cayugas - 41
Cherokees - 22, 67, 71-72, 74, 89, 97, 99, 117, 177, 179, 190, 218, 260, 286-287, 292, 300, 326-327, 329, 333, 347, 352, 359, 361, 388, 395, 397, 406-407, 409-410, 417-419, 425, 431, 445-448, 453-454, 481-482, 509, 545, 547, 557-560
Cheyennes - 454
Chickasaws - 71, 218, 260, 281, 289, 292, 299-302, 304-307, 311, 313, 379, 431, 448, 453, 562
Chippewas - 41, 218, 229, 234, 273, 293, 389, 430, 452, 456, 550, 560- 562, 572, 578, 586
Choctaws - 15, 71, 190, 218, 229, 287, 289, 292, 299-301, 304, 306-307, 311, 313, 346-348, 367, 374, 388-389, 392, 395, 397-399, 402-403, 417, 431, 438-441, 448, 451, 453-455, 481, 483, 535-536, 562-564
Chiweres - 575
Comanches - 299, 323
Creeks (Muscogee) - 13, 15, 41, 71-72, 190, 218, 292, 294, 300, 304, 306, 313, 347, 349-350, 359, 375, 388, 393, 395, 399-400, 402, 406-407, 410, 414-417, 431, 435, 441, 448, 450-451, 453, 481-482, 511-512,

654

Index

Index

Index of Works Cited

Index

Index

Index

Index

Index of Topics

Index

Index

Index

A Choctaw school, circa 1840